A
Langston Hughes
Encyclopedia

A
Langston Hughes
Encyclopedia

Hans Ostrom

GREENWOOD PRESS
Westport, Connecticut • London

Library of Congress Cataloging-in-Publication Data

Ostrom, Hans A.
  A Langston Hughes encyclopedia / Hans Ostrom.
    p. cm.
  Includes bibliographical references (p.   ) and index.
  ISBN 0–313–30392–4 (alk. paper)
    1. Hughes, Langston, 1902–1967—Encyclopedias.   2. Poets, American—20th
  century—Biography—Encyclopedias.   3. Afro-American
  poets—Biography—Encyclopedias.   4. Afro-Americans in literature—Encyclopedias.   I.
  Title.
  PS3515.U274 Z459   2002
  818'.5209—dc21   00–061047
  [B]

British Library Cataloguing in Publication Data is available.

Library of Congress Catalog Card Number: 00–061047
ISBN: 0–313–30392–4

First published in 2002

Greenwood Press, 88 Post Road West, Westport, CT 06881
An imprint of Greenwood Publishing Group, Inc.
www.greenwood.com

Printed in the United States of America

The paper used in this book complies with the
Permanent Paper Standard issued by the National
Information Standards Organization (Z39.48–1984).

10 9 8 7 6 5 4 3 2 1

#44728029

Copyright Acknowledgments

The author and publisher are grateful to the following for granting permission to reprint from their materials:

Arnold Rampersad and David Roessel, eds., *The Collected Poems of Langston Hughes* (New York: Alfred A. Knopf, 1994), reprinted by permission of Alfred A. Knopf, a Division of Random House, Inc. and Harold Ober Associates.

From THE LIFE OF LANGSTON HUGHES, VOLUME 1: 1901–1942: I, TOO, SING AMERICA by Arnold Rampersad, copyright © 1986 by Arnold Rampersad. Used by permission of Oxford University Press, Inc.

Langston Hughes and Ben Frederic Carruthers, trans., *Cuba Libre: Poems by Nicolás Guillén* (Los Angeles, CA: Anderson & Ritchie: The Ward Ritchie Press, 1948), reprinted by permission of Harold Ober Associates.

Contents

Preface

A Langston Hughes Encyclopedia is intended to be useful to undergraduate and graduate students, teachers, scholars, and general readers who are interested specifically in Hughes or in topics somehow connected to him, his work, or his era. Because Hughes produced work in almost every genre imaginable, the encyclopedia contains information potentially significant to those interested in poetry, short fiction, the novel, autobiography, drama, musical theatre, opera, the blues and other popular songs, children's literature, anthologies, and journalism. Individuals engaged in work on the Harlem Renaissance, the Spanish Civil War, folklore, translation, collaborative authorship, American English, African American newspapers, labor history, twentieth-century American history and politics, and Russian, Caribbean, and African cultures may also find the encyclopedia helpful.

A compendium of this sort, to be broadly useful and earn its keep as a reference work, cannot assume the reader has extensive prior knowledge of the subject, so I have written entries chiefly for an audience that is not necessarily familiar with Hughes's life, works, and times. It so happens that Langston Hughes led a vivid, full life in times inundated with crisis and change in the United States and worldwide. By himself he produced a considerable opus, one that includes pioneering work in lyric poetry, short fiction, literary journalism, and theatre, but one that is supplemented by work on which he collaborated with dozens of other gifted individuals, including Zora Neale Hurston, Arna Bontemps, Kurt Weill, Elmer Rice, Jan Meyerowitz, and William Grant Still. He seems, more than thirty years (at this writing) after his death, only to grow in stature as a contributor to American, indeed world, literature.

This well-established but still-growing stature points to the timeliness of an encyclopedia. So do other circumstances. Scholarship and criticism about Hughes and about topics, issues, authors, and works connected to him have poured forth in the last thirty years. Also, new and reprinted collections of his work have regularly appeared, and interest in the Harlem Renaissance has continued to deepen. There is, therefore, a wealth of information to be assimilated and represented. Additionally, and notwithstanding the emergence of this relatively new primary and secondary material, we have only just begun to comprehend fully the breadth of Hughes's achievement. Much work remains in charting, appreciating, and assessing Hughes's accomplishments in songwriting, musical drama, comedic and serious drama, journalism and essay-writing, children's writing, and to some extent even the two parts of his oeuvre on which scholars and critics have concentrated for some time: poetry and fiction.

Although Hughes was a remarkably versatile writer, poetry is indisputably the core of his achievement, as central to his opus as the novel is to that of Henry James. Therefore, the encyclopedia includes a separate entry for each of his published poems, over 850 of them, in addition to entries for different volumes of poetry. In entries on individual poems, I rely on and cite *The Collected Poems of Langston Hughes*, which has become the standard edition. (*Good Morning Revolution: Uncollected Writings of Social Protest by Langston Hughes*, edited by Faith Berry, contains eight poems not included in *The Collected Poems of Langston Hughes*.) Like other scholars working on Hughes, I owe an enormous debt of gratitude to the editors of *Collected Poems*, Arnold Rampersad and David Roessel. In numerous cases, I also cite this volume with regard to revisions poems underwent and noteworthy information about prior publication, including the first appearance of a poem in a periodical. A bracketed number following the title of a poem means that two different poems bear the same title. "Harlem [1]" and "Harlem [2]" are examples. My use of bracketed numbers with titles of poems is based on that of *Collected Poems*. Additionally, David Roessel contributed an entry about Hughes's poetry: **see Revision, Process of, and Hughes**.

The numerous Jesse B. Simple stories called for a principle of coverage different from the one guiding the coverage of the poetry. In these stories, which originally appeared in Hughes's columns for the *Chicago Defender* and, toward the end of the column's run, the *New York Post*, Hughes worked with a recurring cast of characters and developed a relatively consistent narrative style. Therefore, the encyclopedia provides individual entries only for the Simple stories that were later published in book form, and the entries are less detailed than those for individual poems and other short stories. However, a separate entry for the **Simple [Jesse B.] Stories** provides a general overview, and there are entries for each volume of Simple stories, for the *Chicago Defender*, and for Hughes's column in the *Defender*, "Here to Yonder."

Songs for which Hughes wrote lyrics all have separate entries, in which names of composers and publishing information, where available, are included. In the case of poems that were later set to music, information about the resulting song appears in the entry for the poem. However, I have also included an entry on **Songs** that provides a checklist bringing together titles of songs for which Hughes wrote lyrics and of poems subsequently set to music. Entries about songs from musical plays include a cross-reference to the respective musical play, which of course has its own entry as well.

To assist the reader, items in the encyclopedia are cross-referenced by being identified with an asterisk (*). All of Hughes's books, plays, musical plays, operas, oratorios, published poems, published essays, and published short stories have individual entries and are therefore not marked with an asterisk. In addition, many entries are explicitly cross-referenced to other entries with the directives "See" or "See also." "See also" typically suggests a connection between entries that is somewhat less obvious or urgent than one suggested by "See." Titles of books, plays, musical plays, operas, oratorios, recordings, and very long poems are italicized. Titles of poems, stories, chapters, published speeches, songs, and essays appear in quotation marks. Wherever possible, an entry about one of Hughes's works explicitly identifies the genre and scope of the work and often specifies its length as well.

Separate entries also appear for published collections of Hughes's work that were assembled posthumously. These include, for example, *The Collected Poems of Langston Hughes; Arna Bontemps/Langston Hughes: Letters, 1925–1967; Good Morning Revolution: Uncollected Writings of Social Protest by Langston Hughes; The Return of Simple*; and *Langston Hughes: Short Stories*.

Entries summarizing poems, stories, plays, and other works are not intended to provide extensive critical analysis, nor are they meant to substitute for directly experiencing the works themselves. Instead, such entries typically provide a basic sense of the work's scope, form, point of view, subject matter, and essential record of publication. Where appropriate, entries may also provide historical or sociopolitical context, links to other works, facts about critical reception, brief biographical context, and so on. In selected cases, entries point to well-established critical perspectives involving a given work or briefly allude to specific published interpretations; some entries briefly note obvious comparisons or contrasts between works; and some entries discuss briefly how a particular work is clearly unusual. Many entries are followed by a brief bibliography of pertinent secondary sources, and the encyclopedia also includes a general bibliography.

Perhaps even more than other scholars, an encyclopedia author writes mindful of Wordsworth's observation, "We murder to dissect," and, wary of committing textual homicide, presumes not to dissect works for readers but to introduce works to them and to offer links to other information. The entries seek to provide neither the last word about nor a ruinous paraphrase of a work but a quick, clear, informative identification of it.

To more or less conventional encyclopedic items, such as pertinent works, places, people, events, fictional characters, and allusions, I have added entries for several topic areas, including the aforementioned **Revision** and **Songs**, as well as **Ballad, Black Dialect, The Blues, Jazz, Marxism, McCarthyism, Modernism and Hughes, Periodicals** (in which Hughes published work), **Poetics, Politics, Religion, Sexuality and Hughes**, and **Women in Hughes's Writing**, for example. As work on the encyclopedia progressed, such topic areas revealed themselves to be additional useful vantage points from which the book might present information, identify other references, organize material, and anticipate questions to which readers may seek answers in the book. In other words, entries that add synthesis seemed to help advance the main goals of the encyclopedia. Consequently, while I believed that, as noted earlier, each poem Hughes published deserves its own entry, I also believe that in many cases entries should point the reader to closely related poems, and that some subjects were clearly so important to Hughes that they warranted an entry, which would include a reference to individual works on that subject. In this sense, the encyclopedia contains two-way avenues whereby the reader can move from an entry on a single work to entries on related works and then to entries on topics, but can also go in the other direction, from the general to the specific. Therefore, to cite one more example, the encyclopedia includes an entry on **Jim Crow Laws** that concludes with a checklist of works Hughes wrote on the subject.

The choice about whether to use the words "Negro," "black," or "African American" in entries depended upon different historical and rhetorical contexts and respected the ways in which such terminology necessarily changes over time.

It is safe to say that not so very long ago, Langston Hughes was a well-regarded but hardly stellar figure in American literature, generally subordinated in stature to Wallace Stevens and T. S. Eliot, to Ernest Hemingway and Richard Wright, William Faulkner and Ralph Ellison, Amiri Baraka, James Baldwin, and Allen Ginsberg, to mention representative writers roughly contemporary with Hughes. A few readers may still view Hughes as something of a lesser light, and indeed the importance of any writer is always a matter of debate—of criteria, values, predispositions, and opinions. Nonetheless, most students of modern American literature and anyone familiar with African-American literature will have noticed how substantial a figure Hughes has become—will be aware of the extent to which scholars, critics, editors, and teachers have reconsidered the breadth and depth of his work and of the influence his work has had on other writers. To suggest that Hughes has been rediscovered would be a gross overstatement, but to a great degree he has been revalued. The revaluation continues.

The sustained interest in and continuing revaluation of Hughes may spring in part from his having been many writers in one: lyric poet, political poet; poet of solitude and independence, poet of the masses; comic writer, tragic writer; fiction writer, dramatist; loner, collaborator; editor, biographer, journalist, librettist; American and internationalist; Marxist socialist, liberal, polemicist, iconoclast; expatriate, patriot; brash prodigy, avuncular mentor; fierce social critic, bemused social spectator; confirmed Harlemite, restless traveler. The many facets of Langston Hughes resulted less from confusion or impulsiveness on his part and more from his steady growth as a writer, tremendous creative energy, resilience, worldly embrace of political debate, constant attention to the situation of African Americans and working people, and perhaps above all his empathy, which led him naturally not just to speak *for* people but to speak *as* different persons: to inhabit the minds, emotions, and crises of women and men whom he encountered.

In fact, as varied and prolific as his writings are, a coherent set of values supports them. These include an implicit belief that simpler language was often suppler, that the "choice" between art and politics was false, and that—for art and artists—everyday experience was not just a sufficient reservoir of material but a compelling and inexhaustible one.

An awareness of both the varying and constant aspects of Hughes's life and writing, then, necessarily informs this encyclopedia. Certainly, the abundance and complexity of Hughes's work lend themselves to a reference work of this sort; indeed, Hughes is an especially worthy subject for an encyclopedia, one aim of which is to represent complexity and richness by presenting particulars. My hope is, at any rate, that this encyclopedia, as it fulfills its role as a reference work, also implicitly conveys some of what I have discovered or had reconfirmed as I worked on it: namely, that the more one studies Hughes, the more reasons emerge to continue to study him—and, in several senses of the word, to appreciate him.

I have also appreciated the work of other scholars, first and foremost that of Arnold Rampersad, author of a superb two-volume biography of Hughes and, as noted, main editor of *The Collected Poems of Langston Hughes*. Faith Berry, Christopher De Santis, Donald Dickinson, James Emanuel, R. Baxter Miller, and Steven Tracy have all produced important work on Hughes as well. Akiba Sullivan Harper's work on Hughes's short fiction has been nothing short of heroic. The names of other critics and scholars appear in bibliographies throughout the encyclopedia; these individuals have my gratitude and admiration as well. A special word of thanks is due to the founders and members of the Langston Hughes Society, to editors of and contributors to the *Langston Hughes Review*, and to those responsible for building and maintaining collections at the Schomburg Center for Research in Black Culture and the Langston Hughes Papers of the James Weldon Johnson Memorial Collection in the Beinecke Rare Book and Manuscript Library at Yale University.

Four scholars were kind enough to write selected entries for the encyclopedia. Professor William Haltom wrote about **Brown v. Board of Education**, **Herndon v. Lowry**, **The Scottsboro Boys**, and **Robinson and Una Jeffers**. Professor Joseph Deters contributed entries on translations by Hughes of **Cuba Libre: Selected Poems of Nicolás Guillén; Selected Poems of Gabriela Mistral**; **Blood Wedding** and **Yerma** (by Frederico García Lorca; one entry); and **Lorca: Gypsy Ballads** (also by Lorca). Professor Diane Kelley contributed an entry about Hughes's translation, **Masters of the Dew**, by Jacques Roumain. I deeply appreciate the generosity and expertise of Professors Haltom, Deters, and Kelley. As noted earlier, David Roessel, associate editor of *The Collected Poems of Langston Hughes*, contributed the entry on **Revision**, based on a paper he delivered at a Modern Language Association conference.

The rest of the entries are my doing, so any imperfections in them are my responsibility. Fortunately, Langston Hughes and his work attract new readers, critics, editors, and scholars all the time. I hope the encyclopedia will be useful to these new generations even as they add to and correct the work that has come before, my own included.

Librarians at the University of Puget Sound gave the gifts of their time and expertise during the course of this project. Specifically, I want to thank Michael Nanfito, Lorraine Ricigliano, Suzanne Schreiner, and most especially Maureen Kelly. I also appreciate the support of my colleagues Michele Birnbaum and Priti Joshi. Margo Petit Nichols, Associate Arts and Entertainment Editor of the *Carmel Pine Cone*, kindly and expertly responded to my request for information about Noel Sullivan and about Hughes's visits to Carmel, California. At Greenwood Press, George F. Butler has been a patient, perceptive editor. I thank him as well as Charles Eberline, a superb manuscript editor, and Senior Production Editor David Palmer. My son, Spencer Ostrom, helped with several research tasks. My thanks and affection go to him, as well as to his mother, Jacquelyn Bacon Ostrom.

Abbreviations and Short Titles

Berry — Faith Berry, ed., *Good Morning Revolution: Uncollected Writings of Social Protest by Langston Hughes* (New York: Citadel Press, 1992).

CP/Collected Poems — Arnold Rampersad, editor, and David Roessel, associate editor, *The Collected Poems of Langston Hughes* (New York: Vintage Classics, 1994). (In entries, this work is referred to as *Collected Poems*; in bibliographies following entries, it is referred to as *CP*.)

Emanuel — James Emanuel, *Langston Hughes* (New York: Twayne, 1967).

Hicklin — Fannie Ella Frazier Hicklin, "The American Negro Playwright, 1920–1964" (Ph.D. dissertation, Department of Speech, University of Wisconsin, 1965; Ann Arbor: University Microfilms: 65–6217).

Hutchinson — George Hutchinson, *The Harlem Renaissance in Black and White* (Cambridge, MA: Belknap Press of Harvard University Press, 1995).

Lewis, *HRR* — David Levering Lewis, ed., *The Portable Harlem Renaissance Reader* (New York: Penguin, 1995).

Lewis, *WHWV* — David Levering Lewis, *When Harlem Was in Vogue* (New York: Vintage, 1979).

Miller — R. Baxter Miller, *The Art and Imagination of Langston Hughes* (Lexington: University Press of Kentucky, 1989).

Mullen — Edward Mullen, ed., *Critical Essays on Langston Hughes* (Boston: G. K. Hall, 1986).

O'Daniel — Therman B. O'Daniel, ed., *Langston Hughes: Black Genius* (New York: Collier Books, 1971).

Ostrom   Hans Ostrom, *Langston Hughes: A Study of the Short Fiction* (New York: Twayne, 1993).

PEPP   Alex Preminger, Frank J. Warnke, and O. B. Hardison, eds., *Princeton Encyclopedia of Poetry and Poetics*, enlarged ed. (Princeton: Princeton University Press, 1974).

Rampersad, I   Arnold Rampersad, *The Life of Langston Hughes*, vol. 1, *1902–1941* (New York: Oxford University Press, 1986).

Rampersad, II   Arnold Rampersad, *The Life of Langston Hughes*, vol. 2, *1941–1967* (New York: Oxford University Press, 1988).

Tracy   Steven C. Tracy, *Langston Hughes and the Blues* (Urbana: University of Illinois Press, 1988).

Watson   Steven Watson, *The Harlem Renaissance: Hub of African-American Culture, 1920–1930* (New York: Pantheon, 1995).

Wintz   Cary D. Wintz, *Black Culture and the Harlem Renaissance* (Houston: Rice University Press, 1988).

Chronology

1871	James Nathaniel Hughes,* Hughes's father, is born in Charlestown, Indiana.
1873	Carolina Mercer Langston (later known as Carrie Langston Hughes*), Hughes's mother, is born in Lakeview, Kansas, north of Lawrence.
1899	Carrie Langston and James Hughes are married on April 30 in Guthrie, Oklahoma.
1902	James Langston Hughes is born on February 1 in Joplin,* Missouri. Almost from the beginning, and for the rest of his life, he is known as Langston Hughes.* Not long after Hughes's birth, his father moves to Mexico and decides to live there permanently. Except for one brief visit to Mexico, Carrie and Langston Hughes live in the United States apart from James Hughes. Langston will visit his father in Mexico twice later in life.
1903–1915	During these years, Hughes often lives with his maternal grandmother, Mary Sampson Patterson Leary Langston, because Carrie Langston seeks work in several states (*see* "October 16: The Raid"). In his childhood and adolescence, Hughes lives in Buffalo, New York; Cleveland, Ohio; Lawrence, Topeka, and Kansas City, Kansas; and Colorado Springs, Colorado.
1915	Hughes goes to Lincoln, Illinois, to live with his mother and her new husband, Homer Clark.* At what point James and Carrie Hughes were divorced is not known precisely. Because of his mother's second marriage, Hughes gains a step-brother, Gwyn "Kit" Clark.*
1916	Hughes begins to write poetry and becomes the "class poet" of his middle-school class in Lincoln. Later in the year, the family moves to Cleveland, Ohio, where Hughes attends Central High School.* At Central High he reads the work of such writers as Henry Wadsworth Longfellow, Carl Sandburg,* Amy Lowell, and Edgar Lee Masters. He also publishes poetry in the school magazine, the *Belfry Owl*,* and reads philosophy by Nietzsche and Schopenhauer.

1918	Hughes visits Chicago for the first time.
1919	Hughes spends the summer with his father in Mexico. Their relationship is troubled. His father does not endorse Hughes's ambition to be a writer.
1920	Hughes graduates from Central High School.
1921	Hughes visits his father in Mexico once more and briefly teaches English there. In June, his poem "The Negro Speaks of Rivers" is published in *Crisis** magazine. With limited financial support from his father, Hughes enrolls at Columbia University* in the fall. At Columbia he meets Mary Bethune.* He visits Harlem* for the first time.
1922	Partly for financial reasons, Hughes drops out of Columbia University.
1923	Hughes lives in Harlem, works at a variety of jobs, and continues to write and publish poetry. He reads poems publicly for the first time and meets Jessie Redmon Fauset,* Carl Van Vechten,* and other key figures of what will later be called the Harlem Renaissance.* Later in the year, he signs up to work on a freighter, sails to West Africa, and returns to the United States. He becomes increasingly interested in the blues.*
1924	Hughes ships out once more, this time to Europe, where he leaves the ship, deciding to live in Paris. In Paris he works in a restaurant and frequently listens to jazz* bands.
1925	Living in Washington, D.C., with his mother, Hughes works briefly for historian Carter G. Woodson,* performing office duties. In Washington he also meets poet Vachel Lindsay,* who praises his poetry. In April he wins a prize from *Opportunity** magazine for the poem "The Weary Blues." During visits to Harlem, he meets Alain Locke,* who edits an anthology entitled *The New Negro* and a special issue of the magazine *Survey Graphic*, both of which include poetry by Hughes. Locke is sexually attracted to Hughes and will later attempt to seduce him. Hughes also meets Arna Bontemps,* Zora Neale Hurston,* and Wallace Thurman,* and a friendship with Countee Cullen* develops. Cullen and Hughes are perceived to be friendly rivals as young publishing poets.
1926	Hughes's first collection of poetry, *The Weary Blues*, is published by the firm of Alfred A. Knopf,* and his extraordinary essay, "The Negro Artist and the Racial Mountain," intended as a response to an essay by George Schuyler,* appears in the *Nation*. In the middle of the academic year, Hughes enrolls at Lincoln University.*
1927	*Fine Clothes to the Jew* is published. Partly because it includes poems that present an unvarnished view of urban African American life, some reviews of the book are negative. Hughes meets Mrs. Charlotte Osgood Mason,* who will become his patron and that of Zora Neale Hurston.
1929	Hughes graduates from Lincoln University and completes a manuscript of the novel *Not Without Laughter*. The U.S. stock market crashes. The economic catastrophe that ensues hits Harlem extremely hard, contributing to the demise of the Harlem Renaissance.
1930	Hughes visits Cuba and meets writer Nicolás Guillén,* whose book of poems *Cuba Libre* Hughes will later translate. Back in the United States,

Hughes quarrels with Mason, who withdraws her financial support of him. *Not Without Laughter* is published and is awarded the Harmon Foundation Medal. Hughes and Zora Neale Hurston collaborate on the play *Mule Bone*. However, Hughes's break with Mason affects his relationship with Hurston; the two writers quarrel about finances related to the project and about authorship; the project and their friendship ends. The play will not be produced until 1991.

1931   Hughes travels to Haiti, and his writings begin to reflect his growing interest in political ideas influenced by Marxism.* *Dear Lovely Death* is published by the small Troutbeck Press in Amenia, New York. A grant from the Rosenwald Foundation allows Hughes to travel in the South giving poetry readings. He visits the Scottsboro Boys,* who are incarcerated in an Alabama prison. The small Golden Stair Press publishes *The Negro Mother*.

1932   *Scottsboro Limited* is published. Franklin Delano Roosevelt* is elected president of the United States. Joining about twenty other African Americans, Hughes travels to Russia to take part in an ill-fated motion-picture project, *Black and White*.* Although the project disintegrates, he decides to remain in Russia, then travels throughout the Soviet Union and into parts of Asia. He meets Arthur Koestler.* The politically satirical poem "Goodbye Christ" is published in the *Negro Worker* and sparks public outrage.

1933   Hughes returns to the United States, arriving by ship in San Francisco, where he stays at the home of Noel Sullivan* and then lives in Sullivan's cottage in Carmel-by-the-Sea. Hughes is ill and is also depressed by the reaction to "Goodbye Christ." He meets Robinson and Una Jeffers* and works on short stories. Like Arna Bontemps and Carl Van Vechten, Noel Sullivan will become one of Hughes's most constant friends.

1934   Hughes's first collection of short stories, *The Ways of White Folks*, is published by Alfred A. Knopf. Blanche Knopf* continues to be his editor at the firm. Hughes participates in labor protests organized by farm workers and members of the John Reed Club.* Hughes's father dies in Mexico. Hughes travels there to oversee the disposition of his father's small estate.

1935   Unbeknownst to Hughes, his play *Mulatto* (written several years earlier) is in production in New York City. Returning to New York, he is unhappy with how the producers have enhanced the melodramatic aspects of the play. Nonetheless, the production moves forward and enjoys a relatively long run on Broadway.

1936   Hughes receives a Guggenheim Foundation fellowship. He travels to Cleveland and begins writing plays for the Karamu Theatre, which that year produces *Little Ham* and *Troubled Island*. In New York City he meets Ralph Ellison.* Outraged by Italy's invasion of Ethiopia, Hughes publishes such poems as "Broadcast on Ethiopia" and "Call of Ethiopia."

1937   The Karamu Theatre produces *Joy to My Soul*. Hughes travels to Spain to report on the Spanish Civil War for the *Baltimore Afro American*.*

He also makes radio broadcasts, meets up again with Nicolás Guillén, and meets Ernest Hemingway.* His experience in Spain leads to such works as "Letter from Spain," "Hero—International Brigade," "Madrid," and "Spain's Martyred Poet, García Lorca." Later Hughes will translate Lorca's *Gypsy Ballads* and (in a single volume) *Blood Wedding* and *Yerma.*

1938   Back in New York City, Hughes is the driving force behind the creation of the avant-garde Harlem Suitcase Theatre,* which stages his play *Don't You Want to Be Free?* The poetry chapbook *A New Song* is published by the International Workers Order and contains some of the most politically charged, Marxist-influenced poems Hughes will write. *Front Porch* is produced by the Karamu Theatre. Hughes meets Richard Wright.* His mother is stricken with cancer and dies in New York City.

1939   Hughes collaborates with actor, writer, and singer Clarence Muse* on the screenplay for the motion picture *Way Down South,** which stars Bobby Breen* and in which Muse acts. In part, Hughes is motivated to work on the screenplay for financial reasons: he needs to pay for expenses associated with his mother's final illness and her funeral services. Later he returns to Carmel to live in Noel Sullivan's cottage for an extended period and work on an autobiography. "Red Clay Blues," a poem cowritten with Richard Wright, is published in *New Masses* magazine.

1940   Hughes's first autobiography, *The Big Sea*, is published. It includes the chapter "When the Negro Was in Vogue," considered an important depiction of the Harlem Renaissance. Hughes collaborates with composer and musician James P. Johnson* on the innovative blues opera *De Organizer.* (In the 1920s Johnson had cowritten the popular song "Charleston.")

1941   Several of Hughes's poems appear in the *Carmel Pine Cone.*

1942   The United States has declared war on Japan and the Axis powers. Initially Hughes is ambivalent about America's involvement in World War II because he sees a double standard at work in the way the United States opposes tyranny abroad but supports Jim Crow laws* domestically. *The Sun Do Move* is produced by the Skyloft Players in Chicago. *Shakespeare in Harlem* is published. Hughes begins writing a newspaper column, "Here to Yonder,"* for the *Chicago Defender.**

1943   In his newspaper column, Hughes introduces a character first known as "my simple-minded friend," then briefly as Jesse B. Semple, and finally as Jesse B. Simple. Eventually, several volumes of the Simple stories* will be published. Also in the column and in poems such as "Bonds for All," Hughes supports America's involvement in World War II, partly because of Adolf Hitler's racist agenda but also because of Joseph Stalin's pact with Hitler. *Jim Crow's Last Stand* is published. Hughes begins publishing the Madam poems* in magazines.

1944   Hughes goes on a national reading tour.

1945   Hughes begins working on the opera* *Street Scene* with Elmer Rice* and Kurt Weill.*

1946   Poet Countee Cullen dies.

1947   *Street Scene* opens on Broadway. *Masters of the Dew*, a translation by
              Mercer Cook and Hughes of a novel by Jacques Roumain, is published
              by Reynal and Hitchcock. Visiting Kenyon College, Hughes meets poet
              and critic John Crowe Ransom.* *Fields of Wonder* is published. Hughes
              meets composer Jan Meyerowitz.*

1948   Claude McKay* dies. Hughes takes up residence at 20 East 127th Street
              in Harlem.*

1949   The landmark anthology edited by Hughes and Arna Bontemps, *The
              Poetry of the Negro, 1746–1949*, is published. A collection of poetry,
              One-Way Ticket, is published, as is Hughes's translation, *Cuba Libre:
              Poems by Nicolás Guillén. Troubled Island*, an opera based on Hughes's
              play of the same name and for which William Grant Still* composed
              the music, is produced in New York City.

1950   The first collection of Simple Stories, *Simple Speaks His Mind*, is pub-
              lished by Simon and Schuster. *The Barrier*, an opera based on Hughes's
              play *Mulatto* and his short story "Father and Son," is produced at Co-
              lumbia University. Jan Meyerowitz* is the composer, Hughes the li-
              brettist.

1951   Hughes's blues- and jazz-influenced, book-length poem *Montage of a
              Dream Deferred* is published by Henry Holt. His translation of García
              Lorca's poetry, *Gypsy Ballads*, is published.

1952   The collection of stories *Laughing to Keep from Crying* is published.
              Publisher Franklin Watts brings out Hughes's children's book *The First
              Book of Negroes*. Ralph Ellison's monumental novel *Invisible Man* is
              published. Ellison distances himself from Hughes.

1953   Hughes is called to testify about his affiliation with Marxist-influenced
              politics in the 1930s before U.S. Senator Joseph McCarthy's Permanent
              Sub-Committee on Investigations (*see* McCarthyism). The poem "Un-
              American Investigators" will be based on this experience. *Simple Takes
              a Wife* is published. Hughes travels again to Carmel, California.

1954   An oratorio with music by Jan Meyerowitz and text by Hughes, *Five
              Foolish Virgins*, is performed in New York City. The U.S. Supreme
              Court makes its landmark ruling in *Brown v. Board of Education.* *Fa-
              mous American Negroes*, for a juvenile audience, and *The First Book of
              Rhythms*, for children, are published.

1955   *The First Book of Jazz* and *Famous Negro Music Makers* are published.
              The Glory around His Head, an Easter cantata with music by Jan Mey-
              erowitz and text by Hughes, debuts at Carnegie Hall in New York City.
              A book of photographs by Roy DeCarava and an innovative text by
              Hughes, *The Sweet Flypaper of Life*, is published.

1956   *The First Book of the West Indies, I Wonder As I Wander* (Hughes's
              second autobiography), and *A Pictorial History of the Negro in America*
              (with Milton Meltzer as coauthor) are all published. Hughes's good
              friend Noel Sullivan dies suddenly of a heart attack in San Francisco.

1957   The opera *Esther*, with music by Jan Meyerowitz* and libretto by Hughes, debuts at the University of Illinois. Hughes's translation *Selected Poems of Gabriela Mistral*, is published by Indiana University Press.

1958   *The Langston Hughes Reader* is published by Braziller; it contains, among other things, much children's poetry* not previously published. *The Book of Negro Folklore*, which Hughes coedited with Arna Bontemps, appears from Dodd, Mead, as does *Famous Negro Heroes of America* (for juvenile readers). The musical play *Simply Heavenly* debuts off-Broadway.

1959   *Tambourines to Glory*, a "novelization" of a gospel song-play of the same name written in 1956, appears from Jonathan Day Publishers. Ironically, the play will not be produced until 1963. *Selected Poems of Langston Hughes* is published by Knopf and is greeted with a harsh review in the *New York Times Book Review* by James Baldwin.* Hughes contributes the "Introduction"* to a paperback edition of *Pudd'nhead Wilson* by Mark Twain and writes liner notes for Harry Belafonte's* recording of African American spirituals, *My Lord What a Mornin'*.*

1960   A book for children, *The First Book of Africa*, appears from Franklin Watts. Hughes's final collaboration with Jan Meyerowitz, the opera *Port Town*, debuts at the Tanglewood Festival in Massachusetts. Hughes's fellow writer and longtime friend Richard Wright dies in Paris.

1961   Hughes meets poet Robert Frost.* *An African Treasury: Articles, Essays, Stories, Poems by Black Africans*, edited by Hughes, is published. *Ask Your Mama: 12 Moods for Jazz* is published by Knopf, and Hill and Wang publishes *The Best of Simple*. *Black Nativity*, a gospel song-play, debuts on Broadway and is an instant critical and popular success.

1962   Hughes's history of the NAACP,* *Fight for Freedom*, is published. Hughes takes part in the National Poetry Festival in Washington, D.C. One of the poems he reads is "Merry-Go-Round."

1963   *Something in Common and Other Stories* appears from Hill and Wang. *Five Plays by Langston Hughes*, edited by Webster Smalley, is published by Indiana University Press, and the play *Tambourines to Glory* opens on Broadway. A comic musical-drama written some seven years earlier, *Tambourines to Glory* seems out of place in the politically charged 1960s and is not well received by audiences and critics. *Poems from Black Africa*, edited by Hughes, is published by Indiana University Press.

1964   Hughes's play *Jerico-Jim Crow* is produced in Greenwich Village, New York City, and is praised by critics. For a recording by Joan Baez,* Hughes writes liner notes, and for a recording by jazz singer Nina Simone, he writes "The One and Only Nina Simone: A Tribute." Hughes's longtime friend Carl Van Vechten dies.

1965   In a newspaper column, Hughes comments on the writing of LeRoi Jones (Amiri Baraka*). The play *Prodigal Son* opens in New York City and is well reviewed. *Simple's Uncle Sam* is published.

1966   For the *Chicago Defender*, Hughes writes the final Simple story; Simple, it seems, has decided to move from Harlem to "the suburbans."

1967   *The Best Short Stories by Negro Writers*, edited by Hughes, is published by Little, Brown; it includes his story "Thank You, Ma'am." In early May Hughes enters a hospital in New York City, undergoing surgery for a diseased prostate gland. Complications, including an extremely high fever, ensue. He dies on May 22. His funeral* is held on May 24. His best friend Arna Bontemps delivers a brief eulogy, and a jazz band plays "Do Nothing 'Til You Hear from Me," by Duke Ellington.* "Backlash Blues," believed to be the last poem Hughes submitted for publication before his death, is published by *Crisis* magazine. *The Panther and the Lash*, the last collection of poems that Hughes himself assembled, is published posthumously by Knopf. *Black Magic: A Pictorial History of the Negro in American Entertainment* (coauthored with Milton Meltzer) is also published posthumously.

A

"Abe Lincoln." Fourteen-line, free-verse poem in which the persona addresses U.S. President Abraham Lincoln, expressing sympathy for the difficulties and disappointments Lincoln experienced but also praising his hope for humankind. The poem was first published in *Voices* (May–August 1960), 17. *See* "Lincoln Monument: Washington." *See also* Sandburg, Carl.

Bibliography: *CP*, 467; David Herbert Donald, *Lincoln: A Biography* (New York: Simon and Schuster, 1995).

Abortion. The critical event on which the plot of the story "Cora Unashamed" turns.

"Acceptance." Four-line rhymed poem first published in *Beloit Poetry Journal Chapbook* (1950), a collection in honor of Robert Frost.* The acceptance referred to is God's, of human stupidity.

Bibliography: *CP*, 455.

"Addition [1] [2]." Hughes wrote two different poems with this title, both referring epigrammatically to arithmetic in order to invoke larger topics such as love, hate, and jealousy. The first was a four-line poem published in the *Carmel Pine Cone*, 2 May 1941. The second was a seven-line poem published in *Voices*, May–August 1953. *See* Jeffers, Robinson and Una.

Bibliography: *CP*, 229, 443.

"Adventure." Short story, included in the collection *Simple's Uncle Sam*. *See* Simple [Jesse B.] Stories.

"Advertisement for the Waldorf Astoria." Poem of several pages that, in form, plays with the structure of a magazine advertisement and that, in execution, satirizes a Waldorf advertisement Hughes had seen in the magazine *Vanity Fair*. In part, the poem highlights the economic gulf in 1931 between Waldorf patrons and both workers (mostly unemployed) and African Americans (who were not allowed to stay at the hotel, regardless of income). First published in *New Masses* (December 1931), the poem echoes the political and satirical sensibility of several stories in *The Ways of White Folks*. Hughes reprinted the poem in its entirety in *The Big Sea. See* Marxism; Politics; Roosevelt, Franklin Delano.

Bibliography: *The Big Sea*, 320–324; *CP*, 143.

"Advice." Poem of six short lines, reminiscent of American poet Ogden Nash's light verse, advising "folks" to get some "loving" between birth and death. It was first published in *Senior Scholastic Magazine* (April 1946). Later Hughes included it in *Montage of a Dream Deferred*.

Bibliography: *CP*, 400.

"Aesthete in Harlem." Seven-line poem touching on the issue of white, liberal, upper-class New Yorkers visiting Harlem* in the 1920s almost as cultural "tourists." It was first published in *Opportunity** (May 1930).

Bibliography: *CP*, 128; Lewis, *WHWV*.

"Afraid." Six-line, free-verse poem connecting the experience of African Americans in large U.S. cities to that of Africans centuries earlier. It was first published in *Crisis** (November 1924).

Bibliography: *CP*, 41.

"Africa." Poem of fifteen very short lines, the primary trope being to personify Africa. It was first published in the *Long Island University Review* (June 1952).

Bibliography: *CP*, 441.

"African Dance." Song. Hughes composed the lyrics, and Connie Benis and Clarence Muse* composed the music. According to ASCAP,* EMI/Mills, Inc., holds the publishing rights, and the ASCAP registry number is 310084861.

"African Fog." Poem. *See* "Fog."

"African Morning." Short story. In this narrative, a white banker in Africa sends his "mulatto" son on an errand to the waterfront of a city. On the way, the boy is mistaken for a prostitute. He is teased, beaten, and chased. The episode drives the boy to despair at having been born "the color of gold" (*Laughing to Keep from Crying*, 19). His black African mother is dead, and he fears that his white father will abandon him. He leaps into the ocean, wanting to drown, but bobs up and decides to live. With regard to racial issues, the story is related to several other works by Hughes, including "Father and Son," "Mulatto," and the play *Mulatto*. It is also a lyrical story rich in imagery. It was first published under the title "Outcast" in *Pacific Weekly* (August 31, 1936), was included in the collections *Laughing to Keep from Crying* and *Something in Common and Other Stories*, and was reprinted in *Langston Hughes: Short Stories*.

Bibliography: Ostrom, 21–22.

An African Treasury: Articles, Essays, Stories, Poems by Black Africans (New York: Pyramid Books, 1961). 192 pp. Anthology edited by Hughes. The book is out of print at this writing but was issued in microform by Northwestern University in 1997. *See* Anthologies; *Poems from Black Africa*.

Bibliography: Rampersad, II, 238.

Afrika Singt: Eine Auslese neuer Afro-Amerikanischer Lyrik (1929). Anthology, edited and translated by Austrian scholar Anna Nussbaum. The book, published in Germany, included translations of thirty-seven of Hughes's poems, chiefly from *The Weary Blues*.

Bibliography: Rampersad, I, 159.

"Afro-American Fragment." Poem of two twelve-line stanzas concerning Hughes's complicated, powerful emotions toward the conception of Africa. For a summary of the several revisions the poem underwent, see *Collected Poems*. It was first published in *Crisis* (July 1930). It was later set to music by William Earl Averitt; the song is registered with ASCAP,* registry number 310300911. It was also set to music by Frank Proto; the ASCAP registry number for this version is 310378339. Proto's version is published by Liben Music Publishers (Cincinnati, Ohio).

Bibliography: *CP*, 129, 637.

"After Hours." Short story, included in the collection *Simple Speaks His Mind*. *See* Simple [Jesse B.] Stories.

"After Many Springs." Poem of eight lines in free verse. It was first published in *Crisis** (August 1922) and was later included in *The Weary Blues* and *The Dream Keeper*. The first-person speaker is wistful about his or her inability to perceive magical aspects of experience.

Bibliography: *CP*, 28.

"After the Accident." Short story. *See* "Heaven to Hell."

"Again Cousin Minnie." Short story, included in *The Best of Simple*. *See* Simple [Jesse B.] Stories.

Agents, Literary, Hughes's. Hughes's two chief literary agents during his career were Maxim Lieber and Harold Ober.
Bibliography: Rampersad, I, 270; II, 195.

"Ain't It Awful, the Heat." Song, included in *Street Scene*. Hughes and Elmer Rice* wrote the lyrics, and Kurt Weill* wrote the music. The song is registered with ASCAP,* registry number 310016729. *See* "A Boy like You"; "Catch Me If You Can"; "Don't Forget the Lilac Bush"; "I Got a Marble and a Star"; "I Loved Her, Too"; "Ice Cream."

"Air Raid: Barcelona." Two-page poem that is at once lyrical and reportorial. Hughes had traveled to Spain in 1937 to cover the Spanish Civil War for the *Baltimore Afro American** newspaper. The poem was first published in *Esquire* (October 1938).
Bibliography: *CP*, 207.

"Air Raid over Harlem." Two-page poem subtitled "Scenario for a Little Black Movie." "Spoken" by several different voices or characters, including a personified Harlem,* the poem concerns police brutality and other signs of racial tension in Harlem. It hints that a revolution based on economic class differences, not just on ethnic conflict, is imminent. Doreski observes that "[t]he invasion of Ethiopia, the Spanish Civil War, the Second World War inspired poets and journalists alike to meditate upon the promise and reality of democracy in America," and cites this poem as an example. The poem was first published in *New Theatre* (1936).
Bibliography: *CP*, 185; C. K. Doreski, *Writing America Black: Race Rhetoric in the Public Sphere* (Cambridge: Cambridge University Press, 1998), 83.

"Alabama Earth." Poem of three quatrains with rhyming second and fourth lines, written at the invitation of the Tuskegee Institute and first published in the *Tuskegee Messenger* (June 1928). *See* Washington, Booker T.
Bibliography: *CP*, 126.

Aletha, Theresa Belle. A character in the poem "Summer Evening (Calumet Avenue)."

Alka-Seltzer. Brand name of an American over-the-counter remedy for mild stomach discomfort. *See* "Dixie South Africa."

"All in the Family." Short story, included in the collections *Simple Takes a Wife* and *The Best of Simple*. *See* Simple, [Jesse B.] Stories.

"Always the Same." Free-verse poem of about one page, spoken by an exploited, black-worker "Everyman" or collective persona.* Under the title "The Same," it was first published in the *Negro Worker* (Fall 1932). Hughes uses two devices to suggest the international nature of exploitation: one is to mention far-flung sites on the global map, such as banana fields in Central America and diamond mines in South Africa; the other is to mention different currencies, such as dollar, lira, and franc. Not a few readers would find the poem propagandistic, and virtually none would miss the Marxist influence, for the poem predicts an uprising of "the Red Army of the International Proletariat." The poem, in any event, concretely exemplifies the brief but intense Marxist political phase through which Hughes went in the 1930s. *See* Marxism; Politics.
Bibliography: *CP*, 165.

"America." Short-lined, free-verse poem portraying Jewish and African Americans as people naturally aligned by virtue of their "outcast" status in the United States. Midway through the poem, the voice shifts, and a kind of "universal" African American speaks: "I am Crispus Attucks . . . I am Sojourner Truth." (Attucks [1723–1770] escaped slavery, fled to Boston in 1750, and was killed in the Boston Massacre. Truth [1797–1883] was a former slave who became a renowned advocate for abolition of slavery.) The poem concludes optimistically, almost patriotically, by suggesting that while democracy is stained, outcasts have reason to dream, to aspire, and to expect success and acceptance. First published in *Opportunity** (June 1925), the poem represents a stark contrast to "Always the Same" (1932) and other poems of the early 1930s that seem to reject even guarded faith in the American Dream in favor of more radical, class-oriented, internationalist views.
Bibliography: *CP*, 52.

The America First Party. *See* "Goodbye, Christ"; "In Explanation of Our Times."

"American Dilemma." Short story, included in the collection *Simple's Uncle Sam. See* Simple [Jesse B.] Stories.

"American Heartbreak." Poem in six lines, spoken by a collective persona* implicitly representing African Americans. It was first published in *Phylon* (1951).
Bibliography: *CP*, 385.

The American Heritage Foundation. *See* "Freedom Train."

American Mercury. Magazine edited by H. L. Mencken. Mencken published two of Hughes's short stories in the magazine: "Cora Unashamed" (September 1933, 19–24) and "Poor Little Black Fellow" (November 1933, 326–355). *See also* Knopf, Alfred A.

Bibliography: Fenwick Anderson, "Black Perspectives in Mencken's *Mercury,*" *Menckeniana: A Quarterly Journal* 70 (1979), 2–6; Hutchinson, 313–341; Rampersad, I, 426.

American Society of Composers, Authors, and Publishers. *See* ASCAP.

"America's Young Black Joe!" Inelegantly rhymed, balladlike poem spoken by a collective persona* (Young Black Joe) who is variously identified with such athletes as Jesse Owens, who won four gold medals in the 1936 Berlin Olympics, Kenny Washington, an All-American football player at the University of California, Los Angeles, in the 1930s, and Joe Louis,* heavyweight boxing champion. The poem was one of several submitted to the Associated Negro Press (ANP) for distribution to African American newspapers (*see Collected Poems*, 683). Many of these poems appeared in the *Baltimore Afro American.** "America's Young Black Joe!" leaves the impression of having been a quickly written piece of verse intended for a casual audience, with the rhyming being not entirely different from that of "cowboy poetry." All the poems submitted to the ANP for distribution appear in Appendix I (565–593) of *Collected Poems*. Each poem has an entry in this encyclopedia and is cross-referenced to "America's Young Black Joe!" to indicate that these poems form a distinct subset of Hughes's poetic canon. Later the poem was apparently set to music. As "Young Black Joe," it is listed with ASCAP,* with Hughes named as the sole author (both lyricist and composer, that is). No publisher is listed, however, and none of Hughes's biographers mentions the song or a poem titled "Young Black Joe." The song's ASCAP registry number is 550036781.

Bibliography: *CP*, 565.

Anderson, Marian (1897–1993). American classical singer. *See* "Jim Crow's Last Stand."

Anderson, Sherwood (1876–1941). American writer. A native of Ohio, Anderson wrote stories and novels concerned with small-town life in the American Midwest. He left home when he was nineteen to live and work in Chicago; later he enlisted to fight in the Spanish-American War. After the war he attempted to pursue a business career, suffered a nervous collapse in 1912, and thereafter devoted himself primarily to writing. His fourth book, *Winesburg, Ohio* (1919), is his most widely known and respected; it contains a series of interwoven short stories, including the much-anthologized "The Egg." Reviewing *The Ways of White Folks* in the *Nation* (July 11, 1934), Anderson took Hughes to task for using short stories to "get even," for using fiction to advance an excessively pointed, harsh political critique. "Mr. Hughes," wrote Anderson in the review titled "Paying for Old Sins," "my hat off to you in relation to your own race, but not to me and mine."

Bibliography: Mullen, 65; Ostrom, 83–84.

Andrzejewski, Sartur (1902?–?). A friend of Hughes's at Central High School.* He is mentioned in *The Big Sea*.

Bibliography: *The Big Sea*, 30.

Angelo Herndon Jones (1938). Play in one act. Angelo Herndon was a young (age nineteen) American labor activist who organized a multiracial labor demonstration in Atlanta, Georgia, in January 1932. He was arrested for inciting an insurrection, tried, convicted, and sentenced to the state penitentiary for eighteen to twenty years. Herndon's case was eventually reviewed by the U.S. Supreme Court (1937), which ruled that Georgia's anti-insurrection law was unconstitutional. Herndon was released from prison. Hughes's play dramatizes issues involved in the case and the events leading up to it. The play was performed by the Harlem Suitcase Theatre* in May 1938 and was published in *New Theatre Magazine* that year. The play was published again in 2000. In addition, Hughes wrote in *I Wonder As I Wander* about the heroic death of Milton Herndon (Angelo's brother) in the Spanish Civil War. Milton died while attempting to rescue a white comrade. *See* "Ballads of Lenin"; "Black Workers"; "Chant for Tom Mooney"; *Don't You Want to Be Free?*; "Goodbye Christ"; "Good Morning Revolution"; "Kids Who Die"; "Lenin"; "One More 'S' in the U.S.A."; "Revolution"; "Song of the Revolution"; "Wait." *See also Herndon v. Lowry*; Marxism; Politics.

Bibliography: Hicklin; Langston Hughes, *Angelo Herndon Jones*, in *The Political Plays of Langston Hughes*, ed. with introductions and analyses by Susan Duffy (Carbondale: Southern Illinois University Press, 2000), 147–162.

"Angels [sic] Wings." Poem of fourteen lines, intermittently rhymed, in black dialect. The speaker contrasts the pure white of "angels [sic] wings" with his or her own figurative wings, which have been dragged through mud—meaning, presumably, that the speaker has sinned. The poem was first published in *Fine Clothes to the Jew*.

Bibliography: *CP*, 118.

"Angola Question Mark." Irregularly rhymed poem of nineteen short lines, first published in *Black Orpheus* (May 1959). The "I" of the poem is a collective persona*; the "question mark" is rhetorical, concerning why struggles for independence (from colonialism) in emerging African nations were necessary—why, in effect, independence came at such a dear price.

Bibliography: *CP*, 464.

"Anne Spencer's Table." Four-line, free-verse "thing poem" focusing not so much on the table as on a pencil atop it—an unsharpened (and, the suggestion is, unused) one. Anne Spencer* was an important but unprolific Harlem Renaissance* poet and a friend of Hughes. The poem, therefore, offers a quick glance at two different artistic temperaments: Hughes's ceaselessly productive one and Spencer's more reticent, irregular one. The poem hints, at least, that the question "Why doesn't she write more?" may have been on Hughes's mind. See "doorknobs" [*sic*] for another example of a thing poem.

Bibliography: *CP*, 128.

"Announcement." Humorous poem in a four-stanza, modified ballad* form; the persona details troubles with his "gal" that also involve his Buick automobile. The poem was first published in *Shakespeare in Harlem*.

Bibliography: *CP*, 261.

Anonymous publication by Hughes. *See* "Nonette."

"An Anonymous Verse." Poem of eight lines. Hughes translated it "from a Puerto Rican Christmas card." It was first published in *Carol of the Brown King: Nativity Poems by Langston Hughes*.

Anthologies Edited or Coedited by Hughes. *See An African Treasury; The Best Short Stories by Negro Writers: An Anthology from 1899 to the Present; The Book of Negro Folklore; The Book of Negro Humor; Poems from Black Africa; The Poetry of the Negro, 1746–1949: An Anthology.*

Apollo Theatre. One of the most popular theatres in the Harlem Renaissance* and still in operation.

Bibliography: Watson.

The Appeal. The newspaper Hughes sold when he was a boy. He mentions it in *The Big Sea*, calling it the *Appeal to Reason*. *The Appeal* was a Chicago-based newspaper when Hughes sold it but was founded in St. Paul, Minnesota, in 1885 and stayed in business until 1926. Walker describes it as "a four-page paper that initially printed its editorials on the first page." She characterizes the editorials as "militant," indicating that they "denounced lynching* [and] southern atrocities, and expressed 'moral outrage' at social conditions in the South." However, she also notes that as "early as 1897, the *Appeal* aligned itself with Booker T. Washington's* camp, referring to him as 'the Moses of the people' " (20–21). *The Appeal* was edited by brothers John Quincy Adams and Cyrus Adams.

Bibliography: Juliet E. K. Walker, "The Promised Land: The *Chicago Defender* and the Black Press in Illinois, 1862–1970," in *The Black Press in the Middle West, 1865–1985*, ed. Henry Lewis Suggs (Westport, CT: Greenwood Press, 1996), 9–50.

"Apple Strudel." Short story, included in the collections *Simple Takes a Wife* and *The Best of Simple*. *See* Simple [Jesse B.] Stories.

"April Rain." Song. Hughes wrote the lyrics, and Charles Kingsford composed the music. The song is registered with ASCAP,* registry number 310236527. ASCAP lists no publisher.

"April Rain Song." Seven-line, free-verse poem about the joys of rain. *See* Children's Poetry.
Bibliography: *CP*, 597.

Aragon, Louis (1897–1982). French poet who belonged to the literary movement known as surrealism, which began in France, had as its chief spokesperson André Breton, and influenced poetry in many languages after 1924. Among Aragon's better-known books of poetry is *Le mouvement perpetuel* (1926). In *I Wonder As I Wander*, Hughes mentions meeting Aragon in Moscow, Russia.
Bibliography: *I Wonder As I Wander*, 399–402; "Surrealism," in *PEPP*, 821–823.

"Ardella." Six-line, free-verse poem characterizing a young woman. The poem was first published in *The Weary Blues* and was published in *The Dream Keeper* with the title "Quiet Girl."
Bibliography: *CP*, 95.

"Argument." Hughes gave two poems this title. The first was published in *New Masses* (1926) and was written in black dialect*; the second is part of *Montage of a Dream Deferred*.
Bibliography: *CP*, 87, 421.

Arna Bontemps/Langston Hughes: Letters, 1925–1967. Selected and edited by Charles H. Nichols (New York: Dodd, Mead, 1980). 529 pp. The volume reprints 500 letters out of "about 2300" that Hughes and Arna Bontemps* exchanged. In the preface, Nichols cites six criteria for selection, which have to do with literary, political, social, and biographical interest. The first letter reprinted is from Bontemps to Hughes, undated but written in 1925. The last letter is from Bontemps to Hughes, dated May 1, 1967. Nichols's "Prologue" (1–14) discusses the deep friendship that grew between the two writers, the personalities of both men, and the character of the correspondence. The letters are organized into three periods: 1925–1940, 1941–1959, and 1960–1967. The volume also includes a chronology of each man's life, several facsimile letters, and an extensive index. *See* Bernard, Emily, in the general bibliography.

"As Befits a Man." Humorous four-stanza ballad* in which the speaker details what kind of funeral he would like to have, emphasizing his hope that many women will attend. It was first published in *Selected Poems* and was reprinted in *The Block*.

Bibliography: *CP*, 465.

"As I Grew Older." Free-verse poem about a dream; "dream" in the poem refers both to aspiration and a sleeping dream. It was first published in *The Weary Blues*.

Bibliography: *CP*, 93.

ASCAP. Acronym for American Society of Composers, Authors, and Publishers, an organization that, among other things, registers songs and copyrights of songs, lists authorship, and oversees payment of royalties. Most, but not all, of Hughes's songs and poems set to music are registered with ASCAP, each with a registry number, which is provided in this encyclopedia's entries for those individual songs (and for poems later set to music) that are listed with ASCAP at this writing. ASCAP has offices in Atlanta, Chicago, Hato Rey (Puerto Rico), London, Los Angeles, Miami, and New York City, and it has a Website: http://www.ascap.com.

Ashes, Hughes's (disposition of). *See* Funeral, Hughes's.

Ask Your Mama (New York: Knopf, 1961). 59 pp. Subtitled *12 Moods for Jazz*. Book-length poem. *Ask Your Mama* (*AYM*) is arguably Hughes's most experimental work of poetry and certainly one of his most ambitious works in any genre. Like those of *Montage of a Dream Deferred* (*Montage*), its structure, rhythms, and phrasing are influenced by jazz,* but more than that, it was also written as a performance piece: All twelve free-verse sections—or poems within the poem—are printed all in capital letters, with extensive marginal notes to the right, in italics, giving specific directions regarding musical accompaniment. The whole poem is preceded by the printed music (treble clef) of the traditional blues* song "Hesitation Blues" in the key of F. Following these bars of music, Hughes describes the song as the "leitmotif" of the poem and indicates that the marginal notes in the text assume that musicians accompanying the reading of the poem will improvise extensively, "where the voice pauses." Then the eight-note "figurine" of "Shave and a Haircut," popularized in vaudeville, is also printed (treble clef, key of C). Whereas one major organizing principle of *Montage* is the image-collage, a major organizing principle of *AYM* is repetition of phrases (such as "IN THE QUARTER OF THE NEGROES") and allusions to individuals (such as Hughes himself, George Schuyler,* Arna Bontemps,* African leader Jomo Kenyatta, Harlem's U.S. congressman Adam Clayton Powell, singer Dinah Washington, and so on). Titles of the twelve "moods" are "Cultural Exchange," "Ride, Red, Ride," "Shades of Pigmeat," "Ode to Dinah" (that is, singer Dinah Washington, 1924–1963), "Blues in Stereo," "Horn of Plenty," "Gospel Cha-Cha," "Is It True?" "Ask Your Mama," "Bird in Orbit" (referring, in part, to jazz musician Charlie "Bird" Parker, 1920–1955), "Jazztet Muted," and "Show Fare, Please."

The phrase "Ask Your Mama" comes from "the dozens," also known as "the dirty dozens," a kind of game of wordplay, improvised insults, and "one-upmanship" common to working-class, urban, African American neighborhoods and participated in chiefly by young black men. Major notes that "the participants insult each other's relatives—in twelve censures—especially their mothers. The object of the game is to test emotional strength. The first person to give in to anger is the loser" (138). Consequently, Hughes's choice of twelve "moods" is at least partially due to the twelve censures of "the dozens." Major links "the dirty dozens" to the period 1900–1950, but such wordplay still persists in, for example, the form of "trash talk" in athletics. As Major, Gates, and others have suggested, "the dozens" is one example of a broader oral tradition of verbal improvisation known as "Signifying," a term that should not be confused with "signifying," used by structuralist literary theorists. Major defines "Signifying" succinctly as "performance talk" and, more broadly, as "speaking ironically" (416). Gates cites *AYM* as one example of a literary text influenced by the oral tradition of Signifying. Like another of Hughes's long poems, "Prelude to Our Age," *AYM* is at once immediate (or topical) and historical, although the allusions in the latter are sometimes more difficult than those in the former. Recognizing this and, as always, attentive to his audience,* Hughes included "Liner Notes" (a reference to printed remarks accompanying a sound recording) corresponding to each section of *AYM*, explaining some allusions and encapsulating some of his rhetorical and thematic purposes. (The editors of *Collected Poems* provide even more detailed explanatory notes.) Although *AYM* does indeed represent a spectrum of moods, it is by and large a denser, more cynical work than *Montage*, and it often points to the violence and oppression Hughes believes African Americans and persons of color worldwide are forced still to confront. Rampersad suggests that "in 1960 [when he began to write *AYM*], Langston felt for America not the sentimental idealism that mainly had inspired his Depression plea but flaring rage and a mocking, sardonic contempt for the national history of racism and lies" (II, 316). Nonetheless, the poem is also full of celebration, wit, and wry (as well as biting) humor (in keeping with the influence of "the dozens"), and it is Hughes's most thoroughly jazz-inspired work, not least of all in its phrasing, rhythms, and points of reference. *See* The Blues; *National Poetry Festival*; "A New Kind of Dozens."

Bibliography/Discography: Henry Louis Gates, Jr., *The Signifying Monkey: A Theory of Afro-American Literary Criticism* (New York: Oxford University Press, 1988); Patricia A. Johnson and Walter C. Farrell, Jr., "The Jazz Poetry of Langston Hughes: A Reflection," *Minority Voices: An Interdisciplinary Journal* 4, no. 1 (Spring 1980), 11–21; Clarence Major, "Dirty Dozens, The" and "Signifying," in *Juba to Jive: A Dictionary of African-American Slang* (New York: Penguin, 1994), 138, 416; R. Baxter Miller, "Framing and Framed Languages in Hughes's *Ask Your Mama: 12 Moods for Jazz,*" *MELUS: The Journal of the Society for the Study of the Multi-Ethnic Literature of the United States* 17, no. 4 (Winter 1991–1992), 3–13; Charlie Parker, *The Complete Live Performances* [sound recording] (New York: Savoy, 1998): 4 compact discs; Rampersad, II, 312–318; Dinah Washington, *Smoke Gets in Your Eyes* [sound recording] (London: Recall, 1999): box set, 2 compact discs.

"Ask Your Mama." Poem. *See Ask Your Mama.*

"Aspiration." Whimsical two-stanza, rhymed poem, first published in the *Carmel Pine Cone* (March 7, 1941). Two aspirations are identified: to do a cartwheel and to walk a tightrope. The poem was also included in *Shakespeare in Harlem*. Bibliography: *CP*, 225.

Associated Negro Press. *See* "America's Young Black Joe."

"At the Feet o' Jesus." Song, based on the poem "Feet o' Jesus." Two composers each wrote different music for the words. ASCAP* lists "At the Feet *o'* Jesus" (emphasis mine) as having music written by Florence Price; the registry number for this version is 310293028. Southern Music Company is the publisher. It lists "At the Feet *of* Jesus" (emphasis mine) as having music written by Toy Harper; the registry number for this version is 310234261, with the publisher listed as Carl Fischer.

"Atomic Age." Short story, included in the collection *Simple Stakes a Claim*. *See* Simple [Jesse B.] Stories.

"Atomic Dream." Short story, included in the collection *Simple's Uncle Sam*. *See* Simple [Jesse B.] Stories.

Attucks, Crispus. *See* "America"; "Dark Youth of the U.S.A."

Audience. The rhetorical concept of "audience"—referring to the intended, imagined, and actual readers of texts or listeners to speech—is an especially interesting topic to consider in relation to Hughes's writing. First, historical, social, and personal circumstances virtually guaranteed that for Hughes "audience" would almost always be a complex matter. Like most African Americans, he necessarily experienced what W.E.B. Du Bois* labeled "double-consciousness"— that is, the simultaneous awareness of oneself and the awareness of oneself as an African American in a white-dominated society. Arguably, he experienced this double-consciousness more acutely because he was a writer, insofar as writers seek audiences in very particular ways. Second, he was born in the American

Midwest, experienced aspects of both working-class and middle-class life, and was exposed both to Jim Crow* social strictures and to ostensibly more equitable social arrangements (such as an integrated high school). Therefore, he viewed both the American rural South and the industrialized North from the perspective of a nonnative, even if, later in life, he would embrace Harlem* as his literal and spiritual home. Third, he participated in the Harlem Renaissance,* which, for a writer, featured its own complex, sometimes-contradictory set of messages: It was a natural development springing from the northern migration of African Americans and from improved economic conditions, but at the same time it was a contrived cultural project advanced by "the Talented Tenth"* and heavily influenced by wealthy white Americans. In some cases, the art and writing of the Harlem Renaissance examined and celebrated more or less authentic aspects of African American culture and history; in other cases, it trivialized, exploited, distorted, or ignored them; in still other cases, it attempted to avoid such a dichotomy. Indeed, Hughes's essay "The Negro Artist and the Racial Mountain" explicitly addresses the question of what is "authentic" African American culture and the question of how African American writers might perceive and represent such culture. Finally, like most writers—and most humans—Hughes changed; his concept of "self" evolved; he refined and revised his notion of what being a writer means, even if some elements of "self" and "writer" remained constant.

All of these circumstances and others bore directly on Hughes's ideas of audience—of the real and imagined persons to whom and for whom he wrote poems, plays, stories, essays, speeches, and other works. For instance, early in his career Hughes decided that the everyday experiences and language of African Americans were compelling material for literature, as evidenced by the stance he articulated in "The Negro Artist and the Racial Mountain." In announcing and adhering to this stance, however, Hughes put himself in opposition to black readers and critics who desired literature that was more refined, more in keeping with the tenets of an Anglo-American literary tradition; also, he ran the risk of alienating white readers and critics (Sherwood Anderson* being one representative example) who would believe that he was not writing to them; and even white readers who ostensibly supported his work might ultimately recoil from it if the African American experience it represented included portrayals of vicious white racism or of topics deemed, a priori, too vulgar. (His patron Mrs. Charlotte Osgood Mason* is one representative example of such an audience.) The situation appears even more labyrinthine when we recall that Hughes was no different from his contemporaries insofar as he naturally sought publication in what were accepted as the best literary magazines of the time, including *Poetry* or the *New Yorker*, not just in periodicals with primarily black audiences, such as *Crisis** or *Opportunity.** (The sheer range of periodicals in which Hughes published by itself dramatizes the variety of audiences he negotiated in his career; *see* Periodicals in Which Hughes Published.)

Hughes himself further complicated his relationship with audiences by adopting the role of spokesman-writer and teacher-writer (*see* Collective Persona). That is, at different times in his career, he wrote expressly to and for workers; he wrote verse about current issues for newspaper audiences; he wrote biographies and books on music for children. It is difficult to think of another American writer of Hughes's stature in the twentieth century who sought out such diverse audiences, and Hughes usually seemed well aware that what he wrote for one audience might damage his reputation with another. To some degree, the problem of audience for Hughes was complicated owing to forces beyond his control: his ethnic background, his historical moment. By the same token, he was responsible for complicating questions of audience because of what he chose to write about, how he wrote, and how he positioned himself as a writer in society. One choice he made was to try to make a living exclusively from his writing in an era that included the Great Depression and in which African American writers generally had more difficulty than white American writers. One of the first sentences of his second autobiographical book is "This is the story of a Negro who wanted to make his living from poems and stories" (*I Wonder As I Wander*, 3). Finally, the problem of audience became a multifaceted one for him because at times he refused to choose—that is, he refused to limit himself to one genre, or to one style, or to one "school" of writing, or to one carefully circumscribed readership. In any event, the question of audience with regard to Hughes is fascinating and often perplexing, and it is one that critics and scholars have hardly explored exhaustively. Moreover, one way of critiquing easy lables sometimes attached to Hughes, such as "blues* poet" or "folk poet," is to consider how many audiences he wrote for, the risks and problems he faced in doing so, and the cornucopia of genres and styles he used—and mastered—in reaching out to so many different kinds of readers. *See also* "America's Young Black Joe!"; Children's Poetry; "Lincoln Theatre."

Bibliography: François Dodat, "Situation de Langston Hughes," *Présence Africaine* 64 (1967), 47–50; C. K. Doreski, *Writing America Black: Race Rhetoric in the Public Sphere* (Cambridge: Cambridge University Press, 1998); Rena Fraden, "The Unpredictable Audience" (chapter 4), in *Blueprints for a Black Federal Theatre, 1935–1939* (Cambridge: Cambridge University Press, 1994), 136–167; *I Wonder As I Wander*; Ostrom, 69–79.

Audio Recordings of Hughes. *See The Beat Generation; The Glory of Negro History; Jerico-Jim Crow; Langston Hughes Reads and Talks about His Poetry; Langston Hughes Reads: "One-Way Ticket," "The Negro Speaks of Rivers," "Ku Klux Klan," and Other Poems; Langston Hughes: The Dream Keeper; National Poetry Festival; Poetry by Sterling Brown; Simple: Seven Stories from "The Best of Simple" and "Simple's Uncle Sam"; The Story of Jazz; Tambourines to Glory* [sound recording]; *The Voice of Langston Hughes: Selected Poetry and Prose; The Weary Blues* [sound recording]; *Writers of the Revolution. See also The Best of Simple*; NAACP.

"August 19." Poem, subtitled "A Poem for Clarence Norris," first published in the *Daily Worker* (June 28, 1938). A long polemical poem in free verse, "August 19" was intended, according to notes accompanying it (*see Collected Poems*), to be read at meetings or rallies concerning the fate of the Scottsboro Boys,* of whom Norris was one. Oddly enough, the persona Hughes adopts is that of Norris himself, and the title refers to the date Norris was to die in Alabama's electric chair; his sentence was later commuted to life in prison. *See also* "Ballad of Ozie Powell."

Bibliography: *CP*, 204, 647.

Aunt Clew. A woman mentioned in the poem "Young Gal's Blues."

Aunt Hager. *See Not Without Laughter.*

"Aunt Sue's Stories." Free-verse poem, first published in *Crisis** (July 1921), then in *The Weary Blues*. The poem evokes an oral, familial tradition in which older relatives tell younger ones stories. The stories have to do as much with African American history, the poem suggests, as with personal anecdotes. In *The Big Sea* Hughes fondly recalls being read to and told stories by his maternal grandmother, who may have served as the original for the fictional Aunt Sue. *See* "Grandpa's Stories"; Women in Hughes's Writing.

Bibliography: *CP*, 23.

Autobiographies. *See The Big Sea; I Wonder As I Wander.*

"An Auto-Obituary." Short story, included in *The Best of Simple*. *See* Simple [Jesse B.] Stories.

"Autumn Note." Brief lyric poem using cliché images of autumn and slightly antique diction. Hughes published it in the *Messenger* (September 1926) under the mildly parodic pseudonym J. Crutchfield Thompson, so the poem itself was probably intended as a send-up of derivative magazine verse. *See* Dane, Earl; "Poem d'Automne"; "Signs of Spring."

Bibliography: *CP*, 74.

"Autumn Thought." Five-line poem comparing withered, wind-blown flowers to small brown butterflies. It was first published in *Brownie's Book** (November 1921). *See* Children's Poetry.

Bibliography: *CP*, 600.

"Awe." Poem. *See* "Two Somewhat Different Epigrams."

Azikiwe, Benjamin. *See* "Azikiwe in Jail."

"Azikiwe in Jail." Poem in two ballad* quatrains that imagines a dialogue between "the British" (colonialists) and (Benjamin) Azikiwe, who was an anti-colonial political leader in Nigeria during the 1950s and who became the first president of that nation after it gained independence in 1960. The poem was first published in *Lincoln University Poets*,* edited by Waring Cuney. *See* "Draftees"; "Lincoln University: 1954."

Bibliography: *CP*, 445, 677; Waring Cuney, ed., *Lincoln University Poets: Centennial Anthology: 1854–1954* (New York: Fine Editions Press, 1954), 29.

B

"Baby." Short poem preserving a slice of Harlem* dialect spoken by a mother warning her young son, Albert, not to play in the street. It was first published in *Fine Clothes to the Jew*.

Bibliography: *CP*, 120.

Back to Africa. A shorthand term for an African American political movement of the early twentieth century; leaders of and participants in this movement generally believed that racist barriers in the United States would perpetually block the social and economic advancement of African Americans, and therefore that resettling in Africa offered a more sensible alternative to remaining in the United States. *See* Garvey, Marcus.

"The Backlash Blues." Poem of about one page in blues* form but, as the title suggests, focused on politics—specifically, the backlash against gains made by African Americans and other disenfranchised groups during the civil-rights movement. The poem reveals that Hughes saw disproportionately racially divided communities and low wages for blacks, for instance, as evidence of such a backlash. In the poem he adopts a collective persona*—an "I" who is "Brown, Black, Beige, Yellow" and who is speaking "to" another symbolic figure, "Mr. Backlash." Believed to be the last poem Hughes submitted for publication before his death, it was first published posthumously in *Crisis** (June 1967) but was probably written as early as 1966, when it was also turned into a song, music for which was composed by Nina Simone. ASCAP* lists the song as being published by the Rolls Royce Music Company and EMI/Waterford, Inc. The ASCAP registry number is 310234261.

Bibliography: *CP*, 552; Rampersad, II, 354.

"Bad Luck Card." Three-stanza poem in modified ballad* form, with explicit use of black dialect.* The speaker is "weary" and brokenhearted, having visited a Gypsy who, after reading "the cards," advised the man that his lover does not love him anymore. The poem was first published under the title "Hard Luck" in *Opportunity** (October 1926).
Bibliography: *CP*, 78.

"Bad Man." Three-stanza poem in basic blues* form in which the speaker confesses how bad he is, going so far as to admit to beating his wife. First published in *Fine Clothes to the Jew*, the poem exemplifies the ways in which that book deliberately examined unsavory aspects of African American urban culture, an examination that drew a harsh response from many critics but that also demonstrated Hughes's independence and his way of viewing topics, subjects, and themes from a variety of perspectives.
Bibliography: *CP*, 112.

"Bad Morning." Four-line poem, lines two and four rhyming. The speaker's shoes don't fit. First published in *One-Way Ticket*.
Bibliography: *CP*, 365.

Baez, Joan (born 1941). American folksinger and political activist. Hughes wrote liner notes for Baez's fifth recorded album of songs, *Joan Baez/5*, which was released in October 1964 by Vanguard Records. In the notes Hughes compares Baez's musical presence to Colorado mountains, "A peak alone yet planted here among us," and describes her voice as "cool as rippling water, clear as a mountain stream." He recalls meeting Baez at the Newport Jazz Festival in 1960 and assesses almost all of the songs on the recording individually. He also makes the point that although Baez sings songs from many cultures, she does not try to "be" someone from each culture but instead makes each song "her own." The recording contains a song entitled "Birmingham Sunday," also the title of a poem Hughes published, but the lyrics and music were written by Richard Farina and are not an adaptation of Hughes's poem. The album is now in compact-disc form (Vanguard 79160–2) and cassette form (Vanguard 79160–4). *See also My Lord What a Mornin'.*
Bibliography/Discography: Langston Hughes, "Joan Baez: A Tribute," liner notes for *Joan Baez/5* [compact disc] (Santa Monica, CA: Vanguard Records): VMD 79160.

Baldwin, James (1924–1987). American novelist, playwright, and essayist. Baldwin was born and grew up in Harlem,* publishing his first novel, *Go Tell It on the Mountain*, in 1953. His other novels include *Giovanni's Room* (1956), *Tell Me How Long the Train's Been Gone* (1968), and *If Beale Street Could Talk* (1974). His books of nonfiction include *Notes of a Native Son* (1955), *The Fire Next Time* (1963), and *The Price of the Ticket* (1985). Two of Baldwin's plays, *The Amen Corner* and *Blues for Mister Charlie*, were produced on Broadway. Baldwin is generally considered to be one of the most important American writers of the twentieth century, chiefly because of his sustained, complex, and articulate analysis of race relations in the United States, an analysis that cuts across the several genres in which he worked and that is similar to the critique Hughes developed in his writing, at least insofar as it contemplates and represents sexual, religious, and economic factors bearing on racial conflict. Although Baldwin's stature as a novelist is considerable, it will probably always be overshadowed by his achievement in nonfiction. The essays in *The Fire Next Time* constitute a monumental achievement in American nonfiction writing of the twentieth century. Baldwin published a harsh review of Hughes's *Selected Poems*, indicating that he was "amazed" by "how little" Hughes had done with his talent. Rampersad (II, 295) indicates that in the review Baldwin may have been seeking revenge for what he perceived to be an ambivalent review by Hughes of his book of essays, *Notes of a Native Son* (*see* "*Notes of a Native Son*"). Rampersad also discusses generational differences between the two writers that may have affected the review, and he notes that some years later Baldwin expressed regret about his review of *Selected Poems of Langston Hughes*, going so far as to say that he "hadn't really read the book, to tell the truth" (Rampersad, II, 299). Baldwin appears in the *Voices and Visions* (*see Langston Hughes: Dream Keeper*) television documentary about Hughes, commenting particularly on what he perceived to be Hughes's existential "weariness."

Bibliography: James Baldwin, interview with Arnold Rampersad, quoted in Rampersad, II, 299; James Baldwin, "*Selected Poems of Langston Hughes*" [review], *New York Times Book Review* (March 29, 1959), p. 6, col. 1; James Campbell, *Talking at the Gates: A Life of James Baldwin* (New York: Viking, 1991); *Langston Hughes: The Dream Keeper* [videorecording], *Voices and Visions* [6], South Carolina Educational Television Network, 1988, a New York Center for Visual History Production, directed by St. Clair Bourne, produced by Robert Chapman; Quincy Troupe, ed., *James Baldwin: The Legacy* (New York: Simon and Schuster, 1989).

"A Ball of String." Short story, included in the collection *Simple Speaks His Mind. See* Simple [Jesse B.] Stories.

Ballad. *The Collected Poems of Langston Hughes* contains twenty-five poems with "ballad" in the title, and Hughes used the form in many other poems not so explicitly titled. Hughes often modified the form, which is traditionally a short narrative poem or love poem in quatrains rhymed ABCB, often employing iambic trimeter or tetrameter. In some ballads, for example, Hughes "stretched" the quatrains to as many as seven lines by shortening lines. He used some ballads traditionally—to tell a story or to write about love. In others he shifted the mode from narrative or lyric to dramatic, creating speakers who are characters distinct from a third-person narrator, who is often the controlling voice in a traditional ballad. Sometimes Hughes also wrote ballads in black dialect.* Finally, instead of focusing on traditionally lyrical subjects, such as love, he addressed political or social issues—although it is worth noting that some ballads from long ago can also be characterized as "political," and that ballads from the folk-music revival in the United States and elsewhere in the 1960s expressed political views (*see* Baez, Joan). Arguably the most traditional element in Hughes's ballads is their rhetoric, specifically their sense of audience.* In these poems Hughes speaks directly and simply to "the common folk": readers who may not have had extensive literary background but who would have seen themselves, or at least their concerns, in the poems, and who would not have encountered complicated poetic techniques, difficult allusions, or dense language. Indeed, a number of these ballads were first published in newspapers, as opposed to literary magazines. Although Hughes's technical modifications of the ballad form were often deceptively sophisticated, his sense of audience was a throwback to the oral tradition out of which ballads sprang, a tradition predating the poetry of William Wordsworth, whose *Lyrical Ballads* (1798) ostensibly used relatively ordinary language but were, in fact, aimed at a rather sophisticated audience. Although Wordsworth's experiments with ballads are far more renowned in literary history than Hughes's, Hughes was actually even more determined than Wordsworth to "speak to" a nontraditional literary audience. At any rate, it is fair to suggest that in no other works does Hughes position himself more fully as the unofficial poet laureate of African Americans and of working people of all ethnic backgrounds than in the ballads. *See also Lorca: Gypsy Ballads*; Songs.

Bibliography: Alan Norman Bold, *The Ballad* (New York: Methuen, 1979); John Avery Lomax and Alan Lomax, *American Ballads and Folk Songs* (New York: Macmillan, 1934); Ron Padgett, "Ballad," in *A Handbook of Poetic Forms* (New York: Teachers and Writers Collaborative, 1987), 17–20; *PEPP*.

"Ballad of Adam and Eve." Song. Hughes wrote the lyrics, and Elie Siegmeister, with whom Hughes briefly collaborated on an opera that never materialized (*Wizard of Altoona*), composed the music. ASCAP* lists the song as being published by Carl Fischer, Inc. The ASCAP registry number is 320338943. *See* Ballad.

"The Ballad of Booker T." As in "Alabama Earth," in this poem Hughes, whose politics were generally less conciliatory and often more radical than those of Booker T. Washington,* puts aside his own views to a degree and presents positively Washington's ethos of practicality and clearheadedness. The poem was first published in *Common Sense Historical Review* (May 1953). *See* Ballad.
Bibliography: *CP*, 445, 669.

"Ballad of Gin Mary." Six-stanza ballad,* narrated by "Mary," who laments that she must go to jail again for public drunkenness. The ballad was first published in *Fine Clothes to the Jew*. *See* "Bad Man."
Bibliography: *CP*, 114.

"Ballad of Harry Moore." Twenty-stanza ballad,* with a concluding couplet; a third-person narrator describes the murder of NAACP* activist Harry Moore, whose house was firebombed on December 25, 1951, in Mims, Florida. Moore was in Florida representing the NAACP in the Groveland Case, which is briefly described in *Collected Poems*. The ballad was circulated by the Associated Negro Press in 1952. *See* "America's Young Black Joe."
Bibliography: *CP*, 588, 694.

"Ballad of Little Sallie." This ballad* is actually a dialogue poem concerning the courtship of "Jimmy" and "Little Sallie." Jimmy speaks in quatrains one and four; Little Sallie, in quatrain three. Deftly, Hughes gives the characters two lines each in quatrain two. The ballad was first published in *Opportunity** (December 1940).
Bibliography: *CP*, 222.

"The Ballad of Margie Polite." Ballad* of thirteen quatrains, though the last two are "stretched." With a light tone, the poem narrates the true story of one Margie Polite, who quarreled with a policeman in Harlem on August 1, 1943. A black soldier stepped in on Polite's behalf; the policeman shot him. A riot ensued in which four citizens were killed, four hundred injured. The soldier recovered from the gunshot wound. The ballad was first published in the *Amsterdam News* (October 2, 1943).
Bibliography: *CP*, 282, 650; Rampersad, II, 75–76.

"Ballad of Mary's Son." Modified ballad* in four stanzas of seven lines each; the last two lines of the last stanza are broken off to stand alone. Insofar as the poem narrates straightforwardly the crucifixion and resurrection of "Mary's Son" (Christ is not mentioned by name), the poem is unusual for the notoriously areligious, skeptical Hughes, though of course the poem does not necessarily reflect Hughes's personal religious views. The poem was included in the musical play *Black Nativity*. *See* Religion.
Bibliography: *CP*, 462.

"A Ballad of Negro History." Subtitled "(So Much to Write About)." Poem of about two pages in traditional ballad* form, except that Hughes leaves no additional space between the quatrain units. The history covered stretches from the pharaohs to Countee Cullen* and Ralph Bunche, with "My race!" repeated twice to conclude the poem. The poem was first published in *Negro History Bulletin* (February 1952).
Bibliography: *CP*, 434, 676.

"Ballad of Ozie Powell." Poem of eight stanzas that modifies the ballad* form by rhyming lines one and three and using lines two and four to repeat "Ozie

Powell" as a kind of chant. Powell was one of the defendants in the Scottsboro trial.* He was convicted and sentenced to be executed in 1932, but the U.S. Supreme Court, in *Powell v. Alabama*, granted his appeal, citing inadequate counsel. The poem is addressed to Powell, refers to the Alabama sheriff in Scottsboro as "The Law's a Klansman with an evil will," and refers to the U.S. Supreme Court as "Nine old men so rich and wise." The poem was first published in *American Spectator* (April 1936). *See Collected Poems* for notes on an omitted stanza. *See also* "August 19."

Bibliography: *CP*, 188, 645.

"Ballad of Rabbi Henry Cohen." Song. Hughes wrote the lyrics, and Tom Glazer composed the music. ASCAP* lists the song as being published by Songs Music, Inc. The song's ASCAP registry number is 320011750. *See* Ballad.

"Ballad of Roosevelt." Eight-stanza poem in which a refrain is added to the traditional ballad* quatrain. The refrain is "A-waitin' on Roosevelt / Roosevelt, Roosevelt," or slight variations thereof. The poem was first published in the *New Republic* in 1934 (November 14), when Franklin Delano Roosevelt* was in his first term as president and his New Deal policies and other factors had not yet brought substantial relief from the Great Depression. Hence the speaker of the poem is "damn tired o' waitin' on Roosevelt." *See* "Crow Goes, Too"; "Dear Mr. President"; "403 Blues"; "Judge William Hastie."

Bibliography: *CP*, 178–179; John B. Kirby, *Black Americans in the Roosevelt Era: Liberalism and Race* (Knoxville: University of Tennessee Press, 1980).

"Ballad of Sam Solomon." Poem of over one page in traditional ballad* form, except that Hughes included no extra space between quatrains. The poem concerns Samuel Johnson, an NAACP* organizer, who defied an open Ku Klux Klan* threat and led over a thousand African American voters to the polls in Miami in May 1939. The poem was first published in *Jim Crow's Last Stand*.

Bibliography: *CP*, 295.

"Ballad of the Black Sheep." Four-stanza ballad* in which the fourth quatrain is "stretched" to six lines, followed by a concluding line, set off: "Help me, Jesus!" The poem is spoken by a wandering man who contrasts himself unfavorably with his stay-at-home brother. The poem was first published in the *Baltimore Afro American** (August 16, 1941).

Bibliography: *CP*, 569–570.

Ballad of the Brown King (1960). Cantata. Margaret Bonds* composed some music for the piece, which chiefly included traditional gospel songs in the public domain (not copyrighted, that is). Hughes wrote the brief text, which relates the story of the dark-skinned member of the three Magi—or Kings or Wise Men—

from the biblical tale of Christ's birth. One implicit premise of the piece is that the histories of Christianity, Africans, and African Americans are significantly intertwined. The cantata was first produced at the Clark Auditorium of the New York YMCA on December 11, 1960. The following year it was produced by the East Side Development Organization of New York City. Hughes and Bonds dedicated the work to Dr. Martin Luther King, Jr. Some of the musical and textual material of *Ballad of the Brown King* was later used in *Black Nativity*, which was produced more often and drew far more critical acclaim than its predecessor. ASCAP* lists the cantata as being published by Fox Sam Publishing Company, Inc., and the ASCAP registry number is 320011910. It also lists separately the song from *Ballad of the Brown King* "Mary Had a Little Baby," with lyrics by Hughes and music by Bonds, also published by Fox Sam Publishing Company, Inc., ASCAP registry number 430388799. *See* Religion.

Bibliography: Bernard L. Peterson, Jr., *Contemporary Black American Playwrights and Their Plays: A Biographical Directory and Dramatic Index* (Westport, CT: Greenwood Press, 1988).

"Ballad of the Fool." Four-stanza poem in traditional ballad* form, expressing envy toward the fool who is unaware of the world's troubles. The poem was first published in the *Baltimore Afro American** (May 17, 1941).

Bibliography: *CP*, 567.

"Ballad of the Fortune Teller." Eight-stanza poem in traditional ballad* form; the poem turns on the irony of one "Madam" being able to tell others' fortunes but not to predict that a man, "Dave," will do her wrong, even when her friends warn her about him. Whether this "Madam" is the same as the figure featured in "the Madam poems"* remains ambiguous. The poem was first published in *Shakespeare in Harlem*. Later it was turned into a song, with music composed by Albert Hague. ASCAP* lists no publisher for the song, but the ASCAP registry number is 320011965. *See* Ballad. *See also* "Fortune Teller Blues."

Bibliography: *CP*, 255.

"Ballad of the Girl Whose Name Is Mud." Poem in four ballad* stanzas. It concerns a young woman named Dorothy who has an affair with "a no-good man," gets pregnant, is shunned, but is not contrite. The poem was first published in *Shakespeare in Harlem*.

Bibliography: *CP*, 256.

"Ballad of the Gypsy." Poem in five ballad* stanzas, with a concluding couplet, and a one-line interjection (*"Aw, what a lie!"*) between stanzas three and four. The first-person narrator recounts visiting a gypsy fortune teller and asking when his "gal" will return. The gypsy predicts his companion will return "soon," but the narrator believes the fortune teller is lying. The poem was first published in *Shakespeare in Harlem. See* "Madam and the Fortune Teller."

Bibliography: *CP*, 256–257.

"Ballad of the Killer Boy." Seven-stanza poem in traditional ballad* form; the last stanza is broken and "stretched" to five lines. The poem is spoken by a young man who robs a bank in order to satisfy his girlfriend's material desires, which include wanting to own a Packard automobile. In the robbery he kills a guard, is tried, convicted, and sentenced to death, and blames his girlfriend for his fate. The poem was first published in *Shakespeare in Harlem.*

Bibliography: *CP*, 254.

"Ballad of the Landlord." Poem. *See Montage of a Dream Deferred.*

"Ballad of the Man Who's Gone." Seven-stanza poem in traditional ballad* form, first published in *Shakespeare in Harlem.* It describes the difficulties a deceased man's family has trying to pay for his funeral.

Bibliography: *CP*, 258.

"Ballad of the Miser." Short, light poem in ballad* form but with no extra space between quatrains. The miser not only hoards his money but wills it to no one. The poem was first published in *Opportunity** (December 1940).

Bibliography: *CP*, 221–222.

"Ballad of the Pawnbroker." Poem in the form of a modified ballad* with many extremely short lines, first published in *Shakespeare in Harlem.* The poem is a dramatic monologue, spoken by a customer to the pawnbroker, "Mr. Levy." The customer is disappointed by the prices offered for the goods he wishes to pawn and concludes by asking what his "self" is worth.

Bibliography: *CP*, 257.

"Ballad of the Seven Songs." Subtitled "A Poem for Emancipation Day," this is a long free-verse poem (hence not a traditional ballad*) celebrating the emancipation of African American slaves and continuing struggles for civil rights. Hughes links seven figures from African American history with seven folk songs crucial to that history. The figures are Cudjoe, a Jamaican slave who led a revolt; Harriet Tubman and Sojourner Truth, organizers of the Underground Railroad, which helped guide African American slaves to freedom; Frederick Douglass*; Booker T. Washington*; George Washington Carver*; and pioneering American athlete Jackie Robinson. The songs are "Jordan River," "Freedom (Before I'd be a Slave)," "Go Down, Moses," "John Brown's Body," "Battle Hymn of the Republic," "De Cotton Needs Pickin'," and "John Henry." Hughes interweaves lyrics from the songs with his own text. The poem was first published in *Common Ground* (1949). *See* "Love."

Bibliography: *CP*, 343; John Avery Lomax and Alan Lomax, *American Ballads and Folk Songs* (New York: Macmillan, 1934).

"Ballad of the Sinner." Five-stanza poem in traditional ballad* form, narrated by a young man who sees himself going down the "road to Hell," first published in *Shakespeare in Harlem*. A separate, single line ends the poem.

Bibliography: *CP*, 253.

"Ballad of the Two Thieves." Seven-stanza poem in traditional ballad* form, wherein Hughes retells the story of Christ's crucifixion and of the two thieves crucified with him. The poem was first published in *Shenandoah* (Winter 1955).

Bibliography: *CP*, 439.

"The Ballad of Walter White." Short ballad,* rhymed traditionally but with no extra space between quatrains. The poem focuses on the light skin color of the African American civil-rights leader Walter White,* on his ability to "pass" as Caucasian, and most especially on his use of "passing" to investigate lynching* in the South. The poem was first published in the *Baltimore Afro American** (June 28, 1941).

Bibliography: *CP*, 567.

"Ballads of Lenin." Poem of seven quatrains, in which stanzas one, three, five, and seven serve as a kind of refrain in which "Comrade" Vladimir Lenin is urged to "move over" in his tomb to make way for workers; stanzas two, four, and six are spoken, respectively, by Ivan (a Russian peasant), Chico (a black sugar-cane cutter), and Chang (a Chinese foundry worker). The choice of speakers implies that issues of class transcend national boundaries, that such workers are as crucial to the proletarian revolution as its chief architect, and that at this particular moment of his career, Hughes was in his most sympathetic posture toward a Marxist analysis of economic ills. The poem was first published in *Proletarian Literature in the United States* (1935). *See also Angelo Herndon Jones*; "Chant for Tom Mooney"; *Don't You Want to Be Free?*; "Goodbye, Christ"; "Good Morning, Revolution"; "Lenin"; "A New Song"; "One More 'S' in the U.S.A."; "Revolution"; "Song of the Revolution"; "Wait." *See also* John Reed Club; Marxism; Politics.

Bibliography: *CP*, 183; Granville Hicks, ed., *Proletarian Literature in the United States* (New York: International, 1935), 165.

Baltimore Afro American. Newspaper for which Hughes covered the Spanish Civil War in 1937 and that also published several of his poems. The *Afro American* was established in 1892 by the Reverend William Alexander of Sharon

Baptist Church; the first issue, four pages long, appeared on August 13. The weekly was founded in part to address the concerns and meet the interests of Baltimore's large African American population, which totaled at least 25,000 as early as 1860. The *Afro American* grew out of an earlier weekly edited by Alexander, the *National Home Protector*. Founding investors of the *Afro American* included William H. Daly, George W. Reid, V. E. Toney, and F. A. Gains, all Baltimore businesspersons. From the beginning, the paper focused on fighting racism and identifying social and political issues it deemed important to African Americans in Baltimore and nationwide. However, as Hayward Farrar has observed, the *Afro American* practiced sensational journalism (covering crime and scandal in exaggerated ways), particularly in the 1920s and 1930s, in part to appeal to working-class blacks (Farrar, xiv–xv, 7–16). Partly because of sensationalism's appeal, but also because of solid management, the paper survived the Great Depression. Between 1930 and 1940 the paper's circulation grew from about 45,000 to nearly 105,000, and it also added outlets in Pittsburgh, Pennsylvania, Washington, D.C., and Richmond, Virginia, where local stories were integrated into the national edition published in Baltimore.

Hughes published numerous poems in the *Afro American* during his career (*see* "America's Young Black Joe!"), but especially in the 1940s, when he seemed to want to reach a broad audience with several accessible, plainspoken poems in support of U.S. involvement in World War II. However, Hughes's most significant contributions to the paper were his articles about the Spanish Civil War. On August 28, 1937, before his series of articles started, the newspaper ran a notice, "Hughes to Speak from Spain," which announced that "Langston Hughes will be one of the three colored Americans to speak over short-wave radio, over station EAR, direct from Madrid, at 6:30 p.m., Eastern Standard Time" (2). The broadcast began in September. The other speakers were Harry Haywood, "Communist leader," and Walter Gardner, "machine gunner of the Abraham Lincoln Battalion, who was twice wounded." On October 23, 1937, Hughes's first article appeared under the main page-one headline, "Hughes Bombed in Spain." Next to the article and a photograph of Hughes appeared the announcement "Exclusive!!! From war-torn Spain, Langston Hughes, celebrated American novelist and poet, brings exclusively to *Afro American* readers a vivid and accurate picture of the bitter struggle that is now going on. This interesting series and accompanying photos will appear only in the *Afro American*." The subheadlines for the article are "Tells of Terror of Fascist Raid" and "Women, Children Huddled in Fear as Bombs Explode." In the article, Hughes describes his journey by train to Barcelona, accompanied by other Americans and by Cuban poet Nicolás Guillén.* He goes on to recount being awakened by antiaircraft gunfire when he was in his hotel and then hearing and seeing bombs explode near the hotel. He describes dressing quickly, going to Guillén's room, and accompanying Guillén and Guillén's wife outside to seek safer shelter, returning to the hotel in the early morning hours.

On October 30, 1937, a second article appeared with the headline "Hughes

Finds Moors Being Used as Pawns by Fascists in Spain" and with a subheadline, "Colored Sympathizers from Many Lands, However, Aiding People's Army; Oxcarts Still Used in Rural Areas." In this article Hughes writes, "Why had I come to Spain? To write for the colored press. I knew that Spain once belonged to the Moors, a colored people ranging from light dark to dark white. Now the Moors have come again to Spain with the fascist armies as cannon fodder for Franco." (In the poem "Letter from Spain" Hughes explores further the issue of Moors fighting on the side of Franco's forces.) On November 6, 1937, Hughes's article was given the headline " 'Organ Grinder's Swing' Heard above Gunfire in Spain—Hughes." Beside the article is a photograph of Hughes standing with "Captain Basilio Cueria, Cuban-American, N.Y.," a man identified only as "El Campesino, peasant military leader," and "Miss Louise Thompson of N.Y." The four appear to be standing in front of a hotel or other business establishment in Madrid. In the article Hughes writes, "All the colored people of whatever nationality to whom I've talked agree that there is not the slightest trace of color prejudice to be found [in Spain]." He goes on to report that the Cuban and Cuban American volunteers are "exhausted" and describes a conversation with a medical student from Spanish Guinea who has volunteered to fight on behalf of Loyalist forces. The student expresses his hope that if the Loyalists prevail, Spain's colonial relationship with some Latin American countries will improve. The headline concerns Hughes's general discovery that African American music, including recordings by Duke Ellington,* are popular in Spain and his particular report that during one battle he heard the song "Organ Grinder's Swing," as recorded by Jimmie Lunceford, being played in a nearby apartment. In his November 20, 1937, article, Hughes writes, "Time is with the people of Spain. Time, and the moral consciousness of the world." The headline for the article reads, "Madrid Getting Used to Bombing—It's Food Shortage That Hurts." Hughes goes on to write, "The Fascists who bomb women and children, who have put to death Garcia Lorca,* Spain's greatest poet, who deliberately rained explosives on the art museum of El Prado and on the National Library with its priceless books and manuscripts, who use churches for arsenals and bring Mohamedans to battle for 'a Christian ideal,' and who fight for no cause at all except for the forcing of the Spanish people back into economic and spiritual slavery for the sake of a handful of rich men and outworn nobles—these Fascists, Madrid feels, cannot win." In the article appearing on November 27, 1937, under the headline "Madrid's Flowers Hoist Blooms to Meet Raining Fascist Bombs," Hughes writes, "Ruined and lifeless cities are very sad. I've seen them in Mexico. I've seen what remained of Chaipai after the Japanese bombarded it in their attack on Chinese Shanghai some years ago. And lately I've seen Arguelles, that ruined section of Madrid proper." In his last article, appearing on December 18, 1937, under the headline "Soldiers from Many Lands United in Spanish Fight," Hughes writes, "Give Franco a hood and he would be a member of the Ku Klux Klan*—a kleagle. Fascism is what the Ku Klux Klan will be when it combines with the Liberty League and starts using machine guns and airplanes instead of a few yards of rope." He goes on to report that Franco's army includes volunteers from fascist countries such as Germany and Italy but observes that volunteers from those countries and from France, the United States, and Latin America have also joined the Loyalist side.

Hughes's "international" articles seem somewhat out of place in the *Afro American* because the paper focused on such national issues as antilynching legislation, Jim Crow laws,* and the controversial appointment of Hugo F. Black to the Supreme Court. (After President Franklin Roosevelt* nominated Black but before Congress approved the selection, Black's having once been a member of the Ku Klux Klan was revealed.) The paper also continued to run sensational crime stories, stories about black actors in Hollywood, local (Baltimore) stories, "society" stories, and sports stories, especially about Joe Louis* and other black boxers. Hughes's articles reveal the extent to which he perceived the Spanish Civil War in terms of race consciousness and racism worldwide, in terms of labor issues and Marxist politics, in terms of how the war affected ordinary Spanish citizens, and in connection with what he regarded as fascist tendencies in the United States that were expressed by white-supremacist organizations like the Ku Klux Klan. The articles mix personal narrative, travel writing, reportage, and opinion. *See also Cuba Libre: Poems by Nicolás Guillén*; "Hero—International Brigade"; "Letter from Spain"; Marxism; "Spain's Martyred Poet, García Lorca."

Bibliography: *Baltimore Afro American*: August 28, 1937, 2 ("Hughes to Speak from Spain"); October 23, 1937, 1 ("Hughes Bombed in Spain"); October 30, 1937, 1 ("Hughes Finds Moors Being Used as Pawns by Fascists in Spain"); November 6, 1937, 1 (" 'Organ Grinder's Swing' Heard above Gunfire in Spain—Hughes"); November 20, 1937, 3 ("Madrid Getting Used to Bombing—It's Food Shortage That Hurts"); November 27, 1937, 3 ("Madrid's Flowers Hoist Blooms to Meet Raining Fascist Bombs"); December 18, 1937, 9 ("Soldiers from Many Lands United in Spanish Fight"); Gerald T. Dunne, *Hugo Black and the Judicial Revolution* (New York: Simon and Schuster, 1977); Hayward Farrar, *The Baltimore Afro American, 1892–1950* (Westport, CT: Greenwood Press, 1998); Virginia Van der Veer Hamilton, *Hugo Black: The Alabama Years* (Baton Rouge: Louisiana State University Press, 1972); *I Wonder As I Wander*; Rampersad, I, chapter 13, "Earthquake Weather: 1937–1939," 341–372; Tinsley E. Yarbrough, *Mr. Justice Black and His Critics* (Durham: Duke University Press, 1988).

"Baltimore Womens" [*sic*]. Short story, included in the collection *Simple Takes a Wife. See* Simple [Jesse B.] Stories.

"Bang-up End." Short story, included in the collections *Simple Stakes a Claim* and *The Best of Simple. See* Simple [Jesse B.] Stories.

Banjo. Instrument used in blues* music. *See* "Song for a Banjo Dance."

"Banquet in Honor." Short story. The narrative centers on an African American artist who, at a banquet in his honor, drinks excessively and proceeds to attack (verbally) the hosts for not having supported his career when it most needed encouragement. The story was published in *Negro Quarterly* (1941). (*Negro Quarterly* was edited at the time by Angelo Herndon and Richard Wright.*) *See Angelo Herndon Jones.*

Bibliography: Rampersad, II, 30.

"Bar." Poem. *See Montage of a Dream Deferred.*

Baraka, Amiri (born 1934). American poet, playwright, essayist, and novelist. Baraka's original given name was Everett LeRoy Jones. He was born in Newark, New Jersey, and later changed his name to—and published earlier works as—LeRoi Jones. He changed his name to Amiri Baraka in 1967. Baraka was affiliated with the Beat movement, helping to establish the magazine *Yugen* in New York City in the late 1950s. His plays include *Dutchman* (1964), *The Slave* (1964), and *The Toilet* (1964). His volumes of poetry include *Preface to a Twenty-Volume Suicide Note* (1961) and *The Dead Lecturer* (1964). Among his writings on African American music is *The Music: Reflections on Jazz and Blues* (1987). This interest in blues* and jazz* is one link between Hughes and Baraka, as is their exploration of economic imbalance as a circumstance rivaling, even surpassing, racism as a destructive force in African American history. In an essay on Hughes, Baraka wrote, "Hughes's importance, and the strength of his work, lies exactly in the fact that he reflects in his best work the lives and concerns of the black majority. . . . The fact that Hughes was aggressively focused on Black life and speech in his work whether accusingly or humorously or sadly or ecstatically so meant that his work would always be judged by bourgeois critics of whatever skin color as lightweight. As 'Folksy.' " Rampersad discusses Hughes's ambivalent response to Baraka's early work.

Bibliography: Amiri Baraka, *Daggers and Javelins* (New York: Quill Books, 1984), 159, 161; Rampersad, II, 309–311, 375–376, 383–384.

"Barefoot Blues." Three-stanza poem in blues* form in which the speaker is a boy imploring his impoverished father to buy him shoes. The poem was first published as "Don't You See My Shoes?" in *Public Opinion* (Jamaica) (October 1948).

Bibliography: *CP*, 341.

Barnard College. *See* Columbia University.

Barnes, Albert Coombs (1872–1951). American entrepreneur, art collector, and philanthropist. Barnes's great wealth came from sales of an antiseptic, Argyrol, and he used much of that wealth to purchase paintings by Degas, Cézanne,

Seurat, Renoir, and Manet. He also supported the careers of Harlem Renaissance* painters Gwendolyn Bennett and Aaron Douglas, contributed to *Opportunity*,* and supported a vocational training center in New Jersey for African Americans. Although Barnes knew Alain Locke* and Walter White* well, Barnes and Hughes were only acquaintances.

Bibliography: Hutchinson, 44–46, 93, 425–427.

"Barrel House: Chicago." Poem. *See* "Juice Joint: Northern City."

The Barrier **(1950).** Opera. Hughes wrote the libretto, which is based on his play *Mulatto* and his short story "Father and Son." (Regarding the main characters and plot of the opera, see the entries for these works.) Jan Meyerowitz* composed the music. In an article, "From the Blues to an Opera Libretto," that appeared just before the opera debuted, Hughes discussed the origins of the play and short story as lying in his poem "Cross." He described *Mulatto*—and, by implication, *The Barrier*—as "a tragedy of a son's love for his father that turned to murder, caused his mother's madness and his own suicide. Its conflict was motivated by the barrier of race between them. There were no melodies with the spoken words, but I thought of it even then [as he began writing the play in 1929] as the possible basis for a musical drama." He went on to recall Meyerowitz's approaching him in 1948 about turning *Mulatto* into an opera and indicated that he was reluctant to write the libretto because "I had sworn never to have anything more to do with non-commercial theatre, since lecturing and teaching, I had found, met the demands of the landlord so much better." Nonetheless, he reported, Meyerowitz began working on the music, and Hughes ultimately agreed to write the libretto. Hughes recalled drawing up a collaboration agreement with the help of a lawyer (unnamed), who asked, "What, another opera?" To which Hughes remembered responding, "But this will be a very exciting one." *The Barrier* debuted on January 18, 1950, at Columbia University. Felix Brentano directed it. Willard Rhodes conducted the orchestra, and H. A. Condell designed the sets, with assistance from Roger Stevens. Muriel Rhan played the African American mother of Bert, who was played by Robert Gross. Bert's father was played by Paul Elmer. According to Rampersad, the opera "scored a stunning success"; he cites enthusiastic reviews that appeared in the *New York Times* (January 19, 1950), the *New York Herald-Tribune* (January 20, 1950), and *The New Yorker* (January 28, 1950), the latter review written by Virgil Thomson. ASCAP* lists no publisher for the opera, but *The Barrier*'s ASCAP registry number is 320404568. *See also Esther; Five Foolish Virgins; The Glory around His Head; Port Town.*

Bibliography: Langston Hughes, "From the Blues to an Opera Libretto," *New York Times* (January 15, 1950), sec. 2, p. 9, cols. 1–4; Siegmund Levarie, "Jan Meyerowitz," in *The New Grove Dictionary of Opera*, ed. Stanley Sadie and Christina Bashford (London: Macmillan, 1992), vol. 3, 371; Rampersad, II, 175–177.

"Battle Ground." Comic, rhyming poem featuring a dialogue between a soldier and a general, first published in *Amsterdam News* (August 9, 1942).
Bibliography: *CP*, 574.

"Battle Hymn of the Republic." American folk song. *See* "Ballad of the Seven Songs."

Battling Tom McCann. Name of the cat in the poem "Crowing Hen Blues."

"Be Broad-minded, Please!" Short story, included in the collection *Simple Stakes a Claim. See* Simple [Jesse B.] Stories.

"Beale Street." Short lyric poem evoking the nightlife in Harlem,* first published in *Fields of Wonder*.
Bibliography: *CP*, 326.

"Beale Street Love." Poem concerning a man hitting a woman with his fists. It is one example of how Hughes, in *Fine Clothes to the Jew*, presented unsettling, destructive aspects of blues* and jazz* culture in Harlem.* The poem was first published in *Palms* (November 1926). *See* "Evil Woman," which also concerns violence against women.
Bibliography: *CP*, 80.

The Beat Generation (Santa Monica, CA: Rhino Records/Word Beat, 1992). Sound recording on three compact discs. The collection includes Hughes and Leonard Feather reading/performing "Blues Montage." *See also* Audio Recordings.

"Beat It Out Monday." Song, from *Simply Heavenly*. Hughes wrote the lyrics, and David Martin composed the music. ASCAP* lists the song as being published by the Bourne Company, Inc. The ASCAP registry number is 320026511.

"Beaumont to Detroit: 1943." Poem of eight rhymed quatrains that highlights the irony of African Americans fighting Germany on behalf of the United States while still enduring Jim Crow laws* and other forms of racism. From late spring to early summer in 1943, several race riots occurred in the United States, including ones in Detroit, Michigan, and Beaumont, Texas. The poem was first published in *Common Ground* (August 1943).
Bibliography: *CP*, 281.

"Beauty." Three-line, rhyming, epigrammatic poem concerning how beauty received "Adulation" but not "care," first published in *Opportunity** (July 1938).
Bibliography: *CP*, 207.

Be-bop. *See* Jazz.

"Be-Bop Boys." Four-line poem. *See Montage of a Dream Deferred.*

"Bed Time." Poem, one of the seven separate parts of "Seven Moments of Love."

"Beggar Boy." Two-quatrain poem in which the speaker marvels at the moral resolve of a destitute boy on the street. It was first published in *Crisis** (September 1922).
Bibliography: *CP*, 29.

"Being Old." Poem spoken by a symbolic "we" representing all older people to younger people, who still believe (erroneously, the poem suggests) in the significance and endurance of material things. The poem was first published in *Crisis** (February 1927), when Hughes was twenty-five years old. *See* Collective Persona.
Bibliography: *CP*, 109.

Belafonte, Harry. *See My Lord What a Mornin'.*

The Belfry Owl. Literary magazine at Central High School* in Cleveland, Ohio, in which Hughes published writings.
Bibliography: *The Big Sea*, 26–30.

"Belles and Bells." Short story, included in the collection *Simple Takes a Wife.* *See* Simple [Jesse B.] Stories.

"Bells for John Whiteside's Daughter." Poem by American poet John Crowe Ransom.* *See* "Girl."

"The Bells Toll Kindly." Lyric poem written for the popular press and meditating on the passage of time. *See* "America's Young Black Joe!"
Bibliography: *CP*, 581.

"Beloved." Poem. *See* "Nonette."

Benow. Cornet player at the dance in chapter 8 of *Not Without Laughter. See* Mingo.

"Berry." Short story, included in *The Ways of White Folks.* Its main character is Milberry (Berry) Jones, who is roughly twenty years old and from New Jersey. The story takes place at a certain Dr. Renfield's Home for Crippled Children in

New York, where Berry is hired as a handyman. Berry is a big handsome African American whom the narrator compares to "Paul Robeson* at 20." But his personality is naïve and gentle, and the crippled children take to him more than they take to the brusque, overprotective staff. After a minor mishap in which one of the children is frightened but unhurt, Dr. Renfield seizes on the opportunity to fire Berry because he is jealous of Berry's way with the children. Renfield calls him a "fool nigger." Thus the kind, capable, overworked Berry becomes a scapegoat. The title of the collection springs from this story; at one point Berry observes, "The ways of white folks, I mean some white folks, is too much for me." The story was first published in *Abbott's Weekly* (February 24, 1934) and was reprinted in *Langston Hughes: Short Stories*.

The Best of Simple (New York: Hill and Wang, 1961). 245 pp. Illustrated by Bernard Nast. Collection of stories, containing seventy-two stories. A sound recording, featuring Melvin Stewart reading several stories from the volume, also appeared in 1961. The stories read include "Jazz, Jive, and Jam," and "Simple's Platform." The volume was reprinted in 1989 by Hill and Wang. *See* Simple [Jesse B.] Stories.

Discography: *The Best of Simple*, read by Melvin Stewart (New York: Folkways Records, 1961): Folkways FL 9789 [long-playing vinyl record].

The Best Short Stories by Negro Writers: An Anthology from 1899 to the Present (Boston: Little, Brown, 1967). 508 pp. Anthology of short fiction. Hughes edited the anthology and provided an "editor's note" that, with immodesty uncharacteristic of him, describes the book as "the most comprehensive anthology of American Negro short stories to be published anywhere." In the "Introduction" (ix–xiii), he discusses the persistence of racist stereotypes in American culture but focuses on how these stereotypes are (in 1966) conveyed chiefly through films and television shows—media into which, he suggests, African Americans have not made inroads comparable to those they have made into other media and arts. He asserts, however, that in literature, at least, "Negro artists are beginning to reap their sunrise harvest" (xiii). The introduction also mentions the importance of Charles Chesnutt,* novelist Frank Yerby's decision to live abroad, the accomplishments of Ralph Ellison* and Richard Wright,* and stories by Ted Poston, Alice Childress, Zora Neale Hurston,* Lindsay Patterson, and John A. Williams. The anthology contains forty-seven stories (one per author) organized roughly in chronological order, based on the original publication date of stories. Hughes includes one of his own stories, "Thank You, Ma'am." The volume, retitled *The Best Short Stories by Black Writers, 1899–1967: The Classic Anthology* was reissued by Back Bay Books/Little, Brown (Boston) in 1997. In addition to the title change, the publishers updated (but did not change substantially) brief biographical notes on authors that Hughes had written. *See* Anthologies.

Bethune, Mary (1875–1955). American educator, president of the historically black Bethune-Cookman College in Daytona Beach, Florida. Hughes met Bethune at Columbia University,* and it was she who, in 1930, encouraged Hughes to tour the American South giving poetry readings. A likeness of Bethune was featured on a twenty-two-cent stamp issued by the U.S. Post Office in 1985.

Bibliography: Rackham Holt, *Mary McLeod Bethune: A Biography* (Garden City, NY: Doubleday, 1964); "Mary McLeod Bethune," in *I Wonder As I Wander*, 39–41 (see also chapter 1).

"Better." Two-quatrain rhyming poem not unlike a song lyric. The speaker is lovelorn. The poem was first published in *Reflexus*, but this journal has not been found (see *Collected Poems*).

Bibliography: *CP*, 53, 627.

"Better Than a Pillow." Short story, included in the collection *Simple Takes a Wife*. *See* Simple [Jesse B.] Stories.

"Bewilderment." Song. Hughes wrote the lyrics, and Florence Price composed the music. ASCAP* lists no publisher for the song, but the ASCAP registry number is 320475287.

"Bible Belt." Short poem focusing on the irony that some ostensibly Christian churches in the American South were not open to African Americans. The poem was first published in *Crisis** (March 1953) under the title "Not for Publication." *See also* "Goodbye, Christ"; "On the Road."

Bibliography: *CP*, 440.

"Big Buddy." Lyric poem written in the style of a folk song and particularly reminiscent of the American folk song "John Henry." The poem concerns worker solidarity and was first published in *Negro Quarterly* (Spring 1942).

Bibliography: *CP*, 240.

"Big City Prayer." *See* "Prayer [2]."

"Big Meeting." Short story. The narrative captures the ambience of an African American evangelical gathering or "tent meeting." At the periphery of the meeting, white people are seen sitting like spectators in their parked cars, watching the meeting. The story was first published in *Scribner's Magazine* (July 1935), was included in the collection *Laughing to Keep from Crying*, and was reprinted in *Langston Hughes: Short Stories. See* Religion.

Bibliography: Ostrom, 28–29.

"Big Round World." Short story, included in the collection *Simple Stakes a Claim. See* Simple [Jesse B.] Stories.

The Big Sea (New York: Knopf, 1940). 335 pp. Autobiography. It is Hughes's first autobiography, the second being *I Wonder As I Wander*. Hughes begins by depicting himself at age twenty-one, about to ship out on the *S. S. Malone* as a deckhand and cook's assistant, headed for Africa. Describing his actions as "melodramatic," Hughes recounts throwing all of his books "from Columbia [University]"* overboard, demonstrating to himself that he was about to educate himself by traveling. In subsequent chapters Hughes goes back in time to discuss his ancestry, his childhood (including his grandmother, who read to him), and his days at Central High School* in Cleveland. He describes visiting his father twice in Mexico and his short, uncomfortable tenure at Columbia University. Part two of the book concerns chiefly his experiences on board ship and at African ports. Part three concerns the Harlem Renaissance,* which he calls the "Black Renaissance." This part includes what have become some of the most memorable portraits of the Harlem Renaissance in such chapters as "When the Negro Was in Vogue," "Harlem Literati," "Parties" (including famous parties hosted by A'Lelia Walker), "Downtown," "Shows," and "Nigger Heaven." Also included is a chapter on his studies at Lincoln University,* a chapter on writing his novel *Not Without Laughter*, and a chapter about his disagreement with Zora Neale Hurston* over their collaboration on *Mule Bone*. The book has become something of a classic in American and African American autobiography. It was reissued by Hill and Wang (New York) in 1963 and again by Thunder's Mouth Press (New York) in 1986. The latter reissue is still in print at this writing. Amiri Baraka* provided an introduction to the Thunder's Mouth Press edition. He calls *The Big Sea* "an important book," argues that Hughes's essay "The Negro Artist and the Racial Mountain" is "critical to our understanding of the social, aesthetic, and class-conscious development of black literature," and suggests that Hughes is "the most satisfying reporter of the Black Renaissance, its artistic, political, and social significance." Translations of *The Big Sea* include one in Italian by Antonio Ghirelli (Rome: Einaudi, 1948). *See also* The Black Aesthetic.

Bibliography: Amiri Baraka, foreword to *The Big Sea* by Langston Hughes (New York: Thunder's Mouth Press, 1986), i–iii; R. Baxter Miller, " 'For a Moment I Wondered': Theory and Symbolic Form in the Autobiographies of Langston Hughes," *Langston Hughes Review* 3, no. 2 (Fall 1984), 1–6.

"Big Sur." Three-line poem celebrating the natural beauty of this California coastal region, first published in the *Carmel Pine Cone* (July 18, 1941). *See* Jeffers, Robinson and Una; Sullivan, Noel.

Bibliography: *CP*, 235.

"The Big-Timer." A long monologue poem in rhymed quatrains, with notes in the left margin describing a jazz* accompaniment as well as costuming, mood, and motivation for the "character." This semidramatic piece is spoken by a self-proclaimed "Black Sheep," a kind of gangster who, despite the flashy, tough persona he projects, is a lost soul.
Bibliography: *CP*, 153.

"Bird in Orbit." *See Ask Your Mama.*

"Birmingham Sunday." Poem meditating on the bombing of a Baptist church in Birmingham, Alabama, on September 15, 1963. Four African American girls were killed by the blast. The poem was first published in *The Panther and the Lash. See also* "Bombings in Dixie."
Bibliography: *CP*, 557; Juan Williams, *Eyes on the Prize: America's Civil Rights Years, 1954–1965* (New York: Penguin, 1988).

"Birth." Tightly organized twelve-line poem in which lines five and twelve rhyme. The poem associates human birth with inanimate phenomena such as lightning or the birth of stars. It was first published in the *Christian Register, Unitarian* (May 1947).
Bibliography: *CP*, 323.

Birthplace of Langston Hughes. Hughes was born in Joplin,* Missouri, on February 1, 1902.

"Bitter Brew." Poem in five short-lined ballad* stanzas. The speaker of the poem indicates that he is being reduced to a kind of essence of hatred. The poem was first published in *Umbra Anthology* (1967–68), and is included in the second edition of *Collected Poems.*
Bibliography: *CP*, [second edition only], 617–618, 695.

"The Bitter River." Poem that remembers and reacts to the lynching* of two young African American men, Charlie Lang and Ernest Green, from the Shubuta Bridge, which spans the Chickasawhay River in Mississippi. The lynching occurred on October 12, 1942. "Bitter river" in the poem is used flexibly to refer to the actual river, to the flow of racist hatred in the South, and to the upwelling of outrage and impatience in African Americans who have been told to wait for better days in the United States. The poem was first published in *Negro Quarterly* (Autumn 1942). It is dedicated to the memory of the victims.
Bibliography: *CP*, 242.

Black, Hugo F. (1886–1971). U.S. Supreme Court Justice. *See Baltimore Afro American*; "The Mitchell Case."

The Black Aesthetic. Primarily an American literary and critical phenomenon of the 1960s and 1970s, with links to broader cultural developments such as the civil-rights movement and Black Power as well as developments in popular music forms such as blues,* jazz,* and soul. With roots in the Harlem Renaissance,* the Black Aesthetic, also known as the Black Arts movement, denotes a deliberate attempt on the part of African American writers and critics to define and produce literature embodying forms, kinds of language, perspectives on history, and subjects that are distinctly African American, as opposed to European American. Blues, jazz, African American folk and vernacular traditions, and Signifying were among the sources on which this literature and criticism drew. Some of the writing honed a politically aggressive, "antiestablishment" edge, and much of it explicitly addressed particular political, social, economic, and psychological challenges faced by contemporary African Americans. The movement discovered, made visible, and supported numerous younger writers as well as influencing the creation of black studies programs in American universities. Among those associated with the movement were Amiri Baraka,* Lucille Clifton, Sonia Sanchez, Ed Bullins, Ishmael Reed, Larry Neal, and Jayne Cortez. Although the Black Aesthetic movement did not explicitly embrace Hughes's writing as a source of inspiration, the movement's ideas echo many of Hughes's and specifically fulfill aspirations for African American literature that he expressed in "The Negro Artist and the Racial Mountain." *See Ask Your Mama*; Black Panther Party; Poetics; Politics.

Bibliography: LeRoi Jones [Amiri Baraka] and Larry Neal, eds., *Black Fire: An Anthology of Afro-American Writing* (New York: Morrow, 1968); Addison Gayle, *The Black Aesthetic* (Garden City, NY: Doubleday, 1971).

Black and White. Title of the ill-fated and never-completed motion picture in which Hughes and other African Americans were to act and that Hughes was supposed to help write. The motion picture was to have been produced by Russians in Russia but was to have concerned race relations in the United States. Hughes recounts the farcical nature of the project in *I Wonder As I Wander*. He also writes extensively in that book about his travels in Russia following the collapse of the film project (1932).

Bibliography: "Moscow Movie," "Scenario in Russian," and "The Mammy of Moscow," in *I Wonder As I Wander*, 69–86; Rampersad, I, 246–251.

Black Arts Movement. *See* The Black Aesthetic.

"The Black Clown." Monologue poem with notes describing musical accompaniment and costuming for anyone performing the piece. It was first published in *The Negro Mother and Other Dramatic Recitations*. *See* "A Black Pierrot."

Bibliography: *CP*, 150, 640.

"Black Dancers." Two-stanza poem spoken by a collective persona* of black dancers explaining why, philosophically and perhaps existentially, they must dance and sing and laugh. It was first published in *Crisis** (May 1932).

Bibliography: *CP*, 172.

Black Dialect. Because most Africans (later African Americans) came to the American colonies (later the United States) against their will and led lives controlled by English-speaking slaveholders, language has always been a unique issue for African Americans. Complicating it further are at least three other factors: (1) Africa, as opposed to Europe, was black Americans' primary source of native languages, lore, and culture; (2) as slaves, African Americans were often forbidden to learn to read and write (English, that is); therefore, both the importance of oral traditions and the obvious political dimension of language have always attached themselves to the issue; (3) discussions, perceptions, judgments, and definitions of African American speech and writing, language acquisition, expressive style, and related matters have always been shaped by the dominant, chiefly white, and mainly Anglo-American culture; consequently, problems of bias and prejudice and inherent cultural conflict have always complicated the issue. Although, in both social and linguistic contexts, "Black English" is widely considered to be a self-contained language with its own conventions and history, its status remains controversial and constantly debated because of the complicating factors mentioned earlier, because of the social dominance of "standard written English," and because questions of "Black English" often collide with questions of language education, education in general, and language acquisition.

The term "black dialect," which is less precise and less "official" than "Black English," refers in the context of Hughes's writing to his attempts to represent speech with written words. More specifically, it refers to his attempts—in poetry, fiction, songs, and drama—to create literary effects aimed at capturing elements of everyday colloquial speech used by working-class urban and rural African Americans. In this encyclopedia's entries for works written in or making use of "black dialect," then, it is to this literary context that the term refers. In linguistic and literary matters such as these, no term will be wholly satisfactory, but "black dialect" may be preferable to "Black English" because it highlights Hughes's intuitive, unsystematic, and literary approach, as opposed to the systematic, sociolinguistic, and academic approach that "Black English" connotes.

Hughes represented "black dialect" in a variety of works: blues* poems ("Bound No'th Blues," "Blues at Dawn," and "Lonesome Place," for example); monologue poems (the "Madam" poems,* "Still Here," "Too Blue," "Southern Negro Speaks," and "Mazie Dies Alone in the City Hospital," for example); monologue stories ("A Good Job Gone" and the Jesse B. Simple stories,* for example); plays (*Simply Heavenly* and *Mule Bone*, for example); and passages within novels (*Tambourines to Glory* and *Not without Laughter*). Osinubi characterizes this literary representation of dialect as "foregrounding ethnicity," that is, taking pains to mirror and highlight identifying traits—in this case, everyday speech—of a specific ethnic group. In the early "manifesto" "The Negro Artist and the Racial Mountain," Hughes explicitly announces how important it is for African American writers to acknowledge and make literary use of the raw material of African American experience and not to shy away from authentic aspects of this material just because it is different from so-called mainstream American culture. Certain kinds of African American speech—with their particular elements of idiom, slang, pronunciation, vocabulary, and rhythm—are one example of such authentic, raw material. So although Hughes did not use Osinubi's term "foregrounding ethnicity," he certainly anticipated the sense of Osinubi's thesis.

Even a cursory study of works in which Hughes represented black dialect reveals that his purpose was not to provide a transcription of speech—in which, for example, unconventional spelling would dominate a work—but to alter selected elements such as the spelling of certain words, the conventional syntax of certain phrases, or the rhythm of certain phrases. Put more impressionistically, Hughes used a "light touch," especially in contrast to the approach of Zora Neale Hurston* in her fiction, in which a greater volume of alterations occurs. (Hurston was a trained anthropologist and therefore was more inclined toward a transcriptive approach. Moreover, she was immersed in the culture of a very specific region surrounding her hometown of Eatonville, Florida.) In "Homesick Blues," for example, Hughes represents the black-dialect pronunciation of "they" as "de," and he writes, "I wants," creating the effect of a speaker employing an alternate first-person-singular conjugation of "to want," a conjugation common in Black English. He spells "Lord" "Lawd," uses "ma" for "my," and drops the "d" from "and" ("an"). This is a poem that, for Hughes, contains a substantial number of alterations, but even so, most of the spelling, phrasing, and punctuation is in keeping with conventions of standard written English. If Hughes had been more concerned with "transcription" than "effect," he could have, for example, misspelled dozens of words in the poem ("misspelled" according to conventions of standard written English, that is). In "Question [2]," from *Montage of a Dream Deferred*, Hughes misspells no words but uses the word "daddy," which in urban African American slang at the time meant "boyfriend" and was a shortened form of "sugar daddy" (see Major). This single word, then, signals or "foregrounds" the ethnicity of the speaker, a young African American woman in Harlem.* In *Not Without Laughter* the controlling third-person narrative voice is represented by means of standard written English, but within the narration some dialogue, especially that representing the speech of older working-class African American townspeople, contains the effect of black dialect.

Hughes himself, of course, was educated in ordinary midwestern lower and middle schools, in a racially integrated high school (Central High School*), and at Columbia University* and Lincoln University.* His mastery of standard written English was complete, so his use of black dialect in certain works sprang from an artistic choice. In poetry especially, he was preceded most significantly in this choice by Paul Laurence Dunbar* and the poems in Dunbar's *Lyrics of Lowly Life*. As the word "lowly" itself implies, the representation of black dialect inevitably raises questions, judgments, and controversies about social class, ethnicity, subject matter, and "appropriate" literary styles. As Hughes himself knew well, as evidenced by "The Negro Artist and the Racial Mountain," to represent black dialect was an artistic choice with political, social, and professional consequences because the reactions of editors, publishers, readers, reviewers, scholars, teachers, and others to the results of such a choice will vary widely and will often be expressed contentiously. *See also* Audience; Revision, Process of, and Hughes.

Bibliography: J. Dillard, *Black English: Its History and Usage in the United States* (New York: Vintage, 1972); M. Farr and H. Daniels, *Language Diversity and Writing Instruction* (Urbana, IL: National Council of Teachers of English, 1986); V. Harris, "African American Conceptions of Literacy: A Historical Perspective," *Theory into Practice* 31, no. 4 (Winter 1992), 276–286; W. Labov, *Language in the Inner City: Studies in the Black English Vernacular* (Philadelphia: University of Pennsylvania Press, 1972); Clarence Major, "Daddy" and "Sugar daddy," in *Juba to Jive: A Dictionary of African-American Slang* (New York: Penguin, 1994), 128, 457; J. Nembhard, "A Perspective on Teaching Black Dialect-speaking Students to Write Standard English," *Journal of Negro Education* 52, no. 1 (Spring 1983), 75–82; Viktor Osinubi, "African American Writers and the Use of Dialect in Literature: The Foregrounding of Ethnicity," *Journal of Commonwealth and Postcolonial Studies* 4, no. 1 (Fall 1996), 65–77; G. Smitherman, *Talkin' and Testifyin': The Language of Black America* (Boston: Houghton Mifflin, 1977).

"Black Gal." Four-stanza ballad* written in black dialect* and spoken by a woman who describes herself as having very dark skin. She laments that she treats men well, only to be abandoned by them for lighter-skinned African American women. She is especially heartbroken about how one Albert Johnson has mistreated her. Thus the poem bears on an implicit caste system, based on skin color, evident in some African American communities. The poem was first published in *Fine Clothes to the Jew*. *See* "Passing" (short story).

Bibliography: *CP*, 121.

Black Magic: A Pictorial History of the Negro in American Entertainment. (Englewood Cliffs, NJ: Prentice-Hall, 1967). 375 pp. Nonfiction book. Hughes cowrote it with Milton Meltzer, with Hughes being responsible for most of the text and Meltzer for the photographs and illustrations, of which there are hundreds, as the title suggests. On the dedication page, Meltzer writes, "This book was to have had no dedication. . . . On May 22, 1967, shortly after work on the book was completed, and before it could be published, Langston Hughes died." Meltzer then dedicates the book "*To Langston, with love.*" The sixty-one chapters cover such topics as African sources of African American music, "Plantation Days," the blues,* jazz,* the landmark Broadway musical *Shuffle Along*, "The

Federal Theatre," "Drama in Harlem," the Karamu Theatre (*see* "For Russell and Rowena Jeliffe"; *Front Porch*; The Gilpin Players), the renowned production of *Othello* in which Paul Robeson* starred, Lorraine Hansberry's play *A Raisin in the Sun*, off-Broadway productions, "Spotlight on the Sixties," "The Negro in Films," and "Manhattan Milestones." Individuals discussed include Ira Aldridge, Bert Williams, Bill Robinson, Cab Calloway, Eubie Blake, Jelly Roll Morton, W. C. Handy,* Bessie Smith, James Reese "Big Jim" Europe, Marian Anderson,* Leontyne Price, Mahalia Jackson, Fats Domino, the Drifters, Billy Eckstine, Hattie McDaniel, Sidney Poitier, Harry Belafonte, Duke Ellington,* Clarence Muse,* Nora Holt, Lena Horne, Canada Lee, Ossie Davis, Louis Gossett, Ornette Coleman, James Baldwin,* and LeRoi Jones (Amiri Baraka*), among many others. Hughes's text includes description, evaluation, historical encapsulation, biographical sketches, and captions for photographs, which are taken from private collections, museums, production companies, and news sources. *See also Famous Negro Music Makers*; Harlem Suitcase Theatre; *My Lord What a Mornin';* Nonfiction; *A Pictorial History of the Negro in America; The Strollin' Twenties; Way Down South.*

"The Black Man Speaks." Poem in ballad* form in which the speaker asks why American democracy does not apply to African Americans, why Jim Crow laws* still exist, and why, given that the United States is fighting Hitler in order to preserve freedom, freedom is not granted to African Americans immediately. It was first published in *Jim Crow's Last Stand. See also* "How about It, Dixie?"
Bibliography: *CP*, 288.

"Black Maria." Lyric poem in modified blues* form in which the speaker hopes that the Black Maria—nickname for a police van—is not coming for him. It was first published in *Poetry* (1941) and also published in *Shakespeare in Harlem.*
Bibliography: *CP*, 227.

Black Misery (New York: P. S. Eriksson, 1969; New York: Oxford University Press, 1994). 68 pp. (1994 edition). Book for children. Illustrated by Arouni. In an afterword to the reissue, Robert G. O'Meally explains that in 1967 Hughes was approached by Paul Eriksson to write a book that would join a children's-book series begun by Suzanne Heller. Heller's picture-and-caption books were *Misery, More Misery*, and *Misery Loves Company*, all published in the early 1960s. They expressed—accurately but with warm humor—problems children encountered in everyday life. Eriksson wanted Hughes to write captions for a book aimed chiefly at African American children. At first Hughes declined, O'Meally notes, because he believed that the amiable humor with which he wrote for children would not be well received in the tense racial climate in the United States of the late 1960s. However, Hughes changed his mind and began working on the book. Soon thereafter he was struck by what would become a fatal illness, and he even worked on the book in the hospital. At his death Hughes had completed only twenty-seven of a projected fifty captions. The publishers briefly considered asking another author, such as Arna Bontemps,* to complete the captions but decided in the end just to publish a shorter book. Heller was supposed to have illustrated *Black Misery* but declined because, according to O'Meally, she believed that her white suburban background would not allow her to do justice to the book. Therefore, Lynette Logan, who drew under the name Arouni, provided ink-wash illustrations. Hughes's captions, of one sentence each and usually running four to five lines on one page, isolate unpleasant, embarrassing, or disillusioning experiences that African American children were likely to face in a racist society. However, the phrasing is usually matter-of-fact or warmly ironic, not bitter, and some of the experiences, such as having to wear a sweater given to one by a relative, have nothing to do with racism. For the reissue (1994), the Reverend Jesse Jackson wrote an introduction. *See* Children's Poetry.

Bibliography: Robert G. O'Meally, "Afterword," in Langston Hughes, *Black Misery* (New York: Oxford University Press, 1994).

Black Nativity: A Christmas Song Play (1961). Play, often characterized as a gospel song-play, in two acts. Peterson describes the work as a "celebration of the birth of Christ and the spread of the gospel, in the black idiom, with gospel music, spirituals, dance, drama, and narration." The play included material from *Ballad of the Brown King*. It was first produced on December 11, 1961, at the 41st Street Theatre in New York City, moving to the New York Theatre from January 9 to January 28, 1962. The total number of performances was fifty-seven. Vinnette Carrol directed, and Marion Williams was the primary singer, accompanied by the Stars of Faith choir. One of Hughes's most successful musical plays, *Black Nativity* won the Catholic Dove Award at Cannes, France. It was also presented at the Festival of Two Worlds in Spoleto, Italy, in June 1962. Before returning to New York for seven performances at Lincoln Center (December 23–30, 1962), the production toured London (Criterion Theatre), Oslo, Copenhagen, Hamburg, and Brussels. The following year it was presented in Paris (Champs Elysées Théâtre), Italy, Germany, the Netherlands, Belgium, and Sweden. Additional American performances occurred in Boston (October 1963) and Chicago (January 1964). An unpublished script of *Black Nativity* is held in the Schomburg Collection (New York Public Library), and Dramatic Publishers (New York) published the play in 1992. Vee Jay Records produced the cast recording (VJS-8503) on a long-playing vinyl record, which is out of print at this writing. "Inspired by the challenge [presented by a gospel song-play]," writes Rampersad, "Langston worked so long and hard that a two-tone beard blossomed on his cheeks. . . . *Black Nativity* marked a major breakthrough in the gospel musical form." Rampersad also notes that except for "a few melodies set by Alex Bradford, an ordained minister and the musical director of the Greater Abyssinian Church of Newark, New Jersey, all the songs were in the public domain as part of the religious music tradition." The song-play was produced several times in the 1990s and in 2000 by the Intiman Theatre in Seattle, Washington. *See also Ballad of the Brown King; Carol of the Brown King: Nativity Poems by Langston Hughes*; Religion.

Bibliography: Langston Hughes, *Black Nativity* (New York: Dramatic Publishers, 1992); Bernard L. Peterson, Jr., *Contemporary Black American Playwrights and Their Plays: A Biographical Directory and Dramatic Index* (Westport, CT: Greenwood Press, 1988); Rampersad, II, 345–347.

"Black Panther." Twelve-line poem at once empathetic toward and critical of the Black Panther Party,* characterizing its philosophy as "an Eye for an Eye" and calling that perspective one of the "oldest" lies. The poem was first published in *The Panther and the Lash*.

Bibliography: *CP*, 555.

Black Panther Party. Social-activist and political organization founded by Bobby Seale (born 1937) and Huey Newton (1942–1989) in Oakland, California, in 1966. To a degree, the Black Panther Party defined itself in opposition to the nonviolent, direct-action philosophy of Dr. Martin Luther King, Jr., and one of its purposes was to provide armed defense of African Americans whom the party believed to be targets of police harassment in Oakland and other cities. Members of the party often wore black jackets and berets and carried weapons. In an atmosphere of severe racial tension in urban centers across the nation, mainstream media were, of course, intensely interested in this militialike image of the Black Panther Party. The federal government, specifically J. Edgar Hoover, director of the Federal Bureau of Investigation, believed the party to be a threat to national security and devoted resources to investigating its activities. Activists working against the U.S. war in Vietnam were attracted to the party's militant, articulate profile; therefore, intermittent alliances were formed between mostly white, middle-class antiwar activists and the Black Panther Party, which was composed chiefly of working-class African Americans. The University of California at Berkeley was one site of such alliances. The party also worked with the Student Nonviolent Coordinating Committee, headed by Stokely Carmichael. Although the militant, menacing image of the Black Panther Party was the one mainstream American journalists focused on, many of the party's activities, including literacy and food programs, were community oriented, pragmatic, and nonviolent. Chapters of the party organized themselves in many cities, including Detroit and Seattle. However, the infamous trial of the "Chicago Eight" (1969)—eight activists charged with inciting riots during the Democratic Party's 1968 national convention—reinforced the one-dimensional image of the party because Bobby Seale was one of the codefendants and participated in disrupting the trial, which all of the defendants believed to be politically, not legally, motivated. In 1968 Newton was arrested following an armed altercation with the Oakland police in which an officer was killed. He spent two years in prison awaiting trial, but charges were dismissed in 1970. In his absence, the male-dominated party was headed by a woman, Elaine Brown, whose account of the party's development is one of the most engaging. Newton resumed control of the party upon his release. In the late 1970s Newton was accused of misappropriating funds intended for the party's outreach programs, and the party began to disintegrate. Newton was fatally shot outside an Oakland "crack" cocaine house in 1989, allegedly by a drug dealer whom he had attempted to rob. Hughes mainly agreed with the party's political and economic analysis of certain racist aspects of American society but disagreed with militaristic aspects of the party's ethos and rhetoric (*see* "Black Panther"). The title of the last book of poetry Hughes assembled before his death, *The Panther and the Lash*, alludes to the Black Panther Party. Bobby Seale ran unsuccessfully for mayor of Oakland in 1973, later wrote a cookbook (*Barbecuin' with Bobby*, 1986), and at this writing works as a community liaison for Temple University.

Bibliography: "Bobby Seale Pens Cookbook, Starts Foundation," *Jet* 73 (October 26, 1987), 22; Elaine Brown, *A Taste of Power: A Black Woman's Story* (New York: Pantheon, 1992); Paul Chevigny, *Cops and Rebels: A Study of Provocation* (New York: Pantheon, 1972); Frank Gannon, review of *Barbecuin' with Bobby*, by Bobby Seale, *Harper's Magazine* 278, no. 1668 (May 1989), 55; David Hilliard, *This Side of Glory: The Autobiography of David Hilliard and the Story of the Black Panther Party* (Boston: Little, Brown, 1993); Assata Shakur, *Assata: An Autobiography* (Westport, CT: Hill, 1987); U.S. Congress, Joint Committee on Internal Security, *The Black Panther Party: Its Origin and Development as Reflected in Its Official Weekly Newspaper, "The Black Panther"* (Washington, DC: Government Printing Office, 1970); Yohuru R. Williams, "In the Name of the Law: The 1967 Shooting of Huey Newton and Law Enforcement's Permissive Environment," *Negro History Bulletin* 61, no. 2 (April–June 1998), 6–12.

"A Black Pierrot." Three-stanza lyric poem spoken by a black Pierrot, which is a conventional figure in Italian and French pantomime. The poem deliberately plays with the Pierrot convention, for the traditional Pierrot appears in whiteface, as contrasted with the conventional blackface, trouble-making Harlequin. It was first published in the *Amsterdam News* (April 4, 1923). Later, William Grant Still* set the poem to music. ASCAP* lists the song as being published by William Grant Still Music (Flagstaff, Arizona), and the ASCAP* registry number is 320054893. *See also* "The Black Clown"; "The Jester"; "Pierrot." With regard to collaborations with Still, *see also* "Breath of a Rose"; *Troubled Island*.

Bibliography: *CP*, 31, 622; Douglas Hunt and Kari Hunt, *Pantomime: The Silent Theater* (New York: Atheneum, 1964); Maurice Sand, *The History of the Harlequinade* (New York: Blom, 1968).

"Black Seed." Fifteen-line poem using an extended metaphor that compares the African diaspora to the broadcast of seeds to distant, frequently hostile, lands, where often the plants (people) that sprout from the seeds are cut down by white gardeners. It was first published in *Opportunity** (December 1931).

Bibliography: *CP*, 130.

Black Swan Records. One of the first companies to record African American blues* and jazz* artists. It was founded in 1921 by the Pace Phonograph Company in New York City, and Fletcher Henderson served as its chief producer, signing Ethel Waters to the label in the first year. The company helped expand the audience for the blues and jazz during the Harlem Renaissance.*

Bibliography: Lewis *WHWV*, 174–176.

"Black Workers." Five-line poem comparing black workers to bees, whose "work is taken from them." It was first published in *Crisis** (April 1933). *See also Angelo Herndon Jones*; "Ballads of Lenin"; "Chant for Tom Mooney"; *Don't You Want to be Free?*; "Goodbye, Christ"; "Good Morning, Revolution"; "Lenin"; "One More 'S' in the U.S.A."; "Revolution"; "Song of the Revolution"; "Wait." *See also* Marxism; Politics.

Bibliography: *CP*, 172.

"Blessed Assurance." Short story narrated by one "John," who fears that his son is homosexual. The son sings beautifully but, in John's opinion, sounds "like a woman," and John is mortified when the son sings in church. The story was included in the collection *Something in Common and Other Stories* and was reprinted in *Langston Hughes: Short Stories. See* Sexuality and Hughes.

Bibliography: Ostrom, 49.

"Blind." Fourteen-line poem spoken by a blind person who is glad not to see differences in people's skin color. It was first published in *Span* (Fall 1943).

Bibliography: *CP*, 277.

The Block: Collage by Romare Bearden/Poems by Langston Hughes (New York: Viking Press/Metropolitan Museum of Art, 1995). 32 pp. Introduction by Bill Cosby. Children's book. In "picture-book" format, thirteen of Hughes's poems are combined with Bearden's colorful, highly original collages. The poems are "Theme for English B," "Projection," "Late Last Night," "As Befits a Man," "Juke Box Love Song," "Testimonial," "Madam's Calling Cards," "Harlem Night Song," "To Be Somebody," "Corner Meeting," "Note on Commercial Theatre," "Stars," and "Motto." Like that of Hughes, the work of Bearden (1911–1988) was shaped by an interest in the blues* and jazz,* and like Hughes, Bearden was a longtime resident of Harlem.* In the introduction, the American actor Bill Cosby observes that "the poems and the collage in this book present people in all the ways we might see them in real life on one of the busy streets of Harlem. It could be happening today" (6). The poems and collages were selected by Lowery S. Sims and Daisy Murray Voigt. *See Black Misery; Carol of the Brown King: Nativity Poems by Langston Hughes*; Children's Poetry; *Popo and Fifina; The Sweet and Sour Animal Book.*

Blood Wedding and Yerma [one volume]. By Federico García Lorca, translated by Langston Hughes and W. S. Merwin (New York: Theatre Communications Group, 1994). 135 pp. This book is a translation of two of Federico García Lorca's best-known plays, both preceded by an introduction written by Melia Bensussen. Merwin translated *Yerma* and had no part in Hughes's translation of *Blood Wedding*. As Bensussen mentions, Langston Hughes's rendering of *Blood Wedding* (which he had originally titled *Fate at the Wedding*) was unknown until the early 1980s when she and the then executor of the Hughes estate, George Bass, discovered the script in Yale University's Beinecke Library. It appears that after having written the first draft of the translation in Paris in 1937, the American writer abandoned the project, and the text went unnoticed until 1984. In her adaptation of the play, she and Bass edited Hughes's original version and carefully considered the grammatical inaccuracies and misunderstandings, typical of a first draft, to determine which were errors and which were artistic choices of the translator. The end result is quite satisfactory. In the late 1920s the Spanish-born Federico García Lorca had achieved his international fame as author of the collection of poetry titled *Gypsy Ballads*, also translated by Hughes (*see Lorca: Gypsy Ballads*). The poet, however, had always shown an interest in theatre, and his first published drama predates his important books of verse. In 1920 he staged *The Evil-doing of the Butterfly* (*El Maleficio de la mariposa*) in Madrid, where it received poor reviews. In spite of his less-than-promising start, the writer was not discouraged and continued to ruminate on his theatrical ideas throughout the decade. In 1931 Lorca began to work with a government-sponsored university theatre group called La barraca (The Cabin). Its mission was to take theatre to the Spanish countryside using university students as cast and crew. While the group did not present much modern drama, favoring instead the Spanish theatre of the sixteenth and seventeenth centuries by Lope de Vega, Pedro Calderón, and Miguel de Cervantes, Lorca acquired staging and technical expertise as a producer and director with the company. After three years of work with La barraca, he began to withdraw from his position as director to be able to devote more time to writing his own work.

Lorca originally wrote *Blood Wedding* in 1932. It is the first of a trilogy of plays known as the "rural tragedies," as many of the characters and plots were supposedly inspired by incidents reported in Lorca's native Andalusia. The other two plays of this cycle are *Yerma* (1934), also included in this volume, and *The House of Bernarda Alba* (*La casa de Bernarda Alba*), written just before the author's death in 1936. *Blood Wedding* was staged for the first time in Madrid in 1933 and later in Buenos Aires when Lorca traveled to Argentina to give a series of lectures. It was first presented in the United States in 1935 in New York. The play is divided into three acts. The cast consists of four main characters and several minor figures. None of the characters have names except one, Leonardo Felix. The others are referred to as Boy, Mother, and Girl. A pair of especially curious minor characters are the Moon, a young woodcutter dressed all in white, and Death, portrayed as an old beggar woman.

The main themes of the play, death and sensuality, are evidenced early on. In the first scene of act one in the opening dialogue between Boy and Mother, she immediately comments on her murdered husband and son, victims of a blood feud with the Felix family. The conversation becomes even more intense with her admonition to her son not to take a knife to the fields even though he only wants it to be able to cut grapes. Her words recall the violent deaths of her loved ones and also serve as foreshadowing: "A knife! Always a knife! Knives are no good, like the scoundrels that invented them" (5). This conversation is juxtaposed with her son's revelation of his plans to marry Girl. The notion of sensuality becomes apparent when Mother reflects back on her husband, "He was a man, made of good stuff! And your grandfather, he left a baby on every corner" (7). For her, the only favorable aspect to Boy's marriage will be grand-children; "And see if you can't raise me six grandchildren to make me happy. Or as many as you want to, since your father didn't have a chance to give them to me" (8–9). As she sends Boy on his way to work in the fields, she begins to kiss him goodbye but instead says, "Go on with you! You're too big for kisses. Save them for your wife—when she is your wife" (9). These bits of dialogue reveal both the potential for expressing desire and its repression. Together with the mention of the hot temperature, they underscore the passion that lies beneath the surface of the characters. As the scene ends, Mother learns that her daughter-in-law-to-be is the ex-girlfriend of Leonardo Felix, a young son of the family that killed her husband.

The second scene of act one begins and ends with two sections of metered and rhymed lullabies (six-syllable lines with assonant rhyme). Here the Wife and Mother-in-Law of Leonardo, known only by these names, are rocking his son to sleep. While Hughes's renditions of the songs do not preserve the formal aspects of the verses, he skillfully captures the two most important images of the lullaby, the horse and the dagger: "The horse starts to cry. His hooves are bruised and his mane is frozen and between his eyes is a silver dagger. They went to the river. Oh, see them go down where the blood flows fast, faster than the water" (13). While the images of the dagger and blood continue the imagery suggested in scene one, the horse is a new symbol. It is important because it refers to Leonardo himself, who has been tearing around the countryside on his steed at breakneck speeds for weeks. Leonardo, ex-boyfriend of Boy's soon-to-be betrothed, has since married her cousin. The unbridled desire that he still feels for his first love, however, is patently illustrated.

The last scene of act one takes place in Girl's house, where Boy and Mother have traveled to ask for her hand. The speech of the characters and the setting are quite formal. In the conversation between Mother and Girl's father, the attributes of their children, especially purity, are highlighted. Additionally, the

potential for the two families to combine crops, vineyards, and lands is a reminder that the union of marriage will result in an increased fertility and potential for new life. Their discussion is tempered by Mother's somber reminder that
the day of the wedding will also mark the day that her dead son would have
turned twenty-two. Girl is notably less than enthusiastic about the wedding, and
in the last dialogue with her servant, it is revealed that there has been a
horseman, not her fiancé, visiting the window of her room for the past few
nights.

Act two begins with a servant combing Girl's hair for the wedding. The two
women are in petticoats in the courtyard of the house trying to escape the heat.
The prevalent theme of sensuality is manifested by both the revealing dress of
the women and the words of the servant, who reminds Girl that her marriage
will allow her to "hold a man in your arms, to kiss him, to feel his weight on
your body!" (28). As the first guests begin to arrive for the ceremony, Leonardo
appears and cruelly questions the bride's purity and her previous rejection of
him due to his lack of money. Both characters seem to be slowly losing control.
This serious conversation is interrupted by merrymaking as the arriving guests
sing choruses of celebratory songs greeting the bride and wishing her good
fortune on her wedding day. This happy revelry is juxtaposed with the somber,
foreboding attitude of the bride as the ceremony is about to begin.

In scene two the vows have been taken, and the wedding party is beginning.
There is music, dancing, and singing, and everyone seems happy except Girl.
The dialogue is replete with innuendo about the upcoming wedding night, keeping the theme of sensuality ever-present. Mother recalls yet again the death of
her son and expectant hopes for grandchildren. However, the fun comes to an
end when it is discovered that Girl has made off with Leonardo on his horse.
As act two ends, Mother urges her son in pursuit of the couple, declaring, "The
day of blood has come again" (51).

The third act begins with three woodcutters in the forest discussing what has
happened at the wedding and the probable outcome of the chase. That it will
be tragic, they have no doubt. They predict, however, that before the couple is
discovered and killed, "they'll have mingled their blood, and they'll be like two
empty vessels, like two dry streams" (53). The character of Moon enters the
scene and gives a lengthy soliloquy reinforcing what the woodsmen have said:
"The moon leaves a knife hanging in the air, lurking steel for the pain of blood"
(55). The Moon will indeed be an accomplice to the Beggar (Death), who
schemes how to bring about the death of the couple. It is she who ultimately
agrees to show Boy the way to the lovers. At the end of the scene Leonardo
and Girl sense their impending death and lament their inability to have controlled
their desires and actions. Having not obeyed their passion earlier has led to all
of their suffering and anguish that is now reaching its culmination. They have
brought about their own demise. The scene ends with two offstage shrieks.

In the final scene of act three, it is learned that Leonardo and Boy are dead.
As Mother laments the loss of her last son, Girl arrives, professing that although

she deserves to be punished, she dies a virgin. The Mother is unmoved by her arrival and words, and as the play ends, Girl, Mother, and Leonardo's wife mourn the loss of their loved ones.

In general, Federico García Lorca's work has been problematic for translators. This drama, one of the author's most acclaimed, is especially challenging. Not only is Lorca's imagery difficult to convey in English, but many parts of the play are in verse and have to be sung, as was explained in the case of the lullabies in act one. Furthermore, the festivities surrounding the marriage in *Blood Wedding* are particularly Spanish and, moreover, are particularly turn-of-the-century provincial Andalusian. All three of these factors complicate the task of translating. (Indeed, a whole doctoral dissertation considers the various English translations of *Blood Wedding* that exist; see Robie-Theunen). Nonetheless, Langston Hughes's version of the play displays all the dramatic and poetic craft found in the original in an artistic and believable way. The communication of characters' passions, so convincing in the original, comes through in Hughes's version. Finally, the mystery and beauty so representative of Lorca's drama are masterfully captured in this edition. *See Lorca: Gypsy Ballads* for more detailed biographical information about Lorca. *See also* "Spain's Martyred Poet, García Lorca."

Joseph Deters

Bibliography: Brian D. Bethune, "Langston Hughes' Lost Translation of Federico García Lorca's *Blood Wedding," Langston Hughes Review* 15, no. 1 (1997), 24–36; Carl Cobb, *Federico García Lorca* (Boston: Twayne, 1967); Ian Gibson, *Federico García Lorca* (New York: Pantheon Books, 1989); Edward Mullen, ed., *Langston Hughes in the Hispanic World and Haiti* (Hamden, CT: Archon Books, 1977); Nicole Susanne Robie-Theunen, "Norms and Strategies in the English Translations of Federico García Lorca's *Bodas de sangre*" (Ph.D. dissertation, Ohio State University, 1993).

"Blue Bayou." Poem of approximately one page spoken by a man wandering the bayou; he is deeply embittered by his white boss's having taken "his woman." The poem also refers to lynching.* "Greeley" is the white boss's name, and "Lou" is mentioned, but whether Lou is short for Mary Lou and refers to the woman or refers to a lynching victim is unclear. Repeated sun imagery takes on an apocalyptic quality by being linked to blood imagery. The poem was first published in *Jim Crow's Last Stand*.

Bibliography: *CP*, 292.

"Blue Evening." Short story, included in *The Best of Simple. See* Simple [Jesse B.] Stories.

"Blue Monday." Three-stanza lyric poem spoken by a man who is late for work on a Monday, first published in *Selected Poems*. Later, Frederick Koch set the poem to music. ASCAP* lists the song as being published by Barrow Press, and the ASCAP registry number is 320430511.

Bibliography: *CP*, 466.

The Blues. A type of song indigenous to the United States but now written, performed, and recorded worldwide to such an extent that the term can refer more broadly to a whole genre of popular music. Concerning the word "blues," Clarence Major suggests that it is "closely related, in the African-American historical memory, with blackness. The word use may have its origins in the concept of blue-black skin, or black skin that seems to reflect blue light or has a blue cast to it. Although it is pure speculation, the concept of the blues may have its origin in this idea" (48). He adds, "For white speakers in America, as early as the 1800s, 'blue' meant 'drunk,' perhaps because, when intoxicated, one's skin, especially the tip of the nose, might appear blue" (48). Apparently, "the blues" also began, as early as the mid-nineteenth century, to be used in the United States to refer to "feeling down," being sad, or experiencing emotional depression. For instance, David Herbert Donald quotes Abraham Lincoln as using "the Blues" with this connotation in the 1840s, in a conversation with the mother of his good friend Joshua Speed. *Webster's New Riverside Dictionary* refers to this connection between the blues and sadness but suggests that in this context, "the blues" was actually a shortened form of "the blue devils." In any case, the blues as a song form were linked from the beginning with expressions of sadness brought on by lost love (or ill treatment from a lover, wife, or husband), despair, poverty, homelessness, or some combination of these elements. Major writes, "Out of 'Negro' work songs, hollers, and spirituals, this special type of music became popular through the vocal style of W. C. Handy* around 1912" (49). Actually, W. C. Handy, sometimes called "the Father of the Blues," first encountered this type of song while he was visiting the Mississippi Delta—specifically, Tutwiler, Mississippi—in 1895. (Interestingly, Handy had not yet encountered this type of song in his native Alabama.) There he observed an African American man playing the guitar and singing, using a bottleneck on the guitar strings to create a mournful sound and to "bend" notes. At that time, blues songs were created and learned without being written down—strictly through an oral tradition, that is. It was Handy who first wrote down a blues song, the "St. Louis Blues," and in so doing started what would become a revolution whereby the blues were written, performed, adapted, and popularized all over the United States and beyond.

Early blues artists considered crucial to the tradition include Alberta Hunter, Blind Lemon Jefferson, Robert Johnson, Leadbelly, Ma Rainey, Bessie Smith, Clara Smith, and Mamie Smith. As even this brief list suggests, women have always been important in the blues tradition. From the beginning, the blues were more than just a type of song, bringing with them notions of an itinerant, dissolute, and even—in religious rural areas of the South—sinful way of life. Blues lyrics themselves evoked this way of life, so that the blues singer was not just a performer but also a persona, an embodiment of the lifestyle evoked. Many blues lyrics were explicitly sexual (*see* Ball, *The Nasty Blues*). The Mississippi Delta remained the homeland of the blues, but soon different cities became known for their own blues styles: St. Louis, Memphis, Chicago, New York City (Harlem*), and San Francisco.

A traditional blues-lyric stanza contains three lines; line two repeats line one, and line three rhymes with lines one and two. However, a poem based on traditional blues lyrics may shorten the lines, breaking them roughly in half, creating a six-line stanza on the page. Hughes arranges the lines this way in, for example, the poems "Fortune Teller Blues," "Gal's Cry for a Dying Lover," "Hard Luck," "Homesick Blues," "Midwinter Blues," and "Po' Boy Blues." The poem "Curious" consists of one stanza of blues lyrics, arranged in six lines. In the musical tradition of the blues, each of the three lines of lyrics represents four bars of music, creating a twelve-bar song, repeated with each lyric stanza. At the end of the lines, and especially of stanzas, a pause often occurs in which an instrumental "break" may be played. The blues tradition assumes that performers will alter lyrics and improvise upon the basic music, which is based on a three-chord progression built on the first, fourth, and fifth notes (or "degrees") of a key. Often the third and fifth of the key are flatted, creating a dissonance long associated with blues songs. In the key of C, therefore, the essential chords would be C, F, and G, but to the C chord a B-flat might be added, to the F an E-flat, and to the G an F. Many blues songs employ more than three chords, of course. The use of a bottleneck or other "slide" implement on a guitar, which W. C. Handy observed, facilitates the flatting of notes and the "bending" of notes and chords. (*See* Tracy and other secondary sources listed in the Bibliography for more extensive definitions and analyses of the blues.)

Hughes's book *The Weary Blues* was a bona fide path-breaking work because it created literary art out of the oral folk material of the blues. Ironically, however, the title poem of the book is not structurally in traditional blues form. It is chiefly about the spirit, the appeal, and the deceptively complex emotional content of the blues, although it contains "quotations" from blues lyrics, blues-like repetitions of phrasing, and so forth. In Tracy's view, "*Fine Clothes* [*to the Jew*] was an advance over the blues poems of *The Weary Blues* because of its greater variety of stanzas, speakers, subjects, and literary effects" (4). In some poems Hughes uses the language and captures the spirit of the blues but uses a different lyric form, such as ballad* stanzas; the poem "Reasons Why" is an example. Other poems are written in standard English (not in black dialect*) but take "blues culture" as their subject; the poems "Cabaret" and "Young Singer" are examples. With regard to form, perspective on the world, subject matter, and language, the blues lie at the heart of Hughes's achievement as a writer, just as Hughes's achievement helped highlight the extent to which the blues comprise an immensely important, vibrant, adaptable art form. *See also* "Barefoot Blues"; Black Dialect; "The Blues" (poem); "The Blues I'm Playing";

"Bound No'th Blues"; "Crowing Hen Blues"; "Down and Out"; Jazz; Johnson, James P.; "Juice Joint: Northern City"; "Little Green Tree Blues"; "Little Old Letter"; "Lonesome Place"; "Maker of the Blues"; *Montage of a Dream Deferred; Mule Bone*; "The Negro Artist and the Racial Mountain"; "Red Clay Blues"; "Red Roses"; "Six-Bit Blues"; Songs; "Songs Called the Blues"; "To Midnight Nan at Leroy's"; Wright, Richard; "Young Gal's Blues."

Bibliography: Tom Ball, comp., *The Nasty Blues* (Fullerton, CA: Centerstream Publishing, 1995); Samuel Charters, *The Roots of the Blues: An African Search* (New York: M. Boyars, 1981); David Herbert Donald, *Lincoln: A Biography* (New York: Simon and Schuster, 1995), 89; David Evans, *Big Road Blues* (Berkeley: University of California Press, 1982); William Ferris, *Blues from the Delta* (Garden City, NY: Doubleday, 1978); Alan Lomax, *The Land Where the Blues Began* (New York: Pantheon, 1993); Clarence Major, ed., *Juba to Jive: A Dictionary of African-American Slang* (New York: Viking/Penguin, 1994), 47–50; Roger St. Pierre, *The Best of the Blues: The Essential CD Guide* (San Francisco: Collins Publishers, 1993); Derrick Stewart-Baxter, *Ma Rainey and the Classic Blues Singers* (New York: Stein and Day, 1970); Tracy (includes bibliographies and discographies).

"The Blues." Poem. *See* Children's Poetry.
Bibliography: *CP*, 608.

"The Blues." Short story, included in the collection *Simple's Uncle Sam. See* Simple [Jesse B.] Stories.

"Blues at Dawn." Poem. *See Montage of a Dream Deferred.*

"Blues at the Waldorf." Song, from *Simply Heavenly*. Hughes wrote the lyrics, and David Martin composed the music. The ASCAP* registry number for the song is 320069190, but ASCAP lists no publisher.

"Blues Fantasy." Poem in the spirit of the blues* but in a looser, less traditional form. The persona is that of a heartbroken woman who wants to leave town by train. The poem was first published in *The Weary Blues*.
Bibliography: *CP*, 91.

"The Blues I'm Playing." Short story. The narrative concerns Oceola Jones, a young African American woman, and Dora Ellsworth, a wealthy white woman. Oceola is a pianist, and Mrs. Ellsworth becomes her patron. Their relationship begins well, but Mrs. Ellsworth becomes offended by Oceola's interest in a man and by her love for popular forms of music, including the blues* and jazz.* Quietly but firmly, Oceola rebels. In the final meeting between the two, Oceola plays the blues, demonstrating her affinity for that form of music but also expressing her independence. The story can be, but need not be, read as having some connection with Hughes's own problems with his patron, Mrs. Charlotte

Osgood Mason.* Because of its subject matter and subtle narrative form, "The Blues I'm Playing" is widely regarded as one of Hughes's best short stories. It was first published in *Scribner's Magazine* (May 1934), was included in *The Ways of White Folks*, and was reprinted in *Langston Hughes: Short Stories*.

Bibliography: Ostrom, 14–15; Hans Ostrom, "Langston Hughes's 'The Blues I'm Playing,' " in *Reference Guide to Short Fiction*, ed. Thomas Riggs (Detroit: St. James Press, 1999), 770–771.

"Blues in Stereo." Poem. *See Ask Your Mama.*

"Blues Montage." Song. Hughes wrote the lyrics, and Leonard Geoffrey Feather composed the music. ASCAP* lists the song as being published by Model Music. The song's ASCAP registry number is 320071249. *See The Beat Generation* [sound recording].

Discography: *The Beat Generation*, 3 compact discs (Santa Monica, CA: Rhino Records/ Word Beat, 1992). (Includes "Blues Montage.")

"Blues on a Box." Eight-line poem suggesting that playing the blues* is a way to drive off bad luck. "Box" refers to the guitar. The poem was first published in *Poetry* (February 1947).

Bibliography: *CP*, 321.

"Boarding House." Fourteen-line poem that wryly refers to the graveyard as "the cheapest boarding house of all." It was first published in *One-Way Ticket*.

Bibliography: *CP*, 368.

Boatman, David. One of Hughes's pseudonyms. *See* "Autumn Note"; "Mailbox for the Dead"; Pseudonyms used by Hughes.

"Bodies in the Moonlight." Short story, among Hughes's earliest published fiction. The narrative concerns a lovers' triangle in which two sailors in Africa literally fight for the attention of a woman, Nunuma. The story was first published in the *Messenger** (April 1927). Ironically, George Schuyler,* with whom Hughes had disagreed in print about the issue of "Negro art," was editor of the *Messenger* at the time. The story was reprinted in *Langston Hughes: Short Stories*. Other early short stories set in Africa include "The Little Virgin," "Luani of the Jungles," and "The Young Glory of Him." *See also* "The Negro Artist and the Racial Mountain."

Bibliography: Rampersad, I, 139–140.

"Bomb Shelters." Short story, included in the collection *Simple's Uncle Sam*. *See* Simple [Jesse B.] Stories.

"Bombings in Dixie." Two-quatrain, rhyming poem that suggests that mourning and praying do not constitute a sufficient response to the bombings of African American churches in the South. It was first published in *The Panther and the Lash. See* "Birmingham Sunday."

Bibliography: *CP*, 557; Juan Williams, *Eyes on the Prize: America's Civil Rights Years, 1954–1965* (New York: Penguin, 1988).

"Bon-Bon Buddy." Short story for children. It was cowritten by Arna Bontemps* and Hughes in 1935 but was never published. A manuscript is held in the Langston Hughes Papers, James Weldon Johnson Memorial Collection, Beinecke Library, Yale University.

Bibliography: Rampersad, I, 307–308.

Bond, Horace Mann. *See* Lincoln University.

Bonds, Margaret (1913–1972). American composer, pianist, and teacher. Bonds was born in Chicago and began her music education with her mother. In high school she studied music with Florence Price and William Dawson and went on to earn undergraduate and graduate degrees in music from Northwestern University (1933, 1934). In 1932 she won the Wanamaker Prize for a song, "Sea Ghost." In 1933, as a soloist, she performed Florence Price's 'Piano Concerto' with the Chicago Symphony Orchestra, becoming the first African American soloist to appear with that symphony. Soon thereafter she moved to New York and studied at the Juilliard Graduate School with Djane Herz. Later she established the Allied Arts Academy for ballet and music in Chicago and a music program at Mount Calvary Baptist Church in Harlem.* She also taught at the Inner City Institute and the Inner City Repertory Theatre in Los Angeles. Jackson writes that Bonds's "works for orchestra and for piano are programmatic and reflect her strong sense of ethnic identity in their use of spiritual materials, jazz harmonies, and social themes" (256). With Hughes, Bonds collaborated on *Ballad of the Brown King*, and she set "The Negro speaks of Rivers" to music. She also composed music for "Mary Had a Little Baby" and "Three Dream Portraits," songs for which Hughes wrote lyrics. Rampersad notes that in February 1961 Bonds accompanied Hughes on the piano during his reading of *Ask Your Mama* in New York City. Jackson also indicates that Hughes and Bonds collaborated on a "song cycle," "Fields of Wonder," in 1964; this work is not mentioned by Rampersad, nor is it listed by ASCAP.* Overall, her works include four orchestral works, forty-two songs, fourteen popular songs, several spiritual songs, and music for several stage productions in addition to *Ballad of the Brown King*. Her last work, *Credo*, was performed by the Los Angeles Philharmonic Orchestra, directed by Zubin Mehta, posthumously in 1972.

Bibliography: Barbara Garvey Jackson, "Margaret Bonds," in *The New Grove Dictionary of American Music*, ed. H. Wiley Hitchcock and Stanley Sadie, (New York: Grove's

Dictionaries of Music, 1986), vol. 1, 255–256; Rampersad, II, 327; Daryl Taylor, "The Importance of Studying African-American Art Song," *Journal of Singing* 54, no. 3 (January–February 1998), 9–16.

"Bonds for All." Poem that is a versified request, intended to appear in the popular press, asking citizens to purchase U.S. bonds to help finance America's participation in the war against the Axis powers (World War II). *See* "America's Young Black Joe!"; "Bonds: In Memoriam"; "Just an Ordinary Guy."

Bibliography: *CP*, 584.

"Bonds: In Memoriam." Subtitled "Written Especially for the Writers' War Board, War Loan Drives, by Langston Hughes (for ANP)." Like "Bonds for All," this poem is a versified plea for citizens to purchase "war bonds." "ANP" refers to Associated Negro Press. The poem was first published in the *Baltimore Afro American** (June 24, 1942). *See* "America's Young Black Joe!"; "Bonds for All"; "Just an Ordinary Guy."

Bibliography: *CP*, 587.

"Bones, Bombs, Chicken Necks." Short story, included in the collection *The Best of Simple. See* Simple [Jesse B.] Stories.

Bontemps, Arna (1902–1973). American poet, fiction writer, biographer, and editor. A native of California, Bontemps was drawn to the Harlem Renaissance* in 1924. He and Hughes first met late that year, and their acquaintance grew into unquestionably one of the most enduring and important friendships of Hughes's life. The two often accompanied each other on poetry-reading and lecture tours throughout their careers. Their extensive correspondence began in 1925 and ended only with Hughes's death in 1967. A wry wit, unpretentiousness, an acute awareness of political issues, generosity toward younger writers, and literary versatility were among the characteristics the two shared. Also, both developed a lifelong interest in the folk roots of African American culture. Bontemps and Hughes collaborated to write *The Paste-Board Bandit*, a children's story; *Popo and Fifina*, a children's book set in Haiti; and "Boy of the Border," an unpublished short story. Other unpublished works (for children) on which they collaborated are held in the Langston Hughes Papers of the James Weldon Johnson Memorial Collection, Beinecke Library, Yale University. Bontemps's works include *Black Thunder* (1936), a historical novel based on a slave uprising led by Gabriel Prosser; the novel *Drums at Dusk* (1939); biographies of W. C. Handy,* Frederick Douglass,* and George Washington Carver*; numerous novels and histories for young readers; the historical study *We Have Tomorrow: Famous American Negroes* (1954); and three important edited works, *American Negro Poetry* (1963), *Great Slave Narratives* (1969), and *The Harlem Renaissance Remembered* (1972). Bontemps collaborated with Countee

Cullen* on the play *St. Louis Woman* (1946) and taught at the University of Illinois, Yale University, and several colleges. Hughes dedicated *Fields of Wonder* to Arna Bontemps and his wife, Alberta. *See* Funeral, Hughes's.

Bibliography: *Arna Bontemps/Langston Hughes: Letters, 1925–1967*, ed. Charles H. Nichols (New York: Dodd, Mead, 1980).

"Boogie: 1 A.M." Poem. *See Montage of a Dream Deferred.*

The Book of Negro Folklore (New York: Dodd, Mead, 1958). 624 pp. Coedited with Arna Bontemps* (Hughes's name appears first). Collection of folklore (tales, stories, rhymes, poems, songs, and so on). Bontemps's "Introduction" (vii–xv) provides a brief historical overview. The volume is organized according to the following categories (and chapters): "Animal Tales," "Animal Rhymes," "Memories of Slavery," "Sometimes in the Mind" (which includes the tale "High John de Conquer" by Zora Neale Hurston*), "God, Man, and the Devil," "Do You Call That a Preacher?" "Ghost Stories," "Black Magic and Chance,""On the Levee," "Amen Corner," "Spirituals," "Gospel Songs" (which includes "When I Touch His Garment," from *Tambourines to Glory*), "Pastime Rhymes," "Ballads," "Blues," "Work Songs," "Street Cries," "Playsongs and Games," "The Jazz Folk," "Harlem Jive," "The 'Problem,' " "Songs in the Folk Manner," "Poetry in the Folk Manner," and "Prose in the Folk Manner." Unlike *The Book of Negro Humor* (see the entry for that work), *The Book of Negro Folklore* was well received by critics, owing to the variety of sources and texts the two editors used. Contemporary writers whose works Hughes and Bontemps reprinted include Taylor Gordon, Jean Toomer,* Sterling Brown,* Richard Wright,* Ralph Ellison,* St. Clair Drake, Horace R. Cayton, Owen Dodson, Gwendolyn Brooks,* Abram Hill, and Alice Childress. Also represented are Paul Laurence Dunbar,* James Weldon Johnson,* Bert Williams, Robert Hayden, and Melvin B. Tolson.* Bontemps's story "Lonesome Boy" is reprinted, as are several poems by Hughes, including "Young Gal's Blues," "Ma Lord," "Bad Morning," "Motto," "Jam Session," and "Wake." *See also Black Magic: A Pictorial History of the Negro in American Entertainment.*

Bibliography: Rampersad, II, 265–266, 277–278, 290.

The Book of Negro Humor (New York: Dodd, Mead, 1966). 265 pp. Collection of humor, edited by Hughes. Rampersad suggests that part of the material had previously appeared in *The Book of Negro Folklore*, and he notes that before Dodd, Mead accepted the book, Indiana University Press rejected it, finding "the jokes . . . insulting to blacks" (377).

Bibliography: Rampersad, II.

"Bop." Short story, included in *The Best of Simple. See* Simple [Jesse B.] Stories.

"Border Line." Two-quatrain rhyming poem pondering border lines that are metaphysical; first published in *Fields of Wonder*. Later Charles Barrett Griffin set the poem to music. *See* "Distance Nowhere"; "Drum"; "Night: Four Songs"; "Suicide's Note." Ricky Ian Gordon also set the poem to music as part of a song cycle: *see* "Strange Hurt."

Bibliography: *CP*, 325; Earlene Garber, "Form as a Complement to Content in Three of Langston Hughes' Poems," *Negro American Literature Forum* 5 (Winter 1971), 137–139; Charles Barrett Griffin, *Distance Nowhere: 5 Langston Hughes Songs: For Baritone and String Quartet* (Forest Hills, NY: Charles Griffin, 1995).

"The Bottle of Wine." Short story, written in 1941. The narrative concerns a man whose mother has just died; rather than confronting the death emotionally, the man goes on a drinking binge. Later Hughes changed the title to "On the Way Home" and published the story in *Story Magazine* (May/June 1941). Under the latter title, the story is included in the collections *Laughing to Keep from Crying* and *Something in Common and Other Stories* and is reprinted in *Langston Hughes: Short Stories*.

Bibliography: Rampersad, II, 30.

"Bound No'th Blues." Four-stanza poem written in traditional blues* form and in black dialect.* The speaker is delighted to be leaving the small towns in Mississippi. The poem was first published in *Opportunity** (1926). *Collected Poems* includes a note on revisions the poem underwent. For the 1991 production of *Mule Bone*, Taj Mahal set the poem to music, and it is included in Taj Mahal's recording of songs from the play. The song is published by Prankee Music; see the entry for *Mule Bone* for information about the recording.

Bibliography: *CP*, 76, 630.

"Bouquet." Six-line poem. Lines three and six rhyme. *Carpe diem* can be said to be the theme. The poem was first published in *Colorado Review* (Spring–Summer 1957).

Bibliography: *CP*, 457.

Boy, Big. Name of a character in the dialogue-poem "50–50," and of one in the poem "Catch."

"A Boy like You." Song, from *Street Scene*. Hughes wrote the lyrics, and Kurt Weill* composed the music. ASCAP* lists the song as being published by Chappell & Company, and the ASCAP registry number is 320008400. *See also* "Ain't It Awful, the Heat"; "Catch Me If You Can"; "Don't Forget the Lilac Bush"; "I Got a Marble and a Star"; "I Loved Her, Too"; "Ice Cream."

"Boy of the Border." Short story for children. It was cowritten by Arna Bontemps* and Hughes in 1935 but was never published. A manuscript is held in the Langston Hughes Papers, James Weldon Johnson Memorial Collection, Beinecke Library, Yale University.

Bibliography: Rampersad, I, 374.

Boyd, Ananias. Name of the narrator of Hughes's Jesse B. Simple stories.* Boyd is a peripheral narrator of the tales, functioning as a kind of foil or "straight man" for the character Jesse B. Simple. Typically, a few lines of narration in the short tales precede a dialogue between Boyd and Simple, one that Simple dominates. In the tales Boyd comes off as taciturn, unflappable, and reserved, especially in contrast to the extroverted, loquacious Simple. *See* "Here to Yonder."

Bibliography: Akiba Sullivan Harper, *Not So Simple: The "Simple" Stories by Langston Hughes* (Columbia: University of Missouri Press, 1995).

"Boys, Birds, and Bees." Short story, included in the collections *Simple Takes a Wife* and *The Best of Simple*. *See* Simple [Jesse B.] Stories.

"Brand New Clothes." Poem. *See* Children's Poetry.

Bibliography: *CP*, 606.

"Brass Spittoons." Free-verse poem of about one page, spoken by a collective persona* representing different employees in different American cities ordering a "boy" (that is, different African American employees) to clean spittoons. The callous bluster of the persona, the derogatory use of "boy," and the menial task itself combine to symbolize racial and economic injustice. The poem was first published in *New Masses* (December 1926). Later, Murray Bain set the poem to music. ASCAP* lists no publisher for the song, but the ASCAP registry number is 320394042.

Bibliography: *CP*, 86.

Braswell, Duke (Reverend). Pastor of the First Ethiopian Baptist Church in *Not Without Laughter*.

"Breakfast in Virginia." Short story, first published under the title "I Thank You for This" in *Common Ground* (October 1944). The narrative concerns two African American soldiers during World War II. They take a train from their army training facility in the southern United States to Harlem*; the story concerns their experiences in a "Jim Crow" car of the train. The story was included in the collection *Something in Common and Other Stories* and was reprinted in *Langston Hughes: Short Stories*. *See* Jim Crow Laws.

Bibliography: Ostrom, 48.

"Breath of a Rose." Rhyming poem in four quatrains. It features highly conventional poetic diction and imagery and is a kind of throwback to British lyric poetry from earlier centuries, especially in the way it compares the transitory nature of love to that of a rose blossom. It was first published in *The Big Sea*, where Hughes indicates that the poem sprang from a failed romance with a woman named Mary, identified in Rampersad's biography of Hughes as Anne Marie Coussey. Later, William Grant Still* set the poem to music. ASCAP* lists the song as being published by G. Schirmer, Inc., and the ASCAP registry number is 320088053. With regard to collaborations with Still, *see* "A Black Pierrot" and *Troubled Island. See also* "Letter to Anne."

Bibliography: *The Big Sea*, 170–171; *CP*, 305; Rampersad, I, 86–90.

Breen, Bobby (born 1927). Canadian American singer and actor. Breen was born Robert Boruch in Montreal, Canada, the son of Russian immigrants. He took up singing as a young boy and won several amateur contests in Canada. Managed by his sister Sally, Breen moved to Chicago when he was sixteen and appeared at the Oriental Theatre in a revue, one star of which was Milton Berle. He also began appearing on radio programs. In 1934 he moved to New York, where he earned a part in the Broadway musical *Say When*, starring Bob Hope. Shortly thereafter he and Sally moved to Hollywood and began appearing in low-budget musical films produced by Sol Lesser, who used Breen in ways similar to those in which Shirley Temple was used in musicals and melodramas with larger budgets. Breen's first film was *Let's Sing Again* (1936), followed by *Rainbow on the River* (1936), *Make a Wish* (1937), *Hawaii Calls* (1938), *Break the Ice* (1938), *Fisherman's Wharf* (1939), and *Way Down South* (1939), the latter cowritten by Hughes and Clarence Muse.* During this decade Breen also appeared on Eddie Cantor's radio program. When Breen's voice changed, his career in Hollywood faltered, although he did appear in one more film, *Johnny Doughboy* (1943). He attended the University of California, Los Angeles, and served in the U.S. Army during World War II. Later he became a theatrical agent in Miami, Florida.

Bibliography: James Robert Parish and Michael R. Pitts, *Hollywood Songsters* (New York: Garland, 1991), 58.

The Bremen. Name of the ship on which Hughes sailed to the Soviet Union from New York City in June 1932.

Bibliography: *I Wonder As I Wander*, 24.

"Brief Encounter." Three-stanza poem in black dialect,* spoken by a man to a judge. Apparently the man killed a woman. He is explaining his motive for murder to the judge. The poem was first published in *Shakespeare in Harlem*.

Bibliography: *CP*, 247.

"Broadcast on Ethiopia." Poem that creates a collage of voices and texts, including a sarcastic narrator's voice, excerpts from Associated Press wire stories, and mock radio broadcasts, all concerning the invasion of Ethiopia by Italy in 1936. The poem mentions the flight of Haile Selassie (emperor of Ethiopia, 1930–1974) from Addis Ababa (capital of the East African country), as well as Benito Mussolini (dictator of Italy, 1922–1943), who ordered the invasion. The poem was first published in the *American Spectator* (July–August 1936). *See also* "Call of Ethiopia"; "Emperor Hailie Selassie"; "Gangsters"; "Refugee Road"; "Shall the Good Go Down?"

Bibliography: *CP*, 192; Jasper Godwin Ridley, *Mussolini* (New York: St. Martin's Press, 1998); John H. Spencer, *Ethiopia at Bay: A Personal Account of the Haile Selassie Years* (Algonac, MI: Reference Publications, 1984).

"Broadcast to the West Indies." Poem of over two pages, in free verse. Between the title and the text of the poem are the lines, "Radio Station: Harlem/ Wave Length: The Human Heart." The poem is spoken by a collective persona* representing Harlem. The poem stresses the common interests and problems between the people of Harlem and those of Carribean countries and argues that, in spite of its problems, the United States is much preferable to the world envisaged by the Axis Powers in World War II. The poem was first published in *People's Voice* (August 1943).

Bibliography: *CP*, 273.

"Broken Strings." Song, from *Simply Heavenly*. Hughes wrote the lyrics, and David Martin composed the music. ASCAP* lists the song as being published by the Bourne Company, and the ASCAP registry number is 320093065.

Brooks, Gwendolyn (1917–2000). American poet, novelist, and teacher. Brooks was born in Topeka, Kansas, but grew up in Chicago. She began writing poetry in her teen years. During the 1930s, she worked for the NAACP.* Her first collection of poetry, *A Street in Bronzeville* (1945), received critical acclaim. In 1949 Brooks became the first African American writer to win the Pulitzer Prize, which was awarded to her novel *Annie Allen*. Other works include *Selected Poems* (1967), *In the Mecca* (1968), *Riot* (1969), and an autobiography, *Report From Part One* (1972). Brooks taught at several universities. Like much of Hughes's poetry, Brooks's verse often concerns the lives of urban African Americans, and it combines lyric and narrative modes powerfully.

Bibliography: Harry B. Shaw, *Gwendolyn Brooks* (New York: Twayne, 1980); Stephen Caldwell Wright, ed., *On Gwendolyn Brooks* (Ann Arbor: University of Michigan Press, 1996).

"Brotherly Love." Poem in five modified ballad* stanzas. It is subtitled "A Little Letter to the White Citizens of the South." The "writer" of the letter insists that he and other African Americans are determined to love even those white citizens who are aggressively racist. The poem alludes to the Montgomery, Alabama, bus boycott of 1956. The poem was first published in the *Nation* (August 18, 1956) and was reprinted in *The Panther and the Lash*.

Bibliography: *CP*, 453.

"Brothers." Poem. *See Montage of a Dream Deferred.*

"Brothers." Unproduced radio script, written in 1942. A manuscript is held in the Langston Hughes Papers, James Weldon Johnson Memorial Collection, Beinecke Library, Yale University.

Bibliography: Rampersad, II, 39.

Brown, Lord Piggly-Wiggly Wigglesfoot. *See* "Envoy to Africa."

Brown, Ruby. The character in the narrative poem "Ruby Brown."

Brown, Sterling (1901–1989). American poet, scholar of folklore, critic, editor, and teacher. Brown was born and grew up in Washington, D.C., and earned a B.A. from Williams College in 1923. He taught at several universities before joining the faculty at Howard University in 1929, where he taught until he retired in 1969. His book *The Negro in American Fiction* (1937) is a seminal work of criticism. Like Hughes, Brown had a long-standing interest in African American folklore; he contributed pieces to *The Book of Negro Folklore*.

Bibliography: Roger M. Valade III, *The Essential Black Literature Guide* (Detroit: Visible Ink Press, 1996), 59–60.

"Brown America in Jail: Kilby." Essay. The piece sprang from Hughes's visit to the state penitentiary at Kilby, Alabama, where the Scottsboro Boys* were serving sentences. Much of the essay is written in deliberately halting notation form to give Hughes's impressions of the prison. Other parts of the essay directly attack what Hughes believed to be the fierce racism lying behind the Scottsboro prosecution. Additionally, Hughes portrays the Scottsboro Boys as symbols both of "Brown America" and of martyrdom. The essay was first published in *Opportunity* (June 1932) and was reprinted in Berry.

Bibliography: Berry, 58–60.

Brown v. Board of Education. Landmark decisions by the U.S. Supreme Court that revolutionized racial politics and mobilized Hughes and other African Americans. The Board of Education of Topeka, from which Carrie Hughes had secured permission for her son to start first grade at the Harrison Street School rather than a "colored" school in 1908, lent its name to one of the most important decisions issued by the U.S. Supreme Court in the Twentieth century. *Brown v.*

Board of Education is shorthand for two opinions of the Court, four cases from four states (Delaware, Kansas, South Carolina, and Virginia), and a sea change in thinking and speaking about race in America. The two opinions, nicknamed *Brown I* and *Brown II*, augured a racial and constitutional revolution that would reconstitute judicial, executive, legislative, and electoral arrangements through the end of the millennium. The four cases from two border states and two southern states decided at a minimum that states violated the Equal Protection Clause of the Fourteenth Amendment when they mandated public schools separated by race. The sea change in governmental and popular attitudes toward race made it seem possible that segregation might yield to integration or at least desegregation. *Brown I* (announced May 17, 1954) represented the most significant triumph of the Legal Defense Fund (LDF) of the National Association for the Advancement of Colored People (NAACP*). Headed by William Hastie, Charles Houston, and Thurgood Marshall,* the NAACP and its LDF had coordinated litigation against segregation for decades and had achieved notable triumphs. When Chief Justice Earl Warren spoke for a Court that he had marshaled into unanimity, his unadorned opinion awarded the LDF a stunning if circumscribed victory: "We conclude that in the field of public education the doctrine of 'separate but equal' has no place. Separate educational facilities are inherently unequal." The chief justice had constructed an opinion that was spare and simple enough for newspapers to reprint it in its entirety. In a short complement to *Brown I*, the unanimous Court disallowed Congress from segregating public schools in the District of Columbia. This latter opinion, *Bolling v. Sharpe*, found such "Jim Crow" schools to be contrary to the Due Process Clause of the Fourteenth Amendment. To cushion the blow of *Brown I*, the Court postponed its directives regarding implementation of the principles pronounced in the 1954 bombshell. When it issued *Brown II* on May 31, 1955, the Court revealed compromises that underlay its unanimity. Chief Justice Warren's most famous phrase in *Brown II* was that U.S. district courts should remedy Jim Crow schools with "all deliberate speed," a standard in which "deliberate" seemed to take back whatever "speed" might have promised. The remainder of the very short implementation decision was somewhat contradictory as well. On the one hand, the Court directed district courts to devise remedies "to achieve a system of determining admission to the public schools on a nonracial basis." On the other hand, district courts were "to effectuate a transition to a racially nondiscriminatory school system." The latter directive—that schools must be "nondiscriminatory"—might be met once parents could no longer prove that separation of the races was intentional. This might be called a policy of *desegregation*, the ending of overt, official segregation by state legislatures. In contrast, the former directive—that public schools be operated on a "nonracial" basis—might be called a policy of *integration*, for schools might remain recognizably racial even in the absence of formal or informal actions by states. Thus the text of *Brown II* itself reflected an American dilemma between merely ceasing to discriminate and actually beginning to integrate. After *Brown I* and *Brown II*, this ambivalence about racism and discrimination was exacerbated by "massive resistance" in the South and elsewhere. Hughes contested resistance to *Brown I* and waged the new racial politics, mostly through letters and statements. He also participated in a celebrity-studded NAACP tribute on the tenth anniversary of *Brown I*. *See also* "Democracy and Me"; *Fight for Freedom*; "Governor Fires Dean"; Jim Crow Laws; "Little Song on Housing."

William Haltom

Bibliography: *Bolling v. Sharpe*, 347 U.S. 497 (1954); *Brown v. Board of Education*, 347 U.S. 483 (1954); *Brown v. Board of Education*, 349 U.S. 294 (1955); Richard Kluger, *Simple Justice* (New York: Knopf, 1975); Rampersad, II; Gerald N. Rosenberg, *The Hollow Hope* (Chicago: University of Chicago Press, 1991); Mark V. Tushnet, *Making Civil Rights Law: Thurgood Marshall and the Supreme Court, 1936–1961* (New York: Oxford University Press, 1994); Mark V. Tushnet, *The NAACP's Legal Strategy against Segregated Education, 1925–1950* (Chapel Hill: University of North Carolina Press, 1987).

The Brownie's Book. A magazine produced chiefly for African American adolescents in the early 1920s. It was begun by W.E.B. Du Bois*; he oversaw the editing, which was performed mainly by Jessie Fauset.* The magazine published two early short stories by Hughes: "In a Mexican City" and "Those Who Have No Turkey," as well a short play, "Gold Piece," and several poems. *See* Children's Poetry.

"Buddy." Poem. *See Montage of a Dream Deferred.*

"Bulwark." Poem of twenty-four lines, intermittently rhymed. Addressing a certain "You," the speaker indicates that the person had been an emotional "bulwark" but that "you, too, have tumbled down." The poem was first published in *Carolina Magazine* (1927) and was included in the second edition of *Collected Poems*.
Bibliography: *CP* [second edition only], 613.

"Burden." Haunting four-line poem (lines two and four rhyme) about a "song without sound," first published in the *Carmel Pine Cone* (August 14, 1941).
Bibliography: *CP*, 326.

"But I Rode Some." Song, from *Mule Bone*. The lyrics, by Hughes, appear in the published text of the play, and the music for the 1991 production was composed by Taj Mahal. At this writing, the song is not registered with ASCAP*; however, information accompanying the recording of *Mule Bone* songs by Taj Mahal indicates that the song is published by Prankee Music and Golden Foot Music. For additional information about the recording, *see* the entry for *Mule Bone*. *See also* "Bound No'th Blues"; "Crossing"; "Graveyard Mule"; "Hey-Hey Blues"; "Jubilee"; "Me and the Mule."

Butler, Nicholas Murray. *See* Columbia University.

Butler, Sadie. In *Not Without Laughter*, chapter 14, Sadie Butler is one of three African American students—including the main character, Sandy—in a fourth-grade class. She and Sandy move on to fifth grade, but Mary Jones is held back. Sadie sends Sandy a "big heart" on Valentine's Day.

Bynner, Witter (1881–1968). American editor, writer, translator, and patron of the arts. Bynner is perhaps best known now for the foundation bearing his name and supporting programs that promote the writing and reading of poetry. He was educated at Harvard and later gained recognition for his translation of Chinese poetry, especially verse dating from the T'ang dynasty. Bynner praised Hughes's early work but later expressed distaste for Hughes's more politically alert writings.

Bibliography: Rampersad, I, 203.

C

"Cabaret." Six-line poem in which lines two, four, and six rhyme. It concerns the moods of a jazz* band. The poem was first published in *Crisis** (August 1923).

Bibliography: *CP*, 35.

"Cabaret Girl Dies on Welfare Island." Two-quatrain poem spoken by the dying former "cabaret girl," who laments that she cannot die amidst her earlier vivid life and times. It was first published in *Shakespeare in Harlem*. *See* "The New Cabaret Girl."

Bibliography: *CP*, 251.

"Café: 3 a.m." Poem. *See Montage of a Dream Deferred*; Sexuality and Hughes.

Caledonia. A character in the poem "Fired."

"Call of Ethiopia." Two-stanza poem in which the first stanza is spoken to a personified Ethiopia and the second exhorts all of Africa to follow Ethiopia's example of independence. (In 1935 only Ethiopia and Liberia were independent African states, and Italy was about to try to colonize the former.) Doreski has observed that "[t]he invasion of Ethiopia, the Spanish Civil War, and the Second World War inspired poets and journalists alike to meditate upon the promise and reality of democracy in America" and cites this poem as one example. It was first published in *Opportunity** (September 1935). *See also* "Broadcast on Ethiopia"; "Emperor Haile Salassie"; "Gangsters."

Bibliography: *CP*, 184; C. K. Doreski, *Writing America Black: Race Rhetoric in the Public Sphere* (Cambridge University Press, 1998). *See also* bibliography for "Broadcast on Ethiopia."

"Call to Creation." Twenty-six-line poem addressed to "beauty makers," exhorting them to empathize with and assist starving, downtrodden, and oppressed people of the world, with specific reference to such people in India, Africa, and China. It was first published in *New Masses* (February 1931). *See* "Roar China!"
Bibliography: *CP*, 135.

"Canto de Una Muchacha Negra." Song. Hughes wrote the lyrics, and Silvestre Revueltas composed the music. The ASCAP* registry number for the song is 330381850. ASCAP* lists no publisher. The electronic database World Cat lists the song as "Canto" and lists E. B. Marks (New York) as the publisher (1948).

"Capitalism." Poem of seven lines in free verse. It critiques capitalism, described as a "Ship / Going Nowhere." The date of the poem's composition is uncertain, but it may have been written in the 1930s, when Hughes was most influenced by Marxist ideas. It was first published in Berry and is not included in *Collected Poems*. *See* Marxism; Politics.
Bibliography: Berry, 21–22.

Capone, Al (1899–1947). Legendary American criminal who controlled organized crime in Chicago from 1925 to 1931. *See* "Gangsters."

Capstan. A brand of cigarette mentioned in "Sailor."

"Caribbean Sunset." Poem of a single free-verse quatrain comparing the Caribbean sunset to God's having a hemorrhage; out of this startling, potentially reckless comparison, Hughes manages to produce a surprisingly effective image and certainly subverts cliché descriptions of beautiful sunsets. The poem was first published in *The Weary Blues*.
Bibliography: *CP*, 98.

Carmel-by-the-Sea (Carmel). California community. *See* Jeffers, Robinson and Una; Steffens, Lincoln; Sullivan, Noel.

"Carmelita and the Cockatoo." Scenario for a ballet, written in 1941 but unproduced. Hughes wrote it expressly for dancer Katherine Dunham. A playful scenario, it concerns a tropical bird that becomes enamored with a maid.
Bibliography: Rampersad, II, 28.

"Carol of the Brown King." Poem focusing on and forging an identification with the one "brown man" of the three Wise Men who, according to Christian tradition, visited the newborn Jesus in the manger. It was first published in

Crisis* (December 1958). *See Ballad of the Brown King; Carol of the Brown King: Nativity Poems by Langston Hughes.*

Bibliography: *CP*, 461.

Carol of the Brown King: Nativity Poems by Langston Hughes. (New York: Atheneum, 1998). 32 pp. Illustrated by Ashley Bryan. Children's book that includes "Carol of the Brown King," "Shepherd's Song at Christmas," "On a Christmas Night," "On a Pallet of Straw," "An Anonymous Verse," and "The Christmas Story." *See Ballad of the Brown King*; Children's Poetry; *The Glory around His Head; Gospel Glow*; Religion.

"Carolina Balmoral." Song. Hughes wrote the lyrics, and James P. Johnson* composed the music. ASCAP* lists the song as being published by EMI/Mills, Inc., and the song's ASCAP registry number is 330256076.

"Carolina Cabin." Four-stanza poem in which the last words of stanzas one and two rhyme, as do those of stanzas three and four. The poem is restrained in its celebration of coziness, peace, and intimacy in the cabin, but for many readers, it may still seem to gravitate, at least, toward sentimentality. It was first published in *Fields of Wonder*. Later, Jean Berger set the poem to music. ASCAP* lists the song as being published by Broude Brothers, Ltd., and the ASCAP registry number is 330303827. Also, Robert Owens set this poem, "In Time of Silver Rain," "Fulfillment," "Night Song," "Silence," and "Songs" to music in a song cycle, *Silver Rain*.

Bibliography: *CP*, 331; Robert Owens [composer], *Silver Rain: Song Cycle For Tenor and Piano*, op. 11 (Munich: Orlando *Musik-Verlag, 1975*).

Carraway, Michael and Anne. The married couple in the story "Slave on the Block," who are fascinated by African Americans. The first sentence of the story is "They were people who went in for Negroes—the Carraways—Michael and Anne" (*The Ways of White Folks*, 19).

"Carry On, America." Dramatic material. With Norman Corwin and Howard Fast, Hughes collaborated on this script for a pageant, which was one segment of a "Negro Freedom Rally" that took place on June 25, 1944, in Madison Square Garden, New York City. Actors Paul Robeson,* Canada Lee, and Frederic March participated in the rally.

Bibliography: Rampersad, II, 105.

Carver, George Washington (1864–1943). American scientist, agriculturalist, and educator. Carver is best known for his remarkable achievements in developing new methods of plant propagation and farming and for the teaching and research he did at the Tuskegee Institute in Alabama. In *I Wonder As I Wander*,

Hughes mentions meeting Carver at the institute when Hughes came there in 1932 to read poetry. Carver showed Hughes his "private laboratory." *See* Washington, Booker T.

Bibliography: George Washington Carver, *George Washington Carver in His Own Words*, ed. Gary R. Kremer (Columbia: University of Missouri Press, 1987); *I Wonder As I Wander*, 60; Linda O. McMurry, *George Washington Carver: Scientist and Symbol* (New York: Oxford University Press, 1982).

"Castles in the Sand." Short story, included in the collection *Simple Takes a Wife*. *See* Simple [Jesse B.] Stories.

"Casual." Two-stanza poem personifying death as someone who does not know or use the doorbell but, familiarly, just enters. Both the personification and the wry tone are slightly reminiscent of Emily Dickinson's poem "I Could Not Stop for Death." According to the editors of *Collected Poems*, the poem was first published in a magazine called *Hearse*, for which the editors could not find an issue date or volume number. *Hearse* was published by E. V. Griffith from 1957 to 1972. The Stanford University library holds an E. V. Griffith special collection that includes many issues of *Hearse* and an index of poetry in those issues. Neither Hughes nor "Casual" appears in this index.

Bibliography: *CP*, 459, 680.

"Casualty." Poem. *See Montage of a Dream Deferred.*

"The Cat and the Saxophone (2 a.m.)." Poem that interweaves a conversation between a man and a woman with (in all capital letters) parts of a popular lyric. The editors of *Collected Poems* identify the song as "Everybody Loves My Baby, But My Baby Don't Love Nobody But Me," written in 1924 by Jack Palmer and Spencer Williams. The poem was first published in *The Weary Blues*.

Bibliography: *CP*, 89, 632; James A. Emanuel, "The Literary Experiments of Langston Hughes," in O'Daniel, 171–182.

"Catch." Thirteen-line poem that narrates the story of a certain "Big Boy," who is a fisherman and who weds a mermaid. It was first published in *Minnesota Quarterly* (September 1950).

Bibliography: *CP*, 375.

"Catch Me If You Can." Song, from *Street Scene*. Hughes and Elmer Rice* wrote the lyrics, and Kurt Weill* composed the music. ASCAP* lists the song as being published by Chappell, Inc., and the ASCAP registry number is 330281215. *See also* "Ain't It Awful, the Heat"; "A Boy like You"; "Don't

Forget the Lilac Bush"; "I Got a Marble and a Star"; "I Loved Her, Too"; "Ice Cream."

"Celebration for Art Tatum." Song. Hughes wrote the lyrics, and David N. Jex composed the music. ASCAP* lists no publisher for the song, but the ASCAP registry number is 330614705. *See* Jazz.

"Cellophane Bandanas." Short story, included in the collection *Simple Stakes a Claim. See* Simple [Jesse B.] Stories.

"Census." Short story, included in the collection *Simple's Uncle Sam. See* Simple [Jesse B.] Stories.

Central High School, Cleveland, Ohio. The high school from which Hughes graduated in 1920. The first free public high school west of the Allegheny Mountains, it was founded on July 13, 1846, on Prospect Avenue, west of East Ninth Street in Cleveland. In 1856 it moved to the corner of East Ninth Street and Euclid Avenue; it outgrew that facility, and a third complex was built between Wilson Avenue and East 55th Street (2200 East 55th), which is where Hughes attended high school and contributed writings to the school magazine at the time, the *Belfry Owl*. He also published two stories in the *Monthly*, also a publication of the high school: "Those Who Have No Turkey" and "Seventy-five Dollars." Both stories are reprinted in *Langston Hughes: Short Stories*. "Mary Winosky," a story written, as Harper indicates, "for an English assignment in 1915" at Central High, is held in the Langston Hughes Papers of the James Weldon Johnson Memorial Collection at Yale University and has been reprinted in *Langston Hughes: Short Stories*. In 1940 the school moved to its present location at 2225 East 40th Street, and in 1952 it was converted to Central Junior High School, now known as Central Middle School, serving grades six through eight. In addition to Hughes, other notable alumni of Central High (or Middle) School include John D. and William Rockefeller, Laura C. Spelman (Mrs. John D. Rockefeller), Noble Sissle, General Benjamin O. Davis, jurist Anthony O. Celebreeze, Sr., and Congressperson Louis Stokes. *See also* Ingram, Zell; "Swing Time at the Savoy."

Bibliography: Akiba Sullivan Harper, ed., *Langston Hughes: Short Stories* (New York: Hill and Wang, 1996), 219–231; "History of Central Middle School," publication of Central Middle School, 2225 East 40th Street, Cleveland, Ohio 44104, telephone: (216) 431–4410; "Mary Winosky," Langston Hughes Papers (item 666), James Weldon Johnson Memorial Collection, Beinecke Library, Yale University.

Césaire, Aimé (born 1913). Poet, political writer, and politician. A native of the Caribbean island of Martinique, Césaire has long been associated with the idea of "Negritude," a concept that includes an awareness of African cultural roots that many peoples worldwide share, an awareness that transcends nationality. Césaire has also been a proponent of Marxist ideas, or at least of political views that take into account economic power (especially with regard to colonialism), economic conflict, and the situation of working people worldwide. Poets Léon Damas of French Guiana and Léopold Senghor of Senegal also participated in the "Negritude" movement. Césaire, Damas, Senghor, and others saw Hughes's work as an important touchstone for "Negritude," partly because his writing expresses an awareness of African cultural roots and of the international community of "Negroes." Rampersad observes, "To such people [as Césaire, Damas, and Senghor], Langston Hughes had been not only one of the prophets in his calls during the previous decade for black racial pride instead of assimilation, but the most important technical influence in his emphasis on folk and jazz* rhythms as the basis of his poetry of racial pride" (II, 343). Studying in Paris in the 1930s, Césaire helped establish the newspaper *L'Etudiant noir*. Writing in French, he has published several volumes of poetry and a book on colonialism, *Discours sur le colonialisme* (1955), and he wrote an adaptation of Shakespeare's *Tempest* for the stage; the play has been produced worldwide. He has served in the French Parliament for over forty years. *See* "Lumumba's Grave"; *Poems from Black Africa*.

Bibliography: A. James Arnold, *Modernism and Negritude: The Poetry and Poetics of Aimé Césaire* (Cambridge, MA: Harvard University Press, 1981); *Aimé Césaire. The Collected Poems*, translated, with an introduction, by Clayton Eshleman and Annette Smith (Berkeley: University of California Press, 1983); Aimé Césaire, *Discours sur le colonialisme* (Paris: Présence Africaine, 1955); Aimé Césaire, *A Tempest*, transl. Richard Miller (New York: George Borchardt, 1985); Lilyan Kesteloot, "Césaire, Poet and Politician," *Research in African Literatures* 26, no. 2 (Summer 1995), 169–173; Annick Thebia Melsan, "The Liberating Power of Words (Interview with Poet Aimé Césaire)," *UNESCO Courier* (May 1997), 4; Rampersad, II, 343.

"Chalk Marks on the Sidewalk." Song. Hughes wrote the lyrics, and Elie Siegmeister, with whom Hughes collaborated on the *Wizard of Altoona* (unfinished opera), composed the music. ASCAP* lists the song as being published by the Alfred Publishing Company, and the ASCAP registry number is 330262701.

"Change." Eight-line rhyming poem that includes an unusual image of the moon and a surprising comparison between the moon and the speaker's "love." To some extent, the poem subverts the conventional imagery of love poetry. It was first published in *Reflexus*, but see the entry on "Better" for a note on this journal.

Bibliography: *CP*, 54.

"Chant for May Day." Poem intended to be performed by "a Workman" and different configurations of a workers' dramatic chorus, according to notes that appear just below the title. It was first published in *A New Song*.

Bibliography: *CP*, 209.

"Chant for Tom Mooney." Poem rhetorically addressed to Tom Mooney but implicitly aimed at rallying support for him. Mooney (1882–1942) was a labor activist in San Francisco, California, who, in 1916, was arrested for throwing a bomb during a rally held in support of U.S. involvement in the Great War (World War I). He was convicted and sentenced to die, but later perjured testimony was shown to have led to his conviction. His sentence was commuted to life in prison, but he was released in 1939. Ironically, the poem proclaims how famous Mooney will be down through the years as a hero of labor, but he is largely forgotten now and is memorialized chiefly in this poem. It was first published under the title "For Tom Mooney" in *New Masses* (September 1932). *See also Angelo Herndon Jones*; "Ballads of Lenin"; *Don't You Want to Be Free?*; "Goodbye, Christ"; "Good Morning, Revolution"; "Lenin"; "One More 'S' in the U.S.A"; "Revolution"; "Song of the Revolution"; "Wait." *See also* Marxism; Politics.

Bibliography: *CP*, 164; Rampersad, I, 238.

Charlie. A character in the poem "Saturday Night."

"Checking on the Freedom." Song. Hughes wrote the lyrics, and Samuel Edwin Heward, Jr., composed the music. ASCAP* lists the song as being published by Handy Brothers Music Company, and the song's ASCAP registry number is 330041637.

Chesnutt, Charles Waddell (1858–1932). American short-story writer, novelist, and professional court reporter. Chesnutt was born in Cleveland, Ohio, and except for a stint as a public-school principal in North Carolina, spent his life there, working as a court reporter. The appearance of the story "The Gophered Grapevine" in the *Atlantic Monthly* launched his writing career. He went on to publish collections of stories, a biography of Frederick Douglass,* and novels, including *The House behind the Cedars* (1900) and *The Colonel's Dream* (1905). Chesnutt's treatment of racial conflict, including the theme of passing, as well as his grasp of Douglass's intellectual and political importance, made him an especially important literary figure for writers in the Harlem Renaissance.*

Bibliography: Charles Duncan, *The Absent Man: The Narrative Craft of Charles W. Chesnutt* (Athens: Ohio University Press, 1998).

"Chicago." Poem of sixty lines, intermittently rhymed. It celebrates the city of Chicago. First published in *Negro Digest* (September 1964); it is included in the second edition of *Collected Poems*.

Bibliography: *CP* [second edition only], 616, 695.

"Chicago Blues." Subtitled "(moral: go slow)," this seven-stanza poem evokes a despair associated with the blues,* but the form diverges from that of a traditional blues lyric. Stanza seven repeats stanza one exactly, constituting a refrain; stanzas two through six narrate, in the first person, the specific tale leading to despair. The editors of *Collected Poems* found no date or previous publication record for the poem. *See also* "Promised Land."

Bibliography: *CP*, 592, 686.

The *Chicago Defender.* Newspaper. Robert S. Abbott founded the *Chicago Defender* in 1905, the first issue appearing on May 5. Abbott was a graduate of the Hampton Institute in Virginia and also earned a law degree at the Kent School of Law in Chicago. A weekly newspaper for the first fifty-one years of its existence, the *Chicago Defender* was aimed chiefly at an African American readership, although it reported on general news as well as on issues and events bearing directly on African American communities. Abbott was determined to ensure that the newspaper would improve the lives of African Americans in Chicago, the Midwest, and nationwide not just by reporting news that affected them but also by involving itself with specific causes. For example, Abbott urged African Americans living in the southern United States to migrate north, where he believed that more opportunities for employment and social advancement existed. Although many factors influenced the massive migration of African Americans to northern cities in the early part of the twentieth century, Abbott's campaign is generally considered to have had a crucial impact; it may have induced as many as 50,000 African Americans to migrate north in 1915 alone. Eventually, the *Defender* became the first African American newspaper to reach a circulation of 100,000. Walker observes, "In 1910 the *Defender* reached one-tenth of Chicago's black population; some ten years later the *Defender* reached one-tenth of the nation's black population. By 1920 the *Chicago Defender* was the first black newspaper to gain extensive national circulation" (25). Abbott's nephew, John H. Sengstacke, transformed the *Defender* into a daily newspaper (beginning on February 4, 1956), which it remains. (As of this writing, the newspaper's offices are located at 2400 South Michigan Avenue in Chicago). In 1942 then editor-in-chief Metz P. T. Lockhart invited Hughes to contribute a weekly column to the *Defender*, and Hughes agreed, publishing the first installment of "Here to Yonder" (the column's title) on November 21, 1942. The weekly column continued for twenty-three years, the last one appearing on January 8, 1966. It was in "Here to Yonder" that Hughes created the Jesse B. Simple stories, the first one appearing on February 13, 1943. *See Baltimore Afro American*; "Here to Yonder."

Bibliography: Christopher De Santis, ed., *Langston Hughes and the* Chicago Defender: Essays on Race, Politics, and Culture, 1942–62 (Urbana: University of Illinois Press, 1995); Donna Akiba Sullivan Harper, *Not So Simple: The "Simple" Stories by Langston Hughes* (Columbia: University of Missouri Press, 1995); Henry Lewis Suggs, "Conclusion: An Interpretive History of the Black Press in the Middle West, 1865–1985," in *The*

Black Press in the Middle West, 1865–1985, ed. Henry Lewis Suggs (Westport, CT: Greenwood Press, 1996), 349–364; Juliet E. K. Walker, "The Promised Land: The *Chicago Defender* and the Black Press in Illinois, 1862–1970," in *The Black Press in the Middle West*, ed. Henry Lewis Suggs (Westport, CT: Greenwood Press, 1996), 9–50.

"Childhood Memories." Song. Hughes wrote the lyrics, and Elie Siegmeister, with whom Hughes collaborated on the *Wizard of Altoona* (unfinished opera), composed the music. ASCAP* lists the song as being published by Seesaw Music Corporation, and the song's ASCAP registry number is 330327721.

"The Childhood of Jimmy." Short story, published in *Crisis** (May 1927). It concerns the experience of a young man in Harlem.*

Bibliography: Akiba Sullivan Harper, *Short Stories/Langston Hughes* (New York: Hill and Wang, 1996), 293–294.

Children's Poetry. *Collected Poems* contains thirty-three poems Hughes wrote and published primarily for children; these are included in an appendix. Among the topics the poems concern are nature, young love, racism, the blues,* hope, and aspirations. Several of the poems appeared in *Brownie's Book,** edited by Jessie Fauset* in 1921: "April Rain Song," "Autumn Thought," "Fairies," "The Lament of a Vanquished Beau," "Mister Sandman," "Signs of Spring," "Thanksgiving Time," and "Winter Sweetness." Eighteen of the poems, including "The Blues," first appeared in *The Langston Hughes Reader*. Others first appeared in the magazine *Common Ground*, in the *Baltimore Afro American,** and in the anthology *Golden Slippers*, edited by Arna Bontemps* (New York: Harper, 1941). *Black Misery* and *The Block*—both in "picture-book" format—contain short lyric poems for children and were published posthumously. *The Dream Keeper* is an illustrated book of poems for children, but it reprints previously published poems that were not necessarily first intended for children. Thus *The Dream Keeper* points to an interesting issue concerning Hughes's poetry, namely, that its overall accessibility invites a wide range of readers, including children. The poems for children that *Collected Poems* contains do reveal, however, that Hughes made particular choices with regard to topic, vocabulary, and diction when he had a children's audience primarily in mind, but at the same time such choices did not entail a radical shift from his usual approaches to poetry. Consequently, a poem such as "Theme for English B," to cite just one example, is extremely effective for both younger and older readers, even though it was not written primarily for children. *See also* Audience; *The Block*; "Boy of the Border"; *Carol of the Brown King: Nativity Poems by Langston Hughes; Famous American Negroes; Famous Negro Heroes of America; Famous Negro Music Makers; The First Book of Africa; The First Book of Jazz; The First Book of Negroes; The First Book of Rhythms; The First Book of the Caribbean; The*

First Book of the West Indies; The Paste-Board Bandit; Popo and Fifina; The Sweet and Sour Animal Book; Thank You, Ma'am.
Bibliography: *CP*, 595–610.

"Children's Rhymes." Poem. *See Montage of a Dream Deferred.*

"Chippy." Nine-line poem that extends a comparison between a "chippy" (prostitute) and a rose. It was first published in Australia's *Poetry Magazine* (August 20, 1946). *See also* the poem "Midnight Chippie's Lament," in which, obviously, Hughes uses another spelling of the word.
Bibliography: *CP*, 334.

"Chips on the Shoulder." Short story, included in the collection *Simple Stakes a Claim. See* Simple [Jesse B.] Stories.

"Chocolate Sailor." Synopsis for a prospective musical motion picture. Hughes wrote it in 1943. Neither a motion picture nor even a script materialized. *See* "Chocolate Soldier." A manuscript is held in the Langston Hughes Papers, James Weldon Johnson Memorial Collection, Beinecke Library, Yale University.
Bibliography: Rampersad, II, 69.

"Chocolate Soldier." Outline that expressed ideas for a musical motion picture. No synopsis, script, or motion picture resulted from the outline, which Hughes wrote in 1943. A manuscript is held in the Langston Hughes Papers, James Weldon Johnson Memorial Collection, Beinecke Library, Yale University.
Bibliography: Rampersad, II, 63.

"Chord." Poem. *See Montage of a Dream Deferred.*

Christ, Jesus. *See* Religion.

"Christ in Alabama." Fourteen-line poem, unquestionably one of Hughes's most memorable, explosive, and controversial works. It opens with the lines "Christ is a nigger, / Beaten and black." Mary becomes a "mammy," and "God" is the "white master above." One interpretation of these startling comparisons is that the poem intends to portray African Americans as martyrs to white supremacy in the United States. That is, one might reasonably argue that racism, not Christianity, is the "target" of the poem. However, after the poem was published, Hughes experienced a considerable critical backlash, which Rampersad details; the backlash was driven by a belief that the poem was anti-Christian. Regardless of which interpretation seems better supported by the text of the poem itself, the comparisons Hughes employed probably made the severe critical reaction inevitable, roughly in the same way that Jonathan Swift's legendary satire "A Modest Proposal" was destined to be interpreted by many readers not as ironic discourse but as straightforward opinion. Hughes's poem was first published in *Contempo* (December 1931). In *I Wonder As I Wander* Hughes offers his own interpretation of the poem: "It was an ironic poem inspired by the thought of how Christ, with no human father, would be accepted were He born in the south of a Negro mother" (46). In the same passage he describes how the editors of *Contempo*, Anthony Buttita and Miles Abernathy, were "delighted" by the "commotion" created by the publication of Hughes's poem and the essay "Southern Gentlemen, White Prostitutes, Mill Owners, and Negroes." *See* Religion.

Bibliography: *CP*, 143, 640; Mary Beth Culp, "Religion in the Poetry of Langston Hughes," *Phylon: A Review of Race and Culture* 48, no. 3 (Fall 1987), 240–245; James A. Emanuel, "Christ in Alabama: Religion in the Poetry of Langston Hughes," in *Modern Black Poets*, ed. Donald B. Gibson (Englewood Cliffs, NJ: Prentice-Hall, 1973), 57–68; *I Wonder As I Wander*, 46; Rampersad, I, 224–225.

"A Christian Country." Poem of a single quatrain in which God is compared to a drunk in an alley with a gin bottle in his hand, first published in *New Masses* (February 1931). *See* Religion.

Bibliography: *CP*, 136.

Christianity. *See* Religion.

"Christmas Eve: Nearing Midnight in New York." Poem of four quatrains with descriptions of New York City but more concerned with a mood of quiet imminence, playing deftly with the word "almost." *See also* "Harlem Night."

Bibliography: *CP*, 548.

"Christmas Song." Short story, included in the collections *Simple Takes a Wife* and *The Best of Simple*. *See* Simple [Jesse B.] Stories.

"The Christmas Story." Thirty-three-line poem in rhymed couplets, chiefly in trochaic meter, with four stresses in most lines. The poem recapitulates conventional elements concerning Christ's birth. It was first published in the *Catholic Interracialist* (January 1952) and was reprinted in *Carol of the Brown King: Nativity Poems by Langston Hughes*.

Bibliography: *CP*, 432.

Church bombings. *See* "Birmingham Sunday."

"Circles." Poem of ten lines in three stanzas; it is intermittently rhymed. The poem meditates on the circular, cyclical aspects of life and suggests that our lives eventually become circular "jails." The poem was first published in *Fields of Wonder*.

Bibliography: *CP*, 327.

"City." Poem of two quatrains personifying an unnamed city at dawn and at dusk. *See* Children's Poetry.

Bibliography: *CP*, 602.

Clark, George. In *Not Without Laughter* George Clark is a bellman at Drummer's Hotel, where Sandy, the main character, works. In chapter 19, he is also described as "the chief bootlegger [supplier of illegal liquor]" for the hotel.

Clark, Gwyn "Kit" (dates unknown). Hughes's stepbrother, son of Homer Clark.* He was several years younger than Hughes.

Bibliography. *The Big Sea*, 205; Rampersad, I.

Clark, Homer (dates unknown). Hughes's stepfather. Hughes's mother, Carrie Hughes,* married Clark in 1915.

Bibliography: *The Big Sea*; Rampersad, I, 48.

Clay, Samuel (dates unknown). One of Hughes's great-grandparents.

Bibliography: *The Big Sea*, 11–12; Rampersad, I, 10.

Clezie-Anne. First name of Hughes's female companion in Cuba. *See also* Coloma.

Bibliography: *I Wonder As I Wander*, 20–21.

"Closing Time." Fifteen-line poem. In phrasing it is spare and elliptical, but the emotions it evokes are complex insofar as the poem concerns a woman leaving a nightclub, hailing a taxi, but all the while remembering a girl—probably a daughter, perhaps a sister—who drowned in a river. It was first published in *Fine Clothes to the Jew*.

Bibliography: *CP*, 113.

Cocking, Walter. *See* "Governor Fires Dean."

"Cocktail Sip." Short story, included in the collections *Simple Takes a Wife* and *The Best of Simple*. *See* Simple [Jesse B.] Stories.

"Coffee Break." Short story, included in the collection *Simple's Uncle Sam*. *See* Simple [Jesse B.] Stories.

The Collected Poems of Langston Hughes. Edited by Arnold Rampersad and David Roessel (New York: Vintage Classics, 1994). 717 pp. At this writing, the book is considered the standard edition of Hughes's poetry. It includes over 850 poems, presented in chronological order (from 1921 through 1967), except for poems in three appendices: "Poems Circulated by the Associated Negro Press," "Poetry for Children," and (in the second edition) "Additional Poems." References in this encyclopedia to the earliest publication of poems are almost always based on the information in the extensive "Notes to Poems" section of *Collected Poems*. The volume also includes an introduction by Rampersad, a "Chronology of the Life of Langston Hughes," an "Index of First Lines," and an "Index of Titles." All poems included in *Collected Poems* have a separate entry in this encyclopedia. In a review of the book, Taylor writes, "Langston Hughes is one of the essential figures in American literature. . . . By his work and his example, he has enriched our lives." In another review, Vendler writes, "The [*Collected*] *Poems* completes Rampersad's long service to Hughes's memory." The second edition of *Collected Poems* contains six poems that were not included in the first printing of the book (613–618). These are "Bitter Brew," "Bulwark," "Chicago," "Madrid," "Moscow," and "Old Youth." *Collected Poems* does not contain eight poems that appear in Berry. These are "Capitalism," "Cotton," "Easter in Wartime," "Moscow," "Our Spring," "Poem for a Poster on Africa," "The Poor," and "War." Each of these poems also has its separate entry in this encyclopedia. *See also* "Ode to My Simple Minded Friend"; Revision, Process of, and Hughes.

Bibliography: Berry; Ellen Kaufman, review of *The Collected Poems of Langston Hughes, Library Journal* 119 (November 1, 1994), 80; Merle Rubin, review of *The Collected Poems of Langston Hughes, Christian Science Monitor* (December 2, 1994), 10; Donna Seaman, review of *The Collected Poems of Langston Hughes, Booklist* 91 (October 1, 1994), 186; Henry Taylor, review of *The Collected Poems of Langston Hughes, New York Times Book Review* (December 25, 1994), 15; Helen Vendler, review of *The Collected Poems of Langston Hughes, New Republic* 212 (March 6, 1995), 37.

Collections of Poetry. *See* Poetry, Collections of.

Collections of Short Stories. *See* Short Stories, Collections of.

Collective persona. As a poet, Hughes drew on an enormous variety of forms, techniques, levels of diction, and "voices" or personae. One poetic persona he relied on throughout his career, however, was that of an Everyman or collective persona: the voice of the people, a universal spokesperson, or a kind of metonymic voice—"metonymy" being the device whereby a part represents or symbolizes the whole, as in the expressions "all hands on deck" or "the Crown supports the new prime minister." Hughes used the collective persona most often to represent "all" African Americans with the first-person speaker of a poem. "Always the Same," "America," "American Heartbreak," "America's Young

Black Joe!", "Broadcast to the West Indies," "Dixie Man to Uncle Sam," "Do You Reckon," "I, Too," "The Negro Mother," "Southern Negro Speaks," and "Will V-Day Be Me-Day Too?" are among these poems. Hughes manages to employ such a persona without seeming to presume to speak for all African Americans (or all African American soldiers, or all workers, and so on). Nor does he presume that anyone could literally accomplish such a task. Instead, the collective persona tends to have the effect of making an invisible, ignored group visible and authoritative, or to highlight common interests. The persona can also allow Hughes to compress key issues of identity, politics, racism, or economics into a lyric form of poetry without oversimplifying issues. Therefore, while figuratively he may speak as a group, even as a people, the collective persona seems less a presumptuous poetic gesture and more a means to highlight the importance of an issue or to show how a group's interests might intersect with an issue, even if individuals in such a group cannot literally be said to view the issue uniformly. The collective persona—the term being but one way to describe the rhetorical or poetic trope—is by no means unrelated, of course, to the persona of the blues*: the man or woman singing the blues, no matter how specific the lyric's story may be, speaks "for" the brokenhearted, the betrayed, the down-and-out, and the like in general. Indeed, Hughes explicitly joins the blues form with the use of a collective persona in "Backlash Blues." Whether Hughes's early experiments with blues poetry led to the use of this persona or whether a natural affinity for such a rhetorical device made blues poetry an even more attractive form to him are open questions, but we might at least observe how useful Hughes found this poetic persona to be, how well he tailored it to different subjects and poetic forms, and how it appears in all political and literary phases of his career. We might also safely conclude that the collective persona was likely one of several elements in Hughes's poetry that have led many people to regard Hughes as an unofficial poet laureate of African Americans—as a genuine "voice of the people."

"College Formal: Renaissance Casino." Poem. *See Montage of a Dream Deferred.*

"Colleges and Color." Short story, included in the collection *Simple Takes a Wife. See* Simple [Jesse B.] Stories.

Colleges Attended by Hughes. *See* Columbia University; Lincoln University.

Collins, Durwood. Pseudonym under which Hughes published the poem " 'The Jesus.' " *See* Pseudonyms Used by Hughes.

Coloma. First name of the woman with whom Zell Ingram* was romantically involved when he and Hughes lived in Cuba. *See also* Clezie-Anne.
Bibliography: *I Wonder As I Wander*, 20–23.

"Color." Eight-line rhyming poem suggesting that one should be proud of one's (skin) color and "Wear it / Like a banner." It was first published in *Jim Crow's Last Stand*. Therefore, the poem anticipates the "Black is Beautiful" motto popularized in the late 1960s and associated with the Black Aesthetic.* *Collected Poems* contains notes regarding slight revisions the poem underwent.
Bibliography: *CP*, 290, 658.

"Color on the Brain." Short story, included in the collection *Simple Stakes a Claim*. *See* Simple [Jesse B.] Stories.

"Color Problems." Short story, included in the collection *Simple's Uncle Sam*. *See* Simple [Jesse B.] Stories.

"The Colored Soldier." Long poem in rhymed couplets, spoken—as a note preceding the poem describes—by "a young brown fellow who has a vision of his brother killed in France while fighting for the United States of America." The note also describes songs to be played in the background of the "recitation," and notes in the left margin give what amount to stage directions. The poem explores, among other issues, the irony of African Americans fighting on behalf of a nation that has deprived them of basic rights at home. *See* "Moonlight in Valencia: Civil War"; "The Negro Mother"; "War."
Bibliography: *CP*, 147–148.

"Columbia." Poem addressed to a personified United States of America—a woman (Columbia) who is knowing, experienced, powerful, and manipulative, who "consorts" with world powers and intimidates less powerful nations, but who still pretends to be "naive," "coy," and "a virgin." The chief extended comparison of the poem, therefore, is between female sexuality (as viewed by Hughes) and imperialism. The poem was first published in *International Literature* (no. 2, 1933).
Bibliography: *CP*, 168.

Columbia University. American university, the oldest in the state of New York and the fifth oldest in the United States. It was founded in 1754 as King's College under a royal charter of King George II of England. The first location was in a schoolhouse adjoining Trinity (Anglican) Church in an area near what is now lower Broadway Avenue in Manhattan. John Jay, the first chief justice of the United States, and Alexander Hamilton, the first secretary of the Treasury, were among its first students. Because of the American Revolution, the college suspended its operation from 1776 to 1784, when it reopened under the name Columbia College. In 1849 the college moved to 49th Street and Madison Avenue, where it remained for fifty years. It established a law school in 1858, and in 1859 it established the first school of mining in the United States. Seth Low, who became president of Columbia in 1890, centralized its administration. Barnard College became affiliated with Columbia in 1889, and in 1896 the trustees of the college authorized the name "Columbia University," a decision that coincided roughly with Low's decision to move the campus to Morningside Heights in Manhattan, its current location and the campus Hughes attended for one year (1921–22), midway through the university presidency of Nicholas Murray Butler, who served from 1902 to 1945.

Bibliography: Rampersad, I, 51–58.

Column, Hughes's, for the *Chicago Defender*.* *See* "Here to Yonder"; Simple [Jesse B.] Stories.

"Come On." Song, from *Street Scene*. Hughes wrote the lyrics, and Kurt Weill* composed the music. At this writing, the song is not listed with ASCAP.* It is published by Warner Chappell, Ltd. It is not included in the published vocal score (see bibliography).

Bibliography: Booklet accompanying *Street Scene* [compact disc], performed by Kristine Ciesinski, Janis Kelly, Bonaventura Bottone, Richard van Allan, Catherine Zeta Jones, and the Orchestra and Chorus of the English National Opera, conducted by Carl Davis (London: Jay Records, 1996): CDJAY2–1232; *Kurt Weill: Street Scene* [vocal score] (New York: Hal Leonard, n.d.): ISBN 0881880523.

"Comment." Four-stanza, rhyming poem asserting that "man" is more dangerous and murderous than tigers and poisonous snakes. It was first published in *Span* (Winter 1946).

Bibliography: *CP*, 319.

"Comment on Curb." Poem. *See Montage of a Dream Deferred*.

"Comment on War." Nine-line poem that develops an argument claiming that "truth" is merely "war-makers' bait" to entice "youth" to participate in war and to die. The poem is therefore open to being interpreted as isolationist in sentiment with regard to American participation in World War II, but later poems, such as "Broadcast to the West Indies," "Broadcast on Ethiopia," and "Bonds for All," reflect Hughes's support for such participation. The poem was first published in *Crisis** (June 1940). Later, Ned Rorem set the poem to music. The resulting song was part of a song cycle by Rorem, *Evidence of Things Not Seen*, recorded by Monique McDonald (soprano), Delores Ziegler (mezzo-soprano), and Michael Barrett (piano). ASCAP* lists the song as being published by Boosey and Hawkes, and the song's ASCAP registry number is 330578086.

Bibliography: *CP*, 221; *Evidence of Things Not Seen* [compact disc] (New York: New World Records, 1999), 80575–2.

"Commercial Theater." Song. Hughes wrote the lyrics, and Leonard Geoffrey Feather composed the music. ASCAP* lists the song as being published by Model Music, Inc., and the song's ASCAP registry number is 330184724. *See also* "Blues Montage"; "Could Be."

"Communion." Poem of twenty-four short lines. It is addressed ostensibly to a musician with "bebop hands" and "ragtime feet," bemoaning the fact that this musician cannot play a song with a simple blues* or boogie-woogie beat. (Although both boogie-woogie and ragtime piano styles employ syncopation, the former is often considered earthier and more dance oriented, less cerebral than the latter. Similarly, be-bop, a relatively complicated jazz* form that arose in the 1940s and 1950s, is sometimes considered overwrought in contrast to simpler, blues-oriented jazz.) At the end of the poem, the musician is advised that "you aren't so hot," suggesting that technical virtuosity cannot replace the "heart" of blues and boogie-woogie music. The poem was first published in *Free Lance* (1958).

Bibliography: *CP*, 339.

"Concerning 'Goodbye, Christ' " (1941). Essay, written about a decade after the publication of the poem "Goodbye, Christ," which is perhaps Hughes's most controversial work. In the essay Hughes explains the genesis of the poem, recalling that he had traveled extensively in the United States in 1930, witnessing widespread racism, exemplified by lack of voting rights for African Americans, Jim Crow laws* and segregationist policies, lynching,* widespread poverty among African Americans, and lack of educational facilities for African Americans. He then describes visiting the Soviet Union, where he observed comparatively less racism and a society relatively free of severe social-class distinctions. Hughes claims to have written the poem to "shock" Americans into recognizing racism, inequity, and their effects on American society. He notes that the occasion for the essay is that at poetry readings, protestors—including followers of evangelist Aimee Semple McPherson—have distributed copies of the poem and urged boycotts of his appearances. He notes that the reprints of his poem are undated and explains that in ten years both his writing and his politics have changed. The essay is reprinted by Berry, who lists January 1, 1941, as the date of composition but lists no previous publication. *See* "Concerning Red Baiting"; McCarthyism.

Bibliography: Berry, 147–149.

"Concerning Red Baiting." (1963). Essay. Berry characterizes the piece as a "defense," noting that Hughes distributed it to newspapers to counteract attacks on his work and his politics by organizations he terms, in the essay, as "reactionary," "anti-Negro," "anti-Jewish," and "anti-labor." In the essay he notes that the publication of the poem "Goodbye Christ" in 1931 was what first brought him to the attention of such groups. The essay appeared ten years after Hughes's appearance before Joseph McCarthy's Permanent Sub-Committee on Investigations. *See* "Concerning 'Goodbye, Christ' "; McCarthyism. Berry does not specify which periodicals may have published the essay but notes that a manuscript of it is held in the Fisk University Library Special Collections.
Bibliography: Berry, 159–161.

"Concernment." Short story, included in the collection *Simple's Uncle Sam.* *See* Simple [Jesse B.] Stories.

"Confused." Short story, included in the collection *Simple Speaks His Mind.* *See* Simple [Jesse B.] Stories.

Conga. Latin American dance with African origins. The conga, part of which is a line dance, is associated with syncopated rhythms common to African-influenced folk music and folk dance of the Caribbean, Central America, and South America. Referring to his having seen the conga performed in Haiti, Hughes bluntly calls it "a sex dance" (*I Wonder As I Wander*, 22).

Congo. African nation that gained independence from Belgium in 1960, now known as Zaire. *See* "Lumumba's Grave."

"Conservatory Student Struggles with Higher Instrumentation." Three-stanza poem in which the student expresses having a love-hate relationship with the saxophone, which the student sees as being "vulgar" but also irresistible. It was first published under a slightly different title in *Lionel Hampton's Swing Book* (1946). *See* Jazz.
Bibliography: *CP*, 319, 663; Lionel Hampton, *Lionel Hampton's Swing Book* (Chicago: Negro Story Press, 1946), 38.

"Consider Me." Poem in which the speaker describes his hardworking, underprivileged, but nonetheless joy-filled life and the problem of racism that defines much of that life and divides all societies. The poem suggests that all people are descended from the same "mystery," implying that racism is, among other things, irrational. "Consider me" in the poem therefore becomes an imperative statement aimed at making invisible or ignored people visible in their humanity and particular circumstances and at highlighting common humanity. The poem was first published in the *American Scholar* (Winter 1951–1952). *Collected Poems* contains a note on revisions one stanza of the poem underwent. *See* Collective Persona.

Bibliography: *CP*, 385, 672.

Consuelo. A main character in the short story "Tragedy at the Baths."

"The Consumptive." Twelve-line, three-stanza poem describing the latter part of a consumptive man's life. It was first published in *Dear Lovely Death*. A revised version of the poem appeared in *Crisis** (1933). *Collected Poems* includes information about the specific revisions. *See also* Revision, Process of, and Hughes.

Bibliography: *CP*, 157, 640–641.

"Contest." Short story, included in the collection *Simple's Uncle Sam. See* Simple [Jesse B.] Stories.

"Convent." Nine-line poem in which lines three, five, and nine rhyme. The poem is addressed to the convent itself, asking whether "peace" exists behind its walls or an "insistence" that "beckons and appalls." It was first published in *Opportunity** (March 1938).

Bibliography: *CP*, 203.

"Conversation on the Corner." Short story, included in *The Best of Simple. See* Simple [Jesse B.] Stories.

"Cool Saturday Night." Song. Hughes wrote the lyrics, and David Martin composed the music. ASCAP* lists the song as being published by Colgems/EMI, and the song's ASCAP registry number is 330094189. Rampersad indicates that the song was recorded in 1950 by an American group, the Striders. *See also* "Five o'Clock Blues."

Bibliography: Rampersad, II, 178.

"Cora." Seven-line poem in which the speaker—Cora, presumably—cites the trouble she's had with men. It was first published in *Fine Clothes to the Jew*.

Bibliography: *CP*, 119.

"Cora Unashamed." Short story. In the narrative Cora Jenkins is an African American woman working as a housekeeper for a middle-class white family (the Studevants) in a small midwestern city, Melton. Cora grew up in a working-poor family, became pregnant out of wedlock (the father disappearing), and lost the child to whooping cough. The reliable, sweet-tempered Cora becomes a surrogate mother to the Studevants' daughter, Jessie. When the teenaged Jessie

becomes pregnant out of wedlock, Cora is more understanding and supportive than the parents, and she urges Jessie to bear the child and raise it, or at least put it up for adoption. The parents disagree and force Jessie to travel to Kansas City for an abortion. After Jessie returns, she dies of complications from the abortion. At Jessie's funeral Cora expresses outrage and emerges as the moral center of the story. It was first published in the *American Mercury** (September 1933), 19–24; and is included in the collection *The Ways of White Folks*.
Bibliography: Ostrom, 8–11.

Cordelia. A character in the poem "Stony Lonesome."

"Corner Meeting." Poem. *See Montage of a Dream Deferred. See also The Block.*

Correspondence. *See Arna Bontemps/Langston Hughes: Letters, 1925–1967.*

"Cotton." Poem in two short-lined ballad* quatrains. It concerns the exploitation of black workers in cotton fields by "the white man." The date of the poem's composition is uncertain, but the poem may have been written in the 1930s. It was first published in Berry and is not included in *Collected Poems*.
Bibliography: Berry, 13.

"De Cotton Needs Pickin'." American folk song. *See* "Ballad of the Seven Songs."

"Could Be." Poem of four rhyming quatrains in which the speaker laments the loss of a woman and his watch, which the woman pawned. It was first published in *One-Way Ticket*. Later, Leonard Feather set the poem to music. ASCAP* lists the song as being published by Model Music, and the song's ASCAP registry number is 330184733. *See also* "Blues Montage"; "Commercial Theater."
Bibliography: *CP*, 366.

"Country." Ten-line poem spoken by a child whose mother has announced that the family will buy a house in the country; the child predicts with delight that near the house will be a hill to climb. It was first published in *The Langston Hughes Reader. See* Children's Poetry.
Bibliography: *CP*, 605.

Cousin Minnie. Recurring character in the Simple [Jesse B.] stories.* *See* "Again Cousin Minnie"; "Enter Cousin Minnie"; "Minnie Again"; "Minnie One More Time"; "Minnie's Hype."

Coussey, Anne Marie. *See* "Breath of a Rose"; "Letter to Anne."

"Cowards from the Colleges." Essay. Based on observations made during his extensive tour of the American South in 1931, when Hughes gave reading at numerous historically black colleges, Hughes uses the essay to critique viewpoints expressed by leaders of some of those colleges. He objects to "mid-Victorian" attitudes toward men and women socializing, to what he regards as an oppressive emphasis on religion,* to political passivity, and to resistance to allowing students to practice nonviolent protest against Jim Crow laws.* The essay was first published in *Crisis** (August 1934) and was reprinted in Berry, 61–69. *See also* Bethune, Mary; Ingram, Zell.

"Cracker Prayer." Short story, included in the collection *Simple's Uncle Sam.* *See* Simple [Jesse B.] Stories.

"Crap Game." Nine-line poem in black dialect* that reproduces some of what a player says during the dice game craps. It was first published in *Fine Clothes to the Jew.*

Bibliography: *CP*, 114.

Crisis: A Record of the Darker Races. Magazine founded in November 1910 in New York City by W.E.B. Du Bois* with the assistance of publisher Oswald Villard and the financial backing of the NAACP.* The expressed purpose of *Crisis* was to discuss interracial conflict and critique racial prejudice, especially in the United States but also worldwide. Du Bois edited the magazine, wrote for it often, and saw it reach a circulation of over 50,000 by 1918. *Crisis* was the official publication of the NAACP. A politically progressive magazine, it was too radical for some African Americans swayed by the ideas of Booker T. Washington* but too conservative for those influenced by the ideas of Marcus Garvey* or by socialist ideas expressed in such magazines as *New Masses* and the *Messenger.** Therefore, the political stance of *Crisis* at least approximated that of Hughes, especially in the mid-1920s, before he became more interested in Marxism.* Along with the magazines *Opportunity** and the *Messenger, Crisis* contributed enormously to the intellectual character and conflict of the Harlem Renaissance.* Hutchinson discusses the relationship of these magazines to the Harlem Renaissance in detail and argues that "1926 . . . marks the period of *The Crisis*'s relative decline as an influence on the New Negro movement in the arts, as a rift with *Opportunity* opened and the latter magazine grew in influence" (167). Jessie Fauset,* literary editor of *Crisis* in its early years, published "The Negro Speaks of Rivers" in June 1921, which went on to become one of Hughes's best-known poems. Over the course of his career, Hughes published at least eighty-two poems in *Crisis*, more by far than he published in any other periodical and, indeed, nearly 10 percent of the poetry in *Collected Poems*.

Bibliography: Harold Cruse, *The Crisis of the Negro Intellectual* (New York: William Morrow, 1967); W.E.B. Du Bois, *The Autobiography of W.E.B. Du Bois* (New York: International Publishers, 1968); Hutchinson, especially chapter 5, "*The Crisis* and the Nation's Conscience," 137–169; Lewis, *WHWV*; Mullen; Arnold Rampersad, *The Art and Imagination of W.E.B. Du Bois* (Cambridge MA: Harvard University Press, 1976).

"Croon." Three-line poem expressing disdain for "Alabam' "—the state of Alabama. It is part of *Montage of a Dream Deferred*.

Bibliography: *CP*, 394.

"Cross." Poem of three rhyming quatrains spoken by a person whose father was white and whose mother was black. The speaker expresses regret over any "curses" he leveled at his parents; reports that his mother died in a shack, his father in a fine house; and wonders where, "being neither white nor black," he or she will die. Hughes mentions this poem in *The Big Sea*, connecting it to the story "Father and Son" and to *Mulatto*, the play connected to that story. "Cross," therefore, could refer to the speaker's "cross to bear," or to the fact that in racist terms, the speaker is a "cross" between white and black. In an essay published in 1950, "From the Blues to an Opera Libretto," Hughes discusses "Cross" in connection with the opera *The Barrier* (based on *Mulatto*), for which he wrote the libretto. The poem was first published in *Crisis** (December 1925).

Bibliography: *The Big Sea*, 262–263; *CP*, 58.

"Crossing." Twenty-two-line rhyming poem that includes surrealistic imagery and is spoken by someone dying. The control of the voice, the haunting imagery, and the deft rhyming combine to make this, arguably, one of Hughes's most powerful but also underrated poems. It was first published, with a slightly different ending (which, echoing the African American spiritual song, referred to "Crossing Jordan [River]") in *Poetry* (May 1941). It was also published in *Shakespeare in Harlem*. In 1991, when the play *Mule Bone* by Zora Neale Hurston* and Hughes finally debuted, it included several of Hughes's poems set to music and performed by musician and songwriter Taj Mahal. "Crossing" is one of these poems. ASCAP* lists the publisher of the song as Golden Foot Music, and the ASCAP registry number is 330513690. (Taj Mahal's given name is Henry St. Clair Fredericks, which ASCAP lists as the name of record for the composer.) The other poems Taj Mahal (Fredericks) set to music for the play are "Jubilee," "Song for a Banjo Dance," "Hey-Hey Blues," and "Bound No'th Blues." Other lyrics by Hughes appeared in the *Mule Bone* manuscript, and Taj Mahal set these to music as well. They are "Graveyard Mule," "Me and the

Mule," and "But I Rode Some." The songs were recorded (see the Bibliography). *See also Mule Bone.*

Bibliography/Discography: John Beaufort, "*Mule Bone* Debuts after 60 Years," *Christian Science Monitor* (February 26, 1991), 13; *CP*, 251, 653; Taj Mahal, *Mule Bone: Music Composed and Performed by Taj Mahal, Lyrics by Langston Hughes* [compact disc] (Gramavision, distributed by Rhino Records (Santa Monica, CA), 1991): R2 79432.

Crow-for-a-day, Chicken. A character in *Tambourines to Glory* who is the first convert to the church founded by Laura Reed and Essie Belle Johnson in Harlem.*

"Crow Goes, Too." Five-stanza poem addressed to "Uncle Sam" (the United States of America), advising him that Jim Crow laws* contradict the principles for which the United States is fighting in its war against Hitler (World War II). The poem mentions Tom Driberg, member of the British House of Commons, who spoke out in Parliament against the racist attitudes he had observed among American troops stationed in England. It was first published in the *Amsterdam News* (October 17, 1942). *See* "Ballad of Roosevelt"; "Dear Mr. President"; "403 Blues."

Bibliography: *CP*, 576; Francis Wheen, *Tom Driberg: His Life and Indiscretions* (London: Chatto & Windus, 1990).

"Crowing Hen Blues." Humorous poem in traditional blues* form. The speaker complains that he hears his hen crow and his cat, Battling Tom McCann, talk; he inquires as to whether his "baby" (girlfriend) hears the same thing; she responds that she hears only his liquor-induced snoring. The poem was first published in *Poetry* (September 1943).

Bibliography: *CP*, 278.

"Crowns and Garlands." Twenty-line poem that characterizes popular African American figures as crowns and garlands that ordinary African Americans figuratively wear. However, the poem suggests that these sources of pride cannot solve fundamental social or personal problems, including paying the bills. Mentioned are opera singer Leontyne Price, performer Sammy Davis, Jr.,* singer Harry Belafonte, actor Sidney Poitier, "Cassius Mohammed [*sic*] Clay" (boxer Muhammad Ali), and Ralph Bunche. The poem was first published in the *Nation* (January 1967). For a poem that expresses a sharply different view of symbolic figures, *see* "Emperor Hailie Salassie." Regarding Harry Belafonte, *see My Lord What a Mornin'.*

Bibliography: *CP*, 551.

Crowville. Fictional Mississippi town in *Not Without Laughter. See* Sister Johnson.

Cuba Libre: Poems by Nicolás Guillén. Translated by Langston Hughes and Ben Frederic Carruthers (Los Angeles, CA: Anderson and Ritchie: The Ward Ritchie Press, 1948). 98 pp. In this difficult-to-find collection (only 500 copies were printed), the translation by Hughes and Ben Frederic Carruthers captures the language and rhythm of Nicolás Guillén's early poetry. The book has fifty poems divided into eight sections and is illustrated by Gar Gilbert.

Born in 1902 to a mulatto family in Camagüey, Cuba, Nicolás Guillén began to publish his verses in literary magazines at the age of eighteen. Although he entered law school at the University of Havana, he never finished his formal course of study. The young Cuban met Hughes in 1930 for the first time and recorded his impressions of their meeting in a literary supplement of a Havana newspaper later that same year. The two men would remain in contact in the years to come. In 1930 Guillén published *Sound Motifs* (*Motivos de son*), a year later *Sóngoro cosongo*, (Rhythmic Songs) and in 1934, *West Indies Ltd.* In addition to writing poetry during these years, he also worked as an editor for various leftist journals. In 1937 Guillén left Cuba and, after traveling to Mexico, the United States, Canada, and France, eventually arrived in Civil War–torn Spain to attend the Second International Writers Congress for the Defense of Culture. This same year he published *Songs for Soldiers and Sones for Tourists* (*Cantos para soldados y sones para turistas*) and *Spain: A Poem in Four Anguishes and a Hope* (*España: Poema en cuatro angustias y una esperanza*). In 1938 he officially joined the Communist Party and returned home. As Guillén gained prestige in international artistic and academic circles, he began to travel more and more, giving poetry recitals and speaking. He visited South America, Europe, Asia, and the United States and received numerous awards and honorary degrees. His most important later works include *The Dove in Popular Flight* (*La paloma de vuelo popular*) (1948), *I Have* (*Tengo*) (1964), *The Great Zoo* (*El gran zoo*) (1967), *The Daily Daily* (*El diario que a diario*), and *The Gearwheel* (*La rueda dentada*) (1972). Nicolás Guillén died in 1989.

The first section of *Cuba Libre* is titled "Cuban Blues" and consists of nine poems. The translators preserve the poetic style of the poet, omitting syllables not pronounced in Cuban Spanish and relying on phonetic spellings of words in order to capture the speech of Guillén's island homeland. In the same way that Hughes attempted to capture the orality of African American speech in his own poetry, here he is able to translate the same spoken quality from Guillén's Spanish. Especially notable are "Thick-lipped Cullud Boy," which begins, "How come you jumps salty / when they calls you thick-lipped boy, / if yo' mouf's so sweet, / thick-lipped cullud boy?" (5), and "High Brown," "Well, look at yo'self an' see / you ain't no prize to wed. / Yo' mouf' is awful big fo' me, / an yo' naps is short an' red" (6). The second section is "Habaneros" and has four poems that present the themes and symbols of music, work, the moon, and death. All of these elements are present in the poem "Wake for Papa Montero" (18–20), which relates the tale of a musician killed in a knife fight.

"West Indies," also the title of Guillén's third book, has twelve poems. The first six are about the labor, exploitation, cruelty, and suffering of the Negro in Cuba. A particularly poignant example is the short poem "Cane" (23), "Negro / in the cane fields. / White man / above the cane fields. / Earth / beneath the cane fields. / Blood / that flows from us." The idea of exploitation in the sugar-cane fields is explored farther in "Chop It with a Cane Knife!" In this selection Guillén recalls the Spanish domination of the island, which ended in 1898, and the imperial influence of the United States in Cuba so prevalent prior to the Cuban revolution, "When they chew this sugar-cane / with it they'll be chewing you, / just like in the days of Spain, / just like in the days of Spain, / now the Yankee's trampling you!" (30). "Sensemayá" (32) is one of Guillén's best-known compositions and captures the rhythm and language brought by the first Cuban slaves from Africa. The notion that class, in addition to race, is a factor in determining one's stake in life is suggested in the poem "Song in an Havana Bar" (37–38). Here the poetic voice tells the supposedly wealthy Yankee tour-ists, "When you get back to New York / send me some poor folks, / poor like me, / poor like me, / like me. / I can shake hands / with poor folks / and sing *with* them swell—/ for the same songs they know, / I know, as well!" Social class is also the issue in the selection "Two Kids," in which two children, one black and one white, are both described as poor and hungry (39). Yet another portrayal of wealthy tourists oblivious to the poverty and suffering in Cuba is seen in "Sightseers in a Courtyard" (40–42).

"Songs for Soldiers" is the fourth section, and as its title indicates, all seven poems deal with military men. In "Execution" Guillén explores the idea of duty, "They are about to shoot / a man with his arms tied. / Four soldiers / are about to fire. / Four silent soldiers / tied / the same as the man / they are going to kill / is tied" (48). A reminder that soldiers are sometimes sent into action by un-caring generals is evidenced in "Soldiers in Ethiopia" (52–54), and the idea that being a soldier subject to the command of a superior is analogous to a form of slavery surfaces in "That Kind of a Soldier, Not Me" (56–57).

"Here We Are!" is the fifth section of the collection and has five poems. The first four selections explore the communion between nature and her inhabitants, portraying people as products of the rivers, jungles, and sun. This is apparent in "Words in the Tropics": "I owe to you my dark body, / my agile limbs and my crisp hair, / my love for elemental females, / and this indelible blood of mine" (64–66). In the last poem of the section the theme changes as "Little Ode" recounts the tale of a Cuban boxer who has finally "made it" in New York: "Now that the white world / toasts its body in our sun / and looks for rumbas in Havana, / shine in your blackness, kid, / while the crowd applauds. / Envied by the whites, / speak for the blacks indeed!" (68–70).

In the sixth section, "Federico," there are two poems lamenting the death of Spanish poet Federico García Lorca. "Moment with the Muse of García Lorca" (76) is especially noteworthy as a translated piece because the Lorcan imagery in the original has been preserved: "Federico dreamed of spikenard and wax /

and olive and carnation and cold moon. / Federico, his Granada, and the spring-time lax. He slept alone in solitude's abode, / stretched out beneath ambiguous lemon trees / as songs passed down the lonely road."

"Mulatto Poems" is the penultimate section of the book and has five selections that explore the nature of *Mulattismo*. In "Ballad of the Two Grandfathers" (86–88) the poetic speaker, a racial and cultural product of his grandfathers, speculates on his relatives, Federico the Spanish conquistador and Facundo the African slave. In the sonnet "Grandfather," a different look at the same theme is presented: "This angelic dame with Southern eyes, / who lives by rhythms of her Northern blood, / she never knew that deep within that flood / a black man beats a hoarsened drum and sighs. . . . Behold him there beside the virgin shores, / your black grandfather's dulcet shadow flees. / He put the curl in those blond locks of yours" (83).

The six poems of the last section, "Propositions," have no real thematic connection. The selection of the same name, "Proposition," is a short lyrical speculation on the moon: "Tonight / when the moon comes out / I shall change it / into money. / But I'd be sorry if people knew about it / for the moon / is an old family treasure" (95). A second poem of interest in this last part is "Two Weeks" (98), a composition that tells the tale of the frustrated romance of a girl who is too shy to speak to her suitor. As a whole, Hughes's and Carruthers's translation provides a nice overview of the early work of Nicolás Guillén. In *I Wonder As I Wander* Hughes describes traveling with Guillén in Spain during the Spanish Civil War. *See also Baltimore Afro American*; "Soledad"; Translations by Hughes.

Bibliography: Robert Chrisman, "Nicolás Guillén, Langston Hughes, and the Black American/Afro-Cuban Connection," *Michigan Quarterly Review* 33, no. 4 (Fall 1994), 807–820; Martha Cobb, *Harlem, Haiti, and Havana: A Comparative Critical Study of Langston Hughes, Jacques Roumain, Nicolás Guillén* (Washington, DC.: Three Continents Press, 1973); Keith Ellis, *Cuba's Nicolás Guillén: Poetry and Ideology* (Toronto: University of Toronto Press, 1983); Nicolás Guillén, *¡Patria o Muerte! The Great Zoo and Other Poems*, ed. and transl. Robert Márquez (Havana, Cuba: Editorial de Arte y Literatura, 1973); *I Wonder As I Wander*; Edward Mullen, ed., *Langston Hughes in the Hispanic World and Haiti* (Hamden, CT: Archon Books, 1977).

Joseph Deters

"Cubes." Free-verse poem involving a complicated comparison between artist Pablo Picasso's surrealistic cubist paintings and the harsh realities faced by Senegalese immigrants to France, whom the poem depicts as hapless victims who return from France to Senegal carrying chiefly venereal disease. The poem was first published in *New Masses* (March 14, 1934). *See also* "The Dove."

Bibliography: Andrew Francis Clark and Lucie Colvin Phillips, *Historical Dictionary of Senegal*, 2nd ed. (Metuchen, NJ: Scarecrow Press, 1994); *CP*, 175.

Cudjoe. *See* "Ballad of the Seven Songs."

Cullen, Countee (1903–1946). American poet, novelist, essayist, and teacher. The place and precise circumstances of Cullen's birth remain unclear, and Cullen himself did little to clear up the confusion, listing Louisville, Baltimore, and New York City at different times as his birthplace. Nor is it clear precisely when he was adopted by Dr. Frederick A. and Carolyn Belle (Mitchell) Cullen of Harlem.* The adoption apparently occurred between 1914 and 1918, but Early suggests that the adoption may never have been made official (3). In any event, Cullen spent the middle years of his childhood and his adolescence in the secure, if strict, household of the Cullens, and he spent most of the rest of his life in New York City. He produced some of the most accomplished lyric poems of the twentieth century and is considered one of the major figures to emerge from the Harlem Renaissance.* Early states that in "1925 Countee Cullen, at the age of twenty-two, was the most celebrated and probably the most famous black writer in America" (4). In that year his first book of poems, *Color*, appeared and contained at least three of his enduring poems, "Yet Do I Marvel," "Black Magdalens," and "Saturday's Child." Cullen and Hughes achieved success almost simultaneously, but they took sharply different approaches to poetry. Cullen tended to work within an established tradition of Anglo-American literary poetry, with polished, formal diction and traditional rhyme schemes and meter. Meanwhile, Hughes was adapting the blues* to poetry, using black dialect,* modifying traditional forms such as the ballad,* and embracing "Negro" folklore. Consequently, the two young poets were perceived and depicted as "rivals," partly because Cullen was seen by W.E.B. Du Bois,* Alain Locke,* and others as a model of a New Negro* writer, whereas Hughes was perceived to be less predictable and more adventurous in his writing. Cullen was married briefly to Du Bois's daughter, Yolanda. However, Cullen and Hughes themselves were on friendly terms and tended not to see themselves as competitors. Moreover, a closer inspection of their poetry reveals a fair number of similarities in their use of language, their understanding of lyric poetry, and their preoccupations, even as they each carved out distinct niches in American poetry. One complicating factor in their relationship was the presence of Alain Locke, who apparently was attracted sexually to both men. Watson goes so far as to suggest that in 1923 Cullen and Locke "began a campaign to seduce Langston Hughes" (203). Like that of Hughes, Cullen's sexuality has been a topic of considerable speculation. After the appearance of *Color*, Cullen produced several more books rapidly: the collections of poetry *Copper Sun* (1927), *The Ballad of the Brown Girl* (1927), and *The Black Christ and Other Poems* (1929), as well as the novel (set in Harlem) *One Way to Heaven* (1932). He also edited the important anthology *Caroling Dusk* (1927). The Great Depression and the dissolution of the Harlem Renaissance were, of course, difficult for most of the writers associated with the movement, Hughes included, but Cullen's productivity seemed especially affected. However, he went on to publish *The Medea and Some Poems* (1935), two children's books—*The Lost Zoo* (1940) and *My Lives and How I Lost Them* (1942)—and the posthumous collection *On These I Stand: An An-*

thology of the Best Poems of Countee Cullen (1947), which his devoted second wife, Ida M. Cullen, helped see through to publication following Cullen's sudden death in 1946. Cullen completed a master's degree in English at Harvard University and taught middle school in Harlem for many years. He was an innovative teacher, and one of his students was James Baldwin.* An extensive collection of Cullen's papers is held in the Amistad Research Center at Tulane University. The collection includes a letter Hughes sent to Cullen asking for his support of efforts on behalf of the Scottsboro Boys.* *See also* Schomburg, Arthur.

Bibliography: Houston A. Baker, Jr., "A Many-colored Coat of Dreams: The Poetry of Countee Cullen," in his *Afro-American Poetics: Revisions of Harlem and the Black Aesthetic* (Madison: University of Wisconsin Press, 1988), 45–87; Countee Cullen, *My Soul's High Song: The Collected Writings of Countee Cullen, Voice of the Harlem Renaissance*, edited with an introduction by Gerald Early (New York: Anchor Books, 1991); David Kirby, "Countee Cullen's Heritage: A Black Waste Land," *South Atlantic Bulletin* 36, no. 4 (1971), 14–20; Michael Lomax, "Countee Cullen: A Key to the Puzzle," in *The Harlem Renaissance Re-examined*, ed. Victor A. Kramer (New York: AMS Press, 1987), 213–222; Hans Ostrom, "Countee Cullen: How Teaching Rewrites the Genre of 'Writer,' " in *Genre and Writing: Issues, Arguments, Alternatives*, ed. Wendy Bishop and Hans Ostrom (Portsmouth, NH: Boynton/Cook-Heinemann, 1997), 93–104; Watson, 203.

"Cultural Exchange." *See Ask Your Mama.*

Cuney, Waring. *See* Harlem Suitcase Theatre.

"Curious." Six-line rhyming poem in which the speaker asks questions of his "babe" (girlfriend). It was first published in the *Carmel Pine Cone* (April 4, 1941).

Bibliography: *CP*, 226.

"Cycles." Poem. *See* "New Flowers."

D

The Daily Leader. In *Not Without Laughter*, the *Daily Leader* is the newspaper in the town of Stanton.

Dambala. An Afro-Caribbean religious deity. *See* "Death in Africa."

"Dancer." Poem. *See Montage of a Dream Deferred.*

"Dancers." Poem of two short stanzas that characterizes dancers as stealing life from death. It was first published in *Fields of Wonder*. Later, Robert Owens set the poem to music. ASCAP* lists the song as being published by Gema, Inc., and the song's ASCAP registry number is 340133377.
Bibliography: *CP*, 334.

Dane, Earl. One of Hughes's pseudonyms. *See* "For Dead Mimes." *See also* "Autumn Note"; "Mailbox for the Dead"; Pseudonyms Used by Hughes.

"Danse Africaine." Fifteen-line poem evoking images and rhythms of (as the title suggests) an African dance. It was first published in *Crisis** (August 1922). Later, John W. Work set the poem to music. ASCAP* lists the song as being published by Ethel Smith Music, and the song's ASCAP registry number is 340001076.
Bibliography: *CP*, 28.

"Dare." Eight-line poem (lines four and eight rhyme) in which darkness is personified as a gentle human presence and daylight as a kind of bully. It was first published in *Voices* (Winter 1949).
Bibliography: *CP*, 350.

"Dark Youth of the U.S.A." Poem. A note below the title describes the work as a "recitation to be delivered by a Negro boy, bright, clean, and neatly dressed, carrying his books to school." The poem contains four stanzas in limerick form; the fifth is a quatrain. Education as an avenue toward full membership in American society constitutes a main theme of the poem. Crispus Attucks is mentioned (*see* "America"). The poem was first published in *Common Sense Historical Review* (August 1953).

Bibliography: *CP*, 156–57; Ron Padgett, "Limerick," in *A Handbook of Poetic Forms* (New York: Teachers and Writers Collaborative, 1987), 98–99.

Davis, Sammy, Jr. (1925–1990). American entertainer. Davis was one of the most gifted and versatile popular entertainers of the twentieth century, achieving success as a dancer, Broadway actor, singer, concert performer, dramatic and comic film actor, and television performer. *See* "Crowns and Garlands."

Bibliography: "Sammy Davis, Jr." [obituary], *New York Times* (May 17, 1990), 1.

"Day." Fifteen-line poem articulating the ways in which all persons eventually will lose everything and be left to die completely alone.

Bibliography: *CP*, 103.

"Daybreak." Poem, one of the seven separate parts of "Seven Moments of Love."

"Daybreak in Alabama." Twenty-three-line free-verse poem spoken by a person aspiring to be a composer and specifically imagining a musical work that will capture the natural beauty of Alabama but also present a unifying vision of Alabamans from different ethnic backgrounds. It was first published in *Unquote* (June 1940). Later, Kevin Ray Haight set the poem to music. ASCAP* lists no publisher for the song, but the ASCAP registry number is 340387611. Singer Audra McDonald recorded the song. *See also* "Song for a Dark Girl."

Bibliography/Discography: *CP*, 220–221; Audra McDonald, "Daybreak in Alabama," *Way Back to Paradise* [compact disc] (New York: Nonesuch Records, 1998): Nonesuch 79482–2.

De Castro, José Antonio Fernández (1897–?). Cuban journalist and editor. In *I Wonder As I Wander* Hughes mentions him briefly, noting that he worked for the newspaper *Diario de la Marina*, that he edited the weekly magazine *Orbe*, and that he went fishing with Ernest Hemingway.*

Bibliography: "Havana Nights," in *I Wonder As I Wander*, 6–10.

"Dead in There." Poem. *See Montage of a Dream Deferred.*

"Dead Soldier." Poem by Nicolás Guillén* that Hughes translated from the Spanish. It is a eulogy for the dead soldier and is published in *The Langston Hughes Reader. See Cuba Libre.*

Bibliography: *The Langston Hughes Reader*, 141–142.

"Dear Dr. Butts." Short story, included in the collection *Simple Takes a Wife. See* Simple [Jesse B.] Stories.

Dear Lovely Death (Amenia, NY: Troutbeck Press, 1931). Chapbook of poems, printed privately by Amy Spingarn. It includes the poems "Aesthete in Harlem," "Afro-American Fragment," "The Consumptive," "Dear Lovely Death," "Demand," "Drum," "Flight," "Florida Road Workers," "Garden" (under the title "Poem"), "Tower," and "Two Things." *See* Ingram, Zell.

"Dear Lovely Death." Ten-line rhyming poem concerning mutability. It is an unusual Hughes poem inasmuch as it contains antique diction ("taketh," "thy"). It is the title poem of a volume privately published by Amy Spingarn (*see Dear Lovely Death*). The poem was first published in *Opportunity** (June 1930).

Bibliography: *CP*, 127.

"Dear Mr. President." Poem of nine rhyming quatrains organized as a letter to President Franklin Delano Roosevelt* from an African American soldier training in Alabama. The chief purpose of the "letter" is to point out and seek relief for what Hughes believed to be the unjust, racist situation whereby African American soldiers serving their country must ride in the back of public buses and endure other consequences of Jim Crow laws.* (Segregation in the U.S. military itself would not end until 1948, when President Harry Truman removed it by an executive order). The poem was first published in *People's Voice* (July 3, 1943). *See* "Ballad of Roosevelt"; "Crow Goes, Too"; "403 Blues."

Bibliography: *CP*, 271; John B. Kirby, *Black Americans in the Roosevelt Era: Liberalism and Race* (Knoxville: University of Tennessee Press, 1980).

Death, Hughes's. *See* Funeral, Hughes's.

"Death and Laughter in Madrid." Essay that discusses the resilience of Madrid's citizens when the city was being shelled by the artillery of fascist forces during the Spanish Civil War. Published in the *Nation* (October 1938), it reflects some of the observations Hughes reported in his articles written from Spain for the *Baltimore Afro American.** Rampersad notes that *Reader's Digest* subsequently reprinted an excerpt of "Death and Laughter in Madrid."

Bibliography: Rampersad, I, 355.

"Death Chant." Poem. *See* "Stony Lonesome."

"Death in Africa." Sixteen-line free-verse poem describing slow deaths in Africa resulting from poverty, hunger, and colonialism. It mentions the Afro-Caribbean deity Dambala. The poem was first published in *Opportunity** (August 1941).

Bibliography: *CP*, 236–237.

"Death in Harlem." Story-poem of several pages in modified ballad* form. With ironic humor and occasional use of black dialect,* the poem relates the tale of a deadly triangle in a Harlem* nightclub. The main characters are Arabella Johnson and the Texas Kid, with Dixie (a nightclub owner), Lucy (a singer), and Bessie (a nightclub patron) in supporting roles. Arabella murders Bessie in a fit of jealous rage. The poem was first published in *Literary America* (June 1935) and in *Anthology of Magazine Verse*, edited by Alan Pater (New York: New York Poetry Digest Association, 1935), 75–79.

Bibliography: *CP*, 179–81.

"Death in Yorkville." Twenty-line poem subtitled "(James Powell, Summer, 1964)." The poem responds to the murder of sixteen-year-old James Powell by a white police officer in Manhattan's Upper East Side on June 16, 1964. The killing touched off civil unrest in Harlem*; the poem refers to the unrest as "the long hot summer." Rhetorically, the poem asks how many bullets, lynchings,* Emancipation Centennials, and so on it will take before the essential racism of American society disappears. It was first published in *The Panther and the Lash*. *See* "The Ballad of Margie Polite"; "The Harlem Story"; "Harlem III."

Bibliography: *CP*, 554–555.

"Death of an Old Seaman." Ten-line poem in which the first stanza is a quatrain rhymed ABAB and the second stanza is in rhymed couplets. The old sailor's soul speaks to the narrator of the poem on the burial day. The poem was first published in *The Weary Blues*.

Bibliography: *CP*, 99.

"Death of Do Dirty: A Rounder's Song." Poem in seven ballad stanzas with a single-line refrain between stanzas. The narrator praises his dead friend, Do Dirty, for being loyal and generous, if violent toward others both of them knew. (In colloquial usage, "rounder" refers to "a dissolute person or drunkard.") The poem was first published in *Fine Clothes to the Jew*.

Bibliography: *CP*, 115; *Webster's New World Dictionary of the American Language*, 2nd college ed. (Englewood Cliffs, NJ: Prentice Hall, 1986), 1240.

"Deceased." Seven-line poem. The deceased in question died from unwittingly drinking liquor that had been poisoned with lye. The poem was first published in *One-Way Ticket*.

Bibliography: *CP*, 368.

"Declaration." Three-stanza poem not in the form of the blues* but infused with blues spirit. The speaker is telling his troublesome lover that he would leave her—if he were either a sea lion or a rich boy with a car. The poem was first published in *Shakespeare in Harlem*.

Bibliography: *CP*, 246.

The Declaration of Independence. *See* "Freedom Train."

"Deep like the Rivers." Song that alludes to "The Negro Speaks of Rivers." Hughes wrote the lyrics, and Charles A. Harrison composed the music. ASCAP* lists the song as being published by Serocs Music, Inc., and the song's ASCAP registry number is 340350776.

"Deferred." Poem. *See Montage of a Dream Deferred. See also* Revision, Process of, and Hughes.

"Delinquent." Poem of four rhyming quatrains, although the last stanza is "stretched" to five lines. The young delinquent in question is Miss Julie, who is streetwise but who is pregnant out of wedlock, the poem asserts, because no one cares about her. The poem was first published in *Olivant Quarterly* (Summer 1953).

Bibliography: *CP*, 447–448.

"Demand." Eleven-line rhyming poem in which the speaker insistently questions a persona called "dream of utter aliveness," wondering from whence it came, what accounts for it, and so on, and reporting that it has touched the speaker's "body of utter death." The poem was first published under the title "Request to Genius" in *Poetry Quarterly* (Spring 1931).

Bibliography: *CP*, 158.

"Democracy." *See* "Freedom [1]."

"Democracy and Me." Essay based on remarks Hughes made at the Third American Writers' Congress, Carnegie Hall, New York City, in June 1939. The essay argues that "Negro" writers face much greater obstacles than their white counterparts because editors view Negro writers and Negro experience as exotic; because (as one result of "exoticism") the market for Negro writing is limited; and because Negro writers have more difficulty earning a living in areas related to writing, such as lecturing, teaching, and selling novels to Hollywood film producers. The essay acknowledges that all writers face economic hardship, but that racism exacerbates the situation of the Negro writer. It was first published in *Fighting Words*, edited by Donald Ogden Stewart (New York: Harcourt, Brace, 1940), 58–63, and was reprinted in Berry.

Bibliography: Berry, 138–141.

"Democracy, Negroes, and Writers." Essay. Hughes sent it as a speech to be read in his absence at the Fourth American Writers' Congress in New York City (June 1941). The essay specifies ways in which democracy in the United States remains a "paradox" for African Americans. For instance, Hughes notes that although blacks can vote in northern states, they are not allowed to work in airplane factories, and although they can publish newspapers in southern states and thereby exercise the right of free speech, they live in fear of lynching.* Hughes urges the Writers' Congress to continue to try to extend democracy to all Americans. The essay is reprinted in Berry.

Bibliography: Berry, 141–143.

"Demonstration." Twenty-seven-line rhyming poem that begins by evoking images of a civil-rights demonstration, including fire hoses, dogs, tear gas, and guns. Later in the poem, "Your dawn" becomes a refrain, and the poem implies that the powerless shall one day wrest control from the powerful. It was first published in *Negro Digest* (September 1966).

Bibliography: *CP*, 553; Michael S. Durham and Charles Moore, *Powerful Days: The Civil Rights Photography of Charles Moore* (New York: Stewart, Tabori, & Chang, 1991).

"Departure." Nine-line rhyming elegaic poem concerning a woman who was "regal in her bravery," first published in *Free Lance* (no. 1, 1958).

Bibliography: *CP*, 458.

"Depression in the Cards." Short story, included in the collection *Simple Stakes a Claim*. *See* Simple [Jesse B.] Stories.

"Desert." Ten-line poem using images of a desert landscape to represent spiritual and emotional barrenness. It was first published in *Negro Digest* (December 1950).

Bibliography: *CP*, 328.

"Desire." Nine-line poem concerning intense, short-lived sexual desire. It was first published in the *Messenger** (May 1927).

Bibliography: *CP*, 105.

Dessalines, Jean-Jacques. *See Troubled Island* (play).

"Dialogue at Dawn." Short story, unpublished. Rampersad indicates that Hughes was working on it in early 1954. It concerns adultery. A manuscript is held in the Langston Hughes Papers, James Weldon Johnson Memorial Collection, Beinecke Library, Yale University.
Bibliography: Rampersad, II, 234.

Did You Ever Hear the Blues? Long-playing record album recorded by Big Miller (New York: United Artists, 1959). The title song was originally from *Simply Heavenly* (*see* "Did You Ever Hear the Blues?"). The recording is held by the Library of Congress.

"Did You Ever Hear the Blues?" Song, from *Simply Heavenly*. Hughes wrote the lyrics, and David Martin composed the music. ASCAP* lists the song as being published by the Bourne Company, and the song's ASCAP registry number is 340034573. *See Did You Ever Hear the Blues?*

"Dime." Poem. *See Montage of a Dream Deferred.*

"Dimout in Harlem." Five-quatrain poem that, although in free verse, is extremely stylized, sonorous, and improvisational in phrasing. It evokes the surreality of Harlem* streets during a partial failure of electrical utilities there. It was first published in *Panorama* (March 1943).
Bibliography: *CP*, 270.

"Dinner Guest: Me." Twenty-three-line poem describing an experience Hughes himself no doubt had: being invited to dine with wealthy white liberals on Park Avenue in New York City. The poem in part expresses the tedium and frustration Hughes or another African American might feel among superficially well-meaning white liberals who ask the dinner guest questions about "the Negro problem" in the United States. It was first published in *Negro Digest* (September 1965).
Bibliography: *CP*, 547–548.

"Disillusion." Poem of fifteen short lines in which the speaker expresses a desire to be "simple again" and specifically not to know Harlem* as well as he or she does now. It was first published in *Crisis** (December 1925).
Bibliography: *CP*, 60.

"Distance Nowhere." Song. Hughes wrote the lyrics, and Charles Barrett Griffin composed the music. The song's ASCAP registry number is 340402540.

With "Border Line," "Drum," "Night: Four Songs," and "Suicide's Note," it is included in Griffin's *Distance Nowhere: 5 Langston Hughes Songs*.

Bibliography: Charles Barrett Griffin, *Distance Nowhere: 5 Langston Hughes Songs: For Baritone and String Quartet* (Forest Hills, NY: Charles Griffin, 1995).

"Dive." Poem. *See Montage of a Dream Deferred.*

"Dixie Man to Uncle Sam." Three-quatrain poem spoken by a collective persona* who asks "Uncle Sam" (the U.S. government) how he (it) can "shake a fist at tyranny" in Europe while tolerating racism in the South. The persona specifically calls Jim Crow laws* "Hitler-like." The poem was first published in the *Baltimore Afro American** (April 25, 1942). *See* "America's Young Black Joe."

Bibliography: *CP*, 572.

"Dixie South Africa." Seven-line poem addressed to a personified South Africa, comparing the "craziness of [South Africa's] craziness"—namely, apartheid and its effects—to the short-lived chaos of a white dissolving Alka-Seltzer tablet. The poem was first published in *Free Lance* (1958). *See* "Johannesburg Mines"; "Question[1]"; "Question and Answer."

Bibliography: *CP*, 458.

"Do Nothing 'Til You Hear from Me." Song composed by Duke Ellington.* It was played at Hughes's funeral* service. *See* "Request for Requiems."

"Do You Reckon." Four-stanza poem in ballad* form, addressed to "Mr. White Man" and "Miss White Lady" and written in black dialect.* The poem touches on some of the sociosexual ironies of racism in the United States that Hughes explores more comprehensively in *The Ways of White Folks*. For example, Mr. White Man sleeps with an African American man's sister but will not shake hands with the African American man, and Miss White Lady will overwork an African American housekeeper and then sleep with her son. The poem was first published in the magazine *Deer and Dachshund* (no. 6), for which the editors of *Collected Poems* could find no date or place of publication. The library of the University of California lists the magazine's place of publication as "Ranches of Taos, New Mexico" and lists its dates of publication (vol. 1, no. 1–6) as 1952?–1954.

Bibliography: *CP*, 444, 677.

"Dr. Brown's Decision." Short story. *See* "Professor."

"Dr. Sidesaddle." Short story, included in the collection *Simple's Uncle Sam*. *See* Simple [Jesse B.] Stories.

"A Dog and Cat Tale." Short story for children. It is unpublished. A manuscript is held in the Langston Hughes Papers, James Weldon Johnson Memorial Collection, Beinecke Library, Yale University.

Bibliography: Rampersad, II, 257.

"Dog Days." Short story, included in the collection *Simple's Uncle Sam*. *See* Simple [Jesse B.] Stories.

"A Dog Named Trilby." Short story, included in the collection *The Best of Simple*. *See* Simple [Jesse B.] Stories.

Dogberry, Wim. In *Not Without Laughter* Wim Dogberry is a hod carrier for bricklayers building a movie theatre in Stanton. He boards with Aunt Hager* and the main character, Sandy, whose mother has left him to join his father in Detroit.

"Domesticated." Short story, included in the collection *Simple's Uncle Sam*. *See* Simple [Jesse B.] Stories.

"Don't Forget the Lilac Bush." Song, from *Street Scene*. Hughes and Elmec Rice* wrote the lyrics, and Kurt Weill* composed the music. ASCAP* lists the song as being published by Chappell and Company and Hampshire House. The song's ASCAP registry number is 340052651. *See* "Ain't It Awful, the Heat"; "A Boy like You"; "Catch Me If You Can"; "I Got a Marble and a Star"; "I Loved Her, Too"; "Ice Cream."

"Don't You See My Shoes?" *See* "Barefoot Blues."

Don't You Want to Be Free? Play in one act. Hughes described it as "an experimental poetic play in one long act" (Hicklin, 525); he produced and directed it in May 1938 at the Harlem Suitcase Theatre,* West 125th Street and 8th Avenue, New York City. Beginning June 10, 1938, the play ran for 135 performances (three performances per week) on the second floor of the International Workers Order Community Center, 317 West 125th Street, Harlem* (Rampersad, 358–360; Hicklin). The price of tickets was thirty-five cents, and Robert Earl Jones was the primary actor. The first performance of the improvisational play included music—spirituals and blues*—and dance; the accompanist, on piano, was Carroll Tate, who also served as musical director. Subsequently *Don't You Want to Be Free?* has been performed by small dramatic groups and college theatres in Chicago, Los Angeles, New Orleans, and Pittsburgh and at Howard University and Talladega College. The play has two characters: Young Man, an African American who says that "this show is about what it means to be colored in America"; and Overseer, a white man who in different episodes appears as a tenant farmer, a hotel manager, a landlord, a butcher, an editor, a factory foreman, a U.S. Army sergeant, and an insurance broker. Hughes stipulates that except for the bare stage, the set shall include only a hanging lynch rope and a slavery auction block. Rampersad considers the play to be "a major step in the evolution of Hughes as an artist," suggesting that the play's "major criteria . . . came not from the white stage but from Hughes's sense of the distinguishing features of modern, urban black culture and his own poetic gifts." He further characterizes it as "loose-limbed and improvisational" (I, 358). Samuel Hay credits Hughes with "designing New York City's first avant-garde theatre space" under the auspices of the Harlem Suitcase Theatre and specifically for this play, which starkly dramatizes racist encounters between the two symbolic characters and links issues of racism and labor. Hughes was clearly interested in creating severe, even brutal, effects with the staging, but also spontaneous verve with the improvisational style. The play was published in *One-Act Play* magazine (October 1938). *See also Angelo Herndon Jones*; "Ballads of Lenin"; "Chant for Tom Mooney"; "Goodbye, Christ"; "Good Morning, Revolution"; "Lenin"; "A New Song"; "Note on Commercial Theatre"; "One More 'S' in the U.S.A."; "Revolution"; "Song of the Revolution"; "Wait." *See also* John Reed Club; Marxism; Politics.

Bibliography: Samuel A. Hay, *African American Theatre: An Historical and Critical Analysis* (Cambridge: Cambridge University Press, 1994), 173–174; Hicklin; Rampersad, I, 356–360; Maxine Schwartz Seller, ed., *Ethnic Theatre in the United States* (Westport, CT: Greenwood Press, 1983), 51–52.

"doorknobs." Twenty-five-line poem focusing on doorknobs as a "simple silly terror"—a symbol for life's unpredictability and for passages in a lifetime and in generations. This is the only published poem by Hughes that he titled without initial capitalization; however, the capitalization is conventional in the body of the poem. Insofar as it is a "thing poem," "doorknobs" is comparable to "Anne Spencer's Table." It was first published in *Outsider* (Fall 1961).

Bibliography: *CP*, 537.

The Doors of Life. In *Not Without Laughter* the main character Sandy is given this (fictional) book by his Aunt Tempy when he is in high school. It is a Christian-influenced book on how to lead a proper life.

Dorsey, James. *See* Lincoln University.

Douglas, Alta. *See* Harlem Suitcase Theatre.

Douglass, Frederick (1818–1895). American writer, social activist, and orator. Douglass's mother, Harriet Bailey, was a slave at Holme Hill Farm in Maryland. His father was an unidentified white man but was suspected to have been Bailey's owner, Aaron Anthony. Douglass's original given name was Frederick Augustus Washington Bailey. Douglass himself worked, in slavery, as a servant for Hugh and Sophia Auld in Baltimore, and it was Sophia Auld who taught him to read; however, literacy among slaves was generally discouraged, and Hugh Auld put a stop to the reading lessons. Douglass nonetheless continued to read on his own. His remarkable, enduring autobiography, *The Narrative of the Life of Frederick Douglass, Written by Himself* (1845), recounts his experiences in slavery, including a fistfight with one of his "masters," Thomas Covey. Douglass successfully escaped slavery in 1838, changed his name, married Anna Murray, and settled in New Bedford, Massachusetts. Soon thereafter Douglass joined William Lloyd Garrison's antislavery (or "abolitionist") movement and became an enormously effective, popular public speaker. Later his *Narrative* and two subsequent autobiographical installments became popular and critical successes. For example, in just five years, 30,000 copies of the *Narrative* were sold (Baym, 1991). After the Civil War, Douglass worked on behalf of African American civil rights, women's and African American suffrage, and antilynching legislation. Hughes regarded Douglass as a towering intellectual, literary, and political figure. *See* "Frederick Douglass, 1817–1895." *See also* Lynching.

Bibliography: Nina Baym, ed., *The Norton Anthology of American Literature*, 5th ed. (New York: W. W. Norton, 1998), 1990–2075; Frederick Douglass, *Narrative of the Life of Frederick Douglass: An American Slave, Written by Himself*, ed. Benjamin Quarles (Cambridge, MA: Harvard University Press, 1967); Waldo E. Martin, *The Mind of Frederick Douglass* (Chapel Hill: University of North Carolina Press, 1984).

"The Dove." Nine-line poem that interprets in a surprising way a famous painting of a dove by Pablo Picasso, the enormously influential modern Spanish artist. Hughes focuses on the two dominant colors of the poem, white (dove) and brown (background), and instead of viewing the dove conventionally as a symbol of peace, he sees the dominant colors as representing racial conflict and therefore social unrest. The poem was first published in *Outcry* (Summer 1962). *See also* "Cubes."

Bibliography: *CP*, 536.

"Down and Out." Two-stanza poem in modified blues*-lyric form, spoken in black dialect* by a woman who has had her wardrobe seized by "the creditman"; also, her rent is due, she wants to buy "a straightenin' comb" for her hair, and she needs "a dime fo' beer." The poem was first published with an additional stanza (as noted in *Collected Poems*) in *Opportunity** (October 1926). *See also* Revision, Process of, and Hughes.

Bibliography: *CP*, 78, 631.

"Down Where I Am." Four-stanza poem in a short-lined ballad* form. It is spoken by a person who is deeply weary of trying to get ahead in life, and

Hughes juxtaposes symbols of economic upward mobility with effects that are more literal-minded. For example, from "[b]eatin' at the door [of opportunity]," the man has sore fists, and from trying in vain to climb the ladder of advancement, he has broken his ankles. The poem ends with another juxtaposition: surrender and defiance. It was first published in *Voices* (Winter 1950).

Bibliography: *CP*, 375.

The Dozens. *See Ask Your Mama.*

"Draftees." Twenty-four-line rhyming poem with irregular stanzas. Addressed to men drafted to fight in World War II, it provides a playful look at "leaving home," portraying it as a process of saying goodbye to American girlfriends and hello to European ones. It was first published in *Lincoln University Poets* (1954).

Bibliography: *CP*, 445.

Drama. Hughes may legitimately be considered a pioneer in American theatre, and his achievement in drama is varied and significant. He spearheaded the founding of the innovative Harlem Suitcase Theatre,* and his play *Mulatto* was one of the first works by an African American playwright to be produced on Broadway. Hughes's range as a dramatist stretches from tragedy (*Mulatto*) to comedy (*Little Ham*) and from experimental plays (*Don't You Want to Be Free?*, *Soul Gone Home*) to overtly political work (*Angelo Herndon Jones*, *Scottsboro Limited*). In addition, his achievement in musical drama is impressive in its own right. It includes work in opera with Jan Meyerowitz* and William Grant Still,* the "blues opera" *De Organizer*, gospel song plays such as *Black Nativity*, and the elaborate musical play, *Street Scene*, on which he collaborated with Kurt Weill* and Elmer Rice.* *See* "Carry On, America"; *Don't You Want To Be Free?; Drums of Haiti; Emperor of Haiti; Front Porch; "Gold Piece"; Harvest; Limitations of Life; Little Ham; Mulatto; Mule Bone; De Organizer; The Road; Scottsboro Limited; Soul Gone Home; Troubled Island* (play); *When the Jack Hollers. See also* Harlem Suitcase Theatre; Musical Plays; Opera; *The Political Plays of Langston Hughes.*

Bibliography: Rena Fraden, *Blueprints for a Black Federal Theatre, 1935–1939* (Cambridge: Cambridge University Press, 1994); Samuel A. Hay, *African American Theatre: An Historical and Critical Analysis* (Cambridge: Cambridge University Press, 1994); Hicklin, especially 246–259.

"Drama for Winter Night (Fifth Avenue)." One-page poem focusing on homelessness, particularly on how a homeless man is told repeatedly where he may not sleep, on how even God and the Christian church seem to forsake him, and on how emergency services are sent for only because onlookers do not want

the man to clutter the street by dying there. It was first published in *Workers Monthly* (March 1925). *See also* "On the Road."
Bibliography: *CP*, 47.

"Dream." Fourteen-line poem (not a sonnet) in which the speaker's dream of a lost love and the experience of same converge. It was first published in somewhat revised form (as noted in *Collected Poems*) in *Opportunity** (September 1933).
Bibliography: *CP*, 173, 644.

"Dream Boogie." Poem. *See Montage of a Dream Deferred.*

"Dream Boogie: Variation." Poem. *See Montage of a Dream Deferred.*

"Dream Deferred." Song that alludes to *Montage of a Dream Deferred.* Hughes wrote the lyrics, and Paul A. Siskind composed the music. ASCAP* lists the song as being published by Sweet Child Music, and the song's ASCAP registry number is 340377257. Hal Leonard published a work by Siskind entitled "A Dream Deferred"; *see* entry for "Poem."

"Dream Dust." Seven-line poem depicting the source of dream dust as residing in literal dust of clouds, stars, earth, and storms. It was first published in *Fields of Wonder.*
Bibliography: *CP*, 336.

The Dream Keeper. (New York: Knopf, 1932). 77 pp. Book of poetry. The book, which contains fifty-nine poems, was intended for young readers, but instead of writing poems explicitly for children, Hughes selected poems he had already published—in magazines and in *The Weary Blues*—that he believed would be accessible to a younger audience. Consequently, almost all of the poems are more sophisticated and represent a wider range of subject matter than one might expect from a "children's book." Several poems, for instance, address issues of racism rather bluntly. From *The Weary Blues*, poems Hughes chose to reprint include "After Many Springs," "Aunt Sue's Stories," "Beggar Boy," "A Black Pierrot," "Death of an Old Seaman," "Mexican Market Woman," "Mother to Son," "Negro Dancer," "The Negro Speaks of Rivers," "Poem [2]," "Sea Calm," "The Weary Blues," and "When Sue Wears Red." The five sections of the book are "The Dream Keeper," "Sea Charm," "Dressed Up," "Feet o' Jesus," and "Walkers with the Dawn." In addition to the title poem, the "Feet o' Jesus" section contains such gospel-influenced poems as "Judgment Day," "Ma Lord," "Prayer," "Prayer Meeting," and "Sinner." Rampersad notes that the book "appeared from Knopf with generally good reviews" (I, 254), and that Helen Sewell illustrated the book. Rampersad writes, "Langston had begged Sewell to avoid the usual kinky headed caricatures used so often to represent blacks. Her illustrations proved to be very sensitive" (I, 254). Hughes dedicated the book "To My Brother—L. H.": actually his stepbrother, Gwyn Clark,* son of Homer Clark.* In 1994 Knopf reissued the book with new illustrations by Brian Pinkney, who worked in "scratchboard," a technique in which a white board is covered with black ink. The ink is then scratched off with a sharp tool to reveal white underneath" (copyright page). The new edition contains the section "Additional Poems," which adds seven poems not included in the 1932 edition: "Snail," "Stars," "Dream Dust," "Color," "Daybreak in Alabama," "Merry-Go-Round," and "In Time of Silver Rain," which has been set to music at least twice. For the 1994 edition, Lee Bennett Hopkins wrote a brief introduction providing biographical information (x–xi), and Augusta Baker contributed an afterword entitled "A Personal Note" (82–83). In it she indicates that her "husband-to-be" was an instructor at Lincoln University* in 1927, where Hughes "found himself, at age twenty-five, in what must have been a boring English class. [Professor Baker] asked to see a book in which Langston was writing. It was his French-English dictionary, and on the flyleaf, hastily scrawled, was a beautiful poem." The poem turned out to be "Dreams," included in both editions of *The Dream Keeper.*

Bibliography: Langston Hughes, *The Dream Keeper and Other Poems,* illustrated by Brian Pinkney (New York: Knopf, 1994); Rampersad, I, 253–255.

"The Dream Keeper." Eight-line poem addressed to dreamers (aspirants) by the dream keeper, whose task it is to protect dreams from "the too-rough fingers / Of the world." The poem was first published in *Survey Graphic* (March 1, 1925) and was also published in the book of poems *The Dream Keeper.* John James Kreckler set the poem to music. ASCAP* lists no publisher for the song, but the song's ASCAP registry number is 340413501. *See* Locke, Alain.

Bibliography: *CP,* 45.

"Dream of Freedom." Poem of five quatrains in ballad* form (stanza five is "stretched" to five lines); the poem asserts that the dream of freedom must remain a collective vision and pursuit and not disintegrate into private, individual aspirations. It was first published in *Wayne State Graduation Comment* (1964) and the NAACP* *Freedom Journal* (April 1964), which commemorates the tenth anniversary of the U.S. Supreme Court's ruling in *Brown v. Board of Education.**

Bibliography: *CP,* 542.

"Dream Thoughts." Song. Hughes wrote the lyrics, and Noel Da Costa composed the music. ASCAP* lists no publisher for the song, but the ASCAP registry number is 340232671.

"Dream Variations." Rhyming poem of seventeen lines in two stanzas. Ecstatic in tone, it expresses a wish to "dance" and "whirl" in the sun until night arrives "tenderly / Black like me." It was first published in *Crisis* (July 1924). *Collected Poems* contains information about revisions to stanzas and punctuation the poem underwent. William Benjamin Cooper set the poem to music. ASCAP* lists the song as being published by the Dangerfield Music Company, and the song's ASCAP registry number is 340260775. Phyllis Ludens Reed set the poem to music different from that of Cooper's. ASCAP lists no publisher for that song, but its registry number is 340275910.

Bibliography: *CP*, 40, 624.

"Dreamer." Twelve-line poem addressed to an indeterminate listener. The speaker indicates how he or she makes such things as vases and fountains out of his or her dreams, asks if the listener cares about the dreams, and concludes by deciding that whether the listener cares does not matter. The poem was first published in *Ebony and Topaz*, edited by C. S. Johnson (New York: National Urban League, 1927), 36.

Bibliography: *CP*, 111.

"Dreams." Poem of two ballad* quatrains that exhorts the reader/listener to "hold fast to dreams." It was first published in *World Tomorrow* (1923). Later, William Benjamin Cooper set the poem to music. ASCAP* lists no publisher for the song, but the song's ASCAP registry number is 340292900. Lon Beery also set the poem to music, and his version is published by Hal Leonard.

Bibliography: Lon Beery, "Dreams" [text by Langston Hughes], music for choral ensemble (New York: Hal Leonard, 1998), HL 8602141; *CP*, 32.

"Dressed Up." Four-quatrain rhyming poem in black dialect*; the speaker has purchased new shoes and a new hat and has had his clothes cleaned but remains miserable because he "ain't got nobody / For to call [him] sweet." In *I Wonder As I Wander* Hughes mentions that he sometimes began poetry readings with this poem and that it represented "verses written when I was about fifteen." It was first published in *Palms* (November 1926). *See also* "Porter."

Bibliography: *CP*, 80; *I Wonder As I Wander*, 57.

Dreyfus, Alfred (1859–1935). French military officer of Jewish descent. Based on false evidence, Dreyfus was convicted of treason. Known now as "the Dreyfus Affair," the case highlighted problems with anti-Semitism and political corruption in French society. Dreyfus was paroled in 1906. He returned to the military, which faced discredit because of the case, as did the Catholic clergy and the monarchy. Dreyfus is mentioned in Hughes' poem "Final Call."

Driberg, Tom. *See* "Crow Goes, Too."

"Drum." Eighteen-line poem that elaborates on a comparison between death and a relentlessly beating drum. It was first published in *Poetry Quarterly* (Spring 1931). *Collected Poems* contains information about slight revisions the poem underwent. Later Charles Barrett Griffin set the poem to music.

Bibliography: *CP*, 137, 639; Charles Barrett Griffin, *Distance Nowhere: 5 Langston Hughes Songs: For Baritone and String Quartet* (Forest Hills, NY: Charles Griffin, 1995).

Drums of Haiti. Play. *See Troubled Island* (opera); *Troubled Island* (play).

"Drunkard." Poem. *See Montage of a Dream Deferred.*

Du Bois, W.E.B. (1868–1963). American sociologist, political leader, essayist, novelist, and editor. Du Bois was born and grew up in Great Barrington, Massachusetts. He earned a B.A. from Fisk University in 1891 and an M.A. from Harvard University in 1892, after which he studied in Berlin, Germany. In 1896 he became the first African American to earn a Ph.D., which he took at Harvard. From 1899 to 1910 he taught at Atlanta University and conducted path-breaking sociological research. It was, however, his comparatively nonacademic book of essays *The Souls of Black Folk* (1903) that secured Du Bois's reputation as a social philosopher and political thinker. Because the book, in part, argued for political and social change, Du Bois became the political rival of Booker T. Washington,* who emphasized economic self-sufficiency for African Americans and discouraged political activism. Du Bois was cofounder of and the strongest driving force behind the NAACP,* and for many years he edited its chief publication, *Crisis.** As an articulate, forceful leader, a renowned scholar, and a worldly social critic, Du Bois was a primary architect of the Harlem Renaissance,* promoting the idea of the Talented Tenth* and helping Alain Locke* envisage "New Negro" writing and art (*see* The New Negro). To the extent that Hughes embraced the idea that African American writers should be "social" (politically alert) writers, he can be seen as a "disciple" of Du Bois, but as to the specific form such writing should take, the two did not always agree, and Du Bois tended to prefer the poetic example set by Countee Cullen* (among others) to that set by Hughes. *See* Fauset, Jessie; "To Certain Negro Leaders."

Bibliography: Hutchinson; Lewis, *WHWV*; Arnold Rampersad, *The Art and Imagination of W.E.B. Du Bois* (Cambridge, MA: Harvard University Press, 1976).

Du Sable, Jean-Baptist-Point (1750?–1818). French explorer, considered one of the first settlers of what is now Chicago, Illinois, in 1782 or 1783. *See* "Migrant."

Dunbar, Paul Laurence (1872–1906). American poet, novelist, and lecturer. A native of Ohio, Dunbar graduated from high school there and privately published his first book of poems in 1893, *Oak and Ivy*. A second book, *Majors and*

Minors (1895), received good reviews, especially with regard to the poems in black dialect,* and Dunbar's popularity and reputation would come to be based almost entirely on his dialect poetry; however, he also wrote novels, including *The Uncalled* (1898) and *The Sport of the Gods* (1902). Because Dunbar enjoyed a wide readership and used identifiably African American linguistic resources, he was an important literary model for African American writers of the next generation, including Hughes.

Bibliography: Benjamin Brawley, *Paul Laurence Dunbar: Poet of His People* (Chapel Hill: University of North Carolina Press, 1936); John Keeling, "Paul Dunbar and the Mask of Dialect," *Southern Literary Journal* 25, no. 2 (Spring 1993), 24–38.

"Dusk." Thirteen-line, free-verse poem that is not so much about dusk per se as it is about perseverance. It was first published under the title "Poem" in *New Challenge* (June 1936).

Bibliography: *CP*, 193.

"Dustbowl." Taking its title from the term applied to the drought-plagued North American Great Plains during the 1930s, this free-verse poem of thirteen lines is spoken by a farmer who "hears" the land calling him to return. It was first published in *Poetry* (May 1941).

Bibliography: *CP*, 228.

"Duty Is Not Snooty." Short story, included in the collections *Simple Stakes a Claim* and *The Best of Simple*. *See* Simple [Jesse B.] Stories.

"Dying Beast." Thirteen-line rhyming poem, at once stark and lyrical, evoking images of buzzards waiting for an unspecified animal to die. It was first published in *Poetry* (October 1931).

Bibliography: *CP*, 139.

E

The Eagle Rock. An American dance step popular in the 1920s. *See* "Ma Man."

"Early Autumn." Short story. The narrative concerns two former lovers who meet on a street corner, engage in pleasant conversation, but decide not to rekindle romance. The story was included in the collection *Something in Common and Other Stories* and was reprinted in *Langston Hughes: Short Stories*.
Bibliography: Ostrom, 46.

"Early Evening Quarrel." Five-stanza dramatic poem in which "Hattie" speaks stanzas one, three, and five, and "Hammond" speaks stanzas two and four. The couple quarrels about Hammond's not having purchased sugar, but larger issues are refracted through this disagreement. The poem was first published in *Living Age* (June 1941). It was also published in *Shakespeare in Harlem*.
Bibliography: *CP*, 231.

"Earth Song." Fifteen-line rhyming poem, ecstatic in tone and celebrating spring, birth, and "body"; the narrator has "been waiting long / For an earth song." The poem was first published in *Survey Graphic* (March 1925). *See* Locke, Alain.
Bibliography: *CP*, 46.

"Easter in Wartime." Poem in two ballad* quatrains with no stanza breaks. The poem concerns the "Divine Celestial Will" that might be able to "lift" the murderous "soul of man." The date of composition is uncertain. The poem was first published in Berry and is not included in *Collected Poems*. *See* Religion.
Bibliography: Berry, 45.

Eastman, Max (1883–1969). American editor and writer. *See* McKay, Claude; Reed, John.

"Easy Boogie." Poem. *See Montage of a Dream Deferred.*

"Economics." Poem. *See* "Frosting."

Einstein, Albert (1879–1955). German physicist whose theories of time, space, and "relativity" revolutionized the science of physics and influenced science and technology in general, including the development of nuclear weapons. Clark observes that Einstein "radically altered man's ideas of the physical world" (9). Hughes's poem "Not What Was" seems to reveal Einstein-influenced views of time, space, and destiny.

Bibliography: Ronald W. Clark, *Einstein: The Life and Times* (New York: Avon Books, 1971).

"Elderly Leaders." Fifteen-line poem (of which the last five lines are dollar signs) that critiques elderly leaders of African American communities, focusing on the cautiousness of such leaders and their tendency to sacrifice their principles for money and comfort. The poem was first published in *Race* (Summer 1936).

Bibliography: *CP*, 193; James Emanuel, "The Literary Experiments of Langston Hughes," in O'Daniel, 171–182.

"Elevator Boy." Twenty-three line poem, a monologue by an elevator boy at the "Dennison Hotel" in New Jersey. He compares the job with what he regards as other dead-end occupations, such as washing dishes and shining shoes. The poem was first published in *Fire!!** (November 1926). *See* McKay, Claude.

Bibliography: *CP*, 85.

Ellington, Duke (1899–1974). American composer, musician, and orchestra leader. Ellington was born in Washington, D.C., and attended Armstrong High School there. In 1917 he won a scholarship to study music at the Pratt Institute in Brooklyn, New York, but turned it town, preferring to work at odd jobs, study music more informally, and pursue a career as a musician. His most influential teacher was Oliver Perry. Ellington moved to New York City in 1923, organized small orchestras and bands, and played at several clubs in Harlem.* Music publisher Irving Mills, who would write lyrics for many of Ellington's songs, signed Ellington to a publishing contract in 1927 and provided the funding that would allow him to enlarge his orchestra. He also secured a contract for Ellington's orchestra to play at the Cotton Club, which became Harlem's most famous nightclub during the Harlem Renaissance* and which, ironically, did not allow black customers through its doors. Although Ellington was an important figure in the jazz* composed and played during the Harlem Renaissance*, he did not truly begin to forge a national and international reputation until the 1930s and 1940s. He composed the music for some of the most enduring popular American songs, including "Mood Indigo," "Sophisticated Lady," "The A Train," "Satin Doll," "Don't Get Around Much Anymore," "Paris Blues," and "Do Nothing 'Til You Hear from Me." His music is known for its subtlety and complex harmonies but at the same time for being solidly rooted in the blues* and rhythmic jazz. He also composed long suites, jazz symphonies, tone poems, music for ballet, and music for the cinema. He tirelessly toured with his orchestra in the United States and worldwide until his death. Hughes mentions Ellington in the story "A Toast to Harlem." *See* Funeral, Hughes's.

Bibliography/Discography: *The Duke Ellington Centennial Edition: The Complete RCA Victor Recordings* [24 compact discs/boxed set] (New York: RCA Music, 1999); *The Big Sea*; Duke Ellington, *All Time Favorite Classics* [song book] (New York: Warner Books, 1999); John Edward Hasse and Wynton Marsalis, *Beyond Category: The Life and Genius of Duke Ellington* (New York: Da Capo, 1995); Lewis, *WHWV*; Rampersad, I, II; Scott Yanow, with a Foreword by Billy Taylor, *Duke Ellington* (New York: Friedman/Fairfax, 1999).

Ellison, Ralph (1914–1994). American writer and professor. Ellison was born and grew up in Oklahoma City. For three years he studied music at the Tuskegee Institute but moved to New York City in 1936, began to pursue a writing career, met Hughes and Richard Wright,* and worked with the Federal Writers Project. He began publishing short fiction and essays and won fellowships that allowed him to work on a novel, part of which ("Battle Royal") first appeared as a short story in 1947. Eventually the novel, *Invisible Man*, was published in 1952, and almost immediately it was acclaimed as one of the most accomplished, original, and powerful novels of its time. It won the National Book Award in 1953, and its status as a major work has only grown in subsequent years. As Rampersad recounts, Hughes first met Ellison on July 6, 1936, in the lobby of the YMCA in Harlem.* Because Alain Locke* happened to be there as well, Rampersad suggests that Hughes was meeting "the past and the future," Locke representing the former, Ellison the latter (I, 329). Shortly thereafter Hughes loaned Ellison two books, André Malraux's *Man's Fate* and John Strachey's Marxist-influenced book *Literature and Dialectical Materialism* (Rampersad, I, 329). The two writers became friends; Ellison and his wife, Fanny, often visited Hughes's apartment; and Hughes came to see the younger writer as his protégé. After the publication of *Invisible Man*, which appeared in the same year as *Laughing to Keep from Crying*, the relationship changed. Rampersad concludes that "[a]lthough Langston initially was happy for Ellison, the astonishing success of *Invisible Man*, coupled with the growing privacy of the younger writer, slowly antagonized him" (II, 201); nonetheless, Hughes continued to praise the achievement of Ellison's epic novel. Ellison, for his part, distanced himself from Hughes. In 1964 Ellison published *Shadow and Act*, a collection of essays, and in 1970 he became a professor at New York University. In 1986 he published another collection of essays, *Going to the Territory*. The novel *Juneteenth* was published posthumously.

Bibliography: Kimberly W. Benston, ed., *Speaking for You: The Vision of Ralph Ellison* (Washington, DC: Howard University Press, 1990); Ralph Ellison, *The Collected Essays of Ralph Ellison*, ed, with an introduction by John F. Callahan, with a preface by Saul Bellow (New York: Modern Library, 1995); Ralph Ellison, *Flying Home and Other Stories*, ed. John F. Callahan (New York: Random House, 1996); Ralph Ellison, *Going to the Territory* (New York: Random House, 1986); Ralph Ellison, *Juneteenth* ed. John F. Callahan (New York: Random House, 1999); Ralph Ellison, *Invisible Man* (New York: Random House, 1952); Ralph Ellison, *Shadow and Act* (New York: Random House, 1964); Ralph Ellison and Karl Shapiro, *The Writer's Experience* [lectures] (Washington, DC: Library of Congress/Government Printing Office, 1964); Donald B. Gibson, ed., *Five Black Writers: Essays on Wright, Ellison, Baldwin, Hughes, and Le Roi Jones* (New York: New York University Press, 1970); Rampersad, II, 23, 30, 41, 200–202, and elsewhere.

"Em-Fuehrer Jones." *See Limitations of Life.*

"Emperor Hailie Selassie." Nineteen-line rhyming poem subtitled "On Liberation Day, May 5, 1966." Hughes presented the poem in person to Selassie on the twenty-fifth anniversary of Selassie's triumphant return to Addis Ababa after having been exiled during the Italian occupation of Ethiopia. The poem praises Selassie as an important symbol of Negritude (*See* Césaire, Aimé) and as a "King of Kings" in whom ordinary people can invest their pride. In its attitude toward symbolic figures, the poem differs sharply from "Crowns and Garlands." *See also* "Broadcast on Ethiopia"; "Call of Ethiopia."

Bibliography: *CP*, 551.

Emperor of Haiti. Play. *See Troubled Island* (play).

"Empty House." Nine-line rhyming poem in which an empty house becomes a symbol of wretchedness. It was first published in *Buccaneer* (May 1925).

Bibliography: *CP*, 51.

"Empty Houses." Short story, included in the collection *Simple's Uncle Sam*. *See* Simple [Jesse B.] Stories.

"Empty Room." Short story, included in the collections *Simple Takes a Wife* and *The Best of Simple*. *See* Simple [Jesse B.] Stories.

"Encounter." Nineteen-line rhyming poem spoken to a certain "You," whom the speaker meets on this person's "way to death." Soon the poem reveals the "You" to be Christ, and the concluding lines are "But on Your back You carried

/ My own Misery." The poem was first published in *Voices* (Spring 1962). *See* Religion.
Bibliography: *CP*, 534.

"End." Ten-line poem imagining death, first published in *Fields of Wonder*.
Bibliography: *CP*, 328.

"Enemy." Eight-line rhyming poem that combines whimsy with venom; the speaker hopes to meet his or her enemy face-to-face for the first time as the enemy descends to (and the speaker emerges from) Hell. The poem was first published in the *Carmel Pine Cone* (July 11, 1941).
Bibliography: *CP*, 233.

"The English." Thirteen-line free-verse poem depicting the English as eccentric imperialists. *See* "Envoy to Africa"; "Explain It, Please."
Bibliography: *CP*, 129.

"Ennui." Four-line humorous, epigrammatic poem satirizing, from a poor individual's perspective, middle-class ennui, or deep spiritual boredom. It was first published in the *Maryland Quarterly* (1944).
Bibliography: *CP*, 305.

"Enter Cousin Minnie." Short story, included in the collection *The Best of Simple*. *See* Simple [Jesse B.] Stories.

"Envoy to Africa." Eleven-line poem in rhyming couplets that satirizes British diplomacy and imperialism. The poem is spoken by one Lord Piggly-Wiggly Wigglesfoot Brown. It was first published in *Crisis* (August 1953). *See* "The English"; "Explain It, Please."
Bibliography: *CP*, 441.

"Epigram." Poem by Armand Lanusse that Hughes translated from "Louisiana Creole." It concerns a dialogue between a priest and a woman; the subject of the dialogue is the Devil. It was published in *The Langston Hughes Reader*.
Bibliography: *The Langston Hughes Reader*, 136.

"Epitaph [1]." Extremely spare seven-line poem; within the grave, reports the poem's persona, "Lies nothing more / Than I." The poem was first published under the pseudonym J. Crutchfield Thompson in *Crisis* (September 1926). *See* "Autumn Note"; Pseudonyms Used by Hughes.
Bibliography: *CP*, 74.

"Epitaph [2]." Poem. The epitaph is for Uncle Tom, the figure representing African-American docility toward whites and based on the main character of *Uncle Tom's Cabin*, the popular novel by Harriet Beecher Stowe. The poem concludes, "Now, thank God, / Uncle Tom / Is dead." It was first published in the *Amsterdam News* (October 18, 1941). *See* "America's Young Black Joe!"; "Uncle Tom [1]"; "Uncle Tom [2]."

Bibliography: *CP*, 570.

"Equality and Dogs." Short story, included in the collection *Simple Speaks His Mind. See* Simple [Jesse B.] Stories.

Essays. *See* Baez, Joan; *Baltimore Afro American; The Barrier; Chicago Defender; Good Morning Revolution: Uncollected Protest Writings of Langston Hughes*; "The Harlem Story"; "Harlem III"; "Here to Yonder"; "Introduction" to *Pudd'nhead Wilson*; "Jamaica"; *The Langston Hughes Reader; My Lord What a Mornin'*; "The Negro Artist and the Racial Mountain"; Poetics; Politics; Whitman, Walt.

Esther. Opera in three acts and sixteen scenes, with music by Jan Meyerowitz* and a libretto by Hughes. It debuted at the University of Illinois Festival of Contemporary Arts (Champaign-Urbana) on March 17, 1957. Hughes based the libretto closely on the story of Esther (which contains the legend of the feast of Purim) in the Bible. Bruce Foote sang the role of Ahasuerus, Elaine Quint the role of Esther. Howard Talley found Meyerowitz's music uninspired and "the vocal line" mainly "declamatory," but also believed that with a more "sumptuous" production, the opera would provide "a welcome and much-needed novelty for the repertoire of professional companies here [the United States] and abroad." *See also The Barrier; Five Foolish Virgins; The Glory around His Head; Port Town; Street Scene.*

Bibliography: Jan Meyerowitz and others, *Esther: Oper in drei Akten (16 Szenen)* (New York: Associated Music Publishers, 1956); Howard Talley, "Krenek, Meyerowitz Operas Staged in Illinois Festival," *Musical America* 77 (April 8, 1957), 8.

"Evenin' Air Blues." Four-stanza poem in black dialect* and in traditional blues*-lyric form. The speaker is homesick for the American South. The poem was first published in *Common Ground* (Spring 1941).

Bibliography: *CP*, 225.

"Evening Song." Poem. *See Montage of a Dream Deferred.*

"Everybody Loves My Baby, But My Baby Don't Love Nobody But Me." Popular American song. *See* "The Cat and the Saxophone (2 A.M.)."

"Evil." Poem of a single quatrain spoken by a personified "Evil," first published in the *Carmel Pine Cone* (April 24, 1941). It was also published in *Shakespeare in Harlem. See* Religion.

Bibliography: *CP*, 227.

"Evil Morning." Four-quatrain poem in traditional ballad* form spoken by a person who is feeling especially ill and vindictive; first published in *Shakespeare in Harlem.*

Bibliography *CP*, 262.

"Evil Woman." Four-quatrain rhyming poem in black dialect* spoken by an especially vicious man who is thinking of killing his girlfriend, as opposed to mistreating her, a line of thought Hughes has the speaker report without a trace of self-consciousness. Therefore, while the man may be thinking of an "evil woman," Hughes constructs the poem so as to expose the evil man, or the evil in this man. The poem was first published in *Fine Clothes to the Jew. See* "Beale Street Love."

Bibliography: *CP*, 120.

"Exits." Eleven-line poem concerning how and why suicide appeals to some people, first published under the title "Song for a Suicide" in *Crisis** (May 1924).

Bibliography: *CP*, 38.

"Expendable." Ten-line poem that in direct, even brutal, language reduces the soldier's role in war to its most basic element. It was first published in *Voices* (1947).

Bibliography: *CP*, 457.

"Explain It, Please." Sixteen-line rhyming poem in which the speaker adopts mock naïveté and asks why the British are fighting for freedom from Nazi Germany while still maintaining their colonies and thereby oppressing people of color. It was first published in the *Amsterdam News* (June 14, 1941). See "English, The"; "Envoy to Africa." *See also* "America's Young Black Joe."

Bibliography: *CP*, 569.

"Explain That to Me." Short story, included in the collection *Simple Takes a Wife. See* Simple [Jesse B.] Stories.

"Eyes Like a Gypsy." Unpublished short story, written in 1934. A manuscript is held in the Langston Hughes Papers, James Weldon Johnson Memorial Collection, Beinecke Library, Yale University.

Bibliography: Rampersad, I, 301.

F

F. S. Dedicatee of "Poem [2]," to date unidentified.

"Face and Race." Short story, included in the collection *Simple Stakes a Claim. See* Simple [Jesse B.] Stories.

"Face of War." Song. Hughes wrote the lyrics, and Elie Siegmeister, with whom Hughes would collaborate on the *Wizard of Altoona* (unfinished opera), composed the music. ASCAP* lists the song as being published by Carl Fischer, Inc., and the song's ASCAP registry number is 360140170.

"Fact." Poem. *See Montage of a Dream Deferred.*

"Fairies." Five-line poem concerning the mythical winged creatures, first published in *Brownie's Book* (January 1921). *See* Children's Poetry.
Bibliography: *CP*, 597.

"Faithful One." Poem in three short-lined quatrains, spoken by a man who tends to get drunk and stray from home but reports that a certain "she" will always be waiting for him—and let him in—upon his return. It was first published in *Fields of Wonder*.
Bibliography: *CP*, 335.

"Family Tree." Short story, included in *Simple Speaks His Mind* and *The Best of Simple. See* Simple [Jesse B.] Stories.

Famous American Negroes. (New York: Dodd, Mead, 1954). 147 pp. Biography. This volume contains sixteen biographies written for a juvenile audience, part of an extensive series published by Dodd, Mead that included such titles as *Famous Engineers, Famous Scientists, Famous British Novelists*, and *Famous Women of America*. Hughes's subjects are poet Phyllis Wheatley, religious leader Richard Allen, actor Ira Aldridge, freedom fighter Harriet Tubman, educational leader and inventor Booker T. Washington,* physician Daniel Hale Williams, painter Henry Ossawa Tanner, chemist George Washington Carver,* journalist Robert S. Abbott, poet Paul Laurence Dunbar,* blues* musician W. C. Handy, business leader Charles C. Spaulding, labor leader A. Philip Randolph,* political leader Ralph Bunche, concert singer Marian Anderson,* and professional baseball player Jackie Robinson. Hughes did know one of the individuals well—A. Philip Randolph, who edited the *Messenger*,* a magazine in which Hughes published many poems early in his career and on the editorial staff of which Wallace Thurman* worked. Hughes makes clear that the roster of subjects is intended to be representative of African American achievement in general. He also stresses that black contributions to North American history began before the Jamestown colony; he cites the story of Estavancio, who in 1529 was the first European to enter what is now Arizona. His third major point is that in the biographies he intends to show *how* his subjects achieved what they achieved and to describe the extent to which, by being of color, they faced even more difficulties than other people. Hughes's prose is crisp and vivid, and readers would be hard-pressed to find even one instance in which he condescends to his juvenile audience. Nor does he avoid difficult issues; for example, he describes how Booker T. Washington, because of his accommodationist attitudes toward whites, came to be regarded as an "Uncle Tom" by many African Americans (53). *See also* Audience; Children's Poetry; *Famous Negro Music Makers; The First Book of Africa; The First Book of Jazz; The First Book of Negroes; The First Book of Rhythms; The First Book of the Caribbean; The First Book of the West Indies; Popo and Fifina.*

Famous Negro Heroes of America. (New York: Dodd, Mead, 1958). 203 pp. Illustrated by Gerald McGann. Nonfiction book for juvenile readers. The book includes short biographical essays about American revolutionary Crispus Attucks, "mountain man" James P. Beckwourth, explorer Paul Cuffe, air force general Benjamin O. Davis, writer and activist Frederick Douglass,* explorer Esteban, explorer Matthew Henson, soldier Henry Johnson, soldier Dorie Miller, sailor Hugh N. Mulzac, slave-revolt leader Gabriel Prosser, explorer Jean-Baptiste-Point Du Sable, "patriot" (Hughes's term) Robert Smalls, "liberator" (Hughes's term) Harriet Tubman, and soldier Charles Young. *See* Audience; Children's Poetry; *Famous American Negro Music Makers; The First Book of Africa; The First Book of Jazz; The First Book of Negroes; The First Book of Rhythms; The First Book of the Caribbean; The First Book of the West Indies; Popo and Fifina*; "To Captain Mulzac."

Famous Negro Music Makers. (New York: Dodd, Mead, 1955). 179 pp. Illustrated with photographs. Nonfiction book for juveniles. The book features short biographical sketches of the Fisk Jubilee Singers, Bert Williams, Marian Anderson,* Louis Armstrong, James Bland, and Mahalia Jackson. *See The First Book of Jazz*; Jazz.

"Fancy Free." Short story, included in the collection *Simple Takes a Wife. See* Simple [Jesse B.] Stories.

"Fantasy in Purple." Poem in two rhyming quatrains, though the last line of stanza two is broken to add, technically, two additional lines. The speaker is giving directives as to what music should be played at his funeral. The poem was first published in *Vanity Fair* (September 1925), without the broken last line.

Bibliography: *CP*, 56, 627.

"A Farewell." Eight-line rhyming poem with slightly antique diction; the speaker is about to become a vagabond like "sailors and gypsies" and is bidding farewell to someone who "lives between the hills" and "has not seen the sea." The poem was first published in *The Weary Blues*.

Bibliography: *CP*, 96.

"Fascination." Poem of concentrated, vivid imagery and with, for Hughes, an unusual mixture of very short and very long lines (seven lines total). The speaker expresses his fascination with and love for a young woman. The poem was first published in *Crisis** (June 1924).

Bibliography: *CP*, 39.

Fate at the Wedding. *See Blood Wedding* and *Yerma* (one entry).

"Father and Son." Short story, adapted from the play *Mulatto* (1931). The narrative concerns Bert Norwood,* the illegitimate "mulatto" son of Colonel Norwood, a white plantation owner in the American South. Bert returns from college to confront his father, insisting that his father acknowledge him openly. In the denouement, Colonel Norwood collapses and dies when he is faced with the choice of killing Bert or acknowledging him. Bert is falsely accused of killing his father. Bert flees, but a mob hunts him down. Bert commits suicide rather than allow the mob to lynch him. "Father and Son" is one of Hughes's most ambitious treatments of the "tragic mulatto" theme, generating tragedy of classical Greek dimensions. Apparently it also contained material crucial to Hughes, because he reworked *Mulatto* into an opera, *The Barrier*. The story was included in the collections *The Ways of White Folks* and *Something in*

Common and Other Stories and was reprinted in *Langston Hughes: Short Stories. See* Lynching; "Mother and Child"; "Mulatto" (poem); "Passing."

Bibliography: Miller; David Michael Nifong, "Narrative Technique and Theory in *The Ways of White Folks*," *Black American Literature Forum* 15, no. 3 (Fall 1981), 93–96; Ostrom, 14–17, 55–57, 92; Sybil Ray Ricks, "A Textual Comparison of Langston Hughes's *Mulatto*, 'Father and Son,' and *The Barrier*," *Black American Literature Forum* 15, no. 3 (Fall 1981), 101–103.

"Faults of the Soviet Union." Essay. In it Hughes explains why even ardent admirers of the Soviet Union's socialist society must admit that it is not a utopia. He notes the "little things" he missed about the United States while he traveled in the Soviet Union, including wristwatches, good radio programs, and good newspapers. More broadly, he points to social inequities that persist in the Soviet Union. He closes by explaining why, even as he admires aspects of the Soviet Union, he does not leave the United States to live there: "This is my home, the U.S.A. I was born in the very middle of it" (Berry, 96). The essay was first published in the *Chicago Defender** (August 3, 1946). *See* Joplin. *See also* "Here to Yonder"; "The Soviet Union"; "The Soviet Union and Health"; "The Soviet Union and Jews"; "The Soviet Union and Women."

Bibliography: Berry; *The Big Sea; I Wonder As I Wander*; Rampersad, I, II.

Fauset, Jessie Redmon (1884–1961). American editor, novelist, and teacher. Fauset was undebatably one of the most important editors of the Harlem Renaissance,* publishing the work of younger African American writers in *Crisis* * and *The Brownie's Book*.* These writers included Claude McKay,* Nella Larsen,* and Hughes. Fauset was both the first woman to graduate from Cornell University with Phi Beta Kappa honors and the first African American woman to join that honor society. She served as literary editor of *Crisis* from 1919 to 1926, after which she taught at DeWitt Clinton High School in New York. Her novels include *There Is Confusion* (1924), *Plum Bun* (1929), and *The Chinaberry Tree* (1931). In 1921 Fauset published in *Crisis* what was to become one of Hughes's best-known poems, "The Negro Speaks of Rivers." She went on to publish dozens of Hughes's poems in *Crisis* over the next several years, establishing a foundation for a publishing relationship that would last throughout Hughes's life, for the magazine was indisputably crucial not just in Hughes's early development as a poet but in representing a constant forum for his work in all phases of his career. To a great extent, then, it is fitting that Hughes's relationship with the magazine spanned the publication of "The Negro Speaks of Rivers" (1921) and the posthumous publication of "Freedom [3]," which appeared in *Crisis* in 1968. *See also* "Nonette."

Bibliography: Carolyn Wedin Sylvander, *Jessie Redmon Fauset: Black American Writer* (Troy, NY: Whitson, 1981); Lewis, *WHWV*, 121–125.

"Feet Live Their Own Life." Short story, collected in *The Best of Simple. See* Simple [Jesse B.] Stories. *See also Poems by Sterling Brown.*

"Feet o' Jesus." Two-quatrain poem in black dialect,* evoking both the sound and sense of African American hymns. It was first published in *Opportunity** (November 1926). Florence Price set the poem to music, and the printed music—part of "Two Songs by Florence Price"—was published by the Southern Music Company and is held by the Library of Congress (LC). The LC control number is 96751652. The ASCAP* registry number for the song is 310293028. ASCAP lists "At the Feet *of* Jesus" [emphasis mine] as having music by Toy Harper, published by Carl Fischer, with the ASCAP registry number 310234261. *See* "At the Feet o' Jesus"; Religion; Songs.

Bibliography: *CP*, 78.

Fields of Wonder (New York: Knopf, 1947). 116 pp. Book of poetry that contains seventy-four poems, some of which were published for the first time in the book, many of which had appeared earlier in such periodicals as the *Carmel Pine Cone, Crisis,* Harper's Bazaar, Kansas Magazine, New York Herald Tribune, Opportunity,* Poetry, and Poetry Quarterly.* Almost all of the poems in the book are extremely spare and lyrical, inducing many readers to regard the book as Hughes's most lyrical, least political collection. The first section, "Fields of Wonder," includes two poems expressing Hughes's affinity for the California coastal region surrounding Carmel, "Big Sur" and "Moonlight Night: Carmel" (*see* Jeffers, Robinson and Una; Sullivan, Noel). The second section, "Border Line," includes melancholy poems linked to a wide variety of places—the American Midwest, Harlem,* Paris, a desert, a convent, a cemetery ("Dustbowl," "Beale Street," "Montmartre," "Desert," "Convent," "Grave Yard"). "Heart on the Wall," the third section, includes the poems "Heart" and "Havana Dreams." The fourth section, "Silver Rain" includes highly lyrical poems, among them "In Time of Silver Rain" (which at least two composers later set to music), "Songs," "Night Song," and "Carolina Cabin." "Desire," "Dream," "Juliet," and "Man" comprise the fifth section, "Desire." "Tearless," the sixth section, includes poems concerning persons down on their luck; examples include "Vagabonds," "Exits," "Chippy," and "Grief." The penultimate section, "Mortal Storm," includes such poems as "A House in Taos," "Genius Child," "Dream Dust," "Jaime," and "Sailing Date." "Stars over Harlem" is the final section and includes such poems as "Harlem Dance Floor," "Dimout in Harlem," "Refugee in America," "Earth Song," "When the Armies Passed," and "Oppression." Rampersad characterizes the reviews greeting *Fields of Wonder* as mixed but chiefly positive, with several reviewers responding favorably to Hughes's spare, lyrical, muted style in the book. Rampersad himself finds the comparative absence of political and social awareness in the book to be a drawback. He writes, "In spite of its lyric ambitions, *Fields of Wonder* negatively endorses the poetic power of Hughes's racial and political sense, which endowed him with almost his entire distinction as a poet. Nevertheless, the volume is valuable in that it illuminates the gloomy, brackish pool out of which this poetic power emerges, and which it aims mightily to transcend" (II, 133). Miller takes a different approach to the book, cautioning readers not to accept "too readily the distinction between lyric and rhetoric" (162). He adds, "[W]hat generates the lyrical power in *Fields [of Wonder]* conceals the real concern with community. While the persona [of the poems] feigns privacy, he addresses the men and women who would hear him, for the lyric, like the dramatic monologue, implies the respondent" (162). All of the poems in the book are included in *Collected Poems* (and each has its own entry in this encyclopedia), and many are included in both *The Dream Keeper* and *Selected Poems. See also* Politics; Songs.

Bibliography: R. Baxter Miller, " 'Some Mark to Make': The Lyrical Imagination of Langston Hughes," in Mullen, 154–166; Rampersad, II, 131–133.

"Fields of Wonder." Song cycle. *See* Bonds, Margaret.

"50–50." Fourteen-line poem in which a conversation between an unnamed woman and a man named Big Boy is reported. The woman complains about how difficult her life is. Big Boy assures her that he could help her—provided she share her "money" and her "bed." Thus the title of the poem is ironic insofar as Big Boy's contribution to the arrangement seems ill defined, at least. The poem was first published in *Shakespeare in Harlem*.

Bibliography: *CP*, 261.

Fight for Freedom: The Story of the NAACP (New York: Berkeley Books, 1962). 224 pp. Nonfiction book. It covers the history of the National Association for the Advancement of Colored People (NAACP*) from its roots in abolitionist politics and the Niagara movement through the 1950s and up to 1962, when Arthur Spingarn,* who wrote the foreword to the book, was the organization's president and Roy Wilkins served as its executive secretary. Hughes's sympathetic story of the organization is, like his other books of nonfiction, presented in concise, briskly paced chapters. *See* Du Bois, W.E.B. *See also Brown v. Board of Education*; Marshall, Thurgood.

"Final Call." Poem of twenty-six lines, twenty-five of which are completely in capital letters, simulating the print graphics of a telegram. Each line begins with "SEND FOR," followed by the names of figures as diverse as Christ, Abraham Lincoln, U. S. Grant, the Pied Piper, W.E.B. Du Bois,* U.S. Congressman (representing Harlem*) Adam Clayton Powell, Jr., Alfred Dreyfus, and King Arthur. The reason for the urgent request is left unspoken, but the title at least suggests that Apocalypse may be near and may involve race relations, which were extremely volatile in the United States in the mid-1960s. In keeping with the ironic tone of the poem, the last line is "(And if nobody comes, send for me.)." The poem was first published in *American Dialogue* (October 1964).

Bibliography: *CP*, 545.

"Final Curve." Deft four-line poem concerning discovery of the self, first published in *One-Way Ticket*.

Bibliography: *CP*, 368.

"Final Fear." Short story, included in *The Best of Simple*. *See* Simple [Jesse B.] Stories.

"Finale." Song, from *Simply Heavenly*. Hughes wrote the lyrics, and David Martin composed the music. ASCAP* lists the song as being published by the Bourne Company, and the song's ASCAP registry number is 360025081.

"Finaletto." Song, from *Street Scene*. Hughes wrote the lyrics, and Kurt Weill* composed the music. At this writing, the song is not listed with ASCAP.* It is published by Warner Chappell, Ltd.

Bibliography: Booklet accompanying *Street Scene* [compact disc], performed by Kristine Ciesinski, Janis Kelly, Bonaventura Bottone, Richard van Allan, Catherine Zeta Jones, and the Orchestra and Chorus of the English National Opera, conducted by Carl Davis (London: Jay Records, 1996): CDJAY2–1232.

"Fine Accommodations." Short story. The narrative concerns three African American men: a porter on a train and two traveling companions, a college president and a professor at the college. Because the professor behaves in a way that the porter regards as morally weak, the porter compares the professor to a pimp. The story was included in the collection *Something in Common and Other Stories* and was reprinted in *Langston Hughes: Short Stories*.

Fine Clothes to the Jew (New York: Knopf, 1927). 89 pp. Collection of poetry. The book was controversial because many of its poems presented an unvarnished depiction of life in Harlem* and of problems encountered by African Americans. A review by J. A. Rogers in the *Pittsburgh Courier* was especially harsh. Other reviewers, including DuBose Heyward,* praised the book and believed that it demonstrated Hughes's growth as a poet. The book includes several of Hughes's most accomplished blues* poems. The poems in *Fine Clothes to the Jew* are "Angels Wings," "Baby," "Bad Luck Card," "Bad Man," "Ballad of Gin Mary," "Beale Street Love," "Black Gal," "Bound No'th Blues," "Brass Spittoons," "Closing Time," "Cora," "Crap Game," "Death of Do Dirty," "Dressed Up," "Elevator Boy," "Evil Woman," "Feet o' Jesus," "Fire," "Gal's Cry for a Dying Lover," "Gypsy Man," "Hard Daddy," "Hard Luck," "Hey!" "Hey! Hey!"

"Homesick Blues," "Judgement Day," "Lament over Love," "Listen Here Blues," "Ma Man," "Magnolia Flowers," "Midwinter Blues," "Minnie Sings Her Blues," "Misery," "The New Cabaret Girl," "Porter," "Prize Fighter," "Railroad Avenue," "Red Silk Stockings," "Ruby Brown," "A Ruined Gal," "Saturday Night," "Shout," "Sinner," "Sport," "Suicide," "Sun Song," "Workin' Man," and "Young Gal's Blues." Each poem has a separate entry in this encyclopedia, and all are included in *Collected Poems*.

Bibliography: DuBose Heyward, "Sing a Soothin' Song," in Mullen, 48–50; Arnold Rampersad, "Langston Hughes's *Fine Clothes to the Jew*," *Callaloo: A Journal of African-American and African Arts and Letters* 9, no. 1 (Winter 1986), 144–57; J. A. Rogers, review of *Fine Clothes to the Jew*, in Mullen, 47–48.

"Fire." Twenty-five-line poem in black dialect,* spoken by a person convinced that he or she shall be consumed by the fires of Hell. It was first published in *Fine Clothes to the Jew*.

Bibliography: *CP*, 117.

Fire!! Magazine of one issue edited by Claude McKay* and published in Harlem* in 1926. One of McKay's editorial purposes was to feature the work of younger, relatively radical African American writers living in Harlem. Another was to challenge what he perceived to be the Harlem cultural establishment, led by W.E.B. Du Bois* and the self-described Talented Tenth.* McKay included two of Hughes's poems in the issue: "Elevator Boy" and "Railroad Avenue." Some of the New York literati found the magazine to be avant-garde; others thought it scandalous.

Bibliography: Lewis, *HRR*, xxxi–xxxii.

"Fire-Caught." Six-line poem that is a fable involving a gold moth and a gray one, each representing different kinds of love. It was first published in *Crisis** (April 1924).

Bibliography: *CP*, 38.

"Fired." Ten-line poem. The narrator explains how he slept late and got fired from his job as a result, but was more than glad to return to bed with a certain woman named Caledonia. Though it is a relatively little-known poem, it is very characteristic of Hughes's work insofar as it expresses everyday concerns in lyric form and blends sentiment with practicality and wry wit. It was first published in *Shakespeare in Harlem*. Later it was set to music by Elie Siegmeister, with whom Hughes would collaborate on the *Wizard of Altoona* (unfinished opera). ASCAP* lists the song as being published by Carl Fischer, Inc., and the song's ASCAP registry number is 360207723. Under "Performers," ASCAP also indicates the song as having been recorded by the Washington Ensemble but does not list the recording itself.

Bibliography: *CP*, 260.

The First Book of Africa (New York: Franklin Watts, 1960). 82 pp. Nonfiction book for juvenile readers in twenty-two short chapters, beginning with "Unknown Africa," "Africa Today," and "Ancient Africa." Other chapters concern the "great kingdoms" of Africa and early white explorers. David Livingstone and Henry Morton Stanley, Cecil Rhodes, and Albert Schweitzer each receive a chapter, and Hughes includes chapters on "Home Life and Arts in Primitive Africa," "Children in Africa," and "Africa's Governments." Concluding chapters concern separate nations, including Kenya, South Africa, the Belgian Congo, Guinea, Liberia, and Ghana. An appendix, "The Countries of Africa," lists the countries (as identified in 1959), their populations, their land masses, and their capital cities. The book is illustrated with black-and-white photos from news services and from the United Nations. *See also Famous American Negroes; Famous Negro Heroes of America; Famous Negro Music Makers; The First Book of Jazz; The First Book of Negroes; The First Book of Rhythms; The First Book of the Caribbean; The First Book of the West Indies.*

The First Book of Jazz (New York: Franklin Watts, 1955). 65 pp. Nonfiction book for juvenile readers. This sixty-five-page book surveys jazz* historically, profiles major jazz figures (including Louis Armstrong, Bix Beiderbecke, and Duke Ellington*), and discusses different jazz instruments and styles. The book has a keen sense of its audience, is not condescending, and conveys a significant amount of information briskly. It briefly describes jazz's roots in African music, African American work songs and spirituals, and the blues.* It also covers different jazz styles associated with New Orleans, St. Louis, Memphis, Chicago, and New York. It includes photographs. Rampersad indicates that Hughes had the manuscript of the book "carefully scrutinized" by such "jazz experts" as David Martin (with whom Hughes would collaborate on many songs for *Simply Heavenly*), Marshall Stearns, and John Hammond (232). Rampersad characterizes the book itself as "[s]crupulously written and edited, with handsome designs by Clifford H. Roberts," and as having been greeted by "superb reviews" (246), although he does not cite specific ones. The publisher updated and reissued the book in 1976 (nine years after Hughes's death) and included discussions of important jazz horn players Ornette Coleman, John Coltrane, and Miles Davis; the author of this added material is not listed. Ecco Press reissued the book in 1995. *See Famous Negro Music Makers.*

Bibliography: Calvin Reid, "Hughes's 'Jazz' Returns, Via Ecco," *Publishers Weekly* 242, no. 41 (October 9, 1995), 26; Rampersad, II, 232, 246.

The First Book of Negroes (New York: Franklin Watts, 1952). 69 pp. Illustrated by Ursula Koering. Children's book. In short chapters Hughes surveys African

American history, first discussing African heritage. The survey is presented from the point of view of "Terry," an African American child living in contemporary (1952) New York City. The book was favorably reviewed in such periodicals as *Library Journal, Commonweal, Kirkus Reviews*, the *Christian Science Monitor*, and the *New York Times* (November 16, 1952, 32). *See also Famous American Negroes; Famous Negro Heroes of America; Famous Negro Music Makers; The First Book of Africa; The First Book of Jazz; The First Book of Rhythms; The First Book of the Caribbean; The First Book of the West Indies.*

The First Book of Rhythms (New York: Franklin Watts, 1954). 65 pp. Illustrated by Robin King. Children's book. In two-or three-page chapters Hughes discusses "rhythm" in its various incarnations—in handwriting, writing, nature, music, language, athletics, furniture, and so on. He discusses rhythm as both a visual and aural concept, examines its "mysteries," and considers the ways in which it can be "broken" and improvised upon. *See also Famous American Negroes; Famous Negro Heroes of America; Famous Negro Music Makers; The First Book of Africa; The First Book of Jazz; The First Book of Negroes; The First Book of the West Indies.*

The First Book of the Caribbean (London: E. Ward, 1965, c. 1956). 65 pp. Nonfiction book for juvenile readers, introducing them to the history, music, and culture of the Caribbean Islands. It was first published under the title *The First Book of the West Indies. See also Famous American Negroes; Famous Negro Heroes of America; Famous Negro Music Makers; The First Book of Africa; The First Book of Jazz; The First Book of Negroes; The First Book of Rhythms.*

The First Book of the West Indies (New York: Franklin Watts, 1956). 62 pp. Illustrated by Robert Bruce. Nonfiction book for juvenile readers, introducing them to the history and culture of islands in the West Indies. It was republished in 1965 under the title *The First Book of the Caribbean. See also Famous American Negroes; Famous Negro Heroes of America; Famous Negro Music Makers; The First Book of Africa; The First Book of Jazz; The First Book of Negroes; The First Book of Rhythms.*

"First of May." Ten-line poem in which the speaker is self-described as "poor and black" but is full of optimism that his "first of May"—a date associated with the Bolshevik Revolution in Russia—shall liberate him and improve his situation. The poem was first published in *People's Voice* (May 4, 1946). Bibliography: *CP*, 318–319.

Fisher, Rudolph (1897–1934). American physician, writer, and musician. Fisher was born in Washington, D.C. He grew up there and in Providence,

Rhode Island, graduating from Brown University in 1919. He completed an M.D. degree at Howard University and took further medical training at Columbia University.* Fisher began living in Harlem* in 1925, the same year many of his essays began appearing in *Opportunity,* * *Crisis*,* and other magazines. A genuine Renaissance man, Fisher also composed music, arranged African American spirituals, and published fiction. His first novel was *The Walls of Jericho* (1928), and his second was *The Conjure Man Dies* (1932), which is considered to be the first detective novel published by an African American writer. It is widely believed that Fisher's fatal illness was caused by his pioneering work in the use of radiation for medical purposes.

Bibliography: Roger M. Valade III, *The Essential Black Literature Guide* (Detroit: Visible Ink Press, 1996), 139.

Five Foolish Virgins (1954): Oratorio. Hughes wrote the libretto, and Jan Meyerowitz* composed the music. As Rampersad notes, the libretto is based on the Book of Matthew 25:1–13, which concerns five wise virgins who chose to wait for the bridegroom and five who did not, the analogy of the parable being to waiting for "the Son of Man." Rampersad quotes Meyerowitz as remembering that Hughes liked the episode from Matthew because he (Hughes) assumed that the virgins who did not wait had to be "Negro." According to Meyerowitz, when Hughes was asked why this was so, he remarked, "Because they [African Americans] were never on time" (II, 229). The oratorio debuted on February 11, 1954, at Town Hall in New York City and was performed by a choir under the directorship of Margaret Mills. The oratorio was met with harsh criticism, especially with regard to the music; Rampersad (II, 233) refers to this criticism. Meyerowitz wanted to turn the oratorio into a full-scale opera, but the project did not materialize. *Five Foolish Virgins* is registered with ASCAP (registry number 360258624), but no publisher is listed.

Bibliography: Rampersad, II, 229, 233.

"Five o'Clock Blues." Song. Hughes wrote the lyrics, and Elie Siegmeister, with whom Hughes would collaborate on the *Wizard of Altoona* (unfinished opera), composed the music. Rampersad indicates that the song was recorded in 1950 by an American group called the Striders. ASCAP* lists no publisher for this version of the song, but the song's ASCAP registry number is 350154862. For the same lyrics, David Martin wrote a different song, listed by ASCAP as being published by EMI/Colgems (registry number 360087121) and as having been recorded by a group called the All Stars. *See* The Blues; "Cool Saturday Night."

Bibliography: Rampersad, II, 178.

Five Plays By Langston Hughes, edited with an introduction by Webster Smalley (Bloomington: Indiana University Press, 1963.) 258 pp. The collection includes *Little Ham, Mulatto, Simply Heavenly, Soul Gone Home*, and *Tam-bourines to Glory*. In his introduction (vii–xvii), Smalley emphasizes the extent to which Hughes was interested in dramatizing the concerns of ordinary people, discusses Hughes's involvement with the Harlem Suitcase Theatre,* and briefly summarizes and assesses each of the five plays. Smalley does not explicitly discuss why he selected these five plays, but the collection does provide a glimpse of Hughes's range as a playwright by including two tragedies (*Mulatto* and *Soul Gone Home*), two comedies (*Little Ham* and *Simply Heavenly*), and a comic melodrama (*Tambourines to Glory*). *See* Drama; *Political Plays of Lang-ston Hughes*.

Flamenco. Style of folk dance and folk music with origins in Gypsy, or "Rom," culture in Europe, specifically in Spain. In the poem "From Spain to Alabama" Hughes compares the blues* to flamenco.

Bibliography: Timothy Mitchell, *Flamenco Deep Song* (New Haven: Yale University Press, 1994).

"Flatted Fifths." Poem. *See Montage of a Dream Deferred*.

"Flay or Pray?" Short story, included in the collection *Simple's Uncle Sam*. *See* Simple [Jesse B.] Stories.

"Flight." Eight-line poem that represents the fact of lynching* as a constant threat to African American males—especially but by no means exclusively in the South—and that points to a common invented "reason" for lynching: an African American male's having made sexual advances toward a white woman. The poem was first published in *Opportunity** (June 1930). With the poems "Lynching Song" and "Silhouette," this poem appeared as "Three Songs about Lynching" in *Opportunity** (June 1936). *See* "Home"; "Three Songs about Lynching."

Bibliography: *CP*, 127, 637.

"Florida Road Workers." Twenty-line poem spoken by one of the road work-ers to someone driving by ("Hey, Buddy, look! / *I'm makin' a road!*"). He notes that he is too poor to afford a car to drive on the road he is making, but he is nonetheless cheerful, not embittered. Melvin B. Tolson* compared the poem to Archibald MacLeish's poem "Burying Ground by the Ties." It was first pub-lished in the *New York Herald Tribune* (November 23, 1930). *Collected Poems* contains information about slight revisions the poem underwent. *See also* Re-vision, Process of, and Hughes.

Bibliography: *CP*, 158–159, 641; Melvin B. Tolson, "Books and Authors: Let My People Go," *Southwest Journal* 4 (Fall 1948), 41–43.

"Flotsam." Rhyming poem of two quatrains. Spoken in the first person, it relates a kind of existential parable in which the speaker's boat is washed up on the shores of "Nowhere." It was first published posthumously in *Crisis** (June–July 1968). Later, William Mayer set the poem to music. ASCAP* lists no publisher for the song, but the ASCAP* registry number is 360190714.

Bibliography: *CP*, 562.

"Flower of the Air." Song. Hughes translated the lyrics from the original Spanish of Gabriela Mistral. Mistral and Eric Warner Sawyer composed the music. ASCAP* lists no publisher for the song, the ASCAP registry number for which is 360358463. ASCAP* lists "Alcayaga Godoy" as the co-composer. Mistral's given name was Lucila Godoy y Alcayaga. *See* "I am Not Lonely"; *Selected Poems of Gabriela Mistral*.

"Flute Players." Poem by Jean-Joseph Rabearivelo (a writer from Madagascar) that Hughes translated from the French. It is a free-verse poem of about one page that celebrates flute music. It is published in *The Langston Hughes Reader*. *See Poems from Black Africa*.

Bibliography: *The Langston Hughes Reader*, 137.

"Flyer." Song. Hughes wrote the lyrics, and Hall Johnson composed the music. ASCAP* lists the song as being published by Carl Fischer, Inc., and the song's ASCAP registry number is 360210282.

"Flying Saucer Monologue." Song. ASCAP* lists Hughes as the sole author and the Bourne Company as the publisher; the song's ASCAP registry number is 360039316.

"Fog." Eight-line poem spoken to "singing black boatmen" in the fog at Sekundi, port city of Ghana, West Africa. It was first published under the title "African Fog" in the *New York Herald Tribune* (February 14, 1926). In *The Big Sea* Hughes mentions visiting Sekundi.

Bibliography: *The Big Sea*, 106; *CP*, 63.

"The Folks at Home." Short story. *See* "Home."

"For an Indian Screen." Nineteen-line poem in two stanzas. The first stanza imagines a story suggested by the two classic mime figures Pierret and Pierrot. The poem was first published in the *Messenger** (September 1926).

Bibliography: *CP*, 102.

"For Dead Mimes." Nine-line rhyming poem that praises dead mimes. First published in the *Messenger** (September 1926) under the pseudonym Earl Dane.* *See* "Heart"; "Pierrot"; Pseudonyms Used by Hughes.
Bibliography: *CP*, 75, 630.

"For President." Short story, included in the collection *Simple's Uncle Sam.* *See* Simple [Jesse B.] Stories.

"For Russell and Rowena Jelliffe." Thirty-two-line occasional poem, written for a dinner held in honor of the Jelliffes, with whom Hughes first became acquainted when he attended Central High School* and who were founders of the Cleveland cultural center known as Karamu House, which included a theatre at which several of Hughes's plays were performed by the Gilpin Players.* The poem was first published in the *Cleveland Call and Post* (April 6, 1963).
Bibliography: *CP*, 540.

"For Salome." Twelve-line poem that asks rhetorically of Herod's daughter Salome—who ordered the decapitation of John the Baptist, whom she loved—what she hoped to gain. Therefore, while the phrasing of the poem is lyrical and restrained, in essence it applies a practicality characteristic of Hughes to the legend of Salome. Not unreasonably, one might also regard the poem as concerning overpossessive desire in general, not just Salome's extreme variety of it. The poem was first published in the *Messenger** (July 1927).
Bibliography: *CP*, 109.

"For the Sake of Argument." Short story, included in the collection *Simple Speaks His Mind. See* Simple [Jesse B.] Stories.

"For Tom Mooney." Poem. *See* "Chant for Tom Mooney."

"Formals and Funerals." Short story, included in the collections *Simple Takes a Wife* and *The Best of Simple*. See Simple [Jesse B.] Stories.

"Formula." Four-quatrain rhyming poem facetiously arguing that "Poetry should treat / Of lofty things" and not concern itself (for example) with the fact that roses grow in manure. The "greeting-card" style parodies the kind of verse for which the poem disingenuously argues. "Formula" articulates concisely Hughes's insistence that literature ought to concern itself with so-called common experience, should embrace authentic situations, circumstances, problems, and crises, and should not limit itself only to subjects conventionally deemed "poetic" in nature. It was first published in the *Messenger** (September 1926). *See* Poetics.
Bibliography: *CP*, 74.

"Fortune Teller Blues." Three-stanza poem in traditional blues*-lyric form, spoken in black dialect* by a woman who complains that the fortune tellers she visits never tell her "nothin' kind"—do not, that is, give her peace of mind. The poem was first published in *Vanity Fair* (May 1926). *See also* "Ballad of the Fortune Teller."

Bibliography: *CP*, 70.

"Four Choruses after Langston Hughes." Song. Hughes wrote the lyrics, and Conrad De Jong composed the music. ASCAP* lists the song as being published by G. Schirmer and Company, and the song's ASCAP registry number is 360269569.

"403 Blues." Poem in three traditional blues*-lyric stanzas, spoken by a man who is superstitious about killing spiders but may kill one anyway because he is so angry about his girlfriend leaving him just when he received his "403"—a form notifying him that he has been dismissed from his job with the Works Progress Administration (WPA), which was among the federally sponsored employment programs that President Franklin Roosevelt* instituted to try to counteract widespread joblessness created by the Great Depression of the 1930s. The poem was first published in *Fountain* (May 1942). *See* "Ballad of Roosevelt"; "Crow Goes, Too"; "Dear Mr. President."

Bibliography: *CP*, 241.

"Four Preludes." Song. Hughes wrote the lyrics, and Irving Mopper composed the music. ASCAP* lists no publisher for the song (or songs), but the ASCAP* registry number is 360253816.

"Four Rings." Short story, included in the collection *The Best of Simple*. *See* Simple [Jesse B.] Stories.

"Fourth of July Thought." Ten-line poem that encourages people to do their part on the "HOME FRONT" [*sic*] to support the efforts of the U.S. military in World War II. It was first published in the *Amsterdam News* (July 4, 1942). *See* "America's Young Black Joe!"

Bibliography: *CP*, 574.

"Four-Way Celebrations." Short story, included in the collection *Simple Stakes a Claim*. *See* Simple [Jesse B.] Stories.

"Fragments." Six-line, three-stanza poem in which each stanza seems to stand alone, suggesting that Hughes indeed assembled three fragments. Many readers will find a haunting quietness in the surreal effect—a mood similar to that created by effective haiku verse. The poem was first published in *Fields of Wonder*.

Bibliography: *CP*, 328.

"Franco and the Moors." Essay. It is a condensed version of an article that first appeared in the *Baltimore Afro American**: "Hughes Finds Moors Being Used as Pawns in Spain By Fascists." It was first published by Faith Berry.

Bibliography: Berry, 104–107.

Frank, Waldo (1889–1967). American novelist, journalist, and editor. Frank arranged for Claude McKay* to edit the *Liberator*, to which Hughes contributed poems.

"Frederick Douglass 1817–1895." Twenty-two-line poem praising Frederick Douglass,* particularly his fierce commitment to abolishing slavery and his decisiveness. It was first published in the *Liberator* (December 1966). Most scholars now believe that Douglass was born in 1818.

Bibliography: *CP*, 549.

"Free Man." Poem in two rhyming quatrains, spoken by a man to a woman he calls "pretty mama" and asserting that he will remain an untamed wanderer whom domestic life will never control. It was first published in *Shakespeare in Harlem*.

Bibliography: *CP*, 247.

"Freedom [1]." Twenty-one-line poem that argues against the notion that African Americans should patiently wait for freedom and civil rights to be realized. It was first published in *Jim Crow's Last Stand* under the title "Democracy." The title was changed when the poem appeared in *The Panther and the Lash*.

Bibliography: *CP*, 289.

"Freedom [2]." Fourteen-line, free-verse poem asserting that burning books, imprisoning Nehru in India, or lynching* African Americans in the United States will not stop the progress of freedom. Toward the end of the poem, "Freedom" is personified and stands and "laughs in [the] faces of oppressors." The poem was first published in *Jim Crow's Last Stand. See* "Freedom [3]."

Bibliography: *CP*, 290.

"Freedom [3]." Poem of nineteen very short lines. It is a substantially revised version of "Freedom [2]" and was published posthumously in *Crisis** (September 1968). *See* Fauset, Jessie Redmon.

Bibliography: *CP*, 562.

"Freedom Land." Song. *See Jerico-Jim Crow*.

"Freedom Road." Song. ASCAP* lists Hughes as the sole author (of both lyrics and music, that is) and lists no publisher. The song's ASCAP registry number is 360058135.

"Freedom Seeker." Twelve-line poem that personifies freedom as a caged, winged woman. It was first published in *Crisis** (October 1927).
Bibliography: *CP*, 110.

"Freedom Train." Poem of several pages. It reacts ironically, even sarcastically, to a plan (never executed) by the American Heritage Foundation to transport a copy of the Declaration of Independence around the United States by train. The poem asks whether this "Freedom Train" will, for instance, have a Jim Crow* car. It was first published in the *New Republic* (September 1947). Hughes later included it in *Montage of a Dream Deferred*. Later, Charles Davidson set the poem to music. ASCAP* lists the song as being published by EMI/Mills, Inc., and the song's ASCAP registry number is 360081412. *See* Revision.
Bibliography: *CP*, 323, 663.

Freedom's Plow (New York: Musette Press, 1943). 14 pp. Chapbook edition of the poem "Freedom's Plow."

"Freedom's Plow." Free-verse poem of several pages that first speaks in general about how the dream of freedom guides people's lives, then turns to the freedom sought by colonists in North America, and concludes by celebrating the freedom that is owed to and sought by "labor"—that is, all working people. As the editors of *Collected Poems* note, Hughes revised and shortened the poem when he included it in *Selected Poems of Langston Hughes*. It was first published in *Opportunity** (April 1943) and was also published in a limited-edition chapbook (New York: Musette Press, 1943).
Bibliography: *CP*, 263–269, 647; James Presley, "The American Dream of Langston Hughes," *Southwest Review* 48 (1963), 380–386; Rampersad, II, 57–58.

"Friendly in a Friendly Way." Poem for children in four rhyming quatrains. *See* Children's Poetry.
Bibliography: *CP*, 609.

"The Frightened Little Child." Poem. *See* "Migration."

"From an Emir's Harem." Article based on an interview Hughes had conducted with a former wife of the emir of Bokhara during Hughes's extensive travels after visiting Russia. The article was published in *Woman's Home Companion* (1934). Rampersad describes the piece as "titillating."

Bibliography: Rampersad, I, 285.

"From Harlem to Samarkand" (1934). Book manuscript. The unpublished nonfiction work concerns Hughes's extensive travels in Russia after the collapse in Moscow of the motion-picture project *Black and White.** A manuscript is held in the Langston Hughes Papers, James Weldon Johnson Memorial Collection, Beinecke Library, Yale University. Some of the material from this manuscript found its way into *I Wonder As I Wander*.

Bibliography: Rampersad, I, 284.

"From Selma." Fifteen-line, free-verse poem meditating on how "kids" in Selma, Alabama, think and dream of Chicago and New York, how "kids" from those large cities think and dream of Paris and London, but how children in all those large cities do not think and dream of Selma—despite the fact, the poem appears to imply, that Selma is the hub of civil-rights activities that will have global impact. The poem was first published in *Ebony Rhythm*.

Bibliography: *CP*, 343, 665; B. Murphy, ed., *Ebony Rhythm* (New York: Exposition Press, 1948), 88.

"From Spain to Alabama." Poem in four stanzas that connects African American blues* of the South to flamenco* music and dance in Spain. Stanzas two and four function as a "response" to a "call" from stanzas one and three. The poem was first published in *Experiment* (Summer 1949).

Bibliography: *CP*, 352–353.

"From the Blues to an Opera Libretto." Essay. *See The Barrier*.

Front Porch (1938). Play in three acts, first performed by the Gilpin Players* at the Karamu Theatre, Cleveland, Ohio, November 16–21, 1938. The drama concerns a teacher, Mrs. Harper, her daughter, Harriet, and Harriet's boyfriend, Kenneth, who is deeply involved in labor-union issues. The chief conflict is between Mrs. Harper's middle-class aspirations for her daughter and Kenneth's working-class, politically radical sensibilities, with Harriet caught, obviously, between mother and boyfriend. Hughes wrote two endings for the play, although Rampersad indicates that Rowena Jelliffe "apparently" wrote the second ending. In one, Harriet becomes pregnant out of wedlock, Mrs. Harper sends her to Cincinnati to have the baby and give it up for adoption, and Harriet returns in a weakened state and dies soon thereafter (this ending echoes that of the short story "Cora Unashamed"). In the second ending, Kenneth is arrested during a strike and is sent to jail, but upon release returns to Harriet, and the two marry (she is pregnant but refuses to get an abortion). The second ending was the one actually produced on stage. Clearly Hughes was unsure about how severely to represent (for this theatre audience, at any rate) consequences of class conflict among African Americans, and unsure about whether *Front Porch* should center on social comedy or on social tragedy. Nonetheless, he was clear about the *social* focus of the play and its portrayal of political alternatives facing African Americans in the 1930s: optimistic, comparatively apolitical confidence in the middle-class American Dream and a more combative, politically alert insistence on proletarian reform, even revolution. Because Hughes wrote the play during the decade in which his politics were greatly influenced by Marxism,* the fact that *Front Porch*, in both versions, is ultimately biased toward the labor activist Kenneth's point of view comes as no surprise. Hughes wrote *Front Porch* during an extremely active part of his career. Rampersad notes: "Langston had put himself on an impossible schedule" (364). While writing *Front Porch* for the Gilpins, Hughes was collaborating with the composer James P. Johnson* on *De Organizer* (364). As Rampersad also notes, *Front Porch* received mixed reviews from critics at newspapers in Cleveland. The play has not been published but in manuscript form is held in the James Weldon Johnson Memorial Collection at Yale University. *See* "For Russell and Rowena Jelliffe"; *Joy to My Soul; Little Ham; Troubled Island; When the Jack Hollers. See also De Organizer.*

Bibliography: *Cleveland Plain Dealer* (November 17, 1938); *Cleveland Press* (November 17, 1938); Hicklin; Rampersad, I, 363–366.

Frost, Robert (1874–1963). American poet. Although Frost and his poetry are closely associated with rural New England, he was born in San Francisco, California, and lived there until he was eleven years old, when his family moved to Massachusetts. He attended Dartmouth College and Harvard University but dropped out of both schools. He married Elinor Miriam White in 1895 and took up farming, but also taught at Pinkerton Academy. His first book, *A Boy's Will* (1913), was published in England. His second book, *North of Boston* (1914), began to bring him critical attention. He went on to become one of America's best-known poets and cultivated an avuncular public image. His poems often combine compact lyric form and terse phrasing with deceptively cerebral themes, but he also produced remarkable dramatic poems, including "Home Burial." His best-known lyric poems include "Mending Wall," "Stopping by Woods on a Snowy Evening," "Birches," and "The Road Not Taken." In a letter (1961) to Arna Bontemps,* Hughes recalls being seated next to Frost at a dinner hosted by the National Institute of Arts and Letters.

Bibliography: *Arna Bontemps/Langston Hughes: Letters, 1925–1967*, 415.

"Frosting." Poem that compares freedom to "frosting" on a cake and exhorts African Americans to learn how to "bake"—that is, to control their economic fate. The poem is in eight very short lines, but the rhyme scheme is that of a couplet. The poem was first published under the title "Economics" in *Crisis** (December 1966).

Bibliography: *CP*, 550.

Fry, Martha. In *Not without Laughter*, chapter 24, Martha Fry is a high-school teacher who encourages the main character, Sandy, to read William Shakespeare's *Merchant of Venice*. She also organizes an essay-writing contest in which Sandy takes second prize.

"Fulfillment." Twenty-one-line poem in four irregular stanzas. For Hughes, it is a comparatively mystical poem insofar as it concerns a fusion of "earth-meaning" and "sky-meaning" and contains evocative images of light. It was first published in *Fields of Wonder*. Robert Owens set this poem, "In Time of Silver Rain," "Night Song," "Silence," "Carolina Cabin," and "Songs" to music in the song cycle *Silver Rain*.

Bibliography: *CP*, 330; Robert Owens [composer], *Silver Rain: Song Cycle for Tenor and Piano*, op. 11 (Munich: Orlando-Musikverlag, 1975).

"The Fun of Being Black." Essay that explores "many intricate and amusing angles" of "this racial struggle of ours [in the United States]" (499). It was published in *The Langston Hughes Reader*. *See* Van Vechten, Carl.

Bibliography: *The Langston Hughes Reader*, 498–500.

"Funeral." Nine-line poem spoken by the deceased, who first claims that if he were alive, he wouldn't care that his funeral is glum and mundane. Then he changes his mind: "But I would give a damn." The poem, therefore, plays with the notion of "letting go" of life. It was first published in *One-Way Ticket*.

Bibliography: *CP*, 369.

Funeral, Hughes's. On May 22, 1967, Hughes died of septic shock following an operation at Polyclinic Hospital in New York City. His body was removed to the Benta Funeral Home. On May 23 and 24 it was on display there. A memorial service was held at the Benta Funeral Home on May 24. The service included the playing of the song "Do Nothing 'Til You Hear from Me," composed by Duke Ellington.* Arna Bontemps* gave a brief eulogy. Later on May 24, Hughes's body was removed to the Ferncliff Crematory just outside New York City, where it was cremated. The ashes were kept by George Houston Bass, the executor of Hughes's estate. Later some of the ashes were placed beneath a memorial plaque in the Langston Hughes Theatre at the Schomburg Center for Research in Black Culture (Harlem*), and the rest remained in the possession of George Houston Bass.

Bibliography: Rampersad, II, 420–425.

G

"Gal's Cry for a Dying Lover." Poem in three traditional blues* stanzas and spoken in black dialect* by a woman who seems to have foreknowledge of her lover's death and prays to Jesus to keep him alive. It was first published in the *Saturday Review of Literature* (April 19, 1927). *See* Religion.

Bibliography: *CP*, 104.

Gandhi, Mahatma. *See* "Gandhi Is Fasting."

"Gandhi Is Fasting." Poem in five ballad* stanzas, observing that the fasting of Mahatma Gandhi (1869–1948), spiritual and political leader in India, will succeed and lead eventually to the withdrawal of Great Britain from India. The poem also suggests that Indians are being "jim crowed" by Great Britain, just as African Americans are "jim crowed" by white Americans. Gandhi's nonviolent but direct political actions during the 1940s influenced strategies and tactics employed by the Reverend Martin Luther King, Jr., and others in advancing African American social and political equality, so there is an element of prescience in Hughes's poem. It was first published in the *Baltimore Afro American** (November 20, 1943). *See* "America's Young Black Joe"; "Wealth." *See also* Jim Crow Laws.

Bibliography: Joan V. Bondurant, *Conquest of Violence: The Gandhian Philosophy of Conflict*, rev. ed. (Berkeley: University of California Press, 1965); William Borman, *Gandhi and Non-Violence* (Albany: State University of New York Press, 1986); *CP*, 578; Mahatma Gandhi, *Gandhi's Autobiography: The Story of My Experiments with Truth*, transl. Mahadev Desai (Washington, DC: Public Affairs Press, 1948); Martin Luther King, Jr., "Letter from Birmingham Jail," in *Why We Can't Wait* (New York: Harper and Row, 1963), and widely reprinted and anthologized, including in Edward P. J. Corbett, *Classical Rhetoric for the Modern Student*, 3rd ed. (New York and London: Oxford

University Press, 1990), 343–356; Jawaharlal Nehru, *Mahatma Gandhi* (London: Asia Publishing House, 1965).

"Gangsters." Sixteen-line rhyming poem with no stanza breaks. To some extent, it advances an argument: namely that gangsters such as Al Capone* (1899–1947) infamous leader of a criminal organization in Chicago, are "small fry," and that the real gangsters of the world plunder countries; specifically, the poem refers to Ethiopia, which Italy invaded under the orders of dictator Benito Mussolini. The poem was first published in *Crisis** (September 1941). *See also* "Broadcast on Ethiopia"; "Call of Ethiopia"; "Emperor Hailie Salassie."

Bibliography: Laurence Bergreen, *Capone: The Man and the Era* (New York: Simon and Schuster, 1994); *CP*, 237.

García Lorca, Gabriel. *See Blood Wedding* and *Yerma* (one volume); *Lorca: Gypsy Ballads.*

"Garden." Poem of seven short lines, three lines of which consist of the word "strange." The poem focuses on images of a "distorted garden." It was first published under the title "Poem" in *Dear Lovely Death.*

Bibliography: *CP*, 159, 641.

"Garment." Four-line poem comparing clouds to a shawl. The poem is included in the essay "Poetry and Children" in *The Langston Hughes Reader. See* Children's Poetry.

Bibliography: *CP*, 601, 695.

Garvey, Marcus (1887–1940). Jamaican political leader and entrepreneur. Garvey was born and grew up in the town of St. Ann's Bay, Jamaica. He studied briefly in London, where he also worked for the newspaper *African Times and Orient Review.* He came to believe himself to be destined to lead New World descendants of Africans to freedom, and in 1914 he established the Universal Negro Improvement Association (UNIA). He traveled to the United States in 1916 and settled in Harlem,* where he purchased real estate and attracted thousands of African Americans to the UNIA. Soon Garvey promoted the idea that African Americans could realize political and economic freedom only by returning to Africa, and he established the newspaper *The Negro World* in part to promote this notion, which was referred to as the "Back to Africa"* movement. Through subscriptions, he sold shares in the Black Star Line, a shipping business intended to transport African Americans back to Africa. Faulty business practices led Garvey to be indicted for and convicted of mail fraud in 1925. At the same time, Garvey drew the opposition of black leaders such as W.E.B. Du Bois,* Charles S. Johnson,* and A. Philip Randolph,* who strongly objected to Garvey's relationship with the white-separatist organization the Ku Klux Klan.*

In 1927 President Calvin Coolidge pardoned Garvey, who was deported to his native Jamaica. Like Garvey, Hughes was interested in the political and economic predicament of persons of color worldwide, not just in the United States. Unlike Garvey, he did not favor a "Back to Africa" strategy. *See* "To Certain Negro Leaders."

Bibliography: Judith Stein, *The World of Marcus Garvey: Race and Class in Modern Society* (Baton Rouge: Louisiana State University Press, 1986).

"Gate Keeper of My Castle." Song, from *Simply Heavenly*. Hughes wrote the lyrics, and David Martin composed the music. ASCAP* lists the song as being published by the Bourne Company, and the song's ASCAP* registry number is 370004352.

"Gauge." Poem. *See Montage of a Dream Deferred.*

Gay. Concerning Hughes's use of this word, see "Nocturne for the Drums." *See also* Sexuality and Hughes.

"Genius Child." Twelve-line poem of varying stanza lengths, in which the genius child is portrayed as wild, untamed, and therefore ultimately unlovable. It was first published in *Opportunity** (August 1937). Later, Ricky Ian Gordon set the poem to music, and ASCAP* lists the song as being published by Williamson Music Company, as well as indicating that Harolyn Blackwell once recorded it (no recording title or date is given). The song's ASCAP registry number is 370247331. *Collected Poems* contains information about slight revisions the poem underwent. *See* "Strange Hurt."

Bibliography: *CP*, 198, 646; Ricky Ian Gordon, *Genius Child: A Cycle of 10 Songs* (New York: Williamson Music Company, 1992).

"Georgia Dusk." Poem. In contrast to literature that typically celebrates twilight and focuses exclusively on nature imagery, this three-quatrain poem—more with a fatalistic than an embittered tone—links images of dusk with questions of violence, racism, and hatred. It was first published in the *Olivant Quarterly* (Summer 1955).

Bibliography: *CP*, 448.

"Get a Load of That (Gossip Trio)." Song, from *Street Scene*. Hughes and Elmer Rice* wrote the lyrics, and Kurt Weill* composed the music. At this writing, the song is not listed with ASCAP. It is published by Warner Chappell, Ltd.

Bibliography: Booklet accompanying *Street Scene* [compact disc], performed by Kristine Ciesinski, Janis Kelly, Bonaventura Bottone, Richard van Allan, Catherine Zeta Jones, and the Orchestra and Chorus of the English National Opera, conducted by Carl Davis (London: Jay Records, 1996): CDJAY2–1232.

"Get on Board, Little Children." Gospel song sung by the Tambourine Choir in "The Reed Sisters' Tambourine Temple," the church founded by Laura Reed and Essie Belle Johnson in Harlem,* in the novel *Tambourines to Glory*. The song is mentioned in chapter 32 ("Everlasting Arm").

"Get Up Off That Old Jive." Twenty-nine-line poem addressed to "white folks," advising them that African Americans want concrete advances in civil rights. The poem also alludes to President Franklin Roosevelt's* radio speech to the nation in 1941, following the Japanese attack on Pearl Harbor, Hawaii; in the speech Roosevelt said that "the only thing we have to fear is fear itself." Similarly, the poem asserts, African Americans desire to be free from fear and would be better able to fight on behalf of American interests in World War II as a result. "Jive" refers in this instance to empty words offered in support of African American freedom. The poem was first published in the *Amsterdam News* (July 13, 1942). *See* "America's Young Black Joe!".

Bibliography: *CP*, 573.

"Ghosts." Poem. *See* "Ghosts of 1619."

"Ghosts of 1619." Thirty-line poem linking the ghosts of African slaves (slaves first arrived at the Jamestown, Virginia, colony in 1619) to African Americans being able finally to exercise voting rights in the South. The poem subtly conveys the sense in which, via moral authority, the ghosts have exerted a political presence. Many readers may find "Ghosts of 1619" to be one of Hughes's most undeservedly little-known poems. It was first published under the title "Ghosts" in the *Liberator* (July 1964).

Bibliography: *CP*, 543; Peter Kolchin, *American Slavery, 1619–1877* (New York: Hill and Wang, 1993).

"Gifts." *See* "Luck."

The Gilpin Players. An acting troupe connected to the Karamu Theatre in Cleveland, Ohio, that produced several of Hughes's plays in the 1930s. *See Front Porch; Joy to My Soul; Little Ham; Troubled Island; When Jack Hollers.*

"Girl." Poem in five ballad* stanzas, though two are stretched to five lines. It is an elegy for a girl who lived "in sinful happiness," who loved to dance, who died young, but whose spirit seems to reside in flowers, tall trees, and sturdy weeds, all of which dance in the breeze. The restrained rhetoric and traditional form will remind some readers of verse by John Crowe Ransom,* especially

"Bells for John Whiteside's Daughter." When Hughes visited Kenyon College during a reading tour in 1946, he met Ransom, who taught there; the two talked at length. Ransom apparently had discussed Hughes's poetry in a class, and Hughes mentioned that he had long admired Ransom's poetry (see Rampersad). The poem was first published under the title "Mona" in *Opportunity** (June 1927). Regarding a musical adaptation of this poem, see "Heart." *See also* Religion.

Bibliography: *CP*, 106; Rampersad, II, 126; John Crowe Ransom, *Selected Poems*, 3rd ed. revised and enlarged (New York: Knopf, 1969).

"Give Us Our Peace." Poem in six rhyming quatrains and one couplet. The opening line is "Give us a peace equal to our war," and the implied logic of the poem is that now that the Allies—including African American soldiers—have prevailed in World War II, which was fought in part to preserve freedom, African Americans have every right to expect the United States to "fight" in peacetime to secure freedoms, rights, and economic well-being for African Americans. The poem describes many specific expectations. It was first published in the *Chicago Defender** (August 25, 1945). *See* "Get Up Off That Old Jive."

Bibliography: *CP*, 313.

The Glory around His Head (1955). Cantata. Hughes wrote the text (or libretto), and Jan Meyerowitz* composed the music. The piece retells the story of Christ's birth, life, death, and resurrection, focusing chiefly on the resurrection. (The piece is sometimes referred to as an "Easter cantata"). It depicts Jesus as "unwanted" by society, specifically by "the men who hate, . . . the men who cheat, . . . the men who live by the sword, . . . the kings and princes, the robbers and killers." The conclusion of the piece recapitulates the conventional notion that Christ died for humankind's sins. The cantata was performed at Carnegie Hall in New York City on April 14, 1955. Dimitri Mitropoulos directed the New York Philharmonic Orchestra, and Margaret Hillis led the Westminster Choir. Reviewer Olin Downes characterized Hughes's language as "simple and folklike," with "direct dramatic impact." He characterized Meyerowitz's music as "post-Romantic," more "harmonic" than "melodic," and believed that the music "failed to be convincing," noting an apparent disjunction between Hughes's simple, earthy language and Meyerowitz's more cerebral music. Henry Cowell concurred with this assessment of the music, adding, "All manner of dissonant and consonant intervals are treated freely and similarly, with no great sense of formal organization." He went on to observe that when "a melodic inversion development occurs a few measures later [in the song 'My Lord Not Wanted'], it seems exceptionally hardboiled to hear the text 'Jesus Christ not wanted' spat out on such fast and unyielding eights." (In this regard, Hughes himself was known to be dissatisfied in general with the Meyerowitz collaboration—not necessarily with this particular work—believing that the composer's music overwhelmed the text.) The audience reacted favorably to the cantata. Indeed, Rampersad concludes that with *The Glory around His Head*, Meyerowitz and Hughes "scored an authentic hit" (247). Rampersad also quotes Meyerowitz as having remarked of *The Glory around His Head* that "this was probably the most important thing we [he and Hughes] did together" (247). ASCAP* lists the work as being published by Broude Brothers, Ltd., and the work's ASCAP registry number is 370025642.

Bibliography: Henry Cowell, "New York," *Musical Quarterly* 41 (July 1955), 368–370; Olin Downes, review of *The Glory Around His Head, New York Times* (April 15, 1955); 17; Rampersad, II, 247.

The Glory of Negro History. (New York: Folkways, 1958). Sound recording (one long-playing vinyl disc). Hughes is the narrator on this recording. *See The Glory of Negro History: A Pageant. See also* Audio Recordings of Hughes.

The Glory of Negro History: A Pageant (1958). This fifteen-page monologue is chiefly in prose but includes excerpts from spirituals, folk songs, and the blues.* Its two parts are "The Struggle" and "The Glory." It was published in *The Langston Hughes Reader. See The Glory of Negro History* [sound recording].

Bibliography: *The Langston Hughes Reader*, 165–180.

"Go Slow." Twenty-six-line poem in which the speaker, a collective persona,* undermines through relentless questioning the logic behind the "go slow" advice offered to African Americans with regard to progress toward civil rights and economic power in the 1960s. The last five lines of the poem consist entirely of question marks. It was first published in *ETC.* (1964).

Bibliography: *CP*, 538–539; James A. Emanuel, "The Literary Experiments of Langston Hughes," in O'Daniel, 171–182.

God. *See* Religion.

"God." Thirteen-line poem spoken by God, who laments that He is "Alone in [His] purity," envies the young lovers on Earth, and believes—at least momentarily—that it is better to be human than supremely lonely. The poem was first published in *Poetry* (October 1931). *See* Religion.

Bibliography: *CP*, 140.

"God to Hungry Child." Ten-line free-verse poem in which God tells a hungry child that He "didn't make this world for you"; however, the poem seems to depict God as he is perceived by corporate magnates, railroad tycoons, the wealthy in general, and "the will-be-rich." Therefore, to some extent, Hughes juxtaposes what he perceives to be Judeo-Christian values with the values of a society that he sees as being composed of haves and have-nots. Consequently, while the poem rhetorically pretends to depict a callous God, it is in fact an implicit social critique. It was first published in *Workers Monthly* (March 1925). *See* Religion.

Bibliography: *CP*, 48.

Godmother. Nickname of Mrs. Charlotte Osgood Mason,* who briefly supported Hughes's career during the Harlem Renaissance.*

"Gods." Twelve-line poem suggesting that people needlessly fear religious icons because the icons are merely creations of the people. It was first published in the *Messenger** (March 1924). *See* Religion.

Bibliography: *CP*, 37.

"God's Other Side." Short story, included in the collection *Simple's Uncle Sam. See* Simple [Jesse B.] Stories.

"Going South in Russia." Essay. Hughes describes his journey by train in 1932 from Moscow to Soviet Central Asia, as the region was known at that time. He contrasts what he regards as the multicultural, politically progressive "South" of the Soviet Union with the American South, which in his view symbolizes racism, oppression, and—particularly in the context of train travel—Jim Crow laws.* The essay was first published in the *Chicago Defender** (June 1934). It was later reprinted in Berry. In the 1940s Hughes would revisit Soviet Central Asia and write about the region in such essays as "Light and the Soviet Union" and "The Soviet Union and Health."

Bibliography: Berry, 79–84.

"Gold Piece." Brief allegorical play for children. Its main characters are Mexican farmers. It was first published in *Brownie's Book** (June 1921).

Bibliography: Rampersad, I, 48.

"Golden Gate." Short story, included in the collection *Simple's Uncle Sam. See* Simple [Jesse B.] Stories.

"Golfing and Goofing." Short story, included in the collection *Simple Stakes a Claim. See* Simple [Jesse B.] Stories.

"Gone Boy." Nine-line poem about a "Playboy of the dawn" who goes to parties into the wee hours of the morning and does not show up to work. It was first published in *Voices* (January–April 1957).

Bibliography: *CP*, 455.

"Good Bluffers." Four-line poem asking pity for those who are afraid but do not appear to be so. It was first published in *Approach* (Spring 1965).

Bibliography: *CP*, 535.

"Good Ground." Song. Hughes wrote the lyrics, and Clarence Muse* composed the music. It was one of the songs in *Way Down South*. ASCAP* lists no publisher for the song, but the ASCAP registry number is 370040670.

"A Good Job Gone." Short story. Like many stories in the collection *The Ways of White Folks*, this narrative concerns the predicament of an African American who must negotiate conflict between two white Americans—conflict for which he is not responsible. The pragmatic but somewhat naïve narrator works for a white man who is having an affair; the man's marriage is thereby threatened; indirectly, the troubled marriage threatens the narrator's employment. The story was first published in *Esquire* (April 1934) and was reprinted in *Langston Hughes: Short Stories*.

Bibliography: Ostrom, 12–13.

"Good Morning." Poem. *See Montage of a Dream Deferred.*

"Good Morning Revolution." Poem of sixty-five lines in free verse. Spoken by a collective persona* ("Worker"), the poem expresses enthusiasm for a coming revolution of workers in Germany, China, Africa, Italy, Poland, America, and the USSR. It was first published in *New Masses* (September 1932). The editors of *Collected Poems* suggest that the poem might satirically play off of the title of a poem by Carl Sandburg,* "Good Morning, America." *See also Angelo Herndon Jones*; "Ballads of Lenin"; "Chant for Tom Mooney"; *Don't You Want to Be Free?*; "Goodbye, Christ"; *Good Morning, Revolution: Uncollected Writings of Langston Hughes*; "Lenin"; "A New Song"; "One More 'S' in the U.S.A."; "Revolution"; "Sister Johnson Marches"; "Song of the Revolution"; "Wait." *See also* John Reed Club; Marxism; Politics.

Bibliography: *CP*, 162, 641.

Good Morning Revolution: Uncollected Writings of Social Protest by Langston Hughes. Edited by Faith Berry (New York: Citadel Press, 1973). 175 pp. One purpose of the volume is to present previously uncollected "writings of social protest" by Hughes, including short stories, poems, and essays. With regard to short stories and poems, the volume has been superseded by *Collected Poems* and *Langston Hughes: Short Stories*, except for eight poems Berry includes that *Collected Poems* does not include: "Capitalism," "Cotton," "Easter in Wartime," "Moscow," "Our Spring," "Poem for a Poster on Africa," "The Poor," and "War." The book remains a useful source of essays previously published only in journals or newspapers or even unpublished. These essays include "Concerning 'Goodbye Christ,' " "Concerning Red Baiting," "Cowards from the Colleges," "Democracy and Me," "Democracy, Negroes, and Writers," "Faults of the Soviet Union," "Franco and the Moors," "Going South in Russia," "I Remember the Blues," "Langston Hughes Speaks," "Laughter in Madrid," "Light and the Soviet Union," "Moscow and Me," "My Adventures as a Social Poet," "Negroes in Spain," "Revolutionary Armies in China—1949," "Southern Gentlemen, White Prostitutes, Mill Owners, and Negroes," "The Soviet Union," "The Soviet Union and Color" "The Soviet Union and Health," "The Soviet Union and Jews," "The Soviet Union and Women," "Spain's Martyred Poet, García Lorca," "The Task of the Negro Writer as Artist," "To Negro Writers," "Too Much of Race," and "What Shall We Do about the Junkies?" Additionally, the volume coherently organizes poems, stories, and essays focused on a variety of social and political issues. Berry's introduction provides a brief overview of what changed and what remained constant with regard to Hughes's political views over the course of his career. Saunders Redding provided a foreword to the book. *See also Baltimore Afro American; Chicago Defender*; "Here to Yonder"; Marxism; McCarthyism; Poetics; Politics.

"Good Morning, Stalingrad." Poem of over fifty lines spoken by an African American resident of Alabama who regards the Russian city of Stalingrad (now Volograd) as a symbol of the Soviet Union and therefore of hope for freedom of oppressed people. It was first published in *Jim Crow's Last Stand. See* Marxism.

Bibliography: *CP*, 297.

"Good Old Girl." Song, from *Simply Heavenly*. Hughes wrote the lyrics, and David Martin composed the music. ASCAP* lists no publisher for the song, but the song's ASCAP registry number is 370042801.

"Goodbye Christ." Poem of thirty-seven lines in which the speaker claims that Christ is no longer a viable religious figure and has been appropriated by religious hucksters and a commercial society. The speaker further claims that economic liberation is the only authentic salvation. The poem first appeared in the *Negro Worker* (December 1932), but was later published without Hughes's permission in the *Saturday Evening Post* (December 21, 1940), a magazine to which the poem refers derogatorily. The publication in the *Post* sparked an outcry against the poem, its pro-Communist and anti-Christianity sentiments, and its author; the reaction included boycotts (some organized by the America First Party) against Hughes's public readings. Hughes later repudiated some ideas expressed in the poem, which is perhaps the most controversial one of his career. *See also Angelo Herndon Jones*; "Ballads of Lenin"; "Chant for Tom Mooney"; "Concerning 'Goodbye Christ' "; "Concerning Red Baiting"; *Don't You Want to Be Free?*; "Good Morning Revolution"; "In Explanation of Our

Times"; "Lenin"; McCarthyism; "A New Song"; "One More 'S' in the U.S.A.";
"Revolution"; "Song of the Revolution"; "Wait." *See also* John Reed Club;
Marxism; Politics; Religion.

Bibliography: *CP*, 166; Charles H. Nicholls, ed., *Arna Bontemps/Langston Hughes Letters 1925–1967* (New York: Dodd, Mead, 1980), 51; Rampersad, I, 390–395.

"Gospel Cha-Cha." Poem. *See Ask Your Mama.*

Gospel Glory. See Gospel Glow.

Gospel Glow. (1962). Play in one act, with the subtitle *A Passion Play*. Like *Ballad of the Brown King, Black Nativity*, and *Tambourines to Glory* (the play, as opposed to the novel), *Gospel Glow* is a musical play immersed in African American gospel music. In the program notes Hughes described it as "the first Negro passion play, depicting the life of Christ from the cradle to the cross" (Peterson, 256). It was first produced in Brooklyn, New York, on October 26, 1962, running for two nights at the Washington Temple, Church of God in Christ. Soon thereafter productions occurred in Cleveland, Ohio, and Westport, Connecticut. Hughes regarded the production in Westport as a failure, indicating that he had never seen "a more amateurishly and carelessly presented performance" (Rampersad, II, 350). Therefore, he abruptly ended an agreement with producer Alfred Duckett that was planned to have resulted in a recording of the play as well as a television adaptation of it. Apparently the performance in Brooklyn was also marred by technical difficulties. A reviewer wrote, "It is impossible to evaluate Mr. Hughes's work since the dialogue was lost amid the microphones. . . . Theatre in the church is a healthy and significant sign. Our religious organizations should be attuned to the arts and encourage more artists such as Mr. Hughes, [*sic*] to make contributions. But they should also have skilled crewmen to handle the mechanics." The reviewer was, however, pleased with the performance of Mildred Bryant and of the choir. Ernestine Washington and Robert Madison "received billing," according to the reviewer, who also suggested that *Gospel Glow* "might be considered Mr. Hughes's sequel to *Black Nativity*." The performances in the Brooklyn church were for the benefit of the Eastern Christian Leadership conference, described by the reviewer as "a new civil rights agency." Peterson suggests that for the Brooklyn performances, the play was called *Gospel Glory*, but the reviewer refers to it as *Gospel Glow*. Unpublished scripts of *Gospel Glow* are held in the Schomburg Center for Research in Black Culture, in the Manuscript Division of the State Historical Society of Wisconsin, and in the Langston Hughes Papers, James Weldon Johnson Memorial Collection, Beinecke Rare Book and Manuscript Library, Yale University. *See* Religion.

Bibliography: Paul Gardner, "Brooklyn Church Stages Song-Play: Langston Hughes's Gospel Glow Is Performed," *New York Times* (Sunday, October 28, 1962), 18; Bernard

L. Peterson, Jr., *Contemporary Black American Playwrights and Their Plays: A Biographical Directory and Dramatic Index* (Westport, CT: Greenwood Press, 1988), 254–257; Rampersad, II, 350.

"Gospel Singers." Short story, included in the collection *Simple's Uncle Sam. See* Simple [Jesse B.] Stories.

Gospel Song-Plays. *See* Musical Plays.

"Governor Fires Dean." Twenty-six-line poem in rhymed couplets. It reacts to Georgia governor Eugene Talmadge's dismissal in 1942 of a Georgia educator, Walter Cocking (a professor at the University of Georgia), who headed a group that advocated training rural teachers in a racially integrated setting. Talmadge (1884–1946) was governor of Georgia from 1933 to 1937 and from 1940 to 1943; he was governor-elect when he died. Earlier Talmadge had stated that he would dismiss any public educator who advocated either communism or integration. In reaction to Talmadge's decision, the president of the university resigned, and the Board of Regents overturned the decision made by Talmadge, who then fired Cocking once more. Talmadge was defeated in the next gubernatorial election. The poem compares Talmadge's actions to those of Adolf Hitler. Talmadge has long been considered a demagogue in the style of the infamous Louisiana governor Huey Long. The poem was written in 1942 but was first published in *Collected Poems* (1994).

Bibliography: William Anderson, *The Wild Man from Sugar Creek: The Political Career of Eugene Talmadge* (Baton Rouge: Louisiana State University Press, 1975); *CP*, 572, 692–693; [Untitled article on Talmadge's death], *New York Times* (December 22, 1946).

"Graduation." Thirty-two-line poem describing a high-school graduation party for "Mary Lulu Jackson," whose mother has worked tirelessly to arrange the party and who sees her daughter's diploma as a sign that the daughter will have many more opportunities than she. The poem implies that the mother's hopes are, while not essentially unreasonable, perhaps excessively optimistic, and it suggests that in supporting her daughter, she has worked as hard for the diploma as has Mary Lulu. It was first published in *Common Ground* (Autumn 1945).

Bibliography: *CP*, 315.

"Grammar and Goodness." Short story, included in the collection *Simple Stakes a Claim. See* Simple [Jesse B.] Stories.

"Grandpa's Stories." Ten-line poem spoken by an adolescent who enjoys his grandfather's stories, which make the speaker dream better than "pictures on the

television." It was first published in *The Langston Hughes Reader*. *See* "America's Young Black Joe"; "Aunt Sue's Stories." *See also* Children's Poetry.
Bibliography: *CP*, 605.

"Grave Yard." Poem of six lines. It emphasizes the fact that a graveyard is a final resting place. The poem was first published in *Fields of Wonder*.
Bibliography: *CP*, 327.

"Graveyard Mule." Song, from the 1991 production of *Mule Bone*. Hughes wrote the lyrics, and Taj Mahal composed the music, although his original given name, Henry St. Clair Fredericks, is used in the ASCAP* registry (the song's registry number is 370241962). Taj Mahal recorded songs from the 1991 production. Publishers for them are Prankee Music and One Foot Music. *See also* "Bound No'th Blues"; "But I Rode Some"; "Crossing"; "Hey-Hey Blues"; "Jubilee"; "Me and the Mule"; "Song for a Banjo Dance."
Discography: Taj Mahal, *Mule Bone: Music Composed and Performed by Taj Mahal/ Lyrics by Langston Hughes*. [compact disc] (Los Angeles: Gramavision, distributed by Rhino Records, 1991): R2 79432.

"Great But Late." Short story, included in the collection *Simple Stakes a Claim*. *See* Simple [Jesse B.] Stories.

"Great Day." Short story, included in the collection *Simple Stakes a Claim*. *See* Simple [Jesse B.] Stories.

The Great Migration. Name given to the migration of African Americans from the South to the North. *See The Chicago Defender*; The Harlem Renaissance; "Migration."

Green, Ernest. *See* "The Bitter River."

"Green Memory." Seven-line poem, part of *Montage of a Dream Deferred*. It points to the irony of World War II having been good for the American economy.
Bibliography: *CP*, 401.

"Grief." Poem of six lines in two three-line stanzas. The last words of the first stanza rhymes with that of the second. In part the poem concerns the powerlessness of grief. The poem was first published in *Fine Clothes to the Jew*.
Bibliography: *CP*, 334.

Guillén, Nicolás (1902–1989). Cuban poet. *See Cuba Libre: Poems of Nicolás Guillén*. *See also I Wonder As I Wander; The Langston Hughes Reader*.

"Guinea." Poem by Haitian writer Jacques Roumain that Hughes translated from the French. It is twenty lines long and in free verse. It concerns returning to a village in Guinea. Hughes's translation is published in *The Langston Hughes Reader. See Masters of the Dew.*
Bibliography: *The Langston Hughes Reader*, 138.

"Gumption." Short story that concerns class struggle and racism during the Great Depression in the United States. The story is narrated by an elderly African American woman. Rampersad characterizes it as manifesting "pro-communist zeal" (301). It was first published under the title "Oyster's Son" in the *New Yorker* (January 12, 1935), was included in the collection *Something in Common and Other Stories*, and was reprinted in *Langston Hughes: Short Stories*.
Bibliography: Ostrom, 48–49; Rampersad, I, 301.

"The Gun." Short story. The main character, Flora Belle Yates, and her parents are the only African Americans in Tall Rock, Montana. Flora learns that her parents had fled Texarkana, pursued by a lynch mob. Most of the story concerns Flora's restlessness after she decides to leave Montana. She wanders from Tall Rock to Butte, from Butte to Seattle, and from Seattle to several California cities and towns: Monterey, Berkeley, San Diego, Marysville, San Jose, and finally Fresno. In Fresno she contemplates suicide, going so far as to purchase a gun and put it against her chest. She decides against suicide, however, and the decision seems to liberate her; she feels as if she "were no longer a prisoner in the world" (*Something in Common*, 159). The story was included in the collection *Something in Common and Other Stories* and was reprinted in *Langston Hughes: Short Stories. See* Lynching.
Bibliography: Ostrom, 44–45.

Gutierrez, Valerio. The main character in the short story "Spanish Blood."

"Gypsy Man." Poem in four traditional blues* stanzas and in black dialect.* The speaker claims her "man" is a gypsy because he never comes home. She complains of being mistreated in Memphis and reports that a "yellow" (light-skinned African American) man took her money. The poem was first published in *New Republic* (April 14, 1926).
Bibliography: *CP*, 66.

"Gypsy Melodies." Five-line poem concerning songs by gypsies. It was first published in the *Carmel Pine Cone* (July 18, 1941).
Bibliography: *CP*, 235.

H

"Hail and Farewell." A short story—the last of the Simple [Jesse B.] stories* Hughes published.

"Haircuts and Paris." Short story, included in the collection *Simple's Uncle Sam. See* Simple [Jesse B.] Stories.

Hammarskjöld, Dag (1905–1961). Swedish diplomat, secretary general of the United Nations from 1953 to 1961. *See* "Lumumba's Grave."

Hammond. A character in the poem "Early Evening Quarrel."

Handy, W. C. (1873–1958). American musician, composer, and music publisher. Handy is often referred to as the "father" of the blues,* chiefly because he was the first person to systematically collect and transcribe blues lyrics and tunes. In *Not Without Laughter* Jimboy Rodgers (father of the main character, Sandy) is said to have met Handy (in Memphis), who thinks that Jimboy plays and sings the blues well enough to make a living doing so.

Bibliography: W. C. Handy, *Father of the Blues: An Autobiography*, ed. Arna Bontemps, with a foreword by Abbe Niles (London: Sidgwick and Jackson, 1957).

Hansberry, Lorraine (1930–1965). American playwright and essayist. Hansberry is best known for her play *A Raisin in the Sun* (1959), which took its title from a line in Hughes's poem "Harlem [2]" from *Montage of a Dream Deferred*.

"Hard Boiled Mama." Song. Hughes wrote the lyrics, and J. Rosamund Johnson composed the music. ASCAP* lists no publisher for the song, but the song's ASCAP registry number is 380235727.

"Hard Daddy." Poem in three traditional blues* stanzas. It is spoken by a woman whose "daddy" (lover) is callous and unsympathetic toward her. It was first published in *Fine Clothes to the Jew*.

Bibliography: *CP*, 124.

"Hard Luck." Poem, not to be confused with the poem "Hard Luck" in *Fine Clothes to the Jew*. *See* "Bad Luck Card."

"Hard Luck." Poem in three traditional blues* stanzas. It advises those down on their luck to sell their fine clothes "to the Jew" and use the money to get drunk. The poem can be read as stereotyping Jews as merchants or pawnbrokers. The poem also provides a title for the collection in which it was first published, *Fine Clothes to the Jew*.

Bibliography: *CP*, 82.

Harlem. A section of New York City. After Manhattan Island was purchased from Native Americans, the area was eventually settled by Dutch and German settlers, "Haarlem" being the name of a city in the Netherlands. Harlem is located north of 114th Street, west of the Harlem River, east of St. Nicholas Avenue, and south of 156th Street. It takes up roughly two square miles of land. African Americans and immigrants from Africa and the West Indies began resettling in Harlem in the early twentieth century. Among Hughes's several residences in Harlem was a townhouse located at 20 East 127th Street that he purchased in 1948. *See* Harlem Renaissance.

Bibliography: Lewis, *WHWV*; Rampersad, II; Watson.

"Harlem [1]." Twenty-two-line poem in three stanzas expressing the deep frustration of African Americans in economically depressed Harlem,* which the poem describes as being "on the edge of Hell." It was first published under the title "Puzzled" in *One-Way Ticket*.

Bibliography: *CP*, 363–364.

"Harlem [2]." Poem, part of the long poem *Montage of a Dream Deferred*. Other entries for titles within *Montage of a Dream Deferred* refer the reader to the entry for this long work, but "Harlem [2]" is especially noteworthy because it is one of Hughes's most famous poems (often anthologized on its own), it compresses prophetic intensity into an eleven-line lyric, it anticipates the social upheaval in the United States during the 1960s, and it provided the title for what would become a classic, enduring American play, *A Raisin in the Sun*, by Lorraine Hansberry.*

Bibliography: *CP*, 426.

"Harlem Dance Hall." Eight-line poem that suggests that the floor and the people on it have no dignity—until the dancing begins, at which moment the Harlem* venue and the people are transformed. The poem was first published in *Fields of Wonder*.

Bibliography: *CP*, 339.

"Harlem Night." Eleven-line poem that conveys the despair of Harlem* subtly, suggesting that Harlem has a rhythmic but tuneless song and a moonless—but also starless—sky. It was first published under the title "Troubled Night" in *Crisis** (October 1945). *See also* "Christmas Eve: Nearing Midnight in New York."

Bibliography: *CP*, 314.

"Harlem Night Club." Poem in five stanzas, all quatrains except for the first, which is stretched to five lines. The poem evokes the ecstatic atmosphere of the Harlem* nightclub but also focuses on the racially integrated nature of the venue. It was first published in *The Weary Blues*. *See* "Who's Passing for Who?"

Bibliography: *CP*, 90, 632.

"Harlem Night Song." Poem of sixteen lines in free verse. The speaker expresses his love for an unnamed "listener" and entreats the person to wander with him through Harlem.* The poem was first published in *The Weary Blues*. Later, Ricky Ian Gordon set it to music. ASCAP* lists the song as being published by the Williamson Music Company, and the song's ASCAP registry number is 380353608. The poem was also reprinted in *The Block*. *See also* "Harlemer Nachtlied."

Bibliography: *CP*, 94.

The Harlem Renaissance (circa 1920–1930). As historians of the Harlem Renaissance (HR) have observed, it was at once a spontaneous result of changes in American society and the product of conscious orchestration by intellectuals, community leaders, editors, patrons, musicians, artists, publishers, and writers. The northern migration of African Americans from southern states after Reconstruction created in the New York City borough of Harlem* (among other urban centers) a substantial African American population—a "critical mass" of sorts. Immigrants from Africa and the West Indies also lived there. This community was one that experienced comparatively substantial economic well-being, which peaked in the mid-1920s before being undercut by the Great Depression. Therefore, a spirit of renaissance already existed in this new vibrant community, which was by no means homogeneous but which nonetheless shared a sense of history and a sense of new possibilities. Intellectuals like W.E.B. Du Bois,* Charles Johnson,* and Alain Locke,* with their notions of the Talented Tenth and the New Negro,* were determined to shape these possibilities, to channel political, artistic, and literary energy. Some white New Yorkers, driven by a variety of motives, assisted in this attempted orchestration: Carl Van Vechten* and Mrs. Charlotte Osgood Mason* are representative examples. However, as Hutchinson demonstrates, the political, social, and artistic energies were too diverse to manage smoothly, and one of the key elements that drove the HR— the presence of so many talented, determined, opinionated writers, editors, actors, musicians, and others—was also the element that caused the HR to experience as much conflict, disagreement, and ferment as it involved collaboration and common purpose. Moreover, as Hutchinson also points out, the HR did not occur in a vacuum, nor did it concern only African American culture, but it was instead part of a changing, tumultuous American cultural landscape, one that was more complex than the popular label "the Roaring Twenties" suggests.

Hughes's career in some ways is a vivid microcosm of the HR. He was drawn to New York chiefly for his own reasons, namely, to study at Columbia University,* but was swept up in the cultural reformation in Harlem, transfixed by jazz,* and energized by a variety of personalities. He received support from Du Bois, Johnson, Locke, Van Vechten, and Mason; magazines such as *Opportunity,* *Crisis,* and the *Messenger** published his poems; and the publication of his book *The Weary Blues* by Alfred A. Knopf* put him in the limelight. Although he was smitten by Harlem and would live there on and off for the rest of his life, he also found it to be claustrophobic in the 1920s and chose to leave for long stretches. His first autobiography, *The Big Sea*, is at once one of the most important chronicles of the HR and a record of travels inspired by the need Hughes felt to escape Harlem. The chapter "When the Negro Was in Vogue" captures the ambivalence with which Hughes and other writers regarded the social engineering that helped drive the HR and the interest that white Americans suddenly showed in "Negro" culture. His legendary falling-out with his patron Charlotte Osgood Mason and her "lieutenant," Alain Locke, crystallizes many conflicts and complexities inherent in the HR. Nonetheless, the HR also provided Hughes with lifelong friends, a profound connection to his sense of "African Americanness," a heightened sense of politics and history, and a resilient foundation for his literary career. *See also* The Blues; Bontemps, Arna; Cullen, Countee; Fauset, Jessie; Harlem Suitcase Theatre; Hurston, Zora Neale; Larsen, Nella; Marxism; McKay, Claude; Nugent, Richard Bruce; Poetics; Politics; Talented Tenth.

Bibliography: Houston A. Baker, Jr., *Modernism and the Harlem Renaissance* (Chicago: University of Chicago Press, 1987); Faith Berry, *Langston Hughes: Before and Beyond Harlem* (Westport, CT: L. Hill, 1983); *The Big Sea*; Arna Bontemps, ed., *The Harlem Renaissance Remembered* (New York: Dodd, Mead, 1972); Hutchinson; Lewis, HRR; Lewis, *WHWV*; Ostrom; Rampersad I; Watson; Wintz; Cary D. Wintz, ed., *African-American Political Thought, 1890–1930: Washington, Du Bois, Garvey, and Randolph* (Armonk, NY: M. E. Sharpe, 1996).

"The Harlem Story." Essay. On the occasion of civil unrest in Harlem,* it meditates on the history of Harlem as an African American community. It was published in the *New York Post* (July 21, 1964). *See* "Death in Yorkville"; "Harlem III."

Harlem Suitcase Theatre. Theatre group that Hughes cofounded and whose operation he oversaw. In early 1938 Hughes expressed to Louise Thompson his desire to establish a theatre, the purpose of which would be to produce artistically avant-garde and politically radical drama. (Thompson was a graduate of Hampton College, had been married to Wallace Thurman,* and in 1938 was associated with the International Workers Order [IWO], which was a comparatively radical labor organization.) Thompson found a space for the theatre in the IWO's Community Center at 317 West 125th Street in Harlem,* and the first members of the theatre all belonged to the IWO (Rampersad, I, 356). They included Thompson, Mary Savage, Grace Johnson, Edith Jones and her husband, Robert Earl Jones (father of the celebrated actor James Earl Jones), Dorothy Peterson, Alta Douglas, Gwendolyn Bennett, Waring Cuney, Dorothy Maynor, Toy Harper, and Hilary Phillips. The theatre was formally established in February 1938, and Hughes wrote *Don't You Want to Be Free?* expressly as the inaugural production. Owing largely to the success of this play, the Harlem Suitcase Theatre enjoyed a robust first season. Rampersad writes, "By the end of its first season in July [1938], some 3500 persons, about seventy-five per cent of whom were black, would attend thirty-eight performances of the Harlem Suitcase Theatre. In the process, the group had eclipsed its main rival, the Harlem Unit of the Federal Theatre Project" (I, 359–360). Hughes's departure for Paris, his involvement with other theatres, and insufficient financial backing led to the demise of the Harlem Suitcase Theatre after the 1939 season. (In his position as director of the theatre, Hughes earned no money.) Nonetheless, its contribution to Hughes's career as a dramatist, to avant-garde theatre in New York, to radical theatre of the 1930s, and to the history of African American theatre was enormous (*see Angelo Herndon Jones* and *Don't You Want to Be Free?*). *See* "Note on Commercial Theatre."

Bibliography: Samuel A. Hay, *African American Theatre: An Historical and Critical Analysis* (Cambridge: Cambridge University Press, 1994); Rampersad, I, 355–361.

"Harlem Sweeties." Poem of forty-four short lines with a rhyme scheme of ABCBDEFE (even-numbered lines rhyming, that is). It is an exuberant celebration of the beauty and eroticism of women in Harlem,* drawing on a spectrum of comparisons between women and various colors, textures, and flavors of wine, sweet foods, and spices. It was first published in *Shakespeare in Harlem.*

Bibliography: *CP*, 245–246; Davis.

"Harlem III." Essay that concerns civil unrest in Harlem* in 1964 and recalls two other riots in Harlem. It was published in the *New York Post* (July 23,

1964). *See* "Ballad of Margie Polite"; "Death in Yorkville"; "The Harlem Story."

"Harlemer Nachtlied." Song. It is the German version of "Harlem Night Song," with music and translated lyrics by Eric Zeisl, a composer who worked in Hollywood, writing (among other things) music for the films *Abbott and Costello Meet the Invisible Man* and *Abbott and Costello Meet Dr. Jekyll and Mr. Hyde*. ASCAP* lists no publisher for the song, but the song's ASCAP registry number is 380289027.

Harmon Foundation Medal. The award presented to Hughes in 1930 for his novel *Not Without Laughter*. It was accompanied by a prize of four hundred dollars.
Bibliography: Rampersad, 128.

Harper, Toy. *See* Harlem Suitcase Theatre.

Harvest (1934). Play. Hughes co-wrote it with Ella Winter and Ann Hawkins. He and Winter began working on the play in Fall 1933 when he was living with Noel Sullivan* in Carmel, California, becoming involved in labor politics, and in particular associating himself with the John Reed Club.* Through many drafts, the play bore the working title, *Blood on the Fields*. It is based on actual events involving labor unrest among agricultural workers, growers, and local officials in California's San Joaquin Valley in 1932 and 1933. In dramatizing the historical events, Hughes (as lead author), Winter, and Hawkins chose to use over one hundred characters representing Mexican American and white farm workers (cotton pickers), growers, union organizers, law-enforcement officials, and local citizens. The enormous cast required by *Harvest* is one reason the play has not, to date, been produced. Another reason may be that it is Hughes's most topically political play. It was finally published in 2000 in a collection also including *Angelo Herndon Jones*, *De Organizer*, and *Scottsboro Limited*. In her introduction to the play, the collection's editor, Susan Duffy, details the circumstances leading to Hughes's collaboration with Winter and Hawkins, including a fierce reaction in Carmel against Hughes and his politics. Rampersad also discusses background to the writing of the play. *See* Marxism; Politics and Hughes.
Bibliography: Langston Hughes, *Harvest*, in *The Political Plays of Langston Hughes*, ed. with introduction and analyses by Susan Duffy (Carbondale: Southern Illinois University Press, 2000), 68–137; Duffy's introduction to the play, 50–68.

"A Hat Is a Woman." Short story, included in the collection *Simple Takes a Wife*. *See* Simple [Jesse B.] Stories.

Hattie. A character in the poem "Early Evening Quarrel."

"Havana Dreams." Eight-line poem with deliberately fragmentary imagery that reinforces the speaker's claim that the dreams in question are just out of reach, not quite identifiable. It was first published in *Opportunity** (June 1933). Regarding a musical adaptation of the poem. *See* "Heart."
Bibliography: *CP*, 173.

"Heart." Nineteen-line poem that relates a parable describing how "Pierrot"— the traditional French and Italian pantomime character—lost his heart. It was first published in *Fields of Wonder*. Later, Jean Berger set the poem to music. ASCAP* lists the song as being published by Broude Brothers, Ltd., and the song's ASCAP registry number is 380231847. Also, Robert Owens set "Heart," "For Dead Mimes," "Girl," "Havana Dreams," and "Remembrance" to music under the title *Heart on the Wall: 5 Lieder Für Sopran*, with the texts of the songs (poems) translated into German by Erika Berghöfer-Engen (Munich: Orlando-Musikverlag, 1968).
Bibliography: *CP*, 329; S. Marie Yestadt, "True Poets: Their Influence on the Contemporary Art Song," *Xavier University Studies* 10 (Spring 1971), 33–43.

"The Heart of Harlem." Forty-line poem that is unabashedly sentimental, even boosterish, in its praise of Harlem* and of many personages living there at the time, including Joe Louis,* Earl Hines, Dorothy Maynor, Canada Lee, Father Divine, W.E.B. Du Bois,* and Mother Horne. Because the poem was first published in *Hawk's Cry* (August 18, 1945), the newspaper at Tuskegee Army Air Field, where the African American Tuskegee Airmen trained, its chief purpose may have been to reinforce the morale of the fighter pilots toward the end of World War II. *See* "To Dorothy Maynor."
Bibliography: *CP*, 311, 661.

Heart on the Wall: 5 Lieder Für Sopran. See "Heart."

"A Hearty Amen." Short story, included in the collections *Simple Takes a Wife* and *The Best of Simple*. *See* Simple [Jesse B.] Stories.

"Heaven." Poem in three short-lined quatrains. It depicts heaven as a place where many animals, not just birds, sing and where stones talk. It was first published in the *Carmel Pine Cone* (July 4, 1941). *See* Religion.
Bibliography: *CP*, 232–233.

"Heaven to Hell." Short story. It is a monologue spoken by a woman who was in an automobile accident. She speaks from her hospital bed, where she is visited by a woman whom she assumes to be her husband's mistress. The jealousy and religious piety the narrator expresses is, unwittingly on her part, comic. Rampersad cites the story as being published under the title "Heaven to Hell" in *American Spectator* (1935). Harper cites it as being published later under the title "After the Accident" in *Crisis** (June 12, 1943). It is included in the collection *Laughing to Keep from Crying*. Reprinted in *Langston Hughes: Short Stories*.

Bibliography: Akiba Sullivan Harper, ed., *Langston Hughes: Short Stories* (New York: Hill and Wang, 1996), 297; Ostrom, 22; Rampersad, I, 310.

"Helen Keller." Twelve-line poem in praise of Keller (1880–1968), the American writer and teacher who was deaf, blind, and mute. Hughes was asked to contribute a poem, which turned out to be this one, to *Double Blossoms: Helen Keller Anthology*, edited by E. Porter (New York: Copeland Publishers, 1931).

Bibliography: *CP*, 146.

"Hello Harry." Unpublished short story, written in 1934. *See also* "Eyes like a Gypsy"; "Mailbox for the Dead"; "A Posthumous Tale." A manuscript is held in the Langston Hughes Papers, James Weldon Johnson Memorial Collection, Beinecke Library, Yale University.

Bibliography: Rampersad, I, 301.

Hemingway, Ernest (1899–1961). American novelist, short-story writer, and journalist. Hemingway is widely considered to be one of the most important American writers of the twentieth century. He is known for the spare prose style he developed and his depictions of bullfighting, fishing, hunting, enervated modern relationships, and war. He was born in Oak Park, Illinois, and attended schools there. During World War I he served as an ambulance driver in France and Italy. Later he lived in Paris and met such Modernist writers as Ezra Pound and Gertrude Stein. His collections of stories include *In Our Time* (1925) and *The Short Stories of Ernest Hemingway* (1938). His novels include *The Sun Also Rises* (1926), *A Farewell to Arms* (1929), and *For Whom the Bell Tolls* (1940). His novel *The Old Man and the Sea* won the Pulitzer Prize in 1953, and he won the Nobel Prize for Literature in 1954. As Hughes notes in *I Wonder As I Wander*, he met Hemingway in Spain in 1937 when both men were reporting on the Spanish Civil War, and Hemingway helped arrange a farewell party for Hughes just before the latter returned to the United States. *See Baltimore Afro American*; Modernism and Hughes.

Bibliography: Scott Donaldson, ed., *The Cambridge Companion to Ernest Hemingway* (Cambridge: Cambridge University Press, 1996); *I Wonder As I Wander*, 187–188; Kenneth Lynn, *Hemingway* (Cambridge, MA: Harvard University Press, 1995); Jeffrey Meyers, *Hemingway: A Biography* (New York: Harper and Row, 1985); Ostrom; Rampersad, I, 347–348.

"Here Comes Old Me." Short story, included in the collection *Simple Takes a Wife. See* Simple [Jesse B.] Stories.

"Here to Yonder." Newspaper column. Hughes began writing this weekly column for the *Chicago Defender** in 1942, publishing the first one on November 21, 1942. He wrote the column for the next twenty-three years, publishing the last one on January 8, 1966, in the *New York Post*. (In late 1957, he began publishing the column in both the *Chicago Defender* and the *New York Post*, transferring to the *Post* exclusively in 1962). Some columns were occasional essays in the European tradition of Montaigne, Joseph Addison and Richard Steele, Charles Lamb, and William Hazlitt. For example, the column appearing on January 22, 1944, concerned the inadvisability of "cussing in public." More often, however, Hughes concentrated on larger social issues. Numerous columns, for instance, expressed his fierce opposition to Jim Crow laws* and segregationist policies in public transportation, public accommodations, and public schools. He also wrote about the "race riots" in Detroit (the September 11, 1943, column), his support of U.S. involvement in World War II, why Hitler's ideas had to be "defeated," racism in Hollywood, the importance of political solidarity among ethnic minorities in the United States, and segregation in the U.S. armed forces. Hughes's greatest achievement in the column, however, is widely regarded to be the creation of the fictional character Jesse B. Simple, whom Hughes first presented on February 13, 1943. (The character was first called "My Simple Minded Friend," then, briefly, Jesse B. Semple, and finally Jesse B. Simple). From that point on, the Jesse B. Simple stories* would be a staple in the column, Simple would become a fictional folk hero of enormous appeal and, for Hughes, of enormous flexibility, and Hughes would produce enough stories to fill several published volumes. Surveying columns appearing between November 21, 1942, and December 31, 1949, reveals that 235 columns were nonfiction commentaries on a wide spectrum of topics, 118 were Simple stories, 7 were fictional narratives not featuring Simple (*see* Old Ghost), and 1 was a humorous poem about Simple: "Ode to My Simple Minded Friend" (May 15, 1943). (*See* Appendix A in Harper, 219–242.) Rampersad observes that through the column Hughes reached "directly" his "prime audience,* the masses of literate blacks who read the *Chicago Defender*—as he and his grandmother had read the newspaper when he was a boy in Lawrence, Kansas" (II, 55). De Santis has edited a volume containing a generous selection and representative cross-section of Hughes's nonfiction columns. *See also Baltimore Afro American.*

Bibliography: Christopher C. De Santis, ed., *Langston Hughes and the Chicago Defender: Essays on Race, Politics, and Culture, 1942–62* (Urbana: University of Illinois Press, 1995); Donna Akiba Sullivan Harper, *Not So Simple: The "Simple" Stories by Langston Hughes* [critical overview] (Columbia: University of Missouri Press, 1995); Rampersad, II, 53–59; Juliet E. Walker, "The Promised Land: The Chicago Defender and the Black Press in Illinois, 1862–1970," in *The Black Press in the Middle West, 1865–1985*, ed. Henry Lewis Suggs (Westport, CT: Greenwood Press, 1996), 9–50.

Herndon, Angelo. *See Angelo Herndon Jones; Herndon v. Lowry*; "Kids Who Die."

Herndon, Milton. *See Angelo Herndon Jones; Herndon v. Lowry.*

Herndon v. Lowry. U.S. Supreme Court decision in 1937 setting aside a conviction for fomenting insurrection. Angelo Herndon (born on May 6, 1913) recruited for the communist party, organized workers, and agitated on behalf of the Scottsboro Boys.* Herndon was arrested for organizing for the Communist Party and passing out inflammatory leaflets. According to Herndon himself, he was being held incommunicado in jail during the march by unemployed whites and blacks on the Fulton County (Atlanta, Georgia) courthouse for which he was indicted as a leader. Charged with attempting to incite an insurrection under an 1861 law against slave rebellions, Herndon was convicted by a jury of white males in three days (January 16–18, 1933) and sentenced to eighteen to twenty years in state prison because the jury recommended mercy rather than death. Herndon's attorney had moved to stop the proceedings because African Americans were excluded from service on both the grand jury (a large body of citizens who officially charge citizens with crimes) and the trial jury. Radical attorney William L. Patterson, the International Labor Defense, and the Communist Party took charge of the defense in the courts and in the newspapers. The American Civil Liberties Union, the NAACP,* and individuals such as C. Vann Woodward of Georgia Institute of Technology protested the manifest unfairness of the trial, in which Judge Lee B. Wyatt overruled an objection by Herndon's lawyer (Ben Davis, Jr.; John H. Geer was cocounsel) to the arresting policeman's use of "nigger" to refer to the defendant from the witness chair. On appeal, these and other improprieties were condoned by the Georgia Supreme Court. His appeals to Georgia courts exhausted, Herndon challenged his conviction in the U.S. Supreme Court, with Whitney North Seymour as his advocate. In an opinion written by Justice Owen Roberts and over the objections of four justices, the Supreme Court found that the prosecution had introduced at trial too little evidence to justify Herndon's conviction and imprisonment. The Court determined that Georgia had not made membership in the Communist Party illegal or an insurrectionary act in itself and that the vague statute invaded Herndon's freedom of speech by making recruitment and advocacy criminal acts. More important for highlighting the unfairness of Herndon's trial under that statute, the 5–4 majority found in the statute no definition of the standards sufficient to guide the judge and jury in applying the law at trial. Justice Roberts sternly noted that Herndon could have been sentenced to death under a law that "amounts merely to a dragnet which may enmesh any one [*sic*] who agitates for a change of government if a jury can be persuaded that he ought to have foreseen his words would have some effect in the future cause of others." Hughes was moved by Herndon's unjust trial and dehumanizing imprisonment to write the one-act play *Angelo Herndon Jones* (1938). In that play Buddy

Jones is so inspired by Herndon that he shoulders his own responsibilities and resolves to name his soon-to-be-born son after Angelo Herndon. In addition, Hughes wrote in *I Wonder As I Wander* about the heroic death of Milton Herndon (Angelo's brother) in the Spanish Civil War. Milton died while attempting to rescue a white comrade. *Let Me Live*, by the playwright Oyam O (Charles S. Gordon) is based on Herndon's experiences in 1933. It was performed in New York City in 1991 and in Chicago in 1998. *See also* "Kids Who Die."

Bibliography: John C. Edwards and Joseph H. Kitchens, Jr., "Georgia's Anti-Insurrection Law: Slave Justice for Twentieth-Century Negro Radicals," *Research Studies* 38, no. 2 (1970), 122–133; Thomas I. Emerson, "Southern Justice in the Thirties," *Civil Liberties Review* 4, no. 1 (1977), 70–74; Mel Gussow, "Black Leftist's Jail Ordeal in the South in the 1930's" [review of *Let Me Live*], *New York Times*, January 17, 1991, sec. C, col. 1, p. 21; Arthur Garfield Hays, *Trial by Prejudice* (New York: Covici, Friede, 1933), 296–302; Angelo Herndon, *Let Me Live* (New York: Arno Press, 1969); *Herndon v. Lowry, Sheriff*, 301 U.S. 242 (1937); Charles H. Martin, *The Angelo Herndon Case and Southern Justice* (Baton Rouge: Louisiana State University Press, 1976);

William Haltom

"Hero—International Brigade." Forty-four-line poem that uses poetic license to have a dead soldier speak about why he volunteered to travel from his own country (unspecified) to fight with the antifascists in the Spanish Civil War, on which Hughes had reported for the *Baltimore Afro American*.* (The strategy of constructing a monologue spoken by a dead soldier is similar to that of "The Death of the Ball Turret Gunner," Randall Jarrell's widely anthologized poem from World War II.) The poem was first published in the anthology *The Heart of Spain* (1952), according to the editors of *Collected Poems*, who give only the volume's title and date.

Bibliography: *CP*, 431–432, 676.

"Hey!" Six-line blues*-influenced poem in which the speaker, in black dialect,* indicates that the setting sun will induce him to sing the blues. It was first published in *Fine Clothes to the Jew. See* "Hey! Hey!"

Bibliography: *CP*, 112.

"Hey Boy." Song. Hughes wrote the lyrics, and Ernest Waxman composed the music. ASCAP lists no publisher for the song, but the ASCAP* registry number is 380297205.

"Hey! Hey!" Six-line companion poem to "Hey!" The rising sun drives the speaker's blues* away. The poem was first published in *Fine Clothes to the Jew*.

Bibliography: *CP*, 112.

"Hey-Hey Blues." Poem of four stanzas in traditional blues* form, in which "HEY" becomes a marker for the speaker's intensity as a blues singer: water induces a HEY, beer a HEY-HEY, corn liquor a HEY-HEY-HEY. The poem was first published in the *New Yorker* (November 25, 1939). It was also published in *Shakespeare in Harlem*. For the 1991 production of *Mule Bone*, Taj Mahal set the poem to music. It is included in Taj Mahal's recording of the *Mule Bone* songs. At this writing, the song is not registered with ASCAP,* but information accompanying the recording indicates that the song is published. For additional information about the recording, *see* the entry for *Mule Bone*.

Bibliography/Discography: *CP*, 213; Taj Mahal, "Hey-Hey Blues" [lyrics by Langston Hughes], New York [?]: Prankee Music/Golden Foot Music, 1991.

Heyward, (Edwin) DuBose (1885–1940). American novelist, playwright, and poet. Heyward was born in Charleston, South Carolina, and attended schools there. His first novel, *Porgy* (1925), was set in Charleston. Heyward and his wife Dorothy turned the novel into a play in 1927, and in 1935 Heyward collaborated with Ira and George Gershwin to transform the play into an opera, *Porgy and Bess*, which became a classic of American musical theatre. A motion-picture version of the opera was produced in 1959. Heyward's volumes of poetry include *Carolina Chansons* (1922), *Skylines and Horizons* (1924), and *Jasbo Brown and Selected Poems* (1931). His other novels include *Angel* (1926), *Peter Ashley* (1932), and *Star Spangled Virgin* (1939). Heyward wrote favorable reviews of *The Weary Blues* and *Fine Clothes to the Jew*, and *Porgy and Bess* anticipated Hughes's own collaborative work with Jan Meyerowitz,* Kurt Weill,* William Grant Still,* and others in the genre of opera.* Like Hughes, Heyward was a writer of remarkable versatility.

Bibliography: William H. Slavik, *Dubose Heyward* (Boston: Twayne, 1981).

Hibler, Al. Musician who played in one of the jazz* bands conducted by Duke Ellington,* *See* "Jitney."

"High Bed." Short story, included in *The Best of Simple*. *See* Simple [Jesse B.] Stories.

High School Attended by Hughes. *See* Central High School.

"High to Low." Poem. *See Montage of a Dream Deferred*.

"His Last Affair." Short story. The narrative concerns a married white businessman from Terre Haute, Indiana, who travels to New York City and rekindles romance with a former mistress, an African American woman. We learn that according to her, she had once claimed to be pregnant by him and that his parents paid her to keep quiet about the pregnancy. After the New York City tryst, she claims to be pregnant again. The narrative then reveals that in neither case was she in fact pregnant. The story is included in the collection *Something in Common and Other Stories*.

Bibliography: Ostrom, 46–47.

"History." Four-line poem suggesting that the "blood and sorrow" of the past must not be repeated. It was first published in *Opportunity** (November 1934).

Bibliography: *CP*, 179.

"Home." Short story. In this narrative an ailing African American jazz* musician returns from Europe to his hometown in the American South. He encounters his former music teacher, a white woman, and politely tips his hat to her on the street. White townsmen observe this, kidnap him, beat him, and lynch him. Although the story obviously addresses racism and lynching* in an unvarnished way, it does not idealize Europe, for the main character is represented as remembering scenes of despair and poverty during his European travels. The story was first published under the title "The Folks at Home" in *Esquire* (May 1934). It was included in the collection *The Ways of White Folks* and was reprinted in *Langston Hughes: Short Stories*.

Bibliography: Ostrom, 11–12.

"Homecoming." Two-quatrain poem in which the speaker comes home to discover that his lover has moved out. It was first published, with an additional stanza, in *Experiment* (Summer 1949). The additional stanza was deleted in *Selected Poems* but is reprinted in *Collected Poems* (658).

Bibliography: *CP*, 352, 666.

"Homesick Blues." Poem of three stanzas in traditional blues* form and in black dialect.* The speaker is made intensely homesick by a visit to the train station. The poem was first published in *Measure* (June 1926). Later, Sam Raphling set the poem to music. ASCAP* lists no publisher for the song, but the ASCAP registry number is 380191891.

Bibliography: *CP*, 72.

Homosexuality and Hughes. *See* Sexuality and Hughes.

"Honey Babe." Four-quatrain poem in black dialect.* The speaker addresses himself to a woman whom he calls "Honey Babe." She is generous and welcoming to him, he claims, and he is grateful, although he believes that she braids her hair too tightly. The poem was first published in *One-Way Ticket*.

Bibliography: *CP*, 359.

"Hope [1]." Poem of a single quatrain, rhymed ABAB, concerning loneliness and the hope that it will disappear. It was first published in *Shakespeare in Harlem*.

Bibliography: *CP*, 245.

"Hope [2]." Poem. *See Montage of a Dream Deferred.*

"Hope for Harlem." Poem of over two pages in ballad* stanzas. The key image is of a new skyline in Harlem,* and the poem expands it into a representation of prayers answered, of chronic poverty defeated, and of a new economic day for Harlem. It was first published in *Our World* (1952).

Bibliography: *CP*, 436–438.

"Horn of Plenty." Poem. *See Ask Your Mama.*

"A House in Taos." Poem. As Hughes himself noted, this poem is unusual among his works because it evokes Native American mythology, is set in a region—the American Southwest—he had not visited, and seems to have come to him in a dream. It interweaves images of four gods—Sun, Moon, Wind, and Rain—with references to a house in which a lover's triangle takes place. Wealthy patron of the arts Mabel Dodge Luhan later indicated that the poem uncannily seemed to describe her house (in Taos, New Mexico), which Hughes had never seen. "Mailbox for the Dead" is another work inspired by a dream. The poem was first published in *Palms* (November 1926). *See also* "Small Memory."

Bibliography: *The Big Sea*, 260–261; *CP*, 80.

"House in the World." Poem in two rhyming quatrains in which the speaker expresses a desire to live in a house "Where the white shadows will not fall" (i.e., shadows of oppression by white people) but then acknowledges that escape from the white shadows is not possible. The poem was first published under the title "White Shadows" in *Contempo* (September 15, 1931).

Bibliography: *CP*, 138, 639.

Housing Discrimination. *See* Jim Crow Laws; "Little Song on Housing"; "Restrictive Covenants."

"How about It, Dixie?" Poem in six ballad* stanzas in which a collective persona* asks "Dixie" (the American South) whether it will grant African Americans the "Four Freedoms" President Franklin Roosevelt* endorsed—freedoms of speech and worship and from want and fear. The poem refers to Indian leader Mahatma Gandhi and alludes to an assault in Georgia on black singer Roland Hayes. The speaker also observes that "It's hard to beat Hitler / Protecting Jim

Crow," suggesting that the morale needed to defeat Hitler's forces in World War II is undermined by domestic racism. The poem was first published in *Jim Crow's Last Stand*. *See* "Ballad of Roosevelt"; "The Black Man Speaks"; "Gandhi Is Fasting"; Jim Crow Laws; "Warning [1]."

Bibliography: *CP*, 291.

"How Old Is Old?" Short story, included in the collection *Simple's Uncle Sam*. *See* Simple [Jesse B.] Stories.

"How Thin a Blanket." Twenty-four-line rhyming poem that expresses compassion for hungry and impoverished people worldwide but despair concerning how little one person can do to help them. It was first published in *Opportunity** (December 1939).

Bibliography: *CP*, 214–215.

"How to Be a Bad Writer (in Ten Easy Lessons)." Essay. The tongue-in-cheek advice includes the recommended use of clichés, writing ("if you are a Negro") exclusively for a white market, having nothing to say, trying to sound exotic, and drinking a great deal of alcohol. The essay is published in *The Langston Hughes Reader*.

Bibliography: *The Langston Hughes Reader*, 491–492.

Hughes, Carrie Langston (1873–1938). Hughes's mother. Born at the family farm in Lakeview, Kansas (north of Lawrence), she was baptized Carolina Mercer Langston, the daughter of Charles Langston and Mary Leary Langston. When Hughes was young, his mother traveled extensively in search of work, and Hughes was cared for chiefly by his maternal grandmother. Carrie Hughes died of cancer in New York City. *See* Hughes, James Nathaniel (Hughes's father); Langston, James Mercer; "October 16: The Raid"; Tolson, Melvin B.

Bibliography: Rampersad, I, 3–4, 157–167, 360–361, and elsewhere.

Hughes, James Nathaniel (1871–1934). Hughes's father. He was born in Charlestown, Indiana. Rampersad describes him as "a sometime schoolteacher, law clerk, farmer, grocery operator, homesteader, and surveyor's assistant" (I, 10). According to Rampersad, "Carrie Langston and James Hughes were married on April 30, 1899, in Guthrie, Oklahoma" (I, 10). Rampersad also notes that it is uncertain whether "James Hughes was with her [Carrie Langston Hughes] when his son was born on February 1, 1902" in Joplin,* Missouri (I, 11). At any rate, James Hughes decided to live permanently in Mexico shortly after Hughes's birth. Precisely when Carrie Langston Hughes* and James Hughes were divorced is not certain, but James Hughes had virtually no part in raising his son. Hughes visited his father in Mexico three times—once (with his mother) when he was five years old, twice when he was in his late teens. He also returned to Mexico after his father died of a stroke to oversee the dispensation of the estate. James Hughes decided to live in Mexico because of the racism and lack of opportunity he encountered in the United States, and Rampersad suggests that the father's attitude toward the United States influenced Hughes's own political views to some degree, although Hughes, of course, always claimed the United States as his home and never chose to live in exile, even though he was an inveterate traveler. James Hughes was also not supportive of Hughes's writing career.

Bibliography: Rampersad, I, 10–12 ff.

Hughes, Langston (1902–1967). Hughes's full name was James Langston Hughes. It is of note that the main character of the coming-of-age novel *Not Without Laughter* is James "Sandy" Rodgers, who is always called Sandy, just as Hughes was, from the beginning, called Langston. Essential facts of Hughes's life include the following: He was born in Joplin,* Missouri, the only child of Carrie Langston Hughes* and James Nathaniel Hughes.* James effectively abandoned Carrie and Langston shortly after the latter's birth and moved to Mexico. Because Carrie Hughes traveled extensively in search of work, Hughes lived chiefly with his grandmother, Mary Sampson Patterson Leary Langston, early on. Between 1903 and 1915, Hughes lived (and attended schools) in such cities as Buffalo, New York; Lawrence, Kansas; Topeka, Kansas; Colorado Springs, Colorado; and Kansas City, Kansas. His mother married Homer Clark* in 1915, and Hughes gained a half-brother, Gwyn "Kit" Clark.* In 1916 the family moved to Cleveland, Ohio, where Hughes attended Central High School,* graduating in 1920. His first significant publication was that of the poem "The Negro Speaks of Rivers" in *Crisis** (1921). He enrolled at Columbia University* in 1921 but dropped out in June 1922, lived in Harlem,* worked at several jobs, and met Alain Locke,* Countee Cullen,* and numerous other key figures in the Harlem Renaissance.* More poems were published in *Crisis, Opportunity,** the *Messenger,** and other magazines. In 1923 and 1924 Hughes took a job on a freighter and sailed to West Africa, returned to the United States briefly, shipped out twice more, and lived in Paris. He worked briefly for Carter G. Woodson* in 1925, enrolled at Lincoln University* in 1926, and published his first collection of poems, *The Weary Blues*. In 1927 he published *Fine Clothes to the Jew* and met Mrs. Charlotte Osgood Mason,* who would become his patron; he graduated from Lincoln in 1929 and visited Cuba in 1930, meeting Nicolás Guillén (*see Cuba Libre*). Also in 1930 Hughes broke with Mrs. Mason; the break led to a falling-out with Alain Locke and with Zora Neale Hurston,* with whom he had collaborated on *Mule Bone*. Hughes's novel *Not Without Laughter* was published later that year and went on to win the Harmon Foundation Medal.* In 1931 he traveled throughout the American South, accompanied by Zell Ingram,* and traveled to San Francisco for the first time, meeting (and living with) Noel Sullivan.* In 1932 Hughes traveled to Moscow, Russia, and from there he ventured into other parts of the Soviet Union and Asia. *Dear Lovely Death* was published in 1931, *Scottsboro Limited* in 1932 (*see* Scottsboro Boys), and *The Ways of White Folks* in 1934. During this time Hughes was greatly influenced by Marxism.* His play *Mulatto* opened on Broadway in 1935. His plays *Little Ham* (1936) and *Joy to My Soul* (1937) were produced at the Karamu Theatre in Cleveland, Ohio. In 1937 he traveled to Spain and reported on the Civil War there for the *Baltimore Afro American*.* There he met Ernest Hemingway* and other writers. In 1938 Hughes founded the Harlem Suitcase Theatre,* where his play *Don't You Want to Be Free?* was produced. In 1939 he cowrote the screenplay for *Way Down South* with Clarence Muse,* who also acted in the motion picture, the star of which was Bobby Breen.* Much of 1939 and 1940 was spent in Carmel-by-the-Sea, California, where Hughes became acquainted with Robinson and Una Jeffers,* worked on *The Big Sea* (1940), and published poems in the *Carmel Pine Cone*. *Shakespeare in Harlem* was published in 1942, the same year in which Hughes began writing the column "Here to Yonder"* for the *Chicago Defender*,* in which the Simple [Jesse B.] stories* began appearing in 1943. In 1945 Hughes began collaborating with Elmer Rice* and Kurt Weill* on the opera *Street Scene*, which opened in January 1947 on Broadway. The year 1947 also saw the publication of *Fields of Wonder*. The following year Hughes took up more or less permanent residence in Harlem, although he continued to travel extensively. In 1949 the anthology *The Poetry of the Negro, 1746–1949* (coedited with Arna Bontemps*) was published, as was *One-Way Ticket* and *Cuba Libre*; that year the opera *Troubled Island*, on which Hughes collaborated with William Grant Still,* was produced in New York City. In the following year the opera *The Barrier*, on which Hughes collaborated with Jan Meyerowitz,* was produced. *Simple Speaks His Mind* was published in 1950, *Montage of a Dream Deferred* in 1951, and *Laughing to Keep from Crying* in 1952. In 1953 Hughes testified before a U.S. congressional committee chaired by Joseph McCarthy (*see* McCarthyism), and *Simple Takes a Wife* was published. In 1954 the oratorio *Five Foolish Virgins* (cowritten with Jan Meyerowitz) was performed in New York City, and Hughes published *Famous American Negroes* and *The First Book of Rhythms*, followed in 1955 by *The First Book of Jazz* and *Famous Negro Music Makers*. *I Wonder as I Wander* is published in 1956. *Selected Poems of Gabriela Mistral* appeared in 1957.

The musical play *Simply Heavenly* opened off Broadway in 1958, the same year *The Langston Hughes Reader* was published. The year 1959 saw the publication of *Selected Poems*, followed in 1961 by the anthology *An African Treasury*. *Ask Your Mama: 12 Moods for Jazz* also appeared in 1961, the same year in which the musical play *Black Nativity* was produced. Hughes's history of the NAACP,* *Fight for Freedom*, was published in 1962, followed in 1963 by *Something in Common and Other Stories* and the anthology *Poems from Black Africa*. The play *The Prodigal Son* was produced in 1965, which also saw the publication of *Simple's Uncle Sam*. In 1966 Hughes began working with Milton

Meltzer on *Black Magic: A Pictorial History of the Negro in American Entertainment* (1967) and on the anthology *The Best Short Stories by Negro Writers* (1967). In early May 1967 Hughes entered a hospital in New York City; his prostate gland was operated on; complications ensued; and he died on May 22. His funeral* service took place on May 24, 1967. Hughes never married and had no children. He left the Langston Hughes Papers to the James Weldon Johnson Memorial Collection in the Beinecke Rare Book and Manuscript Library at Yale University. The executor of his estate was George Houston Bass. *See* "Aunt Sue's Stories"; "Genius Child"; Langston, James Mercer; "October 16: The Raid"; Papers, Hughes's.

Bibliography: Berry; *The Big Sea; I Wonder As I Wander*; Rampersad, I, II.

"Hughes Bombed in Spain." Newspaper article. *See Baltimore Afro American.*

"Hughes Finds Moors Being Used as Pawns by Fascists in Spain." Newspaper article. *See Baltimore Afro American.*

Hurston, Zora Neale (1891–1960). American writer, anthropologist, folklorist, librarian, and teacher. Hurston was born and grew up in Eatonville, Florida, although she completed her high-school education at Morgan Academy in Baltimore. She earned an associate degree from Howard University in 1924 and began publishing short stories about the same time. Between 1925 and 1927 she studied with the renowned anthropologist Franz Boaz at Barnard College, conducted anthropological field research in Harlem,* and came in contact with Hughes, Wallace Thurman,* Countee Cullen,* Carl Van Vechten,* and other notables, adding her wit, intelligence, talent, and vivid personality to the conversations, conflicts, and social events of the Harlem Renaissance.* Like Hughes, Hurston enjoyed the patronage of Mrs. Charlotte Osgood Mason,* but when Hughes broke with Mason in 1930, Hurston and Alain Locke* took the latter's side. Nonetheless, Hughes and Hurston began to work on the play *Mule Bone*. Arguments about authorship and finances as well as a personality conflict ensued, however, and the play was not produced or published until well after both writers had died. In 1927 Hurston married Robert Sheen (whom she divorced a few years later) and published a study of the African American settlement in St. Augustine, Florida. She also continued to collect folklore in Florida. In the 1930s, after the ill-fated *Mule Bone* collaboration, Hurston wrote fiction, published an article on "Hoodoo [Voodoo] in America," wrote for the theatre, and published *Jonah's Gourd Vine*, a novel. A Guggenheim Fellowship in 1936 enabled her to study spiritual practices in Jamaica and Haiti. She taught drama at North Carolina College in 1939 and published an autobiography, *Dust Tracks on a Road*, in 1942. Hurston continued to publish stories, folklore, and essays until 1959, when she suffered a stroke and, because of financial problems, had to enter a county convalescent hospital. She died in 1960 and became something of a forgotten writer until 1975, when novelist Alice Walker discovered her grave in Eatonville, Florida, and marked it. Walker then wrote about Hurston in *Ms.* magazine. Thereafter, many of Hurston's works were republished. Quickly she came to be regarded as a significant writer of fiction and memoir and a pioneering analyst of folk culture. With Hughes, Hurston shared a deep interest in folklore, working-class people, and Caribbean culture, and both writers shared certain ambivalent views about the Harlem Renaissance.

Bibliography: Robert E. Hemenway, *Zora Neale Hurston: A Literary Biography* (Urbana: University of Illinois Press, 1977); Karla Holloway, *The Character of the Word: The Texts of Zora Neale Hurston* (Westport, CT: Greenwood Press, 1987); Zora Neale Hurston, *Dust Tracks on a Road* (Philadelphia: Lippincott, 1942; New York: Harper Perennial, 1991); Zora Neale Hurston, *Mules and Men* (Philadelphia: Lippincott, 1935; New York: Harper Perennial, 1990); Zora Neale Hurston, *Spunk: The Selected Stories of Zora Neale Hurston* (Berkeley, CA: Turtle Island Foundation, 1985); Zora Neale Hurston, *Tell My Horse: Voodoo and Life in Haiti and Jamaica*, with a foreword by Ishmael Reed (New York: Harper Perennial, 1990); Zora Neale Hurston, *Their Eyes Were Watching God* (Philadelphia: Lippincott, 1937); Adele S. Newson, *Zora Neale Hurston: A Reference Guide* (Boston: G. K. Hall, 1987); Alice Walker, "In Search of Zora Neale Hurston," *Ms.* (March 1975), 74–79, 85–89.

"Hurt." Nine-line poem asserting that no one really cares about another's pain and advising that one remedy for such isolation is to make a jazz* song out of the phrase "Nobody cares." It was first published in the magazine *Harlem* (1928).

Bibliography: *CP*, 126.

I

"I." Poem by a Mexican author identified only as "Francisca" that Hughes translated from the Spanish. The speaker, a young girl, exuberantly expresses interest in a variety of "play" activities, including climbing walls and frightening dogs. The poem was published in *The Langston Hughes Reader. See Blood Wedding* and *Yerma* (one entry); Children's Poetry; *Cuba Libre; Selected Poems of Gabriela Mistral*; Translations by Hughes.

Bibliography: *The Langston Hughes Reader*, 139–140.

"I Am Not Lonely." Song. Hughes translated the lyrics from the original Spanish of Gabriela Mistral. Mistral composed the music. ASCAP* lists the song as being published by Colgems/EMI Music, Inc., and the song's ASCAP registry number is 390378297. ASCAP lists "Alcayaga Godoy" as the composer. Mistral's given name was Lucila Godoy y Alcayaga. *See* "Flower of the Air"; *Selected Poems of Gabriela Mistral*.

"I Been Buked and I Been Scorned." Song. "Buked" is a shortened form of "rebuked." *See Jerico-Jim Crow*.

"I Don't Feel Noways Tired." Song. ASCAP* lists Hughes as being the sole author (both lyricist and composer, that is) but lists no publisher. The song's ASCAP registry number is 90033486.

"I Dream a World." Sixteen-line rhyming poem in which the speaker dreams of a world that is peaceful, equitable, and kind. The poem was part of the libretto for *Troubled Island* and was later published in *Teamwork* (1945). Later, Virginia

Clarke set the poem to music. ASCAP* lists no publisher for the song, but the song's ASCAP registry number is 390239535.

Bibliography: *CP*, 311; 661.

"I Got a Marble and a Star." Song, from *Street Scene*. Hughes wrote the lyrics, and Kurt Weill* composed the music. ASCAP* lists the song as being published by Chappell and Company, Inc., and by Hampshire House Publishers. The song's ASCAP registry number is 390019933. See also "Ain't It Awful, the Heat"; "A Boy like You"; "Catch Me If You Can"; "Don't Forget the Lilac Bush"; "I Loved Her, Too"; "Ice Cream."

"I Got the World by the Tail." Song. Hughes wrote the lyrics, and Albert Hague composed the music. ASCAP* lists the song as being published by Wayfarer Music, and the song's ASCAP registry number is 370048369. ASCAP* lists separately the title "*I've* [emphasis added] Got the World by the Tail" and includes a separate registry number (390075417), but it is presumably the same song. Rampersad indicates that American folksinger Burl Ives recorded the song (with the "I Got" title) in 1950. Possibly the recording to which Rampersad refers is Ives's long-playing record *Ballads and Folk Songs II*, released by Decca Records in 1950.

Bibliography/Discography: Burl Ives, *Ballads and Folk Songs II* (1950): Decca (D1-5013); Rampersad, II, 178.

"I Loved Her, Too." Song, from *Street Scene*. Hughes and Elmer Rice* wrote the lyrics, and Kurt Weill* composed the music. ASCAP* lists the publishers as being Chappell and Company, Inc., and Hampshire House Publishers. The song's ASCAP registry number is 390043791. *See also* "Ain't It Awful, the Heat"; "A Boy like You"; "Catch Me If You Can"; "Don't Forget the Lilac Bush"; "I Got a Marble and a Star"; "Ice Cream."

"I Remember the Blues." Essay. Hughes recalls hearing the blues* all his life, sketches the history of the blues, mentions W. C. Handy,* and reserves special praise for women blues singers—"The three great Smiths" (Mamie, Bessie, and Clara). The essay was first published in the supplement *Panorama* of the *Chicago Daily News* (January 26, 1964) and later in an anthology of Missouri writing. It was reprinted in Berry.

Bibliography: Berry, 164–167; F. L. Mott, ed., *Missouri Reader* (Columbia: University of Missouri Press, 1964), 152–155.

"I Thank You for This." Short story. *See* "Breakfast in Virginia."

"I Thought It Was Tangiers I Wanted." Thirty-three-line poem in free verse. To some extent the poem is a meditation on travel; the speaker reports what he "knows" now about various cities, including Paris, Antwerp, Genoa, Venice, and the Moroccan city of Tangiers, but implies that his real search has been for happiness, not worldly knowledge. Therefore, "wanting" Tangiers turns out to have been an illusory desire for the speaker. The poem was first published in *Opportunity** (December 1927).

Bibliography: *CP*, 110–111.

"I, Too." This eighteen-line, free-verse poem is one of Hughes's most frequently anthologized and therefore best-known works. Its opening line, "I, too, sing America," echoes Walt Whitman's* *Song of Myself* and other parts of *Leaves of Grass*, although in Hughes's poem the "T" is a collective persona* representing African Americans. The foundation of the poem is the extended metaphor of the dinner table, to which African Americans ("the darker brother" of the dining family) have not been invited; they must "Eat in the kitchen." The poem predicts that when the darker brother is one day invited to the table, everyone will realize how "beautiful" he is; therefore, the poem anticipates the Black Aesthetic* movement of the 1960s and one of its credos, "Black is beautiful." The poem was first published in *Survey Graphic* (March 1, 1925). Later the renowned American composer Leonard Bernstein set the poem to music as part of his song cycle *Songfest*. ASCAP* lists the song as being published by Boosey and Hawkes, Inc., and by the Leonard Bernstein Music Company. The song's ASCAP registry number is 390322873. *See* Locke, Alain.

Bibliography: *CP*, 46.

"I Tried to Be a Good Wife to Him." Song, from *Street Scene*. Hughes wrote the lyrics, and Kurt Weill* composed the music. At this writing, the song is not listed with ASCAP.* It is published by Warner Chappell, Ltd.

Bibliography: Booklet accompanying *Street Scene* [compact disc], performed by Kristine Ciesinski, Janis Kelly, Bonaventura Bottone, Richard van Allan, Catherine Zeta Jones, and the Orchestra and Chorus of the English National Opera, conducted by Carl Davis (London: Jay Records, 1996): CDJAY2–1232.

I Wonder As I Wander (New York: Rinehart, 1956). 405 pp. Autobiography. The book is Hughes's second autobiography, the first being *The Big Sea*. To a large degree it is a travelogue, covering in great detail Hughes's trips in the 1930s and 1940s to the Soviet Union, Turkey, Japan, Spain, Haiti, and Cuba, among other places. It discusses his first play to be produced on Broadway (*Mulatto*), his friendships with Zell Ingram,* Arthur Koestler,* Jacques Roumain (*see Masters of the Dew*), Noel Sullivan,* Nicolás Guillén (*see Cuba Libre*), and Mary Bethune,* his intimate relationship with one Natasha in Moscow, the ill-fated Russian film project *Black and White*,* reading tours in the southern states, firsthand experiences with Jim Crow laws,* meeting George Washington Carver,* his first encounters with Richard Wright,* Robinson and

Una Jeffers,* and Ralph Ellison,* his Marxist-influenced politics, his coverage of the Spanish Civil War, the fierce reaction to the publication of his poem "Christ in Alabama," and a variety of other topics and individuals. The volume was reissued by Thunder's Mouth Press (New York) in 1986, with an introduction by Margaret Walker.* This reissued volume remains in print at this writing. *See also Baltimore Afro American*; "Faults of the Soviet Union"; John Reed Club; Marxism; McCarthyism; Politics; "The Soviet Union"; "The Soviet Union and Health"; "The Soviet Union and Jews"; "The Soviet Union and Women."

"Ice Cream." Song, from *Street Scene*. Hughes and Elmer Rice* wrote the lyrics, and Kurt Weill* composed the music. ASCAP* lists the song as being published by Chappell and Company, Inc., and by Hampshire House Publishers. The song's ASCAP registry number is 390089055. *See also* "Ain't It Awful, the Heat"; "A Boy like You"; "Catch Me If You Can"; "Don't Forget the Lilac Bush"; "I Got a Marble and a Star"; "I Loved Her, Too."

"If You Would." Poem of eighteen lines in free verse. It gives a list of things to which "You" could put a halt, including factories, trains, and atom-bomb production; therefore, "You" might include unionized workers, voters, or any large grassroots group capable of exerting political will. The poem was first published in *Rong, Wrong*. The editors of *Collected Poems* did not find a date of publication for this magazine but speculate that it was published in 1961.
Bibliography: *CP*, 533, 686.

"If-ing." Poem of four quatrains in black dialect.* The speaker suggests what he could buy with everything from small change to a million dollars, then announces that he is broke but is contented to continue "If-ing"—dreaming of what he could buy and do *if* he had the money. The poem was first published in the *Carmel Pine Cone* (April 5, 1941). It was also published in *Shakespeare in Harlem*.
Bibliography: *CP*, 226.

"Imagine." Poem of eighteen lines in four stanzas, each of which begins with the word "Imagine" and expresses incredulity that "they" (whites) could fear people (blacks) they label with such dehumanizing epithets as "black dog," "monkey," "donkey," and "nigger." The poem was first published in *Chelsea Eight* (October 1960). *See also* Revision, Process of, and Hughes.
Bibliography: *CP*, 468, 681.

"Impasse." Poem in two short-lined quatrains; the last words of the quatrains rhyme. The poem crystallizes the sense in which those whom the speaker addresses do not want to know him, and in which he no longer cares whether they want to know him. It is arguably one of Hughes's most potent short poems. It was first published under the title "So" in the *Colorado Review* (Spring/Summer 1957).

Bibliography: *CP*, 458.

"In a Mexican City." Short story. *See The Brownie's Book.*

"In a Troubled Key." Poem in two stanzas in traditional blues* form. In the second stanza the speaker threatens violence against his lover. The poem was first published in *Shakespeare in Harlem*.

Bibliography: *CP*, 249.

"In Explanation of Our Times." Sixty-line free-verse poem that explicitly discusses terms loaded with class status, such as "coolie" and "mister," and that more indirectly links the interests of lower-class people in China, India, and the United States. The poem mentions Gerald L. K. Smith, founder of the America First Party, a right-wing political group that boycotted Hughes's poetry readings in the 1940s. Smith was associated with southern Democrats (including Georgia governor Eugene Talmadge; *see* "Governor Fires Dean"), who fiercely opposed the New Deal policies of President Franklin Roosevelt,* who sometimes referred to "New Dealers" as "nigger lovers," and who generally supported Jim Crow laws* (*see* Sitkoff). The poem was first published in *Olivant Quarterly* (1955). *See* "Goodbye Christ."

Bibliography: *CP*, 449–450, 670; Harvard Sitkoff, "A Rift in the Coalition" (chapter 5), in *A New Deal for Blacks: The Emergence of Civil Rights as a National Issue: The Depression Decade* (New York: Oxford University Press, 1978), 102–138, especially 106–108.

"In Henry's Back Yard." Song. Hughes wrote the lyrics, and Tom Glazer composed the music. ASCAP* lists the song as being published by Universal/ MCA Music, and the song's ASCAP registry number is 390122124.

"In the Dark." Short story, included in the collection *Simple Speaks His Mind*. *See* Simple [Jesse B.] Stories.

"In the Mist of the Moon." Nine-line poem addressed to a "Nanette" and celebrating her sensuality and beauty, first published in *Lincoln University News* (1927).

Bibliography: *CP*, 101.

"In the Time of Silver Rain." Song. *See* "In Time of Silver Rain."

"In Time of Silver Rain." Poem of twenty-four short lines. It is one of Hughes's most conventional nature poems, celebrating the restorative powers of spring rain. It was first published in *Opportunity** (June 1938). Later, Jean Berger set the poem to music. ASCAP* lists the song as being published by Broude Brothers, Ltd.; the song's ASCAP registry number is 390379303. ASCAP also lists "In *the* [emphasis added] Time of Silver Rain," with Hughes again as lyricist but with Howard Swanson as composer. This is most likely the same poem with different music. The ASCAP registry number is 390310279, and the publisher is listed as Weintraub Music, Inc. Rampersad mentions yet a third composer who set the poem to music, Edward Ballantine, but Ballantine's version is not listed by ASCAP, nor is additional information about it supplied by Rampersad or other biographers. However, the electronic database World Cat indicates that two manuscript scores of Ballantine's version of this song are held in the collection of the New England Conservatory of Music. Finally, ASCAP lists a song, "Silver Rain," with words by Hughes and music by Robert Owens, but lists no publisher. This song is a fourth musical version of "In Time of Silver Rain"; its ASCAP registry number is 490761576. It is part of a song cycle, *Silver Rain*, in which Owens also set to music "Carolina Cabin," "Fulfillment," "Night Song," "Silence," and "Songs."

Bibliography: *CP*, 203–204; Robert Owens [composer], *Silver Rain: Song Cycle for Tenor and Piano* (Munich: Orlando-Musikverlag, 1975); Rampersad, II, 177.

"Income Tax." Short story, included in *The Best of Simple*. *See* Simple [Jesse B.] Stories.

Ingram, Garnett. Wife of Zell Ingram.*

Ingram, Zell (1909?–?). Friend and traveling companion of Hughes's. As Hughes notes in *I Wonder As I Wander*, he met Ingram at Karamu House (where many of Hughes's early plays were produced by the Gilpin Players*) in Cleveland in 1930. The two struck up a friendship, traveled through the American South together, and ultimately traveled together to Haiti and other Caribbean islands in 1931. Rampersad describes the friendship in some detail, picturing Ingram as "a big, handsome, young black man, about twenty-one years old [at the time he met Hughes], who lived with his mother over a popular Cleveland hot-dog shop" (I, 201). Ingram had graduated from Cleveland's Central High School* some years after Hughes did. Ingram figures significantly in several chapters of *I Wonder As I Wander*. Hughes and Ingram collaborated on the unpublished "Journals: 1931/The Official Daily Log Book—Jersey to the West Indies." The "Journals" are part of the Langston Hughes Papers in the James Weldon Johnson Memorial Collection, Beinecke Rare Book and Manuscript Library, Yale University. Ingram designed a wood-block cover for Hughes's privately printed book of poems, *Dear Lovely Death*. Ingram and his wife, Garnett,* attended the opening of *Street Scene*. *See* Coloma.

Bibliography: *I Wonder As I Wander*, 33, 40–41; Rampersad, I, 200–213; II, 120.

"Inside Us." Short story. *See* "One Friday Morning."

"Interne at Provident." Forty-two-line poem depicting a black medical intern at work in a hospital. The poem also suggests that the intern will one day visit (or return to?) Africa to practice medicine. The poem's diction, phrasing, heavy use of assonance and consonance, and dense imagery are atypical of Hughes's poetry, even if placing a profession against a backdrop of race and class is by no means unusual for him. The poem was first published in *One-Way Ticket*.
Bibliography: *CP*, 373–374.

"Interview." Short story, included in the collection *Simple's Uncle Sam. See* Simple [Jesse B.] Stories.

**"Introduction" to *I Hear the People Singing: Selected Poems of Walt Whitman. See* Whitman, Walt.

"Introduction" to *Pudd'nhead Wilson* by Mark Twain (New York: Bantam, 1959), v–ix. The novel by Twain (1835–1910) was originally titled *Pudd'nhead Wilson and Those Extraordinary Twins* and was published in 1894 (New York: Harper). In the novel Roxana, an African American slave, gives birth to a child fathered by a white man and decides to switch the baby with one just born to her master and his wife. The grimly satiric plot follows the lives of the "twins" but focuses chiefly on Roxana's biological child, Valet de Cambres (Chambers), who, when switched, becomes Thomas a Becket (Tom). Pudd'nhead Wilson, a lawyer whose hobby is collecting fingerprints, ultimately reveals the switch and exposes the false "Tom" as a thief. "Tom" is "sold down the river" as a slave, and "Chambers" becomes a "white" property owner. Hughes calls the book an "ironic little novel" and praises Twain for depicting blacks in ways that are not stereotypical. He also deftly analyzes Twain's adaptation of elements from conventional melodrama in crafting the satiric narrative. Bantam Books (New York) reissued the 1959 edition in 1994 with Hughes's "Introduction."
Bibliography: Mark Twain, *Pudd'nhead Wilson*, introduction by Langston Hughes (New York: Bantam Books, 1994).

"Irish Wake." Eight-line rhyming poem focusing on the cathartic nature of an Irish wake, first published in *The Dream Keeper*.
Bibliography: *CP*, 167.

"Is Hollywood Fair to Negroes?" Essay. As Jemie observes, Hughes's answer to the title question is "an unequivocal 'No' " (107). Jemie adds, "Hollywood, he argues, presents a one-sided picture of blacks: the same age-old stereotypes dating back to minstrelsy." The essay was published in *Negro Digest* (April 1965), 19–21.

Bibliography: Onwuchekwa Jemie, "Hughes's Black Esthetic," in Mullen, 95–120.

"Is It True?" Poem. *See Ask Your Mama.*

"Is Massa Gwine to Sell Us Tomorrow?" Song. *See Jerico-Jim Crow.*

"Island [1]." Poem of four couplets in which island and wave become symbols, respectively, of hope and sorrow; a hint of suicide is noticeable because the speaker fears not being able to reach "the island" before sorrow drowns him. The poem was first published under the title "Wave of Sorrow" in the *Minnesota Quarterly* (1950). *See* Religion.

Bibliography: *CP*, 376.

"Island [2]." Poem. *See Montage of a Dream Deferred.*

"It Gives Me Pause." Four-line epigrammatic poem concerning the wages of sin, first published in the *Carmel Pine Cone* (July 25, 1941). *See* Religion.

Bibliography: *CP*, 235.

"I've Got the World By the Tail." Song. *See* "I Got the World by the Tail."

J

"Jaime." Poem in two quatrains. The title character sits alone on a hill gazing out to sea and beyond to "a mirage-land / That will never be." The poem was first published in *Fields of Wonder*.

Bibliography: *CP*, 336.

"Jam Session." Poem. *See Montage of a Dream Deferred.*

"Jamaica." Essay, a travel article about Jamaica, focusing on the island as a place to take a vacation. It was published in *Ebony* (November 1948).

Jazz. Rooted in the blues,* jazz is a genre of music comprising a variety of musical styles expressed through numerous instruments and combinations thereof. Major suggests that variants of the word "jazz" can be traced back as far as the 1620s and speculates that "jazz" is "very likely a modern word for *jaja* (Bantu), which means to dance, to play music; early variants are 'Jas,' 'jass,' and 'jasy'; a type of black music derived from blues, work songs, spirituals; possibly a Creole version of the Ki-Kongo word *dinza*, and the early New Orleans variant 'jizz' " (255).

"Stride" and "boogie-woogie" styles of piano playing from the early twentieth century are two crucial bridges between blues and jazz; they are rhythmically innovative styles that made blues songs and ballads* more dance oriented. "Ragtime" piano music is also an important link, but it is a more technically formal style. Perhaps the most significant development in early jazz, however, was the rise of the orchestra (or band or "combo"). As early as 1917, the Original Dixieland Jazz Band, which blended the spirit of improvisation and syncopation with a variety of string and horn instruments, as well as drums, developed a distinctive style of jazz.

Like the blues, jazz is indigenous to the United States but represents a complex mixture of African, European, and Caribbean traditions, draws heavily on African American folk and urban culture, and has had enormous impact on popular American culture, musical theatre, symphonic music, and written and visual arts. Jazz was also an integral part of the Harlem Renaissance,* when cabarets, nightclubs, and theatres flourished. It was also primarily responsible for drawing whites to Harlem,* creating situations that were often more than ironic. (Lewis observes, "Until the playhouse and concert hall guided white traffic above Central Park [into Harlem], the New York and national press had deigned to mention Harlem merely to insult, alarm, or ridicule—squibs about primitive hygiene, grisly homicides, religious aberrations" [163]). For example, while the Cotton Club was famous for its jazz and was one venue at which Duke Ellington* and his orchestra played, it only rarely allowed black patrons through its doors. For another example, white performers like Al Jolson would wear dark makeup ("blackface") and perform jazz songs for white audiences. This sort of troubled, ironic, potentially exploitative social and artistic relationship between blacks and whites is one Hughes examines in such works as "Slave on the Block" and "The Blues I'm Playing." Jazz was but the most obvious of many cultural "sites" for such relationships and was often therefore not just a genre of music but also a nexus for social, political, and even economic conflict.

Fletcher Henderson, Duke Ellington, King Oliver, Kid Ory, Bix Beiderbecke, Louis "Satchmo" Armstrong, Bessie Smith, Ethel Waters, James P. Johnson,* and Earl "Fatha" Hines are but a few of numerous performers, composers, and bandleaders now associated with the Harlem jazz scene, even though they may have had stronger musical and social connections to other cities, including Chicago, New Orleans, and, in the case of Ellington, Washington, D.C. Other figures associated with relatively early innovations in orchestral jazz are Jelly Roll Morton, Jack Teagarden, James Miley, and Fats Waller. Benny Goodman, Count Basie, Billie Holiday, Art Tatum, Sidney Bichet, and Charlie "Bird" Parker are among the figures crucial to the development of jazz in the 1930s and 1940s, as were such popular bandleaders as Artie Shaw and Glenn Miller. After World War II the popularity of dance-oriented "swing" jazz began to wane, and experimentation flourished, influenced by soloists such as Miles Davis, Thelonius Monk, Sonny Rollins, Dizzy Gillespie, Oscar Peterson, John Coltrane, Horace Silver, and Charles Mingus. (This period saw the rise of "be-bop" jazz.) Hughes (reading his poetry) collaborated with bass player Charles Mingus and his band on the sound recording *The Weary Blues* (1958).

Because it is driven by improvisation, thrives on innovation, appeals to a spectrum of audiences, and blends with other forms of music, jazz remains an unpredictable, robust, flexible genre—and a controversial one, insofar as performers, composers, discographers, historians, and listeners never cease debating about which eras, forms, and styles of jazz are "purer," better, more or less derivative, more or less pretentious, and so on. In general, Hughes was probably more influenced by the blues than by jazz, though of course the two forms of music are intricately interwoven, so that separating the influence of each on his work is not always possible or even desirable. Nonetheless, many of his works concern aspects of jazz culture, such as the diverse audiences of jazz, the eccentric, often-difficult lives of jazz performers, and the sensuality of jazz. Examples include "Beale Street," "Cabaret," "Cabaret Girl Dies on Welfare Island," "Jazz as Communication," "Jazz Band in a Parisian Café," "Jazz Girl," "Juice Joint: Northern City," "Lady in a Cabaret," "The New Cabaret Girl," and "Nude Young Dancer." He was also alert to conflicts, ironies, and debates (musical and otherwise) caused by or at least located in jazz, as revealed in such works as "Be-Bop Boys," "Conservatory Student Struggles with Higher Instrumentation," "Jazz, Jive, and Jam," and "Rejuvenation through Joy." Moreover, two of his major works, *Montage of a Dream Deferred* and *Ask Your Mama*, are enormously influenced by jazz and can be classified as genuine "jazz poetry." Structural patterns, phraseology, the "collage" or "montage" of imagery, the direct references to songs, sounds, motifs, and terminology of jazz, shifts of mood and tone, and urban themes all suggest the extent to which Hughes understood, appreciated, and drew inspiration from jazz and the extent to which he perceived poetry and jazz to be cognate arts. Indeed, as Rampersad notes, the customarily modest Hughes viewed *Montage of a Dream Deferred* as a "*tour de force*" in part because it seemed to him to fuse jazz and poetry in such original ways (II, 151). Similarly, *Ask Your Mama* was written not just as a long poem to be read on the page but as a jazz performance piece (*see* Bonds, Margaret). Although Jack Kerouac and other members of the Beat Generation would attract more publicity for fusing literature and jazz, Hughes anticipated many of the jazz-influenced innovations in their work (*see* Tracy in the Bibliography). *See also* Audio Recordings of Hughes; Poetics; Songs.

Bibliography/Discography: Amiri Baraka, *Black Music* (New York: Morrow, 1967); David Chinitz, " 'Dance, Little Lady': Poets, Flappers, and the Gendering of Jazz," in *Modernism, Gender, and Culture: A Cultural Studies Approach*, ed. Lisa Rado (New York: Garland, 1997), 319–335; Scott Knowles Deveaux, *The Birth of Bebop* (Berkeley: University of California Press, 1997); Walter C. Farrell, Jr., and Patricia A. Johnson, "Poetic Interpretations of Urban Black Folk Culture: Langston Hughes and the 'Bebop' Era," *MELUS: The Journal of the Society for the Study of the Multi-Ethnic Literature of the United States* 8, no. 3 (Fall 1981), 57–72; *A History of Jazz: The New York Scene* [sound recording] (New York: RBF Records, 1961); Frank Kofsky, *Black Music, White Business: Illuminating the History and Political Economy of Jazz* (New York: Pathfinder, 1998); Gene Lees, *Cats of Any Color: Jazz Black and White* (New York: Oxford University Press, 1994); Lewis, *WHWV*; Leonard Lyons, *The 101 Best Jazz Albums: A History of Jazz on Records* (New York: Morrow, 1980); Clarence Major, "Jazz," in *Juba to Jive: A Dictionary of African-American Slang* (New York: Penguin, 1994), 255; Toni Morrison, *Jazz* (New York: Plume, 1992); Leroy Ostransky, *The Anatomy of Jazz* (Seattle: University of Washington Press, 1964); Brian Priestley, *Mingus: A Critical Biography* (New York: Da Capo Press, 1983); Rampersad, I, II, 149–152; Gunther Schuller,

Early Jazz: Its Roots and Musical Development (New York: Oxford University Press, 1968); Tracy; Mark Tucker, ed. *The Duke Ellington Reader* (New York: Oxford University Press, 1993); Watson.

"Jazz as Communication." Essay that stresses the extent to which jazz is more audience centered than other forms of music, and the extent to which it "speaks to" a wide variety of people. The essay also predicts the demise of rock-and-roll music—music that in Hughes's view, sprang directly from jazz. It was first published in the *Chicago Defender** (date unknown) and was also published in *The Langston Hughes Reader*.

Bibliography: *The Langston Hughes Reader*, 492–494.

"Jazz Band in a Parisian Café." Free-verse poem of twenty-two lines. Early in the poem a speaker exhorts the band to play and suggests how socially diverse the audience is. Later another speaker, seemingly a member of the band, takes over and makes a "pass" at a young woman. The poem was first published in *Crisis** (December 1925). *See* Jazz; Revision, Process of, and Hughes.

Bibliography: *CP*, 60.

"Jazz Girl." Thirteen-line poem spoken by a mellow but dissipated "girl" in a bar. The poem ends, "Sure, go ahead, / Buy a drink for me." It was first published in the *Baltimore Afro American** (May 16, 1942). *See* "America's Young Black Joe"; Jazz.

Bibliography: *CP*, 571.

"Jazz, Jive, and Jam." Short story, included in *The Best of Simple*. *See* Simple [Jesse B.] Stories. *See also* Jive.

"Jazz Songs." This title is listed as a single song by ASCAP*; the ASCAP registry number is 400133173. However, three composers (in addition to Hughes, as lyricist) are listed (Eileen "Betty" Bishop, Stefan De Haan, and Jacqueline Froom), so the listing may in fact represent several songs, but whether they might be previously published poems or new lyrics set to music is unclear because no additional information appears, and Rampersad (for example) does not mention this title. ASCAP lists the publisher of "Jazz Songs" as the Performing Right Society, Ltd., the address of which at this writing is 22/23 Berners Street, London, England W1P 4AA. In 1972, York Edition published *Jazz Songs: For Soprano & Double Bass*, composed by Betty Roe. Among the songs is "Madam and the Minister." Therefore, the ASCAP information about "Jazz Songs" may be inaccurate, Betty Roe may be the Eileen

"Betty" Bishop to which ASCAP refers, and "Madam and the Minister" is probably the only Hughes work in the "Jazz Songs" ASCAP lists.

Bibliography: Betty Roe [composer], *Jazz Songs: For Soprano & Double Bass* (London: York Edition, 1972).

"Jazzonia." Poem in six stanzas, three of which are a refrain. The poem pictures and celebrates a Harlem* "jazz* cabaret," a six-member band, and a dancing girl who is compared to Eve and Cleopatra. It was first published in *Crisis** (August 1923).

Bibliography: *CP*, 34.

"Jazztet Muted." Poem. *See Ask Your Mama.*

"Jealousy." Short story, included in *The Best of Simple. See* Simple [Jesse B.] Stories.

Jeffers, Robinson and Una. Acquaintances and townsfolk of Hughes during his sojourns in Carmel-by-the-Sea, California. Stern skeptic and reclusive realist, John Robinson Jeffers (1887–1962) was a poet and tragedian who portrayed a beautiful and balanced but uncaring and fierce universe in which humans could find their way only by appreciating their own insignificance and shedding their self-absorption. Alfred Kreymborg characterizes Jeffers by opposing forces: "the lover and the hater, the human and the hermit, the man and the superman" (624). Jeffers had compassion for human beings, whom he saw as perpetually troubled or afflicted, but he despised the venality and egoism that led to problems and ills. He assayed humanity by balancing classical (usually Greek) examples against modern Californians, but shunned the company of humans in favor of enduring stone and alluring hawks. His verse was cruelly honest, uncivilly direct, and fiercely unadorned but festooned with residues from his study of Greek, Latin, French, German, the physical sciences, forestry, physiology, philosophy, and theology. Born and raised in Pittsburgh, Jeffers attended a succession of schools on the west coast, where he met Una Call Kuster (1884–1950). She was three years his senior and was studying literature for her bachelor's and master's degrees at the University of Southern California as the wife of a young attorney. After an intermittent affair and her somewhat scandalous divorce, the couple married and moved to Carmel-by-the-Sea. Soon after their arrival, Robinson Jeffers found two refrains that oriented his career and life: horror at human frailty and wretchedness (represented to him most acutely at that time by trench warfare and poison gas in World War I) and Tor House. Tor House was (and is) a house of stone that Robinson, Una, and their twins Donnan and Garth built on a craggy cape overlooking the Pacific Ocean. Nearby was and is Hawk Tower, four stories of stone that Robinson Jeffers built.

Langston Hughes visited both Tor House and Hawk Tower in May 1932 after the Jefferses had attended Hughes's reading in Carmel. After Hughes returned from his fifteen months abroad, he luxuriated in a year of writing at his friend and patron Noel Sullivan's* cottage 'Ennesfree' in Carmel (beginning in September 1933) and thus saw the Jefferses on occasion. Hughes found Jeffers to be as laconic and reserved as his stone tower at first but warmer, if still a bit reticent, upon subsequent visits. Jeffers's oft-expressed contempt for the ordinary run of humanity and his borrowings from Greek tragedy and Nietzschean philosophy ran against Hughes's proclivities, but the two found common ground in poetry, and Jeffers's dislike of the mass of men did not extend to an outstanding individual such as Hughes. Hughes delighted in Una, whom he described as energetic, talkative, pretty, petite, and Republican. Hughes also observed (*I Wonder As I Wander*, 284) that Una guarded the solitude of her "Robin" quite vigorously. She discussed her political opinions freely with Hughes, who found Una quite conservative on national and international issues but harder to predict regarding local politics. Hughes particularly enjoyed a Big Sur beach picnic with Sullivan, "Robin," Una, wine, and salami sandwiches on his thirty-second birthday (*see* a picture between pages 278 and 279 of Rampersad, I). The Jefferses both so encouraged Hughes that he felt almost at home in Carmel despite its "whiteness" and its remoteness from Hughes's experience; the friendship between Hughes and Noel Sullivan was important, too. Hughes was able in Carmel to complete many of his projects, including *The Ways of White Folks* and *The Big Sea*. On the other hand, the Carmel literary community drew so many visiting personages that Hughes was harried by socializing from time to time. More serious harassment came from anti-communist agitation— Hughes was nearly driven from Carmel over his radicalism and involvement in the John Reed Club.* He revisited the Jefferses in Carmel in 1935 and sought Garth Jeffers's advice about herding horses for "Boy of the Border." In September 1940 "Robin" was among the Carmel friends at a "housewarming" of a cottage that Sullivan had constructed for Hughes. Hughes effusively toasted "Robin" on the latter's fifty-fourth birthday and published an appreciation of Jeffers's poetry in the *Carmel Pine Cone*. When Hughes revisited Carmel after the death of Una Jeffers in 1950, he remarked that her widower had greeted him quite warmly.

William Haltom

Bibliography: Robert Brophy, ed., *Robinson Jeffers: Dimensions of a Poet* (New York: Fordham University Press, 1995); Arthur B. Coffin, *Robinson Jeffers: Poet of Inhumanism* (Madison: University of Wisconsin Press, 1971); Bill Hotchkiss, *Jeffers: The Sivaistic Vision* (Newcastle, CA: Blue Oak Press, 1975); Langston Hughes, "Jeffers: Man, Sea, and Poetry," *Carmel Pine Cone* (June 10, 1941); *I Wonder As I Wander*, 284–285; James Karman, *Robinson Jeffers, Poet of California* (Ashland, Or: Story Line Press, 1995); Alfred Kreymborg, *History of American Poetry* (New York: Tudor Publishing Company, 1934), 624–630. Rampersad, I, 278–279; II.

"Jeffers: Man, Sea, and Poetry." Essay. *See* Jeffers, Robinson and Una.

Jerico-Jim Crow. Musical play in one act, first produced by the Greenwich Players, Inc., in coordination with the Congress of Racial Equality (CORE), the NAACP,* and the Student Nonviolent Coordinating Committee (SNCC) at the Sanctuary, 143 West 13th Street, New York. Hicklin lists the play as opening on December 28, 1963, probably because that was the scheduled date of the opening, but Rampersad explains that "following nervous conferences with Langston and the co-directors of the play, Alvin Ailey and William Hairston, Stella Holt postponed the official opening by a few days" (II, 370). In fact the play opened on January 12, 1964, at the Sanctuary, which was actually a basement space in the Greenwich Mews Theatre. The play ran through the spring of 1964. It combines gospel music with issues of racism and nonviolent protest, and Hughes dedicated the play "to the young people of all racial and religious backgrounds who are meeting, working, canvassing, petitioning, marching, picketing, sitting-in, singing and praying to help make a better America for all, especially for citizens of color" (Rampersad, II, 370). The figure of Jim Crow reappears throughout the play as a slave trader, a racist white Southerner, and a policeman. Rampersad argues that "[n]o production of any kind by Hughes ever received more extravagant praise than *Jerico-Jim Crow*" (II, 372). Shepard regarded it as "a rousing production [that] is an unabashedly sentimental and tuneful history of the Negro struggle up from slavery." The main actors were Rosalie King, Joseph Attles, Hilda Harris, Dorothy Drake, and Gilbert Price,* a young baritone with whom Hughes became close friends. (Attles and Drake would also appear in Hughes's musical play *Prodigal Son*, and Attles had appeared in *Tambourines to Glory*, the musical play). Hugh Porter was the musical director. The best-known song from the production is "Freedom Land," for which Hughes wrote the music as well as the words. Other songs are "I Been Buked [Rebuked] and I Been Scorned," "Is Massa Gwine to Sell Us Tomorrow?" "Slavery Chain Done Broke at Last," and "Such a Little King." The music was recorded on a long-playing album. *See Tambourines to Glory* (musical play); *Tambourines to Glory* (novel).

Bibliography/Discography: Hicklin, 183; *Jerico-Jim Crow* (New York: Folkways Records/FL 9671, 1964); Rampersad, II, 369–373; Richard F. Shepard, "Theater: A Rousing 'Jerico-Jim Crow,' " *New York Times* (January 13, 1964), section C, p. 4.

Jesse B. Simple. *See* Simple [Jesse B.] Stories.

"The Jester." Nineteen-line poem that first presents conventional images of the jester (half smiling, half frowning) but then focuses on a "black jester," a figure of ridicule who announces, "Once I was wise. / Shall I be wise again?" The poem was first published in *Opportunity** (December 1925). *See also* "A Black Pierrot"; "Pierrot."

Bibliography: *CP*, 56–57; Douglas Hunt and Kari Hunt, *Pantomime: The Silent Theater* (New York: Atheneum, 1964); Maurice Sand, *The History of the Harlequinade* (New York: Blom, 1968).

"The Jesus." Poem of twenty-eight lines. As Hughes informs the reader in a footnote, "The Jesus" was a ship lent to one John Hawkins by Queen Elizabeth I of England so that he might work in the slave trade, transporting kidnapped Africans to the New World. Although the poem is in free verse, it is one of Hughes's most linguistically rich works, full of internal rhymes and surprising alliteration, one result of which is a kind of gnarled, dense text in keeping with the tortured irony of a ship called "The Jesus" serving the slave trade. It was first published in *Chelsea Eight* (October 1960) under the pseudonym Durwood Collins. *See* Revision, Process of, and Hughes.

Bibliography: *CP*, 468.

"Jim Crow Car." Four-line poem. Alternate lines rhyme. The poem leaps from images of people having lunch on a segregated train car to an apocalyptic concluding image. It was first published in *Selected Poems* under the title "Lunch in a Jim Crow Car." *See* Jim Crow Laws; Religion.

Bibliography: *CP*, 467.

Jim Crow Laws. The term "Jim Crow Laws" refers to laws passed chiefly in states of the former Confederacy, laws aimed generally at curbing the rights of African Americans and specifically at denying African Americans access to public services or segregating services. Consequently, many African Americans in such states were, in effect, not allowed to vote, had to attend separate public schools and be treated at separate hospitals, could purchase homes only in certain parts of towns and cities, had to use "colored" sections of trains (and, later, buses), and so on. The "Black Codes" passed into law during Reconstruction formed the basis of Jim Crow laws, which states started passing in the 1890s, with another wave of similar laws coming about a decade later (Lofgren). Jim Crow laws and segregationist, "separate-but-equal" practices persisted into the 1960s and even influenced national policies. For example, during World War II the armed services of the United States were segregated. Although the federal Civil Rights Act of 1964 was designed, in part, to eradicate Jim Crow laws, much de facto segregation persisted. Major's terse definition of "Jim Crow" is "enforced segregation," and he indicates that the "term comes from the song 'Jim Crow,' featured in a Negro minstrel show by Thomas Rice (1808–1860)." In the poem "Gandhi Is Fasting," Hughes turns the term into a verb, referring both to citizens of India and African Americans as having been "jim-crowed." Hughes was an indefatigable opponent of Jim Crow laws and the beliefs behind them, producing poems, commentaries, and other works directly and indirectly expressing this opposition, often highlighting segregationist laws, regulations, and practices in northern states as well. A checklist of these works follows:

"Advertisement for the Waldorf Astoria"

"American Heartbreak"

"Ballad of Roosevelt"

"Ballad of Sam Solomon"

"Beaumont to Detroit: 1943"

Black Misery

"Colored Soldier"

"Crow Goes, Too"

"Dear Mr. President"

"Dixie Man to Uncle Sam"

"Dixie South Africa"

"Fourth of July Thought"

"Freedom Train"

"Freedom's Plow"

"From Selma"

"Gandhi Is Fasting"

"Get Up Off That Old Jive"

"Governor Fires Dean"

"How about It, Dixie?"

Jerico-Jim Crow

"Jim Crow Car"

"Jim Crow's Funeral"

Jim Crow's Last Stand

"Judge William Hastie"

"Let America Be America Again"

"Little Song on Housing"

"Lynching Song"

"Merry-Go-Round"

"Message to the President"

"The Mitchell Case"

"My Most Humiliating Jim Crow Experience"

"One-Way Ticket"

"Open Letter to the South"

"Poem to Uncle Sam"

"Song after Lynching"

"Southern Negro Speaks"

"Total War"

"Us: Colored"

"Visitors to the Black Belt"

"What Shall We Do about the South?"

"Where Service Is Needed"

"Will V-Day Be Me-Day[,] Too?"

See also Angelo Herndon Jones; Brown v. Board of Education; Don't You Want to Be Free? "Here to Yonder"; *Herndon v. Lowry;* The Scottsboro Boys; *Scottsboro Limited;* "The Soviet Union and Color."

Bibliography: Dwight B. Billings, Jr., *Planters and the Making of a "New South": Class, Politics, and Development in North Carolina, 1865–1900* (Chapel Hill: University of North Carolina Press, 1979); Abraham L. Davis and Barbara Luck Graham, *The Supreme Court, Race, and Civil Rights* (Thousand Oaks, CA: Sage Publications, 1995), especially chapter 1, "From Marshall to Fuller: The Era of White Supremacy and Second-Class Citizenship, 1801–1910," 1–27; Christopher De Santis, ed., *Langston Hughes and the Chicago Defender: Essays on Race, Politics, and Culture, 1942–62* (Urbana: University of Illinois Press, 1995); Eric Foner, *Reconstruction: America's Unfinished Revolution, 1863–1877* (New York: Harper and Row, 1988); "Cuban Color Lines," "Death House at Kilby," and "Tragedy at Hampton" (involving the case of Juliette Derricotte), in *I Wonder As I Wander*, 10–15, 41–44; C. A. Lofgren, *The Plessy Case: A Legal-Historical Interpretation* (New York: Oxford University Press, 1987); Clarence Major, *Juba to Jive: A Dictionary of African-American Slang*, 2nd ed. (New York: Penguin, 1994), 258; C. Vann Woodward, *The Strange Career of Jim Crow*, 3rd ed. (New York: Oxford University Press, 1974) (Woodward also figured in the trial of Angelo Herndon; *see Herndon v. Lowry*).

"Jim Crow's Funeral." Short story, included in the collection *Simple Stakes a Claim. See* Simple [Jesse B.] Stories. *See also* Jim Crow Laws.

Jim Crow's Last Stand (Atlanta: Negro Publication Society of America, 1943). 32 pp. Collection of poetry. It contains the poems "Ballad of Sam Solomon," "The Black Man Speaks," "Blue Bayou," "Color," "Daybreak in Alabama," "Freedom [2]," "Good Morning, Stalingrad," "How about It, Dixie?" "Jim Crow's Last Stand," "Me and My Song," "Motherland," "Note on Commercial Theatre," "Note to All Nazis Fascists and Klansmen" [*sic*], "Red Cross," "Still Here," "To Captain Mulzac," and "Visitors to the Black Belt." Each of these poems has its own entry in this encyclopedia.
Bibliography: Rampersad, II, 130–133.

"Jim Crow's Last Stand." Thirty-two-line poem in rhyming couplets. It is essentially a versified argument as to why Jim Crow laws* cannot survive Japan's bombing of Pearl Harbor (December 7, 1941) because if the United States is to join World War II to fight fascism, it cannot logically support antidemocratic domestic laws. It was first published in *Jim Crow's Last Stand.* Marian Anderson,* Joe Louis,* and Paul Robeson* are mentioned in the poem.
Bibliography: *CP,* 299.

"Jitney." Poem of forty-eight extremely short lines, some of them consisting entirely of street numbers, such as "31st." As well as listing the streets on the route of the (New York City?) jitney (bus), the poem records snatches of conversation between riders. Duke Ellington* is mentioned, as is Al Hibler,* one of the musicians in his band. The poem was first published in *Circuit* (January 1947) and was included in *One-Way Ticket.*
Bibliography: *CP*, 371–372.

Jive. An African American slang word. Major indicates that it may have entered the language as early as 1630 as "jev" or "jew" and that "from the forties [1940s] and fifties [1950s] 'jive' meant deceit, nonsense, [or] to put someone on. Some researchers believe it may be a distortion of the English word 'jibe' " (259–260). Major also indicates that in the 1960s "jive" often referred to marijuana, but Hughes did not use the word in this context. *See* "Get Up off That Old Jive"; "Jazz, Jive, and Jam."
Bibliography: Clarence Major, ed., "Jive," in *Juba to Jive: A Dictionary of African-American Slang*, 2nd ed. (New York: Penguin, 1994), 138.

"Joan Baez: A Tribute." Liner notes for a recording (1964). *See* Baez, Joan.

"Joe Louis [1]." Poem. *See Montage of a Dream Deferred. See also* "Jim Crow's Last Stand"; "Joe Louis [2]"; Louis, Joe.

"Joe Louis [2]." Poem of five quatrains (stanza five is stretched to five lines) in which Joe Louis* is praised for joining the U.S. Army in World War II and for being "a man / for any man to imitate." It was first published in the *Baltimore Afro American** (November 3, 1942). *See also* "America's Young Black Joe."
Bibliography: *CP*, 575.

"Johannesburg Mines." Nine-line poem reporting that 240,000 native Africans work in the (diamond) mines of Johannesburg, South Africa, but also implying that Hughes does not know what to make poetically of this fact, which at the time probably represented—to him and many others—widespread exploitation of cheap labor. Implicitly, it is a poem that ponders the relationship between poetry and social problems. It was first published in four long lines in *Crisis** (February 1925). *See* "Dixie South Africa"; "Question [1]."
Bibliography: *CP*, 43.

"John Henry." Song, from *Simply Heavenly*. Hughes wrote the lyrics, and David Martin composed the music. ASCAP* lists the song as being published by the Bourne Company, and the song's ASCAP registry number is 400016488.

John Reed Club. Network of organizations named after the American writer and activist John Reed.* The clubs were influenced by Marxist ideas and were committed to advancing socialism and improving the status of workers in the United States. With chapters in many regions of the United States, the John Reed Club was active in the 1930s. Hughes became involved with the John Reed Club in Carmel, California, when he and his friend Noel Sullivan* lent support to striking longshoremen in San Francisco and to agricultural workers in California's Central Valley. *See Harvest*; Jeffers, Robinson and Una; Marxism; Politics.
Bibliography: William Phillips, "Histories of the Left," *Partisan Review* 60, no. 3 (Summer 1993), 337–401; Rampersad, I; Rita James Simon, ed., *As We Saw the Thirties: Essays on Social and Political Movements of a Decade* (Urbana: University of Illinois Press, 1967).

Johnny. The nominal "author" of two epistolary poems, "Letter from Spain" and "Postcard from Spain."

Johnson, Alberta K. (Madam). *See* The Madam Poems.

Johnson, Arabella. A character in the poem, "Death in Harlem."

Johnson, Charles S. (1893–1956). American sociologist, college president, professor, editor, and writer. Johnson was born in Virginia and graduated with honors from Virginia Union University. He served in the U.S. infantry in World

War I, seeing action in France. Upon his return from the war, he studied sociology at the University of Chicago under the tutelage of Robert E. Park, who had worked with Booker T. Washington* and was a progressive sociologist but who believed that "racial" groups had distinct essential qualities. (He viewed Jews and "Negroes" as racial groups.) In Chicago Johnson helped write a massive report about race relations in that city, *The Negro in Chicago: A Study of Race Relations and a Race Riot* (1922). Soon thereafter he departed for New York City to work with the National Urban League and edit that organization's magazine, *Opportunity*,* in which Hughes published many works. Lewis characterizes Johnson as a mediator between the competing social philosophies of W.E.B. Du Bois* and Booker T. Washington. Specifically, suggests Lewis, Johnson agreed with Washington's view that African American inequality would persist and needed to be faced with patience, but he agreed with Du Bois's belief that an elite group of African American intellectuals must define and direct African American social advancement. Johnson enacted this belief in part by trying to shape the character of the Harlem Renaissance,* of which he is considered one chief architect. Hutchinson discusses ways in which Johnson was influenced by John Dewey's philosophy of pragmatism. Johnson joined the faculty of Fisk University in 1928 and became president of Fisk in 1946.

Bibliography: "Charles Spurgeon Johnson, 1893–1956" [obituary], *New York Times* (October 28, 1956), 88; Matthew William Dunne, "Next Steps: Charles S. Johnson and Southern Liberalism," *Journal of Negro History* 83, no. 1 (Winter 1998), 1–34; Hutchinson, 50–51; Charles S. Johnson, *The Negro in American Civilization: A Study of Negro Life and Race Relations in the Light of Social Research* (New York: Henry Holt, 1930); Lewis, *WHWV*, 45–49.

Johnson, Essie Belle. One of the main characters in *Tambourines to Glory* (the play and the novel). With Laura Reed, she establishes a church in Harlem,* but unlike Laura, she is sincere about the project.

Johnson, Georgia Douglas (1886–1966). American poet, playwright, and teacher. Johnson (born Georgia Douglas) was born and grew up in Atlanta, where she attended Atlanta University. She also received training at the Oberlin Conservatory of Music. Shortly after marrying, Johnson and her husband moved to Washington, D.C., where she began working for the federal government and publishing poetry. Her books of verse include *The Heart of a Woman* (1918), *Bronze* (1922), and *An Autumn Love Cycle* (1928). At her home in Washington, Johnson cultivated a literary "salon society," hosting such Harlem Renaissance* notables as Alain Locke,* Jean Toomer,* W.E.B. Du Bois,* Jessie Fauset,* and Hughes. Hughes included poems by Johnson in *The Poetry of the Negro*.

Bibliography: Roger M. Valade III, *The Essential Black Literature Guide* (Detroit: Visible Ink Press, 1996), 197–198.

Johnson, Grace. *See* Harlem Suitcase Theatre.

Johnson, James P. (1894–1955). American pianist and composer. Johnson was born in New Brunswick, New Jersey, but when he was a teenager, his family moved to New York City, where he encountered ragtime piano music, the blues,* musical theatre, and classical music. He took piano instruction from Bruto Giannini and learned the ragtime style of piano playing by listening to and working with Eubie Blake and other performers. By 1913 he was performing professionally and composing songs, including "The Harlem Strut" and "Carolina Shout." It is somewhat unusual that Johnson remains underappreciated, because he composed and performed much of the music associated not just with the Harlem Renaissance* but with the Roaring Twenties. For example, the first Broadway musical for which he composed music included "The Charleston," the song that is perhaps the musical symbol of the United States in the 1920s, of an era featuring cosmopolitan mores, and of a dance step that became an immense popular "craze." He is also considered to be the "father" of the enormously influential style of piano playing known as "stride piano," which shaped subsequent styles of jazz* music. In addition to composing popular ragtime, blues, and musical-theatre songs, Johnson also composed ambitious orchestral pieces, including *Yamekraw*, a rhapsody, which William Grant Still* arranged when it was performed at Carnegie Hall in 1927, with the renowned Fats Waller as soloist. In 1940 Johnson and Hughes collaborated on a blues opera, *De Organizer*, path-breaking for its fusion of blues and opera and for its theme, which concerned relatively radical labor politics. Johnson performed as a jazz pianist throughout the 1930s and early 1940s. Then he suffered a series of strokes, one of which incapacitated him in 1951. Among other libraries, the Library of Congress holds numerous recordings of Johnson's music, but it holds neither a recording nor a score of *De Organizer*. In 1992 the Concordia Chamber Symphony of Manhattan performed several of Johnson's works. A compact-disc recording of this music was later released. Hughes, Carlton Moss, and Johnson also began to collaborate on an opera entitled *Pied Piper of Swing* but did not complete it. The unfinished manuscript is held in the Langston Hughes Papers of the James Weldon Johnson Memorial Collection, Beinecke Rare Book and Manuscript Library, Yale University.

Bibliography/Discography: *James P. Johnson: King of Stride Piano* (Giants of Jazz [Italy], 1998); *James P. Johnson, 1921–1928* [compact disc] (New York: Jazz Chronological Classics, 1994); *James P. Johnson, Volume 2* [compact disc] (New York: Jazz Chronological Classics, 1996); *James P. Johnson, 1944–1945* [compact disc] (New York: Jazz Chronological Classics, 1999); Willa Rouder, "James P(rice) Johnson," in *The New Grove Dictionary of American Music*, ed. H. Wiley Hitchcock and Stanley Sadie (New York: Grove's Dictionaries of Music, 1986), vol. 2, 580–581 (includes extensive bibliography and discography); Leslie Stifelman, "James P. Johnson: A Composer Rescued," *Columbia Journal of American Studies* 1, no. 1 (1995), 17–19.

Johnson, James Weldon (1871–1938). American poet, novelist, songwriter, diplomat, political leader, and professor. Johnson was born and grew up in

Jacksonville, Florida, in relatively comfortable, middle-class surroundings. Originally his middle name was William, which he changed to Weldon, believing
that it was less commonplace (Lewis, 146). He attended Atlanta University and,
as a freshman, volunteered to teach rural African American children in Georgia,
an experience he described as life-changing, in part because it made him more
aware of his own African American heritage and made him look at African
American history differently. In 1900 he wrote the song "Lift Ev'ry Voice and
Sing," which soon became—and remains—the unofficial "national anthem" of
African Americans. In 1901 Johnson moved to New York City and made a
living writing songs and librettos, as well as a campaign song for Theodore
Roosevelt, "You're All Right, Teddy." Six years later he changed careers, joined
the diplomatic corps, and went on to serve as U.S. consul in Venezuela and
Nicaragua. The year 1913 brought yet another career change: Johnson returned
to New York to edit the newspaper *New York Age*. His politically oriented
writing for that newspaper resulted in his being asked to serve as chief organizer
for the NAACP,* and in 1920 he became the first African American president
of that organization. (Lewis characterizes him as "a superb public speaker and
an even better arbitrator and politician" [143].) Johnson's literary achievements
are as impressive as his range of expertise. He edited the important anthology
The Book of American Negro Poetry (1922), which, like *The New Negro*, edited
by Alain Locke,* helped forge one coherent perspective on African American
writing. His novel *The Autobiography of an Ex-Colored Man* (1912) remains
an American classic. His best-known book of poetry is *God's Trombones* (1927).

Although the lives and careers of Johnson and Hughes did not intersect extensively, similarities between the two men are several. Both came from middle-
class backgrounds but developed a deep interest in folk traditions and a
commitment to bettering the lives of working people. Both were versatile writers, working in genres ranging from poetry and fiction to popular songs and
journalism, and both contributed significantly to the Harlem Renaissance.* Certainly Johnson was drawn to the world of politics much more intensely than
was Hughes, even as Hughes was much more devoted to writing. Nonetheless,
the vision each had for the United States and for African Americans was remarkably similar. Johnson spent the last years of his life as the holder of the
Spence Chair in Creative Writing at Fisk University. He died in an automobile
accident in 1938. One of the most important collections of African American
literary material is the James Weldon Johnson Collection at Yale University,
which includes the bulk of Hughes's papers, letters, and manuscripts (the Langston Hughes Papers).

Bibliography: Eugene Levy, *James Weldon Johnson: Black Leader, Black Voice* (Chicago: University of Chicago Press, 1973); Lewis, *WHWV*.

Johnson, Marietta. Daughter of Essie Belle Johnson* in *Tambourines to Glory*
(the play and the novel). She visits her mother in Harlem,* having arrived from

the South, where she goes to college. She decides to remain in Harlem and help with the church her mother founded with Laura Reed, and she falls in love with a church musician, C. J. Eventually they marry.

Jones, Buddy. The name of a character in the play *Angelo Herndon Jones* and of a different character in the poem "Stony Lonesome."

Jones, Edith. *See* Harlem Suitcase Theatre.

Jones, Everett LeRoy. *See* Baraka, Amiri.

Jones, James Earl. *See* Harlem Suitcase Theatre.

Jones, LeRoi. *See* Baraka, Amiri.

Jones, Milberry "Berry." The main character in the short story "Berry."

Jones, Oceola. The main character in the short story "The Blues I'm Playing."

Jones, Robert Earl. *See Don't You Want To Be Free?*; Harlem Suitcase Theatre.

Jones, Susanna. The character in the poem "When Sue Wears Red."

Joplin, Missouri. Hughes's birthplace. Named after a clergyman from Tennessee, Joplin began as a settlement near a creek in the Ozark mountains of southwestern Missouri, 134 miles south of Kansas City. Joplin was incorporated as a town in 1871, as a city in 1873. In the 1890s lead and zinc mining expanded considerably in the area, drawing a more diverse population to Joplin. During and after World War II its economy became more factory based, and the mining industry died out. A literacy project known as "the Joplin reading program," instituted in 1953, brought the city national attention. Hughes was born in the city on February 1, 1902. *See* Hughes, Carrie Langston; Hughes, James Nathaniel.

Journals in Which Hughes Published Poems, Stories, Essays, and Articles. *See* Periodicals in Which Hughes Published Poems, Stories, Essays, and Articles.

"Journals: 1931/The Official Daily Log Book—Jersey to the West Indies." Unpublished material (diary/journal), cowritten with Zell Ingram.* It is part of the Langston Hughes Papers held in the James Weldon Johnson Memorial Collection, Beinecke Library, Yale University (LHP 586).
Bibliography: Rampersad, I, 200–213.

"Joy." Nine-line poem in which Hughes, with intentional ambiguity, depicts Joy as a sought-after emotion, a mythic nymph, and a young woman whose boyfriend drives a butcher's cart. It was first published in *Crisis** (February 1926). Later, Howard Swanson set the poem to music. ASCAP* lists the song as being published by Weintraub Music Company, and the song's ASCAP registry number is 400021409. Ricky Ian Gordon also set the poem to music as part of a song cycle that included the Hughes poems "Border Line," "Genius Child," "Kid in the Park," "My People," "Prayer," "Troubled Woman," and "To Be Somebody."

Bibliography: *CP*, 63; Ricky Ian Gordon, *Genius Child: A Cycle of 10 Songs* (New York: Williamson Music Company, 1992).

Joy to My Soul (1937). Play in three acts. Like *Little Ham* and *Troubled Island, Joy to My Soul* was first performed at the Karamu Theatre in Cleveland, Ohio. Put on by the Gilpin Players,* a troupe within the Karamu Theatre, it opened on April 1, 1937. It is a comedy set entirely in a hotel lobby and concerns a wealthy Texan (Buster Whitehead) who has traveled from "Shadow Gut, Texas," to Cleveland to meet a woman he has contacted by letter through a "Miss Lonely Hearts" dating service. She turns out to be twice his age and as worldly-wise as he is provincial and naïve. The comedy turns chiefly on his naïveté but also involves other residents of and visitors to the hotel, including gamblers. Like *Little Ham* and *When the Jack Hollers, Joy to My Soul* is earthy and ribald but is a more contrived "situation" comedy and is more constricted by its setting. Hicklin (255) has observed that it lacks the "folk spirit" of Hughes's other comedies. The play has not been published but in manuscript form is held in the Langston Hughes Papers, James Weldon Johnson Memorial Collection, Beinecke Rare Book and Manuscript Library, Yale University.

Bibliography: Hicklin, 148, 153.

"Joy to the World." Song, from *Black Nativity*. ASCAP* lists Hughes as the sole author (composer and lyricist both, that is) but lists no publisher. The song's ASCAP registry number is 100023378.

Joyce. *See* Lane, Joyce.

"Joyce Objects." Short story, included in the collection *Simple Takes a Wife. See* Simple [Jesse B.] Stories.

Juan. A main character in the short story "Tragedy at the Baths."

"Jubilee." Song. Hughes wrote the lyrics, and several decades later, musician and songwriter Taj Mahal set them to music for the debut of *Mule Bone*, the play written by Hughes and Zora Neale Hurston.* ASCAP lists the song as being published by Prankee Music and Golden Foot Music, and the song's ASCAP registry number is 400149755.

Bibliography/Discography: John Beaufort, "*Mule Bone* Debuts after 60 Years," *Christian Science Monitor* (February 26, 1991), 13; Taj Mahal, *Mule Bone* [compact disc] (New York: Gramavision, distributed by Rhino Records, 1991): R2 79432.

"Judge William Hastie." Seven-line poem implicitly praising Judge Hastie's decision in 1943 to resign his federal judgeship to protest the segregation of the U.S. armed forces. The poem refers specifically to the fact that the air force would not allow African Americans to fly airplanes, a policy that later changed with the creation of the Tuskegee Airmen, which was, however, a segregated unit. Hastie was the first African American appointed to the U.S. federal courts. That appointment, by President Franklin Roosevelt* in 1938, was widely praised by the NAACP* and other civil-rights organizations. As Roosevelt's presidency continued, however, Hastie and other African American leaders believed that Roosevelt's commitment to civil rights was not strong enough. Hastie is also well known for being one of Thurgood Marshall's* teachers and for teaming with Marshall and Charles Houston in designing and executing a strategy to win civil rights for African Americans through the U.S. judicial system (as opposed to legislative and executive systems and nonviolent direct action). The poem was first published in the *Amsterdam News* (March 6, 1942). *See* "America's Young Black Joe!" *See also* "Ballad of Roosevelt"; *Brown v. Board of Education*; "Crow Goes, Too"; "Dear Mr. President"; "403 Blues."

Bibliography: *CP*, 578; Abraham L. Davis and Barbara Luck Graham, *The Supreme Court, Race, and Civil Rights* (Thousand Oaks, CA: Sage Publications, 1995); Harvard Sitkoff, *A New Deal for Blacks: The Emergence of Civil Rights as a National Issue: The Depression Decade* (New York: Oxford University Press, 1978); Gilbert Ware, *William Hastie: Grace under Pressure* (New York: Oxford University Press, 1984).

"Judgement Day." Poem of fourteen lines, with irregular rhyming and stanzas. It is spoken in black dialect* by a person who has died, gone to Heaven, and met Jesus. It was first published in *Measure* (June 1926). *Collected Poems* includes information about slight revisions the poem underwent. *See* Religion.

Bibliography: *CP*, 71, 630.

"Juice Joint: Northern City." Rhyming poem in three stanzas that describes and celebrates a bar frequented by African Americans where beer and gin are served, the blues* and jazz* are played, and patrons dance. The mood of the poem is bittersweet; the "juice joint" is portrayed as a site of brief respite for people enduring hard lives. Each stanza contains twelve lines that are comparatively long for Hughes, followed by a quatrain of short rhyming lines that, while not identical in each stanza, function still as a kind of refrain. The poem was first published in *One-Way Ticket*. An earlier version, titled "Barrel House: Chicago," appeared in *Lincoln University News* in 1928 and *Abbott's Monthly*

(1931). *Collected Poems* reprints the earlier version in an appendix; the editors suggest that Hughes revised it in part because Prohibition was repealed and the earlier version refers to the illegal purchase of liquor. *See* "Puzzlement"; Revision.

Bibliography: *CP*, 362, 666–667.

Juke. This word is now most commonly seen as part of the word "jukebox," describing a coin- or currency-operated machine that plays records or compact discs. In the United States, jukeboxes enjoyed widespread use, especially in bars, taverns, and restaurants of the 1950s, 1960s, and 1970s. Major identifies "juke" as being of African-Gullah origin and as entering the mainstream of African American slang in the 1800s, when it was a rough synonym to "unruly," "loud," and "boisterous." Later it was used by African Americans as a verb to mean "to dance in a whorehouse" and/or "to dance to the music of a jukebox." Hughes tended to use the word in this latter sense, as in the poem "Puzzlement," where he refers to a "juke joint": a nightclub or bar frequented by African Americans where patrons danced. Occasionally one hears it as a verb that means "to fake" or "to fake out" in American football or basketball, as when one player feigns moving in one direction but suddenly changes direction to confuse an opponent. Hughes, however, did not use the word in this way.

Bibliography: "Juke v [erb]," in *Juba to Jive: A Dictionary of African-American Slang*, ed. Clarence Major (New York: Penguin, 1994), 264.

"Juke Box Love Song." Poem. *See Montage of a Dream Deferred. See also The Block.*

"Juliet." Free-verse poem in fifteen very short lines. Although the end of the poem alludes to Shakespeare's *Romeo and Juliet* explicitly, the woman portrayed in the poem appears to be a modern-day woman who frequents bars. The poem was first published under the title "On the Road to Mantova" in *Lincoln University News* (March 1926).

Bibliography: *CP*, 332–333, 664.

"Junior Addict." Poem of about one full page, rhymed irregularly, with—for Hughes—relatively long lines. It first offers a somber analysis of forces driving young African American males to become addicted to drugs, especially heroin, with the lack of economic opportunity being the primary force. Later it points to the fatalism inherent in the nuclear age as another cause of despair. The poem implores the sun to rise, suggesting that a sign of hope is desperately needed. It was first published in the *Liberator* (April 1963). *Collected Poems* includes notes about the genesis of the poem.

Bibliography: *CP*, 539, 687.

"Junkies." Short story, included in the collection *Simple's Uncle Sam. See* Simple [Jesse B.] Stories.

"Just an Ordinary Guy." Poem in nine ballad* stanzas that celebrates everyday working American men who become heroes upon joining the armed forces to fight Germany in World War II. It was first published in the *Amsterdam News* (July 1943). *See* "America's Young Black Joe!"; "Bonds for All"; "Bonds: In Memoriam."

Bibliography: *CP*, 579.

Just around the Corner. Musical play. Abby Mann and Bernard Drew had written a text, and Joe Sherman had composed songs for the project, before the three asked Hughes to collaborate with them in the autumn of 1949. Hughes helped rewrite lyrics of existing songs and wrote lyrics for new ones. The play concerns three naïve young men who arrive in New York City by boxcar, believing that success is "just around the corner." The four collaborators had difficulty finding financial backing for the production. Eventually the play was produced in Ogunquit, Maine, opening on July 29, 1950. The cast included Fred Kelly, brother of the renowned dancer and actor Gene Kelly. According to Rampersad, the opening-night audience was enthusiastic, but the reviews were mixed, with *Variety* praising Hughes's lyrics. The show closed quickly. Producer Mike Todd showed brief interest in transforming *Just around the Corner* into a Hollywood film, but the project never materialized. ASCAP* lists no songs cowritten by Hughes, Drew, Mann, and/or Sherman.

Bibliography: Rampersad, II, 151–152, 181–182; the review cited by Rampersad appeared in *Variety* (August 1, 1950).

"Justice." Poem in a single quatrain in which lines two and four rhyme. It analyzes the conventional feminine image of "blind justice" pejoratively, indicating that she is indeed blind—to the injustices suffered by African Americans. The poem was first published in the *Amsterdam News* (April 25, 1923).

Bibliography: *CP*, 31.

K

Keats, John (1795–1821). British poet, considered one of the most important "romantic poets," author of such widely known poems as "Ode on a Grecian Urn," "To Autumn," and "La Belle Dame sans Merci." In the poem "Metropolitan Museum" Hughes alludes to Keats.

Kerlin, Robert T. *See* Lincoln University.

"Kick for Punt." Short story, included in *The Best of Simple*. *See* Simple [Jesse B.] Stories.

"Kid in the Park." Thirteen-line irregularly rhymed poem addressed rhetorically to a child sitting alone in a city park. Implicitly the poem connects the loneliness of the child with his figurative homelessness or emotional abandonment. It was first published under the title "Waif" in the *Minnesota Quarterly* (Spring 1950). Later Ricky Ian Gordon set the poem to music as part of a song cycle: *see* "Genius Child" and "Joy."
Bibliography: *CP*, 376; Ricky Ian Gordon, *Genius Child: A Cycle of 10 Songs* (New York: Williamson Music Company, 1992).

"Kid Sleepy." Twenty-two-line poem in which the speaker engages in a dialogue with one Kid Sleepy, a lazy person so unmotivated that he won't even get up to move into the shade. The poem was first published in the *Carmel Pine Cone* (May 3, 1941). It was also published in *Shakespeare in Harlem*.
Bibliography: *CP*, 229.

"The Kids in School with Me." Poem of twenty-five lines celebrating the multiethnic diversity of the United States and its public schools. *See* Children's Poetry.
Bibliography: *CP*, 601.

"Kids Who Die." Poem eulogizing persons of different nationalities and ethnic backgrounds who die while trying to advance the cause of workers and other disenfranchised people worldwide. The poem also expresses intense dislike of "the old and rich" who abuse political power and intellectuals with Ph.D.'s who may write about "kids who die" but who never get involved themselves with revolution or even reform. Specifically mentioned are Angelo Herndon, a young American labor organizer, and Karl Liebknecht, a German labor leader and colleague of Rosa Luxemburg (1871–1919), founder of the German Communist Party. Liebknecht and Luxemburg were arrested on June 15, 1919, and were put to death the same day, without trial. The poem was first published in *A New Song. See also Angelo Herndon Jones; Herndon v. Lowry*; "Labor Storm"; "Lenin."

Bibliography: *CP*, 210–211; Elzbieta Ettinger, *Rosa Luxemburg: A Life* (Boston: Beacon Press, 1986); Margarethe von Trotta (script and direction), *Rosa Luxemburg* [videorecording, 122 minutes] (New York: New Yorker Video, 1985).

Knopf, Alfred A. (1892–1984). American editor and publisher. Knopf was born in New York City and graduated from Columbia University* in 1912. He worked for the publishing firm of Doubleday, Page before starting his own publishing business in 1915. The publishing firm of Alfred A. Knopf soon became known for the range and quality of literary work it published. Over the course of Knopf's life, his firm published the work of authors who had won or would go on to win numerous Nobel and Pulitzer prizes for literature. For ten years (1924–1934), Knopf also worked as an editor for the magazine *American Mercury.** Knopf published several of Hughes's books, including *The Weary Blues, The Dream Keeper, Fine Clothes to the Jew, Fields of Wonder, Not Without Laughter, One-Way Ticket, Ask Your Mama*, and *The Panther and the Lash*. Alfred Knopf's wife, Blanche Knopf,* was the primary editor for several of these books. In 1966 the Knopf publishing firm was purchased by Random House.

Bibliography: "Knopf, Alfred A.," *Encyclopaedia Britannica Online, http://www.eb.com: 180/bol/topic?eu=46871&sctn=1*; Randolph Lewis, "Langston Hughes and Alfred A. Knopf, Inc., 1925–1935," *Library Chronicle of the University of Texas* 22, no. 4 (1992), 52–63; Rampersad, I, 107 ff., 334–335.

Knopf, Blanche (1894–1966). American editor and publisher. Blanche Wolf was born in New York City and attended the Gardner School there. She met Alfred A. Knopf* when he was attending Columbia University*; the two were married in 1916, one year after he established his own publishing firm. Blanche Knopf quickly became immersed in the business of the firm, managing day-to-day operations, editing books, creating the Borzoi imprint, and finding new authors. She edited a number of Hughes's books, including *The Weary Blues*. One of her most dramatic successes was securing the publication of Sigmund Freud's *Moses and Monotheism* in 1938. She worked with a wide variety of authors, including William L. Shirer, John Hersey, Jean-Paul Sartre, Albert Camus, Lillian Hellman, and Elizabeth Bowen.

Bibliography: "Knopf, Blanche," *Wilson Biographies Plus/Wilson Web* http://hwwilson web.com; Rampersad, I, 107 ff., II.

Koestler, Arthur (1905–1983). Hungarian-British novelist, journalist, and essayist. Koestler was born and grew up in Budapest, Hungary. He attended the University of Vienna, graduating in 1926. He became a supporter of the Zionist movement and worked as a journalist in Jerusalem beginning in 1927. Later he became a correspondent for several European newspapers and was the only journalist to join the Arctic expedition of the *Graf Zeppelin* in 1931. That same year he joined the Communist Party and traveled to Russia, where he met Hughes. The two became friends and traveled together, as Hughes recounts in *I Wonder As I Wander*. Like Hughes, Koestler later was opposed both to Adolf Hitler and Joseph Stalin. He also served in an ambulance corps during World War II. He became a citizen of Great Britain in 1945. His best-known novel, *Darkness at Noon* (1940), concerns in part the deadly reactionary regime of Stalin. A prolific writer and vibrant intellectual, Koestler published several novels and many books of nonfiction.

Bibliography: *I Wonder As I Wander*, 225–230; Arthur Koestler, *Darkness at Noon*, transl. Daphne Hardy, with a foreword by Peter Viereck (New York: New American Library, 1961); Murray A. Sperber, ed., *Arthur Koestler: A Collection of Critical Essays* (Englewood Cliffs, NJ: Prentice-Hall, 1977).

"Ku Klux." Poem of five stanzas in modified ballad* form. The speaker is an African American man who reports having been kidnapped and abused by members of the Ku Klux Klan.* A powerful poem about blatant, violent racism and white supremacy, it nonetheless exhibits wry humor as well. It was first published in *Shakespeare in Harlem. See Langston Hughes Reads: "One-Way Ticket," "The Negro Speaks of Rivers," "Ku Klux Klan," and Other Poems.*

Bibliography: *CP*, 252–253.

Ku Klux Klan. Secret society established in Pulaski, Tennessee, in late 1865. The Ku Klux Klan (the Klan) was founded by white businessmen enraged by the post–Civil War policies sponsored by Reconstruction. The chief purpose of the Klan was to terrorize African Americans, a purpose it shared with such groups as the Knights of the White Camellia and the Pale Faces. However, Franklin and Moss point out that such groups did not invent but rather intensified racist violence and illegal activism that already existed in southern states after the war. The Klan and other groups were heavily armed and usually attacked African Americans at night. Franklin and Moss note that "Union troops were wholly ineffectual in coping with them. . . . Blacks were run out of communities if they disobeyed orders to desist from voting, and the more resolute and therefore insubordinate blacks were whipped, maimed, and hanged" (275). Federal laws passed in late 1871 helped retard the rise of the Klan and control its violence to some degree. The investigation leading to the federal action revealed, for example, that in 1871, 153 African Americans were murdered by the Klan in one Florida county and 300 in a parish outside New Orleans (Morison, 341). The Klan was revived in 1915, however. Franklin and Moss observe that "[w]ithin a year it grew . . . to a militant union of more than 100,000 white-hooded knights. It declared itself against 'Negroes,' Japanese and other Orientals, Roman Catholics, Jews, and all foreign-born individuals" (385). This second incarnation of the Klan and the resulting violence contributed significantly to the massive northern migration of African Americans, a migration that resulted in significant African American communities in northern cities, including New York City (Harlem*). Hughes regarded the presence of the Klan, like that of Jim Crow laws,* as a direct threat to African American safety, well-being, and citizenship, but also as a symbol of the racism American society still tolerated, in his view. At this writing, the Ku Klux Klan still exists. *See* "Ku Klux"; "Note to All Nazis Fascists and Klansmen" [*sic*]. *See also* Lynching.

Bibliography: John Hope Franklin and Alfred E. Moss, Jr., *From Slavery to Freedom: A History of African Americans*, 7th ed. (New York: McGraw-Hill, 1994), 274–278; Samuel Eliot Morison, Henry Steele Commager, and William Leuchtenberg, *A Concise History of the American Republic*, 2nd ed, vol. 2 (New York: Oxford University Press, 1993).

L

"Labor Storm." Poem of forty-seven lines, with irregular stanza lengths and rhyming. It is addressed to members of labor unions, warning them that a general backlash against labor unions—manifested in particular by strikebreakers and dishonest lawyers—is about to occur. It was first published in *New Masses* (July 30, 1946). *See also Angelo Herndon Jones*; "Ballads of Lenin"; "Chant for Tom Mooney"; *Don't You Want to Be Free?*; "Goodbye, Christ"; "Good Morning, Revolution"; Harvest; "Lenin"; "A New Song"; "One More 'S' in the U.S.A."; "Open Letter to the South"; "Revolution"; "Sister Johnson Marches"; "Song of the Revolution"; "Wait." *See also* John Reed Club; Marxism; Politics.

Bibliography: *CP*, 317.

"Lady in a Cabaret." Seven-line poem in which lines three, six, and seven rhyme. The "lady" in question is extremely world-weary. The poem was first published in the magazine *Harlem* (November 1928).

Bibliography: *CP*, 127.

"Ladyhood." Short story, included in the collection *Simple's Uncle Sam. See* Simple [Jesse B.] Stories.

"Lady's Boogie." Poem. *See Montage of a Dream Deferred. See also* Revision, Process of, and Hughes.

"Lament." Song. Hughes wrote the lyrics, and Samuel Edwin Heyward composed the music. ASCAP* lists the song as being published by PRS—the Performing Right Society, Ltd. (London). The song's ASCAP registry number is 420004408.

"Lament for Dark Peoples." Poem in three stanzas of free verse, although key words are repeated. It is spoken by a collective persona* representing people of color who have been displaced and/or enslaved by white people and "caged" in the "circus of civilization." It was first published in *Crisis** (June 1924).
Bibliography: *CP*, 39.

Lament for Dark Peoples and Other Poems (Amsterdam: H. van Krimpen, 1944). With Hughes's permission, a certain H. Driessen selected previously published poems and wrote an introduction to this limited-edition volume, publication of which Driessen oversaw. Considered a rare book, it is held in the Rare Books and Manuscripts Collection of the Schomburg Center for Research in Black Culture (New York City), call number "Sc Rare F 83–73/Black author." Rampersad mentions only the title and, in an index, refers to the book as a "poetry anthology," but it is in fact this rare selection of Hughes's poetry, published in the Netherlands.
Bibliography: Rampersad, II, 94, 501.

"The Lament of a Vanquished Beau." Twenty-four-line light-verse poem in which the speaker is a young man angry at a certain Willy for stealing his girlfriend away. *See* Children's Poetry.
Bibliography: *CP*, 598.

"Lament over Love." Poem in four traditional blues* stanzas in which the speaker, a woman, is so lovelorn that she is contemplating suicide. It was first published in *Vanity Fair* (May 1926). *Collected Poems* includes information about revisions the poem underwent. As a song, "Lament over Love" is listed by ASCAP,* with Hughes indicated as the sole author (lyricist and composer both, that is). ASCAP lists the song as being published by MCA/Northern Music, Inc., and the ASCAP registry number is 420004917.
Bibliography: *CP*, 69, 629.

"Landladies." Short story, collected in *The Best of Simple. See* Simple [Jesse B.] Stories. *See also Poems by Sterling Brown.*

Lane, Jimmy. Mischievous cohort of the main character, Sandy, in *Not without Laughter.*

Lane, Joyce. Recurring character in the Simple [Jesse B.] stories.* She is almost always referred to just as Joyce. *See* "Joyce Objects." *See also Simply Heavenly.*

Lang, Charlie. *See* "The Bitter River."

Langston, Carrie. *See* Hughes, Carrie Langston.

Langston, James Mercer (1829–1890). American attorney, professor, and U.S. congressman. Langston was born in Louisa, Virginia. His older brother Charles married Hughes's grandmother, Mary Leary, several years after Mary's husband, Sheridan Leary, was killed in the raid on Harper's Ferry, led by John Brown (*see* "October 16: The Raid"). James Langston received a B.A. from Oberlin College in 1849 and completed an M.A. degree there in 1852. Denied admittance to law schools because he was black, Langston studied law on his own and eventually was admitted to the bar in Ohio. Langston supported many political causes, including the Voting Rights Act of 1870 that was intended to expand African American suffrage. He helped establish the law program at Howard University and served as dean of the program from 1868–1875. Despite fierce opposition from the Democratic Party and problems with election fraud, Langston was elected to the U.S. House of Representatives (representing a district in Virginia) in 1890 and served one term in an extremely hostile, racist environment. The town of Langston, Oklahoma, and Langston University (located there) are both named after James Mercer Langston. *See* Tolson, Melvin B.

Bibliography: *Langston University, Langston, Oklahoma*, www.lumet.edu; Rampersad, I, 28.

Langston, Mary Sampson Patterson Leary (1832–1915). Hughes's maternal grandmother. *See* Hughes, Carrie Langston; Hughes, James Nathaniel; Hughes, Langston; Langston, James Mercer; "October 16: The Raid."

The Langston Hughes Reader. (New York: Braziller, 1958). 502 pp. Subtitled *The Selected Writings of Langston Hughes*. Anthology. The book contains short stories from *The Ways of White Folks* and *Laughing to Keep from Crying*, as well as twenty-six Simple [Jesse B.] Stories.* It includes poems from *The Weary Blues*, about ten other poems, and all of *Montage of a Dream Deferred*. Also included are translations by Hughes: "Epigram," by Armand Lanusse; "Verse Written in the Album of Mademoiselle," by Pierre Dalcour; "Flute Players," by Jean-Joseph Rabearivelo; "Guinea," by Jacques Roumain; "She Left Herself One Evening," by Léon Damas; "I," by Francesca [*sic*]; "Opinions of the New Student," by Regino Pedroso; and "Dead Soldier," by Nicolás Guillén. Also of note are "18 Poems for Children" and the essay "Poetry and Children," which emphasizes the need to teach poetry to children, as well as six "Song Lyrics." Excerpts from *The Big Sea* and *I Wonder As I Wander* are reprinted, as well as a chapter ("Guitar") from *Not Without Laughter*. Two plays are reprinted in full: *Soul Gone Home* and *Simply Heavenly*. *The Glory of Negro History: A Pageant* is also reprinted in full. The volume concludes with ten "Articles and Speeches" and a one-page "Bibliography of the Writings of Langston Hughes." By 1971 the volume had gone through four printings. *See* Children's Poetry; Translations by Hughes.

Langston Hughes Reads and Talks about His Poems. (New York: Spoken Arts, 1987). Audiocassette. Under the title *Langston Hughes Reading His Poems with Comment*, the recording—on one reel, not on cassette—is held by the Library of Congress, which dates the recording May 1, 1959. *See* Audio Recordings of Hughes.

Langston Hughes Reads: "One-Way Ticket," "The Negro Speaks of Rivers," "Ku Klux Klan," and Other Poems (New York: Caedmon, 1992). Audiocassette. *See* Audio Recordings of Hughes.

Langston Hughes: Short Stories. Edited by Akiba Sullivan Harper (New York: Hill and Wang, 1996). 299 pp. This collection includes forty-seven short stories previously published by Hughes, most of them, as Harper indicates, having appeared in two out-of-print collections: *Laughing to Keep from Crying* and *Something in Common and Other Stories*. From *The Ways of White Folks* (still in print at this writing), "Cora Unashamed" and "Slave on the Block" are included. Of particular note are four early stories by Hughes, "Mary Winosky," "Those Who Have No Turkey," "Seventy-five Dollars," and "The Childhood of Jimmy." These are included in an appendix, followed by a "Publication History of Hughes's Short Stories," excluding the Jesse B. Simple stories. In an introduction to the volume, Arnold Rampersad observes, "Hughes possessed such a profound interest in and commitment to the art of fiction that even if he had never published a single poem, he would still have a place of relative prominence in African-American literary history as the author not only of two novels . . . but also more than fifty short stories [excluding the Simple stories]" (xiii). *See* Central High School.

"Langston Hughes Speaks" (1953). Statement submitted to and officially accepted by the Permanent Sub-Committee on Investigations in the U.S. Senate (*see* McCarthyism for an account of Hughes's appearance before the subcommittee). Hughes describes the circumstances that led him to have "deep sympathies with certain aims and objectives of . . . leftist philosophies" (Berry, 158). These circumstances, he notes, included the impact of the Great Depression on African Americans and on working people in general; problems faced by people of color worldwide; and the persistence of Jim Crow laws* in the southern United States. He observes that the "red flag" of the Soviet Union represented to him at the time the possibility of freedom for oppressed peoples. He notes that his views have changed considerably and that one cause of the change was the Soviet Union's pact with Nazi Germany. He then summarizes his family's history as it relates to the abolitionist movement prior to the Civil War. Finally, he notes that although the United States still faces "many problems," it is also a significantly democratic nation that is "young, strong, and beautiful" (159). *See also* "Ballads of Lenin"; *The Big Sea*; "Concerning Goodbye Christ"; "Concerning Red Baiting"; John Reed Club; Marxism; "One More 'S' in the U.S.A."; Politics; Robeson, Paul; "The Soviet Union"; "Un-American Investigators."

Bibliography: Berry, 157–159; Rampersad, II, 209–219.

Langston Hughes: The Dream Keeper [videorecording], *Voices and Visions* [6], South Carolina Educational Television Network, 1988, a New York Center for Visual History Production, directed by St. Clair Bourne, produced by Robert Chapman. The *Voices and Visions* series, in which fourteen programs of approximately one hour each focused on one American poet, aired on the Public Broadcasting Service television network in the United States in 1988. The recording includes brief video clips of Hughes reading his poems and conversing.

Lanusse, Armand. *See* "Epigram."

Larsen, Nella (1893–1964). American writer, librarian, and professional nurse. Like that of Countee Cullen,* the background of Larsen is somewhat murky. She probably was born in Chicago, the daughter of an African American man and a Danish woman. She sometimes claimed to have studied at the University of Copenhagen but did not in fact attend that university. After spending a year at Fisk University, Larsen completed a nursing program at Lincoln Hospital Training School in New York City. Later she trained to become a librarian and worked at the Harlem* branch of the New York Public Library (later called the Countee Cullen Branch, and still later named the [Arthur] Schomburg* Center for Research in Black Culture) between 1922 and 1929. Larsen published her first novel, *Quicksand*, in 1928. The following year she published her second novel, *Passing*. She was the first African American woman to win a Guggenheim Fellowship, but her progress and confidence as a writer seemed to be greatly altered by charges that her story "Sanctuary" was partly plagiarized. She did not publish another novel, pursuing instead a remarkable career as a nurse at Gouverneur Morris Hospital in New York City. Alain Locke* and Carl Van Vechten* were mutual friends of Larsen and Hughes.

Bibliography: Nella Larsen, *Quicksand: and Passing* [two novels in one volume], edited and with an introduction by Deborah E. McDowell (New Brunswick, NJ: Rutgers University Press, 1986); Lewis, *HRR*, 410–485.

"Last Call." Poem of fourteen lines in which the speaker, previously areligious, addresses God directly, at least because he is "lost" and distraught and perhaps because he is dying. The title may be intentionally ambiguous insofar as it could refer to the speaker's "last call" (to God) before dying and/or to the phrase used in bars indicating a call for a final order of drinks before closing time; that is, the spiritually adrift speaker may be addressing God from a saloon or tavern, may be extremely despondent, but may not be dying. The poem was first published in *New Poems by American Poets* (no. 2, 1957). *See* Religion.

Bibliography: *CP*, 454.

"The Last Feast of Belshazzar." Poem of one sextet and one quatrain. It is a compact, highly imagistic retelling of the story of Belshazzar from the book of Daniel in the Bible. It was first published in *Crisis** (August 1923). *See* Religion.

Bibliography: John Joseph Collins, *Daniel: A Commentary on the Book of Daniel* (Minneapolis: Fortress Press, 1993); *CP*, 33.

"The Last Man Living." Poem of four ballad* quatrains, although the first quatrain is stretched to five lines. It is spoken in black dialect* by a person imagining what it would be like to be the last man living—and hear a knock on his door. It was first published in *Hearse* (no. 7), for which the editors of *Collected Poems* could find neither a date nor a place of publication. However, the University of California's library catalogue gives the place of *Hearse*'s publication as Eureka, California. *See* "Casual" for additional information about *Hearse*.

Bibliography: *CP*, 460, 680.

Last Poem Hughes Submitted for Publication. *See* "Backlash Blues."

"The Last Prince of the East." Fifteen-line poem addressed to an infant who, according to the speaker, is the last prince of Malaysia but who (the speaker predicts) will not become king because "Revolt," which has put on "a red gown" (symbolizing communism)has already invaded "the rice fields." The poem was first published in *The Panther and the Lash*.

Bibliography: *CP*, 558.

"Last Thing at Night." Short story, included in the collection *Simple Takes a Wife. See* Simple [Jesse B.] Stories.

"Last Whipping." Short story, included in *The Best of Simple. See* Simple [Jesse B.] Stories.

"Late Corner." Poem of eleven lines that compares a streetlight to the Christian cross, except that the light has gone out, implying a crisis of faith. It was first published in *New Poems by American Poets* (no. 2, 1957). *See* Religion.

Bibliography: *CP*, 454.

"Late Last Night." Poem of eleven lines in two quatrains and a triplet. Although it is not written in traditional blues* form, it is very much in the idiom and style of the blues and concerns a broken heart. It was first published in *One-Way Ticket* and was reprinted in *The Block*.

Bibliography: *CP*, 365.

"Laughers." Thirty-two-line poem constructed as a list of workers and talents, including dishwashers, elevator boys, cooks, and comedians, and dancing, singing, telling stories, and (repeated several times), laughing—something the poem, in fact, regards as a gift. Hughes names these jobs and talents as belonging especially to "his people" (African Americans), implying that despite facing limited economic opportunities at the time, "his people's" talents flourish. The poem was first published under the title "My People" in *Crisis** (June 1922).

Bibliography: *CP*, 27.

Laughing to Keep from Crying. (New York: Holt, 1952). 206pp. Collection of stories. Most of the stories in this collection are less harsh, more comic, and less fiercely satiric than those in Hughes's first collection, *The Ways of White Folks*. Nonetheless, many stories concern problematic race relations in the United States. The collection includes one of Hughes's most highly regarded and widely anthologized stories, "On the Road."

Bibliography: Ostrom, 19–30, 110.

"Laughter in Madrid." Essay with the dateline "Madrid, December 15 [1937]." Written by Hughes in Madrid during the Spanish Civil War, the essay concerns the resilience of Madrid's citizens when the city was being shelled by fascist forces. It was first published in the *Nation* (January 29, 1938). Concerning additional reportage on the Spanish Civil War by Hughes, *see Baltimore Afro American. See also* "Air Raid: Barcelona"; "Madrid"; "Moonlight in Valencia: Civil War."

Bibliography: Berry, 114–122.

"The Law." Short story, included in the collection *Simple Speaks His Mind. See* Simple [Jesse B.] Stories.

Lee, Birdie. A character in *Tambourines to Glory* (the play and the novel). She is the second convert to the church founded in Harlem* by Laura Reed and Essie Belle Johnson and plays a key role in the resolution of the plot. In chapter 19 ("God's Marquee"), she describes herself as "a sinner determined to become a saint."

Lee, Cora. A character in the poem "Young Gal's Blues."

"Lenin." Poem in three ballad* stanzas. It speaks admiringly of Vladimir Lenin, leader of the Bolshevik Revolution and later premier of the Union of Soviet

Socialist Republics. The poem suggests that the "red star" of communism is rising worldwide. It was first published in *New Masses* (January 26, 1946). *See Angelo Herndon Jones; Don't You Want To Be Free?*; John Reed Club; "Kids Who Die"; "Labor Storm"; Marxism; McCarthyism; "One More 'S' in the U.S.A."; Politics; "Sister Johnson Marches."

Bibliography: *CP*, 318.

"Lenox Avenue Bar." Free-verse poem of twelve lines. It focuses on "one Jew" who owns the bar and weaves his way among "forty Negroes." It concludes by commenting admiringly about a woven tapestry, which some readers might see as symbolizing a weaving together of cultures. The poem was first published in *The Panther and the Lash.*

Bibliography: *CP*, 554.

"Lenox Avenue: Midnight." Free-verse poem of fourteen lines. It calls the "rhythm" of the avenue a "jazz* rhythm," is addressed to "Honey," and suggests that "the gods are laughing at us." Lenox Avenue runs through the heart of Harlem* in New York City and was especially vibrant during the Harlem Renaissance.* The poem was first published in *The Weary Blues.*

Bibliography: *CP*, 92.

Lesch, Eugene. The main character in the story "Rejuvenation through Joy."

"Less Than a Damn." Short story, included in the collection *Simple Takes a Wife. See* Simple [Jesse B.] Stories.

"Let America Be America Again." Long poem (several pages) with an irregular rhyme scheme and stanza lengths. In a declamatory style the poem urges the United States to live up to its ideals and ensure democracy and economic justice for all of its citizens. In much of the poem Hughes uses a collective persona,* an "I" who variously represents African Americans, Native Americans, immigrants, workers, the unemployed, and farmers. This persona characterizes the economic system of the day as being grossly unjust, "dog eat dog," and causing a cultural "gangster death." In discussing how Hughes "offered the immediate source of inspiration for [Melvin B.] Tolson's* enthusiastic reception of the Russian Revolution," Doreski cites this poem as one source of that influence. It was first published in *Esquire* (July 1936). Later, Joan E. Griffith set the poem to music, titling the song "Oh Let America." ASCAP* lists the song as being published by Pleasing Dog Music, and the song's ASCAP registry number is 450023247. Also according to ASCAP, the One Voice Mixed Chorus performed the song, but no recording is listed.

Bibliography: *CP*, 189–191; C. K. Doreski, *Writing America Black: Race Rhetoric in the Public Sphere* (Cambridge: Cambridge University Press, 1998), 63.

"Let Me Take You for a Ride." Song, from *Simply Heavenly*. Hughes wrote the lyrics, and David Martin composed the music. ASCAP* lists the song as being published by Bourne, Inc., and the song's ASCAP registry number is 420023307.

"Let Things Be Like They Always Was." Song, from *Street Scene*. Hughes wrote the lyrics, and Kurt Weill* composed the music. ASCAP* lists the song as being published by Chappell, Inc., and Hampshire House Publishers, and the song's ASCAP registry number is 420029454.

Let Us Remember (1965). Cantata, written for solo voices, chorus, and orchestra. Hughes wrote the text, "a memorial for all men who have died for freedom and a denunciation of the hate experienced by the Jew and the black" (*Wilson Biographies*, p. 5). David Amram composed the music. The cantata was first performed in San Francisco on November 15, 1965. Herelendy described it as "a work of moving profundity, of nobility, of compassion, and of sincerity." The electronic database WorldCat indicates several libraries hold a (noncommercial?) recording of the November 15, 1965, performance.

Bibliography: "Amram, David," *Wilson Biographies Plus 1998* (http://web.hwwilsonweb. com/cgi.); Paul Herelendy, review of *Let Us Remember, Oakland Tribune* (California), November 16, 1965.

"Let's Ball a While." Song. Hughes wrote the lyrics, and David Martin composed the music. ASCAP* lists the song as being published by Bourne, Inc., and the song's ASCAP registry number is 420029454.

"Letter [1]." Poem. *See Montage of a Dream Deferred*.

"Letter [2]." Poem, one of the seven separate parts of "Seven Moments of Love."

"Letter from Baltimore." Short story, included in *The Best of Simple. See* Simple [Jesse B.] Stories.

"A Letter from Haiti." Essay that discusses Hughes's observations about Haiti, where he traveled in 1931. It focuses on the country's poverty. It was published in *New Masses* (July 1931). Some material from the essay later appeared in revised form in *I Wonder As I Wander. See Masters of the Dew*; "People without Shoes"; *Troubled Island*.

"Letter from Spain." Epistolary poem, signed by "Johnny" and addressed to his "brother at home." The poem is in nine traditional ballad* stanzas. Johnny, a member of the volunteer antifascist army known as the International Brigade, describes taking a wounded "Moor" as a prisoner of war and asking him why he is fighting on the side of the fascists. The Moor, who ultimately dies of his wounds, claims to have been forced to join the profascist army. The poem was first published in *Volunteer for Liberty* (November 15, 1937). In *I Wonder As I Wander*, Hughes describes having visited a military hospital in Spain when he was covering the Spanish Civil War for the *Baltimore Afro American**; there he met a wounded Moorish soldier, an encounter that generated ideas for the poem.

Bibliography: *CP*, 201; *I Wonder As I Wander*, 353.

"Letter to Anne." Twelve-line poem. One of Hughes's most personal poems, it speaks of being haunted by the memory of the addressee, a former lover. The editors of *Collected Poems* believe that the poem is addressed to Anne Marie Coussey, a West African woman. Hughes and Coussey were lovers in Paris in 1924. In *The Big Sea* Hughes suggests that Coussey's family caused the breakup of the relationship, but Rampersad suggests that Hughes himself ended the affair.

Bibliography: *The Big Sea*, 168; *CP*, 101; Rampersad, I, 86–90.

"Letter to the Academy." Prose-poem of four paragraphs and two single lines. In an arch, even sarcastic, tone it invites the "bearded" "gentlemen of the academy" who have written theoretical books to come forward and speak "of the Revolution," presumably Communist revolutions. The speaker suggests that the scholars know nothing of actual revolution. Ironically, poet Karl Shapiro later employed a similarly arranged prose-poem paragraph throughout his book *The Bourgeois Poet* (1964). *See* "Cowards from the Colleges."

Bibliography: *CP*, 169; Karl Shapiro, *The Bourgeois Poet* (New York: Random House, 1964).

Letters. *See Arna Bontemps/Langston Hughes: Letters, 1925–1967*; Papers, Hughes's. *See also* Bernard, Emily, in the general bibliography.

"Letting Off Steam." Short story, included in *The Best of Simple. See* Simple [Jesse B.] Stories.

"Liars." Ten-line free-verse poem, spoken in the first-person plural and self-indicting users of language and people with "civilized souls" as liars. The poem might be read as equating primitivism with "truth," but it could also be read as a critique—in poetic form, ironically—of writing; arguably it is one of Hughes's most perplexing poems. It was first published in *Opportunity** (March 1925).

Bibliography: *CP*, 44.

Library Holdings Related to Hughes. *See* Papers, Hughes's.

Librettos (Opera/Oratorio). *See The Barrier; Esther; Five Foolish Virgins; The Glory around His Head; Port Town; Street Scene; Troubled Island. See also* Johnson, James P.; *Let Us Remember;* Meyerowitz, Jan; Musical Plays; Opera; Orchestral Pieces/Oratorios; Songs; Still, William Grant; Weill, Kurt; *The Wizard of Altoona.*

Liebknecht, Karl. *See* "Kids Who Die."

"Life Is Fine." Poem in three pairs of ballad* quatrains; between each pair is a three-line refrain. The speaker recounts two suicide attempts, at which he failed—deliberately. The poem concludes with his assertion that "life is fine." There is a folk-song quality to the light poem. It was first published in *One-Way Ticket.* Later, Jobe Huntley set the poem to music for the musical play *Tambourines to Glory.* ASCAP* lists the song as being published by Chappell, Inc., and the song's ASCAP registry number is 452160981. *See also* "Scat Cat."
Bibliography: *CP*, 358.

"Light and the Soviet Union." Essay. In it Hughes recounts a visit, in 1946, to a dam site on the Chirchik River "in the storied region of Samarkand and Bokhara" in the Soviet Union (Berry, 96). Hughes perceives the future dam and the figurative and literal light it will produce to be a symbol of the progressive social change he believes the Soviet Union can achieve. The essay was first published in the *Chicago Defender** (August 10, 1946). It was later reprinted in Berry. *See* "Faults of the Soviet Union"; "The Soviet Union"; "The Soviet Union and Color"; "The Soviet Union and Health"; "The Soviet Union and Jews"; "The Soviet Union and Women."
Bibliography: Berry, 96–98.

"Likewise." Poem. *See Montage of a Dream Deferred.*

Limitations of Life. (1938). Dramatic work that consists of three skits: "Little Eva's End," a brief parody of the novel *Uncle Tom's Cabin* by Harriet Beecher Stowe; "Limitations of Life," a parody of the motion picture *Imitation of Life* (1934); and "Em-Fuehrer Jones," at once a satire of Adolf Hitler and a parody of Eugene O'Neill's play *The Emperor Jones.* All three pieces exaggerate, for comic effect, portrayals of African Americans in the works parodied: the long-suffering, deferential Uncle Tom; a black woman "passing" as white (but played by white actress Claudette Colbert); and the "primitive" Emperor Jones. *Limitations of Life* was performed with *Don't You Want to Be Free?* by the Harlem Suitcase Theatre* in 1938. *See* "Lincoln Theatre."
Bibliography: Rampersad, I, 363–364.

"Limitations of Life." *See Limitations of Life.*

"Lincoln Monument: Washington." Free-verse poem in eleven lines. It refers to President Lincoln as "Old Abe" and speaks of visiting him (the monument in Washington, D.C.) as he sits in silence, but also characterizes him as "a voice forever / Against the / Timeless walls." The poem was first published in *Opportunity* * (March 1927). *Collected Poems* contains information about slight revisions the poem underwent. *See* "Abe Lincoln."

Bibliography: *CP*, 103, 634.

"Lincoln Theatre." Fifteen-line rhyming poem describing the bust of Abraham Lincoln overseeing an evening at Harlem's* Lincoln Theatre, where African Americans see a film, listen to a female blues* singer, and dance to jazz.* The Lincoln Theatre was where Hughes saw a performance of Eugene O'Neill's play *The Emperor Jones* that was so poorly received by the audience that the leading actor halted his performance. Perceptively, Hughes attributed the play's failure less to the audience's unreadiness to understand "serious" drama and more to the venue itself, which typically hosted comparatively more lowbrow entertainment referred to in this poem. Extending Hughes's analysis, Fraden suggests that "[t]o the audience at the Lincoln [Theatre], used to talking back to the entertainers on stage, their response to *Emperor Jones* was perfectly legitimate behavior. It was the performance of a tragic Emperor Jones that seemed out of place, incongruous. When someone [in the audience] cried out to the Emperor, 'come back to Harlem where you belong,' at least some of the people in the audience asserted their proprietary rights over the Lincoln Theatre. . . . The audience's laughter could have been a rejection of the premises of O'Neill's or any white man's sense of black tragedy" (149). The poem was first published in *One-Way Ticket. See* Audience; *Limitations of Life*.

Bibliography: *The Big Sea*, 258–259; *CP*, 360; Rena Fraden, *Blueprints for a Black Federal Theatre, 1935–1939* (Cambridge: Cambridge University Press, 1994), 148–150.

Lincoln University. American four-year university, founded on April 29, 1854, as Ashmun Institute. Its eighth president, Horace Mann Bond, described it as "the first institution founded anywhere in the world to provide a high education in the arts and sciences for youth of African descent" (Website). It is located forty-five miles southwest of Philadelphia and fifty-five miles north of Baltimore, Maryland. Hughes applied to Lincoln in October 1924, indicating that he wanted to attend "because I believe it to be a school of high ideals and a place where one can study and live simply" (Rampersad, I, 116). He was admitted soon thereafter and enrolled in February 1925. He joined the Omega Psi Phi fraternity. During his time at Lincoln, Hughes accompanied the university's vocal quartet, led by James Dorsey, on brief tours in the Northeast; he read poetry at these engagements. As Rampersad indicates, Hughes was extremely contented at Lincoln, especially early on. He enjoyed the professors (including Robert T. Kerlin, from whom he took "The Art of Poetry"), his classmates (one of whom was Thurgood Marshall*), the atmosphere, and his fraternity brothers. Later his commitment to poetry-reading tours, to his own writing, and to the emerging vibrant culture in Harlem* made Lincoln somewhat less stimulating. While he was at Lincoln, he published in the *Nation* his landmark essay "The Negro Artist and the Racial Mountain," and his relationship to his patron Charlotte Osgood Mason* became increasingly complicated and eventually untenable. Hughes graduated with a bachelor of arts from Lincoln University in 1929. In subsequent decades he contributed poems to university publications, including *Lincoln University News* (*see*, for example, "Lincoln University: 1954" and "Lover's Return").

Bibliography: Lincoln University Website (http://www.lincoln.edu/pages/about); Rampersad, I, chapter 6, "A Lion at Lincoln," 125–155, and chapter 7, "Godmother and Langston," 156–181.

"Lincoln University: 1954." Twelve-line rhyming poem commemorating the one hundredth anniversary of Lincoln University, from which Hughes graduated in 1929. It was first published in *Lincoln University News* (1954).

Bibliography: *CP*, 444.

Lincoln University Poets: Centennial Anthology: 1854–1954, edited by Waring Cuney (New York: Fine Editions Press, 1954). 72 pp. The editors of *Collected Poems* list Hughes as the sole editor of this anthology, but the Library of Congress (for example) lists Cuney as the sole editor. Rampersad (II) suggests that Hughes helped Cuney and Bruce Wright publish the anthology, which included three poems by Hughes: "Azikiwe in Jail," "Draftees," and "Lincoln University: 1954."

Bibliography: *CP*, 619; Rampersad, II, 238.

Lindsay, Vachel (1879–1931). American poet. Lindsay was born and grew up in Springfield, Illinois. He attended Hiram College in Ohio and, from 1900 to 1903, the Art Institute in Chicago. A deeply religious man, he traveled throughout the United States preaching what he called "the gospel of beauty" and reciting his poetry. His first two books of verse were *General William Booth Enters into Heaven* (1913) and *The Congo and Other Poems* (1914); they earned him critical and popular praise. Hughes met Lindsay while the former was working in a hotel in Washington, D.C., in 1925. Lindsay praised some poems Hughes showed him. Lindsay committed suicide in 1931.

Bibliography: Vachel Lindsay, *Collected Poems* (New York: Macmillan, 1931); Rampersad, I, 28, 119–120; Eleanor Ruggles, *The West-Going Heart: A Life of Vachel Lindsay* (New York: Norton, 1959).

"Liner Notes." *See Ask Your Mama.*

Lionel Hampton's Swing Book. (1946). *See* "Conservatory Student Struggles with Higher Instrumentation."

"Listen Here Blues." Poem in three traditional blues* stanzas. It cautions "sweet girls" not to drink whiskey and not to "fool" with men. It was first published in *Modern Quarterly* (1926).
Bibliography: *CP*, 69.

"Litany." Song. Hughes wrote the lyrics, and Ricky Ian Gordon composed the music. ASCAP* lists the song as being published by Williamson Music Co., and the song's ASCAP registry number is 420439636.

Literary Agents. *See* Agents, Literary, Hughes's.

"Little Cats." Nine-line rhyming poem suggesting that no cats go to hell after they die. First published in *Voices* (January 1959).
Bibliography: *CP*, 463.

"Little Dog." Short story. It was first published in *Challenge* (March 1934) and was included in the collections *The Ways of White Folks* and *Something in Common and Other Stories*. It was reprinted in *The Langston Hughes Reader* and *Langston Hughes: Short Stories*.

"Little Dreams." Poem. *See* "Slum Dreams."

"Little Eva's End." *See Limitations of Life.*

"Little Green Tree." Fifteen-line rhyming poem in three quatrains, a couplet, and a one-line conclusion. The poem is spoken by an old person who feels close to death and who believes that he will be buried beneath a small tree. It was first published under the title "Little Green Tree Blues" in *Tomorrow* (1945). *Collected Poems* includes this earlier blues* version of the poem in an appendix. The "Little Green Tree" version was first published in *One-Way Ticket. See also* Revision, Process of, and Hughes.
Bibliography: *CP*, 323, 663.

"Little Green Tree Blues." *See* "Little Green Tree."

Little Ham. (1936). Play in one act. In this comic play, the protagonist is Hamlet Hitchcock Jones, a shoe-shiner in Harlem who is also a bookie. The exuberant drama features much physical comedy and explores Jones's (Little Ham's) fondness for women and gambling. Hughes's celebration in the play of everyday

Harlem life anticipates the comedy later found in the (Jesse B.) Simple stories. *Little Ham* debuted at Cleveland's Karamu Theatre on March 24, 1936.

Bibliography: Langston Hughes, *Little Ham*, in *Five Plays of Langston Hughes*, ed. with an introduction by Webster Smalley (Bloomington: Indiana University Press, 1963), 14–68.

"Little Lyric (*of Great Importance*)." Poem of seven words in a single rhyming couplet that concerns paying the rent. It was first published in the *Carmel Pine Cone* (March 21, 1941) and was later published in *Shakespeare in Harlem*. Later, Harry Belafonte and Robert R. De Cormier, Jr., set the poem to music, including it in the television program *The Strollin' Twenties*. ASCAP* lists the song as being published by Clara Music Publishers, and the song's ASCAP registry number is 420117313. *See also My Lord What a Mornin'*; "Plaint."

Bibliography: *CP*, 226.

"Little Old Letter." Poem in four traditional ballad* stanzas and containing a hint of black dialect.* The speaker has received a letter that wounds him so much that he compares it to a "gun" or a "knife." He does not reveal its contents, but he indicates that it is anonymous, and he implies that the letter contains racist threats. The poem was first published under the title "Little Old Letter Blues" in *Old Line* (April 1943). The earlier version was in four blues* stanzas and is reprinted in an appendix of *Collected Poems*. ASCAP* lists "Little Old Letter" as a song, with Hughes as the sole author (lyricist and composer both, that is), published by MCA/Northern Music, Inc. The song's ASCAP registry number is 420053552. *See also* Revision, Process of, and Hughes.

Bibliography: *CP*, 271, 655.

"Little Old Letter Blues." *See* "Little Old Letter."

"Little Old Spy." Short story that is a comic tale about a visitor to Cuba whom the reactionary government believes to be a spy. It was first published in *Esquire* (September 1934), was included in the collection *Laughing to Keep from Crying*, and was reprinted in *Langston Hughes: Short Stories*.

Bibliography: Ostrom, 27.

The Little Savoy. Nightclub in Harlem* during the 1920s. *See* "Midnight Dancer."

"Little Song." Poem in two quatrains; alternate lines rhyme. The poem concerns "lonely people." It was first published in *Opportunity** (July 1948).

Bibliography: *CP*, 336; 609.

"Little Song on Housing." Rhyming poem of twenty-eight lines and six stanzas. Stanzas one, three, and five convey the predicament of African Americans who encounter racism when they enter the housing market. Serving as a kind of refrain, stanzas two, four, and six depict whites fleeing neighborhoods into which blacks have moved. The poem was first published in *Phylon* (1955). *See also* "Restrictive Covenants"; "Slum Dreams."

Bibliography: *CP*, 451; Robert Eugene Forman, *Black Ghettos, White Ghettos, and Slums* (Englewood Cliffs, NJ: Prentice-Hall, 1971); Jerome G. Rose and Robert E. Rothman, eds., *After Mount Laurel: The New Suburban Zoning.* (New Brunswick, NJ: Center for Urban Policy Research, 1977).

"The Little Virgin." Short story, first published in the *Messenger** (November 1927) and reprinted in *Langston Hughes: Short Stories*. Other early stories set in Africa include "Bodies in the Moonlight" "Luani of the Jungles," and "The Young Glory of Him."

"Live and Let Live." Poem. *See Montage of a Dream Deferred.*

Liza. A character in the poem "Song for a Banjo Dancer."

Locke, Alain LeRoy (1886–1954). American writer, professor of philosophy, and editor. Locke is remembered largely as one main "architect" of the Harlem Renaissance.* The anthology of poetry and prose he edited, *The New Negro* (1925), introduced the work of younger African American writers to a wider audience but also conceptualized contemporary "Negro" writing, thereby providing one coherent vision of literature for writers in and around Harlem.* Locke featured Hughes's poem "Youth" prominently in that volume. However, his role as teacher and scholar—he was professor of philosophy at Howard University from 1918 to 1953—was just as important, and he wrote essays and book reviews in several fields, from sociology and economics to literature and philosophy. Indeed, Linnemann characterizes Locke as a "modern Renaissance man." Consequently, he also served as a model of "the intellectual life" for younger writers and scholars, and he helped shape conversations and debates on which the Harlem Renaissance thrived. *The New Negro*, for example, was to some degree an explicit manifestation of W.E.B. Du Bois's* concept of "the Talented Tenth."

Locke was born in Philadelphia, graduated with honors from Harvard University in 1907, became the first African American Rhodes scholar (taking a degree in literature from Oxford University), studied philosophy at the University of Berlin, and finally returned to Harvard to earn his Ph.D. in philosophy in 1918. Lewis calls Locke's role in the Harlem Renaissance "unsurpassed" and notes that he was "untiring and long suffering in his efforts to placate, cajole, and flatter Mainstream [*sic*] influentials into supporting the Harlem Renaissance . . . [serving] as virtual chamberlain to the imperious Charlotte Osgood Mason*"

(Lewis, *HRR*, 756). As Rampersad explains in some detail, Locke unsuccessfully pursued a sexual and romantic relationship with Hughes, chiefly through a correspondence with him in 1922 and 1923. Although Locke's aspirations for the relationship did not materialize, the two remained friends, and Locke reviewed several of Hughes's works supportively, including *The Ways of White Folks*, of which he wrote, "These fourteen stories of Negro-white contacts told from the unusual angle of the Negro point of view are challenging to all who would understand the later phases of the race question as it takes on the new complications of contemporary social turmoil and class struggle." *See* The New Negro; "Sea Charm"; "Young Gal's Blues."

Bibliography: Leonard Harris, ed., *The Critical Pragmatism of Alain Locke: A Reader on Value Theory* (Lanham, MD: Rowman & Littlefield, 1999); Lewis, *HRR* 754–757; Lewis, *WHWV*, especially chapter 4, "Enter the New Negro," 89–118; Russell J. Linnemann, ed., *Alain Locke: Reflections on a Modern Renaissance Man* (Baton Rouge: Louisiana State University Press, 1982); Alain Locke, ed., *The New Negro* (New York: Boni, 1925); Alain Locke, untitled review of *The Ways of White Folks, Survey Graphic* 23 (November 1934), 565; Rampersad, I, 66–71.

Lomax, Buddy. A character in *Tambourines to Glory*, introduced in chapter 14 of the novel ("Enter Buddy"). By referring to "Lucky Texts" in the Bible, he helps Laura Reed operate a "numbers racket" (illegal lottery) out of the church she founded with Essie Belle Johnson. Toward the end of the novel, Laura murders Buddy.

"Lonely House." Song, from *Street Scene*. Hughes wrote the lyrics, and Kurt Weill* composed the music. ASCAP* lists the song as being published by Chappell, Inc., and Hampshire House Publishers, and the song's ASCAP registry number is 420065174.

"Lonely Nocturne." Highly lyrical, plaintive rhyming poem of seventeen lines concerning abject loneliness. It was first published in the *Amsterdam News* (October 24, 1942). *See* "America's Young Black Joe."

Bibliography: *CP*, 576–577.

"Lonely People." Song. Hughes wrote the lyrics, and Jean Berger composed the music. ASCAP* lists the song as being published by Broude Brothers, Ltd., and the song's ASCAP registry number is 420268197.

Lonesome Blue. Name of a character in the poem "Midnight Chippie's Lament."

"Lonesome Corner." Poem in two rhyming quatrains. The speaker is lovelorn; the mood and style of the poem are influenced by the blues.* It was first published in *Tomorrow* (July 1945).

Bibliography: *CP*, 314.

"Lonesome Place." Poem in three traditional blues* stanzas and in black dialect.* It speaks of loneliness and weariness. It was first published in *Opportunity** (October 1926).

Bibliography: *CP*, 36–37.

"Long Trip." Ten-line free-verse poem evoking a long voyage, describing the sea as "a wilderness of water," and suggesting several cycles within ocean travel. It was first published in *The Weary Blues*.

Bibliography: *CP*, 97.

"Long View: Negro." Thirteen-line poem that depicts historical perspective as a telescope, so that through one end, the Emancipation Proclamation issued by President Abraham Lincoln in 1865 appears to be a massive event, but from the other end (the present day of the poem), it appears to be "so small." The poem was first published in *Harper's Magazine* (April 1965).

Bibliography: *CP*, 547.

"Look for the Morning Star." Song, from *Simply Heavenly*. Hughes wrote the lyrics, and David Martin composed the music. ASCAP* lists the song as being published by Bourne, Inc., and the song's ASCAP registry number is 420071818.

Lorca: Gypsy Ballads. Translated by Langston Hughes. *Beloit Poetry Journal*, volume 2, number 1 (1951). 40 pp. In the fall of 1951 the *Beloit Poetry Journal* published a chapbook of the Spaniard Federico García Lorca's well-known collection *Gypsy Ballads* (*Romancero gitano*). In addition to the fifteen selections translated by Hughes, there is also a brief introduction by Robert H. Glauber preceding the poems and several illustrations by John McNee, Jr. This collection follows the same order as the original text but omits the last three selections known as the "Historical Ballads." Federico García Lorca was born in a small town near Granada in 1898. The quality and variety of his work, as well as his tragic biography, have defined him as one of the twentieth century's most famous Spanish writers. Lorca spent his early youth in rural Andalusia, and it was not until 1909 that his family moved to the city of Granada. As a young man, he enjoyed a solid education and was a very talented musician. In 1919 Lorca left home for the renowned Student Residence in Madrid. This institution had been founded in 1900 as part of a movement of educational reform in Spain and offered training and instruction for students in the arts and sciences. The

Residence attracted some of the brightest minds in Spain, and it was here that Lorca met future film director Luis Buñuel, eventual Nobel laureates in literature Vicente Aleixandre and Juan Ramón Jiménez, and surrealist artist Salvador Dalí. It was also in Madrid that Lorca met a host of other young poets with whom he would become associated as a member of the Poetic Generation of 1927, including Jorge Guillén, Pedro Salinas, and Rafael Alberti. With such a gifted array of friends and acquaintances, Lorca wasted no time in asserting himself as a talented member of his social circle, publishing his first collection of verse, *Book of Poems* (*Libro de poemas*) in 1921. This was followed in 1927 by the publication of *Songs* (*Canciones*), and in 1928, after four years of revision, he published *Gypsy Ballads*.

While Lorca dedicated much of his time and efforts to writing and working in drama during the 1930s, he also published some important poetic works, including *Poem of the Deep Song* (*Poema del cante jondo*) (1931), which had actually been written in the early 1920s. After a visit to the United States, Lorca wrote his radically different *Poet in New York* (*Poeta en Nueva York*). This book of surrealist poetry was published posthumously in 1940. Finally, one of the Spaniard's best-known selections, *Lament for the Death of a Bullfighter* (*Llanto por Ignacio Sánchez Mejías*), was published in 1934. Sadly, Federico García Lorca was one of the first casualties of the Spanish Civil War; in August 1936 he was taken into custody and executed by Nationalist forces.

Of all of Lorca's works of poetry, *Gypsy Ballads* is perhaps the text most often identified with its author. His choice of the ballad* (*romance*) reflects a long poetic Spanish tradition dating back to before the sixteenth century. As a poetic form, the ballad consists of octosyllabic verses with assonant rhyme in alternating verses. Much of the lyrical magic so plainly evident in Lorca's metered and rhymed verses is not as evident in the English free verses. In most cases, the translations seem overly mechanical, with insufficient thought (from a translator's point of view) given to appropriate phrasing and to Lorca's exquisite use of metaphor and symbols.

A note to Hughes's translation of *Gypsy Ballads* indicates that it was undertaken in consultation with Spanish poets Rafael Alberti and Manuel Altolaguirre while the American was in Madrid at the Alianza de Escritores in 1937. He later finished the work in New York in 1945. Hughes's renderings capture the major themes and some of the images of Lorca's poems. The notions of death, violence, sensuality, and religion are transmitted to the reader through the figures of knife-wielding duelers, the Civil Guard, the ever-present Gypsies, nuns, saints and churches. The evocation of the Andalusian atmosphere is a vital element that underlies the selections of the work, and in the language of Lorca this clearly came very naturally. In the translation, however, the characteristics that define the Spain of the Gypsies, complete with the native plants, rivers, and the stark Andalusian moon, are not conveyed adequately. These deficiencies are evident in virtually all of the poems in Hughes's version. There are some cases that can serve as examples of these deficiencies, including one of the best-known selections, the first poem, "Ballad of the Moon, Moon" (5). As the title makes clear with the repetition of the word "moon," the cadence and rhyme of this poetry are an integral part of its composition. Without sufficient attention to these elements in translation, these important aspects get lost. This is the case in various parts of the poem; "the child looks, looks. / The child is looking," "Fly moon, moon, moon," and "The air veils her, veils her. / The air is veiling her" are examples of verses that all seem forced and prosaic. Since these verses do not fit into a larger rhyme scheme with others of the poem, the obvious repetition detracts from the poetic rendering as a whole. Another popular selection is "The Ballad of the Sleepwalker" (10–12). This is a hauntingly lyrical poem that Hughes probably translates too literally and in so doing preserves a syntax that is extremely awkward in English. This is obvious in the third stanza, "Green as I would have you green. / Under the gypsy moon / things are looking at her / but she can't look back at them" (10). While these verses are difficult enough to interpret in the original Spanish, where the syntax is much more natural and the words form a rhythmic and rhymed whole, in Hughes's translation the task becomes even more complicated. In the poem titled "Faithless Wife" (15), some of the simplest verses are translated in a way that makes them more difficult to understand than they really are. In one case, the verses describe a man making a place for his lover to lay her head down on the ground. In Hughes's version this becomes, "I made her mat of hair / hollow the muddy bank" (15). In another instance, what is meant to be praise for the beauty of the beloved's skin is "unpoetically" phrased: "Neither lilies nor snail shells / have such a lovely skin" (17). Federico García Lorca's *Gypsy Ballads* is arguably the most metaphorically and symbolically charged of all the Spanish poetry that Hughes translated. It is a work that does not lend itself to facile interpretation, much less translation. Even with the help of Spanish friends, both of whom were poets, the lyricism of Lorca's poetry evades Hughes, and the end result is a text that fails to capture the beauty and mystery that is *Romancero gitano*. *See Blood Wedding* and *Yerma* (one volume); *Cuba Libre*; "Spain's Martyred Poet, García Lorca."

Bibliography: Carl W. Cobb, *Lorca's Romancero Gitano: A Ballad Translation and Critical Study* (Jackson: University Press of Mississippi, 1983); Ian Gibson, *Federico García Lorca* (New York: Pantheon Books, 1989); Edward Mullen, ed., *Langston Hughes in the Hispanic World and Haiti* (Hamden, CT: Archon Books, 1974).

Joseph Deters

"Lost Wife." Short story, included in the collection *Simple's Uncle Sam. See* Simple [Jesse B.] Stories.

Louis, Joe (1914–1981). American professional boxer. Louis was born in Lafayette, Alabama, but at age seven he moved with his mother and stepfather to Detroit, Michigan. He took up boxing at age sixteen and in 1934 won the Amateur Athletic Union's national light-heavyweight championship in St. Louis.

After several professional victories, most of them by knockout, he was given the nickname "The Brown Bomber from Detroit," which, shortened to "the Brown Bomber," stuck with him throughout his career. His journey toward the heavyweight championship suffered a setback in June 1936 when German boxer Max Schmeling knocked him out in the twelfth round of their boxing match. For many observers worldwide, the fight took on symbolic importance because of the "racial purity" beliefs espoused by Germany's ruling Nazi Party. In this sense, the Louis-Schmeling rivalry was comparable to African American sprinter Jesse Owens's participation (and victories) in the 1936 Berlin Olympic Games. In *I Wonder As I Wander*, Hughes writes about the importance of Louis to African Americans and about the Louis-Schmeling bouts. The second Louis-Schmeling bout took on even greater importance, especially for African Americans (for whom Louis had become a folk hero), more because of racist circumstances they faced in the United States than because of racist Nazi ideas. Additionally, on June 22, 1937, Louis won the heavyweight championship of the world by defeating James J. Braddock, meaning that his second bout with Schmeling would be a title defense. On June 22, 1938, Louis knocked out Schmeling in the first round. In the United States, Louis's victory made him a national hero. Louis became known as a deliberate, even slow-footed, boxer with devastating punching power and a cool, unflappable demeanor. He successfully defended his title twenty-five times in eleven years. In his career he faced such boxers as Primo Carnera, Max Baer, "Two-Ton" Tony Galento, and "Jersey" Joe Walcott. In an era when many African American professional boxers were managed by whites, Louis's management team made news; his trainer (Jack Blackburn) and his managers (John Roxborough and Julian Black) were all African Americans. *See* "Joe Louis [1]"; "Joe Louis [2]."

Bibliography: "Prelude to Spain," in *I Wonder As I Wander*, 314–321; Chris Mead, *Champion—Joe Louis, Black Hero in White America* (New York: Penguin Books, 1986).

"Louisiana." Song. Hughes wrote the lyrics, and Clarence Muse* composed the music. ASCAP* lists the song as being published by Chappell, Inc., and the song's ASCAP registry number is 420080102. The song was composed for the motion picture *Way Down South*.

"Love." Poem in two ballad* stanzas. The first celebrates the mystery and grandeur of love; the second suggests love's fleeting nature, comparing love to a "spark" from the hammer of John Henry (a mythic American folk hero). The poem was first published in *Shakespeare in Harlem*. *See also* "Ballad of the Seven Songs."

Bibliography: *CP*, 263.

"Love Again Blues." Poem in three traditional blues* stanzas; it concerns the destructive power of love. It was first published in *Poetry* (April 1940) and was also published in *Shakespeare in Harlem*.

Bibliography: *CP*, 216.

"Love Can Hurt You." Song. ASCAP* lists Hughes as the sole author (lyricist and composer both, that is) and lists the song as being published by Anne-Rachel Music Corporation. The song's ASCAP registry number is 420082155.

"Love Is like Whiskey." Song. Hughes wrote the lyrics, and Roger Segure composed the music. ASCAP* lists the song as being published by EMI/Mills, Inc., and the song's ASCAP registry number is 420085385.

"Love Song for Antonia." Free-verse poem in fifteen lines. The speaker expresses his absolute and unconditional love for Antonia. The poem is assumed to have been first published in *American Life* (1925), but the editors of *Collected Poems* were unable to locate this journal. *See* "Pale Lady."
Bibliography: *CP*, 54, 627.

"Love Song for Lucinda." Rhyming poem in three six-line stanzas. The structure of each stanza is the same, with varying line lengths within the stanzas and with "Love" as the first word and line. Each stanza develops a different comparison between love and a natural phenomenon. For Hughes, the rhetoric of this lyric poem is comparatively formal. The poem was first published in *Opportunity** (May 1926). Later, Ricky Ian Gordon set the poem to music. ASCAP* lists no publisher for the song, but the song's ASCAP registry number is 420459829.
Bibliography: *CP*, 68.

"Lovely Dark and Lonely One." Song. Hughes wrote the lyrics, and Harry T. Burleigh composed the music. ASCAP* lists the song as being published by Beam Me Up Music, Inc., and the song's ASCAP registry number is 420094044. ASCAP lists Burleigh as having written or cowritten over thirty gospel songs.

"Lover's Return." Nineteen-line rhyming poem in black dialect.* Narrated by "Mary," the poem tells the story of the return of her "Daddy" (lover), who has, she believes, come home to die. Stanza three, in italics, expresses Mary's general dissatisfaction with men, who *"treats* [*sic*] *women / Just like a pair o' shoes."* The poem was first published in *Lincoln University News* (October 24, 1928) and then in *Poetry* (1931).
Bibliography: *CP*, 125.

"Low to High." Poem. See *Montage of a Dream Deferred.*

"Luani of the Jungles." Short story, among Hughes's earliest published fiction. It concerns a university-educated European white man who is married to a beautiful Nigerian woman, Luani. They return to Africa from Europe. In Africa Luani leaves him and runs away to live in the jungle. The story was first published in

Harlem (November 1928). Other early stories set in Africa include "Bodies in the Moonlight," "The Little Virgin," and "The Young Glory of Him."
Bibliography: Rampersad, I, 139–140.

Lucas, Radcliffe (dates unknown). Lucas was a classmate of Hughes at Lincoln University* and agreed to serve as chauffeur during part of Hughes's poetry-reading tour of the American South in 1931. *See also* Bethune, Mary; Ingram, Zell.
Bibliography: *I Wonder As I Wander*, 42.

"Luck." Poem of two quatrains that feature slant rhymes relatively uncommon to Hughes's verse. The poem is a brief philosophical meditation on luck. The second stanza originally appeared as a separate poem entitled "Gifts" in *Shakespeare in Harlem*. The first stanza, under the title "Luck," appeared in *Fields of Wonder*. The two were combined to form this poem, which first appeared in *Selected Poems*.
Bibliography: *CP*, 333, 664; "Rhyme," in Ron Padgett, *A Handbook of Poetic Forms* (New York: Teachers and Writers Collaborative, 1987), 163–164.

"Lullaby." Subtitled "(For a Black Mother)." Poem of twenty-four lines, spoken by a mother to her "black baby." The lullaby focuses alternatively on the child and on images of a wondrous sky. It was first published in *Crisis** (March 24, 1926), arranged in three stanzas.
Bibliography: *CP*, 64, 629.

"Lullaby." Song, from *Street Scene*. Hughes and Elmer Rice* wrote the lyrics, and Kurt Weill* composed the music. At this writing, the song is not listed with ASCAP.* It is published by Warner Chappell, Ltd.
Bibliography: Booklet accompanying *Street Scene* [compact disc], performed by Kristine Ciesinski, Janis Kelly, Bonaventura Bottone, Richard van Allan, Catherine Zeta Jones, and the Orchestra and Chorus of the English National Opera, conducted by Carl Davis (London: Jay Records, 1996): CDJAY2–1232.

Lulu. A character in the poem "Yesterday and Today."

Lumumba, Patrice. *See* "Lumumba's Grave."

"Lumumba's Grave." Poem in six stanzas, all in ballad* form except for stanza five, which is an unrhymed triplet. The poem eulogizes Patrice Lumumba (1925–1961) and praises his courage and his having resisted colonialists and exploitative interests such as uranium-mining companies. The poem suggests that although Lumumba was buried in an unmarked grave, he will be remembered and his leadership will be celebrated. Lumumba served as the first prime minister of the Congo (now known as Zaire) after it gained complete independence from Belgium in 1960. Lumumba quickly became not just a literal but a symbolic representative of African independence from colonialism, as suggested in Hughes's poem. However, the Congolese military rebelled against Lumumba, and he asked for assistance from the United States. (Dag Hammarskjöld,* secretary general of the United Nations, died in a plane crash en route to the Congo.) General Joseph Mobutu took over power from Lumumba, who was assassinated on February 13, 1961. The poem was first published in a Spanish translation by Manuel Gonzáles entitled "El Sepulcro de Lumumba" in *Magisterio* (Mexico City) (November 1961). *See* "We, Too."

Bibliography: Aimé Césaire, *A Season in the Congo: A Play*, translation by Ralph Manheim of *Saison au Congo* (New York: Grove Press, 1969); *CP*, 533; Patrice Lumumba, *Congo, My Country*, translation by Graham Heath of *Congo, terre d'avenir, est-il menacé?* with a foreword by Colin Legum (New York: Praeger, 1969); Henry M. Stanley (Henry Morton Stanley), *The Congo and the Founding of Its Free State: A Story of Work and Exploration* (New York: Harper and Brothers, 1885).

"Lunch in a Jim Crow Car." Poem. *See* "Jim Crow Car."

Luxemburg, Rosa. *See* "Kids Who Die."

Lynching. The infinitive "to lynch" is of U.S. origin and originally meant "to condemn and punish by lynch law. In early use, implying chiefly the infliction of punishment such as whipping, tarring and feathering, or the like; now only, to inflict sentence of death by lynch law" (*The Oxford English Dictionary* [*OED*], 137). One reference in the *OED* is to Ralph Waldo Emerson, who used the word "lynch" in the book *English Traits* (1837). The precise origin of "lynch law" is disputed, with some etymologists believing that the term was associated with one Charles Lynch, a justice of the peace in Virginia, who was punished for illegally imprisoning members of the Tory Party in 1782. That is, "lynch law" may have come from "Lynch's Law," indicating outlaw justice. Other etymologists believe that "lynch law" can be traced to Lynche's Creek, South Carolina, site of a vigilante-justice uprising in 1768 (see *OED*, 138). From the post–Civil War era through the 1950s, lynching became a persistent form of murderous violence directed by certain white racists against African American males. From that period forward, "lynching" meant hanging but encompassed kidnapping and torture, which usually preceded the hanging itself. Asante and Mattson observe that "the decade between 1890 and 1900 was the most dangerous time in the post Civil War era for an African man [in the United States] to be alive. Nearly 1700 persons were lynched in that decade as compared to 921 in the decade between 1900 and 1910" (93). In American history, examples of "vigilante justice"—citizens' arrest and harsh, usually lethal, punishment of alleged criminals—are abundant. Lynching, however, was much less a form of vigilantism than an act of terror perpetrated by white mobs who believed themselves authorized to brutalize African Americans. Moreover, lynching often did not occur in response to behavior exhibited by its victim but resulted strictly from the unprovoked will of the mob. In other cases, lynching occurred because a victim was alleged to have transgressed against an unwritten racist "code" that assumed that African American males should have little or no contact with white females. It is this sort of case that Hughes dramatizes in the short story "Home," in which an African American man merely tips his hat politely to a white woman (his former music teacher), is seen doing this by white townsmen, and is lynched. To make matters worse for African American communities, local and state law-enforcement authorities, particularly in the southern states, often did not investigate lynchings, thereby lending tacit official approval to murders motivated by racist hatred. A large percentage of lynchings occurred in southern states. For example, between 1889 and 1918, 276 lynchings were recorded in Alabama, 214 in Arkansas, 373 in Mississipi, and 313 in Louisiana. However, lynchings occurred in many regions of the United States. For example, in the same period, 16 lynchings occurred in Washington State, 24 in Wyoming, 24 in Indiana, and 11 in Idaho. In Texas, a southwestern state, 335 lynchings occurred during this period. (One might observe that in all of these states, many unrecorded lynchings may also have occurred.) Asante and Mattson write, "The lynchings of Africans in the South became one of the greatest blots on the American society at the end of the 19th century and the beginning of the 20th" (100). *See The Barrier*; "Father and Son"; "Flight"; "Lynching Song"; *Mulatto*; "Silhouette"; "Song after Lynching." *See also* Jim Crow laws; The Scottsboro Boys.

Bibliography: Molefi K. Asante and Mark T. Mattson, *The African-American Atlas: Black History and Culture*, (New York: Macmillan, 1998), 98–101; *The Oxford English Dictionary* (*OED*), 2nd ed. (Oxford: Clarendon Press, 1989), vol. 9, 137–138.

"Lynching Song." Rhyming poem of fifteen lines that begins by pretending to exhort a lynch mob to "pull at the rope," but ends by depicting the "black boy's" "still body" as a symbol of resistance. It was first published in *Opportunity** (June 1936). *See also* "Flight"; "Silhouette."

Bibliography: *CP*, 214.

"Lynn Clarisse." Short story, included in the collection *Simple's Uncle Sam.* *See* Simple [Jesse B.] Stories.

M

"Ma Lord." Poem of sixteen lines. In this poem, perhaps more than in any other, Hughes attempts not just to create the effect of black dialect* but to transcribe it. The speaker presents a view of "Ma [my] Lord," Jesus, perceiving Christ to be humble ("no stuck-up man"), hardworking, and a "friend through eternity." The poem was first published in *Crisis** (June 1927). *See The Book of Negro Folklore*; Religion.
Bibliography: *CP*, 107.

"Ma Man." Sixteen-line poem in black dialect* and heavily influenced by the blues,* except that the speaker, a woman, celebrates her love for her "man," who in her view is extremely attractive and a fine musician (on the banjo). She wants to dance the "eagle-rock" (a popular dance in the 1920s) with him. The poem was first published in the *New Republic* (April 14, 1926) under the title "My Man." *See* "Song for a Banjo Dance."
Bibliography: *CP*, 66.

Madam Alberta K. Johnson. *See* The Madam Poems.

"Madam and Her Madam." Poem of six modified ballad* stanzas. Narrated by Madam (Alberta K. Johnson), it tells the tale of Madam's work as housekeeper, nanny, laundress, cook, and dog walker for a large white family in New York City. She believes that the wife (*her* "Madam") is trying to turn her into a "pack horse" through overwork. The poem was first published in *Common Ground* (Summer 1943). It was also published under the title "Madam to You" in *Southern Frontier* (December 1943). *See also* The Madam Poems; "The Negro Servant"; "A Song to a Negro Wash-woman."
Bibliography: *CP*, 285, 650; Myriam Diaz-Diocaretz, "Society (Pro)poses, Madam (Dis)poses," *Langston Hughes Review* 6, no. 1 (Spring 1987), 30–36; Dellita L. Martin,

"The 'Madam Poems' as Dramatic Monologue," *Black American Literature Forum* 15, no. 3 (Fall 1981), 97–99, reprinted in Mullen, 148–154.

"Madam and Her Might-Have-Been." Poem of eight stanzas in modified ballad* form and narrated by Madam (Alberta K. Johnson), who tells of having been married three times but of being more concerned about Jackson, the man she almost married and who treated her so well that she did not trust his motives. The poem was first published in *Cross Section* (1945). *See also* The Madam Poems.

Bibliography: *CP*, 309–310. *See also* bibliography for "Madam and Her Madam."

"Madam and the Army." Poem of six stanzas in modified ballad* form, with lines relatively shorter than those in other "Madam" poems. In this monologue Madam (Alberta K. Johnson) pretends to marvel that the U.S. Army has drafted her boyfriend because whenever she asks him to do anything for her, he exhibits a variety of ailments and incapacities. The poem was first published in *Negro Story* (November 1944). *See also* The Madam Poems.

Bibliography: *CP*, 283. *See also* bibliography for "Madam and Her Madam."

"Madam and the Census Man." Poem of eight stanzas in modified ballad* form. It is in this "Madam" poem that we learn Madam's full name, Alberta K. Johnson. She sternly advises the census surveyor with whom she speaks that the "K" is only a "K" and does not stand for a middle name, and she asks him to delete the "Mrs." before her name and replace it with "Madam." The poem was first published in *One-Way Ticket*. Later, Elie Siegmeister set the poem to music, and the song may have been part of "All about Women: A Sequence of Monologues, Poems, and Songs," which, as Rampersad indicates, Hughes "fashioned" for actress Hilda Haynes. (Rampersad does not indicate whether Haynes performed the sequence.) ASCAP* lists the song as being published by Seesaw Music Corporation, and the song's ASCAP registry number is 430313654. The electronic database World Cat lists this sequence under the title *Madam to You: A Song Cycle*, with music by Siegmeister, and lists the poems set to music as being "Madam and the Census Man," "Madam and the Minister," "Mama and Daughter," "Madam and the Rent Man," "Madam and the Fortune Teller," "Madam and the Number Runner," and "Madam and the Wrong Visitor." With Siegmeister, Hughes later collaborated on the *Wizard of Altoona* (unfinished opera). *See also* "Madam and Her Madam"; "Madam and the Minister."

Bibliography: *CP*, 355; Rampersad, II, 247. *See also* bibliography for "Madam and Her Madam."

"Madam and the Charity Child." Poem of eight stanzas in modified ballad* form and narrated by Madam (Alberta K. Johnson), who describes having adopted two children whom she ultimately could not rescue from life on the streets. She laments both the environment into which they were born and the lack of societal support she received after adopting them. The poem was first published in *Poetry* (September 1943). *See also* The Madam Poems.

Bibliography: *CP*, 276–277. *See also* bibliography for "Madam and Her Madam."

"Madam and the Crime Wave." Poem of four stanzas in modified ballad* form. The speaker, Madam (Alberta K. Johnson), meditates on the epidemic of crime in general and on the crimes of robbery and rape in particular. The poem was circulated by the Associated Negro Press in July 1943. *See also* "America's Young Black Joe!"; The Madam Poems.

Bibliography: *CP*, 582–583. *See also* bibliography for "Madam and Her Madam."

"Madam and the Fortune Teller." Poem of six stanzas in modified ballad* form and narrated by Madam (Alberta K. Johnson). The fortune teller (whom Madam calls "Madam") advises her that her good fortune is something that exists within her, not something to be found "on nobody else's shelf." The poem was first published in *One-Way Ticket. See also* "Madam and the Census Man"; The Madam Poems.

Bibliography: *CP*, 354–355. *See also* bibliography for "Madam and Her Madam."

"Madam and the Insurance Man." Poem of six stanzas in modified ballad* form and narrated by Madam (Alberta K. Johnson), who recalls a visit from an insurance agent requesting payment on a policy—payment Madam cannot make. The poem was first published in *Negro Story* (March 1945). *See also* The Madam Poems.

Bibliography: *CP*, 310. *See also* bibliography for "Madam and Her Madam."

"Madam and the Minister." Poem of seven stanzas, the first five of which are modified ballad* quatrains; the remaining two stanzas contain seven and six lines, respectively. Madam (Alberta K. Johnson) narrates, recalling being visited (and interrogated) by a minister, whose questions about her soul she resists. The poem was first published in *Cross Section* (1945). *See* "Madam and the Census Man"; The Madam Poems.

Bibliography: *CP*, 307. *See also* bibliography for "Madam and Her Madam."

"Madam and the Movies." Poem of four stanzas in modified ballad* form. Madam (Alberta K. Johnson) ponders the stark difference between movies, which are filled with romance, and her life, which is not. The poem was first published in *Common Ground* (Summer 1943). *See also* The Madam Poems.

Bibliography: *CP*, 284. *See also* bibliography for "Madam and Her Madam."

"Madam and the Newsboy." Poem of seven stanzas in modified ballad* form. Madam (Alberta K. Johnson) explains the appeal African American newspapers hold for her; she subscribes to the *Chicago Defender*.* She likes the sensational stories and gossip columns especially, but can also read about serious issues such as lynching*—and about Marva (Trotman), wife of Joe Louis.* *See Baltimore Afro American. See also* The Madam Poems.

Bibliography: *CP*, 308–309. *See also* bibliography for "Madam and Her Madam."

"Madam and the Number Runner." Poem. *See* "Madam and the Number Writer."

"Madam and the Number Writer." Poem of eight stanzas in modified ballad* form, narrated by Madam (Alberta K. Johnson), who tells of her compulsion to gamble—specifically, to bet on an illegal lottery with the help of a "number writer," or messenger, who goes between players and the operators of the lottery. Of all the "Madam" poems, this one may be the most superbly structured for comic effect. It was first published under the title "Madam and the Number Runner" in *Contemporary Poetry* (Autumn 1943). *See also* "Madam and the Census Man"; The Madam Poems.

Bibliography: *CP*, 269. *See also* bibliography for "Madam and Her Madam."

"Madam and the Phone Bill." Poem in eleven stanzas, most of which are in modified ballad* quatrains but some of which are broken irregularly. In this poem Madam (Alberta K. Johnson) is talking heatedly to the telephone company about her bill, which includes charges from a collect call placed by a friend of hers in Kansas City. The poem was first published in *One-Way Ticket. See also* The Madam Poems.

Bibliography: *CP*, 353–354. *See also* bibliography for "Madam and Her Madam."

"Madam and the Rent Man." Poem of thirty lines, most of which are in modified ballad* quatrains, some of which have fewer or more than four lines. Madam (Alberta K. Johnson) recalls a visit from her landlord's employee, who wants to collect the rent; she explains to him the repairs to her apartment that were promised but never made. The poem was first published in *Poetry* (September 1943). *See also* The Madam Poems.

Bibliography: *CP*, 275. *See also* bibliography for "Madam and Her Madam."

"Madam and the Wrong Visitor." Poem of seven stanzas in modified ballad* form. Madam (Alberta K. Johnson) tells of a visit from a mysterious stranger who turns out to be "Old Death." She sends him away and wakes from the feverish dream in which she imagined the visit. The poem was first published in *Cross Section* (1945). *See also* "Madam and the Census Man"; The Madam Poems.

Bibliography: *CP*, 308. *See also* bibliography for "Madam and Her Madam."

The Madam Poems. Hughes published eighteen poems featuring the character Alberta K. Johnson. In several poems she refers to herself as Madam, and her creator respected her wishes by including "Madam" as the first word in all the poems' titles. Hence the poems are now known collectively as "the Madam poems." With some variations in stanza lengths, all the poems are in ballad* form (rhyming quatrains) but modified insofar as Hughes often used very short lines and accommodated the form to the voice of Madam, who always narrates, sometimes in a monologue and sometimes in a dramatic monologue, in which the effect of a listener or interlocutor is created (see "Madam and the Minister," for example). "Madam" is by turns tough, acerbic, intentionally ironic and icon-oclastic, unintentionally humorous, combative, sagacious, and sentimental. Ul-timately she emerges in the poems as a kind of archetypal working American woman, survivor of the Great Depression, and resilient African American woman (and resident of Harlem*). In some respects, the values of self-reliance and self-definition she projects anticipate some of those articulated in the women's movement of the 1960s and 1970s, especially those concerning women as viable participants in the economy and women needing to become the primary definers of their identities. In this regard, it is noteworthy that most of Madam's conflicts are with men who attempt (but fail) to exert control over her life: her lover Roscoe, the "rent man," the "insurance man," a minister, and so on. The combination of a personality evoked, deceptively deft and economical story-telling, urban folk humor, and represented details of everyday life in Harlem has made the Madam poems among Hughes's best-known works and has lifted the stature of Madam close to that of Hughes's most famous fictional Harlemite, Jesse B. Simple (*see* Simple [Jesse B.] Stories). The Madam poems therefore constitute one of the most important segments of Hughes's poetic oeuvre and stand out as one of his most significant achievements in the 1940s; he began writing the Madam poems in the summer of 1943. The poems are also one vivid example of the extent to which Hughes used his writing to empathize with, represent, and even celebrate the situation of working-class African American women. Arguably the poems also allowed Hughes one of the most important media through which to manifest his ingenuity as a comic writer. Rampersad writes that the Madam poems sprang from a "creative mischief" in Hughes. "At Yaddo," writes Rampersad, "he began work on a series of verses with an as-sertive, brassy Harlem heroine named Alberta K. Johnson. . . . (Perhaps he meant to tease Arna Bontemps' wife, whose maiden name had been Alberta Johnson, although she was nothing like his creation)" (II, 78). Pieces of Madam's "bi-ography" emerge in the poems. For instance, her obsession with her own name emerges in "Madam and the Census Man"; the nature of her work and her attitude toward work appear in "Madam and Her Madam," "Madam and the Army," and "Madam's Past History"; her perspectives on societal problems appear in "Madam and the Charity Child" and "Madam and the Crime Wave"; her ideas about popular culture emerge in "Madam and the Movies" and "Madam and the Newsboy"; circumstances of her "love life," marriages, family, and attitudes toward men are evident in "Madam and Her Might-Have-Been," "Madam and the Army," "Madam and the Charity Child," and "Madam and the Phone Bill"; certain "facts" of everyday Harlem life are represented in "Madam and the Insurance Man," "Madam and the Number Writer," and "Madam and the Rent Man"; and her attitudes toward larger existential issues can be glimpsed in "Madam and the Fortune Teller," "Madam and the Minister," and "Madam and the Wrong Visitor." Composer Elie Siegmeister set several Madam Poems to music; *see* "Madam and the Census Man." *See* individual entries for each "Madam" poem. *See also* "The Ballad of Margie Polite"; Bontemps, Arna; *National Poetry Festival*; "The Negro Servant"; Women in Hughes's Writing.

Bibliography: Rampersad, II, 78–79. *See also* bibliography for "Madam and Her Madam."

"Madam to You." *See* "Madam and Her Madam."

Madam to You: A Song Cycle. *See* "Madam and the Census Taker."

"Madam's Calling Cards." Poem of five stanzas in modified ballad* form. Madam (Alberta K. Johnson) reports having ordered "calling [business] cards," chiefly because she wanted to see her name in print. She believes that they were too expensive. The printer asked her what style of type she preferred—old English or roman letter. She reports having told him that she wanted "American letter" because she is American. The poem was first published in *Negro Story* (December 1944) and was reprinted in *The Block*. *See also* The Madam Poems.

Bibliography: *CP*, 301–302. *See also* bibliography for "Madam and Her Madam."

"Madam's Christmas (or Merry Christmas Everybody)." Poem of five stanzas in modified ballad* form. Madam (Alberta K. Johnson) expresses regret about not having sent Christmas cards to "Jennie" (a cousin), Joe, and Jack and ends her monologue by wishing everyone a Merry Christmas. The poem was circulated to newspapers by the Associated Negro Press. *See also* "America's Young Black Joe!"; The Madam Poems.

Bibliography: *CP*, 583, 693. *See also* bibliography for "Madam and Her Madam."

"Madam's Past History." Poem of six stanzas in modified ballad* (quatrain) form, although two stanzas are stretched to five lines. Madam (Alberta K. Johnson) briefly explains her history as a businesswoman, having operated a hairdressing parlor and a barbecue stand and having cooked professionally (*see* "Madam and Her Madam"). She reports having sought employment with the Works Progress Administration (WPA), a job-creation program that was part of President Franklin Delano Roosevelt's* New Deal reforms in the 1930s. However, she was turned down by the WPA because she already had a source of income—a decision with which she was contented. The poem was first published in *Negro Story* (October 1944). *See also* "Ballad of Roosevelt"; The Madam Poems.

Bibliography: *CP*, 301. *See also* bibliography for "Madam and Her Madam."

"Madrid." Poem in free verse. Its epigraph is a two-sentence quotation from a "News Item" concerning the shelling of Madrid by fascist forces during the Spanish Civil War. The poem is a kind of lament for the city. It was first published in *Fight for Peace and Democracy* (July 1938) and was subsequently reprinted in *Good Morning Revolution: Uncollected Writings of Protest by Langston Hughes*, under the title "Madrid—1937." It is included in the second edition of *Collected Poems* but not the first. Berry indicates that the poem, in manuscript form, was inscribed "To Arthur Spingarn."* *See Baltimore Afro American.*

Bibliography: Berry, 113–115; *CP* [second edition only], 614, 695.

"Madrid Getting Used to Bombing—It's Food Shortage That Hurts." Newspaper article. *See Baltimore Afro American.*

"Madrid—1937." Poem. *See* "Madrid."

"Madrid's Flowers Hoist Blooms to Meet Raining Fascist Bombs." Newspaper article. *See Baltimore Afro American.*

Magazines in Which Hughes Published Poems, Stories, Essays, and Articles. *See* Periodicals in Which Hughes Published Poems, Stories, Essays, and Articles.

"Magnolia Flowers." Thirteen-line poem in free verse and with a suggestion of black dialect.* The speaker is looking for magnolia flowers but finds only a "corner full of ugliness." The poem was first published in *Fine Clothes to the Jew*.

Bibliography: *CP*, 122.

"Mailbox for the Dead." Unpublished short story, written in 1934. According to Rampersad, Maxim Lieber, Hughes's literary agent, believed the story to be sufficiently "poor" in quality that he and Hughes ultimately agreed to submit it to magazines only as being written by "David Boatman," a pen name. An alternate title for the story was "Postal Box: Love." Rampersad describes the style of the story as "deliberately maudlin." In *I Wonder As I Wander* Hughes describes the dream that led to his writing this story. *See also* "Eyes like a Gypsy"; "Hello Harry"; "A Posthumous Tale." *See also* "A House in Taos," another work inspired by a dream.

Bibliography: Rampersad, I, 300–301.

"Maker of the Blues." Essay in which Hughes briefly discusses the influence of the blues* on his work. It was published in *Negro Digest* (January 1943), 37–38. *See also* "I Remember the Blues"; "Songs Called the Blues."

"Mama and Daughter." Rhyming poem of twenty-one lines, representing a dialogue between a mother and daughter as the daughter is about to leave for the evening to join the man she loves. The mother tells the daughter of having once loved a young man (her husband, the daughter's father), who left her and whom she hopes "rots in hell." The poem was first published in *One-Way Ticket. Collected Poems* contains information about slight revisions the poem underwent. The poem was later included in a song cyle: *see* "Madam and the Census."
Bibliography: *CP*, 356–357, 666.

"Mammy." Poem in three couplets. In a kind of incantation the speaker indicates that he or she is waiting for "ma [my] Mammy—/ She is Death." The poem was first published under the title "Poem" in *Crisis** (August 1924).
Bibliography: *CP*, 40.

"Man." Fifteen-line poem in two stanzas. The speaker discusses what he learned between boyhood and manhood about friendship, loving women, and drunkenness. The poem was first published in *Fields of Wonder*.
Bibliography: *CP*, 333.

"The Man in My Life." Song, from *Simply Heavenly*. Hughes wrote the lyrics, and David Martin composed the music. ASCAP* lists the song as being published by the Bourne Company, and the song's ASCAP registry number is 430050947.

"Man into Men." Free-verse poem of twenty lines in three stanzas. Each stanza concerns a man coming home by way of a busy street. The first stanza is from the point of view of a "nigger," the second from that of a "Negro," the third from that of a "man." The second and third points of view are progressively more self-assured, psychically healthy, and socially empowered. The poem embodies one of the most direct—and arguably most perceptive—expressions of how Hughes viewed the connection between language and one's conception of oneself. The poem was first published in *One-Way Ticket*.
Bibliography: *CP*, 364.

"March Moon." Ten-line free-verse poem in two stanzas. It personifies the moon, depicting it as "naked" but unembarrassed. The poem was first published in *The Weary Blues*.
Bibliography: *CP*, 93.

Marshall, Thurgood (1908–1993). American lawyer and U.S. Supreme Court justice. Marshall was born in Baltimore, Maryland. His father was a Pullman-car porter, and his mother was a teacher. He earned a B.A. from Lincoln University,* which was also Hughes's alma mater. Marshall was denied entrance, on segregationist grounds, to the University of Maryland School of Law, so he studied law at Howard University. Later he worked successfully to desegregate the University of Maryland. Marshall became national legal counsel for the NAACP* in 1938, worked to enhance its Legal Defense Fund, and for over two decades was a key figure in many of the NAACP's successful legal battles, the most renowned of which is the case(s) of *Brown v. Board of Education.** President John F. Kennedy appointed Marshall to a U.S. appellate court. President Lyndon B. Johnson appointed him solicitor general and then nominated him to the Supreme Court in 1967. Marshall served on the Court from that year until his retirement in 1991. Marshall praised Hughes's history of the NAACP, *Fight for Freedom.*

Bibliography: Rampersad, II, 356; *Simple Justice* [video recording] (Alexandria, VA: PBS Video, 1993); Mark V. Tushnet, *Making Constitutional Law: Thurgood Marshall and the Supreme Court, 1961–1991* (New York: Oxford University Press, 1997); Juan Williams, *Thurgood Marshall: American Revolutionary* (New York: Times Books, 1998).

Marx, Karl. *See* Marxism.

Marxism. The term "Marxism" refers to a broad spectrum of ideas espoused by German philosopher and political economist Karl Marx (1818–1883), ideas that appeared in *The Communist Manifesto* (1848), cowritten with Friedrich Engels, in *Capital* (three volumes, 1867, 1887, 1894), and in a number of other publications. Countless other writers, politicians, academics, military leaders, and activists elaborated on, extended, quarreled with, and altered Marx's views, and the rise of communism, led by Vladimir I. Lenin and others in the Soviet Union and then extending globally, shaped particular national, governmental, and militaristic enactments of those ideas. At its most basic, Marxism advances a notion of humanity in which men and women are distinct from other animals not just because of sophisticated language but also because of "creative labor." Marx also perceived human beings to be in constant interaction with the material world, chiefly by means of work. Capitalism, an economic system Marx believed to be exemplified especially by Great Britain in his time, creates a situation in which one social class (the *bourgeoisie*) takes advantage of the creative labor of another social class (the *proletariat*, or "workers"). Marx saw human history as being driven by such conflict between classes; he saw it also as a process that evolved in cycles or spasms of conflict and revolution. "Dialectical materialism" refers, in part, to a fusion of these ideas about humans as "material," laboring creatures and about human history as being driven by conflicts between social classes. "Socialism" refers to a much more general, vague view of history and economics, one influenced by Marxism, but one that has had numerous variations, including the so-called middle way (between capitalism and communism) in Sweden.

Hughes was influenced by Marxist concepts, which were among the rich mix of ideas alive in the Harlem Renaissance,* but he was not a systematic reader of Marx's writings and did not see himself as "*a* Marxist" or "*a* Communist." He believed that he saw clear evidence that African Americans and white working Americans were exploited, and especially in the 1930s, connections between racism and class conflict seemed obvious to him. He expressed these views in essays, plays, poems, and other writings, including *Angelo Herndon Jones, Don't You Want to Be Free?, Front Porch*, and the poetry in *A New Song*. Part of his interest in Marxist ideas sprang from a reaction to the rise of fascism (*see Baltimore Afro American*); therefore, Italy's invasion of Ethiopia, Hitler's acts of war, and Soviet leader Joseph Stalin's pact with Hitler were occurrences that led him eventually to support enthusiastically the Allies' war against Hitler and Mussolini and to revise his views of the Soviet Union. *See* "Ballad of Roosevelt"; "Ballads of Lenin"; "Black Workers"; "Call of Ethiopia"; "Chant for Tom Mooney"; "Concerning Red Baiting"; "Good Morning Revolution"; "Goodbye, Christ"; "Johannesburg Mines"; "Langston Hughes Speaks"; "A New Song"; "One More 'S' in the U.S.A."; "Revolution"; "Song of the Revolution"; "The Soviet Union"; "The Soviet Union and Color"; "The Soviet Union and Health"; "The Soviet Union and Jews"; "The Soviet Union and Women"; "Wait." *See also* Césaire, Aimé; "Here to Yonder"; John Reed Club; McCarthyism; *The Messenger*; Politics; Reed, John; Roumain, Jacques; Sullivan, Noel; Wright, Richard.

Bibliography: Frederic L. Bender, ed., *Karl Marx: Essential Writings* (New York: Harper and Row, 1972); Berry; Hutchinson; Rampersad, I, II.

"Mary Had a Little Baby." Song. *See Ballad of the Brown King*.

"Mary Winosky." Short story. *See* Central High School.

Mason, Mrs. Charlotte Osgood (1854–1946). American socialite and patron of the arts. Mason was one of the most influential patrons of the arts in the Harlem Renaissance,* earning the nickname "Godmother." Her relationship with Alain Locke* was extremely close, and it was Locke who introduced Hughes to her. To some degree, Mason supported both Hughes and Zora Neale Hurston* financially in the late 1920s, but Hughes and Mason had a falling-out, about which Hughes became bitter. One source of the disagreement was conflict between what Mason wanted Hughes to write and what he wanted to write, Mason preferring him to explore "primitive" African perspectives. "She wanted me to be more African than Harlem*—primitive in the simple, intuitive and noble sense of the word," Hughes wrote in *I Wonder As I Wander* (5). Mason did not respond favorably to parts of *Not without Laughter* that Hughes showed her. As

Rampersad explains, Locke and Hurston took Mason's side in the disagreement. Mason withdrew her financial support of Hughes. "So that winter [following the break with Mason] left me ill in my soul" (*I Wonder As I Wander*, 5). Rampersad and Watson discuss Hughes's relationship with Mason and Mason's role in the Harlem Renaissance at some length. *See also* "The Blues I'm Playing"; *The Ways of White Folks*.

Bibliography: *I Wonder As I Wander, 5–8*; Thomas H. Nigel, "Patronage and the Writing of Langston Hughes's *Not without Laughter*: A Paradoxical Case," *College Language Association Journal* 42, no. 1 (September 1998), 48–70; Ostrom, 6–17; Rampersad, I (see especially 185–200); Ralph D. Story, "Patronage and the Harlem Renaissance: You Get What You Pay For," *College Language Association Journal* 32, no. 3 (March 1989), 284–295; Watson.

Masters of the Dew. Novel by Jacques Roumain. Translated by Langston Hughes and Mercer Cook (New York: Reynal and Hitchcock, 1947). 180 pp. Published posthumously in 1944, *Gouverneurs de la rosée* represents the culmination of Jacques Roumain's literary work. Throughout much of his adult life, Roumain worked to promote an accurate literary representation of Haitian peasant culture. In *Gouverneurs de la rosée* Roumain takes into account both the French-speaking audience to which the novel is directed and the Creole-speaking peasants who serve as its inspiration. The task of translating such a work was tackled in 1947 by Langston Hughes and Mercer Cook, who successfully collaborated to present a coherent translation that remains faithful to the lyrical nature of Jacques Roumain's language.

Jacques Roumain was born on June 4, 1907, the eldest of eleven children from a wealthy "mulatto" family in Port-au-Prince, Haiti. His grandfather, Tancrède Auguste, had been president of Haiti for a short time. As was expected for families of his social class, his parents sent him to Europe to complete his education when he was sixteen. After time spent in Switzerland, France, and Germany, he went to Spain with the intention of studying agronomy. Whether or not he ever did is unclear, but he did perfect his fluency in Spanish before returning home to Haiti in 1917. The American military had been occupying Haiti since 1915, and it would remain until 1934. Like most Haitians, the young Roumain was hostile to the foreign presence in Haiti and joined the resistance movement. The American occupation gave rise to a growing pride among the Haitians in their heritage. In 1927 Roumain helped found *La Revue indigène*, a journal dedicated to the promotion and valorization of Haitian national literature. The Indigenist movement, a precursor to Negritude, grew from this publication. From 1927 to 1928, Roumain wrote fourteen poems for *La Revue indigène*. These early poems do not yet constitute what would later be called Roumain's desire to "Haitianize" literature coming from Haiti. Rather, his writings from this period reflect the melancholia of the French fin de siècle poets that he undoubtedly studied during his time in Europe.

Roumain's literary interest in Haitian culture began to surface in the early

1930s. After the publication of two short works, *La Proie et l'ombre* (1930) and *Les Fantoches* (1931), which treat his own social class, Roumain began to focus his writing on the description of Haitian peasant customs with his *La Montagne ensorcelée* (1931). Jean Price-Mars's *Ainsi parla l'oncle* (1928) had ignited in Roumain a lifelong concern for the cultural depiction of Haitian rural life and its African roots. In the same year that he published *La Montagne ensorcelée*, Roumain accepted the position of under secretary of the interior in the government of the new "nationalist" president, Eugène Roy. Soon frustrated with the indifference and stagnation he saw around him, he resigned the same year and turned his efforts to the promotion of communism as a solution for Haiti's social problems. Shortly after the end of the American occupation in 1934, Roumain founded the Haitian Communist Party. During the same year he published his *Analyse schématique*, a Marxist analysis of Haiti's economic conditions. Sténio Vincent, then president of Haiti, had Roumain arrested and imprisoned for treasonous activities. After two years in prison, he was released in 1936 and was sent into exile. During his six years away from Haiti, Roumain traveled widely, studied, and wrote. In Paris he studied at the Institut de paléontologie humaine and the Musée de l'homme. In Europe Roumain did not silence his pen. He was tried and convicted in the French courts for public offense against a chief of state after criticizing the president of the Dominican Republic in his article "La Tragédie haitienne" (*Regards*, November 18, 1937). When World War II chased him out of Europe in 1939, he went to New York, where he studied ethnology at Columbia University. His stay in the United States prompted him to write *Griefs de l'homme noir*, a study of the condition of American blacks (1939). Before his return to Haiti, Nicolás Guillén invited Roumain to Havana, where he continued his anthropological research. In 1941 the newly elected Haitian president, Elie Lescot, invited Roumain to return to his homeland. Once there, Roumain founded the Bureau d'ethnologie haitienne to foster the study of Haitian peasantry and also created the Musée des arts et traditions populaires d'Haiti. The Catholic church was waging a controversial campaign at this time to convert all worshippers of voodoo deities. Roumain reacted by publishing his *A propos de la campagne "anti-superstitieuse,"* calling first for the education of peasants so that they might understand what was happening to them. Lescot appointed Roumain to a diplomatic post in the Haitian Embassy in Mexico in 1943. Afraid that he might be compromising his political principles, Roumain nonetheless accepted so as to be able to promote communism from an influential position. In Mexico Roumain wrote prolifically and completed a collection of poems entitled *Bois-d'ébène*. In 1943 he returned to Port-au-Prince because of poor health. On August 18, 1944, he died there of cirrhosis of the liver. He was thirty-seven.

Roumain had been introduced to the poetry of Langston Hughes in Europe and in Haiti before meeting him for the first time in 1931. In that year Hughes quietly spent several months in Haiti, largely unannounced. The day before his departure, he met with Roumain for one hour. They shared an immediate bond.

Roumain's budding relationship with Langston Hughes and the inspiration of Price-Mars's work led Roumain to change the course of his literary career. His writing passed from introspective analysis to a focus on the collective black experience. Hughes returned home from his trip to Haiti and wrote polemical critiques of class divisions there, directed largely at mulattos such as Roumain who did little to help their black brothers. In 1931 he wrote the article "People without Shoes," which was not translated into French until 1934, when it appeared on the front page of the newspaper *Haiti-Journal* (July 26, 1934) with the caption "Un Nègre Américain nous abîme." This was the year during which Roumain was put on trial for Communist activities, and this perhaps accounts for his silence during the whole debate. Hughes was one of the many intellectuals who wrote and worked for his release from prison.

While Roumain was in exile, he had several opportunities to meet with Hughes, although the extent of their contact is unknown. They were in Paris in June 1937 during the Second Congress of Writers for the Defense of Culture and perhaps met again in December of the same year after Hughes's trip to Spain. Both were in New York in 1939, but the only record of their encounters during that time is that of a banquet in Roumain's honor at the Harlem* YMCA on November 15 at which Hughes was a guest of honor (Fowler, 87). Despite the lack of documentation on their meetings, their professional work often intersected. In 1942 Hughes translated Roumain's newly published "Sur le chemin de Guinée" and "Quand bat le tam-tam" for the Dudley Fitts *Anthology of Contemporary Latin-American Poetry* (Norfolk, CT: New Directions, 1942). Shortly after they originally met in 1931, Roumain published his poem "Langston Hughes" in a Port-au-Prince newspaper, documenting the question of an authentic black identity through Hughes's journeys to Africa and Europe and his return to Harlem.

Shortly before his early death Roumain had completed his capstone novel, *Gouverneurs de la rosée*. One thousand copies were published in the original French in 1944, and a translation of the novel by Hughes and Mercer Cook, a professor of French at Howard University and a scholar of Haitian literature, appeared in 1947. The novel is the story of a young man, Manuel, who returns to the Haitian village where he grew up after many years working on a sugarcane plantation in Cuba. He finds the village drought-stricken and divided by a family feud that had bitterly culminated in bloodshed. He falls in love with the beautiful Annaise, a member of the opposite camp, and together they try to inspire the villagers to unite to bring water to the land. While his earlier novel, *La Montagne ensorcelée*, more objectively treats ethnographic details, *Gouverneurs* offers a metaphor for a larger vision of man as well as a solution to the peasants' plight. Manuel offers a model of an enlightened peasant who brings new ideas but still respects the traditions of his people. The novel relies upon religious symbolism to convey a message of hope embedded in the Communist ideal of the *coumbite*, a collective activity that will result in the irrigation of everyone's fields.

The most remarkable aspect of this work is Roumain's artful manipulation of the peasants' language. Roumain wanted to represent authentic Haitian Creole and at the same time make the work accessible to a wide reading public. The result is a modified French, faithful to peasant speech in rhythm and lyricism, spiced with Creole words, songs, and proverbs. The complexity of Roumain's language becomes problematic for translators. In Hughes and Cook's translation, whenever possible, Creole words from the original text are simply given their English equivalents, disrupting the authenticity of Roumain's linguistic project. For the most part, the artistic integrity of the work is not harmed, and Hughes and Cook succeed in capturing the musical qualities of Roumain's language. J. Michael Dash, in his 1978 introduction, offers praise for the quality of Hughes and Cook's work, but offers one major criticism that reflects the complex task of translating this work. Hughes and Cook translate "nègre" as "negro," but, as Dash points out, "[t]he word 'nègre' in Creole has lost all pejorative or even racial overtones and is best translated as 'man' or 'brother'. Hughes and Cook have consistently translated it as 'negro' often creating a very odd situation when it is used by the peasants" (20). Roumain apparently had great faith in Hughes's skill as a translator, however. Roumain's widow wrote to Hughes soon after her husband's death: "Jacques always thought that you alone were capable of doing this work, let us say of adaptation, from one language to another. I've just learned . . . that you've accepted. . . . the dream Jacques had in Mexico when he finished his novel, of seeing it translated into English and presented to the public by Langston, becomes a reality" (quoted in Fowler, 87). *See also* Marxism.

Bibliography: Herman F. Bostick, "From Romanticism to Militant Optimism: The Poetic Quest of Jacques Roumain," *Langston Hughes Review* 2, no. 2 (Fall 1983): 6–14; Martha Cobb, *Harlem, Haiti, and Havana: A Comparative Critical Study of Langston Hughes, Jacques Roumain, Nicolás Guillén* (Washington, DC: Three Continents Press, 1979); J. Michael Dash, "Introduction" to *Masters of the Dew*, by Jacques Roumain, transl. Langston Hughes and Mercer Cook, Caribbean Writers Series 12 (London: Heinemann, 1978), 5–21; Melvin Dixon, "Rivers Remembering Their Source: Comparative Studies in Black Literary History—Langston Hughes, Jacques Roumain, and Négritude," in *Afro-American Literature: The Reconstruction of Instruction*, ed. Dexter Fisher and Robert B. Stepto (New York: Modern Language Association, 1979), 25–43; Carolyn Fowler, "The Shared Vision of Langston Hughes and Jacques Roumain," *Black American Literature Forum* 15, no. 3 (Fall 1981), 84–88; *I Wonder As I Wander*, 208–210; Jacques Roumain, *Masters of the Dew*, transl. Langston Hughes and Mercer Cook (New York: Reynal and Hitchcock, 1947).

Diane Duffrin Kelley

"A Matter for a Book." Short story, included in the collection *Simple Speaks His Mind. See* Simple [Jesse B.] Stories.

"Maybe." Poem of a single quatrain in which lines two and four rhyme. The phrasing is playful; the subject is "understanding" between two lovers. The poem was first published in *Selected Poems*.

Bibliography: *CP*, 466.

"Mazie Dies Alone in the City Hospital." Poem in two ballad* stanzas, spoken (in black dialect*) by Mazie, who asks God rhetorically why He is allowing her to die in a hospital bed and not "where the band's a-playin' / Noisy and loud." The poem was first published in the magazine *Harlem* (November 1928).

Bibliography: *CP*, 126.

McCarthyism. The word "McCarthyism" now refers to almost any sort of political "witch-hunting," demonization of political opponents, or overreaction to perceived threats. In the United States during the 1950s, it referred specifically to the anti-Communist program and the demagogic tactics of U.S. Senator Joseph McCarthy (1908–1957) and his followers. Partly out of a genuine fear of communism and partly for cynical political reasons, McCarthy used his chairmanship of a committee in the U.S. Congress to expose alleged members of the Communist Party, Communist and Russian "sympathizers" (sometimes called "fellow travelers"), and manipulate individuals to testify against friends and associates. The Cold War with the USSR in general and televised hearings in particular helped boost McCarthy's popularity, but eventually he was shown to be abusive, unfair, and often uninterested in legitimate evidence. McCarthy's reckless investigations of the U.S. State Department and the U.S. Army, as well as his contempt for due process, resulted eventually in his being officially censured by the Senate and in his political demise. Advanced alcoholism caused his death shortly thereafter. Not surprisingly, Hughes, because of his interest during the 1930s in Marxist ideas, labor issues, and the Soviet Union, was called to testify before McCarthy's Permanent Sub-Committee on Investigations in 1953. Rampersad describes Hughes as being "badly shaken" upon receiving the subpoena from a U.S. marshall (209). With advice from attorneys Arthur Spingarn,* Lloyd K. Garrison, and Frank D. Reeves, Hughes first met with members of the subcommittee and their associates to determine the form his testimony would take. Those present included congressional counsel G. David Schine and Roy Cohn and U.S. Senator Everett Dirksen. Rampersad observes that "McCarthy had crushed men of far greater prestige and importance than Langston Hughes" and that the "human cost of the McCarthy investigation was already high—if only by democratic standards" (211). Hughes agreed to answer questions from the subcommittee in an open hearing and provide the subcommittee with a statement concerning his political history and his writings. He appeared before the subcommittee on March 26, 1953, when his statement (*see* "Langston Hughes Speaks") was officially accepted. He was then questioned by both Roy Cohn and McCarthy. A copy of the transcript of the hearing is held in the Langston Hughes Papers in the James Weldon Johnson Memorial Collection at the Beinecke Rare Book and Manuscript Library, Yale University, and Rampersad reprints extensive excerpts from it (II, 215–219). Rampersad notes that unlike Paul Robeson,* writer Dashiell Hammett, and Professor Doxey Wilkerson (of Howard University), all of whom refused to testify before McCarthy's sub-committee, Hughes cooperated, knowing that he would "draw the disapproval, even the contempt, of the white left, but keep more or less intact the special place he had painstakingly carved out within the black community" (II, 219). He chose not to testify against friends or acquaintances but only to answer questions about his own political views and his writings. Rampersad characterizes Hughes's appearance before the Permanent Sub-Committee on Investigations as "a rhetorical *tour de force*" and as a delicate political, legal, and moral balancing act (II, 218–219). He also observes that Hughes's choice to appear before the subcommittee raises interesting questions about Hughes's attitude at the time toward socialist ideas and how those ideas had (and had not) ameliorated the situation of African Americans in the United States. Rampersad also summarizes reactions by individuals (such as Charles S. Johnson*) and the black media (such as the *Amsterdam News*) to Hughes's having testified. *See* "Concerning Red Baiting"; "Democracy and Me"; "Goodbye Christ"; John Reed Club; Marxism; "One More 'S' in the U.S.A."; Politics; "Something to Lean On"; Sullivan, Noel; "This Puzzles Me"; "Un-American Investigators."

Bibliography: Rampersad, II, 209–219; Thomas Rosteck, *"See It Now" Confronts Mc-Carthyism: Television Documentary and the Politics of Representation* (Tuscaloosa: University of Alabama Press, 1994); Ellen Schrecker, *Many Are the Crimes: McCarthyism in America* (Boston: Little, Brown, 1998).

McDillors, Dr. In chapter 10 of *Not Without Laughter*, he is referred to as "Old White Dr. McDillors, beloved of all Negroes in Stanton." He makes a house call to treat Sandy, the main character, who injured his foot at the carnival.

McKay, Claude (1889–1948). American poet, novelist, and political activist. A native of Jamaica, McKay moved to the United States in 1912, planning to study at the Tuskegee Institute, but he left Alabama for Kansas shortly thereafter and then moved to New York City, deciding to become a writer, not an agriculturalist. (In Jamaica he had already published two books of poems.) In New York he found supportive editors in Waldo Frank,* who published his work in the magazine *The Seven Arts*, and Max Eastman, who published his work in *The Liberator*. (Eastman also helped edit *The Masses*, with which John Reed* was affiliated.) McKay was profoundly influenced by Marxist ideology at the time, and although his book *Harlem Shadows* (1922) helped trigger the Harlem Renaissance,* McKay remained aloof from W.E.B. Du Bois* and other key figures of the movement. McKay left for Russia in 1923, returned to Harlem,* and divided his time between the United States, France, and Spain until 1929. In 1926 McKay was the chief editor of the magazine *FIRE!!,* which Hughes helped edit and of which only one issue appeared. One purpose of the magazine was to feature younger, more radical African American writers living in Harlem. Another was to challenge the Harlem cultural establishment led by W.E.B. Du Bois and others. McKay returned to Harlem in 1935, converted to Catholicism in 1944, and taught at the Catholic Youth Organization in Chicago until his death. His other books include the novels *Home to Harlem* (1928) and *Banana Bottom* (1933), *Gingertown* (1932), a collection of stories, and an autobiography, *A Long Way from Home* (1937). Although Hughes and McKay were two of the most successful Harlem Renaissance writers, they were never close associates, let alone friends, partly because of McKay's aloofness but also because both were inveterate travelers and were rarely in Harlem at the same time. Nonetheless, McKay influenced Hughes intellectually. Rampersad goes so far as to say that McKay was the "principal influence among blacks on Langston as a young writer" (II, 144). As writers, they share many similarities, including the capacity to combine lyric gifts with political acumen, as well as a stubborn independence of spirit. Hughes's achievement in poetry outstripped McKay's, even as McKay's achievement as a novelist outstripped Hughes's. McKay committed himself more fully first to Marxism* and then, ironically, to religion* than did Hughes, whose affiliation with Marxism was relatively brief and idiosyncratic and whose skepticism about religion was lifelong. Of McKay, Rampersad writes, "The one-time radical had died in the arms of the Roman Catholic Church. Illness, poverty, and isolation had driven him there. McKay had even died without ever meeting his own daughter, Hope, whom Langston had encountered in Jamaica" (II, 144).

Bibliography: Wayne F. Cooper, *Claude McKay: Rebel Sojourner in the Harlem Renaissance: A Biography* (Baton Rouge: Louisiana State University Press, 1987); James R. Giles, *Claude McKay* (Boston: Twayne, 1976); Lewis, *WHWV;* Rampersad, II, 141–145; Tyrone Tillery, *Claude McKay: A Black Poet's Struggle for Identity* (Amherst: University of Massachusetts Press, 1992).

"Me and My Song." Poem of thirty-four lines in free verse. It is a terse but nonetheless celebratory poem concerning an African American poet's sense of African heritage. Fully half the lines consist of a single word, such as "Black," "Africa," "Rich," "Strong," "Deep," and "Song." The poem was first published in *Jim Crow's Last Stand.*

Bibliography: *CP*, 296.

"Me and the Mule." Poem of two rhyming quatrains. The speaker, a self-described black man, compares himself to a mule with regard to self-assurance and resilience. The poem was first published in *Negro Story* (1942) and also published in *Shakespeare in Harlem. Collected Poems* contains information about slight revisions the poem underwent. Taj Mahal set the poem to music and performed it in the 1991 production of *Mule Bone.*

Bibliography: *CP*, 239, 652; Taj Mahal, *Mule Bone: Music Composed and Performed by Taj Mahal, Lyrics by Langston Hughes* [compact disc] (Grammavision 1991), distributed by Rhino Records (Santa Monica, CA), R2 79432.

"Mean Old Yesterday." Poem in four ballad* quatrains, with a mood and phrasing reminiscent of the blues.* The poem concerns regret as well as bitterness toward a spouse. It was first published in *Olivant Quarterly* (1955).
Bibliography: *CP*, 448–449.

"Meine dunklen Hände." Song cycle. ASCAP* lists this title as a single song, with Hughes and Arna Bontemps* as lyricists, and with Hermann Reutter and Paridan Von De Knesbeck [*sic*] as translators and composers. The ASCAP registry number is 430475480, and Schott Music Corporation is listed as the publisher. However, other databases, including the catalogue of the University of California library, suggest the work is a cycle of five songs by Hughes and Bontemps, with Reutter listed as composer but with Paridan von dem Knesbeck (note spelling changes) as translator of the lyrics from English to German. Additionally, the University of California library catalog lists *My Dark Hands* (English for Meine dunklen Hände) as a song cycle with lyrics by Hughes (Bontemps is not mentioned) and with one Günter Raphael as composer.

"Mellow." Poem. *See Montage of a Dream Deferred*; Revision, Process of, and Hughes.

"Memo to Non-White Peoples." Free-verse poem of twenty-six lines and five stanzas. In the "memo" Hughes advises nonwhite peoples that a collective "they" (powerful, predominantly white nations) want them (nonwhite peoples) to abuse drugs and alcohol and to remain in poverty, and the poem suggests that this situation "is the same" "from Cairo to Chicago, / Capetown to the Caribbean." The poem is plainly one of Hughes's most unvarnished critiques of what he perceived to be the oppression of people of color globally. Published in the 1950s, the poem exhibits the rhetoric and the political focus more in keeping with Hughes's overtly political poems of the 1930s, such as "Advertisement for the Waldorf Astoria," "Good Morning Revolution," and "Goodbye Christ." It was first published in *Africa South* (April 1957).
Bibliography: *CP*, 456–457.

"Memories of Christmas." Essay in which Hughes recalls Christmases during his childhood and during his travels abroad. It was published in *The Langston Hughes Reader*.
Bibliography: *The Langston Hughes Reader*, 485–488.

Mercedes. The female singer to whom the poem "To the Dark Mercedes of 'El Palacio de Amor' " is addressed.

"Merry Christmas." Poem in eight ballad* stanzas. With satiric irony the poem wishes Merry Christmas to a variety of nations that are, according to the speaker's implicit point of view, oppressed by Western nations. The oppressed nations identified include China, India, and Haiti, and the oppressors identified include the United States and England. The poem was first published in *New Masses* (December 1940). *See* Religion.

Bibliography: *CP*, 132.

"Merry-Go-Round." Poem, subtitled "Colored Child at a Carnival," in thirteen lines, with an irregular rhyme scheme. The speaker is an African American child who is asking "mister," a white man, where the Jim Crow seats are on the merry-go-round. Using a naïve point of view, reducing Jim Crow laws* to absurdity, and leaving open the possibility that the merry-go-round might be read as a symbol of repetitive injustice, Hughes arguably achieves one of his most tersely potent critiques, in poetry, of "Jim Crow." The poem was first published in *Common Ground* (Spring 1942). It was also published in *Shakespeare in Harlem. See National Poetry Festival.*

Bibliography: *CP*, 240.

"Message to the President." Rhyming poem. It is structured and phrased as a kind of "open letter" to President Franklin Delano Roosevelt.* Although the poem never mentions his name, the references to Roosevelt's "fireside chats"—radio addresses to the nation—Hitler, the predicament of Jews, and the oppression of Czechoslovakia point obviously to Roosevelt. The "argument" of the poem is straightforward insofar as Hughes asks Roosevelt to apply the same values, democratic ideals, and notions of freedom to the condition of African Americans as he does when he speaks out against Hitler and on behalf of oppressed peoples in Europe. Hughes asks Roosevelt to make speeches denouncing "segregation" and "Jim Crow" in the United States. The editors of *Collected Poems* could not date the poem or establish where it was first published, but they deduce that the poem obviously was written during World War II. Because the poem mentions Czechoslovakia, which Hitler's military invaded before the United States entered World War II, and because it refers to Roosevelt's speeches "to England" (part of Roosevelt's effort to reinforce British morale before the United States entered the war), one might further speculate, at least, that the poem was written in 1940 or 1941. *See* "Ballad of Roosevelt"; "Crow Goes, Too"; "Judge William Hastie"; "Merry-Go-Round." *See also* Jim Crow Laws.

Bibliography: *CP*, 590, 694.

The Messenger. Magazine published in New York City and founded in 1921 by A. Philip Randolph* and Chandler Owen. Like the magazines *Crisis** and *Opportunity,** the *Messenger* helped shape and complicate the intellectual character of the Harlem Renaissance.* Its content was influenced by Marxist-socialist ideas and was therefore considered more politically radical than that of *Crisis* and *Opportunity*, but the magazine also insisted on an American intellectual identity. As Hutchinson demonstrates, the *Messenger*, especially under the editorship of George Schuyler* between 1923 and 1927, expressed skepticism about some ideas of ethnic purity that informed concepts of the New Negro* and the Talented Tenth* promulgated by Alain Locke* and W.E.B. Du Bois,* so its editorial profile was in sharp contrast to that of *Crisis*. (Wallace Thurman* also worked as an editor for the magazine.) Like both *Crisis* and *Opportunity*, however, the *Messenger* provided Hughes with an important early forum for his poetry and was part of the political milieu that influenced Hughes's attraction to socialist ideas in the 1930s. The *Messenger* ceased publication in 1928 but was later "reincarnated" as the *Black Worker*. Among the poems by Hughes published in the *Messenger* are "Autumn Note," "For Dead Mimes," "Formula," "Gods," "Minnie Sings Her Blues," "Poem for Youth," "Steel Mills," and "Wise Men."

Bibliography: Hutchinson, especially chapter 10, "Mediating Race and Nation: The Cultural Politics of the *Messenger*," 289–312; Theodore Kornweibel, Jr., *No Crystal Stair: Black Life and the Messenger, 1917–1928* (Westport, CT: Greenwood Press, 1975).

"Metropolitan Museum." Poem in three three-line stanzas in which lines one and three rhyme. The understated speaker recalls visiting a museum—presumably the Metropolitan Museum of Art in New York City—seeing a Grecian urn, thinking of (John) Keats,* and enjoying a brief epiphany or daydream involving an asphodel flower. Keats (1795–1821) is considered one of the most important British "romantic" poets, and perhaps his best-known poem is "Ode on a Grecian Urn." Although Hughes was well read, he infrequently alludes in his poetry to other poets, and this is the only allusion in his published poetry to Keats. The poem was first published in *Crisis** (December 1966).

Bibliography: *CP*, 550.

"Mexican Market Woman." Seven-line poem in which lines two and seven rhyme. It represents close, rather unvarnished observation of the woman, referring to her as a "hag" but also implicitly honoring the harshness of her life. Regarding the time Hughes spent in Mexico, where he lived with his father for about a year, see Rampersad. As the editors of *Collected Poems* note, this is the only published poem springing from Hughes's experience in Mexico. It was first published in *Crisis** (1922). *See also* "Parisian Beggar Woman."

Bibliography: *CP*, 25, 621.

Meyerowitz, Jan (Hans-Hermann) (1913–1998). German American composer. Meyerowitz was born in Breslau, Germany, now known as Wroclaw, Poland. After attending the Hochschule für Musik in Berlin for several years, he continued his studies in Rome under the tutelage of Ottorino Respighi and Alfredo Casella. Later he traveled to Belgium and France. During World War II Meyerowitz, because of his Jewish background, was forced to live in hiding, aided by friends in the Italian and French resistance movements. After the war he began to receive notice as a composer, and his works were performed by Jean-Pierre Rampal (flutist) and Yvonne Loriod (pianist). In 1946 Meyerowitz moved to New York City and began to establish his reputation as a composer of operas, of which he eventually wrote eight. He became an American citizen in 1951. In collaboration with Hughes as librettist, Meyerowitz created three operas: *The Barrier* (1950), based on Hughes's play *Mulatto*, which Hughes also adapted into the short story "Father and Son"; *Esther* (1957), based on the biblical narrative; and *Port Town* (1960). They also collaborated on an oratorio, *Five Foolish Virgins* (1954), and an Easter cantata, *The Glory around His Head* (1955). In addition to writing operas, choral pieces, and chamber music, Meyerowitz was involved in music education, teaching at the Berkshire Music Center, Brooklyn College, and the City College of New York. Levarie has written that Meyerowitz "adhered to tonality and attempted to build his own style on Classic-Romantic traditions," but that he also used "typically American idioms in his operas on American topics." The fact that Meyerowitz was interested in adapting his music to his adopted country made his collaboration with Hughes a rather logical choice, even if the two grew up and were educated in remarkably different circumstances. Also, both were interested in basic issues of humanity and social justice. The attempt to meld Meyerowitz's "Classic-Romantic" predilections with the interests of a librettist who favored blues,* gospel, and jazz* must have been complicated, however, and Hughes did at one point express disappointment in how inconsistently Meyerowitz's music presented his words (Rampersad, II, 243).

Bibliography: Allan Kozinn, "Jan Meyerowitz, 85, Composer on Moral Subjects" [obituary], *New York Times* (December 26, 1998), late edition, final, sec. C, p. 6, col. 1; Siegmund Levarie, "Jan Meyerowitz," in *The New Grove Dictionary of Opera*, ed. Stanley Sadie and Christina Bashford (London: Macmillan, 1992), vol. 3, 371; Rampersad, II, 243, 320–321.

"Midnight Chippie's Lament." Poem of seven stanzas in traditional blues* form and in black dialect,* including the use of the word "ig" (ignore). The speaker, a prostitute or "chippie," has been insulted by a "Cripple" named "Lonesome Blue." The poem was first published in *Shakespeare in Harlem. See also* the poem "Chippy," in which, obviously, Hughes uses a different spelling of the word.

Bibliography: *CP*, 258–259.

"Midnight Dancer." Poem of ten lines, with lines three and ten rhyming. The dedication beneath the title reads "(To a Black Dancer in 'The Little Savoy')." The highly imagistic poem is rhetorically addressed to the dancer and expresses a kind of awe for her beauty. It was first published under the title "To a Black Dancer at the Little Savoy" in *The Weary Blues* and was included in *Selected*

Poems under the revised title. The Little Savoy was a nightclub in Harlem.*
For a discussion of Harlem nightclubs during the Harlem Renaissance,* see
Lewis.

Bibliography: *CP*, 91; "Nigger Heaven" (chapter 6), in Lewis, *WHWV*, 156–197.

Midnight Nan. The blues* singer in "To Midnight Nan at Leroy's."

"Midnight Raffle." Poem of four stanzas in short-lined ballad* form. The
speaker is experiencing hard times and compares dropping a nickel into the
"subway slot" to playing, and losing, a raffle. The poem was first published in
One-Way Ticket.

Bibliography: *CP*, 366.

"Midsummer Madness." Short story, included in the collections *Simple Takes
a Wife* and *The Best of Simple. See* Simple [Jesse B.] Stories.

"Midwinter Blues." Poem of four stanzas in traditional blues* form and in
black dialect.* It is spoken by a woman whose "man" has left her "on the night
befo' Christmas"—and left the coal bin empty. It was first published in the *New
Republic* (April 14, 1926). *Collected Poems* contains information about slight
revisions the poem underwent. *See* Revision, Process of, and Hughes.

Bibliography: *CP*, 65, 629.

"Migrant." Rhyming poem of forty lines and five stanzas with widely varying
line lengths. It depicts a worker who is always on the move, and it alludes to
the persistence of racism in the United States during the 1940s. Because of the
poem's occasionally cryptic phrasing, and because the "migrant" is referred to
as "Daddy-O" and "Buddy-O," whether the poem concerns an African American
worker exclusively is unclear. The poem refers in passing both to "V-J Day"
(Victory over Japan Day), when Japan surrendered to Allied forces to end World
War II (September 2, 1945), and to Jean-Baptist-Point Du Sable,* whom some
consider to be the first settler of what is now Chicago, Illinois. Du Sable's
mother was of African descent, his father French. The poem was first published
in Australia's *Poetry Magazine* (September 30, 1946).

Bibliography: *CP*, 369, 668.

"Migration." Free-verse poem of seventeen lines and five stanzas. Stanzas one
and five are quatrains; stanzas two through four are triplets. The poem concerns
a child who is part of the great "northern migration" of African Americans, a
migration that began after the Civil War, accelerated, and resulted in a massive
influx of African Americans to northern industrial cities, including Chicago and
New York. The child is called "nigger" by white children but is also ostracized
by African American children whose families have lived in the North longer.

The poem views the possible consequences of such treatment ominously. It was first published under the title "The Little Frightened Child" in *Crisis** (October 1923) and was published as "Migration" in *Fields of Wonder*.

Bibliography: *CP*, 36; Alferdteen Harrison, ed., *Black Exodus: The Great Migration from the American South* (Jackson: University Press of Mississippi, 1991); Joe William Trotter, Jr., ed., *The Great Migration in Historical Perspective: New Dimensions of Race, Class, and Gender* (Bloomington: Indiana University Press, 1991).

"Militant." Fourteen-line rhyming poem with widely varying line lengths. It is spoken by a person who is so tired of eating "the bread of shame," encountering racism, and enduring low pay that he is prepared to use violence to change his situation. It was first published under the title "Pride" in *Opportunity** (December 1930) and was later published as "Militant" in *The Panther and the Lash*. *Collected Poems* contains information about slight revisions the poem underwent.

Bibliography: *CP*, 131, 638.

"Million—and One." Short story, included in *The Best of Simple*. *See* Simple [Jesse B.] Stories.

Mingo. One of Harriet Williams's suitors in *Not Without Laughter*. Sandy, the main character, accompanies Mingo and Harriet to a dance (chapter 8), and there he is first exposed to and impressed by the blues* and jazz* played by a band.

"Minnie Again." Short story, included in *The Best of Simple*. *See* Simple [Jesse B.] Stories.

"Minnie One More Time." Short story, included in *The Best of Simple*. *See* Simple [Jesse B.] Stories.

"Minnie Sings Her Blues." Poem in three modified blues* stanzas and in black dialect.* "Minnie" actually "sings" about being in love and enjoying cabaret nightlife but suggests that without love and dancing, she would have the blues. The poem was first published in the *Messenger** (May 1926).

Bibliography: *CP*, 68–69.

"Minnie's Hype." Short story, included in the collection *Simple's Uncle Sam*. *See* Simple [Jesse B.] Stories.

"Minstrel Man." Two-stanza poem, the meter and rhyme scheme of which are based on the structure of a ballad* quatrain; however, Hughes reorganized what would have been four quatrains into eight-line stanzas. The "minstrel man" who

speaks claims that his glad exterior hides sorrow. The poem was first published in *Crisis** (December 1929). *Collected Poems* contains information about Hughes's use of punctuation in the poem. *See also* "A Black Pierrot."
Bibliography: *CP*, 61, 628.

"Misery." Poem that is an unusual fusion of ballad* and blues* elements. It is in four ballad stanzas, but its repetition of phrasing is like that of the blues, as is the voice of the speaker, who needs to hear the blues to be "soothed." Lines one, three, and four rhyme in each stanza. The poem was first published in *Opportunity** (October 1926). *See also* "Miss Blues's Child."
Bibliography: *CP*, 77.

"Miss Blues's Child." Poem of three stanzas; the first is in traditional blues* form, the other two in ballad* quatrains. The sad speaker dubs herself "Miss Blues's Child." The poem was first published in the *Olivant Quarterly* (1955). Later, David Martin, with whom Hughes collaborated on *Simply Heavenly*, set the poem to music. ASCAP lists no publisher for the song, but the song's ASCAP registry number is 430070792. *See also* "Misery."
Bibliography: *CP*, 447.

"Miss Boss." Short story, included in the collection *Simple's Uncle Sam*. *See* Simple [Jesse B.] Stories.

"Mississippi." Free-verse poem of twenty lines in three stanzas. It is a kind of raw lament in response to the murder of Emmett Till* and the subsequent trial (and acquittal) of his accused murderers in 1955. Till was an African American teenager from Chicago visiting relatives in Mississippi. He was murdered simply for having behaved in a friendly way to a white woman. It was first published in the *Amsterdam News* (October 1, 1955).
Bibliography: *CP*, 452; John Hope Franklin and Alfred A. Moss, Jr., *From Slavery to Freedom: A History of African Americans*, 8th ed. (New York: McGraw-Hill, 2000), 514.

"Mississippi Fists." Short story, included in the collection *Simple Stakes a Claim*. *See* Simple [Jesse B.] Stories.

"Mississippi Levee." Poem in three traditional blues* stanzas and in black dialect.* The speaker is bemoaning the fact that he cannot seem to build a levee high enough to contain the flooding Mississippi River. The poem was first published in *Shakespeare in Harlem*.
Bibliography: *CP*, 249.

"Mississippi Monologue." Song, from *Simply Heavenly*. Hughes wrote the lyrics, and David Martin composed the music. ASCAP* lists the song as being published by the Bourne Company, and the song's ASCAP registry number is 430072905.

"Mister Sandman." Poem in sixteen long-lined rhyming couplets. It concerns the legendary bringer of sleep, the Sandman. It was first published in *Brownie's Book** (August 1921). *See* Children's Poetry.
Bibliography: *CP*, 598–599.

Mistral, Gabriela. *See Selected Poems of Gabriela Mistral.*

Mitchell, Arthur Weigs. *See* "The Mitchell Case."

"The Mitchell Case." Poem of thirty-eight lines with no stanza breaks and with a rhyme scheme similar to that of a ballad.* Arthur Weigs Mitchell was the first African American member of the Democratic Party to be elected to the U.S. Congress. Representing the seventy-fourth district in Illinois (including part of Chicago), Mitchell was elected in 1934. In 1937 he journeyed by train from Chicago to Arkansas, but the train stopped at the Arkansas border, where Jim Crow laws* were in effect, and Mitchell was forced to move from a first-class Pullman car to a "colored" car. Later he sued the Rock Island Railroad, claiming that he had a right to sit in the car for which he had purchased a ticket. As reported in the *Baltimore Afro American*,* named in the suit were "Frank O. Lowden, James E. Gorman, and Luther B. Fleming, trustees of the estate of the Chicago Rock Island and Pacific Railway Co.; Illinois Central Railway Co.; and the Pullman Company." Mitchell lost his case in the lower courts, but the case was argued before the U.S. Supreme Court on March 13, 1941 (313 U.S. 80, No. 577). A relatively new member of the Court then was Hugo F. Black. He had been appointed by Franklin Roosevelt* in 1937, but the appointment became controversial when the Hearst newspapers reported (accurately) that Black had been a member of the Ku Klux Klan* in Alabama. Ironically, Mitchell came to Black's defense during the controversy, saying that "Black is a good man and a true liberal. His Klan membership was a mistake which was rectified." On April 28, 1941, the Court overturned the lower-court decision, ruling in Mitchell's favor. (Chief Justice Charles Hughes, who would retire in June 1941, wrote the opinion.) However, the Court essentially ruled only that railroad companies had to provide first-class cars for African Americans, not that they had to desegregate services. Langston Hughes's poem supports Mitchell's legal victory but suggests that few people can afford to sue and that the U.S. government is morally and legally obligated to eradicate Jim Crow laws, not merely address them on a case-by-case basis. The poem was first published in the *Baltimore Afro American* (June 7, 1941).
Bibliography: *CP*, 568–569, 684; "Klan Is Dead, Says Mitchell," *Baltimore Afro American*, October 16, 1937, 1; "Mitchell Acts against Jim Crow Carrier," *Baltimore Afro*

American, September 11, 1937; *Mitchell v. United States et al.*, 313 U.S. 80, No. 577 (April 28, 1941).

Mitchell v. United States et al. *See* "The Mitchell Case."

"Moan." Rhyming poem of six stanzas each composed of two lines followed by a refrain: "O Lord," or "Lord Jesus," or variations thereof. In black dialect* the speaker expresses to Jesus a need for the "peace" that is in "yo' sky." The editors of *Collected Poems* believe that the poem was first published in *American Life* (July 1926?), but the magazine has not been located. *See also* "Love Song for Antonia"; "Pale Lady." *See* Religion.

Bibliography: *CP*, 118.

Modernism and Hughes. As a literary term, "Modernism," as opposed to the more general terms "modern," "modernism," or "modernity," conventionally refers to a widespread movement in American, British, Canadian, continental, Irish, and Latin American writing between about 1910 and 1939, with parallel developments in other arts, including painting, sculpture, music, and dance. Inevitably, both dates can be viewed as arbitrary. Some critics and historians, for example, often discuss sources of Modernism that appear decades, even centuries earlier, and 1939 relates as much to massive political changes influenced by World War II as it does to specific movements in art and culture, even if these changes were more or less connected to political developments. In fact, another suggested beginning date for Modernism is 1914, when the Great War (later called World War I) began, ushering in political and social changes at least as massive as those springing from World War II.

More agreement and less contentious views exist about which authors (in the case of literary Modernism) are representatively "Modern." Such authors include William Butler Yeats (Irish poet), Ezra Pound (American poet), T. S. Eliot (American poet), Gertrude Stein (American prose writer), William Carlos Williams (American poet), James Joyce (Irish novelist), and Ernest Hemingway,* F. Scott Fitzgerald, and William Faulkner (American novelists).

A degree of consensus also exists concerning several circumstances these and many other so-called Modern writers responded to and reacted against. These phenomena include the crisis of faith caused, in part, by the rise of science and, specifically, the influence of Charles Darwin's hypotheses about biology; widespread industrialism, which created great wealth, great urban centers, and sites of mass employment but also seemed to create a more impersonal, spiritually adrift human condition; the fragmentation of religious and artistic traditions; and the horrors of the Great War, including the carnage of trench warfare, the widespread use of bombs and lethal chemical agents, and a ravaged younger generation of men and women across Europe. Ezra Pound's entreaty to "make it [art] new" perhaps encapsulates most efficiently one important Modernist notion:

that the unprecedented changes in civilization required new art forms, radically different ways of representing reality. Precisely how to "make it new" was a matter of opinion, temperament, and aesthetic outlook, however.

For instance, the spare, closely observed, relatively colloquial writing of William Carlos Williams and Ernest Hemingway certainly qualified as new; their writing was quickly perceived to be a fresh departure from fin de siècle and very early twentieth-century literature. By contrast, the "new" writing of other Modernists was often complicated, fragmented, dense, and highly allusive, as exemplified by *Mrs. Dalloway* (Virginia Woolf), *The Apes of God* (Wyndham Lewis), *The Sound and the Fury* (Faulkner), *Ulysses* and *Finnegans Wake* (Joyce), *The Waste Land* (Eliot), the *Cantos* (Pound), and *The Autobiography of Alice B. Toklas* (Stein). To some degree, then, it seemed as difficult as the civilization it interpreted and critiqued, and therefore it seemed aimed at a relatively narrow audience. Most literary historians tend to associate Modernism with these latter, more difficult representatives, so much so that Modernism is often seen as a movement that alienated itself from much of literature's audience, that, while pushing ahead, in avant-garde fashion, with new styles and forms, perhaps simultaneously left many readers behind.

Hughes was, of course, a contemporary of writers considered to be central to Modernism but is infrequently depicted as one of them or discussed in relation to them. His being an African American writer was no doubt one reason for this circumstance, if only because the Modernist movement perceived itself and was later defined further as an "Anglo," Anglo-Irish, Anglo-American, Canadian, and—to a lesser degree—Latin American movement. Hughes's interest in folk traditions, in working people's lives, and in traditional verse forms can also, at first glance, seem to place him at odds with many Modernists, who tended to focus on bourgeois culture (if only to critique or even satirize it), to reject (or at least to change radically) traditional verse forms, and to ignore folk traditions. One obvious exception is William Carlos Williams, whose plain style, affinity for everyday American life, and spare poetic structures are remarkably similar to those of Hughes, even if his political concerns and frames of reference are not. It is also true that William Butler Yeats and Ezra Pound, for example, attempted to reach back to and draw on Celtic and Chinese cultures, respectively, just as Hughes reached back to African legacies.

Closer inspection complicates the issue of Hughes and Modernism even more. For instance, Hughes's long poems *Montage of a Dream Deferred* and *Ask Your Mama* are as complex, experimental, "new," and alert to contemporary urban civilization as many key Modernist poems, including *The Waste Land*. Also, Hughes's critique of Western society was as intense as critiques by Pound, Eliot, Hemingway, or Yeats. One major difference between the critiques, of course, is that Hughes's focused not so much on decline as on oppression: oppression of working people, of Africans and African Americans, of colonized peoples. Moreover, Hughes embraced democracy, about which Yeats, Eliot, Pound, and

Wallace Stevens were at least ambivalent, with Pound going so far as to embrace fascism. That is, while some Modernists associated "the masses" with the decline of Western culture, Hughes associated elements of Western culture—colonialism, racism, severe economic inequality—with the decline of the masses. Throughout his writing, he implicitly and explicitly exhorts European and American culture to live up to its democratic, Judeo-Christian ideals (at least as he perceived these ideals), especially with regard to persons of color. Hughes's overriding concern, then, is with key flaws in Western culture that keep it from reaching its full potential, not with external threats causing a decline from a height that was, in his view, largely mythical. As many of his poems from the 1940s reveal, however, he clearly saw fascism as a threat to those aspects of Western culture he valued, especially democracy and the promise (if not the reality) it held for a variety of peoples he perceived to be oppressed. In this context, he explicitly defended in his writing elements of Western culture. Hughes often worked in traditional verse forms, including the ballad,* but he improvised extensively, and even poems that at first glance seem to draw on conventional rhyme schemes are, on closer inspection, highly innovative in phrasing, line length, rhythm, and placement of rhymes. Moreover, he constantly adapted the conventional poetics on which he drew to black dialect,* to blues* forms and idioms, to jazz* rhythms, and to his own linguistic idiosyncrasies springing from the regional and economic complexities of his background and from his extensive travels.

Therefore, to whatever degree one might wish to depict Hughes as a traditional poet, one would have to be ready to concede a variety of ways in which Hughes was innovative, experimental, and perhaps even revolutionary. Additionally, because the Modernists themselves were such a varied lot, much of their work turns out to share a great deal with Hughes's writing. William Carlos Williams's loyalty to his New Jersey territory has much in common with Hughes's loyalty to Harlem,* and like Hughes, Williams trusted comparatively simple language, expressed an affinity for ordinary people and everyday situations, and explored the subtleties of American speech and idioms. Arguably, Gertrude Stein was as influenced by jazz—if influenced differently—as was Hughes. There are, then, significant reasons for depicting Hughes's work as being significantly different from that of the Modernists, especially when one considers his frames of reference, the "lenses" through which he looked at politics and society, the vantage points from which he approached questions of literary heritage and cultural legacies. It can certainly be fruitful to read his work "against" the backdrop of Modernism or in contrast to the poetry, fiction, poetics, and implicit literary politics of individual Modernists, as several scholars have done and more will likely continue to do. By the same token, scholars, teachers, and students can usefully allow knowledge of Hughes's work to inform and refresh interpretations of, assumptions about, and perspectives on Modernism. It is worthwhile to reemphasize that implicit and explicit critiques of Western society that appear in Hughes's poetry, drama, short fiction, and essays—critiques that concentrate on his perceptions of colonialism, racism, inconsistently asserted democratic principles, and economic oppression—are as potent and sustained as those of Modernists.

A chief difference is that the Modernists' critiques tended to concentrate on the ills of mass culture, on spiritual chaos and fragmented religious and aesthetic traditions, whereas Hughes tended to be more sanguine—albeit hardly uncritical—than they about the health of cultural tradition, partly because he realized the degree to which African culture had survived, thrived, and evolved in the United States and the Caribbean, and because he was sometimes willing to see "the church" as a strong cornerstone of African American culture. *See Montage of a Dream Deferred*; "Montmartre." *See also* Audience; Poetics; Tolson, Melvin B.

Bibliography: Houston A. Baker, Jr., *Modernism and the Harlem Renaissance* (Chicago: University of Chicago Press, 1987); Malcolm Bradbury and James McFarlane, eds., *Modernism: 1890–1930* (New York: Penguin, 1976); Heyward Ehrlich, ed., *Light Rays: James Joyce and Modernism*, prologue by Richard Ellmann (New York: New Horizon Press, 1984); Andrew Hewitt, *Fascist Modernism: Aesthetics, Politics, and the Avant-Garde* (Stanford: Stanford University Press, 1993); Virginia V. James Hlavsa, *Faulkner and the Thoroughly Modern Novel* (Charlottesville: University Press of Virginia, 1991); Hutchinson; Scott W. Klein, *The Fictions of James Joyce and Wyndham Lewis: Monsters of Nature and Design* (Cambridge: Cambridge University Press, 1994); Louis Menand, *Discovering Modernism: T. S. Eliot and His Context* (New York: Oxford University Press, 1987); Hans Ostrom, *"The Ways of White Folks*, Modernism, and 'Signifying,' "in Ostrom, 5–8; Vincent B. Sherry, *Ezra Pound, Wyndham Lewis, and Radical Modernism* (New York: Oxford University Press, 1993); M. Lynn Weiss, *Gertrude Stein and Richard Wright: The Poetics and Politics of Modernism* (Jackson: University Press of Mississippi, 1998).

"Mona." Poem. *See* "Girl."

"Monotony." Poem of seven lines that explicitly addresses monotony in life, first published in *Crisis** (May 1923).

Bibliography: *CP*, 31.

"Monroe's Blues." Poem in two ballad* stanzas concerning one "Monroe," who sings the blues* because his "woman" and "friend" are dead because he has fallen on "evil ways." It was first published in *One-Way Ticket*.

Bibliography: *CP*, 367.

Montage of a Dream Deferred (New York: Holt, 1951). 75 pp. Book-length poem. Generally considered to be one of Hughes's most important achievements if not his masterwork, *Montage of a Dream Deferred* (*Montage*) is a long poem

(387–429 in *Collected Poems*) and eighty-seven separate (and separately titled) parts or poems-within-the-poem. In a brief introductory note to the poem, Hughes identifies its structural and rhythmic sources as "jazz,* ragtime, swing, blues,* boogie-woogie, and be-bop"—styles of popular music influenced by African American musicians, vocalists, and composers. He also states that the poem concerns "contemporary Harlem,"* which he views as "a community in transition." *Montage*, then, represents Hughes's most comprehensive attempt to allow his literary art to absorb and express influences of popular African American culture—influences affecting vocabulary, diction, rhythm, style, mood, and form.

The word "montage" in the title suggests the composite nature of the poem but also hints at the more modern, cinematic connotation of "montage," one more in keeping with the spirit of jazz than the word "collage." As *The Weary Blues*, and "The Negro Artist and the Racial Mountain" (among other works) suggest, Hughes was from the beginning of his career interested in such a jazz-oriented artistic move, but *Montage* was clearly his most ambitious effort in this regard. In some instances, he explicitly represents the influence of jazz, as when, in "What? So Soon!" he attempts to replicate the sound of a horn in a jazz band: "Figurette / De-daddle-dy! / De-dop!" Chiefly, however, the influences manifest themselves in the intricate organization of poems, an arrangement creating the effect of improvisation, of intermixed (or "syncopated") patterns of rhythm in lines and poems, of abrupt changes in represented voices or points of view, and of a wide array of subjects and images. Although *Montage* may be read—and was obviously intended by Hughes to be read—as a "jazz poem," the concept of "montage" is also every bit as crucial as its appearance in the title suggests. For although the poem is linear, reading from left to right, top to bottom, beginning to end, it also invites nonlinear interpretations, in which poems can be read out of order and in which the whole work can be seen less as representing aural patterns of jazz and more as representing visual patterns analogous to those in collages, mosaics, quilts, and textiles (*see* Thompson).

As multifaceted and artistically ambitious as *Montage* may be, it remains accessible, drawing on colloquial speech, focusing on everyday life in Harlem at mid-twentieth century, open to the casual reader as well as to the scholar. Additionally, while in some sense the poem demands to be read against a backdrop of music and visual art, it is also a poem of politics and ideas, of perspectives on the "dream deferred." From Hughes's point of view, the "dream" in question is the quasi-mythic American Dream, composed of aspirations for liberty, prosperity, contentment, and self-determination; for African Americans, he implies—and sometimes states outright—that realization of the dream has been deferred because of racism, the relative paucity of economic opportunity, and the relative paucity of political power and full citizenship. The New York

City borough of Harlem becomes for Hughes a potent symbol of such "deferment" because in the 1920s it held so much economic and cultural promise for African Americans but then, during and after the Great Depression, went into decline economically and did not recover when most of the United States experienced prosperity, especially just after World War II. How citizens experience, overcome, endure, express, and are sometimes made desperate by the deferred dream is reflected in many of *Montage*'s poems. However, other poems, as well as the style and form of even the harshest poems, celebrate the vibrancy of Harlem (and African American culture in general)—Harlem's social complexity, humor, and especially its culture of jazz and "nightlife." The juxtaposition in *Montage* of a poetic structure that embodies African American achievement in popular music and an overriding theme of social inequity is key to the long poem, which deliberately embraces conflicts, contrasts, and contradictions in Harlem and, by extension, in American culture.

As Hughes observes in his introductory note, the poem "is marked by conflicting changes, sudden nuances, sharp and impudent interjections, broken rhythms." There is virtually no question that *Montage* is a major work of twentieth-century American poetry. As an ambitious, experimental, visionary poetic rendering of working-class and middle-class African American life in Harlem, it earns comparison to T. S. Eliot's long poem *The Waste Land*, which expressed Eliot's view—pessimistic, even satiric—of Anglo-American urban life. The separate parts of *Montage*, unlike those of Eliot's poem, are more easily excerpted, however. Many anthologists, and even Hughes himself, have seen fit since 1951 to select individual poems for republication. "Dream Boogie," "Theme for English B," and "Harlem [2]" have been especially popular in this regard.

In addition to looking backward to compare Hughes with Eliot, if only insofar as they both were focused on urban culture, one might also look ahead to the rest of the 1950s and into the 1960s and compare *Montage* to the work of the Beat Poets, who include Lawrence Ferlinghetti, Allen Ginsberg, Gary Snyder, William Everson, and Amiri Baraka.* In his linguistic and formal experimentation and in his quest to interrogate the myth of the American Dream, Hughes in *Montage* clearly anticipated the work and points of view of such writers. In other words, although *Montage* is on the surface a local, topical poem concerning one community in transition at a specific moment, it is also a coherent long poem with ideas, images, and literary subtleties that have endured and continue to resonate. Following, in alphabetical order, not in the order in which they appear in the book, is a checklist of the separate poems within *Montage of a Dream Deferred*. The checklist is based on the version printed in *Collected Poems*. Numbers in brackets after titles are taken from *Collected Poems* and indicate that another poem which is not part of *Montage* bears the same title:

"Advice"

"Argument [2]"

"Ballad of the Landlord"

"Bar"

"Be-Bop Boys"

"Blues at Dawn"

"Boogie: 1 A.M."

"Brothers"

"Buddy"

"Café: 3 A.M."

"Casualty"

"Children's Rhymes"

"Chord"

"College Formal: Renaissance Casino"

"Comment on Curb"

"Corner Meeting"

"Croon"

"Dancer"

"Dead in There"

"Deferred"

"Dime"

"Dive"

"Dream Boogie"

"Dream Boogie: Variation"

"Drunkard"

"Easy Boogie"

"Evening Song"

"Fact"

"Flatted Fifths"

"Gauge"

"Good Morning"

"Green Memory"

"Harlem [2]"

"High to Low"

"Hope [2]"

"Island [2]"

"Jam Session"

"Joe Louis [1]"

"Juke Box Love Song"

"Lady's Boogie"

"Letter [1]"

"Likewise"

"Live and Let Live"

"Low to High"

"Mellow"

"Motto"

"Movies"

"Mystery"

"Necessity"

"Neighbor"

"Neon Signs"

"New Yorkers"

"Night Funeral in Harlem"

"Nightmare Boogie"

"Not a Movie"

"Numbers"

"125th Street"

"Parade"

"Passing"

"Preference"

"Projection"

"Question [2]"

"Relief"

"Request"

"Same in Blues"

"Shame on You"

"Sister"

"Situation"

"Sliver"

"Sliver of Sermon"

"So Long"

"Street Song"

"Subway Rush Hour"

"Sunday by the Combination"

"Tag"	"Warning [2]"
"Tell Me"	"Warning: Augmented"
"Testimonial"	"What? So Soon!"
"Theme for English B"	"Wine-O"
"Tomorrow"	"Wonder"
"Ultimatum"	"World War II"
"Upbeat"	

See also Ask Your Mama; Modernism and Hughes; Poetics.

Bibliography: David Chinitz, "Rejuvenation through Joy: Langston Hughes, Primitivism, and Jazz," *American Literary History* 9, no. 1 (Spring 1997), 60–78; David Chinitz, " 'Dance, Little Lady': Poets, Flappers, and the Gendering of Jazz," in *Modernism, Gender, and Culture: A Cultural Studies Approach*, ed. Lisa Rado, preface by William E. Cain (New York: Garland, 1997), 319–335; *CP*, 387–429; Emanuel; David R. Jarraway, "Montage of an Otherness Deferred: Dreaming Subjectivity in Langston Hughes," *American Literature* 68, no. 4 (December 1996), 819–847; Rampersad, II, 151–153; Robert Farris Thompson, *Flash of the Spirit: African and Afro-American Art and Philosophy* (New York: Vintage, 1984).

"Montmartre." Poem of six lines and thirteen words comparing the Montmartre/Pigalle sections of Paris (known for a vibrant nightlife) to "a neon rose." The poem is reminiscent of imagist poems by H. D. (Hilda Doolittle) and Amy Lowell and especially brings to mind the imagist poem "A Station of the Metro" by Ezra Pound, which also "glimpses" a Paris scene. The poem was first published in *Fields of Wonder*. *See* Modernism and Hughes; Poetics.

Bibliography: *CP*, 327; "Imagism," in *PEPP*.

"Montmartre Beggar Woman." Poem. *See* "Parisian Beggar Woman."

"The Moon." Short story, included in the collection *Simple's Uncle Sam. See* Simple [Jesse B.] Stories.

"Moon Faced, Starry Eyed." Song, from *Street Scene*. Hughes wrote the lyrics, and Kurt Weill* composed the music. ASCAP* lists the song as being published by Chappell, Inc., and Hampshire House Publishers. The song's ASCAP registry number is 430084901.

"Moonlight in Valencia: Civil War." Poem of seventeen lines in free verse. It explicitly subverts romantic notions of war, partly by linking moonlight in Valencia (during the Spanish Civil War) with bombing raids, which, according to the poem, mean "death. / And not heroic death." The poem was first published in *Seven Poets in Search of an Answer*, edited by Thomas Yoseloff (New York:

B. Ackerman, 1944). *See* "Hero—International Brigade"; "Letter from Spain." *See also Baltimore Afro American.*
Bibliography: *CP*, 306.

"Moonlight Night: Carmel." Eight-line rhyming poem that depicts waves off the coast of Carmel, California, by means of militaristic figures of speech. It was first published in the *Carmel Pine Cone* (June 15, 1934). *See* Sullivan, Noel.
Bibliography: *CP*, 178.

"Morals Is Her Middle Name." Short story, included in the collections *Simple Takes a Wife* and *The Best of Simple. See* Simple [Jesse B.] Stories.

"Morning." Song, from *Street Scene*. Hughes wrote the lyrics, and Kurt Weill* composed the music. ASCAP* lists the song as being published by Chappell, Inc., and Hampshire House Publishers. The song's ASCAP registry number is 430091715.

"Morning After." Poem in three traditional blues* stanzas and in black dialect.* The speaker is recovering from a bout of drinking the night before and is also complaining about how loudly his lover snores. The poem was first published in *Shakespeare in Harlem*. Later, Leonard Geoffrey Feather set the poem to music. ASCAP lists the song as being published by Model Music, and the song's ASCAP registry number is 430205280.
Bibliography: *CP*, 248.

"Mortal Storm." *See Mortal Storm*. (Munich: Orlando Musikverlag, 1969).

Mortal Storm: Fünf Lieder nach Texten von Langston Hughes. Song cycle. Hughes wrote the lyrics, and Robert Owens composed the music. ASCAP* the work as a single song, published by Gema, Inc., and the song's ASCAP registry number is 430315063. Although ASCAP also lists Y. Marcoulescou as a "performer" of "Mortal Storm" [*sic*], it does not list a particular recording.

"Moscow." Poem of eight lines. Lines four and eight rhyme. The poem depicts the "red flags" of Moscow as symbols of a new epoch in history. Probably written in the 1930s, the poem was held in the Langston Hughes Papers of the James Weldon Johnson Memorial Collection in the Beinecke Library, Yale University, until it appeared in Berry. *See The Big Sea*; Marxism; McCarthyism; "Moscow and Me"; Politics.
Bibliography: Berry, 99; *CP*, 614.

"Moscow and Me." Essay that records some of Hughes's experiences in and reflections about Moscow when he lived there during and after working on the ill-fated motion-picture project *Black and White.** At the time, Hughes was generally impressed by Russian society. The essay was published in *International Literature* (no. 3, 1933). Much of the material in this essay later appeared in *I Wonder As I Wander*. It was later published in Berry. *See* "From Harlem to Samarkand"; Koestler, Arthur; Marxism, "Negroes in Moscow"; "The Soviet Union and Color."

Bibliography: Berry, 71–79; *I Wonder As I Wander*, 119 and ff.; Rampersad, I, 266–267.

"Mother and Child." Short story. The story concerns the ways in which a white community and an African American community react to the birth of a child out of wedlock; the mother is white and the father is black. The white community is horrified, but the black community—as represented by women in the "Salvation Rock Ladies Missionary Society for the Rescue o' the African Heathen"—react self-righteously as well. The story is told entirely through the dialogue between and among these "ladies." The story was included in the collection *The Ways of White Folks* and was reprinted in *Langston Hughes: Short Stories*. *See* "Mother and Child" (1965).

Bibliography: Ostrom, 15–16.

"Mother and Child" (1965). Described by Peterson as a "theatre vignette" in one act. Hughes adapted the short story "Mother and Child" into this vignette, which was produced off-Broadway in 1965 at the American Place Theatre in New York City. Woodie King, Jr., directed "Mother and Child." It was published in *Black Drama Anthology* (1972). *See* Drama.

Bibliography: Woodie King and Ron Milner, eds., *Black Drama Anthology* (New York: Columbia University Press, 1972); Bernard L. Peterson, Jr., *Contemporary Black American Playwrights and Their Plays: A Biographical Directory and Dramatic Index* (Westport, CT: Greenwood Press, 1988).

"Mother in Wartime." Rhyming poem of fifteen lines in one stanza. It describes a woman who has a sanitized, almost romantic notion of war. The poem is less brutal than "Moonlight in Valencia: Civil War," but like that poem, it implicitly insists on confronting the harsher realities of armed conflict. It was first published in *The Panther and the Lash*. *See* Women in Hughes's Writing. *See also* "The Colored Soldier"; "War."

Bibliography: *CP*, 558.

"Mother to Son." Poem of twenty lines, chiefly in free verse but including two strategically placed rhymes. In black dialect* the speaker tells her son how hard she has worked to overcome obstacles and exhorts him to continue to struggle. The poem contains a frequently quoted line: "And life for me ain't been no crystal stair." It was first published in *Crisis** (December 1922). Later, Hall

Johnson set the poem to music. ASCAP* lists the song as being published by Carl Fischer, Inc., and the song's ASCAP registry number is 430476078. *See also* "The Negro Mother," in which Hughes uses the symbol of "the stair" once more. *See also* Women in Hughes's Writing.
Bibliography: *CP*, 30.

"Motherland." Poem of one ballad* quatrain concerning "Africa imprisoned." It was first published in *Jim Crow's Last Stand*.
Bibliography: *CP*, 292.

"Motto." Poem. *See Montage of a Dream Deferred.*

"Movies." Poem. *See Montage of a Dream Deferred.*

"Mulatto." Poem of forty-five lines concerning the "bastard boy [son]" of a white man and a black woman; spoken alternately by the son and the father, the poem expresses mutual hatred and shame and also implicitly addresses the objectification and sexualization of black women by white men. Thematically, the poem is strongly linked to the short story "Father and Son," the play *Mulatto*, and the opera *The Barrier*. It was first published in the *Saturday Review of Literature* (January 29, 1927).
Bibliography: *CP*, 100.

Mulatto. (1931). Play. The chief conflict is between a white plantation owner in the American South, Colonel Norwood, and his "mulatto" son, Robert (Bert), the offspring of an affair between the colonel and his African American house-keeper, Cora. The setting is sometime during the first quarter of the twentieth century. Bert returns to the plantation from college and demands that the colonel fully acknowledge him as his son. The conflict smolders until Bert, in a fit of rage, kills his father. Bert flees into a swamp, is hunted by a lynch mob, and commits suicide rather than allowing himself to be lynched. *Mulatto* is a melo-dramatic tragedy exploring issues of racism, sexuality, violence, and power. It was both the first play of Hughes's produced and the first of his plays produced on Broadway. As Rampersad suggests, however, the version of *Mulatto* that appeared on Broadway differed from Hughes's. In 1935, when Hughes was traveling in Mexico, his theatrical agent, John W. Rumsey, arranged for the play to be produced by an amateur company in Dobbs Ferry, New York, as a way to attract interest from Broadway producers. The tactic worked, and producer Martin Jones showed interest but asked whether a cowriter could be hired to rewrite the third act. Hughes agreed. Soon thereafter, Hughes returned from Mexico and was surprised to find that the play was already in production and that Jones himself had rewritten the third act. Disturbed by the rush to produc-tion and Jones's revision, Hughes nonetheless agreed to let the play go forward because of the chance to see his work performed on Broadway. Jones sensationalized the play, in part by including a gratuitous rape scene. *Mulatto* debuted on October 24, 1935, and was met the next day by harsh reviews, criticizing Hughes chiefly for the structural problems and sensational elements Jones had introduced. Rampersad includes a complete account of the production and quotes extensively from reviews, and Plum offers a historical reconstruction of the production, but one basic point to stress is that what had promised to be a rewarding debut on Broadway became for Hughes a critical and personal disaster. Rampersad describes Hughes as being "bitter and ashamed because of the reviews" and goes on to observe that Hughes's version of "*Mulatto* is, properly approached, a harrowing orchestration of Hughes's prophetic fear that the great house of America would be brought down by racial bigotry" (315). Smalley cautions, "While reading *Mulatto*, one should remember when it was written. It is very much a play of the thirties, an era when sociopolitical plays dominated American drama." Smalley adds, "Its [*Mulatto*'s] impact is stark and uncomplicated, and it is a difficult play to forget" (xi–xii). Restored to the version Hughes had written before 1935, the play is included in *Five Plays by Langston Hughes*. Somewhat ironically, the short story "Father and Son," adapted from *Mulatto*, actually appeared in print before the play was produced. Eventually Hughes collaborated with Jan Meyerowitz to adapt the play into an opera, *The Barrier*.

Bibliography: Jay Plum, "Accounting for the Audience in Historical Reconstruction: Martin Jones's Production of Langston Hughes's *Mulatto,*" *Theatre Survey: The Journal of the American Society for Theatre Research* 36, no. 1 (May 1995), 5–19; Rampersad, I, 311–315, 317–340; Sybil Ray Ricks, "A Textual Comparison of Langston Hughes's *Mulatto*, 'Father and Son,' and *The Barrier*," *Black American Literature Forum* 15, no. 3 (Fall 1981), 101–103; Webster Smalley, "Introduction" to *Five Plays by Langston Hughes* (Bloomington: Indiana University Press, 1963), vii–xvii.

Mule Bone: A Comedy of Negro Life (New York: HarperCollins, 1991). Play, cowritten with Zora Neale Hurston,* edited with introductions by George Houston Bass and Henry Louis Gates, Jr., with "the complete story of the *Mule Bone* controversy." *Mule Bone* is based on a short story by Hurston, "Bone of Contention," which is reprinted in this 1991 volume. Hughes and Hurston cowrote the play chiefly during 1930, with some work occurring intermittently over the following four years. Set in Hurston's hometown of Eatonville, Florida, *Mule Bone* is immersed in the rural, southern, African American culture with which much of Hurston's fiction and nonfiction are concerned. In the play two men, Jim and Dave, quarrel over the affections of a woman, Daisy. (Jim is a singer and guitar player, Dave a dancer.) Jim strikes Dave with a mule bone, and while he does not injure Dave permanently, the assault causes the town to erupt, with Methodist and Baptist factions taking sides. Written in black dialect,* full of earthy comedy and sharp satire, and displaying the several talents of both writers, *Mule Bone* promised to be a landmark play in American and African American theatre history. Moreover, because it took shape in 1930, it also promised to be a symbol representing the richness of the Harlem Renaissance.* Ironically, however, the real "bone of contention" lay between Hughes and Hurston, not Jim and Dave. The two writers quarreled over authorship, financial arrangements, and their own complicated personal history, which was connected to the patronage of Charlotte Osgood Mason.* With regard to *Mule Bone* itself, the quarrel resulted in the play's not being produced for some sixty years, until long after Hughes and Hurston had died. In his introduction, Gates calls the Hughes-Hurston disagreement "the most notorious literary quarrel in African-American cultural history" (7), and he further observes, "A more natural combination for a collaboration among writers of the Harlem Renaissance, one can scarcely imagine." Also included in the volume are Hughes's account of the falling-out with Hurston (from *The Big Sea*); Hurston biographer Robert Hemenway's account; Rampersad's account; and correspondence between Hughes and Carl Van Vechten,* Hughes and Hurston, and Hughes and Arthur Spingarn.* With the support of a grant from, ironically, the Fund for New American Plays, *Mule Bone* debuted at the Ethel Barrymore Theatre on Broadway in New York City in February 1991. Kanfer describes the play as being "as elemental as a recipe for collard greens" and praises its energy and wit. In the production Kenny Neal played Jim, Eric Ware played Dave, and Akosua Busia played Daisy. Michael Schulz directed. The cast of twenty-nine also included Sonny Jim Gaines, Theresa Merritt, and, in a cameo appearance, Robert Earl Jones (*see* Harlem Suitcase Theatre). For the production, Taj Mahal composed the score, which consists chiefly of Hughes's poems set to music, and made a recording of the music. *See also* "Bound No'th Blues"; "But I Rode Some"; "Crossing"; "Song for a Banjo Dance."

Bibliography/Discography: John Beaufort, "*Mule Bone* Debuts after 60 Years," *Christian Science Monitor* (February 26, 1991), 13; *The Big Sea*; Robert E. Hemenway, *Zora Neale Hurston* (Urbana: University of Illinois Press, 1977); Stefan Kanfer, review of *Lost in Yonkers*, by Neil Simon, and *Mule Bone*, by Hughes and Hurston, *New Leader* 74, no. 3 (February 11, 1991), 22; Rampersad, I, 311–318; Taj Mahal, *Mule Bone: Music Composed and Performed by Taj Mahal/Lyrics by Langston Hughes* [compact disc] (Gramavision, distributed by Rhino Records, 1991): (Santa Monica, CA) R2 79432.

"The Murder." Song, from *Street Scene*. Hughes wrote the lyrics, and Kurt Weill* composed the music. At this writing, the song is not listed with ASCAP.* It is published by Warner Chappell, Ltd.

Bibliography: Booklet accompanying *Street Scene* [compact disc], performed by Kristine Ciesinski, Janis Kelly, Bonaventura Bottone, Richard van Allan, Catherine Zeta Jones, and the Orchestra and Chorus of the English National Opera, conducted by Carl Davis (London: Jay Records, 1996): CDJAY2–1232.

Muse, Clarence (1889–1979). American actor, writer, and songwriter. Muse was born and grew up in Baltimore. He graduated from Dickinson School of

Law in Philadelphia but pursued a career in acting, joining troupes in the South and then in New York City. In 1930 Muse went to Hollywood and landed small comic parts in the movies *Hearts* (1930) and *A Royal Romance* (1930). In 1931 he played Jim in a film version of Mark Twain's *Huckleberry Finn*. For renowned director Frank Capra, Muse acted in three films: *Rain or Shine* (1930), *Dirigible* (1931), and *Broadway Bill* (1934), costarring in the latter film with Warner Baxter. Bogle indicates that in the mid-1930s Muse "appeared in an array of films" (53), and he suggests that Muse was forced to play a version of the stereotypical character commonly referred to as "Uncle Tom," alluding to Harriet Beecher Stowe's novel *Uncle Tom's Cabin*. However, Bogle suggests that in *So Red the Rose* (1935), directed by King Vidor, Muse "appeared as a resurrected old mythic type, the black brute" (54). With Hughes, Clarence Muse cowrote the screenplay for *Way Down South** and cowrote songs for the film, in which he also acted. The songs, "Good Ground" and "Louisiana," were sung in the film by Bobby Breen* and the Hall Johnson Choir. *See* "Uncle Tom [1]"; "Uncle Tom [2]."

Bibliography: Donald Bogle, *Toms, Coons, Mulattoes, Mammies, and Bucks: An Interpretive History of Blacks in American Films*, 3rd ed. (New York: Continuum, 1994), 53–56.

Musical Plays. *See Ballad of the Brown King; Black Nativity; Gospel Glow; Jerico-Jim Crow; Just around the Corner; Mule Bone; Prodigal Son; Simply Heavenly; The Sun Do Move; Tambourines to Glory* (play). *See also* Drama; Harlem Suitcase Theatre; Opera; Orchestral Pieces/Oratorios.

"Must Have a Seal." Short story, included in the collections *Simple Takes a Wife* and *The Best of Simple*. See Simple [Jesse B.] Stories.

"My Adventures as a Social Poet." Essay. Wry in tone, it describes the trouble into which Hughes's political and blues* poetry has gotten him: being detained in Japan because he was suspected of spying for the Soviet Union; being deported from Cuba because he had read political poems there; being asked by a minister never to read blues poems in the minister's church again; not being paid an agreed-upon honorarium at a college in the South because college administrators had been offended by some of his poems; and receiving threatening letters from a member of the Ku Klux Klan.* The essay was first published in *Phylon* (Fall 1947). *See also* "Concerning 'Goodbye Christ' "; "Concerning Red Baiting"; McCarthyism; Politics.

Bibliography: Berry, 151–157; *I Wonder As I Wander*; Rampersad, I, II, 129.

"My America" (1943). Essay. In it Hughes acknowledges many faults of the United States but also praises its strengths, which he sees as including "the voice of democracy" and freedom of the press. It was first published in the *Journal*

of Educational Sociology, volume 16, and was also published in *The Langston Hughes Reader. See* "Democracy and Me"; "Langston Hughes Speaks."
Bibliography: *The Langston Hughes Reader*, 500–501.

"My Beloved." Free-verse poem of four lines. It consists of questions asked by a poet of his "beloved" about whether the beloved one wants to be immortalized in poetry. Whether the questions are rhetorical or not is unclear. The poem was first published in *Crisis** (March 1924).
Bibliography: *CP*, 36.

"My Lord Not Wanted." Song. *See The Glory around His Head.*

My Lord What a Mornin' (1960). Sound recording, long-playing album. American singer Harry (Harold) Belafonte (born 1927) made this recording of African American spirituals and folk songs in 1960. Hughes wrote the "liner notes" (brief comments about the recording) for the album. In his commentary about the recording, Hughes discusses the origins of spirituals in African American slave communities in the South. He suggests that some spirituals were "disguised songs of earthly freedom" and, as such, were "the only kind of protest that in slavery days could be made without great physical danger." Hughes praises the range of songs represented by Belafonte's selection, his versatility as a singer, and his "innate sense of the dramatic value of a song." In its original format, the recording is held by the Library of Congress (LC control number r 60000159). It was released by RCA Victor and rereleased in compact-disc form in 1995. The performers on the recording are Belafonte and the "Belafonte Folk Singers," and the producer was Bob Corman. Songs on the recording are "Wake Up Jacob," "My Lord What A Mornin'," "Ezekiel," "Buked And Scorned," "Stars Shinin' (By 'n By)," "Oh Freedom," "Were You There When They," "Oh Let Me Fly," "Swing Low," "March Down to Jordan," "Steal Away," "All My Trials," "Go Down Emanuel Road," "In My Father's House," and "Goin' Down Jordan." *See also* Baez, Joan; "Little Lyric (*Of Great Importance*)"; "The One and Only Nina Simone: A Tribute"; *The Strollin' Twenties.*
Bibliography/Discography: Harry Belafonte, *My Lord What a Mornin'* [long-playing record] (New York: RCA Victor, 1960): LSP 2022, rereleased on compact disc (1995): ASIN Number B000006 SUV; Rampersad, II, 438.

"My Loves." Poem in three ballad* stanzas, expressing, in conventional terms, admiration for certain aspects of nature, such as the white moon and the blue sky, as well as for the speaker's "lady love." It was first published in *Crisis** (May 1922).
Bibliography: *CP*, 25.

"My Man." Poem. *See* "Ma Man."

"My Most Humiliating Jim Crow Experience." Essay. In it Hughes recalls an experience from his high-school days in Cleveland, Ohio, when he was grossly overcharged at a restaurant simply because he was black. It was first published in *Circuit Magazine* (date unknown) and was also published in *The Langston Hughes Reader*. *See* Central High School; Jim Crow Laws.

Bibliography: *The Langston Hughes Reader*, 488–489.

"My People." Poem in three free-verse couplets concerning the "beauty" of African American people and of their "souls." "My People" was first published under the title "Poem" in *Crisis** (August 1923). Later, Noel Da Costa set the poem to music. ASCAP* lists no publisher for the song, but the song's ASCAP registry number is 430475435. Ricky Ian Gordon also set the poem to music. "My People" (the poem) is also included in *Pictorial History of the Negro in America*. Another poem first titled "My People" was later given the title "Laughers" by Hughes (see "Laughers"). *See* "Genius Child."

Bibliography: *CP*, 36; Ricky Ian Gordon, *Genius Child: A Cycle of 10 Songs* (New York: Williamson Music Company, 1992).

"Mysterious Madame Shanghai." Short story. The narrative concerns a former circus performer, Madame Shanghai, and her husband, whose relationship consists chiefly of cruelty. The story is set in a New York City boardinghouse. It was first published in *Afro Magazine* (March 15, 1942), was included in the collection *Laughing to Keep from Crying*, and was reprinted in *Langston Hughes: Short Stories*. *See* Women in Hughes's Writing.

Bibliography: Ostrom, 26–27; Rampersad, II, 29.

"Mystery." Poem. *See Montage of a Dream Deferred.*

N

NAACP (National Association for the Advancement of Colored People).
Civil-rights organization in the United States. It was established in 1909 (the
centennial of the birth of Abraham Lincoln) chiefly because of the efforts of
Mary White Ovington, who had done research on impoverished African Americans in New York City; William English Walling, a journalist; and Henry Mos-
kowitz, a social worker. W.E.B. Du Bois* was also a key founding member of
the organization, the official publication of which was *Crisis,** which Du Bois
edited for many years. Other founding members were Ida Wells-Barnett and
Oswald Villard. The founders issued a "Call to Action" nationwide to community leaders, social activists, social workers, and legal professionals, urging
them to join forces under the aegis of the NAACP. From the beginning, one
major strategy of the NAACP was to advance the cause of civil rights for
African Americans and other persons of color through legal means, chiefly (but
not exclusively) civil suits concerning voting rights, ethnic segregation of public
schools, and other civil-rights issues. Arthur Spingarn* and Thurgood Marshall*
were key figures in this legal strategy, the most renowned success of which
occurred in the case(s) of *Brown v. Board of Education.** Marshall strengthened
the organization's Legal Defense Fund in the 1930s and 1940s; Spingarn served
as vice president from 1911 to 1940 and as president from 1940 to 1965. In
1939, when the Daughters of the American Revolution refused to allow renowned singer Marian Anderson* to perform in its Constitution Hall because
of segregationist policies, the NAACP sponsored an outdoor performance by
Anderson near the Lincoln Memorial in Washington, D.C. Seventy-five thousand people attended the concert. Hughes wrote a history of the organization,
Fight for Freedom. At this writing, the NAACP has 2,200 branch offices in all
fifty states, and its membership is roughly 500,000. Its stated mission is to
promote "the political, educational, social, and economic equality of minority
group citizens in the United States" (quoted from the Website of the NAACP,

1999). The Library of Congress holds an extensive collection of "Audio Materials, 1956–1977" concerning the NAACP. Hughes is cross-listed to this material, but no additional information about recordings of him in connection with the NAACP is given. The material is contained on 140 reels; the Library of Congress control number for the material is 92779133. *See* "NAACP" (poem); White, Walter.

Bibliography: Web site of the NAACP: http://www.naacp.org.

"NAACP." Rhyming poem of twenty-eight lines. It is an occasional poem concerning an imminent meeting of the NAACP* in Houston and presents versified encouragement to the organization in the struggle against Jim Crow laws* and segregation in the U.S. military. It was first published in *Crisis** (June 1941). *See* "Crow Goes, Too"; "Dear Mr. President"; *Fight for Freedom: The Story of the NAACP; Jerico-Jim Crow; Jim Crow's Last Stand*; "The Mitchell Case."

Bibliography: *CP*, 230.

"Name in Print." Short story, included in *The Best of Simple. See* Simple [Jesse B.] Stories.

"Name in the Papers." Short story. It is a short comic monologue spoken by a man who is lying in a hospital bed after having been shot by a man whose wife was having an affair with the speaker of the story. The wounded man expresses more concern with the likelihood that his name will appear in the newspaper than with his gunshot wound. This version, in which the man is not named, is included in the collection *Laughing to Keep from Crying.* An earlier version, first published in the *Chicago Defender** (February 21, 1948), identifies the man via the original title ("Simple Plays with Fire") as (Jesse B.) Simple. *See* Simple [Jesse B.] Stories.

Bibliography: Ostrom, 25–26.

"Natcha." Poem of seven lines concerning a prostitute, "Natcha," who is "offering love" for "ten schillings." It was first published in *The Weary Blues. See also* "Beale Street Love"; "The New Cabaret Girl"; "Port Town"; "A Ruined Gal."

Bibliography: *CP*, 98.

National Association for the Advancement of Colored People. *See* NAACP.

National Poetry Festival (1962). Sound recording. With numerous other American poets, Hughes was invited to read his poetry at a festival in Washington, D.C. Editor and poet Louis Untermeyer organized the event at the Library of Congress to celebrate the fiftieth anniversary of *Poetry* magazine. Other poets in attendance were John Berryman, R. P. Blackmur, Louise Bogan, Gwendolyn

Brooks, Richard Eberhart, Robert Frost, Randall Jarrell, Robert Lowell, John Crowe Ransom,* Kenneth Rexroth, Muriel Rukeyser, Delmore Schwartz, Karl Shapiro,* Mark Van Doren, and Robert Penn Warren. Jacqueline Kennedy hosted a reception for the poets at the White House. Because of the Cuban missile crisis, President Kennedy did not attend the reception. Hughes read "American Heartbreak," parts of *Ask Your Mama*, one of the Madam poems, "Merry-Go-Round," and "The Negro Speaks of Rivers." Festival sessions on October 24, 1962, were recorded on four sound-tape reels, which are held by the Library of Congress (the control number for the recording is mm 73040774). *See* Audio Recordings of Hughes. *See also* Periodicals.

Bibliography: Rampersad, II, 356–357.

"The Naughty Child." Poem in what is essentially one ballad* quatrain that has been arranged in eight short lines. The poem concerns a child who drowned while picking flowers near a pond, but its ironic references to the "very nice town" add a cryptically satiric element. It was first published in the *Messenger** (June 1927).

Bibliography: *CP*, 106.

"The Necessaries." Short story, included in the collection *Simple Takes a Wife*. *See* Simple [Jesse B.] Stories.

"Necessity." Poem. *See Montage of a Dream Deferred*.

Negritude. *See* Césaire, Aime; *Poems from Black Africa*.

"Negro." Free-verse poem of nineteen lines in six stanzas, all of which are in three lines except the four-line fourth stanza and begin with the words, "I've been." Spoken by a collective persona,* the poem glimpses "Negro" history panoramically, and the persona has been, by turns, a slave, worker, singer, and victim. The poem refers specifically to slavery in the United States ("I brushed the boots of Washington"), contemporary racism in the United States ("they lynch me still in Mississippi"), and colonialism in Africa ("the Belgians cut off my hand in the Congo"). It was first published under the title "The Negro" in *Crisis* (January 1922). It later appeared under the title "Proem" in *The Weary Blues. Collected Poems* contains information about slight revisions the poem underwent. *See also* "Flight"; "Lumumba's Grave"; "Lynching Song"; "The Negro Speaks of Rivers"; "Silhouette."

Bibliography: *CP*, 24, 620.

"The Negro Artist and the Racial Mountain." Essay. It was first published in the *Nation* (June 1926). Hughes wrote it at the invitation of one of the magazine's editors, Freda Kerchway, and in response to an essay (appearing earlier in the magazine) by George Schuyler,* "The Negro-Art Hokum." Whereas Schuyler's essay critiques attempts by African American writers and artists to express authentic "Negro" experiences, Hughes in his essay argues that such attempts are crucial and encourages "Negro" writers to draw upon language, history, folk traditions, and social predicaments with which they are familiar. The essay is considered a key piece of criticism in the Harlem Renaissance.*

Bibliography: Lewis, *HRR*, 91–95, 96–99; Ostrom, 69–71.

"Negro Dancers." Poem of fifteen lines in four stanzas. Stanzas one and four are spoken in black dialect* by someone who does the dance step the Charleston with his or her "baby" (companion). The middle two stanzas are not in dialect and describe the cabaret scene, in which "white folks" are spectators who "laugh" and "pray." Rampersad refers to a letter Hughes wrote to Countee Cullen* about the poem, a draft of which he had sent to Cullen. The poem was first published in *Crisis* *(March 1925). See also "Cabaret;" "Dancer" "Dancers"; "Danse Africaine"; "Juice Joint: Northern City"; "Midnight Dancer."

Bibliography: *CP*, 44; Rampersad, I, 89.

"The Negro Faces Fascism." Speech. Hughes gave the speech before the Third United States Congress against War and Fascism on January 3, 1936. In the speech he criticized the "New Deal" programs of President Franklin Delano Roosevelt,* praised Russian society, and expressed wariness toward America's military buildup. Several years later, when the United States entered World War II, Hughes would become an outspoken supporter of the Allies' war against Germany and Italy. The text of the speech is held in the Langston Hughes Papers, James Weldon Johnson Memorial Collection, Yale University (item 2994). *See also Baltimore Afro American*; "Ballad of Roosevelt"; "Dear Mr. President"; "Hero—International Brigade"; "Message to the President"; "Moscow and Me;" "Out of Work."

Bibliography: Rampersad, I, 322–323.

"Negro Ghetto." Poem of two ballad* quatrains but in a single stanza. The speaker closely observes a street scene in the "ghetto"—presumably Harlem*—and is filled with pity for people he sees but also regards them as "far-too-humble." The poem was first published in *New Masses* (March 1931).

Bibliography: *CP*, 137.

Negro Lament: For Contralto, Alto-Saxophone, and Piano, opus 49 (Amsterdam: Donemus, 1954). Song cycle. Marius Flothius is the composer. In the work he set the following Hughes poems to music: "Proem," "Harlem Night Song," "Troubled Woman," "The White Ones," "Roland Hayes Beaten (Georgia: 1942)," and "Epilogue." ASCAP* lists "Negro Lament on Poems of Langston Hughes" as being composed by M. H. Flothuis, does not list the poems, and lists the publishers of the work as Theodore Presser Company and Buma, Inc. The work's ASCAP registry number is 440154398.

"The Negro Mother." Poem of fifty-two lines in rhyming couplets. It is spoken by a collective persona,* a universal "Negro mother" who charts "her" long history of hardship, courage, and survival from Africa to North America. She describes herself as a source of fertility and nourishment and of integrity and resistance. She exhorts her "children"—subsequent generations of Africans and African Americans—to follow her example and to progress toward freedom. Hughes recapitulates the image of stairs that appears in "Mother to Son," using it once more as a symbol of a long climb to liberation. The poem provided the title to the chapbook in which it first appeared, *Negro Mother and Other Dramatic Recitations.*

Bibliography: *CP*, 155–156.

Negro Mother and Other Dramatic Recitations (New York: Golden Stair Press, 1931). 20 pp. Illustrated by Prentiss Taylor. Chapbook of poems. In *I Wonder As I Wander* Hughes describes putting the chapbook together in order to sell it on a poetry-reading tour in the American South, and he mentions that Prentiss which Taylor designed the book, which includes "The Big-Timer," "The Black Clown," "Broke," "Dark Youth of the U.S.A.," "The Negro Mother," and "The Colored Soldier." Rampersad indicates that partly because Hughes conducted a reading tour upon the book's release, it went through seven printings and sold about 1,700 copies, a remarkable number for a chapbook from a small press. Later "The Colored Soldier" appeared in a book edited by John Henry Williams. The book was reissued by Books for Libraries Press (Freeport, New York) in 1971, by Beaufort Books (New York) in 1977, and by the Ayer Company (Salem, New Hampshire) in 1984, 1987, and 1990. *See* Women in Hughes's Writing.

Bibliography: *CP*, 632; *I Wonder As I Wander*, 47–50; Rampersad, I, 221–223; John Henry Williams, ed., *A Negro Looks at War* (New York: Workers Library Publishers, 1940), 2–3.

"The Negro Servant." Poem of nineteen lines, chiefly in free verse with a few rhymes. It contrasts the workday of an African American woman, who must be "polite" to the whites for whom she works, with her nightlife in Harlem* and with references to the legacy of African tribal celebrations. It was first published in *Opportunity** (December 1930). *See* "Madam and Her Madam"; Women in Hughes's Writing.

Bibliography: *CP*, 131.

"The Negro Speaks of Rivers." Poem of thirteen lines in five stanzas. Excepting juvenilia (*see The Belfry Owl*), this is Hughes's first published poem. It is spoken by a collective persona,* a kind of universal "Negro" who ties together

African and African American history by naming rivers (Euphrates, Congo, Nile, Mississippi) and who observes that the Negro's "soul" "has grown deep like the rivers." Hughes went on to use the device of a collective persona in numerous poems (one example being "The Negro Mother") and to compose other poems that express a panoramic glimpse of history and culture. The poem was first published in *Crisis* * (June 1921), thereby inaugurating one of the most important publishing relationships in his career, for *Crisis* would publish more of Hughes's poems by far than any other periodical. Later, William R. Mayer set the poem to music. ASCAP* lists no publisher for the song, but the song's ASCAP* registry number is 440239001. ASCAP* lists separately a song to which the poem was set, composed by Margaret Bonds,* with whom Hughes collaborated on *Ballad of the Brown King*. The publisher of this song is Handy Brothers Music, Inc., and the song's ASCAP registry number is 440007225. In *The Big Sea* Hughes briefly describes how he came to write the poem. *See Langston Hughes Reads: "One-Way Ticket," "The Negro Speaks of Rivers," "Ku Klux Klan," and Other Poems; National Poetry Festival. See also* Revision, Process of, and Hughes.

Bibliography: *The Big Sea*, 55; *CP*, 23.

"Negro Writers and the War." Essay. It acknowledges the persistence of racism and segregation in the United States but also praises the freedoms of speech and press, from which (the essay argues) African American writers benefit. It was published in the *Chicago Defender* * (August 24, 1942).

Bibliography: Rampersad, II, 49.

"Negroes and Vacations." Short story, included in the collection *Simple Stakes a Claim. See* Simple [Jesse B.] Stories.

"Negroes in Moscow." Essay that concerns the comparative freedom from racism African Americans enjoyed in Moscow. Specifically, it refers to the group, composed mainly of African Americans and of which Hughes was a member, that traveled to Russia to work on the ill-fated motion-picture project *Black and White.** Much material from this essay appeared later in *I Wonder As I Wander*. It was published in *International Literature* (no. 4, 1933). *See also* "Moscow and Me."

Bibliography: *I Wonder As I Wander*, 119 and ff. Rampersad, I, 246–251.

"Negroes in Spain." Essay. In it Hughes remarks on how many American "Negroes" and persons of color from other nations he has seen in Spain—all of them, except for "the Moors," fighting against Franco's Fascist forces in the Spanish Civil War. Hughes argues that the African Americans and other persons of color realize that if Fascism were to spread worldwide, persons of color would be among its chief victims. The essay was first published in *The Volunteer for Liberty* (September 13, 1937) and later reprinted in Berry.

Bibliography: Berry, 107–109.

"Neighbor." Poem. *See Montage of a Dream Deferred.*

"Neon Signs." Poem. *See Montage of a Dream Deferred.*

"Never No More." Short story, included in the collection *Simple Takes a Wife.* *See* Simple [Jesse B.] Stories.

"Never Room with a Couple." Short story, first published in *Laughing to Keep from Crying*, included later in the collection *Something in Common and Other Stories*. The brief narrative concerns the comic situation implied by the title.

"The New Cabaret Girl." Poem in six short-lined ballad* stanzas, spoken in black dialect* by a patron of the cabaret, who focuses on the young woman's skin color ("little yaller [yellow] gal") and her sadness. It was first published under the title "The New Girl" in *New Masses* (December 1926). *See also* "Beale Street Love"; "Cabaret Girl Dies on Welfare Island"; "Natcha"; "Port Town"; "A Ruined Gal."

Bibliography: *CP*, 87.

"New Flowers." Poem in two ballad* quatrains that concerns new spring flowers. It was first published under the title "Cycles" in *Golden Slippers*, edited by Arna Bontemps* (New York: Harper, 1941). *See* Children's Poetry.

Bibliography: *CP*, 604.

"The New Girl." Poem. *See* "The New Cabaret Girl."

"A New Kind of Dozens." Short story, included in the collection *Simple Stakes a Claim. See* Simple [Jesse B.] Stories. *See also Ask Your Mama.*

"New Moon." Free-verse poem of seven lines and three stanzas. It compares the new moon to a rider, to a "sprightly creature," and finally to a young virgin. It was first published in *Crisis** (March 1922).

Bibliography: *CP*, 25.

The New Negro. A phrase that began appearing in African American newspapers just before 1920 and that was especially potent during the Harlem Renaissance.* It encapsulated a sense in which African Americans (or "Negroes") had begun to redefine themselves, assert their civil rights more forcefully, speak out against lynching* and other destructive, racist practices, organize politically, gain greater political power, articulate artistic and intellectual agendas, and so on. To Alain Locke,* who in 1925 edited an anthology that took the phrase as its title, it referred to writers who, in his view, produced works of good literary quality that also represented African American ("Negro") experience accurately and appropriately. To intellectuals like W.E.B. Du Bois* and Charles Johnson,* it evoked the notions of the Talented Tenth*, signaled the rise of an African American intelligentsia, and served as a kind of cultural rallying cry. To writers such as Wallace Thurman*, Zora Neale Hurston,* and Hughes, the phrase and concepts it represented were to be regarded with some ambivalence because although these writers viewed themselves as being both "Negro" and "new" in a variety of meaningful ways, they also resisted definitions of "New Negro Writing" (for example) that were too confining, paternalistic, and/or pretentious. Consequently, Thurman and Hurston used the ironic term "Niggerati" (a play on the word "literati") to satirize more confining, pretentious aspects of the enthusiasm engendered by concepts of the New Negro and of a "renaissance" in Harlem. Similarly, Hughes titled a chapter of *The Big Sea* "When the Negro Was in Vogue" to suggest, with irony, ways in which "the New Negro" was partly an invention of white Americans temporarily infatuated with Harlem* culture and ways in which a "New Negro" agenda had been naïvely optimistic, especially in the face of the Great Depression, Jim Crow laws,* and other adversities. Nonetheless, given how much lasting work and how many influential ideas the Harlem Renaissance produced, Hughes and others by no means dismissed outright the political will and cultural energy symbolized by the phrase.

Bibliography: Hutchinson; Lewis, *WHWV*; Rampersad, I, 105 and ff.; Wintz.

New Negro Poets, U.S.A. (Bloomington: Indiana University Press, 1964). 127 pp. Anthology edited by Hughes and including work from thirty-seven African American poets, including Mari Evans, Robert Hayden, Ted Joans, Helen Johnson, and Le Roi Jones (Amiri Baraka*). Poet Gwendolyn Brooks* contributed a foreword to the volume. *Arna Bontemps/Langston Hughes Letters 1925–1967* contains correspondence in which Hughes discusses his work on the anthology.

"A New Song." Poem of fifty-six lines, chiefly in free verse. It is one of Hughes's most explicitly Marxist poems, envisaging a time when the "white" world and the "black" world will unite in a "workers' " revolution. It exhorts workers to "Revolt! Arise!" *Collected Poems* contains information on slight revisions the poem underwent. It was first published in *Opportunity** (January 1933). *See* Marxism; Revision; Politics. *See also Angelo Herndon Jones*; "Ballads of Lenin"; "Black Workers"; Chant for Tom Mooney"; *Don't You Want to Be Free?*; "Goodbye Christ"; "Good Morning Revolution"; "One More 'S' in the U.S.A"; "Revolution"; "Wait."

Bibliography: *CP*, 170–172.

A New Song. (New York: International Workers Order, 1938). 31 pp. Book of poems. Introduction by Michael Gold. Frontispiece by Joe Jones. It includes several of Hughes's more politically radical poems and poems concerned with labor issues. Gold characterizes the poems as revealing a "voice crying for justice for all humanity" (8). The book includes "Ballad of Ozie Powell," "Ballads of Lenin," "Call of Ethiopia," "Chant for May Day," "Chant for Tom Mooney," "Good Morning Revolution," "History," "Kids Who Die," "Let America Be America Again," "Lynching Song," "A New Song," "One More 'S' in the U.S.A.," "Park Bench," "Revolution," "Sister Johnson Marches," "Song for Ourselves," "Song of Spain," and "Song of the Revolution." *See* Marxism; Politics.

Bibliography: Rampersad, I, chapter 13, "Earthquake Weather," 341–372.

"New Year." Six-line poem in free verse. It is a fatalistic poem that compares years passing to leaves falling. It was first published in the *Messenger** (September 1926).

Bibliography: *CP*, 73.

"New Yorkers." Poem. *See Montage of a Dream Deferred.*

Newspaper Column, Hughes's, for the *Chicago Defender*. *See* "Here to Yonder"; Simple [Jesse B.] Stories.

Newspapers in Which Hughes Published Poems, Stories, Essays, and Articles. *See* Periodicals in Which Hughes Published Poems, Stories, Essays, and Articles. *See also Baltimore Afro American; Chicago Defender.*

"Nickel for a Phone." Short story, included in the collection *Simple Speaks His Mind. See* Simple [Jesse B.] Stories.

"Night: Four Songs." Poem of seven lines in free verse. The title refers not to four song structures within the poem but to four songs, all titled "Sorrow." Cryptically, the poem also refers to the night of "two moons" and "seventeen stars." It was first published in *Fields of Wonder*. Later Charles Barrett Griffin set the poem to music. *See* "Border Line"; "Distance Nowhere"; "Drum"; "Night: Four Songs"; and "Suicide's Note."

Bibliography: *CP*, 326; *Distance Nowhere: 5 Langston Hughes Songs: For Baritone and String Quartet* (Forest Hills, NY: Charles Griffin, 1995.

"Night Funeral in Harlem." Poem. *See Montage of a Dream Deferred.*

"Night in Harlem." Short story, included in the collection *Simple Takes a Wife. See* Simple [Jesse B.] Stories.

"Night Song." Poem in three short-lined stanzas of seven lines each. It person-ifies dusk as "short" and as a singer; it personifies day as a "lady" who faints. The poem was first published in *Fields of Wonder*. Later, Howard Swanson set the poem to music, and ASCAP* lists the song as being published by Weintraub Music Company, Inc. The song's ASCAP registry number is 440002120. Also, Robert Owens set this poem, "In Time of Silver Rain," "Fulfillment," "Silence," "Carolina Cabin," and "Songs" to music in the song cycle *Silver Rain*.

Bibliography: *CP*, 330; Robert Owens [composer], *Silver Rain: Song Cycle for Tenor and Piano* (Munich: Orlando-Musikverlag, 1975).

"Night Time." Song. Hughes wrote the lyrics, and Roger Segure composed the music. ASCAP* lists the song as being published by EMI/Mills Catalog, Inc. The song's ASCAP registry number is 440020424.

"Nightmare Boogie." Poem. *See Montage of a Dream Deferred*.

"No Alternative." Short story, included in *The Best of Simple*. *See* Simple [Jesse B.] Stories.

"No Place to Make Love." Short story. The brief comic narrative concerns a couple who, because they have "no place to make love," get married and have several children. It was included in the collection *Something in Common and Other Stories* and was reprinted in *Langston Hughes: Short Stories*.

Bibliography: Ostrom, 47.

"No Regrets." Poem in two short-lined quatrains. The last word of the first stanza rhymes with that of the second. The speaker is "out of love" but claims, somewhat unconvincingly, to have "no regrets" about being so. The poem was first published in the *Saturday Review of Literature* (January 26, 1952).

Bibliography: *CP*, 433.

"No Tea for the Fever." Short story, included in the collections *Simple Takes a Wife* and *The Best of Simple*. *See* Simple [Jesse B.] Stories.

"Nocturne for the Drums." Rhyming poem of fifteen short lines. It concerns "gay little devils" who are responsible for making African-American men and women mischievous and ecstatic during "the red hour" just before nightlife quickens in Harlem* cabarets. Because the definitions of the word "gay" changed significantly toward the end of Hughes's career, one might note that in the context of this poem, "gay" should probably be read as connoting "spirited" because of when the poem was written and published and because, even in the latter part of his career, Hughes did not use the word as a synonym for "ho-mosexual." In fact, in "Café: 3 A.M.," part of *Montage of a Dream Deferred* (published much later than "Nocturne for the Drums"), Hughes uses the word "fairies" to describe gay men but probably did not regard it as a derogatory or homophobic reference because in that poem he argues that "God made them [homosexual persons]" that way—argues implicitly, that is, not just for tolerance but for acceptance. "Nocturne for the Drums" was first published in the *Messenger** (July 1927). *See* Sexuality and Hughes.

Bibliography: *CP*, 108.

"Nonette." Poem of eight long lines and three stanzas. It contains conventionally exaggerated romantic rhetoric; for instance, the speaker claims that "Nonette's" beauty and love are poisonous and lethal. The poem was first published anonymously in *Crisis** (June 1928). Apparently the poem was part of a backlog of Hughes's poems the magazine had on file. According to Rampersad, Hughes no longer believed these poems to be worthy of publication and advised the editors of *Crisis* accordingly. In the case of "Nonette," the magazine ignored his wishes but did not attribute the poem to him. Later, however, Hughes circulated the poem via the Associated Negro Press (*see* "America's Young Black Joe") under the title "Beloved." *See* Fauset, Jessie Redmon; Women in Hughes's Writing.

Bibliography: *CP*, 125; Rampersad, I, 161.

Nonfiction. *See* Autobiographies; Essays. *See also Arna Bontemps-Langston Hughes: Letters, 1925–1967; Black Magic; Famous American Negroes; Famous Negro Heroes of America; Famous Negro Music Makers; Fight for Freedom; The First Book of Africa; The First Book of Jazz; The First Book of Negroes; The First Book of Rhythms; The First Book of the Caribbean; The First Book of the West Indies; The Langston Hughes Reader; My Lord What a Mornin'*; "The One and Only Nina Simone: A Tribute"; *A Pictorial History of the Negro in America*.

"Northern Liberal." Rhyming poem of twenty-four short lines spoken by a collective persona* representing northern liberals in general. The speaker is self-indicting, suggesting that northern liberals take delight in reports of Jim Crow laws* and other racist practices and policies in the American South because the reports confirm the liberals' views of the South. But the speaker also suggests that the same liberals do not venture south to help with efforts at reform. The poem was first published under the title "Northern Liberal: 1963" in the *Liberator* (July 1963). *See* "Sweet Words on Race."

Bibliography: *CP*, 541.

"Northern Liberal: 1963." Poem. *See* "Northern Liberal."

Norwood, Robert (Bert). The tragic protagonist of both the short story "Father and Son" and the play *Mulatto*.

"Not a Movie." Poem. *See Montage of a Dream Deferred.*

"Not Colored." Short story, included in the collection *Simple's Uncle Sam. See* Simple [Jesse B.] Stories.

"Not Else—But." Poem of fifteen short lines in free verse. The speaker is a free spirit whose "Hip boots" are "Deep in the blues,"* but he is joyful and praises Jesus at the end of the poem. It was first published in *Voices* (1959) and was later published as a stanza in a poem ("Shades of Pigmeat") that is part of the long poem *Ask Your Mama. See also* Religion.
Bibliography: *CP*, 464, 680.

"Not for Publication." Poem. *See* "Bible Belt."

"Not Often." Poem of fourteen lines with very playful rhymes. It concerns animals and a person (a great-grandfather) the speaker of the poem has not seen. The poem was first published in *The Langston Hughes Reader. See* Children's Poetry.
Bibliography: *CP*, 607.

"Not What Was." Poem of twenty-one lines in free verse. It links poetry, a symbolic rose, and the infinite universe in ways that are, for Hughes, extremely mystical and that refer obliquely to an Einstein*-influenced view of time and space. It was first published in the *Massachusetts Review* (Winter 1965). *See* Religion.
Bibliography: *CP*, 546.

Not Without Laughter (New York: Knopf, 1930). 304 pp. Reprinted, with an introduction by Arna Bontemps* (New York: Collier Macmillan, 1969). Reprinted, with an introduction by Maya Angelou and a foreword (formerly the introduction to the 1969 reprint) by Bontemps (New York: Scribner's, 1995). *Not Without Laughter* (*NWL*), one of two novels written by Hughes, took shape over several years; in fact, Arna Bontemps observed that "it was overdue, because the wandering poet had been inveigled into returning to school [Lincoln University*]. Otherwise, it might have been published as early as 1927" (ix, Collier Macmillan edition). The novel appeared, then, in what many regard as the last year of the Harlem Renaissance* and just before Hughes broke with his patron, Mrs. Charlotte Osgood Mason.* There is, therefore, some irony surrounding the publication date because it represented a major step in Hughes's writing career but also inaugurated a decade of personal, national, and international crises—a decade that made Hughes's career more difficult than anyone would have predicted based on the success he had enjoyed in the 1920s and based on the bright early years of the Harlem Renaissance.

The novel remains in print today, a fact that itself points to the success of Hughes's first foray into long fiction. (He wrote and published only one other novel, *Tambourines to Glory*, but that narrative is adapted from an earlier play of the same title.) *NWL* certainly takes its place among the first-rate novels produced by Harlem Renaissance writers, including Jean Toomer,* Carl Van Vechten,* Nella Larsen,* and Wallace Thurman.* Nonetheless, Hughes's novel remains one of his lesser-known works, and one might reasonably argue that it is probably still an undervalued book. *NWL* is a coming-of-age story, the main character of which is James "Sandy" Rodgers, who is about nine years old when the narrative begins and eighteen when it ends. Sandy and his mother, Anjee, live with her mother, whom family, friends, and acquaintances all call Aunt Hager (Williams), in a simple mortgaged house in Stanton, a small Kansas town, early in the twentieth century. Anjee's younger sister, Harriet Williams, also lives with them. Aunt Hager washes clothes for white Stantonites, Anjee works as a cook for a wealthy white family (the Rices), and Harriet waits tables at the Stanton County Country Club; these jobs account for the family's income. Sandy's grandfather has died, and his father, Jimboy Rodgers, is in Kansas City when the narrative opens; ostensibly he is looking for work there. The novel is told in the third person, but the perceptions, reactions, and experiences of Sandy form the lens through which most of the action is filtered. To a large extent, however, Aunt Hager represents the moral center of the novel in her role as firm matriarch and devout, forgiving Christian, and in a novel that involves numerous complicated relationships, the bond between Aunt Hager and Sandy is in many ways the strongest, most significant one.

NWL opens sensationally: a "cyclone" (tornado) hits Stanton, damaging Aunt Hager's house, killing two white neighbors, and terrifying everyone, especially Sandy. To some extent the scene is anomalous because no narrative action thereafter is nearly as chaotic or physically extreme. In another way, though, the scene inaugurates a pattern, for throughout the narrative Sandy will be thrown into situations that are personally or socially disruptive, he will tend to recover from imbalance quickly and become a keen, stoic observer, and often what he will observe, learn from, and benefit from is the courage and tenacity of women. In the aftermath of the tornado, neighbors seek Aunt Hager's practicality and levelheadedness, her selflessness, and her capacity to see past divisions of race and respond to need. Efficiently she helps her family and neighbors recover their equilibrium.

Superficially, at least, Sandy's subsequent experiences are ordinary insofar as, like most children, he becomes aware of family problems, begins to understand the effect of economic pressures, makes friends and discovers the opposite sex, and negotiates his way within such institutions as church, school, and labor, all of which are shaped by turn-of-the-century, racist American society. In this

regard, the novel can appear almost mundanely naturalistic, favoring verisimil-
itude over tragic or melodramatic narrative patterns. Hughes clearly takes the
advice he gave other writers in "The Negro Artist and the Racial Mountain"—
not to look beyond but in fact to embrace the circumstances of African American
life and lives. Implicitly, *NWL* suggests that a clear picture of African American
life in a small Kansas town in the early twentieth century is as valuable as
literature that operates on a grander scale or has mythic aspirations. Furthermore,
on closer inspection, the novel begins to render the dichotomy between naturalistic and mythic approaches to fiction weak, if not altogether false, for in
many ways, Sandy's coming of age becomes a microcosm representing the mac-
rocosmic situation of African Americans, at least as Hughes perceived it and
lived it himself. Sandy, for instance, learns that in general, economic opportunities for African Americans are, in contrast even to those for white residents
of small midwestern towns, severely limited. He learns that because of this
economic disparity, his father must be absent in order to pursue employment in
larger northern cities. In his mother, her sister Harriet, and her other sister
Tempy, Sandy sees examples of the three main pathways open to African American women. They can, like his mother, rely on an extended family and relatively
menial labor to piece together a living. They can, like Harriet, pursue a low-
paying, itinerant entertainment career. (Harriet runs off with a carnival minstrel
show, then works in honky-tonk bars and is even arrested for "street-walking"
before finally achieving a measure of success in a Chicago revue.) Or they can,
like Tempy, begin to edge into the middle class by owning a home and associating with those African Americans who have begun to join the professions
of medicine, law, and education; but from Sandy's perspective late in the book,
middle-class life seems to bring with it snobbishness, oppressive piety, and the
loss of folk ways, folk wit, and unvarnished intensity—qualities that characterize
the vivid matriarch, Aunt Hager. Therefore, Sandy's coming of age seems in
part to involve a coming to awareness of economic, social, and racial realities;
that is, the character of Sandy provides one key bridge between the seemingly
"small," naturalistic plot of *NWL* and more "global" questions that Hughes was
pondering in and around the crucial year 1930.

It is important to keep in mind that Hughes was writing the novel "to" both
white and black Americans (*see* Audience). Therefore, especially for his white
readers, the naturalism would hardly be mundane, for in many chapters and
scenes, such readers would be seeing realities of African American life represented accurately for the first time. Undoubtedly, Hughes wrote *NWL* guided in
part by the notion that he was educating his readership. In chapter 5 ("Guitar"),
for example, Sandy's father Jimboy has returned to Stanton, and one evening
he plays guitar and sings blues* songs with Sandy's Aunt Harriet. In the course
of Sandy's maturation, such a moment is crucial because the boy becomes aware
of an important side of his father—an artistic side. Additionally, he begins to
see crucial differences between his mother, Anjee, who is hardworking and
serious, and his Aunt Harriet, who is enchanted by blues culture and cannot

wait to travel and perform. Also, Jimboy talks about the blues as well as singing them, so he educates Sandy about one crucial aspect of African American culture, one with roots in both the slaveholding South and in Africa. Oddly enough, many white readers in 1930 would have been in Sandy's place, "hearing" blues lyrics, learning about blues history, and seeing one example of how blues played a part in everyday life beyond the stylized clubs of Harlem.* In this way, seemingly plain, straightforward naturalism turns out, therefore, to be rather complicated, operating on several levels. Similarly, chapters 7 ("White Folks"), 18 ("Children's Day"), and 20 ("Hey, Boy!") provide concrete representations of racism, of how these affect a bright, serious child like Sandy, and of debates among African Americans about how to respond to racist hatred. Jimboy, for instance, favors meeting hatred with hatred, but Aunt Hager remains firm in her reading of Christianity, which tells her to love and forgive. Sandy encounters racism, reacts, responds, sees others reacting and responding, and comes of age in extraordinarily complicated, often-oppressive circumstances. Therefore, readers of *NWL*—now and in 1930—learn about racism in a manner unique to naturalistic fiction.

Another aspect of *NWL* that warrants attention is its connections to Hughes's own childhood. Naturally, the success of the novel in no way depends on the audience's prior knowledge of Hughes's biography, and readers must be cautious about reading autobiography "into" works of fiction. Nonetheless, we can observe that like Sandy, Hughes was born and grew up in the American Midwest; his father, too, was largely absent, having sought his fortune in Mexico, and so Hughes was reared by his mother and grandmother, knew economic hardship, and experienced the sometimes-subtle, sometimes-overt racism of the Midwest. Sandy Rodgers is very much a self-contained fictional representation; nonetheless, it is hardly inappropriate to ponder the ways in which Hughes forged the raw material of his own coming of age into the fictional alloy of *NWL*. The denouement of Sandy's maturation is particularly interesting in this regard. Throughout the narrative Sandy has had access to reading material: books at school, Christian-oriented books and the Bible at Aunt Hager's house, and magazines such as *Crisis** and the *Chicago Defender** at the barbershop and hotel where he holds his first jobs. Reading becomes part of his identity, gives him access to the world beyond Stanton, and makes him aware of America, Americans, and African Americans on a broader scale. In the latter part of the novel, however, when Aunt Hager dies, his mother has moved to Chicago, and he must live with his Aunt Tempy, Sandy's encounter with books intensifies. Indeed, a whole chapter (34, "A Shelf of Books") is devoted to this encounter. A teacher shows a special interest in him, and he takes second place in an essay contest, the subject of which is Shakespeare's play *The Merchant of Venice*. Also, Tempy's house is filled with books, and Tempy engages him on ideas. In this chapter she sings the praises of W.E.B. Du Bois,* calling him a great man. Sandy asks if Du Bois is as great as Booker T. Washington,* to which Tempy replies, "Teaching Negroes to be servants, that's all Washington did!" Sandy neither agrees nor disagrees with her, but more important, he feels the impact of living in a house where ideas matter, where "reading" and "life" connect. He begins to see himself as "a student," and when he rejoins his mother in Chicago, he is determined to make higher education his pathway out of the difficulties he has encountered in life. Therefore, to some degree, *NWL* recapitulates Hughes's having embraced literacy and ideas in his own life, so that while *NWL* can be read as a naturalistic depiction of working-class African American life, it can simultaneously be read as a parable of literacy, in which reading may not be an omnipotent saving force but may nonetheless be a crucial source of identity, understanding, and power. For Sandy, as for Hughes, coming of age means, in part, growing into a world of books, ideas, reflection, and expression.

NWL is a briskly paced novel in which the chapters rarely take up more than ten pages each. The chapters evoke moments in young Sandy's life or changes in his family that affect him significantly. As in Hughes's short fiction, the prose style is clear and spare. In several chapters, however, Hughes lets characters deliver themselves of monologues; most of these are spoken by Aunt Hager or her contemporaries, so that Hughes is representing an oral tradition, a culture of talk, as well as advancing the narrative by means of what the characters expound upon or observe. In crafting these monologues, Hughes displays a fine ear for black dialect* and for capturing it unsentimentally, subtly, and purposefully. Perhaps the best example of this technique occurs in chapter 16 ("Nothing But Love"), in which Aunt Hager recounts for Sandy her memories of being a young girl in slavery when the Civil War broke out. Quoted blues lyrics and scenes in which the dozens (*see Ask Your Mama*) are played add texture and depth to the narrative, too, as well as serving a variety of plotting and character-development purposes. In a review, V. F. Calverton observed that "*Not Without Laughter*, continues the healthy note begun in Negro fiction by Claude McKay and Rudolph Fisher. Instead of picturing the Negro of the upper classes, the Negro who in too many instances has been converted to white norms, who even apes white manners and white morality and condemns the Negroes found in this novel as 'niggers,' McKay, Fisher, and Hughes have depicted the Negro in his more natural and more fascinating form." Although these many years later the novel may not seem as path-breaking as it seemed to a reader like Calverton, *NWL* is remarkably mature, confidently crafted, and virtually free of mannerisms or self-indulgences that sometimes plague even very good first novels. *NWL* remains in print (at this writing) not just because of its author's reputation but probably also because its story and the questions it implicitly takes up remain pertinent and because its spare, deft style wears well even some seven decades later.

Bibliography: Hirschel Bickell, "A Poet's Debut as Novelist," *Saturday Review of Literature* 7 (August 23, 1930), 69; Johnnie Brown, "The Major Theme in Langston Hughes's *Not Without Laughter,*" *College English Association Critic* 32, no. 6 (March

1971), 8–10; Sterling Brown, *The Negro in American Fiction* (Washington, DC: Associates in Negro Folk Education, 1937); Barbara Burkhardt, "The Blues in Hughes's *Not Without Laughter,*" *Midamerica: The Yearbook of the Society for the Study of Midwestern Literature* 23 (1996), 114–123; V. F. Calverton, untitled review of *Not Without Laughter, Nation* 31 (August 6, 1930); Walt Carmon, "From Harlem," *New Masses* (October 6, 1930), 17–18; Karen Jackson Ford, "Do Right to Write Right: Langston Hughes's Aesthetics of Simplicity," *Twentieth Century Literature: A Scholarly and Critical Journal* 38, no. 4 (Winter 1992), 436–456; Thomas H. Nigel, "Patronage and the Writing of Langston Hughes's *Not Without Laughter*: A Paradoxical Case," *College Language Association Journal* 42, no. 1 (September 1998), 48–70; James Presley, "The American Dream of Langston Hughes," *Southwest Review* 48 (Autumn 1963), 380–386; Ralph D. Story, "Patronage and the Harlem Renaissance: You Get What You Pay For," *College Language Association Journal* 32, no. 3 (March 1989), 284–295.

"Note in Music." Epigrammatic poem in a single modified ballad* quatrain that compares music to life. It was first published in *Opportunity** (April 1937).

Bibliography: *CP*, 200.

"Note on Commercial Theatre." Poem of twenty lines in free verse. The speaker, a collective persona* representing African Americans, gently accuses "you"—white American commercial theatre—of putting "me"—African Americans—in productions of Shakespeare's *Macbeth* and "Swing Mikados," and of adapting blues* and jazz* to symphony music but of not producing theatre that is actually by African Americans or about their experiences. The speaker concludes that it is up to him (that is, African American writers) to create such theatre, as Hughes had already begun to do with such works as *Angelo Herndon Jones, Front Porch, Little Ham*, and *Don't You Want to Be Free?*, as well as in his involvement with the Harlem Suitcase Theatre.* The poem was first published in *Crisis** (March 1940) and was reprinted in *The Block, Jim Crow's Last Stand*, and *One-Way Ticket*.

Bibliography: *CP*, 215.

"Note to All Nazis Fascists and Klansmen." Poem. (The title appears here as Hughes wrote it, without commas separating elements of the series.) It is in two short-lined quatrains, with lines two and four rhyming in both stanzas. The poem expresses defiance of those named in the title. It was first published in *Jim Crow's Last Stand*.

Bibliography: *CP*, 291.

"Notes of a Native Son." Review of a collection of essays, *Notes of a Native Son*, by James Baldwin* (Boston: Beacon Press, 1955). In the review Hughes praises Baldwin's talents as an essayist and characterizes the book as "thought-provoking." He also suggests that Baldwin has not sufficiently integrated his "American" and "Afro-American" points of view. Hughes's review was published in the *New York Times Book Review* (February 26, 1956), page 36, column 4. Concerning Baldwin's subsequent review of Hughes's *Selected Poems,* *see* Baldwin, James.

"Nothing But a Dog." Short story, included in the collection *Simple's Uncle Sam. See* Simple [Jesse B.] Stories.

"Nothing But Roomers." Short story, included in the collection *Simple Takes a Wife. See* Simple [Jesse B.] Stories.

Novels. Hughes published two novels, *Not Without Laughter* and *Tambourines to Glory.*

"Nude Young Dancer." Poem in two ballad* quatrains. It asks rhetorical questions of the dancer that implicitly celebrate her exoticism and allure as well as revealing that the speaker associates her dance movements and appearance with tribal dancing. The poem was first published in *The New Negro* (1925) edited by Alain Locke.* *See* The New Negro.
Bibliography: *CP*, 61.

Nugent, Richard Bruce (1906–1987). American poet and graphic artist, by all accounts one of the most vivid, self-dramatizing figures of the Harlem Renaissance.* Nugent was born and grew up in Washington, D.C. He ran away from his middle-class family at age fourteen, settling in New York City and working at odd jobs. Lewis suggests that Nugent also became the "mascot" of actor Rudolph Valentino and the "intimate friend" of Alain Locke,* Claude McKay,* Wallace Thurman,* and Hughes (757). He also describes Nugent as a "professional bohemian." Some of his poems appeared in *Caroling Dusk*, the anthology edited by Countee Cullen.* Nugent also contributed illustrations to *FIRE!!**
Bibliography: Lewis, *HRR*, 569–584.

"Number." Poem of twelve lines in free verse in which the last three lines consist entirely of question marks. It is a cryptic poem that hints of apocalypse and the occult. The poem was first published in *South and West Review* (Summer 1962). *See* Religion.
Bibliography: *CP*, 536, 687.

"Numbered." Rhyming poem in two stanzas, one of four lines and one of two. The speaker, addressing his lover, believes that his "days are numbered" and uses this belief to justify spending as much time as he can with his lover. The poem was first published in *Hearse.* The editors of *Collected Poems* could find no date or volume number for the magazine but estimated that the issue appeared in 1958; see entry for "Casual."

Bibliography: *CP*, 460.

"Numbers." Poem. *See Montage of a Dream Deferred.*

Nunuma. The name of a character in the short story "Bodies in the Moonlight." She is a beautiful woman over whom two sailors fight.

O

"October 16: The Raid." Poem of thirty-six lines in free verse, spoken to African Americans who are "now free" and reminding them to remember abolitionist John Brown (1800–1859), his raid on Harpers Ferry, his trial and execution, and—the poem implies—his moral courage. The first husband of Hughes's maternal grandmother, Mary Langston, was Lewis Sheridan Leary, who was a member of John Brown's group and was killed during the raid (October 16, 1859). Hughes's grandmother later married Charles Langston, also an abolitionist, and moved with him to Kansas. Hughes and his mother lived with the Langstons in Lawrence, Kansas, between 1902, the year of Hughes's birth, and 1908. The poem was first published under the title "October the Sixteenth" in *Opportunity** (October 1931). *See* Langston, James Mercer.

Bibliography: *CP*, 141; W.E.B. Du Bois, *John Brown* (New York: International Publishers, 1962); Paul Finkelman, ed., *His Soul Goes Marching On: Responses to John Brown and the Harpers Ferry Raid* (Charlottesville: University Press of Virginia, 1995); Stephen B. Oates, *Our Fiery Trial: Abraham Lincoln, John Brown, and the Civil War Era* (Amherst: University of Massachusetts Press, 1979); Rampersad, I, 218, 352.

"October the Sixteenth." Poem. *See* "October 16: The Raid."

"Ode to Dinah." Poem. *See Ask Your Mama.*

"Ode to My Simple Minded Friend." Poem, published in Hughes's newspaper column "Here to Yonder," May 15, 1943, not subsequently reprinted nor included in *Collected Poems*.

"Office Building: Evening." Rhyming poem of eleven lines in stanzas of varying line lengths. Chiefly it is spoken to, and quietly honors the work of, a "cleaning lady," whom we know is African American because of the single line of black dialect* she utters. The poem was first published in *The Panther and the Lash*.

Bibliography: *CP*, 555.

"Official Notice." Poem of fourteen lines. It improvises on the rhetoric of letters from the military notifying families of sons' deaths in action. The poem is "addressed" to "Dear Death" and is spoken by the mother of a dead soldier. It was first published in *The Panther and the Lash*.

Bibliography: *CP*, 558.

"Oh Let America." Song. *See* "Let America Be America Again."

"Oh Officer." Song, from *Street Scene*. Hughes wrote the lyrics, and Kurt Weill* composed the music. At this writing, the song is not listed with ASCAP.*

Bibliography: Booklet accompanying *Street Scene* [compact disc], performed by Kristine Ciesinski, Janis Kelly, Bonaventura Bottone, Richard van Allan, Catherine Zeta Jones, and the Orchestra and Chorus of the English National Opera, conducted by Carl Davis (London: Jay Records, 1996): CDJAY2–1232.

"Old Age." Poem in three ballad* quatrains and a triplet. Rhetorically addressed to a "you" who is old, the poem evokes wonders, chiefly of nature, that the person has witnessed, suggesting that the memories of these will suffice but that new wonders may nonetheless manifest themselves. It was first published in *Borderline* (January 1965). Hughes was almost sixty-three years old when the poem was published.

Bibliography: *CP*, 545.

"Old Dog Queenie." Humorous poem in a single quatrain about a dog, first published in *The Langston Hughes Reader*. *See* Children's Poetry.

Bibliography: *CP*, 608.

Old Ghost. A third-person persona Hughes occasionally adopted in his newspaper column. *See* the *Chicago Defender*; "Here to Yonder."

"Old Sailor." Rhyming poem in a single stanza of twenty very short lines. It celebrates the life of the sailor, who now "sits paralyzed," thinking of all the women he once knew. The poem was first published in *Fields of Wonder*.

Bibliography: *CP*, 335.

"Old Walt." Poem in eleven lines and two stanzas. It expresses homage to American poet Walt Whitman* (1819–1892), depicting him as a person who went "finding and seeking." The poem was first published in the *Beloit Poetry Journal Chapbook* (no. 3, 1954), a volume dedicated to Walt Whitman.

Bibliography: *CP*, 446.

"Old Youth." Poem of eleven lines in free verse. It concerns a child with an "old" face. The poem was first published in *A Little Book of Central Verse* (1928) and was included in the second printing of *Collected Poems*. *See* Central High School.

Bibliography: *CP*, [second edition], 613.

"On a Christmas Night." Rhyming poem of sixteen lines in a single stanza that recapitulates conventional elements of the biblical narratives concerning Christ's birth in a manger. It was first published in *Crisis** (December 1958). It was also included in *Black Nativity* and was reprinted in *Carol of the Brown King: Nativity Poems by Langston Hughes*. *See* "On a Pallet of Straw." *See also* Religion.

Bibliography: *CP*, 462.

"On a Pallet of Straw." Rhyming poem of twenty lines in a single stanza that recapitulates conventional elements of the biblical narratives concerning the Magi, or Three Wise Men, who attended Christ's birth in Bethlehem. It was first published in *Crisis** (December 1958). It was also included in *Black Nativity* and was reprinted in *Carol of the Brown King: Nativity Poems by Langston Hughes*. *See* "On a Christmas Night." *See also* Religion.

Bibliography: *CP*, 460.

"On the Road." Short story. The plot is spare and parablelike, concerning an African American man, Sargeant, who is trying merely to survive during the Great Depression in the United States. Wandering the streets in a snowstorm, Sargeant happens upon a church and, hoping for a warm place to sleep, knocks on the large door. Christ seems to come down from the cross and converse with Sargeant, and the story proceeds toward a somewhat surprising ending. "On the Road" is widely considered to be one of Hughes's most successful short stories. It was first published under the title "Two on the Road" in *Esquire* (January 1935), was included in the collection *Laughing to Keep from Crying*, and was reprinted in *Langston Hughes: Short Stories*. *See* Religion.

Bibliography: Ostrom, 28–29, 53, 75.

"On the Road to Mantova." Poem. *See* "Juliet."

"On the Warpath." Short story, included in the collections *Simple Takes a Wife* and *The Best of Simple*. *See* Simple [Jesse B.] Stories.

"On the Way Home." Short story. *See* "The Bottle of Wine."

"Once in a Wife-Time." Short story, included in the collections *Simple Takes a Wife* and *The Best of Simple*. See Simple [Jesse B.] Stories.

"One." Poem in two short-lined stanzas and in free verse. It compares loneliness to the wind on the "Lincoln Prairies" and to a solitary bottle of "licker" (liquor) on a table. The poem was first published in the *Carmel Pine Cone* (July 18, 1942).

Bibliography: *CP*, 234.

"The One and Only Nina Simone: A Tribute." Liner notes (commentary) for a recording. Hughes wrote this brief essay for *Nina Simone: Broadway, Blues, Ballads* (New York: Philips/Verve, 1964), a long-playing record album later re-released on compact disc by Polygram. With affection, Hughes describes the jazz* singer and pianist Nina Simone (born 1935) as "strange," "far-out," and "different." He notes that Billie Holiday was and Mort Sahl (comedian) and Willie Mays (professional baseball player) are also "different." He praises the unpretentiousness and authenticity of her singing, observes that she "has flair, but no air," and asserts that she plays the piano both "SIMPLY" and "COMPLICATEDLY." The recording was reissued by Polygram Records on compact disc. Songs on the recording include "Don't Let Me Be Misunderstood," "Don't Take All Night," "Of This I'm Sure," "See-Line Woman," and "The Last Rose of Summer." "A Monster" is included on the 1993 compact disc. *See also* Baez, Joan; *My Lord What a Mornin'*.

Bibliography/Discography: Booklet accompanying *Nina Simone: Broadway, Blues, Ballads* [compact disc] (New York: Polygram, 1993): 314518190–2.

"One Christmas Eve." Short story, first published in *Opportunity** (December 1933), included in the collection *The Ways of White Folks*, and reprinted in *Langston Hughes: Short Stories*.

Bibliography: Ostrom, 3–18.

"One Friday Morning." Short story. The narrative concerns an African American high-school girl who wins an award for her art. When the judging committee discovers that she is black, they withdraw the award, but at the awards ceremony, the girl stands, recites the Pledge of Allegiance to the U.S. flag and republic, and thinks to herself, "That is the land we must make" (95). The story was first published under the title "Inside Us" in *Crisis** (January 1939), was included in the collection *Laughing to Keep from Crying*, and was reprinted in *Langston Hughes: Short Stories*.

Bibliography: *Laughing to Keep from Crying*, 91–96; Ostrom, 24–25.

"125th Street." Poem. *See Montage of a Dream Deferred.*

"One More 'S' in the U.S.A." Poem of six stanzas, each in seven or eight lines and rhymed in the manner of ballad* stanzas. "One more 'S' in the U.S.A." recurs as a kind of chorus to this folk-song–like poem, which explicitly advocates socialism, attacks bankers and other representatives of capitalism, and is perhaps Hughes's most obviously Marxist-influenced poem. The additional "S," the poem makes clear, will make the United States "Soviet"—that is, the poem envisages a union of socialist states in the manner of the Union of Soviet Socialist Republics at the time. It was first published in the *Daily Worker* (April 2, 1934). *See also Angelo Herndon Jones*; "Ballads of Lenin"; Chant for Tom Mooney"; *Don't You Want to Be Free?*; "Goodbye, Christ"; "Good Morning, Revolution"; "Lenin"; "A New Song"; "Open Letter to the South"; "Revolution"; "Song of the Revolution"; "Wait." *See also* John Reed Club; Marxism; Politics.

Bibliography: *CP*, 176.

One-Way Ticket (New York: Knopf, 1949). 136 pp. With six illustrations by Jacob Lawrence. Collection of poetry, notable not least of all for the first appearance in book form of twelve of the Madam Poems.* In addition to the twelve "Madam" poems, the book includes "Bad Morning," "The Ballad of Margie Polite," "Boarding House," "Could Be," "Curious," "Daybreak in Alabama," "Deceased," "Final Curve," "Freedom [1]," "Funeral," "Harlem [1]" (under the title "Puzzled"), "Honey Babe," "Interne at Provident," "Jitney," "Juice Joint: Northern City," "Late Last Night," "Life Is Fine," "Lincoln Theatre," "Little Green Tree," "Lynching Song," "Mama and Daughter," "Man into Men," "Midnight Raffle," "Migrant," "Monroe's Blues," "Note on Commercial Theatre," "One-Way Ticket," "Raid," "Request for Requiems," "Restrictive Covenants," "Seashore through Dark Glasses (Atlantic City)," "Song for Billie Holiday," "S-sss-ss-sh!" "Stranger in Town," "Summer Evening (Calumet Avenue)," "Third Degree," "Warning [1]" (under the title "Roland Hayes Beaten [Georgia 1942]"), "What?" (under the title "White Felts in Fall"), and "Who But the Lord?" The book was actually copyrighted in 1948 and came out in December of that year. The American painter Jacob Lawrence (1917–2000) went on to become a world-renowned artist.

Bibliography: Rampersad, II, 161–163; Ellen Harkins Wheat, *Jacob Lawrence: American Painter* (Seattle: University of Washington Press, 1990).

"One-Way Ticket." Poem of twenty lines in three stanzas. The speaker explains that because of Jim Crow laws* and lynching,* he will move from the American South, live anywhere but there, and never return. The poem was first published

in *One-Way Ticket. See Langston Hughes Reads: "One-Way Ticket," "The Ne-gro Speaks of Rivers," "Ku Klux Klan," and Other Poems.*
Bibliography: *CP*, 361.

"Only Human." Short story, included in the collection *Simple Stakes a Claim. See* Simple [Jesse B.] Stories.

"Only Woman Blues." Poem in four traditional blues* stanzas and in black dialect.* The speaker relates his feelings about his "used-to-be" (former lover), whom he found to be "de meanest woman / I ever did see." The poem was first published in *Shakespeare in Harlem.*
Bibliography: *CP*, 250.

"Open Letter to the South." Poem of two pages with widely varying line and stanza lengths and an improvised rhyme scheme. It is spoken by a collective persona*: "I am the black worker." The poem calls on all workers of the American South to join with black workers everywhere to advance the interests of the working class. It also explicitly disagrees with the notion of Booker T. Washington* that blacks and whites should remain socially separate. Like "One More 'S' in the U.S.A.," this poem is an obvious manifestation of Hughes's interest at the time in Marxist ideas. It was first published under the title "Red Flag over Tuskegee" (the Tuskegee Institute was founded by Booker T. Washington*) in the *Baltimore Afro American** (June 25, 1932). *See* John Reed Club; Marxism; Politics.
Bibliography: *CP*, 160–61.

"Opening Blues." Song. Hughes wrote the lyrics, and Leonard Geoffrey Feather composed the music. ASCAP* lists the song as being published by Model Music, Inc., and the song's ASCAP registry number is 450095791.

Opera. *See The Barrier; Esther; De Organizer; Pied Piper of Swing; Port Town; Street Scene; Troubled Island*; "Uncle Tom's Cabin"; *The Wizard of Altoona. See also* Drama; Johnson, James P.; Meyerowitz, Jan; Musical Plays; Orchestral Pieces/Oratorios; Still, William Grant; Weill, Kurt.

"Opinions of the New Student." Poem by Cuban-Chinese writer Regino Pedroso, translated by Hughes from the Spanish. A free-verse poem of about one page, it concerns the student's increasing interest in revolutionary politics. It was published in *The Langston Hughes Reader.*
Bibliography: *The Langston Hughes Reader*, 140–141.

Opportunity: A Journal of Negro Life. Magazine. Founded in 1923 by the National Urban League and edited during its heyday by Charles S. Johnson,*

Opportunity quickly became a social, political, and artistic force and exerted as much influence over the Harlem Renaissance* as did the powerful magazine *Crisis,* the chief publication of the NAACP.* Hutchinson writes, "Whereas the NAACP undertook direct action and immediatism [to advocate for African Americans and against racism], the Urban League tended toward diplomacy and gradualism" (171). He goes on to explain the intellectual and ideological roots of the Urban League's and *Opportunity*'s ethos and shows how Johnson and Alain Locke* used the magazine to advance a comparatively conservative idea of the "New Negro* Aesthetic." Johnson and Locke did not see Hughes's work as being in complete agreement with their view of this "aesthetic." Hughes's politics were generally much closer to those expressed by *Crisis*, and his poetry was often not as refined as these two men desired "Negro" poetry to be. Nonetheless, Johnson and Locke were early supporters of Hughes's career, and *Opportunity* published numerous poems by Hughes, especially in the 1920s and 1930s. Indeed, in the first decade or more of Hughes's career, *Opportunity* was arguably one of the three magazines most important to his development, the other two being *Crisis* and the *Messenger.* *See also* Audience; Mason, Mrs. Charlotte Osgood.

Bibliography: Hutchinson, 168–175; Hortense E. Simmons, "Sterling A. Brown's 'Literary Chronicles' [in *Opportunity*]," *African American Review* 31, no. 3 (Fall 1997), 443–447.

"Oppression." Poem of fourteen short lines in two stanzas. It describes how "dreams" (aspirations) are "not available" to many people in lands where "night" and "cold steel [p]revail" but predicts that one day such people will recover their aspirations. It was first published in *Fields of Wonder*.

Bibliography: *CP*, 340.

Orchestral Pieces/Oratorios. *See Ballad of the Brown King; Five Foolish Virgins; The Glory around His Head; Let Us Remember.*

"Organ Grinder's Swing' Heard above Gunfire in Spain—Hughes." Newspaper article. *See Baltimore Afro American.*

De Organizer (1940). Blues* opera in one act. Hughes wrote the libretto, and James P. Johnson* composed the music. Rouder writes, "*De Organizer*, a one-act 'blues opera' . . . , received one performance at Carnegie Hall in 1940. A true assessment of this music is hampered by the loss of many of the scores, but some commentators have questioned the success of Johnson's orchestral compositions" (580). As an opera, *De Organizer* was path-breaking in at least two ways: It attempted to combine the blues with operatic form, and it attempted to address labor issues from a comparatively radical perspective. Rampersad indicates that in 1940 a performance of the blues opera was also held for the

International Ladies Garment Workers Union. The blues opera was published in 2000. *See* Marxism; Politics. *See also Don't You Want to Be Free?; Front Porch.*

Bibliography: Langston Hughes, [text of] *De Organizer*, in *The Political Plays of Langston Hughes*, ed. with introductions and analyses by Susan Duffy (Carbondale: Southern Illinois University Press, 2000), 177–190 [Duffy's introduction to the work: 163–176]; Rampersad, I, 363–365, 384; Willa Rouder, "James P. Johnson," in *The New Grove Dictionary of American Music*, ed. H. Wiley Hitchcock and Stanley Sadie (New York: Grove's Dictionaries of Music, 1986), vol. 2, 580–581.

"Our Land." Rhyming poem of seventeen lines in four stanzas of varying length. An epigraph reads, "Poem for a Decorative Panel," but such a panel has not been identified. The poem describes what "our land" should be, evoking chiefly tropical images and contrasting it to the land in which, for example, birds are gray. It was first published in *World Tomorrow* (May 1923).

Bibliography: *CP*, 32.

"Our Spring." Poem of thirty-seven lines in free verse. Defiant in tone, it is spoken by a collective persona* representing a variety of workers and antifascist persons worldwide. The poem mentions Italian-born political activist Bartolomeo Vanzetti (1888–1927) as well as antifascist Bulgarian Georgi Dimitrov (1882–1949), who was among those accused by Adolf Hitler's regime of burning the Reichstag in Berlin, Germany, in 1933. The poem suggests that figuratively, spring has arrived for socialists worldwide. It was first published in *International Literature* (no. 2, 1933). It is not included in *Collected Poems*, but is reprinted in Berry. A significantly different version of the poem, "The Underground," was published in 1943 and has its own entry in this encyclopedia. *See* Marxism; Politics.

Bibliography: Berry, 5–6; Rampersad, I, 115.

"Our Wonderful Society: Washington." Essay. Rampersad characterizes it as a "stinging" assessment of "the black middle-class in Washington, D.C." Hughes wrote it while he was studying at Lincoln University.* It was published in *Opportunity** (August 1927).

Bibliography: Rampersad, I, 146.

"Out-Loud Silent." Short story, included in the collection *Simple Stakes a Claim. See* Simple [Jesse B.] Stories.

"Out of Work." Poem in four traditional blues* stanzas and in black dialect.* The speaker details the effects of his being out of work and his thwarted attempts to find work, including being turned away, because of a local-residency requirement, by the WPA (Works Progress Administration), one of the employment-stimulus programs of Franklin Delano Roosevelt's* "New Deal." The poem was first published in *Poetry* (April 1940). It was also published in *Shakespeare in Harlem. See* "Ballad of Roosevelt"; "Dear Mr. President"; "Message to the President"; "The Negro Faces Fascism."

Bibliography: *CP*, 217.

"Outcast." Short story. *See* "African Morning."

"Oyster's Son." Short story. *See* "Gumption."

P

"Pair in One." Poem of eight short lines in a single stanza; lines four and eight rhyme, as do lines five and six. It is a supremely compact, subtly phrased meditation on life, which the poem associates with "the stranger," and death, which the poem associates with the "strangeness." It is arguably one of Hughes's most undeservedly little-known poems. The poem was first published in *Approach* (Spring 1962).

Bibliography: *CP*, 535.

"Pale Lady." Rhyming poem of thirteen lines in a single stanza. It is a rather straightforward love poem in which the speaker proposes marriage and concludes with the exclamation "How I love you!" The editors of *Collected Poems* speculate that the poem was first published in *American Life* (June 1926), but the journal has not been located. *See* "Love Song for Antonia."

Bibliography: *CP*, 72.

The Panther and the Lash (New York: Knopf, 1967). 101 pp. Collection of poetry. The last collection of his poetry with which Hughes would be involved, the book chiefly reprints poems from previous volumes, including *Fields of Wonder, One-Way Ticket*, and *Scottsboro Limited*. The poems were chosen with an eye toward the civil unrest in the United States at the time, and the *Panther* of the title was a reference to the Black Panther Party.* The volume includes many of Hughes's political poems, for example, "Christ in Alabama," "Daybreak in Alabama," "Jim Crow Car," "Ku Klux," "Northern Liberal," and "Un-American Investigators," but also includes poems about Harlem,* Africa, and other subjects. Poems previously unpublished in book form include "Angola Question Mark," "Bible Belt," "Dinner Guest: Me," "Final Call," "Frederick Douglass 1817–1895," "Junior Addict," "The Last Prince of the East," "Lenox

Avenue Bar," "Little Song on Housing," "Long View: Negro," "Mother in War-time," "Office Building: Evening," "Official Notice," "Prime," "Question and Answer," "Special Bulletin," "Stokely Malcolm Me" (referring to activists Stokely Carmichael and Malcolm X), "Sweet Words on Race," "Un-American Investigators," "Undertow," "War," and "Where? When? Which?" The book was reissued by Vintage Classics (New York) in 1992, with a new cover featuring a pastel portrait of Hughes painted by Winold Reiss in 1925. *See* Politics.

Bibliography: Rampersad, II, 409–412.

Papers, Hughes's (and Related Research Material). The most important collection of Hughes's materials is the Langston Hughes Papers, part of the James Weldon Johnson Memorial Collection in the Beinecke Library at Yale University, New Haven, Connecticut; apart from the Langston Hughes Papers, the Johnson Memorial Collection itself also includes Hughes material. Manuscripts, correspondence, and other materials are also held in the Amistad Research Center, Tulane University, New Orleans, Louisiana (see especially the Countee Cullen* Papers held there); in the Bancroft Library, University of California, Berkeley; the Berg Collection of the New York Public Library; the Carl Van Vechten* Papers in both the Yale University Library and the New York Public Library; the Frank Porter Graham Papers, Fisk University; the archives of the *Carmel Pine Cone*, Carmel, California; the archives of the *Chicago Defender**; the Joel Elias Spingarn Papers in the New York Public Library; the Jean Toomer* Papers at Fisk University; the Moorland-Spingarn Research Center, Howard University; the Library of Langston University, Langston, Oklahoma; the Library of Lincoln University*; the Noel Sullivan* Papers, University of California, Berkeley; various departments of the New York Public Library; the Library of Old Dominion University; the Ralph Ellison* Branch of the Oklahoma City Library; the Schomburg Center for Research in Black Culture, 515 Malcolm X Boulevard, New York City; the W.E.B. Du Bois* Papers, University of Massachusetts, Amherst; and the Walter White* Papers at the Library of Congress, Washington, D.C. *See also Collected Poems; Good Morning Revolution: Uncollected Writings of Protest by Langston Hughes; Langston Hughes: Short Stories.*

Bibliography: Donald C. Dickinson, *A Bio-Bibliography of Langston Hughes, 1902–1967* (Hamden, CT: Shoe String Press, 1967); R. Baxter Miller, *Langston Hughes and Gwendolyn Brooks: A Reference Guide* (Boston: G. K. Hall, 1978); Rampersad, I, 439–443; II, 483–487.

"Parade." Poem. *See Montage of a Dream Deferred.*

Parents, Hughes's. *See* Hughes, Carrie Langston; Hughes, James Nathaniel. *See also* Clark, Homer.

"Parisian Beggar Woman." Poem in three ballad* stanzas. Rhetorically, it is addressed to the woman, who, the speaker speculates, was once beautiful but will now only be kissed by "death." It was first published under the title "Montmartre Beggar Woman" in *Crisis** (November 1927). *See also* "Mexican Market Woman."

Bibliography: *CP*, 110.

"Park Bench." Poem in three short-lined ballad* stanzas. The speaker lives on a park bench and addresses an unnamed "You" who lives on Park Avenue, known as a wealthy area of Manhattan in New York City. The poem briefly contrasts their lives. It was first published in *New Masses* (March 6, 1934).

Bibliography: *CP*, 183.

"Park Benching." Poem of sixteen short lines in free verse, spoken by someone who has sat on park benches in New York City and Paris, hungry and in need of work. It was first published in *Workers Monthly* (April 1925).

Bibliography: *CP*, 49.

"Party in the Bronx." Short story, included in the collection *Simple Takes a Wife*. *See* Simple [Jesse B.] Stories.

"Passing." Poem. *See Montage of a Dream Deferred*.

"Passing." Short story. By means of a first-person epistolary (letter) narrative, Hughes represents a conflict between a young African American man who chooses to "pass" as white (he is light-skinned, obviously) and his mother, whom he passes on the street but—because he is "passing"—refuses to acknowledge. In the letter the son tries to explain his actions and choices to his mother. The issue, theme, and complexity of passing find their way into much American literature, much African American literature, and much writing from the Harlem Renaissance,* including Hughes's story and the novel *Passing* by Nella Larsen.* The story was included in the collection *The Ways of White Folks* and was reprinted in *Langston Hughes: Short Stories*. *See also* "Who's Passing for Who?"

Bibliography: Juda Bennett, *The Passing Figure: Racial Confusion in Modern American Literature* (New York: Peter Lang, 1996); Elaine K. Ginsberg, *Passing and the Fictions of Identity* (Durham: Duke University Press, 1996); Ostrom, 11–12; Werner Sollors, *Neither Black nor White Yet Both: Thematic Explorations of Interracial Literature* (New York: Oxford University Press, 1997).

The Paste-Board Bandit (New York: Oxford University Press, 1997). 96 pp. Cowritten with Arna Bontemps.* Introduction by Alex Bontemps. Illustrated by Peggy Turley. Children's book. An adventure tale for children, written as a short story in 1935 but unpublished until 1997. *See* "The Paste-Board Bandit." *See also Black Misery; The Block; Carol of the Brown King: Nativity Poems by Langston Hughes*; Children's Poetry; Nonfiction; *Popo and Fifina; The Sweet and Sour Animal Book.*

"Paste-Board Bandit, The." Short story for children. It was cowritten by Hughes and Arna Bontemps* in 1935 and remained unpublished until 1997, when it was turned into a book for young adults. *See The Paste-Board Bandit.*
Bibliography: Rampersad, I, 307–308.

"Pastoral." Rhyming poem of nine lines. It refers to shepherds who believe, mistakenly, that their "Saviour," Christ, has returned. It was first published in *The Langston Hughes Reader. See* Religion.
Bibliography: *CP*, 463.

"Pathological Puzzle." Poem in a modified limerick form. It takes a lighthearted look at the numerous diseases to which humans are susceptible. It was first published in the *Baltimore Afro American** (April 1942). *See* "America's Young Black Joe."
Bibliography: *CP*, 572.

"Patron of the Arts." Short story. It is a mild satire of the artist/patron relationship. It was first published in *Something in Common and Other Stories.*
Bibliography: Ostrom, 60–63.

"Payday." Poem, one of the seven separate parts of "Seven Moments of Love."

"Peace." Rhyming poem in two short-lined quatrains that meditates on the futility of war. It was first published in *Opportunity** (Summer 1948).
Bibliography: *CP*, 341.

"Peace Conference in an American Town." Poem of thirty-two lines (in four stanzas), thirteen of which are "At the back fence calling." The poem depicts back-fence conversations as an avenue of building unity across lines of age, ethnicity, and gender. It was first published in *Common Ground* (Winter 1946).
Bibliography: *CP*, 316.

Pen Names, Hughes's. *See* Pseudonyms Used by Hughes.

"Pennsylvania Station." Poem. Hughes wrote numerous poems of sonnet length and often employed techniques connected to that venerable lyric form, but this poem for him is unusual because it is a strict Shakespearian sonnet, and its diction is restrained, even formal. It depicts Pennsylvania Station, a main railway terminus in New York City, as a "basilica" where, even as they are bustling, travelers may be engaged in soul-searching. The poem is a very accomplished sonnet, and Hughes sometimes uses slant rhymes reminiscent of those in William Butler Yeats's poetry, for example, "York / dark" and "old / soul." The poem was first published in *Crisis** (February 1932). "Ph.D." and "Search" are also sonnets. *See also* "Seven Moments of Love," which Hughes subtitled "An Un-sonnet Sequence in Blues." *See* Modernism; Religion.

Bibliography: *CP*, 159; "Sonnet," in *PEPP*, 482–485.

"People without Shoes." Essay that concerns the abject poverty and severe social-class divisions in Haiti. It was first published in *New Masses* (October 1931). Much material from the essay later appeared in *I Wonder As I Wander*. *See also* "A Letter from Haiti"; *Masters of the Dew; Troubled Island*.

Bibliography: *I Wonder As I Wander*; Rampersad, I, 215.

Percy, William Alexander (1885–1942). American poet and prose writer. Percy was a native of Mississippi. In *I Wonder As I Wander* Hughes describes meeting him in the spring of 1932, when Percy was "chairman" of Hughes's poetry-reading program at "a Negro church" in Greenville, Mississippi. Hughes then remembers receiving several "beautiful letters" from Percy over the years and regrets not having met more "gentlemanly [white] Southerners" on his reading tour of the South in 1931–1932. At the reading, Percy gave Hughes an inscribed copy of his autobiography, *Lanterns on the Levee*.

Bibliography: *I Wonder As I Wander*, 52; William Alexander Percy, *The Collected Poems of William Alexander Percy*, with a foreword by Roark Bradford (New York: Knopf, 1944); William Alexander Percy, *Enzio's Kingdom and Other Poems* (New Haven: Yale University Press, 1924); William Alexander Percy, *Lanterns on the Levee: Recollections of a Planter's Son* (New York: Knopf, 1941).

Periodicals in Which Hughes Published Poems, Stories, Essays, and Articles. Following is a checklist of magazines, journals, and newspapers in which Hughes's work appeared. With regard to his career as a poet, four periodicals in particular stand out. These are *Crisis,** in which he published at least eighty-two poems; *Opportunity,** in which he published at least fifty-one poems; *Poetry* magazine (Chicago), in which he published at least twenty poems; and the *Baltimore Afro American,** in which he published at least twelve poems as well as several articles. Periodicals marked** have not been located.

Abbott's Weekly	*American Mercury**
Africa South	*American Scholar*
Afro Magazine	*American Spectator*
American Dialogue	*Amsterdam News*
American Life**	*Anvil*

Approach

Baltimore Afro American

*Belfry Owl** (Central High School,* Cleveland, Ohio)

Beloit Poetry Journal

Black Orpheus

Bookman

Borderline

Brooklyn Daily Eagle

Brownie's Book

Buccaneer

Carmel Pine Cone

Carolina Magazine

Catholic Interracialist

Challenge

Chelsea Eight

*Chicago Defender**

Christian Register, Unitarian

Circuit Magazine

Cleveland Call and Post

Colorado Review

Columbia University Spectator

Common Ground

Common Sense Historical Review

Communist

Contempo

Contemporáneos

Contemporary Poetry

Les Continents (Paris)

Crisis

Cross Section

Current Opinion

Daily Express (Cleveland, Ohio)

Daily Worker

*Deer and Dachshund***

Ebony Rhythm

Epworth Era

Esquire

ETC.

Experiment

Fight against War and Fascism

*FIRE!!**

Fountain

Free Lance

Freedom Journal (NAACP*)

Harlem

Harlem Quarterly

Harper's Bazaar

Harper's Magazine

Hawk's Cry

Hearse

Herald News (Newark, New Jersey)

Home Quarterly

International Literature

Journal of Educational Sociology

Kansas Magazine

Labor Herald

Liberator

Library

Lincoln University News

Lincoln University Poets

Literary Digest

Literary Review of Fairleigh Dickinson University

Living Age

Long Island University Review

Magisterio

Maryland Quarterly

Massachusetts Review

Measure

*Messenger**

Metropolis

Midwest Journal

Minnesota Quarterly

Modern Quarterly

Monthly (Central High School, Cleveland, Ohio)

Nation

Negro Digest

Negro History Bulletin

Negro Quarterly

Negro Story

Negro Worker

New Masses

New Orlando Review

New Republic

New Theatre

New York Herald Tribune

New York Journal American

New York Post

New York Times

New York Times Book Review

New Yorker

Nocturne

Old Line

Olivant Quarterly

One-Act Play

Opportunity

Our World

Outcry

Outsider

Pacific Weekly

Palms

Panorama

Partisan

People's Voice

Phylon

Players

Poetry (Chicago)

Poetry Magazine (Australia)

Poetry Quarterly

Political Affairs

Présence Africaine (Paris)

Public Opinion

Race

Reader's Digest

Reflexus**

Renaissance

Rong, Wrong

Saturday Evening Post

Saturday Review of Literature

Scribner's Magazine

Senior Scholastic

Shenandoah

South and West Review

Southern Frontier

Southern Workman

Span

Story Magazine

Survey Graphic

Tomorrow

Trend

Umbra Anthology

Unquote

Vanity Fair

Voices

Volunteer for Liberty

Wayne State Graduate Comment

Welcome News

Woman's Home Companion

Workers Monthly

World Tomorrow

"Personal." Poem of six lines. It might aptly be described as a sly poem because the speaker reports having received a letter from (and responding with a letter

to) God, but discloses nothing about the contents of the correspondence. The poem was first published in *Crisis** (October 1933). *See* Religion.
Bibliography: *CP*, 173.

"Ph.D." Poem. Although Hughes published numerous poems of sonnet length and employed techniques related to that form, he rarely published sonnets. As a Shakespearian sonnet, then, "Ph.D." is, with regard to form, a rare poem for him. It focuses on the extent to which the unnamed holder of a Ph.D. has been so immersed in academia that he cannot function in or comprehend "all the human world." The poem was first published in *Opportunity** (August 1932). "Pennsylvania Station" and "Search" are also sonnets. "Seven Moments of Love" is subtitled "An Un-sonnet Sequence in Blues" and features seven separate poems that improvise on the sonnet form. *See also* "Cowards from the Colleges"; "Poem for an Intellectual on the Way Up to Submit to His Lady"; "Snob."
Bibliography: *CP*, 161–162; "Sonnet," in *PEPP*, 543–546.

A Pictorial History of the Negro in America. (New York: Crown Publishers, 1956). 316 pp. Nonfiction book, coauthored with Milton Meltzer. The chapters represent well-accepted epochs of African American history, beginning with the slave trade, moving to African Americans' role in revolutionary America, and including chapters on the Civil War and Reconstruction, the abolitionist movement, turn-of-the-century politics, the Harlem Renaissance,* the civil-rights movement, and other events. Across these chapters, Hughes emphasizes little-known or underrepresented contributions of African Americans to all aspects of and institutions in the United States, including science, religion,* manufacturing, government, law, the military, and the arts. The book includes Hughes's poem "My People." Presumably Meltzer was responsible for the illustrations, which include photographs, drawings, reprinted editorial cartoons, facsimiles of posters, and reproductions of portraits. Revised editions of the book appeared in 1963, 1968, 1973, and 1983. Beginning with the 1968 edition, C. Eric Lincoln became a coauthor of the book, the title of which was changed to *A Pictorial History of Black Americans*.

"Picture for Her Dresser." Short story, included in the collections *Simple Takes a Wife* and *The Best of Simple*. *See* Simple [Jesse B.] Stories.

"Pictures to the Wall." Poem in three ballad* quatrains. It is spoken by an older person who asks questions rhetorically of a younger person about whether the speaker ought to talk about disappointments ("bitter, forgotten dreams") and thereby disillusion the younger person. Hughes published the poem when he was twenty-four years old. It was first published in *Palms* (1926).
Bibliography: *CP*, 79.

Pied Piper of Swing. Unfinished opera* in manuscript form. *See* Johnson, James P.

"Pierrot." Songlike poem in six stanzas of varying length. It contrasts "Simple John," a pious, hardworking, loyal person, with Pierrot, the traditional figure of French and Italian pantomime and—as represented in this poem—a shiftless, pleasure-seeking, sinful person who is unfaithful to his lover, Pierrette. It was first published in *The Weary Blues*. *See also* "A Black Pierrot"; "The Jester."

Bibliography: *CP*, 95–96; Douglas Hunt and Kari Hunt, *Pantomime: The Silent Theater* (New York: Atheneum, 1964); Maurice Sand, *The History of the Harlequinade* (New York: Blom, 1968).

"Piggy-Back." Poem in a single rhyming quatrain. The speaker, a child, reports on who in the family will and will not give "piggy-back" rides. The poem was first published in *The Langston Hughes Reader. See* Children's Poetry.

Bibliography: *CP*, 605.

"Plaint." One of Hughes's shortest poems, a couplet consisting of six words. It contrasts money and art. The poem was first published in *Voices* (Fall 1955). *See also* "Little Lyric (*of Great Importance*)."

Bibliography: *CP*, 451.

Plays. *See* Drama; Harlem Suitcase Theatre; Musical Plays; Opera.

"Po' [Poor] Boy Blues." Poem in four traditional blues* stanzas and in black dialect.* It is spoken by a young man who moved from the South to the North, is heartbroken, and feels "weary." It was first published in *Poetry* (November 1926).

Bibliography: *CP*, 83.

"Poem." Title of the first publication of "Dusk," "Garden," "Mammy," "My People," and "Youth."

"Poem." Song (?). ASCAP lists Paul A. Siskind as the composer and Hughes as lyricist but does not specify which poem Siskind set to music. G. Schirmer, Inc., is listed as publisher of the song, the ASCAP* registry number of which is 460282211. The G. Schirmer database does not list such a work. However, Hal Leonard, Inc., publishes a choral work by Siskind, with "text" by Hughes, entitled "A Dream Deferred." Therefore, the "Poem" listed by ASCAP might be "Harlem [2]." *See* "Dream Deferred."

Bibliography: Paul Siskind, "A Dream Deferred," text by Langston Hughes (New York: Hal Leonard, 1993), HL 50483190.

"Poem [1]." With an epigraph, "For a portrait of an African boy after the manner of Gauguin," the poem is spoken by the boy, who indicates how immersed he is in tropical African culture and how afraid he is "of this Civilization," which he characterizes as "cold," "hard," and "strong." Paul Gauguin (1848–1903) was a French painter, classified as a "postimpressionist" artist and best known for earthy, vivid, sensual representations of indigenous people on the island of Tahiti, to which he moved in 1891. The painting to which Hughes refers in the epigraph has not been identified, nor has the painter. The poem was first published in *World Tomorrow* (May 1921).

Bibliography: *CP*, 32.

"Poem [2]." Six-line poem dedicated to "F. S." The speaker expresses love for a "friend" (male) and reports that the friend "went away from me." The editors of *Collected Poems* note that "F. S. has not been plausibly identified." The poem was first published in *Crisis** (May 1925).

Bibliography: *CP*, 52, 626.

"Poem [3]." Nine-line poem in two stanzas with a subtitle, in parentheses, that is repeated as the first line: "When young spring comes." Spring is depicted as an innocent season, summer as one in which "the old god of Love" must be pleased. The editors of *Collected Poems* speculate that the poem first appeared in *Reflexus* (1925) but note that the magazine has not been located. *See also* "Better."

Bibliography: *CP*, 54, 627.

"Poem [4]." Twenty-one-line poem dedicated "To the Black Beloved." Insofar as it uses antique diction ("Thou art not beautiful / Yet thou hast / A loveliness," for example) it is for Hughes an unusual poem. It was first published in *Crisis** (December 1925).

Bibliography: *CP*, 58.

"Poem for a Poster on Africa." Poem of forty-six lines in free verse. It critiques both colonialist forces in Africa and well-meaning but ineffectual scholars who take an interest in Africa from afar. The poster for which the poem was written has not been identified, nor has the poem's date of composition. It was first published in Berry and is not included in *Collected Poems*.

Bibliography: Berry, 11–12.

"Poem for an Intellectual on the Way Up to Submit to His Lady." Poem in four ballad* quatrains, with rhymes and phrasing very much like those of a popular song. It is spoken by an "intellectual-to-be" who indicates that he might one day become a "Ph.D.," a "Rev.[erend]," or a "judge" and instructs his "lady" not to refer to him by professional titles he might earn but instead by pet names, such as "Turtle Dove." The poem was first published in *Contemporary Poetry* (August 1944). *See* "Ph.D."

Bibliography: *CP*, 300.

"Poem for Youth." Poem of twenty-three lines in three stanzas. Addressed rhetorically to "Wise old men," the poem confronts the reader with images of a vibrant new age of jazz,* which is compared to "sun-filled rain / Drowning yesterday." It was first published in the *Messenger** (June 1927).

Bibliography: *CP*, 105.

"Poem to a Dead Soldier." Rhyming poem of thirty-two lines in four stanzas. Its epigraph, set in quotation marks, is "Death is a whore who consorts with all men." The poem reiterates this comparison and views skeptically the ways in which society honors dead soldiers (with speeches and statues, for example). It was first published in *Workers Monthly* (April 1925).

Bibliography: *CP*, 48–49.

"Poem to Uncle Sam." Rhyming poem of twelve short lines. Addressed to "Uncle Sam" (the U.S. government), it encourages "him" to "vanquish" Jim Crow laws* before trying to defeat Adolf Hitler (in World War II). It was first circulated by the Associated Negro Press in November 1943. *See* "America's Young Black Joe!"; "Dear Mr. President"; "Message to the President."

Bibliography: *CP*, 585–586.

"Pòeme d'Automne." Poem of fifteen lines in free verse (two stanzas). The imagistic depiction of autumn works against conventional depictions, portraying autumn as a sluggish season and winter as more intense, even erotic. The poem stands in sharp contrast to "Autumn Note." It was first published in *The Weary Blues*.

Bibliography: *CP*, 92–93.

Poems (New York: Everyman, 1999). 256 pp. Edited by David Roessel (coeditor of *Collected Poems*). A selection of Hughes's poetry. *See also* Revision, Process of, and Hughes.

Poems by Sterling Brown (New York: Folkways Records, 1952). Sound recording. On the long-playing album Hughes is recorded reading the stories "Feet Live Their Own Life," "Landladies," "Simple Prays a Prayer," and "Wooing the Muse." *See* Audio Recordings of Hughes.

Poems from Black Africa (Bloomington: Indiana University Press, 1963). 160 pp. Anthology. Hughes included over seventy poems by thirty-eight different writers from Sierra Leone, Nyasaland, Kenya, Ghana, Liberia, Nigeria, Mozambique, Madagascar, Congo, and Senegal. Most of the poets are English-speaking, but one Portuguese-speaking poet (Valente Malangatama) and six French-speaking poets (Jean-Joseph Rabearivlo, Flavien Ranaivo, Tchicaya U Tam'si, Patrice Lumumba, Léopold Sédar Senghor, and David Diop) are included. Also represented are "Oral Traditionals," translated anonymous poems from oral literatures of several tribes, regions, and countries. In his introduction Hughes stressed the role of the "lyric historian," the poet who records images and emotions connected to important historical epochs in a nation's (and, in this case, a continent's) history (11). Because Africa was emerging from colonialism and negotiating complexities of nationalism, Hughes regarded the epoch to which these contemporary poets belonged as crucial. He added, however, that these "black poets" were "not so much propagandists for African nationalism as they are spokesmen for variations of *negritude*," which Hughes defined as an expression of "pride in and love of the African heritage physically, spiritually, and culturally" (11). What Hughes, probably out of modesty, did not mention is that the writers who advanced the concept of Negritude (including Senghor) drew enormous inspiration from Hughes's work, partly owing to the consciousness of "African heritage" it consistently expressed. In addition to Senghor, other writers in the anthology of special interest are Patrice Lumumba, the first president of the Republic of the Congo (Congo), and Nigerian writer Wole Soyinka, who went on to receive the Nobel Prize for Literature. Rampersad notes that the anthology was "launched with a remarkable, free publicity boost—a fullpage spread of selections from it in the current issue of *Time* magazine, in further testimony to Africa's new significance" (II, 367). In 1961 Hughes had attended a luncheon for Senghor at the White House, hosted by President John F. Kennedy. *See also An African Treasury*; Anthologies; Césaire, Aimé; *The First Book of Africa*; "Lumumba's Grave"; Poetics.

Bibliography: Rampersad, II, 367; Janice S. Spleth, *Léopold Sédar Senghor* (Boston: Twayne Publishers, 1985); "Where God Is Black: Excerpts from 'Poems from Black Africa'," *Time* 82 (September 6, 1963), 22–23.

Poems/Langston Hughes (New York: Knopf, 1999). 252 pp. Edited by David Roessel (coeditor of *Collected Poems*). A selection of Hughes's poetry. *See* Revision, Process of, and Hughes.

"Poet to Bigot." Poem of seventeen lines in four stanzas, chiefly in free verse. Addressing the bigot, the poet draws contrasts between the two and claims that the bigot has more power, but implies that his (the poet's) future is more promising. The poem was first published in *Phylon* (Spring 1953).

Bibliography: *CP*, 443.

"Poet to Patron." Poem in three short-lined ballad* stanzas. It is not so much addressed to a patron as it is crafted to be a complaint about patronage, specifically about how patrons tend to dictate what the poet (in this case) should write. Published several years after Hughes's breakup with his patron, Mrs. Charlotte Osgood Mason,* the poem can nonetheless be read as commenting indirectly on that relationship. It was first published in *American Mercury** (June 1939). *See* "The Blues I'm Playing."

Bibliography: *CP*, 212.

Poetics, Hughes's. Unlike many, if not most, other major writers who were his contemporaries, Hughes did not articulate, by means of literary criticism, a comprehensive poetics or "philosophy of poetry." Especially in contrast to W. B. Yeats, T. S. Eliot, Ezra Pound, William Carlos Williams, Randall Jarrell, Marianne Moore, and any number of poets writing at about the same time as Hughes, he appears relatively quiet on the subject, at first glance uninterested in explicitly educating a readership concerning his view of literature and writing or, more pointedly, concerning how he desires his poetry to be read and evaluated. The most obvious exception to this apparent reticence is the essay "The Negro Artist and the Racial Mountain," which sets out many firm ideas about writing, especially about writing as an African American. Additionally, Hughes wrote book reviews and edited anthologies—endeavors that reflect literary values (*see* "*Notes of a Native Son*" [Hughes's review of a collection of essays by James Baldwin*] and *Poems from Black Africa* for examples). He also wrote a discerning introduction to an edition of Mark Twain's novel *Pudd'nhead Wilson* and an introduction to an edition of selected poems by Walt Whitman.* Still, full-blown literary criticism in the mode of T. S. Eliot's, Ezra Pound's, or Randall Jarrell's is not part of Hughes's "canon." Of two premises we can, however, be reasonably certain: (1) Hughes was more than capable of producing such criticism, as is evident by his other achievements in nonfiction, including *The Big Sea* and *I Wonder As I Wander*, the newspaper column "Here to Yonder," and a variety of essays, such as "From the Blues to an Opera Libretto." (2) He did not fail at a major critical project—that is, no false starts or fragments of a comprehensive work of criticism exist, and no mention of such a project appears in his letters, such as those to Arna Bontemps.*

We might reasonably assume, then, that Hughes chose not to produce the kind of literary criticism so many of his contemporaries published, and that he chose chiefly to let the poetry itself transmit his poetics implicitly. Consequently, we might also suggest that choosing to let his poems implicitly express his poetics was, paradoxically, a key feature of his poetics. That is, amid an age of criticism, Hughes defined himself as a poet who largely let his poems speak for themselves; in this case, as in others, he went against the grain. Additionally, there is reason to believe that when Hughes chose to write nonfiction prose, he chose mainly to address social and political issues, not issues of poetics and literary criticism. Over the course of his career, such topics as Jim Crow laws,* the Scottsboro Boys,* the plight of Ethiopia, the Spanish Civil War, Russian society, the community of Harlem,* and the like apparently seemed more pressing than topics in poetics. Finally, we should not overlook practical economic considerations. "This is the story of a Negro who wanted to make his living from poems and stories," Hughes writes in *I Wonder As I Wander*. That is, he was determined to live by his writing, and indeed, the careers in publishing and academia with which white American writers could financially reinforce their careers as writers were not as welcoming to black writers through most of Hughes's life. He did supplement his income with fees from lecturing; he wrote popular songs and one screenplay; and he wrote books for juvenile readers. Nonetheless, by choice and by circumstances, Hughes made "his living from poems and stories," so to some degree, criticism was a genre he could not afford to write.

With regard to his implicit view of poetic art, Hughes is generally considered to be a rather "simple," folk-oriented poet, but a thorough examination of his poetry reveals a wider range of poetic technique than is apparent in the poems that are frequently anthologized, such as "Theme for English B" or "The Negro Speaks of Rivers." Blues,* ballads,* and other shorter lyric forms constitute a significant part of his poetic oeuvre, but there are also a large number of longer forms and poems that use techniques of surrealism, as well as monologues, dialogues, "dramatic recitations," and so on. He worked extensively both with free verse and traditional forms and also modified traditional forms substantially (*see* The Blues; Ballad). The almost legendary "simplicity" of Hughes's poetry, however, is probably misleading, and one more productive starting point from which to study his poetry is to assume that it is deceptively accessible, surprisingly varied, and significantly innovative. Additionally, even alleged "simplicity" itself is no simple matter when one is approaching Hughes's work. As Rampersad observes, "[F]or Hughes, as for all serious poets, the writing of poetry was virtually a sacred commitment. And while he wished to write no verse that was beyond the ability of the masses of people to understand, his poetry, in common with that of other committed writers, is replete with allusions that must be respected and understood if it is to be properly appreciated. To respect Hughes's work, above all one must respect the African American people and their culture, as well as the American people in general and their national culture" ("Introduction," 5). Also, Hughes's implicit "poetics of a social poet" emerge piecemeal in such essays as "Democracy, Negroes, and Writers," "How To Be a Bad Writer (in Ten Easy Lessons)," "Introduction" to *Poems from Black Africa*, "Langston Hughes Speaks," "My Adventures as a Social Poet," "The Negro Artist and the Racial Mountain," "Spain's Martyred Poet, García Lorca," "Task of the Negro Writer as Artist," and "To Negro Writers." *See* Modernism and Hughes. *See also Good Morning Revolution: Uncollected Writings of Protest by Langston Hughes*; Revision, Process of, and Hughes.

Bibliography: Berry (including the introduction, xix–xxii); Martha Cobb, "Langston Hughes: The Writer, His Poetics, and the Artistic Process," *Langston Hughes Review* 2, no. 2 (Fall 1983), 19–23; Klaus Ensslen, "Plain Living and Plain Talk in Langston

Hughes' 'Mother to Son': A Poetics of the Black Folk Voice," *Anglistick und Englisch-unterricht* (Heidelberg, Germany) 53 (1994), 87–96; Aaron D. Gresson, "Beyond Selves Deferred: Langston Hughes' Style and the Psychology of Black Selfhood," *Langston Hughes Review* 4, no. 1 (Spring 1985), 47–54; Theodore R. Hudson, "Langston Hughes's Last Volume of Verse," *College Language Association Journal* 11, no. 4 (1968), 345–348; Charles S. Johnson, "Jazz Poetry and Blues," in Mullen, 143–148; Delita Martin, "The 'Madam Poems' as Dramatic Monologue," in Mullen, 148–154; Miller; R. Baxter Miller, *Langston Hughes and Gwendolyn Brooks: A Reference Guide* (Boston: G. K. Hall, 1978); Wilson Jeremiah Moses, "More Stately Mansions: New Negro Movements and Langston Hughes's Literary Theory," *Langston Hughes Review* 4, no. 1 (Spring 1985), 40–46; Erskine Peters, "Rhythmic Manipulation and Instrument Simulation in *Montage of a Dream Deferred*," *Literary Griot: International Journal of Black Expressive Cultural Studies* 5, no. 1 (Spring 1993), 33–49; Arnold Rampersad, "Introduction" to *CP*, 3–5; Arnold Rampersad, "Langston Hughes and Approaches to Modernism in the Harlem Renaissance," in *The Harlem Renaissance: Revaluations*, ed. Amritjit Singh, William Shiver, and Stanley Brodwin (New York: Garland, 1989), 49–71; Philip M. Royster, "The Poetic Theory and Practice of Langston Hughes" (Ph.D. dissertation, Loyola University [Chicago], 1974).

"Poetry and Children." Essay. *See The Langston Hughes Reader.*

Poetry, Collections of. *See Ask Your Mama: 12 Moods for Jazz; The Collected Poems of Langston Hughes; Dear Lovely Death; The Dream Keeper; Fields of Wonder; Fine Clothes to the Jew; Freedom's Plow; Jim Crow's Last Stand; Montage of a Dream Deferred; The Negro Mother and Other Dramatic Recitations; A New Song; One-Way Ticket; The Panther and the Lash; Poems; Poems/Langston Hughes; Scottsboro Limited: Four Poems and a Play; Selected Poems of Langston Hughes; Shakespeare in Harlem; The Weary Blues.*

The Poetry of the Negro, 1746–1949: An Anthology (Garden City, NY: Doubleday, 1949). 429 pp. Hughes coedited the anthology with Arna Bontemps.* Doubleday published another edition of the book, "revised and expanded" by Hughes and Bontemps, in 1970. Rampersad states that "*Poetry of the Negro*, which sold briskly from the start, was a historic anthology that would not become outmoded in the lifetime of its editors, who had shown an internationalist understanding of blackness, and a deep pride in their race without a limiting chauvinism" (II, 160). Although Hughes and Bontemps did indeed assemble a historical anthology, the bulk of the poems were first published between 1920 and 1945. They also included the work of such Caribbean writers as Frank Collymore, Edgar Mittelholzer, V. S. Naipaul, A. J. Seymour, and Derek Walcott. Rampersad notes that because of the internationalist approach, the inclusion of chiefly modern poetry, and the inclusion of poems by white writers about black experience, critics' responses to the anthology were mixed. The revised and expanded edition included poems by such up-and-coming African American writers as Lucille Clifton, Mari Evans, Sarah Fabio, LeRoi Jones (Amiri Baraka*), Audre Lorde, Paule Marshall, Loften Mitchell, Raymond Patterson, and Ishmael Reed. *See also* Anthologies; The Black Aesthetic; Poetics.

The Political Plays of Langston Hughes (Carbondale: Southern Illinois University Press, 2000). 221 pp. Edited by Susan Duffy. The book includes *Scottsboro Limited; Harvest*, early drafts of which were titled *Blood on the Fields; Angelo Herndon Jones*; and *De Organizer*. In her general introduction, Duffy discusses Hughes's drama* in general and, in particular, his fusion of politics and theatre. The text of each play is preceded by a substantial introduction as well.

Politics and Hughes. Hughes was one of the most political American poets of the twentieth century. As a person, Hughes exhibited a lifelong interest in a wide range of political issues, including racism, voting rights, housing rights, fascism, socialism, war, the predicament of Third World nations, and other concerns. As a writer, he often explicitly addressed such issues in his poetry, fiction, drama, songs, and nonfiction prose. Like most writers, he went through phases, but none of them was particularly more "political" than another. Rampersad notes that chiefly because of his age, Hughes was personally less politically energetic in the late 1950s and in the 1960s. Even so, Hughes's last collection of poetry, *The Panther and the Lash*, is an extremely politically alert book.

In his early twenties Hughes exhibited this political awareness and was attentive to economic, social, and political obstacles faced by African Americans. Early on he also clearly viewed literary art as an appropriate medium through which to articulate such alertness. For example, poems in his first book, *The Weary Blues*, show no implicit belief in a gulf between "art" and "politics"; one might point specifically to "Cross," "Lament for Dark Peoples," "Our Land," and "The South." Because the Harlem Renaissance* was driven, in part, by the competing views of its leaders (community leaders, editors, publishers, and patrons), writers connected to the movement could hardly avoid, and in most cases embraced, politics, literary and otherwise. To some degree, then, those aspects of the Harlem Renaissance that were political dovetailed with Hughes's predisposition.

In the 1930s Hughes went through his most radical political phase, as evidenced by his poetry, fiction, nonfiction, and drama published during and not long after that decade, including *The Ways of White Folks, A New Song, Jim Crow's Last Stand, Front Porch, Don't You Want To Be Free?, Scottsboro Limited*, "Chant for Tom Mooney," "Labor Storm," "Ballads of Lenin," "Lenin," "Good Morning Revolution," "Goodbye Christ," "One More 'S' in the U.S.A.," "Christ in Alabama," "Sister Johnson Marches," and "Song of the Revolution." Rampersad suggests that the rise of fascism worldwide (and specifically Italy's invasion of Ethiopia) was one cause of Hughes's increased radicalism. Although World War II—America's involvement in which Hughes ultimately supported (*see*, for example, "Bonds for All")—and the Soviet Union's pact with Nazi

Germany altered Hughes's attitudes toward Marxism* and the Soviet Union, Hughes's writing continued to concern itself frequently with the plight of workers, with Jim Crow laws* in the United States, and with those he perceived to be disenfranchised peoples worldwide. Indeed, one characteristic of Hughes's politics is its refusal to concentrate on American or African American issues at the expense of a global perspective; he held fast, for example, to antifascist views.

In the 1950s and 1960s Hughes remained intellectually engaged with politics and with the civil-rights movement in particular, although Rampersad depicts him as being personally less energetic and more of an interested observer. Hughes quibbled with the harshness of works by younger writers such as Amiri Baraka* (LeRoi Jones) and James Baldwin,* and with some of the specific tactics of the Black Panther Party,* but he agreed generally with their diagnosis of social ills. In fact, as noted earlier, his last collection of poetry, *The Panther and the Lash*, contains some of his most potent political poetry, demonstrating that unlike many writers in their sixth or seventh decades, Hughes had not become significantly more conservative. Although most of the poems in the book had been previously published, not all of them had, and the fact remains that Hughes chose to reprint politically acute poems late in his life.

Several factors are likely influences on Hughes's politics, the most obvious being his personal circumstances: He was a person of color in a nation whose laws and attitudes were demonstrably racist; he was an early reader and read such publications as the *Chicago Defender** at home (*see* "The Soviet Union and Jews"); his father's views about the shortcomings of the United States were sharp and rigid; and he attended a racially integrated, if mainly white, high school (Central High School* in Cleveland, Ohio). Rampersad especially points to Hughes's father's attitudes toward the United States (and toward literature) as having influenced Hughes's political development. Hughes's difficulties with his patron, Charlotte Osgood Mason,* his association with W.E.B. Du Bois,* Alain Locke,* Carl Van Vechten,* and others, and his wanderlust all contributed, doubtlessly, to the depth and texture of his political views.

Hughes was not politically naïve. He read and traveled widely, he addressed political issues in poetry, fiction, and drama over several decades, and for twenty-three years he wrote a newspaper column that was often political in nature (*see* "Here to Yonder"). By the same token, he was—and saw himself as—a writer first and a "political animal" or "activist" second; and despite his deep interest in socialism in the 1930s, he was not especially drawn to political theory or to systematic, academic political thought (*see* "Cowards from the Colleges"). He was chiefly pragmatic and mainly focused on what he regarded as basic social fairness. These qualities can be seen in his relentless attacks on Jim Crow laws, which he viewed as being morally wrong but which he also viewed as obstacles to African Americans' concrete, functional social and economic progress. His use of the collective persona,* especially in poetry, positioned him as a populist writer, a literary "spokesperson," a genuine poet of the masses, and yet pragmatism, a sense of fairness, and an interest in specific issues, events, persons, and crises seem to be the main threads running through his political thinking. (*See* "Ballad of Roosevelt," "Dear Mr. President," "Governor Fires Dean," and "Little Song on Housing," for instance.) Perhaps these qualities, especially the pragmatism, also identify him as an American writer as well; and as Hutchinson notes, the philosophy of pragmatism promulgated by John Dewey informed the intellectual life of the Harlem Renaissance to some degree. Although Berry's edition of Hughes's "uncollected" writings (*Good Morning Revolution*) emphasizes his most reformist and radical work, it also provides a fairly comprehensive view of his politics and how they changed, as does De Santis's edition of Hughes's writing for the *Chicago Defender** (*see* "Here to Yonder"). Hutchinson discusses competing ideologies within the Harlem Renaissance and the connection of Hughes to them. *See also Baltimore Afro American*; Césaire, Aimé; *Crisis; Good Morning Revolution: Uncollected Writings of Protest by Langston Hughes*; "Hero—International Brigade"; John Reed Club; Johnson, Charles S.; "Langston Hughes Speaks"; Marxism; McCarthyism; *The Messenger*; "Northern Liberal"; "Note to All Nazis Fascists and Klansmen" [*sic*]; "Opinions of the New Student"; *Opportunity; Poems from Black Africa*; "The Poor"; "Postcard from Spain"; Randolph, A. Philip; Roosevelt, Franklin Delano; Sullivan, Noel.

Bibliography: Hutchinson; Lewis, *WHWV*; Joseph McLaren, "From Protest to Soul Fest: Langston Hughes' Gospel Plays," *Langston Hughes Review* 15, no. 1 (Spring 1997), 49–61; David Chioni Moore, "Local Color, Global 'Color': Langston Hughes, the Black Atlantic, and Soviet Central Asia, 1932," *Research in African Literatures* 27, no. 4 (Winter 1996), 49–70; Hans Ostrom, "*The Ways of White Folks*, Modernism, and 'Signifying,' " in Ostrom, 5–8; Rampersad, I, II; Michael Thurston, "Black Christ, Red Flag: Langston Hughes on Scottsboro," *College Literature* 22, no. 3 (October 1995), 30–49; Cary D. Wintz, ed., *African-American Political Thought, 1890–1930: Washington, Du Bois, Garvey, and Randolph* (Armonk, NY: M. E. Sharpe, 1996).

"The Poor." Poem of fourteen lines in free verse. Spoken by a collective persona* representing "the poor" worldwide, it suggests that the poor are climbing a "hill" of economic oppression. It was written in 1939 but was first published in Berry and is not included in *Collected Poems*.

Bibliography: Berry, 26–27.

"Poor Girl's Ruination." Poem in four short-lined ballad* stanzas, spoken by a young woman who was "nearly ruined" when she moved to Chicago. She moves to Detroit at age twenty-one, reporting, "What Chicago started / Detroit's done." "Ruined" presumably refers, in part, to a life of prostitution. The poem was circulated by the Associated Negro Press in September 1943. *See* "America's Young Black Joe!." *See also* "Beale Street Love"; "Natcha"; "The New Cabaret Girl"; "Port Town"; "A Ruined Gal."

Bibliography: *CP*, 585.

"Poor Little Black Fellow." Short story. In this narrative a wealthy New England couple adopts the orphaned black child of their former servants; the father was killed in the Great War (World War I), and the mother died of pneumonia. Initially the adoption is portrayed as an act of good will, but the family's trip to Paris exposes the racism of the adoptive parents, and the child, now a young man, decides to remain in Paris, where he feels more comfortable than he does in New England. To a degree, then, "Poor Little Black Fellow" is a coming-of-age story. It was first published in the *American Mercury** (November 1933), 326–335, was included in the collection, *The Ways of White Folks*, and was reprinted in *Langston Hughes: Short Stories*.
Bibliography: Ostrom, 13–14.

"Poor Rover." Seven-line rhyming poem concerning a dog, first published in *The Langston Hughes Reader. See* Children's Poetry.
Bibliography: *CP*, 608.

Popo and Fifina: Children of Haiti (New York: Macmillan, 1932). 100 pp. Children's book. An adventure story for children, the narrative is set in Haiti. Hughes cowrote the story with Arna Bontemps.* It was republished with an introduction by Arnold Rampersad and illustrations by E. Simms Campbell (New York: Oxford University Press, 1993). A translation was published in Tokyo in 1957. *See also Black Misery; The Block; Carol of the Brown King: Nativity Poems by Langston Hughes*; Children's Poetry; *The Paste-Board Bandit; The Sweet and Sour Animal Book*.

"Poppy Flower." Poem in six couplets, with the second lines of all the couplets rhyming with each other, and with the third couplet being a repetition of the first. The poem concerns the death of a poppy flower. It was first published in *Crisis** (February 1925).
Bibliography: *CP*, 42.

Port Town (1960). Opera.* Hughes wrote the libretto, based on his poem of the same title, and Jan Meyerowitz* composed the music. The opera debuted at the Tanglewood Festival in Massachusetts in August 1960. Rampersad notes that as with his other collaborations with Meyerowitz, Hughes was disturbed by the extent to which the music made his words virtually inaudible, and *Port Town* was the last collaboration between Hughes and Meyerowitz.
Bibliography: Rampersad, II, 320–321.

"Port Town." Poem in four short-lined ballad* stanzas. The first-person narrator is apparently a prostitute trying to entice sailors. The poem was first published in *The Weary Blues*. Later, Ricky Ian Gordon set the poem to music. ASCAP* lists the song as being published by the Williamson Music Company, Inc., and

the song's ASCAP registry number is 460336207. *See also* "Beale Street Love"; "Natcha"; "The New Cabaret Girl"; *Port Town*; "A Ruined Gal."
Bibliography: *CP*, 87.

"Porter." Poem of thirteen lines in free verse (three stanzas). It is spoken by the porter, who is apparently African American, and who is weary of having to be deferential to "the rich old white man" who "owns the world." The poem was first published in *Fine Clothes to the Jew*. In *I Wonder As I Wander* Hughes mentions that he often read this poem in his poetry readings. *See also* "Dressed Up."
Bibliography: *CP*, 116; *I Wonder As I Wander*, 57.

"Pose-Outs." Short story, included in the collection *Simple's Uncle Sam*. *See* Simple [Jesse B.] Stories.

"Possum, Race, and Face." Short story, included in the collection *Simple Speaks His Mind*. *See* Simple [Jesse B.] Stories.

"Postal Box: Love." *See* "Mailbox for the Dead."

"Postcard from Spain." Poem, subtitled "Addressed to Alabama." Like "Letter from Spain," it is an epistolary poem, constructed as if it were written from "Johnny," in this case to "Dear Folks at Home." Johnny explains how differently he is treated in Spain, meaning that he does not encounter the racism he encounters at home (in Alabama). The postcard includes a "return," which appears above the greeting, in the right margin: "Lincoln-Washington Brigade/April 1938." The Lincoln-Washington Brigade was composed of volunteers from the United States and other countries who fought on the side of Republicans against the forces of Francisco Franco, leader of fascist forces. One of Hughes's articles in the *Baltimore Afro American*,* written while he was in Spain, addresses his view of Spain as being comparatively free of racism. The poem was first published in *Volunteer for Liberty* (April 9, 1938). *See* "Hero—International Brigade."
Bibliography: *CP*, 202.

"A Posthumous Tale." Unpublished short story, written in 1934. *See also* "Eyes like a Gypsy"; "Hello Harry"; "Mailbox for the Dead."
Bibliography: Rampersad, I, 301.

"Powder-White Faces." Short story. The narrative concerns a young Chinese American man who jumps aboard a "tramp" steamship and tells, in monologue, about how he murdered a white woman with whom he was romantically involved. His explanation for the murder is that he became enraged when the woman made fun of him and called him "China boy." The story was included in the collection *Laughing to Keep from Crying* and was reprinted in *Langston Hughes: Short Stories*.

Bibliography: Ostrom, 26–27.

"Prayer." Poem. *See* "Two Somewhat Different Epigrams."

"Prayer [1]." Rhyming poem of nine short lines. It is composed chiefly of questions asked of God concerning what paths to take in life. It was first published in *Buccaneer* (May 1925). *See* Religion.

Bibliography: *CP*, 51.

"Prayer [2]." Rhyming poem of two six-line stanzas. It asks God to "gather up" "In the arms of your pity" the downtrodden. It was first published in *Contemporáneos* (October 1931) and was also published in *Opportunity** (October 1940) under the title "Big City Prayer." Ricky Ian Gordon set the poem to music as part of a song cycle. *See* "Genius Child"; Religion.

Bibliography: *CP*, 138–139; Ricky Ian Gordon, *Genius Child: A Cycle of 10 Songs* (New York: Williamson Music Company, 1992).

"Prayer for a Winter Night." Poem of thirteen lines in free verse that asks the "Great God of Cold and Winter" to freeze all poor people to death so that they may enter Heaven. It was first published in the *Messenger** (May 1924).

Bibliography: *CP*, 38.

"Prayer Meeting." Poem of nine lines, in free verse. It depicts the joyful, ecstatic prayers of a woman in the Ebecaneezer [*sic*] Baptist Church in Harlem. *See also* "Big Meeting"; *The Big Sea*; "Rock, Church"; *Tambourines to Glory*.

Bibliography: *CP*, 35.

"Preference." Poem. *See Montage of a Dream Deferred*.

"Prelude to Our Age." Poem. Except for the book-length *Ask Your Mama* and *Montage of a Dream Deferred*, "Prelude to Our Age" ("Prelude") is Hughes's longest poem, running about five pages and mixing free verse and units of formal verse, including ballad* stanzas. One major thread of coherence is the narrative voice, which is that of a collective persona,* self-identified as "Negro." The poem, subtitled "A Negro History Poem," presents a panorama of black history, with reference both to individuals whom Hughes believes to be exemplary "Negroes" and to particular geographical areas—continents, regions, nations, cities, districts within cities, and historical sites. As the title of the poem suggests, one of Hughes's implicit purposes appears to be to place contemporary African and African American circumstances in relief against an extensive, rich historical background. Another unmistakable purpose is to educate readers about the breadth and depth of "Negro" achievement in all areas of human endeavor. As the editors of *Collected Poems* note, Hughes, in pursuing these purposes, used *Story of the Negro* (1948) by Arna Bontemps* as a major source of information. As factual, informative, and educational as the poem may be, it remains extremely lyrical; it is as casual as it is sincere in tone. It was first published in *Crisis** (February 1951).

Bibliography: *CP*, 379–384.

"Present." Poem. The title refers to a gift. In black dialect* the first-person narrator, who works for a white family, describes an incident in which the husband misinterprets the wife's request for "a robe o' love" and buys her "a fur coat." The poem was first published in *Shakespeare in Harlem*.

Bibliography: *CP*, 247.

"Present for Joyce." Short story, included in the collections *Simple Takes a Wife* and *The Best of Simple*. *See* Simple [Jesse B.] Stories.

Price, Gilbert (1942–1991). American singer and actor. Price, a baritone, performed in *Jerico-Jim Crow* in 1964 and became a close friend of Hughes. He went on to win widespread acclaim for his performance in *The Roar of the Greasepaint, the Smell of the Crowd* on Broadway, at the Shubert Theatre, in 1965. His performance of the song "Feeling Good" was particularly memorable. During his career he received four Tony nominations for roles in *Lost in the Stars* (1972), *The Night That Made America Famous* (1975), *1600 Pennsylvania Avenue* (1976), and *Timbuktu* (1978). Price graduated from Erasmus Hall High School in Brooklyn, New York, in 1960. He died in Vienna.

Bibliography: "Gilbert Price, 48, Broadway Baritone," *New York Times Biographical Service* 22, no. 1 (January 1991), 21.

"Pride." Poem. *See* "Militant."

"Prime." Rhyming poem of eleven lines spoken by a young black man who lives in Harlem,* contrasts its poverty with what he perceives to be the wealth and excess of the United States in general, and explains that Harlem is where, "in the section of the niggers," he comes into his prime. The rhetoric of the poem expresses a smoldering rage. It was first published in *The Panther and the Lash*.

Bibliography: *CP*, 554.

"Prize Fighter." Poem of seven lines in free verse spoken by a boxer, who opines that only "dumb guys fight" and that he could save more money if he worked on the docks instead of fighting professionally. It was first published in *Fine Clothes to the Jew*.

Bibliography: *CP*, 113.

"Problems." Poem in four short-lined rhyming couplets. It playfully combines aspects of simple arithmetic and difficulties in social relationships. It was first published in *The Langston Hughes Reader*. *See* Children's Poetry.

Bibliography: *CP*, 606.

Prodigal Son (1965). Musical play, first produced at the Greenwich Mews Theatre, 141 West 13th Street, New York City, in May 1965 (opening May 20), on a bill with Bertolt Brecht's play *The Exception and the Rule*. It ran for fifteen performances. *Prodigal Son* was billed as "a gospel song-play" and mixed traditional gospel songs with new ones written by Hughes, creating an exuberant rendering of the biblical parable. In a review Taubman noted that the play "uses few spoken words. . . . It is impossible to resist the. . . . high spirits of . . . Mr. Hughes's uncomplicated telling of the ancient parable in song and dance." Stella Holt, Beverly Landau, and Henrietta Stein produced the play, which was directed by Marion Franklin, choreographed by Sylvia Fort, and staged by Vincent Carroll. The cast included Dorothy Drake, who had performed in *Jerico-Jim Crow* a year earlier, as Sister Lord, Robert Pinkston as Brother Callius, Phillip A. Stamps as Prodigal Son, Ronald Platts as Father, Joseph Attles, who had also performed in *Jerico-Jim Crow*, as Exhorter, and Glory Van Scott as Jezebel. The production was taken on tour in Europe in the fall of 1965. It played in Belgium, England, France, and the Netherlands. The play was published in *Players* magazine (December 1967–January 1968).

Bibliography: Bernard L. Peterson, Jr., *Contemporary Black American Playwrights and Their Plays: A Biographical Directory and Dramatic Index* (Westport, CT: Greenwood Press, 1988), 48; Howard Taubman, "Theater: Brecht and Langston Hughes," *New York Times* (May 21, 1965), section C, p. 2.

"Proem." Poem. *See* "Negro."

"Professor." Short story. The narrative concerns Dr. Brown, a professor at a historically black college in the southern United States. Brown visits an unspecified "Midwestern" city, stays (significantly) at the Booker T. Washington* Hotel, and meets with a wealthy, philanthropic white couple, the Chandlers. They behave condescendingly toward Brown, but he suffers them patiently in order to acquire money for his impoverished campus. The story was first published under the title "Dr. Brown's Decision" in the *Anvil* (May/June 1935), was included in the collection *Laughing to Keep from Crying*, and was reprinted in *Langston Hughes: Short Stories*.

Bibliography: Ostrom, 24–25.

"Projection." Poem. *See Montage of a Dream Deferred. See also The Block.*

"Promised Land." Poem of two ballad* quatrains. It suggests that the Promised Land cannot ever quite be reached. The editors of *Collected Poems* were unable to determine where and when this poem was first published and when it was written. *See* Religion. *See also* "Chicago Blues."
Bibliography: *CP*, 592.

"Promulgations." Short story, included in the collection *Simple's Uncle Sam. See* Simple [Jesse B.] Stories.

Pseudonyms Used by Hughes. Hughes published the poem "For Dead Mimes" under the pseudonym Earl Dane, he published the poem "Autumn Note" under the pseudonym J. Crutchfield Thompson, he distributed for publication the story "Mailbox for the Dead," under the pseudonym David Boatman, and he published the poem " 'The Jesus' " under the pseudonym Durwood Collins.

"Psychologies." Short story, included in the collection *Simple Takes a Wife. See* Simple [Jesse B.] Stories.

Pudd'nhead Wilson. *See* "Introduction" to *Pudd'nhead Wilson.*

"Puerto Ricans." Short story, included in *The Best of Simple. See* Simple [Jesse B.] Stories.

"Pushcart Man." Short story. It is a brief narrative without a conventional plot, providing a slice of Harlem* street life and focusing chiefly on conversations, snippets of monologues, arguments, sales pitches, and the like heard on the street as a man pushing a cart full of goods makes his way along a crowded street. It was included in the collection *Laughing to Keep from Crying.*
Bibliography: Ostrom, 24–25; Aaron Siskind, *Harlem: The [19]30s: Photographs by Aaron Siskind—A Book of Postcards* (Washington, DC: National Museum of American Art/Smithsonian Institution, n.d. [circa 1990]) (includes photographs of Harlem pushcart vendors).

"Puzzled." Poem. *See* "Harlem [1]."

"Puzzlement." Poem in two ballad* quatrains. The speaker contrasts what he and an unnamed interlocutor do in "jook joints" with what "rich folks" do in their "clubs." The poem was circulated by the Associated Negro Press in July 1943. *See* "America's Young Black Joe." *See also* "Juice Joint: Northern City"; Juke.
Bibliography: *CP*, 581.

Q

"Question [1]." Poem of eight lines in free verse. It personifies "Death" as "a junk man" and asks, rhetorically, whether the junk man will value the corpse of a "white multi-millionaire" more than the "black torso" of a "Negro cotton-picker." It was first published in *Crisis** (March 1922). *See* "Dixie South Africa"; "Johannesburg Mines."
Bibliography: *CP*, 24.

"Question [2]." Poem. *See Montage of a Dream Deferred.*

"Question and Answer." Poem of sixteen lines, intermittently rhyming. It is a dialogue poem, with terse answers in response to questions about why people take the trouble to engage in protest in such places as "Durban, Birmingham / Cape Town, Atlanta / Johannesburg, Watts": cities in South Africa and the United States, respectively. Thus Hughes draws a parallel between racism in the United States and apartheid in South Africa, as he does in "Dixie South Africa." The poem was first published in *Crisis** (October 1966).
Bibliography: *CP*, 549.

"Question Period." Short story, included in the collection *Simple Speaks His Mind. See* Simple [Jesse B.] Stories.

"Quiet Girl." Poem. *See* "Ardella."

R

"Race Relations." Short story, included in the collection *Simple Speaks His Mind*. *See* Simple [Jesse B.] Stories.

Radio Broadcasts from Spain by Hughes. *See Baltimore Afro American*.

"Radioactive Redcaps." Short story, included in *The Best of Simple*. *See* Simple [Jesse B.] Stories.

"Raid." Poem of eleven lines in five stanzas. It concerns a raid by police ("The man") on a nightclub. The reason for the raid is unclear, but the poem was written and published well after the repeal of Prohibition, so one might infer that serving alcohol illegally may not have been the reason. The poem was first published in *One-Way Ticket*. *See also* "Juice Joint: Northern City"; "Puzzlement."
Bibliography: *CP*, 367.

"Railroad Avenue." Poem of thirty short lines in free verse. It concerns a neighborhood near railroad tracks, a boy watching a girl go by, and the girl's magical laughter. The address "942" is given, but the poem has not been linked to an abode in which Hughes lived. It was first published in *Fire!!* (November 1926). *See* McKay, Claude.
Bibliography: *CP*, 84.

Randolph, A. Philip (1889–1979). American editor, publisher, labor leader, and political activist. Randolph was born in Crescent City, Florida. His family moved to Harlem* in 1911, and soon thereafter he became involved in labor politics, helping to organize black workers. He attended the City College of

New York. With Chandler Owen, he founded the magazine the *Messenger*,* which published many of Hughes's poems in the 1920s. In 1925 Randolph became the founding president of the Brotherhood of Sleeping Car Porters, secured its affiliation with the Congress of Industrial Organizations, and eventually negotiated its contract with the Pullman Company. Randolph also worked tirelessly against discrimination in federal hiring practices and policies. In contrast to other intellectuals and activists who helped shape the Harlem Renaissance,* such as W.E.B. Du Bois,* Charles S. Johnson,* and Alain Locke,* Randolph was intently focused on labor issues and was influenced, to a degree, by Marxist ideas. The politics represented by the *Messenger* contributed to Hughes's own political viewpoints. *See* Garvey, Marcus; Marxism; Politics; "To Certain Negro Leaders"; Thurman, Wallace; Washington, Booker T.

Bibliography: Hutchinson; Rampersad, I, 51, 217; Cary D. Wintz, ed., *African-American Political Thought, 1890–1930: Washington, Du Bois, Garvey, and Randolph* (Armonk, NY: M. E. Sharpe, 1996).

Ransom, John Crowe (1888–1974). American poet, critic, editor, and college professor (at Kenyon College in Gambier, Ohio). In addition to publishing acclaimed volumes of poetry and editing literary magazines, Ransom also wrote the enormously influential book *The New Criticism* (Norfolk, CT: New Directions, 1941). *See also* "Girl."

Bibliography: Miller Williams, *The Poetry of John Crowe Ransom* (New Brunswick, NJ: Rutgers University Press, 1972).

"Reason and Right." Short story, included in the collection *Simple Stakes a Claim. See* Simple [Jesse B.] Stories.

"Reasons Why." Poem in two ballad* quatrains and in black dialect.* The speaker compares his amorous feelings toward his lover to the fluttering of butterflies and of aspen leaves. The poem was first published in the *Columbia University Spectator* (May 1922). *See* Columbia University.

Bibliography: *CP*, 167.

"Reckless Blues." Rampersad lists this title in an index as a song cowritten by Hughes and Richard Wright,* but it is a misprint and actually refers to a mention in Rampersad's text to the poem "Red Clay Blues," on which Hughes and Wright did in fact collaborate.

Bibliography: Rampersad, I, 462 [index].

"Red Clay Blues." Poem cowritten with Richard Wright.* It consists of four traditional blues* stanzas in black dialect* and concerns nostalgia for the state of Georgia, specifically for its renowned red clay. It was first published in *New Masses* (August 1, 1939). *See* "Reckless Blues."

Bibliography: *CP*, 212.

"Red Cross." Poem in a single quatrain; lines two and four rhyme. It comments obliquely but critically on the American Red Cross's policy (at that time) of segregating blood donated by whites and blacks. It was first published in *Jim Crow's Last Stand*. *See* Jim Crow Laws.

Bibliography: *CP*, 290.

"Red Flag over Tuskegee." Poem. *See* "Open Letter to the South."

"Red-headed Baby." Short story. The main character is a drunken, dissolute sailor who visits a young African American woman upon his return, from a voyage, to the Florida coast. The woman has given birth to their illegitimate baby. The narrative makes clear that the man will not remain with the woman or take responsibility for the infant. With regard to narrative form, Hughes experiments with a dramatic monologue; that is, the sailor is the first-person narrator who addresses a specific but unnamed "listener" or narratee within the frame of the story. It was included in the collection *The Ways of White Folks* and was reprinted in *Langston Hughes: Short Stories*.

Bibliography: Ostrom, 13; Gerald Prince, "Introduction to the Study of the Narratee," in *Narrative/Theory*, ed. David H. Richter (White Plains, NY: Longman, 1996), 226–242.

"Red Roses." Poem in three traditional blues* stanzas and in black dialect* that expresses a yearning for springtime. It was first published in *Poetry* (November 1926).

Bibliography: *CP*, 83–84.

"Red Silk Stockings." Poem in two quatrains and a couplet. It is spoken in black dialect* to a young "Black gal" by an indeterminate older person, probably a parent, who advises the young woman that because there "ain't nothin' to do fo' [her] nohow / Round this town," she should don red stockings to attract attention from "de white boys." The speaker predicts that the young woman will get pregnant and give birth to "a high yaller [yellow] child." The poem was first published in *Fine Clothes to the Jew*. In *The Big Sea* Hughes suggests that the poem was intended to be read ironically, and he defends himself against critics of the poem and of the book who believed that he portrayed African Americans too negatively. *See* "Ruby Brown"; "A Ruined Gal"; Women in Hughes's Writing.

Bibliography: *The Big Sea*, 266; *CP*, 122–123.

"Red Sun Blues." Song. Hughes wrote the lyrics, and Albert Hague composed the music. ASCAP* lists the song as being published by Summit Music Corporation and by the Song Writers Guild. The song's ASCAP registry number is 480087941.

Reed, John (1887–1920). American journalist, political activist, and poet. Reed was born in Portland, Oregon, and went to school at Portland Academy before attending Harvard University, where he wrote for and helped edit the *Harvard Monthly* and the *Harvard Lampoon.* After graduating from Harvard, he traveled in Europe, returning to the United States in 1911 and, with the assistance of Lincoln Steffens, joining the editorial staff of *American Magazine.* The following year he published what was to become his best-known poem, "Sangar." In 1914 Reed covered the Mexican revolution for *Metropolitan Magazine,* spending four months with Pancho Villa and his forces. For the same magazine he covered the outbreak of World War I, but many of his stories were considered so biased against Allied interests that editors did not publish them. He married journalist Louise Bryant in 1917. The two traveled to Russia that year and reported on the Bolshevik Revolution from St. Petersburg (Petrograd). His pro-Communist articles for *The Masses* were one reason for that magazine's editors (Max Eastman and Floyd Dell) and Reed being tried for sedition; all were eventually acquitted. Reed's disagreements with other American radicals and reformers led him to establish the Communist Labor Party in 1919, and for the party he edited *Voice of Labor.* That year also saw the publication of his most famous work, a book about the Bolshevik Revolution, *Ten Days That Shook the World.* Charged once more with sedition, Reed fled to Finland but was arrested, held in prison for several months, and finally exchanged for Finnish prisoners held by Russia. In Moscow he contracted typhoid fever and died shortly thereafter. He was buried, with a state funeral, in the Kremlin. The motion picture *Reds* is based on Reed's life. Hughes did not meet John Reed but was influenced indirectly by his politics, with which he became familiar by means of reading *Ten Days That Shook the World* at Central High School* and later reading (and publishing poetry) in the *Liberator,* which Max Eastman also edited. *See Harvest;* Marxism; McKay, Claude; John Reed Club.

Bibliography: Max Eastman, *Heroes I Have Known: Twelve Who Lived Great Lives* (New York: Simon and Schuster, 1942); Barbara Gelb, *So Short a Time: A Biography of John Reed and Louise Bryant* (New York: Norton, 1973); Granville Hicks, *John Reed: The Making of a Revolutionary* (New York: Macmillan, 1936); Rampersad, I, 30; *Reds* [motion picture]: screenplay by Warren Beatty, directed by Warren Beatty (Paramount Pictures, 1981); John Reed, *The Education of John Reed: Selected Writings* (New York: International Publishers, 1955); John Reed, *Ten Days That Shook the World* [first published 1919], foreword by V. I. Lenin, introduction by Granville Hicks (New York: Modern Library, 1935); Robert A. Rosenstone, *Romantic Revolutionary: A Biography of John Reed* (New York: Knopf, 1975).

Reed, Laura. One of the main characters in *Tambourines to Glory* (novel and play). She joins with Essie Belle Johnson* to start a church in Harlem, but she is the cynical partner and never quite gives up her addictions to gambling and alcohol. The chief crisis in the plot hinges on her love affair with "Big-Eyed" Buddy Lomax.*

"Refugee." Poem in two rhyming quatrains with highly variable metrical patterns and a very short concluding line (line eight). The poem is spoken by the refugee, who expresses "loneliness terrific." Hughes rarely employed such old-fashioned reversed syntax but obviously liked the phrasing because he repeats it in the poem. It was first published in the *Carmel Pine Cone* (July 18, 1941). *See* "Remembrance."
Bibliography: *CP*, 235.

"Refugee in America." Poem. *See* "Words like Freedom."

"Refugee in America." Song, based on the poem "Words like Freedom." Charles Kingsford composed the music. ASCAP* lists no publisher for the song, but the song's ASCAP registry number is 480183433.

"Rejuvenation through Joy." Short story. The main character is Eugene Lesch, a former circus performer and inveterate huckster. With the help of his manager, Sol, Lesch forms the Colony of Joy, which promises to "rejuvenate" rich, white patrons by means of "primitive" "Negro" culture, including dancing. The comic, satiric story therefore concerns the trivialization of African American culture that was regarded as one chronic problem during the Harlem Renaissance.* At thirty pages, "Rejuvenation through Joy" is the longest story in the collection *The Ways of White Folks*. It was reprinted in *Langston Hughes: Short Stories*. *See* Religion; Robeson, Paul; "Rock, Church."
Bibliography: David Chinitz, "Rejuvenation through Joy: Langston Hughes, Primitivism, and Jazz," *American Literary History* 9, no. 1 (Spring 1997), 60–78; Ostrom, 12–13.

"Relief." Poem. *See Montage of a Dream Deferred.*

Religion. Hughes's writings reveal no single attitude toward religion and certainly no systematic expression of his religious views, his faith, his lack of faith, or his notions of such concepts as sin, redemption, afterlife, evil, and so on. Indeed, his writings articulate a broad spectrum of attitudes and notions, so broad that with regard to several key religious questions, one can find works that essentially contradict each other, even if they do not necessarily point to self-contradiction in Hughes, for any given work does not necessarily express a personal religious view. In this regard, we should note that in poetry, fiction, and drama, Hughes often embodied views, perspectives, and personae that were not his own (*see* Collective Persona). Nonetheless, the topic of religion figures significantly in his writing during all phases of his career. In its numerous guises, expressions, and forms, religion was something that clearly interested him deeply. Perhaps Hughes's best-known piece on religion is the chapter of *The Big Sea* entitled "Salvation," wherein he recounts a childhood experience during a Christian "tent meeting," aimed at "revival" of faith and evangelism, during which he felt pressured to pretend to undergo a religious conversion, only to go home and, ironically, feel afraid and guilty about the deception he carried out. To some extent, the chapter is characteristic of Hughes's religious thinking, at least insofar as it shows both a temperamental skepticism and a willingness to try to understand faiths that others seem more capable than he of embracing.

In some works the skepticism leads Hughes to satirize religious practices and types of religious figures. In the story "Rejuvenation through Joy," for instance, he satirizes religious fakery of the 1930s, a fraudulence that also exploited a fashionable interest in what was perceived as the exoticism and primitivism of African Americans. In the poems "Bible Belt," "Birmingham Sunday," "Bombings In Dixie," "Brotherly Love," and "A Christian Country," he contrasts the stated tenets of Christianity with the practices of those white Southerners who claim to be Christians but who support Jim Crow laws,* express or at least tolerate racist hatred, and even take part in racist violence and murder. Connected to these works are such poems as "Christ in Alabama" and "Cross," which establish an analogy between Christ's suffering and the suffering of African Americans. The story "On the Road" presents a broader implicit critique of Christianity in the United States, specifically aimed at the extent to which it might better fulfill its commitment to the impoverished and disenfranchised. Similarly, the poem "God to Hungry Child" savagely contrasts what Hughes perceives to be genuine Judeo-Christian values with what he regards as the corrupt values of a capitalist society that only pretends to belong to that tradition; and "Goodbye Christ," perhaps the most controversial work Hughes produced, intensifies the indictment even further. The poem "Jim Crow Car" depicts a segregated dining car on a train and ends with an apocalyptic image. The poems "Merry Christmas" and " 'The Jesus' " broaden the critique to envelop, with bitter irony, Christianity worldwide, and the poem "Gods" is iconoclastic in the strict religious sense of the term.

Overarching all of the aforementioned works is Hughes's sustained interest in religion as a social force, and throughout his career he pondered the connections between religion and other kinds of group behavior—legal, political, regional, national, economic, racist, and so on. Interestingly, in most of these works Hughes implicitly approves of what he perceives to be Christian ideals (including charity and egalitarianism), and his skepticism or disapproval is leveled at those who, in his view, only pretend to believe, or whose actions do not follow logically from stated belief. However, another set of works celebrates, or at least reflects, Judeo-Christian experiences, with no hint of critique; these include the poems "Ballad of Mary's Son," "Ballad of the Two Thieves," "Christmas Eve: Nearing Midnight In New York," "The Christmas Story," "Communion," "Encounter," "The Last Feast of Belshazzar," and "Pastoral." One might place within or beside this category those works that immerse themselves in or attempt to express specific sorts of African American Christianity, spiritual practice, or religious ceremony. The poems, "Feet o' Jesus," "It Gives Me Pause," "Judgement Day," "Moan," "Night Funeral in Harlem" (from *Montage of a Dream Deferred*), "Not Else—But," and "Tambourines" belong in this group, as do the plays *Black Nativity, Prodigal Son*, and *Tambourines to Glory* (novel and play), as well as the aforementioned "Salvation" (from *The Big Sea*), the chapters of *Not Without Laughter* entitled "Rock, Church," "Feet o' Jesus," and "Fire," and the short story "Big Meeting."

Unrelated to or only tangentially related to Judeo-Christian thought are works that appear to emerge from basic spiritual or existential questions—questions about a search for essential meaning in life, about life after death, about good and evil. Poems such as "Circles," "Convent," "Crossing," "Drum," "Evil," "Island [1]," "Last Call," and "Mystery" are good examples in this regard. Arguably, in the poems "Prayer [1]" and "Prayer [2]" Hughes expresses personal religious attitudes that, at least momentarily, go against the grain of the temperamental skepticism he seems to have maintained most of the time, most of his life. The poem "Girl" seems to reflect a pantheistic theology, and the poem "God" wryly suggests that God is supreme but also supremely lonely and may envy "young lovers" on Earth. The poem "Not What Was" seems to reflect an Einstein*-influenced view of time, space, and destiny. "Number," a cryptic poem, contains hints of apocalypse and the occult. If one asks why Hughes produced works that represent such a wide spectrum of religious, spiritual, and existential views, many of which contradict each other, his characteristic skepticism itself may account largely for the breadth, for the autobiographies, Hughes's writing in general, and the Rampersad biography depict a writer who was genuinely skeptical, who lived in and with religious doubt, but who doubted consistently (if not systematically) in this sense: he questioned even atheism and agnosticism. (It is worth noting, in this regard, that in *I Wonder As I Wander* Hughes describes his father as having been a "confirmed atheist.") The doubt seems to have enabled him to embody, inhabit, express, explore, question, and hold accountable a variety of religious points of view; in a significant number of works it seems to have allowed him, by means of prose, poetry, and drama, to engage religion and faith in many sites, situations, and frames of reference. One plausible panoramic view of Hughes and religion, then, pictures him as a religious and philosophical explorer who was intellectually and spiritually curious, even adventurous, but even at the end of his life unsettled, in doubt, undecided. *See also Carol of the Brown King: Nativity Poems by Langston Hughes; The Glory around His Head*; "God's Other Side"; "Sunday Morning

Prophecy"; "There"; "To a Little Lover-lass, Dead"; "To Certain 'Brothers' ";
"Two Somewhat Different Epigrams"; "Wealth"; "Who But the Lord?"

Bibliography: Mary Beth Culp, "Religion in the Poetry of Langston Hughes," *Phylon: A Review of Race and Culture* 48, no. 3 (Fall 1987), 240–245.

"Remember That I Care." Song, from *Street Scene*. Hughes wrote the lyrics, and Kurt Weill* composed the music. ASCAP* lists the song as being published by Chappell, Inc., and by Hampshire House Publishers. The song's ASCAP registry number is 480017934.

"Remembrance." Poem in a single ballad* quatrain that expresses epigrammatically the view that the remembered fragrance of roses is preferable to cutting them. For Hughes the diction is uncharacteristically formal, even old-fashioned. The poem was first published in *Fields of Wonder*. Regarding a musical adaptation of this poem, see "Heart." *See also* "Refugee."

Bibliography: *CP*, 329.

Renfield, Dr. The exploitative doctor in the short story "Berry" who directs a home for crippled children in New York.

"Rent Party Shout: For a Lady Dancer." Rhyming poem of twenty-two lines spoken by a woman who claims to be so angry at her lover that she threatens to assault him with a pistol or a razor, but her hyperbole is ironic and playful, as are the rhymes and rhythms of the poem, which might indeed have been "shouted"—spoken in unison—by a group at a "rent party." As the editors of *Collected Poems* note, parties for which a small entry fee was charged to help pay for apartment rental were common in Harlem at the time. Watson also discusses "rent parties." Hughes describes them in *The Big Sea*. The poem was first published in the *Amsterdam News* (August 20, 1930).

Bibliography: *The Big Sea*, 263–268; *CP*, 130; Watson, 130–131.

"Request." Poem. *See Montage of a Dream Deferred.*

"Request for Requiems." Poem in two ballad* stanzas. The speaker requests that his "requiems," or funeral music, include two blues* songs, "St. Louis Blues" and "St. James Infirmary." (At Hughes's funeral,* incidentally, the song "Do Nothing 'Til You Hear from Me," composed by Duke Ellington,* was played.) The poem was first published in *One-Way Ticket. See* Funeral, Hughes's; "Wake."

Bibliography: *CP*, 368.

"Request to Genius." Poem. *See* "Demand."

Research Material. *See* Papers, Hughes's (and Related Research Material).

"Restrictive Covenants." Poem of seventeen lines with varying stanza lengths and rhyme schemes. Spoken by a collective persona,* an "I" representing African Americans, the poem concerns neighborhood covenants that prevented African Americans from buying or renting homes in certain areas; specifically, Chicago is mentioned, but the practice was commonplace throughout the United States until the mid-1950s. The poem was first published in *One-Way Ticket*. *See* "Little Song on Housing"; "Slum Dreams."
Bibliography: *CP*, 361.

The Return of Simple, ed. Akiba Sullivan Harper, introduction by Arnold Rampersad (New York: Hill and Wang, 1994). 218 pp. The volume contains sixty-two Simple [Jesse B.] stories* organized in four parts: "Women in Simple's Life" (3–66); "Race, Riots, Police, Prices, and Politics" (67–142); "Africa and Black Pride" (143–178); and "Parting Lines" (179–215). In her preface, Harper writes, "Readers who know the five [previously] published volumes [of Simple stories] will be surprised by the previously uncollected episodes, which are sprinkled throughout the four sections" (ix). In the introduction, Rampersad observes, "Langston Hughes liked to pretend that there was no art involved in creating Simple. . . . Nothing could be further from the truth" (xix).

"Return to Sea." Poem in two ballad* quatrains in which the speaker feels rejuvenated upon going to sea again, presumably on a freighter or passenger liner, and has fond memories of earlier voyages. The poem was first published in the *Baltimore Afro American** (May 9, 1942).
Bibliography: *CP*, 571.

"Reverie on the Harlem River." Poem in three ballad* quatrains, although Hughes breaks up the third quatrain into seven lines. The poem is composed chiefly of rhetorical questions and concerns a visit to the Harlem River at 2:00 A.M., with the first-person narrator meditating on the death of his or her mother and the departure of a lover. He or she briefly contemplates suicide but remarks, "Who would miss me if I left?" The poem was first published in *Shakespeare in Harlem. See also* "Suicide"; "Suicide's Note."
Bibliography: *CP*, 262.

Revision, Process of, and Hughes. In his first autobiographical volume, *The Big Sea*, Langston Hughes offered the following account of the composition of "The Negro Speaks of Rivers" during a journey by train from Cleveland to Mexico City:

Now it was just sunset, and we crossed the Mississippi, slowly over a long bridge. I looked out of that Pullman at the great muddy river, flowing down to the heart of the

South, and I began to think of what that river, the old Mississippi, had meant to Negroes in the past. . . . Then I began to think of other rivers in our past, the Congo, and the Niger, and the Nile in Africa—and the thought came to me: "I've known rivers," and I put it down on the back of an envelope I had in my pocket, and within the space of ten or fifteen minutes, as the train gathered speed in the darkness, I had written this poem which I called "The Negro Speaks of Rivers." No doubt I changed a few words next day, or maybe crossed out a line or two. But there are seldom many changes in my poems, once they're down. Generally the first two or three lines come to me from something I'm thinking about, or looking at, or doing, and the rest of the poem (if there is to be a poem) flows from those first few lines, usually right away. If there is a chance to put the poem down then, I write it down. If not, I try to remember it until I get to a pencil and paper; for poems are like rainbows: they escape you quickly. (41–42)

Hughes intentionally presented himself as the antithesis of the high Modernist poetic craftsman—the image of "il migliore fabro," as T. S. Eliot called Ezra Pound. Instead, we have Langston Hughes, folk poet, who "finds" poems nearly complete and has to write them down quickly before they disappear. Hughes returned to this self-construction at the end of *The Big Sea*. "Literature is a big sea full of many fish. I let down my nets and pulled. I'm still pulling" (335).

Hughes's description of his method of composition in *The Big Sea* misled, and continues to mislead, readers. Two poems that Hughes published in *Chelsea Eight* for October 1960 illustrate how Hughes controlled his public image. "Imagine," with its simple language and its repeating lines, has many characteristics that are recognizably "Hughes." " 'The Jesus,' " on the other hand, which employs words never used out on the street (e.g., "shaftsteel" and "weptwashed") and an intricate, dense series of metaphors (e.g., "the balloon dreams of grabber kings"), reads like a poem that has been labored over for days. Hughes himself realized that " 'The Jesus' " was not what the public expected of "Langston Hughes, folk poet," so he printed it under the pseudonym* Durwood Collins.*

Hughes did in fact revise some of his work after it had initially appeared, for despite Hughes's claim that he hardly ever altered his poems "once they were down," he often took the opportunity to change the text when a poem was reprinted. A striking example is the poem "When Sue Wears Red." In *Crisis** for February 1923, the poem read as follows:

> When Susanna Jones wears red
> Her face is like an ancient cameo
> Turned brown by the ages.
>
> When Susanna Jones wears red
> A queen from some time-dead Egyptian night
> Walks once again.
>
> And the beauty of Susanna Jones in red
> Wakes in my heart a love-fire sharp like pain.

What is missing from this early version is immediately recognized—all those wonderful trumpets for which the poem is now famous. They were added when the poem appeared in Hughes's first volume, *The Weary Blues*. Dating the Harlem Renaissance* is a tricky business, but I would suggest that from a literary standpoint, we could plausibly fix upon the point in 1924 when Hughes began to add the trumpets to manuscripts of "When Sue Wears Red." Hughes himself obscured the history of the text when, in *The Big Sea*, he implied that he wrote the 1926 version of the poem when he was a high-school student in Cleveland. His account of the creation of "When Sue Wears Red" should give pause to anyone who thinks that "The Negro Speaks of Rivers" was composed when Hughes crossed the Mississippi on a train at sunset.

A similar example of a careful recrafting of an already-existing text occurred in *Montage of a Dream Deferred*. In the 1951 version of Hughes's "long poem," "Freedom Train" appeared between "Lady's Boogie" and "Deferred." While the lengthy "Freedom Train" is a strong poem in its own right, Hughes realized that it did not quite fit into the theme and overall tone of the sequence of *Montage of a Dream Deferred* and deleted it from the version that was printed in *The Langston Hughes Reader* (1958). For *Selected Poems* a years later, he inserted a new poem, "So Long," which was specifically written to take the place in *Montage* formerly occupied by "Freedom Train."

> *So long*
> is in the song
> and it's in the way you're gone
> but it's like a foreign language
> in my mind
> and maybe I was blind
> I could not see
> and would not know
> you're gone so long
> so long.

On its own, "So Long" hardly has the power of "Freedom Train." Still, in my view, it functions much better within the whole of *Montage of a Dream Deferred*. There are thematic and verbal echoes with both "Lady's Boogie" and "Deferred" (which begins "This year, maybe do you think I can graduate? / I'm already two years late") as well as to poems elsewhere in the sequence—it has a special resonance with "What? So Soon!" another poem about relationships.

One strategy that Hughes employed on more than one occasion was to drop a weak final stanza of a poem and end with a repetition of the last line of the next-to-last stanza. The first version of "Down and Out" concluded as follows:

> Oh, talk about yo' friendly friends
> Bein' kind to you—
> Yes talk about yo' friendly friends

Bein' kind to you—
Just let yo'self get down and out
And then see what they'll do.

This was replaced simply by the repeated line "I need a dime fo' beer." Hughes performed the same surgery on "Six-Bit Blues." The last stanza in that poem, which he later deleted, originally read as follows:

Oh, there ain't no place in
This world to rest a-tall.
Ain't no place for
A man to rest a-tall—
That's why I go to be a-saying
Goodbye to you all.

Not all of Hughes's revisions were as felicitous as the ones just discussed. "Jazz Band in a Parisian Cafe" originally concluded with the open-ended question and answer "Can I?" "Sure." This was superior, at least in my view, to the more direct "Can I go home wid you?" in the later version, which restricts the reader's imagination.

With regard to Hughes's revisions of titles, here is one example. The following poem appears in *Montage of a Dream Deferred*:

Into the laps
of black celebrities
white girls fall
like pale plums from a tree
beyond a high tension wall
wired for killing
which makes it
more thrilling.

In successive drafts, Hughes gave this effort the title "High Tension Wire," then "Pale Plums," until he finally settled on "Mellow."

Hughes certainly did not revise every poem, nor did he always compose slowly and with care. Yet the image of Hughes as a poet who jotted things down quickly on the back of a matchbook errs too far in the other direction. It suggests, perhaps, a bias that the kind of poetry that Hughes writes, "When Sue Wears Red," for example, does not employ the craftsmanship of other verse.

But many of Hughes's revisions are more problematic because the motivating factor appears to be not aesthetic improvement, but rather audience appeal. For example, the poem "Midwinter Blues" appeared in the *New Republic* on April 14, 1926, without the black dialect* forms for "and," "the," and "my." Dialect forms were used when the poem appeared in *Fine Clothes to the Jew* and *Four Negro Poets*, the latter edited by Alain Locke* (New York: Simon and Schuster, 1927). For *Selected Poems*, however, Hughes reverted to the *New Republic* text with its standard orthography. In fact, in *Selected Poems* Hughes consistently "corrected" most of the black dialect in his earlier poems, especially those of *Fine Clothes to the Jew*.

Which of these two versions of "Midwinter Blues" has a greater claim to "authenticity"? The later version, without the dialect forms, has, according to traditional editorial practice, a certain authority as the last text that the author himself approved for publication. Yet the early version might be considered more authentic because of the black dialect. Should the principle of choosing the last published text still hold if the author had simply made his poem more acceptable to a mainstream audience? Probably not, but can we be sure that black dialect was not added to poems in *Fine Clothes to the Jew* and *Four Negro Poets* because Hughes thought that readers expected dialect in those volumes?

Hughes changed more than dialect for *Selected Poems*; on occasion he altered the blues* structure of the original composition. "Little Old Letter Blues" was retitled "Little Old Letter." The first version read as follows:

> It was yesterday morning
> That I looked in my box for mail.
> Yesterday morning
> I looked in my box for mail.
> The letter that I found there
> Made me turn snow pale.
>
> Just a little old letter
> That wasn't but one page long.
> A little old letter—
> One little old page long,
> But it made me wish I
> Was in hell and gone.
>
> I turned the letter over,
> Nary a word writ on the back.
> Turned it over,
> Nothing on the back
> I never felt so lonesome
> Since I was born black.
>
> Just a pencil and a paper,
> You don't need no gun or knife,
> A pencil and a paper,
> Don't need no gun or knife—
> Cause a little old letter
> Can take a person's life.

The "blues" was taken out of the poem and the title, and the stanzas became ballad quatrains. Hughes changed "Little Green Tree Blues" in precisely the same way. The "blues" versions of these poems were published in predominantly white little magazines, *Old Line* and *Tomorrow*, so the audience in both cases was, for the most part, white. In this case Hughes was clearly not writing one version for an African American audience and another for a white audience, even though "Little Old Letter Blues" might seem a more authentically ethnic poem.

In some instances, Hughes removed or watered down some of his language. "Visitors to the Black Belt," for example, originally ended "Who're you rich folks / Ask me who I am." "Rich folks" later became "outsider." Then there is the strange phenomenon of the vanishing adjective "white." In the first version of "Florida Road Workers," lines nine to eleven read "I'm making a road / For the rich old white men / To sweep over in their big cars." Hughes later referred simply to "rich old men."

Nor did Hughes only make revisions in an attempt to attract a mainstream white audience. In the 1930s he changed some of his poems to make them more acceptable to the left. The ending of "A New Song" in *Opportunity** for January 1933 read as follows:

> Take care!
>   Black world
>   Against the wall,
>   Open your eyes—
>
> The long white snake of greed has struck to kill!
>   Be wary and
>   Be wise!
>
>   Before the darker world
>   The future lies.

In the volume *A New Song*, the poem was given a whole new conclusion:

>   The Black
>   And White World
>   Shall be one!
>   The Worker's World!
>   This is past done!
>
>   A new dream flames
>   Against the
>   Sun!

Both of these endings represent "authentic" Hughes at different points of his life. Choosing one version over another hardly does justice to Hughes. Nor does the view that he was really a poet whose poems suddenly came to him whole and had to be written down quickly before they escaped him. *See* Modernism; Poetics.

David Roessel

"Revolution." Poem of eighteen lines, intermittently rhymed. It exhorts workers worldwide to rise up against capitalism, as represented by a symbolic man "of iron and steel and gold." The poem was first published in *New Masses* (March 13, 1934). *See Angelo Herndon Jones*; "Ballads of Lenin"; Chant for Tom Mooney"; *Don't You Want to Be Free?*; "Goodbye, Christ"; "Good Morning Revolution"; *Harvest*; "Lenin"; "A New Song"; "One More 'S' in the U.S.A."; "Song of the Revolution"; "Wait." *See also* John Reed Club; Marxism; Politics.

Bibliography: *CP*, 175.

"Revolutionary Armies in China—1949." Essay that appeared first in Hughes's column for the *Chicago Defender** (*see* "Here to Yonder") on October 8, 1949. The essay is supportive of the revolutionary forces, which Hughes perceives to be anticolonialist in nature. It was reprinted by Berry, who gave the essay its title. *See also* "Roar China!"

Bibliography: Berry, 129–130.

Rice, Elmer (1892–1967). American playwright and attorney. Rice's given name was Elmer Leopold Reizenstein. He was born in New York City into a working-class family; his parents had immigrated from Russia. Rice worked as a law clerk before entering the New York School of Law in 1910; one year later he joined the New York State bar. He began writing plays shortly thereafter, and the first one to be produced on Broadway was *On Trial*, which became an unexpected commercial success in 1914. Many more of Rice's one-act and three-act plays were produced over the next several years, but the next significant critical and commercial success was *The Adding Machine*, a play in eight scenes, which debuted in New York City in March 1923. Six years later Rice won the Pulitzer Prize for his naturalistic play *Street Scene*. In 1946 Rice, Kurt Weill,* and Hughes collaborated on the operatic version of *Street Scene*. Hughes and Rice both died in May 1967 in New York City.

Bibliography: Frank Durham, *Elmer Rice* (New York: Twayne, 1970).

"Ride, Red, Ride." Poem. *See Ask Your Mama*.

"Right Simple." Short story, included in the collection *Simple Speaks His Mind*. *See* Simple [Jesse B.] Stories.

"The Ring." Poem in twelve lines. It is highly lyrical and compares love to a ringmaster at a circus. The speaker expresses fear of love and of its "sharp, stinging" ringmaster's "whip." The poem was first published in *Crisis** (April 1926).

Bibliography: *CP*, 65.

"Rise and Shine and Give God the Glory." Gospel song sung by the Tambourine Choir in the "Reed Sisters' Tambourine Temple," the church founded in Harlem by Laura Reed and Essie Belle Johnson in the novel *Tambourines to Glory*. The song is mentioned in chapter 23 ("Lucky Texts").

"Rise Up Shepherd and Follow." Song, from *Black Nativity*. ASCAP* lists Hughes as the sole author (lyricist and composer both, that is). However, Alex Bradford was known to have written some melodies for *Black Nativity*. Also, for that musical play, some material from *Ballad of the Brown King* was adapted, and composer Margaret Bonds* collaborated with Hughes on that project. ASCAP lists no publisher for the song, but the song's ASCAP registry number is 180027830. *See Carol of the Brown King: Nativity Poems by Langston Hughes; Gospel Glow*.

"Rising Waters." Poem of eleven short lines, rhetorically addressed to "You rich ones," who are compared to "Foam on the sea." It was first published in *Workers Monthly* (April 1925).
Bibliography: *CP*, 48.

Roach, Lizzie. She is part of the minstrel show at the carnival in chapter 9 of *Not without Laughter*. The impresario describes her as "champeen [*sic*] coon-shouter of Georgia."

The Road. Unfinished play. Rampersad describes it as a "playlet" involving "arguments over politics and money." Hughes worked on the play toward the end of 1935 but never completed it, nor have fragments of it been published. A manuscript is held in the Langston Hughes Papers, James Weldon Johnson Memorial Collection, Beinecke Library, Yale University.
Bibliography: Rampersad, I, 319.

"Roar China!" Poem of two pages, intermittently rhymed, addressed to a per-sonified China and also to representative persons within China, such as "little coolie boy" and "Red [Communist] general." "Roar China!" is one of Hughes's most manic political poems; it exhorts China to revolt against European nations and the United States, which through military action had forced China to ac-quiesce to free-trade agreements and accept foreign residents. Judging from the context of the poem, one might conclude that Hughes used the term "little coolie boy" naïvely, unaware of the extent to which the reference might appear con-descending. The poem was first published in *Volunteer for Liberty* (September 6, 1938). *See* "Call to Creation."
Bibliography: *CP*, 198–200.

Robeson, Paul (1898–1976). American singer, actor, athlete, and attorney. Robeson was born and grew up in Princeton, New Jersey. His father had escaped slavery, and his mother's background was, in part, Native American. Robeson attended Rutgers College, excelling in academics and in four sports: track, football, basketball, and baseball. He was named an "All-American" football player in 1917 and 1918. After graduating from Rutgers, Robeson completed a degree in law at Columbia University* and began working for attorney Louis W. Stotesbury in New York City. Soon thereafter he won roles in two plays, Augustin Duncan's *Taboo* and Eugene O'Neill's *Emperor Jones*. He was so successful in these roles that he decided to abandon law and pursue acting full-time. As well as being a gifted actor, Robeson was a talented singer. In his column, journalist Heywood Broun wrote about hearing Robeson and Lawrence Brown sing at the home of Walter White,* and soon Robeson's career as both an actor in musical drama and a performer of spirituals flourished. He performed in *Show Boat, Porgy and Bess, Othello*, and *The Hairy Ape*. His deep baritone rendition of "Old Man River" from *Show Boat* is still considered unsurpassed. He also performed in such motion pictures as *King Solomon's Mines, Show Boat, Dark Sands, Jericho*, and *Song of Freedom*. Robeson spoke out forcefully against racism in the United States and in support of labor unions. Such political activism made him a target of McCarthyism* in the 1950s. Partly because of McCarthyism, Robeson chose to live abroad much of the time in the latter part of his life. He is considered one of the most multitalented performers in the history of American theatre. In "Berry" Hughes compares Berry's physical attractiveness to that of Robeson. Hughes tried to interest Robeson in a motion-picture project based on the short story "Rejuvenation through Joy" and one based on the dramatic recitation "The Negro Mother." Neither project materialized. Rampersad suggests that Hughes did not include a profile of Robeson in *Famous Negro Music Makers* because politically, Robeson was too controversial. Hughes and Robeson both visited Spain during the Spanish Civil War (*see Baltimore Afro American*), and both were interested in the efforts of China to break away from colonialism. *See* Heyward, DuBose; "Langston Hughes Speaks"; "Roar China!"

Bibliography: Martin Duberman, *Paul Robeson: A Biography* (New York: New Press, 1995); Rampersad, II, 28–29, 259–260; Paul Robeson, *Here I Stand* (Boston: Beacon Press, 1988).

Rock. One of the main characters in *The Sun Do Move*.

"Rock, Church." Short story. The narrative concerns the rise and fall of an ambitious, acquisitive minister in Harlem,* Elder William Jones. The story was included in the collection *Something in Common and Other Stories* and was reprinted in *Langston Hughes: Short Stories*. *See* "Rejuvenation through Joy"; Religion.

Bibliography: Ostrom, 49.

Rodgers, Anjee. The mother of the main character (James "Sandy" Rodgers) in *Not Without Laughter*.

Rodgers, James "Sandy." The main character in *Not Without Laughter*. He is referred to as Sandy throughout the book.

Rodgers, Jimboy. The father of the main character (James "Sandy" Rodgers) in *Not Without Laughter*.

"Roland Hayes Beaten (Georgia 1942)." Poem. *See* "Warning [1]."

"Room." Epigrammatic poem in two short-lined quatrains in which the second and fourth lines rhyme. The poem concerns how rooms in an abode should be configured, depending upon whether there is one resident or two. It was first published in *Voices* (Summer 1943).

Bibliography: *CP*, 443–444.

Roosevelt, Franklin Delano (1882–1945). President of the United States from 1933 to 1945. Born in Hyde Park, New York, Roosevelt was the only child of James and Sara Delano Roosevelt. He grew up in Hyde Park but also frequently accompanied his parents on trips to Canada and Europe. He attended Groton School in Massachusetts and then Harvard College, where he edited the student newspaper and from which he graduated in 1903. He married a distant cousin, Eleanor Roosevelt, in 1905. (She would become one of the most influential "first ladies" in U.S. history, a political and moral force in her own right.) He attended the law school of Columbia University* and earned a degree in 1907. In 1910 he was elected to the state senate in New York and was reelected in 1912. For the presidential administration of Woodrow Wilson, Roosevelt served as assistant secretary of the navy from 1913 to 1920. As a vice presidential candidate, he unsuccessfully ran with Democratic presidential candidate James M. Cox in the election of 1920. A year later he contracted poliomyelitis, which left his legs paralyzed for the rest of his life. Undaunted by his disability, Roosevelt continued his career in politics, associating himself with New York governor Alfred E. Smith. Roosevelt succeeded Smith as governor in 1929. Later that year the U.S. stock market crashed, one of many economic disruptions that led to the Great Depression, to President Herbert Hoover's political demise, and to Roosevelt's election to the presidency in 1932.

The effectiveness and character of Roosevelt's presidency will always be matters of debate. The sheer presence of Roosevelt as a political force in American politics is beyond dispute, however, owing to several facts. First, he served as president for over twelve years. Second, he was president during two colossal events in U.S. and world history: the Great Depression and World War II. Third, he was an activist president who expanded the influence of the federal government enormously and energized the executive branch. Fourth, he helped transform the Democratic Party into one associated with liberalism. Finally, by the time he died in office, the United States was on the threshold of becoming a political "superpower." Matters of debate include precisely what impact Roosevelt's "New Deal" policies had on economic recovery; how appropriate his timing in involving the United States in World War II was; his response to information about events later known as the Holocaust; his military acumen; whether (had he lived) he would have allowed the U.S. Army Air Corps to drop nuclear bombs on Japan; his decisions regarding the internment of Japanese Americans during World War II; and other issues.

Hughes viewed Roosevelt's presidency with ambivalence. Like most African Americans interested in politics, he hoped that Roosevelt would improve the economic, social, political, and legal standing of African Americans and working people in general. Also, he viewed a "northern" Democrat as obviously preferable to a "southern" one. Hughes was, however, disappointed in and even angered by Roosevelt's sluggishness, even inactivity, in overturning Jim Crow laws* and in including African Americans in plans for economic recovery. On "America's Town Meeting of the Air," a radio program broadcast nationally in 1944, Hughes took part in a debate about segregation and what he regarded as Roosevelt's insufficient response to the problem. Hughes also perceived a moral and political inconsistency to exist between Roosevelt's willingness to fight tyranny abroad and his toleration of oppression of African American citizens "at home." *See* "Ballad of Roosevelt"; "Crow Goes, Too"; "Dear Mr. President"; "Message to the President"; "Will V-Day Be Me-Day, Too?"

Bibliography: Kenneth S. Davis, *FDR* [with different subtitles], 4 vols. (New York: Putnam, 1972, Random House, 1985, 1986, 1993, 2000); Ted Morgan, *FDR: A Biography* (New York: Simon and Schuster, 1985); Rampersad, I, II; Harvard Sitkoff, *A New Deal for Blacks: The Emergence of Civil Rights as a National Issue* (New York: Oxford University Press, 1978).

"Roots and Trees." Short story, included in the collection *Simple's Uncle Sam. See* Simple [Jesse B.] Stories.

"Rouge High." Short story. The narrative concerns two prostitutes and the violence they encounter. The story was included in the collection *Laughing to Keep from Crying* and was reprinted in *Langston Hughes: Short Stories*.

Bibliography: Ostrom, 26.

"Ruby Brown." Free-verse poem of twenty-eight lines in four stanzas. It is a narrative poem, the main character of which is Ruby Brown, who is a young working-class woman living in a small town in the southern United States. She is depicted as deliberately choosing to become a prostitute, patronized by white men, because she sees the occupation as the only viable economic opportunity in the town. The poem was first published in *Crisis** (August 1926). *See* "Red Silk Stockings"; "A Ruined Gal"; Women in Hughes's Writing.

Bibliography: *CP*, 73.

"Rude Awakening." Short story, including in the collection *Simple's Uncle Sam*. *See* Simple [Jesse B.] Stories.

Rueda, Senora. A main character in the short story "Tragedy at the Baths."

"A Ruined Gal." Poem of eighteen lines, with stanzas that mix conventions of ballad* and blues* forms. In black dialect* the speaker, a young woman, expresses a desperation so deep that it is suicidal. She sees herself as having "gone wrong" morally and as being someone no man will want. The poem was first published in *Fine Clothes to the Jew*. *See* "Red Silk Stockings"; "Ruby Brown"; Women in Hughes's Writing.
Bibliography: *CP*, 120–121.

Rumba. A Cuban folk dance with African origins. Hughes comments on the dance in *I Wonder As I Wander*.
Bibliography: Yvonne Daniel, *Rumba: Dance and Social Change in Contemporary Cuba* (Bloomington: Indiana University Press, 1995); "Havana Nights," in *I Wonder As I Wander*, 6–10.

S

"Sad Song in de Air." Song. Hughes wrote the lyrics, and Jacques Wolfe composed the music. ASCAP* lists the song as being published by EMI/Robbins Catalogue, Inc., and the song's ASCAP registry number is 490001913. *See* Black Dialect.

Sadie. A character in the poem "Saturday Night."

"Sail Sail Sail" [*sic*]. Song. Hughes wrote the lyrics, and Albert Hague composed the music. ASCAP* lists the song as being published by Summit Music Corporation and by the Song Writers Guild. The song's ASCAP registry number is 490003831.

"Sailing Date." Poem of twenty-one lines in three stanzas, intermittently rhymed. It portrays veteran sailors as they are about to board a ship once more, their lives "Twisted and strange" but their hunger to sail undiminished. It was first published in *Fields of Wonder*.
Bibliography: *CP*, 337.

"Sailor." Poem in two ballad* stanzas, providing a closely observed portrait of a sailor, his taboos, and his cigarette—a "Capstan." It was first published in *Poetry* (October 1931).
Bibliography: *CP*, 139.

"Sailor Ashore." Short story set in Los Angeles, chiefly on the waterfront, where a sailor and a prostitute—both African American—seek solace in one another's company but ultimately cannot escape the sense of hopelessness they both feel. The story was included in the collection *Laughing to Keep from*

Crying and was reprinted in *Langston Hughes: Short Stories. See* "The Star Decides."

"Salute to Soviet Armies." Poem of twenty lines in rhymed couplets of variable meter. It praises the armies of the Union of Soviet Socialist Republics as they battle German Nazi forces on the eastern front of World War II. The poem was first published in *New Masses* (February 14, 1944). It was published under the title "To the Red Army" in *Soviet Russia Today* (July 1944).

Bibliography: *CP*, 299–300.

The Salvation Rock Ladies Missionary Society for the Rescue o' the African Heathen. An organization that figures centrally in the short story "Mother and Child."

Sambo and Rastus. Comedy team in the minstrel show at the carnival in chapter 9 of *Not Without Laughter*. Although they are African American, they play to a largely white audience, and their comedy is based on stereotypes of "foolish" blacks. The narrator parenthetically comments, "(The [white] audience thought it [the comedy routine] screamingly funny—and just like niggers)."

"The Same." Poem. *See* "Always the Same."

"Same in Blues." Poem. *See Montage of a Dream Deferred.*

Sandburg, Carl (1878–1967). The son of Swedish immigrants, Sandburg was born in Galesburg, Illinois. He dropped out of school in the eighth grade and later enlisted in the U.S. Army, serving in Puerto Rico during the Spanish-American War. He attended Lombard College but did not finish a degree. Sandburg worked at a variety of odd jobs and also traveled extensively on freight trains, experimenting with the life of a "hobo." Later he worked for the Socialist Democratic Party. His first book of poems, *In Reckless Ecstasy*, was published in 1904, but not until 1914, when several of his poems appeared in *Poetry* magazine, did Sandburg begin to attract critical and popular attention as a writer. Sandburg is known for building upon the legacy of Walt Whitman* by producing expansive free-verse works and celebrating "the common people" of the United States. His best-known poems include "Chicago" and "Grass." He is also remembered for his six-volume biography *Abraham Lincoln* (1926, 1939). As a young writer, Hughes drew inspiration from Sandburg's work and his populist tendencies. Sandburg's influence can be seen in the free verse of "The Negro Speaks of Rivers." The editors of *Collected Poems* suggest that "Good Morning

Revolution" may deliberately play off of Sandburg's poem "Good Morning, America."

Bibliography: *CP*, 641; Carl Sandburg, *The Complete Poems*, 2nd ed., revised (New York: Harcourt Brace Jovanovich, 1970).

"Saratoga Rain." Short story. This one-page narrative concerns two lovers, both gamblers, who wake up one morning and, despite instances of adultery in the past, decide—for the moment, at least—to salvage their relationship. It was first published in *Negro Story* (March/April 1945), was included in the collection *Laughing to Keep from Crying*, and was reprinted in *Langston Hughes: Short Stories*.

Bibliography: Ostrom, 22.

"Saturday Night." Poem of twenty-eight very short lines, with alternate lines rhyming. The voice of the poem, in black dialect,* is garrulous, creating the effect of inebriation as it exhorts a certain "Charlie" (a "gambler") to drink and dance. Also mentioned is "Sadie," a "whore." The poem was first published in *New Masses* (December 1926).

Bibliography: *CP*, 88.

The Save Lidice Committee. *See* "Shall the Good Go Down?"

"Scat Cat." Song, from the musical play *Tambourines to Glory*. Hughes wrote the lyrics, and Jobe Huntley composed the music. ASCAP* lists the song as being published by Chappell, Inc., and the song's ASCAP registry number is 490388177. *See also* "Life Is Fine."

Schomburg, Arthur (1874–1938). American book collector, attorney, and writer. Schomburg was born and grew up in San Juan, Puerto Rico. After studying at St. Thomas College in the Virgin Islands, Schomburg came to the United States in 1891 and began working as an attorney in New York City. He also began collecting literature and other material relating to Africa, African Americans, and people of African ancestry in the Caribbean. He cofounded the Society for Historical Research in 1911. In 1922 the Carnegie Corporation helped the New York Public Library purchase Schomburg's massive collection of books, manuscripts, pamphlets, and artworks. Later the collection was held in the Harlem* branch of the New York Public Library. For a time this branch was called the Countee Cullen* Branch, but later it was renamed the Schomburg Center for Research in Black Culture, the address of which is 515 Malcolm X Boulevard, New York City. Although the bulk of Hughes's papers are held in the James Weldon Johnson Collection in the Beinecke Library at Yale University, the Schomburg Center also contains important Hughes material. *See* Papers, Hughes's (and Related Research Material).

Bibliography: Lewis, *HRR*, 61–67, 761–762.

Schuyler, George (1895–1977). American novelist, journalist, and editor. Schuyler was born in Rhode Island, went to school in upstate New York, and served in the U.S. Army during World War I. He moved to New York City in 1922. There he met A. Philip Randolph,* editor of the literary and political monthly periodical the *Messenger,** and joined Randolph's editorial staff. The *Messenger*, at which Schuyler worked from 1922 to 1928, had enormous influence in shaping the Harlem Renaissance.* In this editorial capacity Schuyler was chiefly responsible for publishing many of Hughes's earlier poems as well as three short stories, "Bodies in the Moonlight," "The Little Virgin," and "The Young Glory of Him." In connection to Hughes, however, Schuyler is best known for having published the essay "The Negro-Art Hokum" in the *Nation* (June 16, 1926). In this essay Schuyler expresses skepticism about the value of, even the existence of, an African American cultural identity separable from an American cultural identity. In the next issue of the *Nation*, Hughes published "The Negro Artist and the Racial Mountain," which urged black writers to embrace their own experiences, sense of history, and sense of language, and which implicitly critiqued Schuyler's argument. What turned out to be Hughes's most important, influential essay, then, was intended chiefly as a response to Schuyler's specific point of view. An inveterate iconoclast, Schuyler published the book *Black No More* (1931), which satirized many aspects of the Harlem Renaissance. Lewis observes that Schuyler and H. L. Mencken were close friends and that Schuyler "clearly came to model his writing on those of the acerbic 'sage of Baltimore' [Mencken]" (761).

Bibliography: Howard J. Faulkner, "A Vanishing Race" [article on *Black No More*], *College Language Association Journal* 37, no. 3 (March 1994), 274–292; Jane Kuenz, "American Racial Discourse, 1900–1930: Schuyler's *Black No More*," *Novel: A Forum on Fiction* 30, no. 2 (Winter 1997), 170–192; Lewis, *HRR*, 761; Ostrom, 69–71; Michael Peplow, *George S. Schuyler* (Boston: Twayne, 1980).

"Science Says It's a Lie." Short story, included in the collection *Simple Takes a Wife*. *See* Simple [Jesse B.] Stories.

"Scottsboro." Poem of twenty-eight lines, intermittently rhymed. It compares the Scottsboro Boys* to more or less famous figures in history who are widely regarded as martyrs or whom Hughes believes to be martyrs and heroes. The poem refers to Christ, John Brown, the "mad mob" that "tore the Bastille down" (in France, 1789), Moses, "Jeanne d'Arc" (Joan of Arc), Nat Turner, Lenin, Gandhi, and others. The poem was first published in *Opportunity** (December

1931). *See* "Ballads of Lenin"; "Brown America in Jail: Kilby"; "Gandhi Is Fasting"; The Scottsboro Boys; *Scottsboro Limited.*

Bibliography: *CP,* 142.

The Scottsboro Boys. Focal figures of three Alabama rape trials and two important U.S. Supreme Court decisions. The earliest rape trial shocked Hughes into literary and political action. In the fall of 1931 he penned *Scottsboro Limited,* a one-act play that used rhyme and rhythm to dramatize accusations and denials in the shadow of a single raised chair awaiting those convicted of rape. *Opportunity** in December published Hughes's poem "Scottsboro," which asked, "Eight black boys and one white lie. / Is it much to die?" Hughes was inflamed by the condemnation of innocents and excoriated the National Association for the Advancement of Colored People (NAACP)* for moving too slowly, worrying about white opinion too much, and refusing to cooperate with the International Labor Defense (ILD) and the Communists. He also visited the boys at the death house on January 24, 1932 (*see* "Brown America in Jail: Kilby"). He found the eight condemned boys listless and unmoved by his reading of his poetry (except for Andy Wright, who thanked him). Hughes was aghast that one of the accusers, Ruby Bates, let it be known around Huntsville that she had falsely accused the defendants and that there had been no rape. His plans to speak to Bates were stymied by warnings that he would imperil his life by interviewing her. In 1934 Hughes returned from his tour of the Soviet Union and participated in a fundraiser for the Scottsboro Boys in San Francisco. Numerous artists, including members of the arts community in Carmel-by-the-Sea, where Hughes was staying, contributed paintings and drawings for an auction. James Cagney served as auctioneer.

The facts of the case seared Hughes and many Americans. In 1931 nine African American youths—Olen Montgomery, Clarence Norris, Haywood Patterson, Ozie Powell, Willie Roberson, Charley Weems, Eugene Williams, Andy Wright, and Roy Wright—hopped a freight train, fought with several white males, and impelled six white men from a "gondola" car. The rousted whites complained to authorities, resulting in the nine African Americans' being detained when the train reached Paint Rock (Jackson County, Alabama). When two white women, Victoria Price and Ruby Bates, claimed that the nine had raped them, the youths were arrested and taken to Scottsboro, the county seat. The Jackson County sheriff kept a lynch mob at bay on the night of the arrest (March 25), but the accused had no other visitors despite the declaration of Judge Alfred E. Hawkins that all seven members of the bar of Scottsboro serve as defense counsel. Until the opening of the trial (April 6), the boys met with defense lawyers for at most half an hour.

The commencement of the trial only exacerbated the disregard of due process. The counsel for the boys were Milo C. Moody, nearing seventy and occasionally scattered, and Stephen R. Roddy, a Chattanooga attorney unfamiliar with Alabama courts, criminal defense work, or sobriety. Prosecution and judge easily had their way with these ineffective counsel and their clients, so that multiple trials of the defendants in small groups consumed less than a day each. The prosecution of Roy Wright reached a mistrial when the all-white jury insisted on his execution despite Alabama's prohibition of putting a thirteen-year-old to death for rape. With little more concern for fairness and propriety, the older eight Scottsboro Boys were sentenced to death. Represented by George W. Chamlee and Joseph R. Brodsky of the International Labor Defense and embraced by a Communist Party hoping to impress African Americans, the eight appealed to the Alabama Supreme Court. Although Chamlee and Brodsky noted the intimidating setting in Jackson County and especially outside the courthouse and the systematic dearth of African Americans on Alabama juries and jury pools, they emphasized the ineffective assistance of counsel to indigent, ignorant, and largely illiterate defendants in capital cases. The Alabama Supreme Court negated the conviction of Eugene Williams because he should have been tried as a juvenile but let stand the other seven convictions. The Supreme Court of the United States saved the seven from execution in the landmark case *Powell v. Alabama* (1932). For the first time, the Court disallowed a state-court conviction because the trial court had not appointed or allowed defendants effective counsel. Writing for a 7–2 Court, Justice George Sutherland noted Judge Hawkins's casual manner in appointing counsel, the absence of legal advice or serious consultation before the trial began, and the requirements of due process of law imposed on the trial court by the Fourteenth Amendment to the U.S. Constitution. Taken together, these factors convinced seven justices (James McReynolds and Pierce Butler dissented) that Judge Hawkins had failed to provide the minimal procedural guarantees due defendants on trial for their lives. Therefore the first trial was disallowed.

For the retrial in 1933, the International Labor Defense secured the services of Samuel Leibowitz, an accomplished criminal defense attorney. Leibowitz poked holes in the prosecution's case, suggested that Price and Bates were prostitutes, and endured anti-Semitic slurs from the prosecution. Although Bates denied on the stand that a rape had occurred, the jury returned capital verdicts. Judge James E. Horton then disallowed that verdict as clearly contrary to the evidence presented and ordered a third trial, thereby securing his electoral defeat in the next year's judicial election. A third trial was rife with judicial error but elicited the same guilty verdicts. Leibowitz appealed this third defeat to the U.S. Supreme Court, which disallowed the results due to Alabama's refusal to permit African Americans to serve as jurors. Chief Justice Charles Evans Hughes, in *Norris v. Alabama* and *Patterson v. Alabama*, found for a unanimous Court (McReynolds, a dissenter in *Powell v. Alabama*, did not participate in the later cases) that the dearth of black jurors in Alabama contradicted the "equal protection of the laws" mandated by the Fourteenth Amendment to the U.S. Constitution. This back and forth between the Supreme Court and Alabama ended only with an agreement between defense and prosecutors that four of the Scottsboro Boys be released while five would get short stretches in prison. Alabama reneged on the agreement. The last of the boys was released in 1950, although Clarence Norris was technically a fugitive because he had violated his parole by leaving Alabama. George Wallace pardoned Norris in 1976.

Bibliography: Dan T. Carter, *Scottsboro: A Tragedy of the American South*, rev. ed. (Baton Rouge: Louisiana State University Press, 1979); Arthur Garfield Hays, *Trial by Prejudice* (New York: Covici, Friede, 1933), 25–153; Gerald Horne, *Powell v. Alabama: The Scottsboro Boys and American Justice* (New York: Franklin Watts, 1997); Charles H. Martin, *The Angelo Herndon Case and Southern Justice* (Baton Rouge: Louisiana State University Press, 1976); Michael Thurston, "Black Christ, Red Flag: Langston Hughes on Scottsboro," *College Literature* 22, no. 3 (October 1995), 30–49.

William Haltom

Scottsboro Limited (1932). Play in one act, written in 1931, published the following year. Although both the directions for its staging and the episodic structure are similar to those of the successfully performed *Don't You Want to Be Free?*, *Scottsboro Limited* was never performed, probably because its subject is more topical and its point of view even more baldly political than that of *Don't You Want To Be Free?*, but also because Hughes perceived it to be chiefly a work to be read—a "play in verse," which is the subtitle he gave it. The characters include the nine Scottsboro Boys,* eight white workers, a white man, and two white women. Audience participation is also written into the play. The only set design stipulated, beyond the bare stage, is a chair on a raised platform, symbolizing the electric chair used in executions. Written in verse, the dialogue is sometimes in rhymed couplets and at other times in alternately rhymed lines. The play recapitulates events leading up to the arrest of the Scottsboro Boys, represents Hughes's notion of their incarceration, and re-creates parts of the trial. However, the play is much less historical than political or activist in its rendering, for it suggests that communism will overturn the racism and class exploitation that Hughes believed, at the time, to lie behind such events as the Scottsboro trial. Some critics have referred to the play as propagandistic. It was published in *Scottsboro Limited: Four Poems and a Play in Verse*. It was republished in 2000. *See also* Jim Crow Laws; Lynching.

Bibliography: Hicklin, 38–40; Langston Hughes, *Scottsboro Limited*, in *The Political Plays of Langston Hughes*, ed. with introduction and analyses by Susan Duffy (Carbondale: Southern Illinois University Press, 2000), 37–49 [Duffy's introduction to the play, 24–36]; Rampersad, I, 215–254; Michael Thurston, "Black Christ, Red Flag: Langston Hughes on Scottsboro," *College Literature* 22, no. 3 (October 1995), 30–49.

Scottsboro Limited: Four Poems and a Play in Verse (New York: Golden Stair Press, 1932). Illustrations by Prentiss Taylor. 20 pp. Book. It contains the play *Scottsboro Limited* and the poems "Justice," "Christ in Alabama," "Scottsboro," and "The Town of Scottsboro." An autographed copy of this relatively rare book is held by the Schomburg Center for Research in Black Culture in Harlem,* the collection of which is part of the New York Public Library system. *See Political Plays of Langston Hughes;* The Scottsboro Boys.

Screenplay. *See Way Down South.*

"Sea Calm." Six-line lyric poem expressing a sense in which the calm of the sea is foreboding. It was first published in *The Weary Blues.* Later, William Benjamin Cooper set the poem to music. ASCAP* lists the song as being published by Dangerfield Music Company, and the song's ASCAP registry number is 490560364.
Bibliography: *CP,* 97.

"Sea Charm." Eleven-line lyric poem. It presents a kind of argument that suggests that the "sea's children" know many of the sea's capacities and powers but not its "charm." Whether these "children" are sailors or sea creatures is unclear. The poem was first published in *Survey Graphic* (March 1, 1925), a special issue edited by Alain Locke.*
Bibliography: *CP,* 44.

"Search." Poem. It represents one of the few times Hughes employed a strict sonnet form, and he went so far as to use strict iambic pentameter and formal, even antique, diction ("goeth," for example). The poem depicts life as a ceaseless process of yearning and searching. Surprisingly, the poem was published in the 1930s, when one might expect Hughes to have been least likely to use such a form because he was producing so much work concerning contemporary political issues and was often working in less refined verse forms. It was first published in *Opportunity** (July 1937). Later, Robert Convery set the poem to music. ASCAP* lists no publisher for the song, but the song's ASCAP registry number is 490950326. *See* "Pennsylvania Station"; "Ph.D."; "Seven Moments of Love"; Sonnet.
Bibliography: *CP,* 200.

"Seascape." Poem in two ballad* stanzas recording what is seen from a ship off the coast of Ireland. It was first published in *The Weary Blues.*
Bibliography: *CP,* 98.

"Seashore through Dark Glasses (Atlantic City)." Poem of thirteen lines in four stanzas, intermittently rhymed. It provides glimpses of some of the people on the seashore and in its establishments, but it also touches on racism, so the "Dark Glasses" of the title begin to take on symbolic meaning. The poem was first published in *Poetry* (February 1947).
Bibliography: *CP,* 322–323.

"Second Generation: New York." Poem of thirty-three lines in six stanzas, rhyming infrequently. It concerns the ways in which Irish and Polish second-generation individuals are attached to the United States and New York City while their parents' fondest memories are of Ireland and Poland. It was first published in *Common Ground* (Spring 1949).

Bibliography: *CP*, 351–352.

"Second-Hand Clothes." Short story, included in the collection *Simple Takes a Wife. See* Simple [Jesse B.] Stories.

"Seeing Double." Short story, included in *The Best of Simple. See* Simple [Jesse B.] Stories.

Selected Poems of Gabriela Mistral (Bloomington: Indiana University Press, 1957). 119 pp. In this collection Hughes includes seventy-four poems he translated from the major works of Gabriela Mistral. The poems have been organized into seven thematically divided sections, and all of the Chilean poet's major works are represented in the volume. Gabriela Mistral (1889–1957) began working as a schoolteacher in rural Chile when she was fifteen years old. Her given name was Lucila Godoy y Alcayaga. After some moderate success as a young poet, Mistral received a gold medal in Chile's 1915 national poetry contest for her *Death Sonnets*. These sonnets were written after a man with whom she had fallen in love committed suicide. Although these poems do not appear in his translation, Hughes explains his decision to omit them in the Introduction: "When I feel I can transfer only literal content, I do not attempt a translation. For that reason I have not translated the three *Sonetos de la Muerte*. They are very beautiful, but very difficult in their rhymed simplicity to put into an equivalent English form. To give their meaning without their word music would be to lose their meaning" (11). After she received this award, Mistral became recognized as not only one of Chile's most important poets but also one of the nation's most important teachers. In her many travels during the rest of her life as artist, educator, and diplomat, she visited and resided in Latin America, the United States, and Europe. In 1922 she published *Despair (Desolación), Tenderness (Ternura)* in 1924, *Felling (Tala)* in 1938, and finally *Winepress (Lagar)* in 1954. A few minor works were published posthumously. Some of the most prevalent themes in her work are love, death, maternity, childhood, religion, and nature. In 1945 Gabriela Mistral was awarded the Nobel Prize for Literature, the first Latin American to receive the prestigious honor.

It is notable that Mistral achieved her prominence as a writer and educator at a time when women's voices, especially in Latin America, were confined almost exclusively to the margins of public discourse. It was, in part, Mistral's distinctly feminine voice that made Hughes think twice before deciding to translate her work; "since her poetry is so intensely feminine . . . I hesitated to attempt translations myself, hoping that a woman would do so" (10).

Despite his initial hesitancy, as this book testifies, Hughes indeed went on to translate Mistral's work. The first section of the book is "Cradle Songs." Here some of Mistral's most frequently anthologized poems are found. As these "lullabies" are presented, the reader realizes that these poetic songs are just as important to the poet/singer as they are for the infant to whom they are directed. In many of the translations Hughes has preserved the rhyme and rhythm of the verses so that they retain their musical quality. The popular selections "I Am Not Lonely," and "Cradle Song" are particularly well rendered. The theme of childhood is intensified and expanded in "Poems for Mothers," where the selections describe the sacred nature of pregnancy, the sisterhood among all women, and the bond between mother and child. The third section, "For the Saddest of Mothers," consists of two poems, "Thrown Out" and "Why Did You Come?" These selections portray how a mother's love for her child can overcome the social stigma associated with pregnancy out of wedlock and even abandonment by the father/husband. The title of the fourth section, "Grain Divine," is taken from the last stanza of the second selection, "Poem of the Son." Hughes reminds us in his introduction that this poem and "Prayer," also found here, were written by Mistral after the suicide of the man with whom she had fallen in love as a young woman. While the latter is an invocation asking for the pardon of her lover's soul, the former is a two-part poem that laments the son that they never had. The resignation of the poetic voice is evident: "I taught the children of others, trusting only in You / to fill my granary with grain divine. / Our Father Who art in heaven, lift up this beggar. / Should I die tonight, let me be Thine" (63). For Mistral, heaven will not be a place filled with angels, but rather with children. In "Earth and Women," the notion of the divine evidenced in the preceding section is expanded. Here the idea of a distant god to whom one prays is recast as a tangible presence that unites humankind and nature. In the poem "The Stable" the speaker presents a version of the birth of the Christ child in the manger in which several of Mistral's thematic elements harmoniously merge together: the spiritual and the natural, humanity and divinity, and the celestial and terrestrial. Throughout the section the poetic imagery is composed primarily of flora and fauna.

In the penultimate section one flower in particular, the rose, continues to be a prevalent image. In the first poem, "Richness," which is the name of the section as well, the poetic speaker cries: "I have a true happiness / and a happiness betrayed, / the one like a rose, / the other like a thorn" (93). The tone of these verses is reflective of the entire section. While life is not perfect, there is joy to be had and beauty to be enjoyed. In keeping with the same imagery and theme in "The Rose," the poetic voice later reveals: "The treasure at the heart of the rose / is your heart's own treasure. / Scatter it as the rose does: / Your pain becomes hers to measure. / . . . Do not resist the rose / lest you burn in its fire" (104). For the poet, there is indeed richness to be had in life. The last section of the work is titled "Country with No Name." This is without a doubt the most somber part of the book, and nearly all of the poems deal with the theme of mortality. There is a subtle acceptance of human finitude in nearly all of the poems, a notion perhaps best represented in the first line of "Song," the final poem of the collection: "A woman is singing in the valley. The shadows falling blot her out, but her song spreads over the field" (119). Hughes captures the tonal quality of yearning that is so prevalent in Mistral's poetry in the original Spanish, and his choice of poetic vocabulary has enabled him to accurately reproduce the literal content, emotion, and style that he intended to portray. While this translation can be viewed more as a poetic exercise than as one that represents a personal relationship with Mistral, the end product is very satisfactory. With this collection, Hughes has offered a coherent introduction to the poetry of this important Latin American poet. *See* "Flower in the Air"; "I Am Not Lonely."

Bibliography: Elizabeth Horan, "Gabriela Mistral: Language Is the Only Homeland," in *A Dream of Light and Shadow: Portraits of Latin American Women Writers*, ed. Marjorie Agosín (Albuquerque: University of New Mexico Press, 1995), 119–142; Gabriela Mistral, *Selected Poems of Gabriela Mistral*, transl. Doris Dana (Baltimore, MD: Johns Hopkins Press, 1971); Edward Mullen, ed., *Langston Hughes in the Hispanic World and Haiti* (Hamden, CT: Archon Books, 1977).

Joseph Deters

Selected Poems (New York: Knopf, 1959). 297 pp. For the book Hughes selected poems from *The Weary Blues, Fine Clothes to the Jew, Shakespeare in Harlem, Fields of Wonder, Montage of a Dream Deferred*, and *Dear Lovely Death*, as well as including some poems previously unpublished in books. Instead of organizing the poems chronologically (according to publication dates of the books listed here), Hughes arranged them in categories. "Afro-American Fragments" (3–17) contains eleven poems reflecting perspectives on African heritage, including "The Negro Speaks of Rivers." "Feet o' Jesus" (18–32) includes poems related to religion.* "Shadow of the Blues" (33–48) contains blues* poems and blues-oriented poems, including "The Weary Blues" and "Bad Luck Card." "Sea and Land" (49–80) features poems springing from Hughes's extensive travels. "Distance Nowhere" (81–106) includes "dream" poems and meditative verse. "After Hours" (107–120) contains more blues poems. "Life Is Fine" (121–142) is an ironically titled section containing poems concerning a variety of hardships and heartaches. "Lament for Love" (143–156) contains poems about love lost and unrequited love. "Magnolia Flowers" (157–176) includes poems that critique racism in the American South, including "Ku Klux," "Silhouette," and "Roland Hayes Beaten (Georgia 1942)." "Name in Uphill Letters" (177–200) includes more poems concerning racism, segregation, and ethnic politics. "Madam to You" (201–220) reprints twelve Madam poems.* Pages 221–274 reprint *Montage of a Dream Deferred*. "Words like Freedom" (275–295) contains eleven poems, including "I, Too," "Freedom Train," "The Negro

Mother," and "Freedom's Plow." Notably absent from the book are Hughes's more heavily Marxist-influenced poems, such as "Ballads of Lenin," "Good Morning, Revolution," and "One More 'S' in the U.S.A." The book was reprinted in 1998 (New York: Vintage Classics) and is in print at this writing.

Selected Songs for High Voice (New York: Southern Music, 1995). 50 pp. Musical score by John Musto. It includes music for two songs with lyrics written by Hughes: "Shadow of the Blues" and "Silhouette" (*see* separate entries for these works). The printed score is held by the Library of Congress. *See also* Songs.

"Self-Protection." Short story, included in the collection *Simple's Uncle Sam.* *See* Simple [Jesse B.] Stories.

Semple, Jesse B. *See* Simple [Jesse B.] Stories.

"Seven Moments of Love." Poem, subtitled "An Un-sonnet Sequence in Blues." The poem consists of seven parts, each in highly modified sonnet form, with improvised rhythms instead of the traditional iambic pentameter, and with some sonnets running to fifteen or sixteen lines. Titles of the separate parts are as follows: "Twilight Reverie," "Supper Time," "Bed Time," "Daybreak," "Sunday," "Payday," and "Letter [2]." The narrator of the poems, Jack, moves from murderous rage against his lover's having left him to less fierce anger to loneliness and regret and finally to an apologetic state in which he writes a letter to "Cassie" (his former lover), asking her to return. The poem was first published in *Esquire* (May 1940). See "Pennsylvania Station"; "Ph.D."; Sonnet.
Bibliography: *CP*, 217–220.

"Seven Rings." Short story, included in the collections *Simple Takes a Wife* and *The Best of Simple*. *See* Simple [Jesse B.] Stories.

"Seventy-five Dollars." Short story. *See* Central High School.

"Sex in Front." Short story, included in the collection *Simple Stakes a Claim.* *See* Simple [Jesse B.] Stories.

Sexuality and Hughes. In connection with the study of Hughes and his work, the topic of sexuality is pertinent for at least four reasons. First, in a variety of ways, it informs Hughes's work. It appears in more or less traditional love poems, in poems that are more directly sexual, and in stories that connect issues of race, sexuality, and power (such as "The Blues I'm Playing" and "Slave on the Block"). In his poetry, fiction, drama, songs, and autobiographies, Hughes treats sexuality tragically, comically, ironically, matter-of-factly, even coyly— representing it, that is, from a wide spectrum of vantage points. Second, sexuality is a topic important to an understanding of the Harlem Renaissance.* Sexual liberation, resistance to American "puritanical" ideas, the sexualizing of African Americans by whites, sexual relations between blacks and whites, the concepts of the "mulatto" and "passing," homosexuality, and the sexuality associated with the blues* and jazz* all figured into the Harlem Renaissance and the epoch of "the Roaring Twenties" in the United States. Third, sexual tension, for lack of a better term, clearly informed, or at least had the potential to influence, some of Hughes's most important relationships, including those with Carl Van Vechten,* Alain Locke,* Countee Cullen,* Richard Bruce Nugent,* Zora Neale Hurston,* and Noel Sullivan.* The extent to which such individuals were (or were not) sexually attracted to Hughes and the extent to which he was (or was not) sexually attracted to them are at least debatable; nonetheless, in all of these relationships, sexuality was certainly among the constellation of elements defining the interaction between Hughes and these individuals. Fourth, Hughes's own sexuality has been a topic of interest to critics and scholars for some time. Whether he was heterosexual, bisexual, homosexual, and/or asexual, how he himself viewed such categories, and the extent to which his sexuality should affect one's interpretation of his work have all been sources of speculation, argument, and controversy. In the story "Blessed Assurance," Hughes treats the issue of homosexuality in ways that might be construed as callously comic, but in the poem "Café: 3 a.m.," part of *Montage of a Dream Deferred*, he implicitly criticizes New York City vice squad policemen for looking at homosexual (Hughes uses the term "fairies") men sadistically. The poem further suggests that homosexuals are not "degenerates" but were "made" by "God or Nature."

Biographer Faith Berry seems to conclude that Hughes was bisexual. Biographer Arnold Rampersad concludes that for the most part Hughes was asexual. Critic Charles I. Nero regards Rampersad's interpretation as an example of "homophobic textuality." British film-maker and actor Isaac Julien's film *Looking for Langston* (1989) concerns homosexuality in the Harlem Renaissance and African American homosexuality in general, mixing drama, narrative, and documentary and operating from the premise that Hughes was indeed gay. Since Hughes's death, studies of the Harlem Renaissance, African American studies, feminist criticism, gay and lesbian studies, and queer theory have all increased the number of interpretive avenues and expanded the critical vocabulary whereby sexuality is discussed in connection with almost all writers and their work, including American writers, writers of the Harlem Renaissance, and Hughes. Hughes's varied, sometimes-direct, sometimes-humorous, but often-subtle treatment of sexuality is but one element that continues to make his oeuvre interesting to study and reevaluate. Similarly, the question of Hughes's own sexuality is one of many elements that make his personality seem mercurial, his life complex, and any biographer's task challenging. *See* Women in Hughes's Writing.

Bibliography: Berry; Manthia Diawara, "The Absent One: The Avant-Garde and the Black Imaginary in *Looking for Langston*," in *Representing Black Men*, ed. Marcellus Blount and George P. Cunningham (New York: Routledge, 1996), 205–224; Isaac Julien, director/actor, *Looking for Langston* [motion picture; 45 minutes], London: water Bearer/ Channel Four, (1989): available on videocassette at this writing; Charles I. Nero, "Re/ Membering Langston: Homophobic Textuality and Arnold Rampersad's *Life of Langston Hughes*," in *Queer Representations: Reading Lives, Reading Cultures*, ed. Martin Duberman (New York: New York University Press, 1997), 188–196; Rampersad, I and II.

"Shades of Pigmeat." Poem. *See Ask Your Mama. See also* "Not Else—But."

"Shadow of the Blues." Short story, included in the collections *Simple Takes a Wife* and *The Best of Simple. See* Simple [Jesse B.] Stories.

"Shadow of the Blues." Song. Hughes wrote the lyrics, and John Musto composed the music. ASCAP* lists the song as being published by Southern Music Publishing Company, Inc., and the song's ASCAP registry number is 490645675. *See Selected Songs for High Voice.*

"Shake Your Brown Feet, Honey." Song. Hughes wrote the lyrics, and John Alden Carpenter composed the music. ASCAP* lists the song as being published by G. Schirmer, Inc., and the song's ASCAP registry number is 490043119.

Shakespeare in Harlem (New York: Knopf, 1942). 124 pp. With drawings by E. McNight Kauffer. Collection of poetry. It includes the poems "Announcement," "Aspiration," "Ballad of the Fortune Teller," "Ballad of the Girl Whose Name Is Mud," "Ballad of the Gypsy," "Ballad of the Killer Boy," "Ballad of the Man Who's Gone," "Ballad of the Pawnbroker," "Ballad of the Sinner," "Black Maria," "Brief Encounter," "Cabaret Girl Dies on Welfare Island," "Crossing," "Declaration," "Early Evening Quarrel," "Evil," "Evil Morning," "50–50," "Fired," "Free Man," "Gifts" (which Hughes later made the second stanza of "Luck"), "Harlem Sweeties," "Hey-Hey Blues," "Hope [1]," "If-ing," "In a Troubled Key," "Kid Sleepy," "Ku Klux," "Little Lyric (*of Great Importance*)," "Love," "Love Again Blues," "Me and the Mule," "Merry-Go-Round," "Midnight Chippie's Lament," "Mississippi Levee," "Morning After," "Only Woman Blues," "Out of Work," "Present," "Reverie on the Harlem River," "Shakespeare in Harlem," "Six-Bit Blues," "Snob," "Southern Mammy Sings," "Statement," "Stony Lonesome," "Wake," "West Texas," "Widow Woman," and "Young Negro Girl." Each of the poems has its own entry in this encyclopedia. *See also* Ballad; The Blues.

Bibliography: Rampersad, II, 34–35, 40–42.

"Shakespeare in Harlem." Poem in two ballad* stanzas, mixing phrases from Elizabethan songs with colloquial language from Harlem.* To some extent, this relatively slight poem makes a profound implicit point—namely, that the cultural energy of Harlem in Hughes's era is as productive and substantial as that of the Elizabethan age, Shakespeare's era. The poem was first published in *Shakespeare in Harlem.*

Bibliography: *CP*, 260.

"Shall the Good Go Down?" Poem of twenty-seven lines in seven stanzas. The poem asks whether certain oppressed peoples deserve their fate or are victims not just of oppressors but of the indifference of others. It also explicitly critiques those who regard politically topical poetry as propaganda, and it specifically mentions Spain, the civil war there about which Hughes wrote extensively, and Lidice, a town in Czechoslovakia that the Nazi military destroyed after the assassination of a Nazi commander, Reinhard Heydrich. Hughes was a member of the Save Lidice Committee, which provided assistance to the townspeople following the Nazis' act of retribution. The poem was first published in *Span* (Fall 1943). *See Baltimore Afro American*; "Hero—International Brigade"; "Letter from Spain."

Bibliography: *CP*, 278.

"Shame on You." Poem. *See Montage of a Dream Deferred.*

Shapiro, Karl (1913–2000). American poet, editor, and professor. *See* Ellison, Ralph; "Letter to the Academy."

"Share-Croppers." Poem in four ballad* stanzas, spoken by a collective persona* representing black sharecroppers, who are described as "[j]ust a herd of Negroes," and explaining that because they own no land, the sharecroppers cannot advance economically. It was first published in *Proletarian Literature.*

Bibliography: *CP*, 185; Granville Hicks, *Proletarian Literature* (New York: International, 1935), 167.

"She Left Herself One Evening." Poem by Léon Damas (a writer from French Guiana) that Hughes translated from the French. It is twelve lines long and concerns a woman, the speaker's love, who is "like a mad dog." It was published in *The Langston Hughes Reader.*

Bibliography: *The Langston Hughes Reader*, 138–139.

"She Shouldn't Be Staying Out Nights." Song, from *Street Scene.* Hughes wrote the lyrics, and Kurt Weill* composed the music. At this writing, the song is not listed with ASCAP.* It is published by Warner Chappell, Ltd.

Bibliography: Booklet accompanying *Street Scene* [compact disc], performed by Kristine Ciesinski, Janis Kelly, Bonaventura Bottone, Richard van Allan, Catherine Zeta Jones, and the Orchestra and Chorus of the English National Opera, conducted by Carl Davis (London: Jay Records, 1996): CDJAY2–1232.

"Shearing Time." Poem in a single ballad* quatrain that offers a humorous comment on sheep being sheared. It was first published in *The Langston Hughes Reader*. *See* Children's Poetry.

Bibliography: *CP*, 606.

"Shepherd's Song at Christmas." Poem in three stanzas of seven lines each, followed by a four-line chorus. The poem is spoken by a "poor shepherd boy" and recapitulates conventional elements of the biblical stories concerning Christ's birth. It is the last poem printed in *Collected Poems*. It was first published in *The Langston Hughes Reader* and was reprinted in *Carol of the Brown King: Nativity Poems by Langston Hughes*. *See* Children's Poetry.

Bibliography: *CP*, 610.

Short Stories, Collections of. See *The Best of Simple; Langston Hughes: Short Stories; Laughing to Keep from Crying; The Return of Simple; Simple Speaks His Mind; Simple Stakes a Claim; Simple Takes a Wife; Simple's Uncle Sam; Something in Common and Other Stories; The Sweet Flypaper of Life; The Ways of White Folks*; Simple [Jesse B.] Stories.

"Shout." Poem of three lines that captures an exclamation that might be heard in an African American church. It was first published in *Brownie's Book* (August 1921) and was included in *Fine Clothes to the Jew*. *See* "Sinner."

Bibliography: *CP*, 117.

"Show Fare, Please." Poem. *See Ask Your Mama*.

"Sick Bed." Poem of six lines in free verse, personifying "Life" and "Death" as two lovers, in between whom a dying woman sleeps. It was first published in *The Weary Blues*.

Bibliography: *CP*, 99.

"Signifyin' Natives." Song. ASCAP* lists Samuel R. Delaney, Audre Lorde, and Bill Lowe as cowriters with Hughes but lists no publisher. The song's ASCAP registry number is 490818703.

"Signs of Spring." Poem in three rhyming couplets. It evokes conventional indications of spring's arrival. It was first published in *Brownie's Book* (1921). *See* "Autumn Note"; children's Poetry.

Bibliography: *CP*, 597.

"Silence." Poem of eight short lines in free verse. The first and third stanzas contain three lines; the second, two. Addressed to "you," the poem partly concerns the eloquence of silence. It was first published in the *Carmel Pine Cone*

(July 18, 1941). Later, Robert Owens set this poem, "In Time of Silver Rain," "Fulfillment," "Night Song," "Carolina Cabin," and "Songs" to music in a song cycle, *Silver Rain*.

Bibliography: *CP*, 234; Robert Owens [composer], *Silver Rain: Song Cycle for Tenor and Piano* (Munich: Orlando-Musikverlag, 1975).

"Silent One." Poem of twelve lines in free verse. It is a cryptic, even mystical, poem about a metaphysical "son," composed of (among other things) "all the atoms in the sun." It was first published in the *New York Times* (November 9, 1962).

Bibliography: *CP*, 536.

"Silhouette." Poem of fourteen lines in four stanzas, intermittently rhymed. It is a brutally ironic poem addressed to a "Southern Lady," telling her not "to swoon" and advising her, with mock politeness, that a black man has been lynched "to protect her Southern womanhood." It was first published in *Opportunity* (June 1936). Later the poem was set to music. ASCAP* lists the composer as John Musto and the publisher as Southern Music, Inc. The song's ASCAP registry number is 490716982. *See* "Home"; *Selected Songs for High Voice*.

Bibliography: *CP*, 305–306.

"Silly Animals." Poem in a single ballad* quatrain that playfully describes a dog, a cat, and a mouse. It was first published in *The Langston Hughes Reader*. *See* Children's Poetry.

Bibliography: *CP*, 608.

"Silver Rain." Song. *See* "In Time of Silver Rain."

Silver Rain: Song Cycle for Tenor and Piano. *See* "Carolina Cabin"; "Fulfillment"; "In Time of Silver Rain"; "Night Song"; "Silence"; "Songs."

Simple, Jesse B. *See* Simple [Jesse B.] Stories.

"Simple and His Sins." Short story, included in *The Best of Simple*. *See* Simple [Jesse B.] Stories.

Simple John. A character in the poem "Pierrot."

"Simple on Indian Blood." Short story, included in *The Best of Simple*. *See* Simple [Jesse B.] Stories.

"Simple on Military Integration." Short story, included in *The Best of Simple*. *See* Simple [Jesse B.] Stories.

"Simple Pins on Medals." Short story, included in the collection *Simple Speaks His Mind. See* Simple [Jesse B.] Stories.

"Simple Plays with Fire." Short story. *See* "Name in the Papers."

"Simple Prays a Prayer." Short story, collected in *The Best of Simple. See* Simple [Jesse B.] Stories. *See also Poems by Sterling Brown.*

"Simple Santa." Short story, included in the collection *Simple Takes a Wife. See* Simple [Jesse B.] Stories.

Simple: Seven Stories from "The Best of Simple" and "Simple's Uncle Sam" (London: Caedmon, 1968). Audio recording of Ossie Davis reading the stories. The recording is held by the Library of Congress and is identified as Caedmon TC 1222. *See* Simple [Jesse B.] Stories. *See also* Audio Recordings of Hughes.

Simple Speaks His Mind (New York: Simon and Schuster, 1950). 231 pp. Collection of forty-four short stories. A limited edition of this book was published by the small publisher Aeonian Press in 1947. *See* Simple [Jesse B.] Stories.

Simple Stakes a Claim (New York: Rinehart, 1957). 191 pp. Collection of forty short stories. A limited edition of this book was published by the small press Amereon House (Mattituck, NY) in 1953. *See* Simple [Jesse B.] Stories.

"Simple Stashes Back." Short story, included in the collection *Simple Stakes a Claim. See* Simple [Jesse B.] Stories.

Simple [Jesse B.] Stories. Short tales featuring the character Jesse B. Simple, who in the first several tales was Jess Semple, then briefly Jesse B. Semple, and finally Jesse B. Simple, as the character is known in the vast majority of the tales (see Harper, 87–89). Hughes began writing a weekly newspaper column for the *Chicago Defender** on November 21, 1942 (*see* "Here to Yonder"). For several weeks the columns featured Hughes's reflections on a variety of subjects. On February 13, 1943, however, Hughes published a column in which he mentioned his "simple minded friend," recording some remarks this friend made about Nazism. Soon thereafter Hughes transformed the columns featuring this "simple minded friend" into fiction: tales in which a certain "Ananias Boyd" narrates but which are dominated by the talk of Jesse B. Simple. Over the next seven years Hughes published about 120 of these tales in his column and continued to publish an average of about fifteen of them per year until January 8, 1966, when "Hail and Farewell," the last Simple story, appeared in the *New York Post* (see Harper, 219–242). (In 1957 Hughes began publishing his column in both the *Defender* and the *Post*, and in 1962 he stopped submitting his column to the *Defender*.)

No doubt Hughes himself did not realize in 1943 that he had created a character who would reappear in so many short tales and who would become one of the most remarkable comic characters in the history of American fiction. Part of the tales' success springs from the suppleness that seems to have resulted from the uncomplicated narrative structure. Typically the nominal narrator, the college-educated, taciturn Ananias Boyd, briefly mentions a recent encounter with his friend, Simple, often in a neighborhood bar in Harlem.* (The tales rarely mention Boyd's first name.) Just as typically, the rest of the tale consists of a dialogue between Boyd and Simple. Simple usually dominates the dialogue to such a degree that it becomes a monologue, within which he may muse on a topical issue of the day; describe an argument with his estranged wife, his strong-willed girlfriend Joyce, his party-going girlfriend Zarita, or his Cousin Minnie; recall a specific misfortune; complain about "money problems"; offer opinions about such national topics as segregation or "black pride"; and otherwise "hold forth." Speaking in standard American English, Boyd functions as a kind of "straight man"; speaking in black dialect,* Simple often uses malapropisms and slang but often only feigns "simplicity," regularly showing himself to be something of a "sly fox," much wiser and more calculating than his garrulous, "uneducated" conversation at first suggests. The deceptive complexity of Simple parallels that of the stories themselves. As Harper suggests, "[T]he premise of the Simple stories appeals as the primary step in the human quest for peace, understanding, and common ground: two men from different educational backgrounds meet on an equal plane, exchange ideas, develop a friendship, and bridge the gap between them" (7). Another critic observes, "Drawing on several sources, including the blues,* the 'dozens,' vaudeville, folktales, and his own trained ear, Hughes invented a sub-genre of short fiction distinctively his own. In a sense, Simple was—to use a musical analogy—a deceptively sophisticated folk instrument with which Hughes was to achieve virtuoso status" (Ostrom, 35). Rampersad suggests that the Simple tales allowed Hughes one more way by which to raise the consciousness of the "black masses" about social and political issues affecting them—beginning (with the very first Simple story) by "leading the black masses to see their destiny linked to the fate of the Allies' fight against the Axis [in World War II]" (II, 62). Hughes himself saw the character Simple and the tales that feature him as one medium through which to represent everyday life in Harlem. "The facts are," he wrote, "that these tales are about a great many people—although they are stories about no specific persons as such. But it is impossible to live in Harlem and not know at least a 100 Simples, 50 Joyces, 25 Zaritas, a number of Boyds, and several Cousin Minnies—or reasonable facsimiles thereof" (Foreword, vii). Harper's book-length study examines the genesis and development of the Simple stories in detail, generates a detailed critical analysis, lists (in Appendix A) the topics of all the "Here to Yonder" columns between 1942 and 1950, and (in Appendix B) lists the table of contents of the first collection of Simple stories (*Simple Speaks His Mind*), with the corresponding dates of columns in which the stories first appeared. Harper also discusses the process whereby Hughes revised Simple stories and collected them in several books. In alphabetical order, the books are as follows: *The Best of Simple* (New York: Hill and Wang, 1961); *The Return of Simple*, edited by Akiba Sullivan Harper (New York: Hill and Wang, 1994); *Simple Speaks His Mind* (New York: Simon and Schuster, 1950); *Simple Stakes a Claim* (New York: Rinehart, 1957); *Simple Takes A Wife* (New York: Simon and Schuster, 1953); and *Simple's Uncle Sam* (New York: Hill and Wang, 1965). Harper's introduction to her edition, *The Return of Simple*, provides a good brief overview of the Simple stories, and the volume organizes the selected tales thematically: "Women in Simple's Life," "Race, Riots, Police, Prices, and Politics," "Africa and Black Pride," and "Parting Lines." The book also reprints the final Simple story, "Hail and Farewell," in which, with a characteristic malapropism, Simple announces to Boyd that he is moving from Harlem to "the suburbans." For the contents of particular volumes, see Ostrom. Each individual Simple story that was later collected in a book has its own entry in this encyclopedia as well, and the entry notes in which collection the story may be found. *See Simply Heavenly.*

Bibliography: Julian C. Carey, "Jesse B. Semple [*sic*] Revisited and Revised," *Phylon* 32 (Summer 1971), 159–163; Donna Akiba Sullivan Harper, *Not So Simple: The "Simple" Stories by Langston Hughes* (Columbia: University of Missouri Press, 1995); Lucia Shelia Hawthorne, "A Rhetoric of Human Rights as Expressed in the 'Simple Columns' by Langston Hughes" (Ph.D. dissertation, Pennsylvania State University, 1971); Langston Hughes, "Foreword" to *The Best of Simple*; Blyden Jackson, "A Word about Simple," in O'Daniel, 110–119; Hans Ostrom, "The Jesse B. Simple Stories and *Something in Common*," in Ostrom, 31–50; Rampersad, II; Carl Van Vechten, "Dialogues—But Barbed," in Mullen, 74–75.

Simple Takes a Wife (New York: Simon and Schuster, 1953). 240 pp. Collection of fifty-eight short stories. *See* Simple [Jesse B.] Stories. *See also* Van Vechten, Carl.

"Simple's Platform." Short story, included in the collections *Simple Stakes a Claim* and *The Best of Simple*. *See* Simple [Jesse B.] Stories.

Simple's Uncle Sam (New York: Hill and Wang, 1965). 180 pp. Collection of forty-six short stories. *See* Simple [Jesse B.] Stories. The book was reprinted in 1977 (Mattituck, NY: Aeonian Press). A revised edition appeared in 2000 (New York: Hill and Wang, 180 pp.). It is "revised" insofar as it includes an introduction by Akiba Sullivan Harper.

Simply Heavenly (1958). Musical play in two acts. Hughes wrote the script and lyrics for the songs, and David Martin composed the music. The play opened on May 21, 1958, at the United Order of the True Sisters Building in New York City. Stella Holt produced the play, Melvyn Stewart played the role of Jesse B. Simple, and Claudia McNeill played Joyce. Joshua Shelley directed. In August it enjoyed another run at the 48th Street Playhouse, and guitarist/singer Brownie McGhee joined the cast. Later in the year the play opened in London, produced by British actor Laurence Harvey, who had seen the New York production. The London production lost money. In 1959 producer David Susskind presented a televised version of the play on *Play of the Week*, a program on Channel 13 in New York City. The play is based on the Simple stories Hughes had begun writing in the 1940s and had collected in several volumes. The comic plot involves Simple's complicated relationships with the stable, no-nonsense Joyce and the wilder Zarita. The mild-mannered, urbane Boyd serves as Simple's advisor and comic "straight man," and a number of working-class Harlemites add texture to the story. These characters include the landladies Madame Butler and Mrs. Caddy, Hopkins, Pianist, Boddidly, Gitfiddle, Arcie, John Jasper, Ali Baba (a "root doctor" or homeopath), a policeman, and a nurse. The play was a success because audiences found it to be a warm, earthy comedy of Harlem,* but some critics found the characters too stereotypical (see Rampersad, II, 271–275). Smalley observes that "[t]hough its plot is of the slenderest comic fabric, its characters and straightforward humor make *Simply Heavenly* the definitive folk comedy of life in Harlem" (xv). *See* Simple [Jesse B.] Stories. *See also* "Beat It Out Monday"; "Did You Ever Hear the Blues?" "John Henry"; *Mule Bone*; "Simply Heavenly" (song).

Bibliography: Langston Hughes and David Martin [composer], *Simply Heavenly* (New York: Dramatists Play Service, 1959); Langston Hughes, *Simply Heavenly*, in *Five Plays by Langston Hughes*, edited with an introduction by Webster Smalley (Bloomington: Indiana University Press, 1963); Rampersad, II; Happy Traum, "Last Chorus: Brownie McGhee (1915–1996)," *Sing Out! The Folk Song Magazine* 41, no. 1 (May–July 1996), 28–29.

"Simply Heavenly." Short story, included in the collection *Simple Takes a Wife*. *See* Simple [Jesse B.] Stories.

"Simply Heavenly." Song, from *Simply Heavenly*. Hughes wrote the lyrics, and David Martin composed the music. ASCAP* lists the song as being published by the Bourne Company, and the song's ASCAP registry number is 470064034.

"Simply Love." Short story, included in the collections *Simple Takes a Wife* and *The Best of Simple*. *See* Simple [Jesse B.] Stories.

"Simply Simple." Short story, included in the collection *Simple's Uncle Sam*. *See* Simple [Jesse B.] Stories.

"Sinner." Five-line poem in black dialect.* Lines one and five are identical: "Have Mercy, Lord!" The speaker "confesses" to being "po' " (poor) and "black" as well as to being a sinner. Like "Shout," the poem represents a spontaneous utterance that might be heard in an African American church. It was first published in *Fine Clothes to the Jew*.

Bibliography: *CP*, 119.

"Sister." Poem. *See Montage of a Dream Deferred.*

Sister Johnson. In *Not Without Laughter* Sister Johnson is a neighbor of the Williams family in Stanton. In chapter 7 ("White Folks") she narrates a harrowing tale of racial backlash and violence that occurred while she lived in a town, nicknamed Crowville by whites, near Vicksburg, Mississippi.

"Sister Johnson Marches." Poem of three ballad* quatrains and a single concluding line, all in black dialect* and spoken by the title character, who is marching in a May Day (May 1) parade, celebrating the achievements of and remaining challenges faced by the "working class." It was first published in *Fight against War and Fascism* (May 1937).

Bibliography: *CP*, 197.

"Situation." Poem. *See Montage of a Dream Deferred.*

"Six-Bit Blues." Poem in two traditional blues* stanzas and in black dialect.* It works with two topics common to the blues: traveling and a short-term love affair. (A "bit" in this context refers to twelve and one-half cents; thus six bits is seventy-five cents, the cost—according to the poem—of a ticket on a "train that runs somewhere"). The poem was first published with an additional stanza in *Opportunity** (February 1939). It was also published in *Shakespeare in Harlem*. *Collected Poems* includes the additional stanza in an appendix. *See also* Revision, Process of, and Hughes.

Bibliography: *CP*, 211.

"Sketch for TV." Short story, included in the collection *Simple Stakes a Claim*. *See* Simple [Jesse B.] Stories.

"Slave." Poem of fourteen lines, intermittently rhymed. The implied first-person speaker appears to be a seller of heroin who "rides" to "the market of death" to pick up a "slave"—that is, a slave to heroin, an addict. The poem was first published in *Renaissance* (Winter 1962). *Collected Poems* includes information about slight revisions the poem underwent.

Bibliography: *CP*, 535.

"Slave on the Block." Short story. In this story an upper-middle-class white couple living in Harlem* in the late 1920s hire a young African American man to pose for a sculpture that the woman, Anne Carraway, is creating. It is titled "Slave on the Block," referring to an African slave being sold at auction in the American South. Anne and her husband Michael view themselves as enlightened with regard to race relations but are revealed to be interested only in exotic, even erotic, stereotypes of African Americans. The poem was first published in *Scribner's Magazine* (September 1933), 141–144. It was included in the collection *The Ways of White Folks* and was reprinted in *The Langston Hughes Reader* and *Langston Hughes: Short Stories*.

Bibliography: Ostrom, 10–11.

"Slave Song." Poem of twelve lines in four stanzas spoken by an African American slave who perceives stars in the East and West as providing no solace or guidance but who sees the North Star as a "guiding" star—that is, as representing the northern United States and freedom from slavery. It was first published in *Voices* (Winter 1949).

Bibliography: *CP*, 351.

"Slavery Chain Done Broke at Last." Song. *See Jerico-Jim Crow*.

"Sleep." Poem of eleven lines in free verse that concerns deep, peaceful sleep following lovemaking. It was first published in *Fields of Wonder*.

Bibliography: *CP*, 332.

"Slice Him Down." Short story set in Reno, Nevada. The narrative concerns two older African American men. They know each other well and are drinking together in a bar, but they argue, and the argument flares into a knife fight. Both men are so inebriated and so layered in clothing, however, that their knives are ineffectual. Rampersad notes that Arnold Gingrich, editor of *Esquire*, wanted to purchase the story. When Hughes was in Chicago in the spring of 1936, he met with Gingrich in the *Esquire* offices, where the editor offered him $150 for the story if Hughes would "tone down" the ending of the story. Hughes agreed to revise the ending but would not accept the money in person (even though his bank account was down to thirty-three cents). He instructed Gingrich to send the money to his (Hughes's) agent, Maxim Lieber (Rampersad, I, 324). The harmless knife fight, creating a comic ending to the story, may be the result, then, of Gingrich's suggestion. The story appeared later that spring in *Esquire* (May 1936) and is included in the collection *Laughing to Keep from Crying*. It was reprinted in *Langston Hughes: Short Stories*. *See also* "Something in Common."

Bibliography: Rampersad, I, 324.

"Sliver." Poem. *See Montage of a Dream Deferred.*

"Sliver of Sermon." Poem. *See Montage of a Dream Deferred.*

"Slum Dreams." Poem of twelve very short lines, intermittently rhymed. It represents dreams (aspirations) in a slum as being naïve, fragile, and ultimately not sustainable. It was first published under the title "Little Dreams" in the *New York Times* (May 8, 1964). *See* "Little Song on Housing"; "Restrictive Covenants."
Bibliography: *CP*, 541.

"Small Memory." Poem of thirteen short lines with one rhyme: "fine / mine." Narrated in the first person, the poem describes a dreamlike memory that includes "seven trees" and "winds that have / No ecstasies." The poem has a haunting, mysterious quality somewhat similar to that found in "A House in Taos." It was first published in *Renaissance* (August 1964).
Bibliography: *CP*, 542.

"Snail." Poem of two ballad* quatrains, except that the lines of the second quatrain are broken so as to stretch it to five lines. The poem is addressed rhetorically to a snail, which "knows" only "weather and rose." It was first published in the *Carmel Pine Cone* (July 18, 1941), with the standard number of lines in the second quatrain. *See also* "Snake."
Bibliography: *CP*, 233.

"Snake." Poem of seven lines. Lines two and four rhyme. The speaker admires the snake and feels guilty about wanting to kill it. The poem was first published in *Poetry Quarterly* (Spring 1931) and later included in *Shakespeare in Harlem*. *See* "Snail."
Bibliography: *CP*, 137.

"Snob." Poem of eight lines in a single stanza, intermittently rhymed. It is spoken to the snob, advising him or her not to "snub" "the other fellow" because such haughtiness might result in the loss of (the snob's) "good reputation." It was first published in the *Carmel Pine Cone* (June 27, 1941). It was also published in *Shakespeare in Harlem*. *See* "Ph.D."; "Poem for an Intellectual on His Way Up to Submit to His Lady."
Bibliography: *CP*, 232.

"So." Poem. *See* "Impasse."

"So Long." Poem. *See Montage of a Dream Deferred*; Revision, Process of, and Hughes.

"So Tired Blues." Poem in four stanzas that combine a ballad* quatrain with a refrain, " 'Cause I'm Tired / Tired as I can be," and variations thereof. It was first published in the *Amsterdam News* (November 1941). *See also* "America's Young Black Joe!"; "The Weary Blues."
Bibliography: *CP*, 570.

Sold Away (1938). Play. Hughes began writing *Sold Away* in 1938, the same year in which he wrote the plays *Front Porch* and *De Organizer*. *Sold Away* was to have concerned slavery. Hughes did not complete it. A manuscript is held in the Langston Hughes Papers, James Weldon Johnson Memorial Collection, Beinecke Library, Yale University.
Bibliography: Rampersad, I, 364.

"Soldiers from Many Lands United in Spanish Fight." Newspaper article. *See Baltimore Afro American.*

"Soledad." Poem, subtitled "A Cuban Portrait." Addressed rhetorically to a young woman, Soledad, the poem depicts her as "deeply scarred" emotionally, her eyes "full" of "passion and pain" and "lies." It was first published in *Opportunity** (December 1925). In *The Big Sea* Hughes describes some of his experiences in Cuba. See *Cuba Libre*; Rumba.
Bibliography: *CP*, 57.

"Some Day." Poem of twenty-four lines, intermittently rhymed, in three stanzas, although the second stanza consists of one line only. The first part of the poem bemoans the arrival of another war (World War II), but the second half predicts that one day humans will evolve beyond war. The poem was first published in *Span* (July 1941).
Bibliography: *CP*, 236.

"Somehow I Never Could Believe." Song, from *Street Scene*. Hughes wrote the lyrics, and Kurt Weill* composed the music. ASCAP* lists the song as being published by Chappell, Inc., and by Hampshire House Publishers. The song's ASCAP registry number is 490100726.

"Something in Common." Short story. It is a brief comic tale set in a Hong Kong bar. An elderly black man and an elderly white man—both American—get into a scuffle. The British bartender breaks up the fight and kicks them out of the bar. The two then join forces, return, and confront the bartender—nationalism winning out over racism for the moment. The story was included in the collections *Laughing to Keep from Crying* and *Something in Common and Other Stories* and was reprinted in *Langston Hughes: Short Stories*. *See also* "Slice Him Down."

Something in Common and Other Stories (New York: Hill and Wang, 1963). 236 pp. Collection of short stories. It includes many stories previously published in *The Ways of White Folks* and *Laughing to Keep from Crying*. Stories it contains that were not previously published in book form include "Blessed Assurance," "Breakfast in Virginia," "Early Autumn," "Fine Accommodations," "Gumption," "The Gun," "His Last Affair," "No Place to Make Love," "Rock, Church," and "Sorrow for a Midget." Each of these stories has its own entry in the encyclopedia. See also *Langston Hughes: Short Stories*.

Bibliography: Ostrom, 44–50.

"Something to Lean On." Short story, included in the collection *Simple Speaks His Mind*. *See* Simple [Jesse B.] Stories.

"Sometimes I Wonder." Short story, included in the collections *Simple Takes a Wife* and *The Best of Simple*. *See* Simple [Jesse B.] Stories.

"Song." Poem of two quatrains in rhyming couplets, although Hughes breaks off the last two words of stanza two to create a fifth line. Addressed rhetorically to a "Lovely, dark, and lonely" young woman, the poem encourages her to liberate herself by living fully and making demands of life. It was published in *Survey Graphic* (March 1, 1925). *See* Locke, Alain.

Bibliography: *CP*, 45.

"Song after Lynching." Poem in five ballad* stanzas. It critiques "white folks[']" use of words such as "democracy," "liberty," and "justice" (which appear in boldface in the poem), a use the poem portrays as hypocritical in an era that tolerates Jim Crow laws* and lynching.* The poem was circulated by the Associated Negro Press in July 1943. *See* "America's Young Black Joe!"; "Song for a Dark Girl."

Bibliography: *CP*, 584.

"Song for a Banjo Dance." Poem of twenty-seven lines in three stanzas, intermittently rhymed and in black dialect.* It is "sung" by the minstrel and is addressed to "Liza," exhorting her to dance. Taj Mahal set the poem to music and performed it in the 1991 production of *Mule Bone*. Although folk or "delta" blues* are often associated with the acoustic guitar, partly because of Robert Johnson's unprecedented use of that instrument in the 1920s and 1930s, the banjo in fact figured significantly in early blues music, and this poem represents the exuberance of banjo blues music, especially as it might have been played in "juke* joints" (rural nightclubs). The poem was first published in *Crisis** (October 1922). *See* "Juice Joint: Northern City"; "Ma Man"; *Mule Bone*.

Bibliography/Discography: *Black Banjo Songsters* [audio compact disc] (Washington, DC: Smithsonian Folkways, 1998): ASIN B000001DJP; *CP*, 29; Taj Mahal, *Mule Bone:*

Music Composed and Performed by Taj Mahal, Lyrics by Langston Hughes [compact disc] (Grammavision, 1991; distributed by Rhino Records, Santa Monica, CA), R279432.

"Song for a Dark Girl." Poem in three ballad* stanzas, each beginning with the lines "Way down South in Dixie / (Break the heart of me)." The poem is narrated by a young woman, presumably the "dark girl," whose lover has been lynched in the South. It was first published in the *Saturday Review of Literature* (April 19, 1927). Later, Ricky Ian Gordon set the poem to music. ASCAP* lists the song as being published by the Williamson Music Company; the song's ASCAP registry number is 490974408. Audra McDonald recorded the song. *See* "Daybreak in Alabama"; Lynching; "Song after Lynching."

Bibliography/Discography: *CP*, 104; Audra McDonald, "Song for a Dark Girl," in *Way Back to Paradise* [compact disc] (New York: Nonesuch Records, 1998): Nonesuch 79482-2; Audra McDonald, *Way Back to Paradise* [musical score] (Milwaukee: Hal Leonard, 1999).

"Song for Billie Holiday." Poem of twenty lines in three stanzas that are structurally quite distinct from one another. The narrator addresses his or her own "sadness" and refers indirectly (not by name) to Billie Holiday and her music. The editors of *Collected Poems* note that the poem was written after Holiday's first arrest for possession of illegal drugs (probably heroin). It was first published in *One-Way Ticket*.

Bibliography: *CP*, 360.

"Song for Ourselves." Twelve-line poem that links (and expresses despair concerning) the fates of Czechoslovakia, Ethiopia, and Spain, three nations that, at the time, had been taken over by fascist forces, the first two via invasion, by Germany and Italy, respectively, the third by means of civil war. It was first published in the *New York Post* (September 19, 1938). *See Baltimore Afro American*; "Broadcast on Ethiopia"; "Call of Ethiopia;" "Emperor Hailie Salassie"; "Gangsters"; *I Wonder As I Wander*, (320 and ff.); "Letter from Spain"; "Shall the Good Go Down?"; "Song of Spain."

Bibliography: *CP*, 207.

"Song for a Suicide." Poem. *See* "Exits."

"Song of Adoration." Poem of thirty-two lines in six stanzas that are essentially based on a limerick structure, except with longer lines. The poem is deeply ironic insofar as the speaker wishes to be "a white man" and lists the activities that would thereby be open to him, all of which are racist. It was circulated by the Associated Negro Press in 1943. *See* "America's Young Black Joe!"

Bibliography: *CP*, 587; "Limerick," in Ron Padgett, *A Handbook of Poetic Forms* (New York: Teachers and Writers Collaborative, 1987), 98–99.

"Song of Spain." Poem of eighty-four lines in free-verse stanzas of widely varying length. The rhetoric of the poem is also mixed, shifting from lyrical to reportorial to colloquial to ecstatic as the speaker struggles to decide how to fashion a song of Spain, in so doing showing Spain to be a country of baffling contradictions in art, politics, and culture. The poem was first published in *International Literature* (no. 6, 1937). *See also Baltimore Afro American*; "Hero— International Brigade"; *I Wonder As I Wander* (338); "Letter from Spain"; Robeson, Paul; "Shall the Good Go Down?"; "Spain's Martyred Poet, García Lorca."

Bibliography: *CP*, 195.

"Song of the Refugee Road." Poem of thirty lines, chiefly in rhymed couplets but in lines of varying length and rhythm. There are no stanza breaks. Spoken by a collective persona* representing Chinese, European Jewish, and Ethiopian refugees in particular but all political refugees in general, the poem expresses despair and alienation. It was circulated by the Associated Negro Press in 1940. *See* "America's Young Black Joe!" *See also* "Broadcast on Ethiopia"; "Call of Ethiopia"; "Emperor Hailie Salassie"; "Here to Yonder"; "Roar China!" "Shall the Good Go Down?"

Bibliography: *CP*, 565.

"Song of the Revolution." Poem in five traditional ballad* stanzas. It expresses idealistic hope for a worldwide revolution of "the masses" that will liberate workers and break "the bonds of the darker races." It was first published in *Negro Worker* (March 1933). *See also Angelo Herndon Jones*; "Ballads of Lenin"; "Chant for Tom Mooney"; *Don't You Want to Be Free?; Front Porch*; "Goodbye Christ"; "Good Morning Revolution"; "Lenin"; "A New Song"; "One More 'S' in the U.S.A"; "Revolution"; "Sister Johnson Marches"; "Wait." *See also* John Reed Club; Marxism; Politics.

Bibliography: *CP*, 170.

"Song to a Negro Wash-woman." Free-verse poem of forty-five lines. In an unusual variation on his use of a collective persona,* Hughes has the speaker of this poem address "a" Negro wash-woman who is actually many such women the speaker has seen in his travels. She/they are portrayed as selfless, hardworking, religious figures, unrecognized as significant pillars of African American communities because of their perseverance, faith, and strength, but the poem also represents them as symbols of limited economic opportunity for blacks in the United States. It was first published in *Crisis** (January 1925).

Bibliography: *CP*, 41.

Songs. There are at least 135 works with which Hughes was involved that qualify as "songs," not necessarily including poems with "song" in the title that may or may not have been set to music. These songs can be sorted into roughly three categories: (1) poems by Hughes that were later set to music by a composer; (2) songs for which Hughes wrote original lyrics; and (3) songs for which Hughes wrote original lyrics but that were part of a larger work, such as an opera or musical play. Hughes almost never wrote the music for song versions of his poems or for original lyrics he wrote. Regarding Hughes's meager capacity to write music, *see* Rampersad (II, 372). However, Hughes's interest in music, his understanding of songwriting, and his ability to work well with a wide variety of composers were profound and lifelong. Especially for American lyricists and composers, ASCAP* is the most comprehensive, reliable source of information about authorship, but no source contains complete information about Hughes's extensive, almost tireless, work as a lyricist and as a poet deeply interested in song forms. (Ironically, the one song Rampersad cites as probably having music written by Hughes is not listed with ASCAP—"Freedom Land," from *Jerico-Jim Crow*.) The following checklist, though by no means complete, nonetheless reflects Hughes's considerable achievement both as a lyricist and as a poet whose work attracted a wide variety of composers. It also represents the vast majority of titles with which Hughes is associated as a coauthor of record. The checklist contains titles of songs from musical plays, including *Mule Bone*, *Simply Heavenly*, and *Street Scene*. All titles on the list have their separate entries elsewhere in the encyclopedia, although in the case of poems later set to music, information about the resulting song appears in the entry for the poem. Entries include the names of Hughes's cowriters and, where applicable, of a song's publisher(s). Many but not all entries also include the registry number for each title listed with ASCAP—the ASCAP registry number being, especially for works by American songwriters, a rough counterpart to an ISBN number for published books. In entries for a song that is known to have been recorded, information about the recording is also given wherever possible. *See* Bonds, Margaret; Drama; Johnson, James P.; Musical Plays; Operas; Orchestral Pieces/ Oratorios; *Selected Songs for High Voice*; Still, William Grant; Weill, Kurt.

Checklist of Song Titles (Including Poems Set to Music)

"African Dance"

"Afro-American Fragment"

"Ain't It Awful, the Heat"

"April Rain"

"At the Feet o' Jesus"

"Backlash Blues"

"Ballad of Adam and Eve"

"Ballad of Rabbi Henry Cohen"

Ballad of the Brown King

"Ballad of the Fortune Teller"

"Beat It Out Monday"

"Bewilderment"

"A Black Pierrot"

"Blue Monday"

"Blues at the Waldorf"

"Blues Montage"

"Bound No'th Blues"

"A Boy like You"

"Brass Spittoons"

"Breath of a Rose"

"John Henry"

"Joy"

"Joy to the World"

"Jubilee"

"Lament"

"Lament over Love"

"Let Me Take You for a Ride"

"Let Things Be (Like They Was)"

"Let's Ball a While"

"Life Is Fine"

"Litany"

"Little Lyric (*of Great Importance*)"

"Little Old Letter"

"Lonely House"

"Lonely People"

"Look for the Morning Star"

"Louisiana"

"Love Can Hurt You"

"Love Is like Whiskey"

"Love Song for Lucinda"

"Lovely Dark and Lonely One"

"Lullaby"

"Madam and the Census Man"

"Madam and the Fortune Teller"

"Madam and the Minister"

"Madam and the Rent Man"

"Madam and the Wrong Visitor"

"Madam to You"

"Madam and Daughter"

"Mary Had a Little Baby"

"Me and the Mule"

"Meine dunklen Hande"

"The Man in My Life"

"Miss Blues's Child"

"Mississippi Monologue"

"Moon Faced, Starry Eyed"

"Morning"

"Morning After"

"Mortal Storm"

"Mother to Son"

"The Murder"

"My Lord Not Wanted"

"My People"

"Negro Lament on Poems of Langston Hughes"

"The Negro Speaks of Rivers"

"Night Song"

"Night Time"

"Oh Let America"

"Oh Officer"

"Opening Blues"

"Poem"

"Port Town"

"Red Sun Blues"

"Refugee in America"

"Remember That I Care"

"Rise Up Shepherd and Follow"

"Sad Song in de Air"

"Sail Sail Sail" [*sic*]

"Scat Cat"

"Sea Calm"

"Search"

"Shadow of the Blues"

"Shake Your Brown Feet Honey"

"She Shouldn't Be Staying Out Nights"

"Signifyin' Natives"

"Silhouette"

"Silver Rain"

"Simply Heavenly"

"Slavery Chain Done Broke at Last"

"Somehow I Never Could Believe"

"Song for a Dark Girl"

"Songs of O"

"Songs through the Long Summer Day"

"Songs to a Dark Virgin"

"Strange Hurt"

"Strollin' "

"Such a Little King"

"Swing Time at the Savoy"

Symphonische Gesänge (Opus 20)

"Tambourines to Glory"

"Tell Me Your Story"

"Testament"

"Three by Langston"

"Three Dream Portraits"

"Three Songs on Poems of Langston Hughes"

"To a Dead Soldier"

"Torch Song"

"Wait for Me"

"Waltz"

"The Weary Blues"

"We'll Go Away Together"

"What Good Would the Moon Be?"

"When a Woman Has a Baby"

"When I'm in a Quiet Mood"

"The Woman Who Lived Up There"

"Words like Freedom"

"Wouldn't You Like to Be on Broadway?"

"Wrapped in a Ribbon, Tied in a Bow"

"[America's] Young Black Joe"

"Songs." Eight-line poem in three stanzas written in free verse. The first two lines—"I sat there singing her / Songs in the dark"—may be read two ways: singing songs that belong to "her" or singing songs to her. The poem was first published in *Fields of Wonder*. Later, Robert Owens set this poem, "In Time of Silver Rain," "Fulfillment," "Carolina Cabin," "Night Song," and "Silence," to music in the song cycle, *Silver Rain*.

Bibliography: *CP*, 332; Robert Owens [composer], *Silver Rain: Song Cycle for Tenor and Piano* (Munich: Orlando-Musikverlag, 1975).

"Songs Called the Blues." Essay that offers a brief appreciation of the blues.* It was first published in *Phylon* (1941) and was reprinted in *The Langston Hughes Reader*. *See also* "I remember the Blues"; "Maker of the Blues."

"Songs of O." Song. ASCAP* lists this as a single title and lists the following cowriters, not distinguishing between lyricists and composers: Hughes, Warren Frank Benson, Archibald MacLeish, Louise Bogan, Shirley Schoonover, and Kenneth Patchen. (Hughes, MacLeish, Bogan, and Patchen are well-known twentieth-century American poets.) The exact nature of Hughes's contribution is unclear. ASCAP* lists no publisher for the song, but the ASCAP registry number is 490501650.

Songs through the Long Summer Day. Compilation of songs by Jay Anthony Gach. This title is given a single entry by ASCAP.* Authors listed are Hughes, Gustav Mahler, Ezra Pound, James Whitcomb Riley, Charlotte Mew, and Virgil. The Hughes poem set to music in the compilation is "Childhood Memories."

No publisher is listed, but the ASCAP registry number for *Songs through the Long Summer Day* is 490687184. The research library of the New York Public Library holds a manuscript of the musical score.

"Songs to the Dark Virgin." Song. Hughes wrote the lyrics, and Florence Price composed the music. ASCAP* lists no publisher for the song, but does list "Y. Marcoulescou" as having performed it, although no information about a recording is provided. The song's ASCAP registry number is 490114604. The Research Library of the New York Public Library contains "Songs, Piano and Organ Music" by Florence Price, and "Songs to the Dark Virgin" is included in this material.

Sonnet. Hughes published three sonnets, "Pennsylvania Station," "Ph.D.," and "Search." "Seven Moments of Love" is subtitled "An Un-sonnet Sequence in Blues" and features seven separate poems that improvise extensively on the traditional sonnet form. *See* "Shakespeare in Harlem."

"Sorrow for a Midget." Short story. It is narrated by an unnamed, unsentimental man who has been employed by a bedridden woman to take care of her. To him she looks like "a dried-up child," and he dubs her "Countess Midget." Her long-lost son—adopted, it turns out—shows up, chiefly interested in an inheritance, and the narrator meditates cynically on the situation. The story was included in the collection *Something in Common and Other Stories* and was reprinted in *Langston Hughes: Short Stories*.

Bibliography: Ostrom, 45–46.

"Soul Food." Short story, included in the collection *Simple's Uncle Sam. See* Simple [Jesse B.] Stories.

Soul Gone Home (1937). Play in one act. Only four pages long, the play features two main characters, "Son" and "Mother." The son has died in the mother's apartment, which Hughes describes as being in a "tenement" and as being "bare, ugly, dirty." Although the son is dead, he speaks; one way to interpret the play is that the mother imagines that he speaks. Smalley suggests that the play mixes fantasy and naturalism to comment indirectly on the plight of impoverished, oppressed African Americans. He writes, "The dominance of the white culture is suggested only by the arrival of ambulance attendants, who are white as the mother knew they would be. The tragedy is of a people so repressed that they can no longer love, and the ironic implications build to a shocking climax" (xii). The play was first published in *One Act Play* magazine (July 1937). It was produced by the Burlap Summer Theatre at Club Baron, 437 Lenox Avenue, New York City, on July 9, 1953.

Bibliography: Hicklin, 39–41; Langston Hughes, *Soul Gone Home*, in *Five Plays by Langston Hughes*, edited with an introduction by Webster Smalley (Bloomington: Indiana University Press, 1963); Rampersad, I, 355.

"The South." Poem of twenty-eight lines, intermittently rhymed. It is spoken by a first-person narrator, a collective persona* representing African Americans. The South (southern United States) is personified as a woman who is at once beautiful and cruel, seductive and diseased. The poem was first published in *Crisis** (June 1922) and was included in *The Weary Blues*.

Bibliography: *CP*, 26.

"Southern Gentlemen, White Prostitutes, Mill Owners, and Negroes." Essay that is one of several expressions of protest Hughes wrote in response to the plight of the Scottsboro Boys.* There was reason to believe that the women the Scottsboro Boys were falsely accused of raping were prostitutes. One of Hughes's points in the essay, therefore, is that low wages paid to white women by mill owners in the South created a greater likelihood of women turning to prostitution. As in much of his writing during the 1930s, then, Hughes connects issues of race and class struggle in the essay. It was first published under the title "Southern Gentlemen, White Women, and Black Boys" in *Contempo* (November 1931). In *I Wonder As I Wander* Hughes describes the circumstances whereby the essay appeared in *Contempo* and mentions the editors of the magazine, Miles Abernathy and Anthony Buttita. *See also* "Christ in Alabama"; "Scottsboro"; *Scottsboro Limited*.

Bibliography: *I Wonder As I Wander*, 45; Rampersad, I, 224–225.

"Southern Gentlemen, White Women, and Black Boys." *See* "Southern Gentlemen, White Prostitutes, Mill Owners, and Negroes."

"Southern Mammy Sings." Poem in four stanzas of six lines each: a ballad* quatrain followed by a two-line refrain. In black dialect* the speaker, an African American woman, expresses deep frustration toward "white folks" because of their propensity toward violence (specifically lynching*) and their apparent lack of "heart." The poem was first published in *Poetry* (May 1941). It was also published in *Million* (no. 1, 1944), under the title "Southern Mammy Song," and in *Shakespeare in Harlem*, under the title "Southern Mammy Sings."

Bibliography: *CP*, 227, 650.

"Southern Mammy Song." *See* "Southern Mammy Sings."

"Southern Negro Speaks." Poem of twenty lines in black dialect and in ballad* quatrains but with no stanza breaks. The collective persona,* representing "Southern Negroes" in general, is puzzled that the United States fights in Europe (in World War II) for freedom but does not fight for African American freedom at home. The poem was first published in *Opportunity** (October 1941).

Bibliography: *CP*, 238.

"The Soviet Union." Essay in which Hughes concedes that the Soviet Union is "no paradise" and emphasizes that he is not a Communist, but—based on firsthand observations in his travels there—praises the Soviet Union for having universal health care, no equivalent to Jim Crow laws,* almost no prostitution, fairness for workers, and almost no anti-Semitism. He harshly criticizes a speech by William Fulbright, U.S. senator from Arkansas, who attacked the Soviet Union's lack of freedom. Hughes observes that African Americans in Arkansas have fewer freedoms and less opportunity than Soviet citizens. The essay was first published in *Crisis** (June 1, 1946) and was reprinted in Berry.

Bibliography: Berry, 84–86.

"The Soviet Union and Color." Essay in which Hughes suggests that since the Bolshevik Revolution, the Soviet Union has attempted with great success to overturn racist laws, practices, and policies, including the equivalent of Jim Crow laws,* one effect of which had been to segregate, according to race and/or ethnic background, public transportation. The short essay is based on observations Hughes made while he traveled in the Soviet Union (*see The Big Sea*). It was first published in the *Chicago Defender** (June 15, 1946) (*see* "Here to Yonder") and was reprinted in Berry.

Bibliography: Berry, 88–90.

"The Soviet Union and Health." Essay. Hughes recounts a visit, in 1946, to the Republic of Uzbekistan in the Soviet Union. He describes an effective free health clinic there, one overseen by "a young and quite beautiful Russian nurse" (Berry, 92). He also recalls receiving treatment for a toothache—without charge, by virtue of his temporary membership in the Soviet Writers' Union. Hughes contrasts Soviet health care with that in the United States. He argues that American health care is undermined by racism that excludes many patients from certain hospitals and many potential doctors from medical schools. The essay first appeared in the *Chicago Defender* (July 20, 1946). It was later reprinted in Berry. *See* "Faults of The Soviet Union"; "Light and the Soviet Union"; "The Soviet Union and Color"; "The Soviet Union and Jews"; "The Soviet Union and Women."

Bibliography: Berry, 92–94.

"The Soviet Union and Jews." Essay. Hughes begins by recalling how, even as a child, he was aware of anti-Semitism in Europe, chiefly because his grand-mother would read him accounts in newspapers of hate crimes against Jews in Russia and Poland. He further remembers thinking that African Americans and Jews shared parallel histories of discrimination. The rest of the essay praises what he perceives, based on his travels to the Soviet Union, as its significant efforts to outlaw anti-Semitism and protect the rights of all ethnic groups. The essay was first published in the *Chicago Defender** (June 8, 1946) and was reprinted in Berry.

Bibliography: Berry, 86–88.

"The Soviet Union and Women." Essay. Hughes reports the extent to which women's lives have improved under Soviet Socialist government. Specifically, he discusses improvements in employment opportunities, education, and the arts. He also discusses the dissolution of harems in Soviet Central Asia. The essay was first published in the *Chicago Defender* (July 20, 1946) and was reprinted in Berry. *See* "Faults of the Soviet Union"; "Light and the Soviet Union"; "The Soviet Union and Color"; "The Soviet Union and Health"; "The Soviet Union and Jews"; Women in Hughes's Writing.

Bibliography: Berry, 90–92.

"Spain's Martyred Poet, García Lorca" (1936). Radio broadcast/essay. Reporting from Madrid in 1936 during the Spanish Civil War, Hughes announces the death of Lorca, provides an overview of his career, describes his poetry, and—relying on an alleged eyewitness account—describes the murder of Lorca. As Berry points out, however, subsequent research has revealed that the precise circumstances of Lorca's death remain cloudy, although there is no doubt that he died at the hands of Franco's fascist soldiers. Reprinted in Berry as an essay, the broadcast (during which Hughes also read translations of several Lorca poems) is an interesting mixture of reporting, eulogy, and criticism. *See Baltimore Afro American; Blood Wedding* and *Yerma* (one entry); *Lorca: Gypsy Ballads.*

Bibliography: Berry, 114–117.

"Spanish Blood." Short story that concerns the difficulties of a young African American named Valerio Gutierrez, whose Puerto Rican father abandoned the family when Valerio was very young. Valerio begins to make his way in Harlem* by dancing at private parties to which many white New Yorkers come, but he runs afoul of organized crime. The story was first published in *Metropolis* (December 29, 1934), was included in the collection *Laughing to Keep from Crying*, and was reprinted in *Langston Hughes: Short Stories.*

Spanish Civil War, Hughes's Coverage of. *See Baltimore Afro American*; "Laughter in Madrid." *See also* "Air Raid: Barcelona"; *I Wonder As I Wander;*

"Madrid"; "Moonlight in Valencia: Civil War"; "Spain's Martyred Poet, García Lorca."

"Speaking of Food." Poem of eighteen lines in four ballad* stanzas and a concluding couplet. Its implied argument is that U.S. citizens should not complain about food shortages during World War II but should think first of the food needed by the military. It was first published in the *Baltimore Afro American** (April 3, 1943). *See* "America's Young Black Joe."

Bibliography: *CP*, 580–581.

"Special Bulletin." Poem of twenty-three short lines in free verse. It develops an explicit comparison between the Ku Klux Klan* and German Nazis. It was first published in *The Panther and the Lash*.

Bibliography: *CP*, 556.

Spencer, Anne (1882–1975). American poet and librarian. Spencer was a native of West Virginia and graduated from the Virginia Seminary and College in Lynchburg, Virginia. Because she was not a prolific poet and because she resided in Lynchburg, Spencer was artistically and geographically at the periphery of the Harlem Renaissance.* Nonetheless, her poem "Lady, Lady" appeared in the important anthology *The New Negro*, edited by Alain Locke.* She also developed a lasting friendship with W.E.B. Du Bois.* She worked as a librarian at Dunbar High School in Lynchburg, retiring from that position in 1943. *See* "Anne Spencer's Table."

Bibliography: J. Lee Greene, *Time's Unfolding Garden: Anne Spencer's Life and Poetry* (Baton Rouge: Louisiana State University Press, 1977) (includes previously uncollected poems, 175–197); Anne Spencer, "Lady, Lady" [poem], in Lewis, *HRR*, 299.

Spingarn, Arthur (1878–1971). American lawyer and civil-rights activist. Spingarn was born in New York City, his father having already accumulated considerable wealth in the tobacco industry. He graduated from Columbia University* in 1897 and took a degree in law from Columbia's School of Law three years later. From 1911 to 1940 he served as vice president of the NAACP* and directed its strategy for combating racism through legal means. He served as president of the NAACP from 1940 to 1965. Along with Thurgood Marshall,* Spingarn is considered to have been the driving force behind the NAACP's numerous legal victories in the area of civil rights, including successful arguments before the Supreme Court in the *Brown v. Board of Education** decisions. Spingarn and Hughes were good friends, and Spingarn advised Hughes during the latter's disagreement with Zora Neale Hurston* over *Mule Bone* and when Hughes was called to testify by Senator Joseph McCarthy's Permanent Sub-Committee on Investigations (*see* McCarthyism). The NAACP's annual award-

ing of the Spingarn Medal, recognizing individuals who work on behalf of social equality and civil rights, first occurred in 1914. Hughes won the award in 1959.
Bibliography: Lewis, *HRR*, xxv–xxviii.

Spingarn Medal. An award Hughes received from the NAACP.* *See* Spingarn, Arthur.

"Spirituals." Poem of sixteen lines in stanzas of varying length. It pays homage to African American spirituals, their long history and deep cultural roots, and their power. The line "Song is a strong thing" is repeated. The poem was first published in *Bookman* (February 1927). *See also The Book of Negro Folklore; My Lord What a Mornin'*; Religion.
Bibliography: *CP*, 102.

"Sport." Poem of sixteen lines in free verse. "Sport" in this case refers to a man who enjoys nightlife and cabarets. The poem suggests that the man sees everything—including death and eternity—in terms of his "sporting life." It was first published in *Fine Clothes to the Jew. See* Religion.
Bibliography: *CP*, 116.

"Spring for Lovers." Poem of six lines in one stanza, a ballad* quatrain followed by a rhyming couplet. The speaker, addressing his or her lover, suggests that notions of love's permanence are delusional. The poem was first published in *Crisis** (July 1930).
Bibliography: *CP*, 128.

"Springtime." Short story, included in *The Best of Simple. See* Simple [Jesse B.] Stories.

"S-sss-ss-sh!" Rhyming poem of twenty-one lines in seven stanzas. It concerns an out-of-wedlock pregnancy, which the mother and baby believe is "fun," but which scandalizes the family and the community. It was first published in *One-Way Ticket. See also* "Cora Unashamed."
Bibliography: *CP*, 357.

"Staggering Figures." Short story, included in the collection *Simple Takes a Wife. See* Simple [Jesse B.] Stories.

"Stalingrad: 1942." Poem of over two pages, intermittently rhymed. It exhorts the reader to assist the Russian city of Stalingrad, which had been attacked by German Nazi forces, and it upbraids countries—implicitly including the United States—for not opening a "second [European] front" in World War II. The poem also refers to other countries besieged by fascist forces: Ethiopia, Spain, and

Czechoslovakia. It was first published in *War Poems of the United Nations*, edited by Joy Davidman (New York: Dial Press, 1943), 321–324. *See also Baltimore Afro American*; "Call of Ethiopia"; "Hero—International Brigade"; "Letter from Spain"; Politics.

Bibliography: *CP*, 285–288.

"The Star Decides." Short story. It is one of several stories written in 1941 that Rampersad characterizes as "illuminations of the blues* ideal" and that emphasize "the mediation of violence by humor." *See* "Mysterious Madame Shanghai"; "Sailor Ashore"; "Two at the Bar."

"Star Seeker." Poem of ten lines in two stanzas. The speaker is a self-described "star seeker" or person who had grand dreams, for which he has only burned hands and scars to show. The poem was first published in the *New York Herald Tribune* (February 14, 1926).

Bibliography: *CP*, 64.

"Stars." Poem of eleven lines in free verse. The speaker implores a young "dark boy" living in Harlem* to "reach up" and "take a star." The poem was first published in *Lincoln University News* (November 1926) and was reprinted in *The Block*.

Bibliography: *CP*, 85.

"Statement." Poem of three lines and a total of eleven words. It concerns urban violence. It was first published in *Shakespeare in Harlem*.

Bibliography: *CP*, 247.

"Statement in Round Numbers Concerning the Relative Merits of 'Way Down South.' " *See Way Down South*.

"Statutes and Statues." Short story, included in the collection *Simple's Uncle Sam. See* Simple [Jesse B.] Stories.

"Steel Mills." Poem of fourteen short lines in free verse that focuses chiefly on how the mills "grind away the lives" of the mill workers. It was first published in the *Messenger** (February 1925). In *The Big Sea* Hughes reports having written the poem while he was in high school.

Bibliography: *The Big Sea*, 29; *CP*, 43, 625.

Still, William Grant (1895–1978). American composer and conductor who was the first African American to conduct a major symphony orchestra. Still was a native of Mississippi. He studied at Wilberforce University, Oberlin College, and the New England Conservatory of Music. He won both Rosenwald and

Guggenheim fellowships. His other credits include Phi Beta Sigma's George Washington Carver Achievement Award and the National Association for American Composers Achievement Award. He played in the orchestra for the landmark Broadway musical *Shuffle Along*, on which Noble Sissle (an alumnus of Cleveland's Central High School,* which Hughes attended) and Eubie Blake collaborated. His music compositions included the ballet *Sahdji, Afro American Symphony*, and *A Bayou Legend*, an opera. He composed the music for *Troubled Island*, the opera based on Hughes's play of the same title, and he set Hughes's poems "A Black Pierrot" and "Breath of a Rose" to music. Still died on December 4, 1978, in Los Angeles. Concerning the relationship between Hughes and Still, *see Troubled Island* (opera).

Bibliography: Catherine Parsons Smith, " 'Harlem Renaissance Man' Revisited: The Politics of Race and Class in William Grant Still's Late Career," *American Music* 15, no. 3 (Fall 1997) 381–406.

"Still Here." Rhyming poem of eight lines, with a hint of black dialect.* The speaker refers to some of the hardships he has endured and concludes by reasserting his resilience. The poem was first published in *Jim Crow's Last Stand* and was revised slightly before appearing in *One-Way Ticket* and *The Panther and the Lash*. The editors of *Collected Poems* note these revisions and published the later version.

Bibliography: *CP*, 295, 659.

"Stokely Malcolm Me [sic]." Poem of twenty-one lines in three stanzas. It features the rare use in Hughes's poetry of "i" in place of "I" for the first-person pronoun. The speaker is upset but confused and speaks directly to "Stokely" (Carmichael), the political activist, toward the end of the poem. Although the title of the poem alludes to Malcolm X, he is not mentioned in the poem. The last three lines consist entirely of question marks. The poem was first published in *The Panther and the Lash*.

Bibliography: *CP*, 561.

"Stony Lonesome." Poem of twenty-one lines in black dialect,* with phrasing influenced by the blues.* The speaker mourns the death of "Cordelia," who has gone to the graveyard, otherwise known as "stony lonesome ground," leaving behind Buddy Jones to "struggle by his self." The poem was first published under the title "Death Chant" in the *Carmel Pine Cone* (March 2, 1941). It was also published in *Shakespeare in Harlem*.

Bibliography: *CP*, 230.

The Story of Jazz (New York: Folkways Records, 1955). Audio recording (long-playing vinyl record). It features Hughes narrating selections from *The First Book of Jazz*. The recording was intended as a companion to the book. It was reissued in audiocassette format in 1985 (serial number FC-7312) and on compact disc in 1999. *See* Audio Recordings of Hughes.

Bibliography: Rampersad, II, 243.

"Strange Hurt." Poem of fifteen lines in three stanzas with a subtle rhyme scheme. Arguably one of Hughes's most haunting poems, it concerns a woman whose "strange" emotional pain drives her to prefer "rain" to "shelter from rain" and otherwise behave in ways that seem irrational or at least counterintuitive. It was first published in the *New York Herald Tribune* (February 14, 1926) under the title "Strange Hurt She Knew." Later, Ricky Ian Gordon set the poem to music. ASCAP* lists the song as being published by the Williamson Music Company, and the song's ASCAP registry number is 490783767. The published score contains a short and a long version of the song. *See* "Genius Child."

Bibliography: *CP*, 63; Ricky Ian Gordon, *Genius Child: A Cycle of 10 Songs* (New York: Williamson Music Company, 1992).

"Strange Hurt She Knew." Poem. *See* "Strange Hurt."

"Stranger in Town." Rhyming poem of eighteen lines in three stanzas, with phrasing influenced by the blues.* The speaker is new in town, lonely, and "nobody's beau." He asks his boardinghouse landlady if he has "privileges," referring to permission to entertain female guests in his room. She replies "No," but the speaker admits that he has no one to invite to his room anyway. The poem was first published in *One-Way Ticket*.

Bibliography: *CP*, 359.

Street Scene (1946). Opera/musical play, cowritten with Elmer Rice* and Kurt Weill.* Rice wrote the dramatic script, based on his earlier play of the same title. For the numerous songs, Hughes wrote some lyrics and co-wrote others with Rice, and Weill composed the music. *Street Scene* is set entirely in the "exterior of a 'walk-up' apartment house in a mean quarter of New York" (Rice, 65). At the core of the plot is an adulterous affair between the married Anna Maurrant and a milkman, Steve Sankey. Ultimately the two are murdered by Anna's husband, Frank Maurrant. To a great extent, however, the tragic "lovers' triangle" is secondary to the naturalistic presentation of multiethnic, working-class life in New York City in the late 1920s. Clearly in *Street Scene* Rice was interested in examining the reality of the mythic "melting-pot" experience, and the apartment-house setting allowed a realistic way in which to feature characters of German American, Jewish American, Swedish American, Italian American, and African American background. Hughes was drawn to the project not just because of the reputations of Rice and Weill but also because of the multiethnic, working-class subject matter. Although he and Weill obviously came from widely different national, ethnic, and educational backgrounds, they were both eclectic, adaptable artists, and both were interested in the way the blues* and jazz* afforded opportunities to blend a variety of lyric forms musically and linguistically. Hughes entered the collaboration guardedly but found Weill, albeit a perfectionist, a delightful composer with whom to work, and he found Rice cooperative, too. When Rice's nonmusical version of *Street Scene* debuted in New York City (January 10, 1929), it was not expected to succeed. It turned into a critical and commercial success, however, and won the Pulitzer Prize in drama. *Street Scene*, the opera, debuted in Philadelphia on December 16, 1945: —a debut Rice described as "cataclysmic" (Rampersad, II, 124). The opera was revised and opened in New York City on January 9, 1947, at the Adelphi Theatre. Maurice Abravanel conducted the orchestra, Charles Rice directed, and Dwight Wiman was the producer. The performers included Polyna Stoska, Norman Cordon, Anne Jeffreys, Creighton Thompson, and Brian Sullivan. Rice, Weill, Hughes, and Wiman were full of trepidation, but the audience responded enthusiastically, and critics wrote rave reviews. *Street Scene* ran for over 140 performances, and although it never became a commercial success, it earned a permanent place in the history of American musical theatre. Subsequent performances took place in Los Angeles and in Germany, and the New York City Opera revived the production in 1959. *Street Scene*, the opera, was again revived in a cooperative production by the English and Scottish National operas in 1989, with a trial performance in 1987 at a fundraising gala. The 1989 English production received favorable reviews. Reviewing a 1992 performance (also by the English National Opera), Greer was probably correct in noting a conflict in the opera between Rice's "naturalism" and Weill's "spontaneity"—a conflict that Hughes no doubt had to negotiate as he composed lyrics. A recording of the 1989 performance was released in 1991, 1995, and 1996. *See also* Meyerowitz, Jan; Musical Plays; Opera; Songs.

Bibliography/Discography: Herb Greer, review of *Street Scene, National Review* (London) 44, no. 13 (July 6, 1992), 55; Rampersad, II, 112–114, 122–127; Elmer Rice, *Street Scene*, in *Elmer Rice: Three Plays* (New York: Hill and Wang, 1965), 63–158; *Street Scene* [compact disc] (New York: Sony Classics, 1988); *Street Scene* [compact disc] (London: TER classics, 1991); *Street Scene* [compact disc] (Ocean, NJ: Musical Heritage Society, 1995); *Street Scene* [two compact discs], as performed by the English National Opera, 1989 (London: Jay Records, 1996), ASIN: B000005B6J; Kurt Weill, *Street Scene* [vocal score] (New York: Chappell, distributed by Hal Leonard Publishing, 1948).

"Street Song." Poem. *See Montage of a Dream Deferred.*

"Strictly for Charity." Short story, included in the collection *Simple Takes a Wife. See* Simple [Jesse B.] Stories.

"Strollin'." Song, from *The Strollin' Twenties*. Hughes wrote the lyrics, and William Hughes Eaton, Jr., composed the music. ASCAP* lists the song as being published by the Clara Music Corporation, and the song's ASCAP registry number is 490237642.

The Strollin' Twenties (1966). Television program, broadcast in the United States in February 1966. Hughes was the chief drafter of the script for this "variety" program thematically focused on Harlem* in the 1920s. According to Rampersad, singer and actor Harry Belafonte had come up with the idea for the show after reading *The Big Sea*. Performers on the program included Belafonte, orchestra leader Duke Ellington,* actress Diahann Carroll, singer, actor, and dancer Sammy Davis, Jr.,* and actor Sidney Poitier. *See also My Lord What a Mornin'*.
Bibliography: Rampersad, II, 392, 398.

The Studevants. The family for whom Cora Jenkins, the main character in the story "Cora Unashamed" works.

"Suburban Evening." Poem essentially constructed of rhyming couplets, except that Hughes breaks them into nine short lines with no stanza break. The poem describes how a quiet night in the suburbs is suddenly made "weird" by the howling of a dog. It was first published in *Crisis** (April 1967), 131.
Bibliography: *CP*, 553.

"Subway Face." Poem in two quatrains. An interior monologue, it is spoken by a person silently admiring a stranger at a subway stop. The speaker claims to have been "looking [f]or you" (the stranger) "all my life." The two then take separate trains. The poem was first published in *Crisis** (December 1924).
Bibliography: *CP*, 40.

"Subway Rush Hour." Poem. It is part of *Montage of a Dream Deferred*.
Bibliography: *CP*, 423.

"Subway to Jamaica." Short story, included in the collections *Simple Takes a Wife* and *The Best of Simple*. *See* Simple [Jesse B.] Stories.

"Success." Poem of fifteen lines in four stanzas and in free verse. The speaker guiltlessly enjoys his success. The poem was first published in the *Messenger** (July 1927).
Bibliography: *CP*, 108.

"Such a Little King." Song. *See Jerico-Jim Crow*.

Suicide. Theme in Hughes's work. *See* "Father and Son"; "The Gun"; *Mulatto*; "Reverie on the Harlem River"; "Suicide"; "Suicide's Note"; "Ways."

"Suicide." Poem in three traditional blues* stanzas and in black dialect.* The female speaker contemplates suicide. The poem was first published in *Poetry* (February 1926). *See* "Suicide's Note"; "Ways."

Bibliography: *CP*, 82.

"Suicide's Note." Poem of three lines in free verse that conveys a seductive quality of suicide. It was first published in *Vanity Fair* (September 1925). Later Charles Barrett Griffin set this poem, "Border Line," "Distance Nowhere," "Drum," and "Night: Four Songs" to music. *See* "Suicide"; "Ways."

Bibliography: *CP*, 55; Charles Barrett Griffin, *Distance Nowhere: 5 Langston Hughes Songs: For Baritone and String Quartet* (Forest Hills, N.Y.: Charles Griffin, 1995).

Sullivan, Noel (1890–1956). American philanthropist, art collector, and singer. Sullivan belonged to a pioneer California family, his grandfather (John Sullivan) having settled in the Sierra Nevada (Calaveras County) in 1844, then moving some years later to the community of Yerba Buena, later known as San Francisco. John Sullivan was the first president of the Hibernia Bank of San Francisco. Noel Sullivan's uncle was James Phelan, a California state senator, mayor of San Francisco, and well-known community leader. Sullivan studied art and music in Paris when he was in his twenties and during World War I served in the Ambulance Corps. In 1930, upon the death of Phelan, he became director of the San Francisco Art Association. In 1937 he moved from San Francisco to the California coastal town of Carmel-by-the-Sea, was active in many philanthropic activities there, and served on the boards of directors for the Carmel Music Society and the Monterey County Symphony Orchestra. He also sang in Bach festivals in Carmel.

As Hughes recounts in *I Wonder As I Wander*, he read poetry in the spring of 1932 at Arkansas A and M College and met an instructor, Arthur Williams, who, upon hearing that Hughes intended to go to California, encouraged him to visit Sullivan in San Francisco. According to Hughes, upon arriving in Los Angeles, he received a letter from Sullivan inviting him to his home. However, Rampersad suggests that although Hughes no doubt received the letter in 1932, he did not actually accept the invitation until August 1933 because he decided to return to the Soviet Union. Therefore, Hughes's description in *I Wonder As I Wander* probably represents a conflation of events but nonetheless records his first impressions of Sullivan. At any rate, Rampersad indicates that on August 9, 1933, Hughes was driven by chauffeur from the San Francisco piers to Sullivan's home at 2323 Hyde Street on Russian Hill—the former home of writer Robert Louis Stevenson. Hughes stayed with Sullivan there briefly and then moved to Sullivan's home—sometimes called "Ennesfree," sometimes "Hollow Hills"—in Carmel. At Sullivan's San Francisco home Hughes met a wide variety of notables, including singer/actor Nelson Eddy and actor Ramon Navarro. While Hughes was in Carmel, Sullivan paid for all his expenses. Over the years

Hughes returned to San Francisco and Carmel several times. In 1948 he told an interviewer, "Carmel is one of the most American of communities, in the best sense of the word" (Upton, 1). His friendship with Sullivan became one of the most important in his life, even as profound as his friendships with Carl Van Vechten* and Arna Bontemps.* Sullivan supported Hughes's career chiefly by giving him time to write and to rest in Carmel, and he apparently never expected anything in return. Although the two shared an interest in the plight of working people and the disenfranchised, Sullivan's philanthropy and activism took place in the context of his Catholic faith, and he sometimes disagreed with Hughes's more radical pronouncements, especially in the 1930s. However, Sullivan's view of Hughes's politics apparently never influenced his generosity toward Hughes. During his visits to Carmel, Hughes became acquainted with Robinson and Una Jeffers,* Lincoln Steffens, and other writers. Rampersad indicates that some mutual acquaintances of both men speculated that Hughes and Sullivan were involved sexually, but citing the opinions of other mutual acquaintances, Rampersad dismisses the idea. Sullivan died suddenly of heart failure at the Bohemian Club in San Francisco in September 1956. In remembering Sullivan, Jeffers wrote, "We think of Noel Sullivan's goodness, his kindness and compassion, and his wide and deep sympathies." In the same publication Hughes wrote, "We who had the good fortune to share his [Sullivan's] friendship knew that he lived so beautifully he had no fear of going and he leaves in our hearts memories that will glow always although we cannot help but miss him greatly. I wish I were there to sorrow with those close to him in Carmel." According to Rampersad, Hughes was unable to travel from New York to Carmel for the funeral because he was "broke." Rampersad observes, "Sullivan's death, though not unexpected, was a blow. With his passing, Langston had lost a haven he had perhaps outgrown, but one which had served him in times of personal crisis ever since his return from his year in the Soviet Union in August 1933" (II, 256). Even in death, Sullivan was generous to Hughes, bequeathing him over two thousand dollars, "as executed by the Crocker Anglo National Bank of California" (Rampersad, II, 262). *See* Sexuality and Hughes.

Bibliography: Langston Hughes, "Telegram from Langston Hughes/New York," *Carmel Pine Cone* (September 20, 1956), 2; Robinson Jeffers, "In Appreciation of Noel Sullivan," *Carmel Pine Cone* (September 20, 1956), 2; Rampersad, I, 276–284; II, 256, 262; John Upton, "Carmel American in Best Sense, Says Langston Hughes, Here on Visit," *Carmel Pine Cone* (April 30, 1948), 1.

"Summer Ain't Simple." Short story, included in *Simple Speaks His Mind. See* Simple [Jesse B.] Stories.

"Summer Evening (Calumet Avenue)." Poem of thirty-four lines in free verse. It captures the sights, sounds, and varieties of people associated with an ordinary evening on Calumet Avenue in Chicago, Illinois. One character it focuses on is

Theresa Belle Aletha. It was first published in *Poetry Quarterly* (London) (Winter 1947).

Bibliography: *CP*, 320.

The Sun Do Move (1942). Musical play, first produced in Chicago by the Skyloft Players, opening on April 24, 1942. The play concerns Rock, an African American slave who is sold and thereby separated from his wife and son, Mary and Little Rock. Twice Rock attempts to return to his family and lead them into freedom. After the first attempt, Little Rock dies while attempting to protect Mary from the mistress of the plantation. Rock's second attempt is successful, and he takes Mary to the North, where they are helped by Quakers. At the end of the play Rock is carrying the U.S. flag and has joined the Union Army to fight in the Civil War. Music for the play consisted chiefly of traditional spirituals, including the "Battle Hymn of the Republic." Rampersad suggests that *The Sun Do Move* is in "the style of Thornton Wilder's *Our Town* and Clifford Odets's *Waiting for Lefty*," especially insofar as it "aimed for the continuity of a motion picture or a radio drama, with no scenery or intermission" (II, 42). Rampersad also notes that *The Sun Do Move* was Hughes's "first play with a religious theme, and his first full-length musical drama (apart from his opera)" (II, 43). Turner finds "Hughes's characteristic interpolations of irreverent low comedy" to constitute a flaw but concludes that *The Sun Do Move* "is much more forceful and dramatically interesting" than *Don't You Want to Be Free?* Turner also maintains that the "dispassionate historicity of the pageant is emotionalized by Hughes's focus upon Mary and Rock, struggling to live as human beings rather than chattel"(90).

Bibliography: Hicklin, 28–30; Rampersad, II, 41–44; Darwin Turner, "Langston Hughes as Playwright," in O'Daniel, 81–95.

"Sun Song." Poem of seven lines, celebrating the sun and songs it inspires. The speaker of the poem addresses "Dark ones of Africa." The poem was first published in *Fine Clothes to the Jew*.

Bibliography: *CP*, 122.

"Sunday." Poem, one of the seven separate parts of "Seven Moments of Love."

"Sunday by the Combination." Poem. *See Montage of a Dream Deferred.*

"Sunday Morning Prophecy." Poem of forty-three lines in five stanzas. It represents the end of a sermon preached by an evangelical minister. The sermon ends with an appeal to the congregation for money. The poem was first published in the *New Yorker* (June 20, 1942). *See* Religion.

Bibliography: *CP*, 241.

"Sunset—Coney Island." Poem of thirteen lines that deliberately creates an unsavory picture of the recreational area. It was first published in *New Masses* (February 1928).

Bibliography: *CP*, 124.

"Sunset in Dixie." Poem of ten short lines in free verse. It predicts that the sun "is gonna go down" figuratively "in Dixie," spelling the end, implicitly, of a racist society. It was first published in *Crisis** (September 1941).

Bibliography: *CP*, 237.

"Supper Time." Poem, one of the seven separate parts of "Seven Moments of Love."

"Surprise." Short story, included in the collection *Simple Speaks His Mind. See* Simple [Jesse B.] Stories.

Swank's Combined Shows. The name of the carnival that comes to Stanton in *Not Without Laughter*. It competes with the revival tent meeting held by the Reverend Duke Braswell.* Harriet Williams* joins the carnival and runs away.

The Sweet and Sour Animal Book (New York: Oxford University Press, 1994). 48 pp. Introduction by Ben Vereen. Afterword by George P. Cunningham. Illustrated by students from the Harlem* School of the Arts. Book for children. For each letter of the alphabet, Hughes wrote a short poem about an animal: ape for "A," "Jocko" (a monkey) for "J," yaks for "Y," and so on. As early as 1951, Hughes unsuccessfully circulated to publishers the manuscript, which Rampersad, exaggerating for effect, describes as being already "ancient" (II, 203) at the time. Hughes had completed the book in 1936. This 1994 edition, therefore, is the first. The union of Hughes's whimsical short poems and the inspired illustrations by children make for a lively volume in traditional "picture-book" format. In his introduction, singer/actor/dancer Ben Vereen remembers appearing in Hughes's *Prodigal Son* in 1965 at the Greenwich Mews Theatre. There he met Hughes by accident. Vereen admits to being a bit gruff with Hughes owing to being preoccupied with production problems, but Hughes immediately won him over by inviting him to dinner. "We became very close at that time," writes Vereen, "though we later lost contact with each other. . . . When we talked, he would go on and on about Harlem and how it had changed. I think he was disappointed at Harlem at that time because of all that had gone downhill, but he wasn't leaving" (1). Vereen also pays tribute to the Harlem School of the Arts, which was founded, ironically, in 1964, just a year before Vereen and Hughes met. In his afterword, Cunningham, professor of Africana studies at Brooklyn College, provides an overview of Hughes's career. He also writes, "Like The Negro Mother and the warm persona that Hughes presented in his lectures, *The Sweet and Sour Animal Book* meets his audience—in this case the youngest that he ever wrote for—halfway. This volume is one of perhaps a dozen projects that Langston Hughes, sometimes in collaboration with Arna Bontemps,* created especially for children" (45–46). The unpublished manuscripts to which Cunningham refers are held in the Langston Hughes Papers of the James Weldon Johnson Memorial Collection, Beinecke Library, Yale University. The last pages of the book include black-and-white photographs of each child who worked on the illustrations as well as photographs of the children as they worked on the illustrations. *See also Black Misery; The Block; Carol of the Brown King: Nativity Poems by Langston Hughes*; Children's Poetry; The *Paste-Board Bandit; Popo and Fifina.*

Bibliography: Rampersad, II, 202–203.

"Sweet Chariots of This World." Essay that is a wry survey of different modes of transportation Americans and African Americans have enjoyed over time. It was first published in *Negro Digest* (volume and date unknown) and was also published in *The Langston Hughes Reader*.

Bibliography: *The Langston Hughes Reader*, 494–496.

The Sweet Flypaper of Life (New York: Simon and Schuster, 1955; reprinted, New York: Hill and Wang, 1967). 96 pp. This is a book that is difficult to characterize. It is composed chiefly of black-and-white photographs by Roy DeCarava, whose name precedes Hughes's on the cover and title page. The photographs are of African American men, women, and children in Harlem* during the 1950s. Some photographs are posed, but not formally; most are candid—taken in apartments, bars, restaurants and churches and on streets. Instead of providing traditional captions for the photographs, Hughes wrote a narrative, "spoken" by an older African American woman, so that many of the individuals photographed become "characters" in "Sister Mary's" monologue about her extended family, pleasures, and hardships in Harlem, her life, and other matters. Standing alone, the photographs offer an array of images from everyday Harlem life, but interwoven with segments of Hughes's fictional monologue, they take on an added coherence. Therefore, they can be interpreted as "objective" journalistic images, or as images in a tale, or both. Because photographs, not text, dominate the page, they cannot truly be said to illustrate Sister Mary's tale. Instead, the text enhances the photographs or improvises upon them in a jazz-like composition. The last (full-page) photograph is of an older African American woman. Above it are the words "ever so once in a while, I put on my best clothes." Below it, "Here I am." *See also* Jazz.

Bibliography: Thadious M. Davis, "Reading the Woman's Face in Langston Hughes's and Roy DeCarava's *Sweet Flypaper of Life*," *Langston Hughes Review* 12, no. 1 (Spring 1993), 22–28; Maren Stange, " 'Illusion Complete within Itself': Roy DeCarava's Photography," *Yale Journal of Criticism* 9, no. 1 (Spring 1996), 63–92.

"Sweet Words on Race." Poem of fifteen lines in a single stanza, with occasional rhymes. The speaker expresses distaste for "sweet words" in support of racial harmony, especially when they are uttered when "danger is so near." The poem was first published in *The Panther and the Lash. See* "Northern Liberal."
Bibliography: *CP*, 560.

"Swing Time at the Savoy." Song. Hughes wrote the lyrics, and Eubie Blake and Noble Sissle composed the music. ASCAP lists no publisher for the song. The song's ASCAP* registry number is 490182586. Blake and Sissle collaborated on the landmark 1920s musical *Shuffle Along*, and, coincidentally, Sissle, like Hughes, was a graduate of Central High School* in Cleveland.

"Sylvester's Dying Bed." Poem of thirty lines in seven and one-half ballad* stanzas. It is one of Hughes's best-known monologue poems. Although Sylvester is dying, he has lost neither his interest in women nor his high regard for himself as a lover of them. The poem was first published in *Poetry* (October 1931).
Bibliography: *CP*, 140–141.

"Sympathy." Short story, included in the collection *Simple's Uncle Sam. See* Simple [Jesse B.] Stories.

***Symphonische Gesänge* (Opus 20).** Alexander Zemlinsky is the composer. According to the ASCAP listing for this work, the symphony draws on works by Countee Cullen,* Jean Toomer,* Frank Horne, and Hughes. "Danse Africaine" is the Hughes poem that is set to music in this work. The score is published by European American Music. The ASCAP registry number is 490814992.

T

Tabulations. In the novel *Tambourines to Glory, Tabulations* is the name Laura Reed mistakenly calls the Book of Revelation from the Bible (Chapter 5 "When Sap Rises").

"Tag." Poem. *See Montage of a Dream Deferred.*

"Tain't So." Short story. It concerns "Miss Lucy," who is from the American South but lives in Los Angeles. She is, among other things, astonished to find out that a certain "faith-healer" in Los Angeles is "treating darkies." Her racist attitudes run deep, but the story portrays her more as anachronistic than as malevolent. The story was first published in the magazine *Fight against War and Fascism* (May 1937), was included in the collections *Laughing to Keep from Crying* and *Something in Common and Other Stories*, and was reprinted in *Langston Hughes: Short Stories.*

The Talented Tenth. A concept promoted by W.E.B. DuBois* and others in the 1920s. It refers to the ten percent of the African American population that DuBois hoped would set an example for African Americans by means of artistic, intellectual, and economic achievement. The concept influenced aspects of the Harlem Renaissance.*

Talmadge, Eugene (1884–1946). American politician, two-time governor of the state of Georgia. *See* "Governor Fires Dean."

"Tambourines." Poem of fourteen lines in three stanzas. Six of the lines consist entirely of the word "Tambourines!" As the editors of *Collected Poems* reveal, on the manuscript of the poem Hughes noted that the poem was written "to fill in" an empty page on the "proofs" for *Selected Poems of Langston Hughes*, in which the poem was first published. The poem contains the phrase "Tambou-rines to Glory!" which is the title of a novel and of a play Hughes also wrote.

Bibliography: *CP*, 465, 680.

Tambourines to Glory (New York: Jonathan Day Publishers, 1958; Copyright 1959). Novel. The book is the second of two novels published by Hughes, the first being *Not Without Laughter*. However, it can also be characterized as a "novelization" of the musical play *Tambourines to Glory*, with music by Jobe Huntley, written in 1956 but, ironically, not produced until 1963, well after the novel had appeared. Consequently, there is an argument to be made that *Not Without Laughter* represents Hughes's only "pure" foray into longer fiction. Indeed, in structure the short novel *Tambourines to Glory* (188 pages) is a kind of long scenario, with thirty-six brief chapters dominated by comic dialogue and including little of the texture, imagery, or psychological depth found in *Not Without Laughter*. In fact, several chapters are titled with what amount to stage directions: "Enter Birdie Lee" (chapter 9), "Enter Buddy" (chapter 14), "Enter Marty" (chapter 15), and "Enter Marietta" (chapter 21). Hughes clearly intended the book to be a brisk comic, often-satiric, study of religion* in Harlem.* Ram-persad suggests that behind "his [Hughes's] almost unseemly conversions of *Tambourines to Glory* was an urgent need for cash" and goes on to describe Hughes's financial straits at the time (II, 255–257).

   Hughes's motives aside, the "novelization" of the play is readable and hu-morous. Two friends, Essie Belle Johnson and Laura Reed, decide to become street-corner preachers, Essie because she is sincerely religious, Laura because she needs the money. Laura is addicted to gambling and alcohol. The street-corner services become so successful that the two are able to found a church, "The Reed Sisters' Tambourine Temple," located, as we learn in chapter 11 ("Ethiopian Eden"), in "an old first-floor apartment between Lenox [Avenue] and the West 130's" in Harlem. The first two converts are a woman, "Birdie Lee," and a man, "Chicken Crow-for-a-Day," followed by a young musician, C. J.; Essie Belle's daughter, Marietta, who arrives from the South, where she is attending college; and "Big-Eyed" Buddy Lomax, a street hustler who is involved in the "numbers racket" (an illegal lottery), a version of which he runs out of the church, with Laura Reed's assistance and without Essie Belle's knowl-edge. Laura and Buddy operate the lottery by referring to "Lucky Texts" (the title of chapter 23) in the Bible. C. J. and Marietta fall in love and eventually marry. Laura falls in love with Buddy, who is not faithful to her. Laura even-tually stabs Buddy to death and claims that Essie Belle murdered him. Essie Belle is arrested, but Birdie Lee testifies against Laura, who eventually confesses fully, apologizes sincerely to Essie Belle, and shifts the money from her (Laura's) bank account to the church's, thereby saving the church and Essie Belle. The novel received mildly praiseworthy critical notices and sold moder-ately well, but the musical play received very negative critical reviews and closed quickly. (The main objection to the play was what critics viewed as its mocking point of view toward black culture in Harlem; *see* the entry for *Tambourines to Glory*, the play). Although the novel does satirize aspects of religion in Harlem, the larger target is human weakness in general—or, in religious terminology, "temptations" of the flesh, of greed, of overindulgence. Also, while the novel possesses a sharp satiric edge, its whole spirit is comic. Its plot, like that of traditional dramatic comedies, ends in marriage; the sincere Essie Belle is rescued, and the church survives; and there is a warmth to the farcical elements of the novel. As he does in other works concerning religion, Hughes depicts not so much a contradiction between faith and baser human impulses but a connection; that is, implicitly, *Tambourines to Glory* suggests that religion exists and is necessary because humans are weak, and that because humans are weak, they sometimes exploit religion.

Bibliography: Rampersad, II, 255–258.

***Tambourines to Glory* (1963).** Musical play, first written in 1956, with songs by Jobe Huntley. Hughes revisited and revised the play several times, turned it into a novel in 1958–1959, and finally saw the play produced for the first time in 1963. The plot of the play closely follows that of the novel (*see* the entry for *Tambourines to Glory*, the novel). The play opened on November 3, 1963, at the Little Theatre on 44th Street near Broadway in New York City. The cast included Joseph Attles, Anna English, Louis Gossett, Hilda Simms, and Rosetta LeNoire. Nikos Psacharopoulos directed. In serving as the company manager, Dick Campbell became the first African American to occupy that role on Broadway, and Otis Young, in serving as stage manager, became the first African American in that position on Broadway. The play drew a generally harsh critical response that Rampersad, among others, attributed chiefly to timing; that is, with the civil-rights movement gaining momentum nationwide, neither black nor white audiences were particularly amenable to a broadly comic, even satiric, treatment of the African American church. Conflicts between the theatre management and the producers as well as complaints from the stagehands' union also affected rehearsals and, therefore, the production, which closed only three weeks later, on November 23. According to Rampersad, the play lost $125,000, $2,000 of which was Hughes's own money. *See The Glory around His Head; Jerico-Jim Crow*; "Life Is Fine"; Religion; "Scat Cat."

Bibliography: Rampersad, II, chapter 14, "Blues for Mr. Backlash," 364–385.

"Tambourines to Glory." Song, from *Tambourines to Glory* (musical play). Hughes wrote the lyrics, and Jobe Huntley composed the music. This version of the song is not listed with ASCAP,* whereas as "Life Is Fine" and "Scat Cat," also from the musical play, are. However, ASCAP lists another version of the song, with music composed by Undine Moore. The publisher listed is Warner Brothers Music, whereas the publisher for "Life Is Fine" and "Scat Cat" is Chappell Music, Inc. The ASCAP registry number for the Hughes/Moore collaboration is 500539242. And finally, *Tambourines to Glory*, a Masters in Music thesis by Adrienne C. Alexander (Michigan State University, 1985) that features songs for unaccompanied choir, includes another version of "Tambourines to Glory."

Tambourines to Glory (New York: Folkways, 1964). Sound recording (one long-playing vinyl disc) of the musical play *Tambourines to Glory*. *See also* Audio Recordings of Hughes.

"Tapestry." Poem in two modified ballad* quatrains with no stanza break. The poem presents a bemused point of view on the chivalrous figures depicted in the tapestry. It was first published in *Crisis** (July 1927).
Bibliography: *CP*, 107

"The Task of the Negro Writer as Artist." Essay that argues that "Negro writers" have "a social as well as a literary responsibility." It was first published in *Negro Digest* (April 1965) and was reprinted in Berry. *See* Poetics.
Bibliography: Berry, 171.

"Teacher." Poem in four ballad* stanzas. It is spoken from the grave by a teacher who expresses doubts about the efficacy of his life's work. The terse diction and irony of the poem are reminiscent of works by Edgar Lee Masters, Edwin Arlington Robinson, and A. E. Housman. It was first published in *Opportunity** (May 1926).
Bibliography: *CP*, 67.

"Telegram from Langston Hughes/New York" (1956). Brief memorial piece. *See* Sullivan, Noel.

Television Program about Hughes. *See Langston Hughes: The Dream Keeper.*

"Tell Me." *See Montage of a Dream Deferred.*

"Tell Me Your Story." Song. Hughes wrote the lyrics, and Albert Hague composed the music. ASCAP* lists the song as being published by Wayfarer Music, and the song's ASCAP registry number is 500023334.

"Temptation." Short story, included in *The Best of Simple. See* Simple [Jesse B.] Stories.

"Ten Thousand Beds." Essay. In it Hughes claims to have slept in ten thousand beds, and he explains how quickly he can fall asleep and how well he can sleep

in almost any venue. The essay was first published in the *Chicago Defender**
(date unknown) and was also published in *The Langston Hughes Reader*.

Bibliography: *The Langston Hughes Reader*, 489–490.

"Testament." Poem in twelve lines, intermittently rhymed. The speaker asks
and answers questions about what he will leave to his family when he dies. The
answers are venomously bitter. The poem was first published in *New Poems by
American Poets #2*, edited by Rolfe Humphries (New York: Ballantine, 1957).
Later, Leonard Geoffrey Feather set the poem to music. ASCAP* lists the song
as being published by Model Music, Inc., and the song's ASCAP registry number is 500209045.

Bibliography: *CP*, 455.

"Testimonial." Poem. *See Montage of a Dream Deferred*.

The Texas Kid. A character in the poem "Death in Harlem."

Thank You, Ma'am (Mankato, MN: Creative Education Press, 1991). 30 pp.
Illustrated book for children, using the text of the story "Thank You, Ma'am."
The book is held by the Library of Congress and other libraries.

"Thank You, Ma'am." Short story, published in *Something in Common and
Other Stories*. In the narrative a young African American boy tries to steal the
purse of an African American woman, Luella Bates Washington Jones. Luella
foils the attempted theft easily, takes the boy (Roger) home, has him wash his
face, feeds him, and gives him some instructions about right and wrong.

"Thanksgiving Time." Poem in three stanzas of fourteen lines that are, for
Hughes's poetry, extremely long. The poem evokes traditional images and customs associated with autumn and the American holiday, Thanksgiving. It was
first published in *Brownie's Book* and reprinted in *The Langston Hughes Reader*.
See Children's Poetry.

Bibliography: *CP*, 600.

"That Powerful Drop." Short story, included in the collection *Simple Takes a
Wife. See* Simple [Jesse B.] Stories.

"That Word Black." Short story, included in the collection *Simple Takes a
Wife. See* Simple [Jesse B.] Stories.

"Theme for English B." Poem, part of *Montage of a Dream Deferred*. It deserves an entry of its own, however, because it is one of Hughes's best-known
poems. The young black speaker who fulfills his white teacher's assignment

does so with wisdom and self-awareness, pointing to potential chasms of misunderstanding between a black student and a white teacher, but also expressing gracefully his hope in the potential of education. The poem was reprinted in *The Block*, and it is often anthologized.

Bibliography: *CP*, 409–410.

"There." Poem of eleven lines in free verse. It meditates on death, "Divinity," and "Infinity." It was first published in *Fields of Wonder*. *See* Religion.

Bibliography: *CP*, 337.

"There Ought to Be a Law." Short story, included in *The Best of Simple*. *See* Simple [Jesse B.] Stories.

"There's Always the Weather." Poem in four ballad* quatrains. The language and tone are playful. The poem was first published in *The Langston Hughes Reader*. *See* Children's Poetry.

Bibliography: *CP*, 603.

"These Bad New Negroes: A Critique on Critics." Essay. Responding to harsh criticism from African American writers leveled at *Fine Clothes to the Jew*, Hughes in the essay defends the style and subject matter of poems in that volume, accusing some black critics of snobbery and of being too concerned with whites' opinions of blacks. As well as being a defense of *Fine Clothes to the Jew*, the essay builds on many of the ideas expressed in "The Negro Artist and the Racial Mountain." It was published in the *Pittsburgh Courier* (April 16, 1927).

Bibliography: Rampersad, I, 145.

"They Come and They Go." Short story, included in the collections *Simple Takes a Wife* and *The Best of Simple*. *See* Simple [Jesse B.] Stories.

"Third Degree." Poem of eighteen lines in free verse. "Third degree" in this case refers to interrogation by the police. The speaker of the poem is being beaten by the police and forced to confess to a crime, one he probably did not commit. The poem was first published in *One-Way Ticket*. *See* "Who But the Lord?"

Bibliography: *CP*, 370.

"This Puzzles Me." Rhyming poem of thirty lines with no stanza breaks. The speaker notes how African Americans are stereotyped as "simple" and childlike and observes that those who perpetuate the stereotypes are in fact simple insofar as they try to solve problems unimaginatively by means of war, for example. The poem also mentions Eugene Talmadge,* governor of Georgia (*see* "Governor Fires Dean"), and Martin Dies, a member of the U.S. Congress from 1931 to 1945. Many regarded Dies as a reactionary politician. He chaired the U.S. House of Representatives' Committee on Un-American Activities, a precursor to a congressional committee before which Hughes would later be called to testify (*see* McCarthyism). The poem was first published in the *Southern Frontier* (November 1941). *See* Politics.

Bibliography: *CP*, 238–239.

Thompson, J. Crutchfield. One of Hughes's pseudonyms. *See* Pseudonyms Used by Hughes.

"The Thorn." Poem of ten lines in two stanzas, intermittently rhymed. It is a dramatic monologue—evoking, that is, a specific listener "within" the poem. The last six lines are printed in italics. The poem is cryptic but seems to suggest that social change does not necessarily depend upon a cause célèbre but will spring from broad social circumstances. "Thorn," therefore, refers in part to "thorn in the side," or the cause of social change. The poem was first published in *Voices* (Autumn 1954).

Bibliography: *CP*, 452.

"Those Who Have No Turkey." Short story, published in *Brownie's Book** (November 1921). *See also* Central High School.

"Three by Langston." Song. ASCAP* lists this as a single title. Ricky Ian Gordon is the composer. Gordon set three of Hughes's poems to music, "Joy," "Luck," and "New Moon." Gordon wrote the songs for the 1998 Manhattan Choral Festival. The publisher listed is the Williamson Music Company, and the song's ASCAP registry number is 500583702.

"Three Dream Portraits: Poems from *The Dream Keeper* by Langston Hughes" (New York: G. Ricordi, 1959). Songs. Hughes wrote the lyrics, and Margaret Bonds,* with whom Hughes also collaborated on *Ballad of the Brown King*, composed the music. ASCAP* lists no publisher for the songs. The songs' ASCAP registry number is 500291143.

"Three Songs About Lynching." Three previously published poems—"Flight," "Lynching Song," and "Silhouette"—were published under this title in *Opportunity* (June 1936).

Bibliography: *CP*, 648.

"Three Songs on Poems of Langston Hughes." Songs. ASCAP* lists this as a single title and does not specify which poems were set to music by the composer, Kevin Lowell Scott; also, no publisher is listed. The songs' ASCAP registry number is 500492275.

Thurman, Wallace (1902–1934). American editor, novelist, and journalist. Thurman was a native of Utah but later moved to Los Angeles, California, where he graduated from the University of Southern California and became acquainted with Arna Bontemps.* In 1924 Thurman moved to New York City. Because of his editorial work on the periodicals *Fire!!* and the *Messenger* and his friendship with Hughes, Zora Neale Hurston,* Bontemps, and others, Thurman became an important figure in The Harlem Renaissance.* Thurman's nonfiction book about racism in the United States, *The Blacker the Berry*, was published in 1929. Two novels—*The Interne* and *The Infants of the Spring*—appeared in 1932. Thurman died of tuberculosis in 1934.

Bibliography: Lewis, *HRR*, 629–654; Wallace Thurman, *The Blacker the Berry* (New York: The Macaulay Company, 1929); Wallace Thurman, *Infants of the Spring* (New York: The Macaulay Company, 1932); Wallace Thurman, *The Interne* (New York: The Macaulay Company, 1932).

"Tickets and Takers." Short story, included in the collection *Simple Takes a Wife. See* Simple [Jesse B.] Stories.

"Tied in a Bow." Short story, included in the collections *Simple Takes a Wife* and *The Best of Simple. See* Simple [Jesse B.] Stories.

"Tired." Poem of two modified ballad* quatrains with no stanza breaks. The speaker is "tired of waiting" for "the world to become good." The poem was first published in *New Masses* (February 1931).

Bibliography: *CP*, 135.

"To a Black Dancer in the Little Savoy." Poem. *See* "Midnight Dancer." *See also* "Swing Time at the Savoy."

"To a Dead Friend." Poem of thirteen lines in four stanzas. The diction and imagery of the elegy are relatively conventional. The poem was first published in *Crisis** (May 1922).

Bibliography: *CP*, 26.

"To a Dead Soldier." Song. Hughes wrote the lyrics, and Dale R. Jergenson composed the music. ASCAP* lists the song as being published by M. Baker Publishers, and the song's ASCAP registry number is 500506223.

"To a Little Lover-lass, Dead." Poem of twelve lines in three stanzas. The dead young woman is described as a "waif" wandering the streets of heaven, and the speaker expresses the hope that "God's kiss" will be "sweet." The poem was first published in *The Weary Blues. See* Religion.

Bibliography: *CP*, 89.

"To Artina." Eleven-line poem in free verse. Addressing Artina, the speaker expresses an all-consuming love for her and wants to be "like God" with regard to her. The poem was first published in *Selected Poems of Langston Hughes.*

Bibliography: *CP*, 466.

"To Be Somebody." Poem of twenty-three lines in free verse. It depicts a boy and a girl, presumably African American, who dream of achieving greatness— he in boxing, she in music (piano). Singer/performer Hazel Scott (1920–1981) is mentioned, as is Joe Louis.* The poem was first published in *Phylon* (1950). It was reprinted in *The Block.*

Bibliography: *CP*, 374.

"To Beauty." Poem of twenty-four lines in free verse. It concerns worshipping at the "Altar of Beauty" and is constructed chiefly of infinitive phrases (for example, "To thrill at the wonder"). It was first published in *Crisis** (October 1926).

Bibliography: *CP*, 75.

"To Captain Mulzac." Poem of two pages in free verse. It is based on the true story of Hugh Nathaniel Mulzac, the first African American to serve in the U.S. Merchant Marine. Late in his career he was given command of a ship, the *Booker T. Washington*, with an ethnically integrated crew. Hughes depicts the ship as a symbol of ethnic harmony, especially between workers. Hughes profiled Mulzac in *Famous Negro Heroes of America*. The poem was first published in *Jim Crow's Last Stand. See* Washington, Booker T.

Bibliography: *CP*, 293–294.

"To Certain 'Brothers.' " Poem of ten lines in free verse that chastises certain Christians whom the speaker regards as hypocritical. It was first published in *Workers Monthly* (July 1925). *See* Religion.

Bibliography: *CP*, 55.

"To Certain Negro Leaders." Poem of seven lines in free verse that critiques leaders whom the speaker regards as too accommodationist in their relationships with whites. It was first published in *New Masses* (February 1931). The editors of *Collected Poems* suggest that the poem may have been implicitly addressed to W.E.B. Du Bois,* A. Philip Randolph,* and Marcus Garvey,* who were not as impressed as Hughes was at the time with Marxism.* *See* Washington, Booker T.

Bibliography: *CP*, 136, 638.

"To Dorothy Maynor." Poem of six lines in free verse that pays homage to the talents of Dorothy Maynor (1910–1996), a classical singer whom Hughes also mentions in "The Heart of Harlem." It was first published in *Crisis** (July 1948).

Bibliography: *CP*, 341; William Grimes, "Dorothy Maynor" [obituary], *New York Times* (February 24, 1996), 12.

"To Make Words Sing." Poem of a single quatrain with two rhyming couplets, first published in *The Langston Hughes Reader. See* Children's Poetry.

Bibliography: *CP*, 602.

"To Midnight Nan at Leroy's." Poem of five short-lined ballad* stanzas with a hint of black dialect* in the diction. It is addressed to a female blues* singer and suggests that she is too inconstant, perhaps even promiscuous, to be satisfied with (and by) one man. It was first published in *Vanity Fair* (September 1925).

Bibliography: *CP*, 57.

"To Negro Writers." Speech/essay read in Hughes's absence at the American Writers' Congress in New York City in April 1935. The speech urges "Negro" writers to use their work to protest racism, politicize African Americans, and critique African American leaders who are (in Hughes's view) too accommodating to whites. Rampersad characterizes the essay as an "extremely militant," "lacerating" statement. The essay was reprinted in Berry. *See* "Too Much of Race."

Bibliography: Berry, 135–137; Rampersad, I, 304–305.

"To the Dark Mercedes of 'El Palacio de Amor.' " Poem of eight lines in free verse. It is addressed to a singer, Mercedes, and advises her to perform in a venue where she will be better paid and appreciated. It was first published in *The Weary Blues*.

Bibliography: *CP*, 99; Rampersad, I, 76–77.

"To the Little Fort of San Lazaro on the Ocean Front, Havana." Poem of seventeen lines in three stanzas, intermittently rhymed. It suggests that the fort survived the age of pirates but will not survive modern times, as represented by the "National City Bank," which presumably wants the site for a resort. The poem was first published in *New Masses* (May 1931).

Bibliography: *CP*, 136.

"To the Red Army." Poem. *See* "Salute to Soviet Armies."

"To You." Rhyming poem of ten lines. The speaker exhorts all "who are dreamers" to help him "make our world anew." The editors of *Collected Poems* note that Hughes wrote the poem to be used on a greeting card issued by the Congress of Racial Equality. It was first published in the *Amsterdam News* (January 30, 1965).
Bibliography: *CP*, 546, 689.

"A Toast to Harlem." Short story, included in *The Best of Simple. See* Simple [Jesse B.] Stories.

"Today." Poem of five lines that concerns "earthquake weather"—a time of social upheaval. It was first published in *Opportunity** (October 1937).
Bibliography: *CP*, 201.

Tolson, Melvin B. (1898–1966). American poet, critic, and community leader. Tolson was born in Missouri and grew up in small towns there and in Iowa. His father was a Methodist Episcopal minister. Like Hughes, Tolson graduated from Lincoln University* (1922). Tolson taught English and coached debate at Wiley College in Texas for several years. In 1931 he began pursuing graduate work in comparative literature at Columbia University,* living in Harlem* and meeting many writers, including Hughes, associated with the Harlem Renaissance.* Tolson's M.A. thesis at Columbia, "The Harlem Group of Negro Writers," includes a study of Hughes, whom Tolson describes as "the idealistic wanderer and defender of the proletariat, . . . the most glamorous figure in Negro literature" (120). His first book of poems, *Rendezvous with America* (1944), was well received by critics; the poetry exhibited many qualities associated with the strain of Modernism* inspired by Ezra Pound and T. S. Eliot. As Valade suggests, Tolson's second volume of poetry, *Libretto for the Republic of Liberia* (1953), exhibits even more Modernist characteristics (358). Additional works include *Harlem Gallery: Book I: The Curator* (1965) and the posthumously published *A Gallery of Harlem Portraits* (1979). In 1947 Tolson began teaching at Langston University in Langston, Oklahoma, where he also ran successfully for mayor in 1952. He served four terms as mayor of Langston. In 1948 he was appointed poet laureate of the nation of Liberia.
Bibliography: Melvin B. Tolson, "[Langston Hughes]," in Mullen, 120–126; Roger M. Valade III, *The Essential Black Literature Guide* (Detroit: Visible Ink Press, 1996), 357–358.

"Tomorrow." Poem. *See Montage of a Dream Deferred.*

"Tomorrow's Seed." Poem of twenty lines, intermittently rhymed. Its extended metaphor compares soldiers who died fighting fascists in the Spanish Civil War to seeds, from which a new world will grow. It was first published in *The Heart of Spain*, edited by Alvah C. Bessie (New York: Veterans of the Abraham Lincoln Brigade, 1952). *See Baltimore Afro American*; "Hero—International Brigade"; "Letter from Spain"; "Spain's Martyred Poet, García Lorca."
Bibliography: *CP*, 431.

"Too Blue." Poem of seventeen lines in four stanzas in black dialect.* The speaker complains of having "the weary blues," contemplates suicide, but is "too blue to look for a gun." The poem was first published in *Contemporary Poetry* (Autumn 1943). *See* The Blues; "The Gun"; "The Weary Blues."
Bibliography: *CP*, 280.

"Too Much of Race." Essay that is the printed version of a speech Hughes gave at the Second International Writers' Congress in Paris in 1937. In the essay Hughes suggests that fascist governments in Spain and Germany, as well as nations such as Great Britain that sometimes, in his view, behave repressively, fear that people of color are developing a sense of solidarity with which to confront racism worldwide. The essay was reprinted in Berry. *See* "To Negro Writers."
Bibliography: Berry, 101–104; Rampersad, I, 344–345.

Toomer, Jean (1894–1967). American novelist, poet, and playwright. Toomer was born in Washington, D.C. His father was a white farmer from Georgia, his mother African American. As a young man, Toomer traveled around the United States extensively, worked at many jobs, and for a short time was a "body builder." In 1919 he moved to Greenwich Village in New York City, where he met writers Edwin Arlington Robinson and Waldo Frank.* In 1923 Toomer published one of the most enduring works to be associated with the Harlem Renaissance,* *Cane*, a stylish, lyrical, exquisitely wrought novel-in-stories. Thereafter Toomer produced nothing approaching the quality and stature of *Cane*, eventually abandoned writing, and even disavowed his African American ethnic background.
Bibliography: Nellie Y. McKay, *Jean Toomer, Artist: A Study of His Literary Life and Work, 1894–1936* (Chapel Hill: University of North Carolina Press, 1984).

"Torch Song." Song. Hughes wrote the lyrics, and Martin Hennessy composed the music. ASCAP* lists the song as being published by Maisie Light Publishing, and the song's ASCAP registry number is 500557151. Also, Heidi Skok is listed as having performed the song, but no information about a recording is provided.

"Total War." Poem, rhymed intermittently, of sixteen lines in three stanzas. Its "argument" is that Jim Crow laws* exist because "Dixie" (the southern United States) was not defeated "properly" in the Civil War and that, therefore, in World War II Adolf Hitler should be defeated totally. The poem was first published in the *Baltimore Afro American** (February 1943). *See* "America's Young Black Joe."

Bibliography: *CP*, 577.

"Tower." Poem in one ballad* quatrain that compares death to a tower. It was first published in *Crisis** (July 1930).

Bibliography: *CP*, 128.

"The Town of Scottsboro." Poem of one ballad* quatrain that depicts the site of the trial of the Scottsboro Boys* as a "weak," "small" town. It was first published in *Scottsboro Limited: Four Poems and a Play in Verse*.

Bibliography: *CP*, 168.

"Tragedy at the Baths." Short story. The narrative, set in Mexico, concerns an ill-fated love triangle including "Juan," "Consuelo," and Consuelo's husband at a hotel run by a certain Senora Rueda. It was included in the collection *Laughing to Keep from Crying* and was reprinted in *Langston Hughes: Short Stories*.

Bibliography: Ostrom, 27.

Translations by Hughes. *See Blood Wedding* and *Yerma* (one entry); *Cuba Libre; The Langston Hughes Reader; Lorca: Gypsy Ballads; Masters of the Dew; Selected Poems of Gabriela Mistral*; "Troubled Lands." Also, the Langston Hughes Papers in the James Weldon Johnson Memorial Collection at the Beinecke Rare Book and Manuscript Library, Yale University, contains unpublished translations by Hughes of works by Iulian Anisimov, Louis Aragon,* Jean Cocteau, Nellie Campobello, Pierre Dalcour, Léon-Gontran Damas, Eliseo Grenet, Armand Lanusse, Anthony Lespes, Vladimir Mayakovsky, Boris Pasternak, Regino Pedroso, Rubén Salazar Mallén, and Xavier Villaurrutia.

"Tribute to Ralph Bunche" (1964). Manuscript of an unpublished essay. Bunche (1904–1971) was an American political scientist and diplomat whose work includes *A World View of Race* (1936). Bunche contributed material to *An American Dilemma* (1944) by Swedish sociologist Gunnar Myrdal, a study of race relations in the United States. Interviews with African Americans he conducted in the South were published posthumously in *The Political Status of the Negro in the Age of FDR* [Franklin Delano Roosevelt*] (1973). Bunche held posts at the U.S. State Department before serving in the United Nations, for which he directed the Palestine Commission, beginning in 1948. The manuscript is held in the Langston Hughes Papers, James Weldon Johnson Memorial Collection, Beinecke Rare Book and Manuscript Library, Yale University (item 3787).

Bibliography: Roger M. Valade III, *The Essential Black Literature Guide* (Detroit: Visible Ink Press, 1996), p 65.

"Trip: San Francisco." Poem in one ballad* stanza that compares the bridges of San Francisco, California, to cobwebs. It was first published in *Golden Slippers*, edited by Arna Bontemps* (New York: Harper, 1941). *See* Children's Poetry; Sullivan, Noel.

Bibliography: *CP*, 600.

Tropics after Dark (1940). Musical revue. Hughes wrote lyrics for the revue, but financial problems and disagreements between sponsors and producers resulted in the revue's being "stripped" (as Rampersad phrases it) of Hughes's lyrics, rearranged hastily, and performed at the American Negro Exposition in Chicago, July 12, 1940.

Bibliography: Rampersad, I, 386–387.

"The Trouble with Angels." Short story. The narrative concerns a touring black theatre troupe that must confront segregation. The story was published in *New Theatre* magazine (July 1935), was included in the collections *Laughing to Keep from Crying* and *Something in Common and Other Stories*, and was reprinted in *Langston Hughes: Short Stories*.

Bibliography: Ostrom, 27–28.

Troubled Island (1938–1949). Opera in three acts, with a libretto by Hughes and music by William Grant Still.* As early as 1938, before he departed for Spain (*see Baltimore Afro American*), Hughes began to transform his play *Troubled Island* into an opera libretto, collaborating with Still. As Rampersad notes, a documentary film about Still mistakenly credits Verna Arvey with having produced much of the work on the libretto. Rampersad points to a *New York Times* interview in which Arvey herself clearly credits Hughes with having written the piece (Rampersad, II, 158). In 1944 Leopold Stokowski, musical director of the New York City Center, expressed enthusiastic interest in producing the opera, but funding did not materialize, and soon thereafter Stokowski married Gloria Vanderbilt, retired from the City Center, and departed for Europe. Next Still and Hughes unsuccessfully offered the work to the Metropolitan Opera of New York City. Ultimately the City Center agreed to produce the opera, which premiered on March 30, 1949. Rampersad notes that the premiere was "a historic event in race relations—the first opera written by blacks to be produced by a major American company." George Balanchine and Jean Leon Destine choreographed the opera. Robert Weede, a white man, sang the role of the black Haitian Jean-Jacques Dessalines. Although, according to Rampersad, "the audience applauded madly," critics reacted negatively, with Irving Kolodin of the *New York Sun* describing the opera as a "turgid, confused mishap." Throughout the collaboration between Hughes and Still, their working relationship had been strained, and after the critical failure of *Troubled Island*, Still chose to break off communication with Hughes, a choice Rampersad links in part to politics, describing Still as "a profoundly religious man and a dedicated anti-communist" who regarded Hughes as a "leftist." ASCAP* lists the opera as being published by Southern Music Publishing Company, Inc., and the work's ASCAP registry number is 500347851.

Bibliography: Irving Kolodin, review of *Troubled Island, New York Sun* (April 1, 1949), as cited in Rampersad, II, 166–169; Rampersad, II, 157–158.

Troubled Island (1936). Play in three acts. The play premiered at the Karamu Theatre in Cleveland, Ohio, on November 18, 1936. Running until November 23, it was performed by the Gilpin Players,* a troupe within the Karamu Theatre. The work dramatizes the life of Jean-Jacques Dessalines (1758–1806), who rose from slavery to lead a revolt against French colonialists and to become emperor of Haiti. In *I Wonder As I Wander* Hughes describes visiting the Citadel, the fortress built by Dessalines's successor, Henri Christophe, and becoming more interested in Dessalines's story. As perceived by Hughes, Dessalines's tragic flaw is his having rejected his wife in favor of a beautiful mulatto woman who subsequently plots Dessalines's overthrow and assassination. Retitled *Drums of Haiti*, the play was performed in Detroit in 1937, and retitled *Emperor of Haiti*, it was performed in New York City, with four performances at the St. Martin's Episcopal Church Theatre and four at the Joseph P. Kennedy Memorial Centre for the Theatre. In yet one more incarnation, it served as the libretto for an opera, *Troubled Island* (1938–1949), with music by William Grant Still* (*see* the entry for *Troubled Island*, the opera). The play has not been published, but a microfilm copy of the original manuscript is held in the New York Public Library.

Bibliography: Robert J. Alexander, ed., *Biographical Dictionary of Latin American and Caribbean Political Leaders* (Westport, CT: Greenwood Press, 1988); "People without Shoes," in *I Wonder As I Wander*, 26–29; David Nicholls, *From Dessalines to Duvalier: Race, Colour, and National Independence in Haiti* (New Brunswick, NJ: Rutgers University Press, 1996).

"Troubled Lands: Stories of Mexico and Cuba." (1935). Manuscript of a collection of stories Hughes translated from the Spanish. It is held in the Langston Hughes Papers in the James Weldon Johnson Memorial Collection, Beinecke Rare Book and Manuscript Library, Yale University (item 3796). At this writing, the manuscript remains unpublished.

Bibliography: Rampersad, I, 303.

"Troubled Night." Poem. *See* "Harlem Night."

"Troubled Water." Poem in three ballad* stanzas. It is addressed to a "loved one." Between the speaker and the loved one lies a "sea of troubled water." The poem was first published in the *Amsterdam News* (October 24, 1942). *See* "America's Young Black Joe."
Bibliography: *CP*, 577.

"Troubled Woman." Poem of twelve lines in free verse that contains a highly imagistic description of the woman, who is "Bowed by / Weariness and pain." It was first published in *Opportunity** (February 1925).
Bibliography: *CP*, 42.

"Trumpet Player." Poem of forty-four lines in six stanzas that provides a rich, complicated portrait of an African American jazz* trumpet player. It was first published in *Fields of Wonder* under the title "Trumpet Player: 52nd Street."
Bibliography: *CP*, 338.

"Trumpet Player: 52nd Street." Poem. *See* "Trumpet Player."

"Twilight Reverie." Poem, one of the seven separate parts of "Seven Moments of Love."

"Two at the Bar." Short story, one of several stories written in 1941 that Rampersad characterizes as "illuminations of the blues* ideal" and that emphasize "the mediation of violence by humor." It has not been published, but a manuscript of it is held in the Langston Hughes Papers, James Weldon Johnson Memorial Collection, Beinecke Library, Yale University. *See* "Mysterious Madame Shanghai"; "Sailor Ashore"; "The Star Decides."
Bibliography: Rampersad, II, 30.

"Two Brothers: Dos Hermanos" (1953). Manuscript of a libretto for a ballet. It is held in the Langston Hughes Papers in the James Weldon Johnson Memorial Collection, Beinecke Rare Book and Manuscript Library, Yale University (item 3801), and is listed as "A Ballet by Katherine Dunham, with lyrics and notes by Langston Hughes." There is no record of the ballet's being performed, but Rampersad indicates that Hughes was paid for his work on the libretto. *See* Opera.
Bibliography: Rampersad, II, 259.

"Two Loving Arms." Short story, included in the collections *Simple Takes a Wife* and *The Best of Simple*. *See* Simple [Jesse B.] Stories.

"Two Old Books New to the Reader: A Comparison." Manuscript of a paper Hughes wrote in college (Lincoln University*?). It is undated. The paper compares the Book of Genesis with the *Odyssey*. The manuscript is held in the Langston Hughes Papers in the James Weldon Johnson Memorial Collection, Beinecke Rare Book and Manuscript Library, Yale University (item 3802).

"Two on the Road." Short story. *See* "On the Road."

"Two Sides Not Enough." Short story, included in the collections *Simple Stakes a Claim* and *The Best of Simple*. *See* Simple [Jesse B.] Stories.

"Two Somewhat Different Epigrams." Poem in two rhymed couplets, numbered with Roman numerals. Both epigrams concern God and "the human race." Couplet I was first published under the title "Prayer" in *Voices* (December 1955). Couplet II was first published under the title "Awe" in *Black Orpheus* (May 1959). *See* Religion.

Bibliography: *CP*, 453.

"Two Things." Poem of ten lines in two stanzas that concerns death and another (unnamed) powerful thing. It was first published in *Dear Lovely Death*.

Bibliography: *CP*, 158.

U

"Ultimatum." Poem. *See Montage of a Dream Deferred.*

"Ultimatum: Kid to Kid." Poem of four ballad* stanzas in which two children argue. It was first published in *Shenandoah* (Winter 1953). *See* Children's Poetry.

Bibliography: *CP*, 439.

"Un-American Investigators." Poem of twenty-three lines, intermittently rhymed. It implicitly concerns the members of the Permanent Sub-Committee on Investigations (U.S. Senate) before which Hughes was called to testify (*see* McCarthyism). The poem focuses on what Hughes regards as the investigators' anti-Semitism and suggests satirically that the committee "shivers" in "manure." It was first published in *The Panther and the Lash*. *See* "Concerning Red-Baiting"; "Langston Hughes Speaks."

Bibliography: *CP*, 560.

"Uncle Sam." Short story, included in the collection *Simple's Uncle Sam*. *See* Simple [Jesse B.] Stories.

"Uncle Tom [1]." Poem of fourteen lines, irregularly rhymed. It concerns the traditional figure of African American slavery and docility Uncle Tom, based on the chief character of the novel *Uncle Tom's Cabin* by Harriet Beecher Stowe (1811–1896), which first appeared in serial form in the periodical *National Era* and then in book form in 1852 and was adapted to the stage in 1853. The poem characterizes the figure of Uncle Tom as one belonging wholly to the past. *See* "Epitaph [2]."

Bibliography: *CP*, 302; Harriet Beecher Stowe, *Uncle Tom's Cabin*, with an introduction by Russel B. Nye (New York: Washington Square Press, 1962).

"Uncle Tom [2]." Poem of twelve short lines that depicts the figure of Uncle Tom conventionally—as, among other things, "obsequious." It was first published in *Selected Poems of Langston Hughes*. *See* "Uncle Tom [1]."

Bibliography: *CP*, 467.

"Uncle Tom's Cabin: [An Opera]" (1955). Manuscript of an uncompleted libretto for an opera. The manuscript, described as a "draft of an opening scene," is held in the Langston Hughes Papers in the James Weldon Johnson Memorial Collection, Beinecke Rare Book and Manuscript Library, Yale University (item 6805).

Bibliography: Rampersad, II, 253.

"The Underground." Poem of thirty lines, intermittently rhymed, in four stanzas. It is spoken by a collective persona* representing members of underground, anti-German resistance forces in several European countries during World War II. The poem expresses defiance. It was first published in *New Masses* (September 28, 1943). A significantly different version of the poem was published separately as "Our Spring," which has a separate entry in this encyclopedia.

Bibliography: *CP*, 279–280.

"Undertow." Poem of fourteen short lines. It depicts the "country club set" as feeling its world slipping away from it between "Selma" and "Peking." "Selma" refers to Selma, Alabama, site of civil-rights protests in the 1950s; "Peking" refers to the capital city of (Communist-controlled) China. The poem was first published in *The Panther and the Lash*. *See* Marxism.

Bibliography: *CP*, 561.

"Union." Poem of twelve lines, intermittently rhymed. It expresses support for organized labor and the hope labor unions represent for solidarity between white and black workers. It was first published in *New Masses* (September 1931). *See* Politics.

Bibliography: *CP*, 138.

"Up-Beat." Poem. *See Montage of a Dream Deferred.*

"Us: Colored." Five-line poem concerning the "strange" predicament of African Americans. It was first published in *Free Lance* (no. 1, 1955).

Bibliography: *CP*, 447.

V

"Vacation." Short story, included in *The Best of Simple. See* Simple [Jesse B.] Stories.

"Vagabonds." Poem of nine lines spoken by a collective persona* representing "hungry" homeless persons. It was first published in *Opportunity** (December 1941).

Bibliography: *CP*, 239.

Van Vechten, Carl (1880–1964). American novelist, music critic, dance critic, photographer, and archivist. Van Vechten was born and grew up in Cedar Rapids, Iowa, where he attended Cedar Rapids High School. He graduated from the University of Chicago in 1903 and moved to New York City shortly thereafter. He began working as a music and dance critic for *Broadway* magazine, edited by Theodore Dreiser, and the *New York Times*. He was among the first critics to analyze and praise the innovative music of Igor Stravinsky and Arnold Schönberg and the experimental dances of Isadora Duncan. In his capacity as critic, friend of writers, and a writer himself, he supported the careers of Gertrude Stein, Wallace Stevens, and James Purdy, among others. Hughes met Van Vechten at a party in Harlem* on November 10, 1923 (Rampersad, I, 97). Van Vechten had become fascinated by the cultural transformation Harlem was experiencing, immersed himself in Harlem nightlife, and became involved— chiefly as a generous supporter of young writers—in the literary politics of what would later be called the Harlem Renaissance.* Van Vechten supported Hughes's career, helped place *The Weary Blues* with the publishing firm of Alfred A. Knopf,* and, perhaps most important, understood Hughes's particular gifts as a writer. The two became lifelong friends; indeed, perhaps only Hughes's friendships with Noel Sullivan* and Arna Bontemps* were as constant. Van

Vechten's novel *Nigger Heaven* (1926) is considered one of the most stylish and wry works about Harlem in the 1920s. Van Vechten published several more novels and books of criticism as well as a classic book about cats, *The Tiger in the House* (1920). In a review of *Simple Takes a Wife*, Van Vechten wrote that "Langston Hughes laughs with, cries with, and speaks for the Negro (in all classes) more understandingly, perhaps, than any other writer. Harlem is his own habitat, his workshop, and his playground." *See* Bernard, Emily, in the general bibliography.

Bibliography: Lewis, *WHWV*, 74–83; Rampersad, I, 96–98; II; Carl Van Vechten, "In the Heart of Harlem" [review of *Simple Takes a Wife*], *New York Times* (May 31, 1953), 5; Watson.

"Vari-colored Song." Poem in four ballad* stanzas, using color as a device by which to represent problems with racism in the American South. It was first published in *Phylon* (1952).

Bibliography: *CP*, 434.

"Verse Written in the Album of Mademoiselle." Poem by Pierre Dalcour that Hughes translated from "Louisiana Creole." Four lines long, it is a fairly conventional love poem. It was published in *The Langston Hughes Reader*. *See* Translations by Hughes.

Bibliography: *The Langston Hughes Reader*, 136.

"A Veteran Falls." Short story, included in *The Best of Simple*. *See* Simple [Jesse B.] Stories.

"Vicious Circle." Short story, included in the collection *Simple Stakes a Claim*. *See* Simple [Jesse B.] Stories.

Video Recording Concerning Hughes. *See Langston Hughes: The Dream Keeper.*

"Vigilantes at My Door." Essay in which Hughes severely criticizes right-wing political groups, especially those aligned against the Scottsboro Boys.* It was published in *New Masses* (September 1934).

Bibliography: Rampersad, I, 296.

"Visitors to the Black Belt." Poem of eighteen lines in six stanzas. It is spoken by a collective persona* representing African Americans who live in the "black belt": predominantly African American communities such as Harlem* and the South Side of Chicago. In part, the poem instructs (white) "outsiders" to ask who "I" (African Americans) "am." It was first published in *Opportunity** (January 1940). *See also* Revision, Process of, and Hughes.

Bibliography: *CP*, 215.

The Voice of Langston Hughes: Selected Poetry and Prose (Washington, DC: Smithsonian Folkways, 1995). Audio recording that features Hughes reading poetry from *The Dream Keeper and Other Poems*, stories from *Simple Speaks His Mind*, and prose from *The First Book of Jazz, The First Book of Rhythms*, and *The Glory of Negro History: A Pageant*. This recording is a compilation of material from earlier recordings. *See* Audio Recordings.

Discography: *The Voice of Langston Hughes: Selected Poetry and Prose* [compact disc] (Smithsonian Folkways 47001).

Voices and Visions. Video series that included a program about Hughes. *See Langston Hughes: The Dream Keeper*.

W

"Waif." Poem. *See* "Kid in the Park."

"Wait." Poem of thirty-six lines in free verse. The main text is bordered on the left, right, and bottom by lists of words referring to specific oppressed peoples, places, groups, and nations. It is one of Hughes's most militant Marxist-influenced poems. The poem was first published in *Partisan* (Los Angeles, California) (December 1933). *See* Marxism; Politics.

Bibliography: *CP*, 174.

"Wait for Me." Song. Hughes wrote the lyrics, and Maria A. Niederberger composed the music. ASCAP* lists no publisher for the song. The song's ASCAP registry number is 530444207.

"Wake." Poem in one ballad quatrain. The speaker instructs mourners at his funeral to "wear red." The poem was first published in the *New Yorker* (June 10, 1944). It was also published in *Shakespeare in Harlem*. *See* "Request for Requiems." *See also* Funeral, Hughes's.

Bibliography: *CP*, 250.

Walker, Alice Malsenior (born 1944). American novelist, poet, and essayist. Walker was born in Eatonville, Georgia. She attended Spelman College and Sarah Lawrence College and became a teacher and lecturer. In the anthology *Best Short Stories by Negro Writers* (1967), Hughes included Walker's story, "To Hell with Dying." This story and "Everyday Use" were widely anthologized in subsequent years. Her best-known work is the epistolary novel *The Color Purple* (1982), which earned Walker the Pulitzer Prize. It also formed the basis for a motion picture directed by Steven Spielberg. Other novels include *Merid-*

ian (1976) and *The Temple of My Familiar* (1989). In 1989 Walker published an essay about Hughes, "Turning into Love: Some Thoughts on Surviving and Meeting Langston Hughes."

Bibliography: Henry Louis Gates, Jr., and K. A. Appiah, eds., *Alice Walker: Critical Perspectives Past and Present* (New York: Amistad, 1993); Alice Walker, "Turning into Love: Some Thoughts on Surviving and Meeting Langston Hughes," *Callaloo: An Afro-American and African Journal of Arts and Letters* 12, no. 4 (Fall 1989), 663–666; Donna Haisty Winchell, *Alice Walker* (New York: Twayne, 1992).

Walker, Margaret (1915–1998). American poet and professor. In *I Wonder As I Wander* Hughes recounts visiting Straight College in New Orleans (February 1932), where, after his poetry reading, "a teen-age girl came up with a sheaf of poems. . . . I saw that these poems showed talent, so I spent an hour after the reading going over them with the girl and pointing out to her where I thought they might be improved." The girl was Margaret Walker. Her book of poems *For My People* won the Yale University Younger Poets Award in 1942. In 1966 Walker published the acclaimed historical novel *Jubilee*, and in 1989, *This Is My Century: New and Collected Poems*. For the 1986 reissue of *I Wonder As I Wander*, Walker wrote an introduction in which she notes that the meeting in 1932 marked "the beginning of a friendship that lasted thirty-five years until Langston's death in May 1967." She remembers that Hughes kept in touch with her no matter where he traveled, and she writes that *I Wonder As I Wander* captures "the kaleidoscopic nature of his [Hughes's] mind and experience." For many years Walker was professor of English at Jackson State University in Mississippi.

Bibliography: Margaret Walker, *For My People*, with a foreword by Stephen Vincent Benet (New Haven: Yale University Press, 1942); Margaret Walker, *How I Wrote Jubilee and Other Essays on Life and Literature*, ed. Maryemma Graham (New York: Feminist Press at the City University of New York, 1990); Margaret Walker, Foreword to *I Wonder As I Wander*, by Langston Hughes (New York: Thunder's Mouth Press, 1986), xi–xii; Margaret Walker, *Jubilee* (Boston: Houghton Mifflin, 1966); Margaret Walker, *This Is My Century: New and Collected Poems* (Athens: University of Georgia Press, 1989).

"Walkers with the Dawn." Poem of six lines in free verse spoken by "walkers with the dawn," who are unafraid. It was first published in *Survey Graphic* (March 1, 1925). *See* Locke, Alain.

Bibliography: *CP*, 45.

"Walls." Poem in two ballad* stanzas that concerns different emotions "four walls" can figuratively contain. It was first published in *Palms* (November 1926).

Bibliography: *CP*, 79.

"Walt Whitman and the Negro." Brief essay concerning images of African Americans in the poetry of Walt Whitman.* It was published in *Nocturne* (Brooklyn College, New York, 1955), 9.

"Walt Whitman's Darker Brothers." *See* Whitman, Walt.

"Waltz." Song, from *The Barrier*. Hughes wrote the lyrics that formed this part of the libretto. Jan Meyerowitz* composed the music. ASCAP* lists no publisher for the song or for *The Barrier*. The song's ASCAP registry number is 530009017.

"War." Eight-line poem, intermittently rhymed. It presents a matter-of-fact depiction of war, emphasizing war's basic destructiveness. The date of composition is uncertain. The poem was first published in Berry and is not included in *Collected Poems*, although an entirely different poem of the same title is. *See also* "The Colored Soldier"; "Mother in Wartime."
Bibliography: Berry, 45.

"War." Poem of twenty-five lines in two stanzas. War, personified, speaks, suggesting that its only real aim is to kill. The poem was first published in *The Panther and the Lash*.
Bibliography: *CP*, 559.

"War and Peace." Manuscript, undated, of drafts for a "dramatic skit" that was never completed. The manuscript is held in the Langston Hughes Papers in the James Weldon Johnson Memorial Collection, Beinecke Rare Book and Manuscript Library, Yale University (item 3821).

"Warning [1]." Poem of ten lines in two stanzas. The warning concerns a coming time when "Negroes" will no longer be "sweet" and "docile." The poem was first published under the title "Roland Hayes Beaten (Georgia 1942)" in *One-Way Ticket*. Hayes (1887–1977), a classical singer, is also mentioned in "How about It, Dixie?"
Bibliography: *CP*, 365.

"Warning [2]." Poem. *See Montage of a Dream Deferred.*

"Warning: Augmented." Poem. *See Montage of a Dream Deferred.*

Washington, Booker T. (1856–1915). American teacher, school administrator, social philosopher, and writer. Washington was born into slavery at a farm near Roanoke, Virginia. His mother, also a slave, worked as a cook for the planter James Burroughs. Washington's white father is unknown but was likely related to Burroughs. After the Civil War and freed from slavery, Washington moved with his mother to West Virginia, where he worked in coal mines. A self-taught student, Washington entered Hampton Institute in 1872, graduated in 1875, and returned to West Virginia to teach. Soon thereafter he was recommended as a candidate for the directorship of a new school for blacks, the Tuskegee Normal and Industrial Institute in Alabama. So new was the school that it had no land, no buildings, and little money. Washington accepted the directorship (and the challenge), borrowed money to purchase land, and began teaching in temporary buildings. Eventually he turned the school, known more familiarly as the Tuskegee Institute into an internationally respected center of industrial-arts education. Simultaneously, he promoted a social philosophy that encouraged African Americans to emphasize economic independence over advocacy for civil rights and social equality. Washington's 1895 speech, now known as "The Atlanta Compromise," defined his approach as "accommodation." This philosophy was in sharp contrast to that of his contemporary, W.E.B. Du Bois,* especially as Du Bois became more committed to social change in the 1920s. Somewhat ironically, however, the two collaborated on the book *The Negro in the South: His Economic Progress in Relation to His Moral and Religious Development* (1907). Because Washington's views were so well known and, in contrast to other emerging political viewpoints, conservative, American and African American intellectuals and leaders tended to use Washington, in varying ways, as a point of reference. Washington's autobiography, *Up from Slavery* (1901), which he cowrote with journalist Bennett Thrasher, quickly became a widely read, even classic, American autobiography, taking its place beside the *Narrative* of Frederick Douglass* and *The Education of Henry Adams*. The political views of Hughes were far closer to those of Du Bois (for example) than to those of Washington; nonetheless, his two poems concerning Washington, "Alabama Earth" and "The Ballad of Booker T.," are sympathetic and respectful. *See* Carver, George Washington; "Heart of Harlem"; "To Certain Negro Leaders."

Bibliography: Donald Gibson, "Strategies and Revisions of Self-Representation in Booker T. Washington's Autobiography," *American Quarterly* 45, no. 3 (September 1993), 370–393; Louis R. Harlan, *Booker T. Washington: The Wizard of Tuskegee, 1901–1915* (New York: Oxford University Press, 1983); Booker T. Washington, *Up from Slavery: An Autobiography* (New York: Doubleday, Page, 1901).

"Watch Out, Papa." Poem of fourteen lines in three stanzas, intermittently rhymed. It warns the reader about certain signs (including nostalgia) of aging. It was first published in the *Carmel Pine Cone* (June 13, 1941).
Bibliography: *CP*, 232.

"Water-Front Streets." Poem in two ballad* quatrains contrasting the rough environs of the waterfront with the dreams and aspirations that the people there (including sailors) can hold. It was first published in *The Weary Blues*.
Bibliography: *CP*, 96.

Watson, Madame Caledonia. Singer in the minstrel show at the carnival in chapter 9 of *Not Without Laughter*. The impresario refers to her as "the Dixie songbird."

"Wave of Sorrow." Poem. *See* "Island [1]."

Way Down South (1939). Motion picture (62 minutes). Hughes cowrote the screenplay with Clarence Muse,* who also acted in the musical drama, which was directed by Bernard Vorhaus and produced by Sol Lesser. Bobby Breen* starred in the film. Donald Bogle writes, "Essentially an Old South melodrama, *Way Down South* told the story of an orphaned white Southern lad (Bobby Breen) and his devotion to the slaves his deceased father had treated so humanely" (56). Bogle groups the film with others Muse acted in, and he describes the roles for which Muse had to settle as "the inhibited, humanized [Uncle] Tom" (53). Muse and Hughes also cowrote the songs "Good Ground" and "Louisiana" for the film; they were performed by Breen and the Hall Johnson Choir. As Rampersad notes, Muse and Hughes saw the project as a way to break into writing for the screen, and Hughes especially was in difficult financial straits at the time. Rampersad also suggests that Hughes was naïve about the financial arrangements and found the working conditions humiliating; he notes that reviewers from *Variety*, the *New York Times*, and the *Los Angeles Times* liked the film but that some of Hughes's friends were highly critical of his participation in a film project that perpetuated racial stereotypes. Angry at such criticism, Hughes composed an unpublished "STATEMENT IN ROUND NUMBERS CONCERNING THE RELATIVE MERITS OF 'WAY DOWN SOUTH.' " In part, the statement indicates that Hughes used money he earned from writing the script to pay for his mother's doctors' bills and then expenses for her funeral (I, 365–366, 370). At this writing, the film is available in videocassette format. A copy of the screenplay is held in the Langston Hughes Papers in the James Weldon Johnson Memorial Collection, Beinecke Rare Book and Manuscript Library, Yale University (items 3899–3901).

Bibliography: Donald Bogle, *Toms, Coons, Mulattoes, Mammies, and Bucks: An Interpretive History of Blacks in American Films*, 3rd ed. (New York: Continuum, 1994), 53–56; Rampersad, I, 365–370 (Reviews of *Way Down South* cited by Rampersad: *New York Times*, June 5, 1939; *Variety*, July 19, 1939; *Los Angeles Times*, June 5, 1939.)

"Ways." Poem of five lines in free verse that concerns methods (ways) of committing suicide. It was first published in *Buccaneer* (May 1925). *See* "Suicide"; "Suicide's Note."

Bibliography: *CP*, 51.

"Ways and Means." Short story, included in the collection *Simple Speaks His Mind. See* Simple [Jesse B.] Stories.

The Ways of White Folks (New York: Knopf, 1934). 248 pp. Hughes's first collection of short stories. As Hughes notes in *I Wonder As I Wander*, part of the impetus for writing many of these stories came from his having read a volume of stories by D. H. Lawrence and realizing that short fiction might be one especially powerful genre through which to represent issues of (and connections between) race, social class, and sexuality in the United States. Rampersad and Ostrom comment on how Hughes adapted Lawrence's approach to short fiction to his purposes. The collection was widely reviewed and was generally well received, but was also controversial (*see* Anderson, Sherwood). It includes at least two stories that are considered classic examples of Hughes's short fiction: "Cora Unashamed" and "The Blues I'm Playing." It also includes several stories set in Harlem* during the Harlem Renaissance*; these include "Slave on the Block," "The Blues I'm Playing," and "Rejuvenation through Joy." The remaining stories are "Home," "Passing," "A Good Job Gone," "Redheaded Baby," "Poor Little Black Fellow," "Little Dog," "Berry" (which includes the sentence from which the title of the collection is taken), "Mother and Child," "One Christmas Eve," and "Father and Son." Each story has its own entry in this encyclopedia. The collection is still in print at this writing.

Bibliography: *I Wonder As I Wander*, 37–40; Ostrom, 3–19; Rampersad, I, 282–293.

"We, Too." Rhyming poem of twenty-one lines expressing kinship between African Americans and Africans, the latter represented specifically by a symbolic "Congo Brother." Line nine includes the unusual word "encarnadine," which *The Oxford English Dictionary* lists as a variant of "incarnadine." As an adjective, the word describes a dark-red or cinnamon color. As a verb, which is how Hughes uses it ("we encarnadine the sky"), it means "to redden" or to "dye" something a cinnamon color. The poem was first published in *New Orlando Anthology* (1963). *See* "Lumumba's Grave."

Bibliography: *CP*, 538, 687; *The Compact Oxford Dictionary of the English Language*, 2nd ed., revised (Oxford: Clarendon Press, 1991), 829.

"Wealth." Poem of fourteen lines in free verse. Referring to Christ, St. Francis of Assisi, and Mahatma Gandhi, the poem suggests that "goodness" is the most genuine form of wealth. It was first published in *Public Opinion* (October 9, 1948). *See* "Gandhi Is Fasting"; Religion.

Bibliography: *CP*, 342.

The Weary Blues. (New York: Knopf, 1926). 110 pp. Introduction by Carl Van Vechten.* Hughes's first collection of poetry. It contains fifty-nine poems in seven sections that take their titles from poems within the sections: "The Weary Blues," "Dream Variations," "The Negro Speaks of Rivers," "A Black Pierrot," "Water-front Streets," and "Our Land." These sections are preceded by the poem "Proem" (later given the title "Negro"), which stands alone. *The Weary Blues* is a remarkable book for several reasons. By almost any measure, the poems it contains represent a variety of subject matter, a maturity of style, and a range of innovation that are all the more impressive for Hughes's having been only twenty-three years old when the book went to press. In his introduction, Van Vechten observes, "At the moment I cannot recall the name of any other person whatever who, at the age of twenty-three, has enjoyed so picturesque and rambling an existence as Langston Hughes" (9). Also, the extent to which and the effectiveness with which Hughes incorporated a blues* idiom in his poetry were genuinely path-breaking. Steven C. Tracy observes, "It is doubly significant that Hughes gave his[first] volume the title of this poem and that it is the first poem (following 'Proem') in the volume. It suggests that the entire volume begins with and is informed by the 'weary blues,' and the tradition with which one must come to grips" (220). Additionally, the book almost immediately came to symbolize several characteristics of the Harlem Renaissance*: its youthful spirit; the several ways in which, in various forms, it attempted to forge new and "authentic" "Negro" art; its use of different modes of African American "language," meaning idioms, slang, speech patterns, black dialect,* phrasings, and rhythms; and its profound interest in an urban African American experience. "Here is a poet with whom to reckon," wrote Countee Cullen* in a review (Mullen, 37). Reviews by Jessie Fauset* and Alain Locke* both noted the apparent emergence of an exceptional new voice in American poetry, while a review by DuBose Heyward* raised an issue that would be linked to Hughes's writing throughout his whole career: the presence in his writing of politics,* which to some readers inevitably raised (and raises) the specter of "propaganda." Heyward wrote, "In one or two places in the book the artist is obscured by the propagandist. Pegasus has been made a pack-horse" (Mullen, 43). Heyward did not specify in which poems this transformation occurred, and at any rate, other readers and writers (Hughes included) might have quarreled with the premise that poetry expressing political views is necessarily a kind of propaganda. *Opportunity* magazine gave Hughes an award for the book in 1926. Among the book's poems that became instantly associated with Hughes's distinctiveness are the title poem, "The Negro Speaks of Rivers," "When Sue Wears Red," "Aunt Sue's Stories," and "Mother to Son." "Jazzonia," "Negro Dancer," "Cabaret," "Harlem Night Club," "Nude Young Dancer," "Lenox Avenue: Midnight," "To a Black Dancer in the Little Savoy," and "Harlem Night Song," and the title poem are indelible evocations of Harlem* in the 1920s. "Cross," "The South," "Our Land," "Lament for Dark Peoples," "The White Ones," and "Mother to Son" signal what would be Hughes's career-long preoccupation with the unique situation of African Americans, with difficulties faced by people of color worldwide, and with specific problems associated with racism in the United States. All of the poems in the book are reprinted in *Collected Poems*, and many are reprinted in *The Dream Keeper* and *Selected Poems. See also* Songs.

Bibliography: Countee Cullen, "Poet on Poet," *Opportunity* 4 (March 1926), 73 (reprinted in Mullen, 37–39); Arthur P. Davis, "The Harlem of Langston Hughes' [*sic*] Poetry," in

Mullen, 135–142; Jessie Fauset, ["Review of *The Weary Blues*"], *Crisis* 30–31 (March 1926), 239 (reprinted in Mullen, 39–41); DuBose Heyward, "The Jazz Band's Sob," *New York Herald Tribune Books* (August 1926), 4–5 (reprinted in Mullen, 42–44); Charles S. Johnson, "Jazz Poetry and Blues," in Mullen, 143–147; Alain Locke, ["Review of *The Weary Blues*"], *Palms* 4 (1926–1927); 25–27 (reprinted in Mullen, 44–46); Rampersad, I, 110–118, Tracy.

"The Weary Blues." Poem of thirty-five lines in two stanzas. It is the title poem of Hughes's first collection of poems. It is also frequently associated with Hughes's opus of blues* poems, but ironically it is not a blues poem per se, although it does quote a stanza from the traditional "Weary Blues." The poem's speaker, wandering through Harlem,* hears someone performing the blues. Later, Dorothy Rudd Moore set the poem to music, although "The," was dropped from the title. The song's ASCAP* registry number is 530251433. The song was published by American Composers Alliance (New York) in 1972.

Bibliography: *CP*, 50.

The Weary Blues (New York: Uni/Verve, 1958). Sound recording. It features the music of Charles Mingus and his band and Hughes reading from *The Weary Blues*. The recording was rereleased in compact-disc form in 1990 (Polygram 841–660–2). *See* Jazz.

"Weight in Gold." Short story, included in the collection *Simple's Uncle Sam*. *See* Simple[Jesse B.] Stories.

Weill, Kurt (1900–1950). German American composer. Weill was born in Dessau, Germany, and studied at the Staatliche Hochschule für Musik in Berlin. Before he was twenty years old, he was conducting orchestras at Dessau and Ludenscheid. Returning to Berlin, he studied with Ferruccio Busoni (1866–1924), and subsequently his first opera, the one-act *The Protagonist*, was performed in Berlin, followed by *Royal Palace* in 1927. He gained wide acclaim and notoriety with the *Rise and Fall of the Town of Mahagonny*, on which he collaborated with Bertolt Brecht. In 1928 the two collaborated on *The Three-Penny Opera*, an adaptation of John Gay's *The Beggar's Opera* that became a landmark achievement in musical theatre and demonstrated Weill's ability to blend his classical training with popular song forms, including American "ragtime" music. "Mack the Knife," from *The Three-Penny Opera*, became an enormously popular song worldwide. The satiric, innovative work for which Weill became known and his Jewish background made him an unwelcome composer in Nazi Germany. Ultimately Weill and his wife, performer Lotte Lenya, moved to the United States, settled in New York City, and became American citizens. In New York Weill successfully composed Broadway musicals, including *Johnny Johnson* (1935), *Knickerbocker Holiday* (1938), and *Lady in the Dark* (1941), the latter a collaboration with Moss Hart and Ira Gershwin. In 1943 he collaborated with S. J. Perelman and Ogden Nash on *One Touch of Venus*, and he collaborated with Elmer Rice* and Hughes on *Street Scene*.

"We'll Go Away Together." Song, from *Street Scene*. Hughes wrote the lyrics, and Kurt Weill* composed the music. ASCAP* lists the song as being published by Chappell, Inc., and by Hampshire House Publishers. The song's ASCAP registry number is 530020736.

"We're All in the Telephone Book." Poem in four ballad* stanzas that depicts the telephone book as a symbol of American democracy. It was first published in *Common Ground* (1947). *See* Children's Poetry.

Bibliography: *CP*, 602.

"West Texas." Poem in four innovative stanzas of five lines; the last words of stanzas one and two rhyme, as do those of stanzas three and four. The speaker is an African American man whose girlfriend is named "Joe." They both want to leave West Texas because of racism. *Collected Poems* contains information about revisions the poem underwent between its publication in *Shakespeare in Harlem* and its inclusion in *Selected Poems of Langston Hughes*. *See* Revision, Process of, and Hughes.

Bibliography: *CP*, 252, 653–654.

"[Western Reserve University: Commencement Address]." Manuscript of an address Hughes gave at commencement ceremonies of Adelbart College, Western Reserve University (later known as Case Western Reserve University), Cleveland, Ohio, on June 10, 1964. Hughes received an honorary degree from the college that day. The manuscript is held in the Langston Hughes Papers of the James Weldon Johnson Memorial Collection, Beinecke Rare Book and Manuscript Library, Yale University (item 3822).

Bibliography: Rampersad, II, 378.

"What?" Poem of eight lines in two stanzas that concerns pimps. It was first published under the title "White Felts in Fall" in *One-Way Ticket*.

Bibliography: *CP*, 367.

"What Can a Man Say?" Short story, included in the collections *Simple Takes a Wife* and *The Best of Simple*. *See* Simple [Jesse B.] Stories.

"What Good Would the Moon Be?" Song, from *Street Scene*. Hughes wrote the lyrics, and Kurt Weill* composed the music. ASCAP* lists the song as being published by Chappell, Inc., and by Hampshire House Publishers. The song's ASCAP registry number is 530039404.

"What I Think." Poem of twenty-six lines that expresses anticolonialist sentiments. It was first published in the *Amsterdam News* (March 27, 1943). *See* "America's Young Black Joe."

Bibliography: *CP*, 579.

"What Makes the Negro Press Worthwhile." Essay commemorating an anniversary of the *Chicago Defender** and praising the strengths of African American newspapers such as the *Defender* and the *Baltimore Afro American.** It was first published in the *Chicago Defender* (May 1955), but was apparently written in 1935. A manuscript of the essay is held in the Langston Hughes Papers of the James Weldon Johnson Memorial Collection, Beinecke Rare Book and Manuscript Library, Yale University.

"What Shall We Do about the Junkies?" Brief essay about the problem of drug addiction, specifically addiction to heroin, in Harlem.* Hughes expresses concern that the Federal Bureau of Investigation and other law-enforcement agencies are indifferent to the problem. The essay was published in *Afro Magazine* (August 10, 1963) and was reprinted in Berry.

Bibliography: Berry, 168–169.

"What Shall We Do about the South?" Essay concerning the need to abolish Jim Crow laws* and to make other reforms to counteract the effects of racism on African Americans in the southern United States. It was published in *Common Ground* (Winter 1943).

"What? So Soon!" Poem. *See Montage of a Dream Deferred.*

"What the Negro Wants." Essay expressing the view that "the Negro" (African Americans) "wants" chiefly the same economic opportunities and social status afforded to other American citizens. It was published in *Common Ground* (1941).

"When a Man Sees Red." Short story, included in the collection *Simple Speaks His Mind. See* Simple [Jesse B.] Stories.

"When a Woman Has a Baby." Song, from *Street Scene*. Hughes and Elmer Rice* wrote the lyrics, and Kurt Weill* composed the music. ASCAP* lists the song as being published by Chappell, Inc., and by Hampshire House Publishers. The song's ASCAP registry number is 530047717.

"When I'm In a Quiet Mood." Song, from *Simply Heavenly*. Hughes wrote the lyrics, and David Martin composed the music. ASCAP* lists the song as being published by the Bourne Music Company, and the song's ASCAP registry number is 530051337.

"When Sue Wears Red." Poem of thirteen lines in six stanzas. With the exuberant, humorous use of religious rhetoric ("Blow trumpets, Jesus!"), it celebrates the beauty of Susanna Jones. The poem is read by an actor in the documentary *Langston Hughes: The Dream Keeper.** It was first published in *Crisis** (February 1923), but *Collected Poems* includes information about changes made to the poem before it was subsequently published in *The Weary Blues.* As the editors of *Collected Poems* also note, Hughes in *The Big Sea* recalls having written the first version of the poem for a young woman he knew at Central High School* in Cleveland, Ohio. *See also* Revision, Process of, and Hughes.

Bibliography: *The Big Sea,* 15; *CP,* 30, 621.

"When the Armies Passed." Poem of twenty-two lines that features a dialogue between "Mama" and "Son," who talk about caps of dead soldiers. The caps have "red stars" (representing the Soviet Union). The poem was first published in *Fields of Wonder.*

Bibliography: *CP,* 340.

When the Jack Hollers (1936). Play in three acts, cowritten by Arna Bontemps* and Hughes, who jointly described it as a "Negro folk comedy." The play was premiered by the Gilpin Players* (connected with the Karamu Theatre) in Cleveland, Ohio, on April 28, 1936. It is set in the Mississippi Delta in spring and draws its comedy from the lives of black sharecroppers. Insofar as the play treats working-class African American life comedically and makes use of African American colloquial speech, it is similar to *Little Ham* and *Mule Bone,* but no reviewer or critic has regarded it to be as successful as these two plays. *When the Jack Hollers* is arguably less unified than these two related works because its impulses are several: satiric, comic, and sentimental—sentimental because the dialogue sometimes seems forced into advocating racial harmony. Hicklin describes its language as "frequently coarse, wordy, and non-dramatic" (253). In a broader overview, Rampersad notes that a tension existed between Hughes's radical political views of the 1930s and the "commercial" nature of *Little Ham* and *When the Jack Hollers.* Rampersad speculates that "[a]t thirty-four, he[Hughes] was probably tired of being poor; the death of his father had perhaps removed the single most important pressure that had driven him toward radicalism and his version of bohemianism. . . . His Karamu playwriting, from one angle a venture in commercialism, was perhaps also part of his renewal of racial bonding. Black audiences wanted to laugh at little Hamlet Jones[in *Little Ham*], not to agonize with *Angelo Herndon Jones*" (I, 322). *When the Jack Hollers* has not been published; a manuscript of it is held in the Langston

Hughes Papers in the James Weldon Johnson Memorial Collection, Beinecke Rare Book and Manuscript Library, Yale University.

Bibliography: Hicklin, 253; Rampersad, I, 322.

"Where Service Is Needed." Poem in five ballad* stanzas. It concerns Jim Crow laws* that prevented African American men and women from participating fully in the U.S. armed services during World War II. It was first published in the *Daily Express*, an African American newspaper in Cleveland, Ohio (February 17, 1951). *Collected Poems* includes additional information regarding publication of the poem. *See* Roosevelt, Franklin Delano.

Bibliography: *CP*, 384, 671.

"Where? When? Which?" Poem of sixteen lines that concerns segregationist policies in the United States and apartheid in South Africa. It was first published in the *Colorado Review* (Winter 1956–1957).

Bibliography: *CP*, 456.

White, Walter (1893–1955). American novelist, essayist, and political leader. White was born and grew up in Atlanta, Georgia, and graduated from Atlanta University. A light-skinned African American, White chose not to "pass" as a white person and, moreover, became committed to political and civil-rights issues early on, becoming executive secretary of the NAACP* in 1918. In this position White was an effective organizer and political strategist. In 1919, passing as a white person (for strategic reasons) under extraordinarily dangerous circumstances, White associated with Ku Klux Klan* chapters in the South to investigate lynching* and other acts of mob violence. His article " 'Massacring Whites' in Arkansas" was based on this investigation and appeared in the *Nation* (December 6, 1919). During the Harlem Renaissance* White was closely associated with James Weldon Johnson,* Charles S. Johnson,* Jessie Redmon Fauset,* and W. E .B. Du Bois.* He also advised such writers as Nella Larsen,* Claude McKay,* and Rudolph Fisher* and became acquainted with Hughes. White published his first novel, *Fire in the Flint*, in 1924 and his second, *Flight*, in 1926. His nonfiction book *Rope and Faggot* (1929) is a landmark study of lynching. *See* "The Ballad of Walter White"; Robeson, Paul.

Bibliography: Roger M. Valade III, *The Essential Black Literature Guide* (Detroit: Visible Ink Press, 1996), 378–379.

"White Felts in Fall." Poem. *See* "What?"

"White Folks Do the Funniest Things." Humorous essay about relations between black and white Americans, published in *Common Ground* (Spring 1944).

"White Man." Poem of thirty-three lines in free verse. It is spoken by a collective persona* representing "Negroes" and is addressed to a collective "listener" within the poem, the "White Man." The poem alludes to Mussolini's invasion of Ethiopia (*see* "Call of Ethiopia"), to white music publishers profiting exploitatively from black musicians, and to what the speaker regards as the racist nature of capitalism. It was first published in *New Masses* (December 1936). *See* Marxism.

Bibliography: *CP*, 194–195.

"White on Black: A Century of Distinguished Short Stories by White Americans about Black Americans" (1965). Manuscript of notes and titles for a proposed anthology to be edited by Hughes and Lindsay Patterson. The project was not completed. The manuscript is held in the Langston Hughes Papers of the James Weldon Johnson Memorial Collection, Beinecke Rare Book and Manuscript Library, Yale University (item 3839). Hughes included a story by Patterson in *The Best Short Stories by Negro Writers: An Anthology from 1899 to the Present.*

"The White Ones." Poem of seven lines in free verse. The speaker indicates that he does not "hate" white people, that he believes that their faces are "beautiful, too." But he wonders why whites seem to hate blacks. The poem was first published in *Opportunity** (March 1924).

Bibliography: *CP*, 37.

"White Shadows." Poem. *See* "House in the World."

Whitehead, Buster. The main character in the play *Joy to My Soul*.

"Whiter Than Snow." Short story, included in the collection *Simple Takes a Wife*. *See* Simple [Jesse B.] Stories.

Whitman, Walt (1819–1892). Whitman was born on Long Island, New York, but his family moved to Brooklyn when he was still a boy. He attended school there, worked as a clerk, and eventually edited the newspaper the *Brooklyn Daily Eagle*, in which Hughes, coincidentally, would later publish work. In 1847 Whitman began working on *Leaves of Grass*, a book of poems he published himself in 1855. He continued to revise, supplement, and republish the collection over the course of his career. Because of his innovative use of free verse, his enormous linguistic gifts, and his exuberance, Whitman is generally viewed as a towering figure in American literature and, indeed, as one of the first writers to craft works that broke sharply from British literary traditions. "Crossing Brooklyn Ferry," "When Lilacs Last in the Dooryard Bloom'd," and "Song of Myself" are among Whitman's best-known works. Hughes appreciated Whitman's innovative verse and his populist perspective, which are also reflected in the work of Carl Sandburg,* by whom Hughes was also influenced. Hughes expressed his affinity for Whitman's work in the poem "Old Walt," in a speech he gave to the Walt Whitman Foundation in 1927 (*see* Rampersad I, 144–146), and in an introduction he wrote for a selected edition of Whitman's poetry. Leonard Bernstein included works by Whitman and Hughes ("I, Too, Sing America") in his song cycle *Songfest*. Hughes had planned to edit an anthology of early African American poetry entitled "Walt Whitman's Darker Brothers." An undated draft of the plan is held in the Langston Hughes Papers of the James Weldon Johnson Memorial Collection, Beinecke Rare Book and Manuscript Library, Yale University (item 3840).

Bibliography: Leonard Bernstein, *Songfest: A Cycle of American Poems for Six Singers and Orchestra*, corrected ed. (New York: Jalni Publications, 1988); Langston Hughes, "Introduction" to *I Hear the People Singing: Selected Poems of Walt Whitman* (New York: International Publishers, 1946); Rampersad, I, 145–146; Walt Whitman, *Leaves of Grass*, ed. Harold W. Blodgett and Sculley Bradley (New York: New York University Press, 1965).

"Who but the Lord?" Poem of twenty-three lines in four stanzas. The speaker reports having seen the police come down the street, knowing they will beat him. He asks God to protect him, but God does not. The speaker asks, rhetorically, who will save people who are "poor and black" from "police brutality" if "the Lord" does not save them. The poem was first published in *Poetry* (February 1947). *See* Religion; "Third Degree."

Bibliography: *CP*, 322.

"Who's Passing for Who?" Short story. The narrative is set in a bar, presumably in Harlem,* and explores the issue of light-skinned African Americans "passing" as white. Unlike the story "Passing" from *The Ways of White Folks*, however, "Who's Passing for Who?" treats the issue comically, not tragically. An altercation in a bar reveals that one man's gallantry extends to women only if they are white, and that the man's friends have been passing as white. The effect is deliberately farcical. One unusual narrative technique in the story is Hughes's use of a first-person-plural narrator. The story was included in the collection *Laughing to Keep from Crying*.

Bibliography: Ostrom, 19–20.

"Why, You Reckon?" Short story. The mildly satiric narrative concerns a wealthy young white man who is "mugged" in New York City by young black men. The black men are befuddled because the white man seems delighted to have been mugged because he considers the occurrence to represent firsthand experience with African American culture. The story was first published in the *New Yorker* (March 17, 1934), was included in the collections *Laughing to Keep*

from Crying and *Something in Common and Other Stories*; and was reprinted in *Langston Hughes: Short Stories*.
Bibliography: Ostrom, 25–26.

"Wide River." Poem in three traditional blues* stanzas and in black dialect.* The speaker is a woman who is separated from her lover by a wide river. The poem was first published in *Measure* (June 1926).
Bibliography: *CP*, 71.

"Wide Wide River: A Folk Opera." Manuscript of a draft of a libretto for an opera based on the play *The Scuffletown Outlaws* by William Norment Cox. (There is no comma after the first "Wide" in the title.) Granville English was to have composed music for the opera, which never materialized. The manuscript is held in the Langston Hughes Papers of the James Weldon Johnson Memorial Collection, Beinecke Rare Book and Manuscript Library, Yale University (item 3848).

"Widow Woman." Poem in three traditional blues* stanzas, although Hughes separates the last two lines from the final stanza and puts them in italics. The speaker, a widowed woman, meditates on death and loneliness. The poem was first published in *Shakespeare in Harlem*.
Bibliography: *CP*, 259–260.

"Wigs for Freedom." Short story, included in the collection *Simple's Uncle Sam*. *See* Simple [Jesse B.] Stories.

"Will V-Day Be Me-Day, Too?" Poem of eighty-five lines with added epistolary material above and below the body of the poem, which is subtitled "(A Negro Fighting Man's Letter to America)." The soldier asks the United States whether it will abolish Jim Crow laws* and otherwise improve the legal, social, and economic conditions of African Americans upon his return from fighting on behalf of the United States in World War II. The poem was first published in the *Chicago Defender** (December 30, 1944). *See also* "Crow Goes, Too"; "Dear Mr. President"; "Letter from Spain"; "Message to the President."
Bibliography: *CP*, 303.

Williams, Hager. The grandmother of James "Sandy" Rodgers,* who is the main character in *Not Without Laughter*. Everyone, including Sandy, calls her Aunt Hager. She is a strong, matriarchal figure, wise and opinionated.

Williams, Harriet. Sister of Anjee Williams Rodgers* in *Not Without Laughter* and thus an aunt to James "Sandy" Rodgers,* the main character.

"Wine-O." Poem. *See Montage of a Dream Deferred.*

"Winter Moon." Poem of three long lines that describes a "ghostly moon." It was first published in *Crisis** (August 1923).
Bibliography: *CP*, 35.

"Winter Sweetness." Poem of one ballad* quatrain that describes a gingerbread house. It was first published in the *Brownie's Book** (January 1921). *See* Children's Poetry; Fauset, Jessie Redmon.
Bibliography: *CP*, 597.

"Wisdom." Poem in two quatrains, although the rhyme scheme and rhythm are those of rhymed couplets. The speaker is skeptical about how wise humans are. The poem was first published in the *Saturday Evening Post* (January 30, 1943).
Bibliography: *CP*, 268–269.

"Wisdom and War." Poem of fourteen lines in four stanzas, intermittently rhymed. The poem regards war as resulting from an absence of wisdom on the part of mankind. It was first published in *Span* (October 1946).
Bibliography: *CP*, 342–343.

"Wise Men." Poem of nine lines in two stanzas. In part, it concerns the "dead eyes" of alleged "wise men." It was first published in the *Messenger** (June 1927).
Bibliography: *CP*, 107.

"With All Deliberate Speed." Short story, included in the collection *Simple Stakes a Claim. See* Simple [Jesse B.] Stories.

"Without Benefit of Declaration." Poem of nineteen lines in four stanzas, intermittently rhymed. It concerns a soldier dying in an undeclared war and may refer to the Korean War. It was first published in *Free Lance* (no. 1, 1955).
Bibliography: *CP*, 446.

Wizard of Altoona (1950). Opera on which Hughes (as librettist) and composer Elie Siegmeister (1909–1991) began to collaborate. It was to be a folk opera set in Pennsylvania, but the project did not materialize. Hughes and Siegmeister did, however, collaborate successfully on such songs (or poems adapted to songs) as "Face of War," "Fired," "Madam and the Minister," and "Madam to You."
Bibliography: "Elie Siegmeister" [obituary], *Opera News* 56, no. 1 (July 1991), 44; Rampersad, II, especially 181–182.

"The Woman Who Lived Up There." Song, from *Street Scene*. Hughes wrote the lyrics, and Kurt Weill* composed the music. ASCAP* lists the song as being published by Chappell, Inc., and by Hampshire House Publishers. The song's ASCAP registry number is 530103227.

Women in Hughes's Writing. One of Hughes's earliest and one of his latest published poems are about women: "Aunt Sue's Stories" (1921), which to some extent draws on Hughes's memories of his grandmother telling and reading him stories, and "Mother in Wartime" (1967), concerning a mother's naïveté about politics and warfare. In the decades between the publication of these poems, Hughes wrote frequently about women, expressing a spectrum of attitudes (his own and others') toward them, often attempting to empathize with and validate their experiences, and making them a part of works in all the genres in which he wrote. The sheer abundance of works he produced that significantly concern women in itself sets him apart from most of his male contemporaries; the subtlety and range of these works distinguish him further from other male writers of his era; and the several ways in which his work anticipates "gender issues" of later decades make him virtually unique. Certainly his perspectives on women were hardly free of prejudices, conventions, and limitations one might expect from a male American writer of his generation; nonetheless, his literary interest in women was profound, sustained, and often subtle. In addition to the two examples already noted, other poems concerning women (many spoken by women personae) include "Anne Spencer's Table," "Ardella," "Bad Man" (which gives an unvarnished depiction of domestic violence), "Ballad of Gin Mary," "The Ballad of Margie Polite," "Ballad of the Girl Whose Name Is Mud," "Beale Street Love" (also concerning violence against women), "Black Maria," "Cabaret Girl Dies on Welfare Island," "Cora," "Evil Woman," "For Salome," "Gal's Cry for a Dying Lover," "Hard Daddy," "Helen Keller," "Jazz Girl," "Juliet," "Lady's Boogie," "Love Song for Antonia," "Love Song for Lucinda," the Madam poems,* "Mama and Daughter," "Mazie Dies Alone in the City Hospital," "Mexican Market Woman," "Midnight Chippie's Lament," "Midnight Dancer," "Minnie Sings Her Blues," "Miss Blues's Child," "Mother to Son," "The Negro Mother," "Nonette," "Pale Lady," "Parisian Beggar Woman," "Poor Girl's Ruination," "Red Silk Stockings," "Ruby Brown," "A Ruined Gal," "Sister Johnson Marches," "Song for a Dark Girl," "Song for Billie Holiday," "Song to a Negro Washwoman," "Songs to a Dark Virgin," "Southern Mammy Sings," "To Artina," "To Midnight Nan at Leroy's," "To the Dark Mercedes of 'El Palacio de Amor,' " "Troubled Woman," "When Sue Wears Red," "Young Bride," "Young Gal's Blues," "Young Negro Girl" and "Young Prostitute." Many of Hughes's short stories contain significant women characters, perhaps the most memorable story being "The Blues I'm Playing." The Simple stories* contain the recurring characters Joyce, Zarita, and Cousin Minnie. The character Aunt Hager is but one of the crucial women characters in the novel *Not Without Laughter*, and the two main characters in the play and novel

Tambourines to Glory are women. The plays *Front Porch, Mule Bone*, and *Soul Gone Home* feature important female characters, as do the musical plays *Simply Heavenly* and *Street Scene*. Both of Hughes's autobiographies, *The Big Sea* and *I Wonder As I Wander*, show the extent to which he believed women to have figured significantly in his life, the variety of female friends he had, the degree to which Mrs. Charlotte Osgood Mason* became (in his view) a nemesis, and—to be sure— the extent to which he resisted permanent romantic commitments to women. The essay "The Soviet Union and Women" is particularly revealing of his interest in women's rights. As an editor of anthologies, Hughes was evidently quite interested in discovering the talents of women writers; see especially *The Best Short Stories by Negro Writers: An Anthology from 1899 to the Present*. Topics that cut across the genres of Hughes's writing include racism and women, domestic violence, women and war, women and work, the sexual exploitation of women, women and the arts, the inconstancy of men, women and workers' rights, women and sexuality, women as matriarchs (particularly in African American families), and women and religion.* *See* Sexuality and Hughes.

Bibliography: Anne Borden, " 'Heroic Hussies' and 'Brilliant Queers': Gender-racial Resistance in the Work of Langston Hughes," *African American Review* 28, no. 3 (Fall 1994), 333–345; David Chinitz, " 'Dance, Little Lady': Poets, Flappers, and the Gendering of Jazz," in *Modernism, Gender, and Culture: A Cultural Studies Approach*, ed. Lisa Rado (New York: Garland, 1997), 319–335; Myriam Diaz-Diocaretz, "Society (Pro)poses, and Madam (Dis)poses," *Langston Hughes Review* 6, no. 1 (Spring 1987), 30–36; Joyce Ann Joyce, "Race, Culture, and Gender in Langston Hughes's *The Ways of White Folks*," in *Langston Hughes: The Man, His Art, and His Continuing Influence*, ed. C. James Trotman (New York: Garland, 1995), 99–107; Delita L. Martin, "The 'Madam Poems' as Dramatic Monologue," in Mullen, 148–154; R. Baxter Miller, " 'No Crystal Stair': Unity, Archetype, and Symbol in Langston Hughes's Poems on Women," *Negro American Literature Forum* 9 (1975), 109–114; Ostrom; Cheryl A. Wall, "Whose Sweet Angel Child? Blues Women, Langston Hughes, and Writing during the Harlem Renaissance," in *Langston Hughes: The Man, His Art, and His Continuing Influence*, ed. C. James Trotman (New York: Garland, 1995), 37–50.

"Wonder." Poem. *See Montage of a Dream Deferred*.

Woodson, Carter G. (1875–1950). Woodson's parents were former slaves. He was born and grew up in New Canton, Virginia, and graduated from Berea College. He earned an M.A. at the University of Chicago and a Ph.D. from Harvard University. In 1915 he established the Association for the Study of Negro Life and History and later founded the *Journal of Negro History*. He taught at Harvard University and West Virginia State College, organized the first Negro History Week, and published *The Negro in Our History* (1922). He is often referred to as the "Father of Negro History." Hughes worked for Woodson briefly in 1925.

Bibliography: Rampersad, I ; Roger M. Valade III, *The Essential Black Literature Guide* (Detroit: Visible Ink Press, 1994), 385.

"A Wooing." Poem of thirteen lines in three stanzas. It is spoken by a man to a woman; he wants to woo her with "big things" such as "flaming love," but she apparently desires money instead. The editors of *Collected Poems* suggest that the poem appeared in *American Life* (July 1925), but they were unable to locate the journal. *See* "Love Song for Antonia."
Bibliography: *CP*, 55, 619.

"Wooing the Muse." Short story, included in *The Best of Simple. See* Simple [Jesse B.] Stories.

"A Word from 'Town and Country.' " Short story, included in the collection *Simple Speaks His Mind. See* Simple [Jesse B.] Stories.

"Words Like Freedom." Poem in two ballad* quatrains. The speaker expresses a deep regard for "words like" "freedom" and "liberty." The poem was first published under the title "Refugee in America" in the *Saturday Evening Post* (February 6, 1943) and was also published under that title in *Fields of Wonder*. The title of the poem was changed when the poem was included in *The Panther and the Lash*. Later, Audrey Snyder Brown set the poem to music. ASCAP* lists the song as being published by Beam Me Up Music, and the song's ASCAP registry number is 530404198.
Bibliography: *CP*, 269.

"Work" (1966). Manuscript of an unpublished essay that Hughes had planned to submit to an organization called the Behavioral Research Laboratories. The manuscript is held in the Langston Hughes Papers of the James Weldon Johnson Memorial Collection, Beinecke Rare Book and Manuscript Library, Yale University (item 3849).

"Workin' Man." Poem in four ballad* stanzas and in black dialect.* The speaker describes the harshness of his working life and describes his wife as a " 'hore." The poem was first published in *Fine Clothes to the Jew.*
Bibliography: *CP*, 119.

"World War II." Poem. *See Montage of a Dream Deferred.*

"Worriation." Poem of two ballad stanzas with no stanza breaks. The poem concerns "Aryans" and "Negroes." It was circulated by the Associated Negro Press in June 1948. *See* "America's Young Black Joe."
Bibliography: *CP*, 588.

"Wouldn't You Like to Be on Broadway?" Song, from *Street Scene*. Hughes and Elmer Rice* wrote the lyrics, and Kurt Weill* composed the music.

ASCAP* lists the song as being published by Chappell, Inc., and by Hampshire House Publishers. The song's ASCAP registry number is 530110719.

"Wrapped in a Ribbon and Tied in a Bow." Song, from *Street Scene*. Hughes and Elmer Rice* wrote the lyrics, and Kurt Weill* composed the music. ASCAP lists the song as being published by Chappell, Inc., and by Hampshire House Publishers. The song's ASCAP registry number is 530111129.

Wright, Richard (1908–1960). American novelist and essayist. Wright was born in Natchez, Mississippi, but owing to the itinerant lifestyle of his mother, who eventually abandoned him, he grew up in several southern states. After his freshman year in high school, Wright decided to live on his own, residing briefly in Memphis before moving to Chicago. Subsequently he enthusiastically embraced Marxist political views, publishing poems in the magazine *Left Front*. His first book, *Uncle Tom's Children* (a collection of short stories), was published in 1936, one year after he had moved to New York City and begun writing for the magazines *New Masses* and the *Daily Worker*. His remarkable first novel, *Native Son* (1940), was widely acclaimed and is regarded as one of the most important works of twentieth-century American fiction. Hughes and Wright collaborated to write the poem "Red Clay Blues," and Rampersad concludes that "Hughes liked Richard Wright. Their professional relationship was excellent" (I, 383). Rampersad indicates the extent to which Hughes applauded Wright's success with *Native Son*, even though, privately, he did not like the novel, in part because he believed that the novel "bared Wright's almost unrelieved distaste for blacks on one hand, and his evident love-hatred of whites, on the other" (I, 383). Wright's autobiography, *Black Boy* (1945), also earned critical acclaim. After World War II Wright moved to Paris, partly at the urging of writer Gertrude Stein, and became increasingly interested in existential philosophy. His later novels are *The Outsider* (1953) and *The Long Dream* (1958). A book of essays, *Black Power*, appeared in 1954. Hughes visited Wright shortly before the latter's death in 1960. "As they talked of Harlem and Chicago," Rampersad writes, "his [Wright's] spirit revived until he seemed to Langston the Richard Wright of old—charming, effervescent, modest" (II, 327). Hughes departed for London and two days later was shocked to hear a radio broadcast that gave news of Wright's death from a heart attack. *See also* Modernism.

Bibliography: Addison Gayle, *Richard Wright: Ordeal of a Native Son* (Garden City, NY: Doubleday, 1980); Yoshinobu Hakutani, *Richard Wright and Racial Discourse* (Columbia: University of Missouri Press, 1996); M. Lynn Weiss, *Gertrude Stein and Richard Wright: The Poetics and Politics of Modernism* (Jackson: University Press of Mississippi, 1998); Richard Wright, *Black Boy* (New York: Harper, 1945); Richard Wright, *Lawd Today!*, with a foreword by Arnold Rampersad (Boston: Northeastern University Press, 1993); Richard Wright, *The Long Dream* (Garden City, NY: Doubleday, 1958); Richard Wright, *Native Son* (New York: Harper, 1940); Richard Wright, *Uncle Tom's Children* (New York: Harper, 1938).

Writers of the Revolution (Detroit: Black Forum, 1970). Sound recording. It is held by the Library of Congress. The recording is of Hughes and Margaret Danner reading and discussing their poems. The recording is on one sound disc (long-playing record) that runs forty-six minutes. The Library of Congress control number is 92788680. The recording is also held by the University of Washington libraries and other libraries. *See* Audio Recordings of Hughes.

Bibliography/Discography: Margaret Esse Danner, *The Down of the Thistle: Selected Poems, Prose Poems, and Songs*, introduction by Samuel Allen, illustrations by Fred L. Weinman (Waukesha, WI: Country Beautiful, 1976); *Writers of the Revolution* [sound recording; long-playing record] (Detroit: Black Forum, 1970), Black Forum H-1725.

"The Writer's Position in America." (1957). Speech/essay. Hughes gave the speech at the National Assembly of Authors and Dramatists Symposium, held at the Alvin Theatre in New York City on May 7, 1957. Reprinted in *The Langston Hughes Reader*, the speech/essay reiterates many points concerning African American writers that Hughes made in "Democracy and Me," "Democracy, Negroes, and Writers," and "To Negro Writers." Concerning "blacklisting," one result of McCarthyism,* Hughes writes, "We Negro writers, just by being black, have been on the blacklist all our lives" (483).

Bibliography: *The Langston Hughes Reader*, 483–485.

Y

"Yachts." Short story, included in the collection *Simple's Uncle Sam. See* Simple [Jesse B.] Stories.

Yates, Flora Belle. The main character in the short story "The Gun."

"Year Round." Poem in five short-lined ballad* stanzas that concerns the four seasons. It was first published in *The Langston Hughes Reader. See* Children's Poetry.
Bibliography: *CP*, 604.

"Yesterday and Today." Poem in three ballad* stanzas and in black dialect.* The speaker bemoans the departure of his lover, Lulu. The poem was first published in *Poetry* (February 1947).
Bibliography: *CP*, 321.

Yoseloff, Thomas. *See* "Moonlight in Valencia: Civil War."

"Young Black Joe." Song (?). *See* "America's Young Black Joe."

"Young Bride." Poem of seven lines, intermittently rhymed. It concerns a woman who "died of grief." It was first published in *Vanity Fair* (September 1925).
Bibliography: *CP*, 56.

"Young Gal's Blues." Poem in four traditional blues* stanzas and in black dialect.* The speaker's friend, "Cora Lee," has died, and her "Aunt Clew" lives in a "po' [poor] house." The poem was first published in *Four Negro Poets*, edited by Alain Locke* (New York: Simon and Schuster, 1927). It was also published in *Fine Clothes to the Jew*.

Bibliography: *CP*, 123.

"The Young Glory of Him." Short story, among Hughes's earliest published fiction. The narrative concerns a young woman, the daughter of missionaries, who is on her way by ship to Africa. She falls in love with a sailor who does not love her, and ultimately she commits suicide. The story was first published in the *Messenger** (June 1927). Ironically, George Schuyler,* with whom Hughes had disagreed in print about the question of "Negro art," was editor of the *Messenger* at the time. The story was reprinted in *Langston Hughes: Short Stories*. Other early stories set in Africa include "Bodies in the Moonlight," "The Little Virgin," and "Luani of the Jungles." *See also* "The Negro Artist and the Racial Mountain."

"Young Negro Girl." Poem of nine lines in two stanzas. It describes—and is addressed to—the girl. It was first published in the *Carmel Pine Cone* (July 18, 1941). It was also published in *Shakespeare in Harlem*.

Bibliography: *CP*, 234.

"Young Prostitute." Poem of five lines describing the prostitute. It was first published in *Crisis** (August 1923). *See also* "Red Silk Stockings"; "Ruby Brown"; "A Ruined Gal"; Women in Hughes's Writing.

Bibliography: *CP*, 33.

"Young Sailor." Poem of twenty lines in three stanzas. It describes one sailor but also evokes the worldview of all sailors. It was first published in *Palms* (January 1926).

Bibliography: *CP*, 62.

"Young Singer." Poem of eight lines describing a young female cabaret singer in Harlem,* first published in *Crisis** (August 1923).

Bibliography: *CP*, 35.

"Youth." Poem of nine lines in four stanzas. It expresses profound hope in the future. The last line, "We march!" evokes a spirit of labor politics. The poem was first published under the title "Poem" in *Crisis** (August 1924), then in *Survey Graphic* (March 1, 1925). *See* Locke, Alain.

Bibliography: *CP*, 39.

Z

Zarita. Recurring character in the Simple [Jessie B.] Stories.* She also appears in *Simply Heavenly*. In the list of "Characters" for *Simply Heavenly*, Hughes describes Zarita as "a glamorous goodtimer" (Smalley, 114).

Bibliography: Webster Smalley, ed., *Five Plays by Langston Hughes* (Bloomington: Indiana University Press, 1963).

Zelli's. The name of a nightclub Hughes frequented when he was living in Paris in 1924.

Bibliography: Rampersad, I, 98.

General Bibliography

Baker, Houston A., Jr. *Blues, Ideology, and Afro-American Literature: A Vernacular Theory*. Chicago: University of Chicago Press, 1984.

Barksdale, Richard K. *Langston Hughes*. Chicago; American Library Association, 1977.

Bernard, Emily, ed. *Remember Me to Harlem: The Letters of Langston Hughes and Carl Van Vechten, 1925–1964*. New York: Knopf, 2001.

Berry, Faith, ed. *Good Morning Revolution: Uncollected Writings of Social Protest by Langston Hughes*. New York: Citadel Press, 1992.

Bruck, Peter, ed. *The Black American Short Story in the 20th Century: A Collection of Critical Essays*. Amsterdam: Grüner, 1977.

Dace, Trish, ed. *Langston Hughes: The Contemporary Reviews*. Cambridge: Cambridge University Press, 1997.

Davis, Arthur P. *From the Dark Tower: Afro-American Writers' (1900 to 1960)*. Washington, DC: Howard University Press, 1974.

Davis, Ossie. *Langston, A Play*. New York: Delacorte Press, 1982.

De Santis, Christopher, ed. *Langston Hughes and the Chicago Defender: Essays on Race, Politics, and Culture, 1942–62*. Urbana: University of Illinois Press, 1995.

Dickinson, Donald C. *A Bio-Bibliography of Langston Hughes, 1902–1967*. 2nd ed., revised. Hamden, CT: Archon Books, 1972.

Elliott, Emory, general editor. *Columbia Literary History of the United States*. New York: Columbia University Press, 1988.

Emanuel, James. *Langston Hughes*. New York: Twayne, 1967.

Franklin, John Hope, and Alfred A. Moss, Jr. *From Slavery to Freedom: A History of African Americans*. 8th edition. New York: McGraw-Hill, 2000.

Gibson, Donald B. *Five Black Writers: Essays on Wright, Ellison, Baldwin, Hughes, and Le Roi Jones*. New York: New York University Press, 1970.

Gilroy, Paul. *The Black Atlantic: Modernity and Double Consciousness*. Cambridge, MA: Harvard University Press, 1993.

Harper, Akiba Sullivan, ed. *Langston Hughes: Short Stories*. New York: Hill and Wang, 1996.

————. *Not So Simple: The "Simple" Stories by Langston Hughes*. Columbia: University of Missouri Press, 1995.

————, ed. *The Return of Simple*. New York: Hill and Wang, 1994.

Hicklin, Fannie Ella Frazier. "The American Negro Playwright, 1920–1964." Ph.D. dissertation. Department of Speech, University of Wisconsin, 1965. Ann Arbor: University MicroFilms: 65–6217.

Huggins, Nathan. *Harlem Renaissance*. New York: Oxford University Press, 1971.

Hughes, Langston. *The Big Sea*. With a foreword by Amiri Baraka. New York: Thunder's Mouth Press, 1986.

————. *I Wonder As I Wander*. With a foreword by Margaret Walker. New York: Thunder's Mouth Press, 1986.

————. *The Langston Hughes Reader*. New York: Braziller, 1958.

————. *Not Without Laughter*. Introduction by Maya Angelou. New York: Scribner, 1995.

————. *The Panther and the Lash*. New York: Vintage Classics, 1992.

————. *Selected Poems of Langston Hughes*. New York: Knopf, 1959; New York: Vintage, 1974.

————. *The Ways of White Folks*. New York: Vintage Classics, 1990.

Hughes, Langston, and Zora Neale Hurston. *Mule Bone: A Comedy of Negro Life*. Edited with introductions by George Houston Bass and Henry Louis Gates, Jr. New York: Harper Perennial, 1991.

Hutchinson, George. *The Harlem Renaissance in Black and White*. Cambridge, MA: Belknap Press of Harvard University Press, 1995.

Ikonne, Chidi. *From DuBois to Van Vechten: The Early New Negro Literature, 1903–1926*. Westport, CT: Greenwood Press, 1981.

Jemie, Onwuchekwa. *Langston Hughes: An Introduction to the Poetry*. New York: Columbia University Press, 1976.

Lewis, David Levering, ed. *The Portable Harlem Renaissance Reader*. New York: Penguin, 1995.

————. *When Harlem Was in Vogue*. New York: Oxford University Press, 1989.

Mandelik, Peter, and Stanley Schatt. *A Concordance to the Poetry of Langston Hughes*. Detroit: Gale Research, 1975.

Miller, R. Baxter. *The Art and Imagination of Langston Hughes*. Lexington: University Press of Kentucky, 1989.

————. *Langston Hughes and Gwendolyn Brooks: A Reference Guide*. Boston: G. K. Hall, 1978.

Mullen, Edward, ed. *Critical Essays on Langston Hughes*. Boston: G. K. Hall, 1986.

O'Daniel, Therman B., ed. *Langston Hughes: Black Genius*. New York: Morrow, 1971.

Ostrom, Hans. *Langston Hughes: A Study of the Short Fiction*. New York: Twayne, 1993.

Rampersad, Arnold. *The Life of Langston Hughes*. 2 vols. New York: Oxford University Press, 1986, 1988.

Rampersad, Arnold, and David Roessel, eds. *The Collected Poems of Langston Hughes*. New York: Vintage Classics, 1994.

Smalley, Webster, ed. *Five Plays by Langston Hughes*. Bloomington: Indiana University Press, 1963.

Thompson, Robert Farris. *Flash of the Spirit: African and Afro-American Art and Philosophy*. New York: Random House, 1983.

Tracy, Steven C. *Langston Hughes and the Blues.* Urbana: University of Illinois Press, 1988.

Watson, Steven. *The Harlem Renaissance: Hub of African-American Culture, 1920–1930.* New York: Pantheon, 1995.

Wintz, Cary D. *Black Culture and the Harlem Renaissance.* Houston: Rice University Press, 1988.

Note: As of this writing, the University of Missouri Press plans to publish the *Collected Works of Langston Hughes* in eighteen volumes.

Index

About the Author and Contributors

HANS OSTROM is Professor of English and Co-Director of African-American Studies at the University of Puget Sound in Tacoma, Washington. His other books include *Langston Hughes: A Study of the Short Fiction* (1993), the novel *Three to Get Ready* (1991), and *Lives and Moments: An Introduction to Short Fiction* (1991). With Wendy Bishop he edited *Genre and Writing: Issues, Arguments, Alternatives* (1997). *Subjects Apprehended: Poems* appeared in 2000.

JOSEPH DETERS is Assistant Professor of Spanish at the University of Puget Sound. He earned his doctorate from the University of Arizona in 1997. His areas of research are contemporary Spanish poetry and Latino literature written in the United States.

WILLIAM HALTOM is Professor of Politics and Government at the University of Puget Sound. He earned a Ph.D. from the University of Washington in 1984. He is author of *Reporting on the Courts* (1998). His current project concerns tort reform and mass media.

DIANE DUFFRIN KELLEY is an Assistant Professor of French at the University of Puget Sound. She earned a Ph.D. from the University of California, Los Angeles, in 1998, writing a dissertation on "Narrative Strategies of Seduction and Subversion in the Nouvelles of Lafayette, Bernard, and Tencin." She is completing research on *La Princesse de Clèves*.

DAVID ROESSEL is Associate Editor of the *Collected Poems of Langston Hughes* and the co-editor of the forthcoming *Selected Letters of Langston Hughes*. He has taught at Howard University and the Catholic University in Washington, D.C. He is currently working on a biography of Mike Gold.